M000191792

Study Guide

Introduction to Psychology

NINTH EDITION

Rod Plotnik
San Diego State University

Haig Kouyoumdjian
University of California, Berkeley Extension

Prepared by

Matthew Enos
Harold Washington College

How English Works section by

John Thissen
Harold Washington College

WADSWORTH
CENGAGE Learning™

Australia • Brazil • Japan • Korea • Mexico • Singapore • Spain • United Kingdom • United States

WADSWORTH
CENGAGE Learning

ISBN-13: 978-0-495-90840-1
ISBN-10: 0-495-90840-1

Wadsworth
20 Davis Drive
Belmont, CA 94002-3098
USA

Cengage Learning is a leading provider of customized learning solutions with office locations around the globe, including Singapore, the United Kingdom, Australia, Mexico, Brazil, and Japan. Locate your local office at: **www.cengage.com/global**

Cengage Learning products are represented in Canada by Nelson Education, Ltd.

To learn more about Wadsworth, visit **www.cengage.com/wadsworth**

Purchase any of our products at your local college store or at our preferred online store **www.CengageBrain.com**

Printed in the United States of America
1 2 3 4 5 6 7 14 13 12 11 10

Contents

Introduction

Welcome to the Exciting World of Psychology

You are taking a challenging course. I think you will enjoy it, because psychology is one of the most exciting and relevant fields of college study today. An explosion of new ideas and research in psychology is creating a vast accumulation of knowledge that is radically changing the way we understand other people and ourselves. To participate fully and effectively in today's world, we need a kind of psychological literacy, just as we need computer literacy, Internet literacy, and other new technological abilities. This course can help you acquire the skills and information you need to become psychologically literate.

Let's Work Together

Forgive me for using the personal pronoun "I" in this Study Guide. As a teacher, I can't help imagining you working your way through beginning psychology. I'd like to help, so I want to speak to you as directly as I can. Even though I don't know you personally, I am sure I have had a student very much like you in my own classes. Happily, we can get to know each other — through e-mail. Throughout the Study Guide, I invite you to e-mail me [Matthew Enos] at <**profenos@mac.com**>.

"Why Can't All *Textbooks Be Like This?"*

I am confident that you are going to enjoy using your new psychology textbook. My own students often ask, "Why can't *all* textbooks be like this?" (Not just psychology textbooks — but textbooks in every course!) What they mean is that Rod Plotnik and Haig Kouyoumdjian's *Introduction to Psychology* is so readable and clear that using it is a pleasure. Two knowledgeable, experienced, and interesting teachers are talking to you in a direct and personal way that makes you even more eager to learn. They know that the psychology course you are taking is important to your success in the modern world, and they are determined to make sure you benefit from using their textbook.

You'll find that *Introduction to Psychology* is as fresh as your morning newspaper or your favorite talk show. At the same time, you'll see that it is a work of solid scholarship. It covers the major areas of psychology, introduces you to the most important theories, and carefully explains the relevant research in the field. It's how Plotnik and Kouyoumdjian tell it that I think you will find especially rewarding.

Their textbook is different. As experts in learning psychology, Plotnik and Kouyoumdjian know that we *understand* what we can visualize in a picture and *remember* what we can organize into a story. That's why they filled their textbook with attractive pictures and compelling stories.

Excellent as this book is, I wouldn't want you to passively agree with everything its authors say. Instead, try to become actively involved in a dialogue with the book. You'll notice how often Plotnik and Kouyoumdjian *ask you a question*. Argue with them. Write notes in the margins. Highlight the important stuff. Make reading and studying this new textbook an adventure.

Plotnik and Kouyoumdjian's "Introduction to Psychology" (9th Edition)

Dr. Rod Plotnik, a psychologist and professor at San Diego State University, is a veteran teacher and writer who sees examples of psychology's importance everywhere he looks and loves sharing his observations with us. When he set out to write an introductory psychology textbook a number of years ago, Plotnik knew he wanted something different for students.

In the previous edition of *Introduction to Psychology*, Plotnik was joined by co-author Dr. Haig Kouyoumdjian, professor of psychology at Mott Community College in Flint, Michigan. Kouyoumdjian has worked with Plotnik for a number of years as a student, fellow teacher, researcher, and writer. He earned his doctorate in clinical psychology and has worked as a psychologist in an outpatient medical center providing mental health services to youths, adults, and families. His two primary areas of research have been child maltreatment and teaching methods. He has used the Plotnik textbook in psychology courses he taught at several schools. Kouyoumdjian's strengths have made a great textbook even better.

If you would like to learn more about the individual stories of Rod Plotnik and Haig Kouyoumdjian, please read the Acknowledgements section at the front of the textbook (page xxxvii). Throughout the textbook itself, the authors share interesting stories (marked R.P. and H.K.) from their own lives that illustrate the feature of psychology they are discussing

What Is a Module?

You may have noticed that Plotnik and Kouyoumdjian call their units "modules" instead of "chapters," and that there are more of them than in most textbooks. The authors want their book to be as flexible as possible, so instructors and students can adapt it to their own needs.

Each module tackles an important aspect of psychology. If you mastered everything in every module, you would have a near-perfect understanding of modern psychology (you also might flunk your other courses!). When you read a single module, you learn the main facts and ideas about one area of interest in psychology.

Please remember that there's no law against reading an unassigned module that interests you. *Hint: when you do, tell your professor about it and you'll make a good impression.*

How This Study Guide Works

The bottom line for this Study Guide is that it must help you earn the grade you want in your psychology course. I tried to include materials that have worked for my own students. Some information is highly specific, aimed straight at getting more questions right on the next exam. There are observations about the field of psychology, because, as I explain in my Study Guide introduction for Module 1, if you can't see the forest because of the trees, you're lost. Still other parts have the general goal of helping you become a more effective student (and where better than in a psychology course?). The Study Guide is organized as follows:

Module Introduction

Each module in the Study Guide begins with an observation I think may help you tackle the module in the textbook more successfully. These introductions are not summaries, but thoughts about how to orient yourself toward understanding what you are reading in the textbook.

Effective Student Tip

Next, you'll find a specific tip on how to become a more effective student. Some effective student tips tell you how to study better, but most are general ideas about the psychology of effectiveness. Please read Tip 1 (on page 7), which explains more about this feature of the Study Guide.

Learning Objectives

There are seven learning objectives for each module that should help you understand what is most important in the module. You will notice that the first one attempts to place the subject of the module into the broad sweep of psychology. I hope these first objectives will help you understand how the subject matter of that module fits into the story of psychology.

Key Terms

Rod Plotnik and Haig Kouyoumdjian have carefully selected the words or phrases they believe are the most important for beginning psychology students to learn. They put each key term in **boldface** type in the text and provide a brief, clear definition of the term (the key term and its definition are in blue print). These terms are also listed at the end of each module and collected in a glossary at the end of the textbook.

If you did nothing but memorize the definition for each of the key terms, you would pass most psychology exams and have a pretty decent command of the vocabulary of the discipline. Of course, it wouldn't be much fun that way, and you need the story to understand psychology in any depth. Still, I can't stress enough the importance of learning the basic vocabulary.

To help you focus on these key terms, I've placed them (in alphabetical order) in the Study Guide right before my outline of the module. I've also included each key term in the outline and placed it in **boldface** type so you won't miss it.

Outline

Each module in the Study Guide includes a topic outline of the module in the text. My outlines stick very close to the book's organization. I think working with the outline will help you read and master the textbook.

There is one thing wrong with my outlines: I wrote them instead of you. Much of the benefit of an outline comes from the process of building it. Therefore, your job is to turn each outline into your own product by writing all over it and revising it as you study. Make each outline a personal set of notes that will help you prepare for your exams. If you add your own notes and details to my outlines, you will have an excellent summary of each module.

Notice that throughout the outlines I've scattered questions for you to think about and answer. Each is preceded by a check box, to draw your attention to it. Why not write your answers right on the outline?

How English Works

Following each outline, there's a special section on language prepared by my colleague Professor John H. Thissen of Harold Washington College. Dr. Thissen wrote this section not only for non-native speakers, but also for *all* students who wish to strengthen their skills with the English language. We hope every user of the Study Guide will try the "How English Works" materials. Since English is such a powerful and complicated language, anyone who reads these pages will gain greater insight into the intricacies of our wonderful language.

Even if you are proficient in English, I can assure you that going through the special language exercises that John Thissen has prepared will improve your skills and deepen your understanding of how the English language works. We hope every student will try them.

Thissen wrote a special introduction (see Module 1, page 12) to help you make the best use of his exercises. Please read it. This material is too good to miss!

Self-Tests

Each module has six sets of questions that will help you review and give you an idea of how well you are studying. These self-tests are the most immediate and practical part of this Study Guide, so be sure to use them.

- **The Big Picture**: This quiz is intended to test your overall understanding of the importance of the module. It presents you with five general summary statements (well, four, really, as you will see!). Which statement best expresses the larger significance of the module?
- **True-False**: Ten true-false questions are intended to indicate how well you understand important ideas in the module.
- **Flashcards 1** and **Flashcards 2**: Two sets of ten matching questions each test your recall of the more important key terms in the module. I have quoted Plotnik's and Kouyoumdjian's definitions as closely as possible, so your results will be a good check on how well you know them. I call these questions "flashcards" in the hope that you will study and test yourself on the key terms more than once.
- **Multiple Choice**: Twenty-five multiple-choice questions explore the important facts, concepts, and theories presented in the module. The multiple-choice questions are especially important because many of you will be taking multiple-choice exams in the course. In fact, some of my questions will be included in the test bank from which your instructor may construct exams.
- **Short Essay:** Five short essay questions (designed for answers of about 75 words) will allow you to show your grasp of the material — or cruelly expose gaps in your learning. Short essay questions can be the toughest of all to answer. They don't allow much "wiggle" room, but don't chicken out! Give them a try. *Hint: Even if you don't write out answers to the short essay questions, I suggest that you read the sample answers. They are condensed summaries of important topics in psychology and should help you understand the module.*
- **"For Psych Majors Only..." and other special quizzes**: In several modules, you will find a special quiz. Some of these quizzes are serious, some not so much. The purpose of these exercises is to go a bit beyond what your course requires. I hope psychology majors will be interested. As you may have guessed, I won't mind a bit if an English major or chemistry major tries these materials! I hope you enjoy them.

Answers Section

The last section of each module in the Study Guide is an unusual answers section. It deserves special attention. The correct answers are given, of course, but there is more. For *incorrect* answers you might have chosen, I've given a brief indication why that alternative is not correct. Since textbook page numbers are given with the correct answers, you can go back to the textbook to make sure you really understand the material.

Feedback Form

At the end of the Study Guide you will find a special mail-in form by which you can let us know how well this Study Guide worked for you and what suggestions you have for helping us make it better. Please send it in to Wadsworth, the publisher. We would love to hear from you. (See below for how to give me more immediate feedback.)

Enjoy Your Study Guide

I hope you enjoy working with the Study Guide. Think about the effective student tips as you write your responses to them. Make real flashcards for the key terms, if you have time. Add your own notes and comments to the outlines.

By the way, if an occasional question or comment of mine makes you laugh, *I'll be delighted!* I don't believe learning has to be deadly serious all the time. So when I was writing and couldn't take it any longer, I sometimes indulged myself in what I hoped would be a bit of humor. The results may be too corny, but you be the judge.

Can We Talk?

I would love to have immediate feedback about the Study Guide. Use my e-mail address to ask questions, share your thoughts, make suggestions for improvements, and, darn it, tell me about those inevitable mistakes I know some of you will find (see box below). It will be fun to share ideas with you. My e-mail address is <**profenos@mac.com**> and I am eager to hear from you!

Wanted!

On the first day of class, I pass out a corny "Wanted" poster urging my students to look for any errors I make in writing (factual, spelling, grammar, formatting). I offer a payoff to students who find an error.

Some students enjoy this challenge, and I thought you might, too. *Can you find any mistakes in this Study Guide?* I can't ask your instructor to pay off (it's my mistake, after all), but I will send you an e-mail you can show your teacher. Might make a good impression!

Please e-mail me if you find a mistake — any mistake, no matter how small! Write to me at <**profenos@mac.com**>.

Module 1

Discovering Psychology

An Explosion of Knowledge

One day I found a box of my old college books. I was delighted to discover the textbook I used when I took my first psychology course, years ago. Would you believe I still remembered some of the pictures and lessons?

I was shocked, though, to see how slender a book it was. It had a chapter on the eye, another on the ear, and others on the rest of the senses. There was some material on Sigmund Freud, but not much on anyone else. I was struck by how much less knowledge there was in the field of psychology back then.

The explosion of research and thinking in psychology has created a problem for teachers and students. Textbooks are four times as thick, yet authors apologize for leaving material out. In the newer textbooks, such as the one by Rod Plotnik and Haig Kouyoumdjian that you are using, the writing is lively and the graphics are superb, but there still is much more material to cover. The problem is that colleges and universities, which change very slowly, still expect you to master it all in one semester!

How to Tell the Forest from the Trees

My experience as a teacher says the single greatest problem of introductory psychology is that the sheer mass of information thrown at students overwhelms them, no matter how diligently they study. What is really important? Where are the connections between all these facts and ideas and names? What must I remember for the exams? The study of introductory psychology presents a classic example of the old problem of not being able to see the forest because of the trees.

The solution is to develop a conceptual framework for understanding psychology. If you have an overview of what questions psychology attempts to answer, how it goes about seeking answers, and what the dominant themes in the answers have been, you will be able to fit any new fact, idea, or name into a coherent picture.

That's where Module 1 comes in. In addition to describing the kinds of work psychologists do, Plotnik and Kouyoumdjian give you an important tool: the six major theoretical approaches to psychology. (They also present two new ways of looking at psychology, but I see these as recent trends within the major approaches.) As a student and consumer of psychology, you need to know how the great pioneers in the field have tried to answer the most important questions about human behavior. Module 1 is the road map for an exciting journey.

Effective Student Tip 1

Take a Tip from Me

I have been teaching psychology for many years, but that's not what makes me so smart (ahem!). I have learned from experience. The next tip, for example, owes a lot to my own checkered past. Have you ever heard of the "reformed drunk syndrome"? Guess who you call on if you want a really convincing lecture about the evils of Demon Rum? When I talk about the importance of good attendance, do as I say, not as I did!

But there's more to it. Not only does my experience as both a student and a teacher tell me that every student wants and needs to be effective (I tell you what the professor wants and needs in Tip 18), but I think the psychology of motivation says we all desire effectiveness in every aspect of our lives.

Meanwhile, I hope you will read all these "Effective Student Tips," even the ones in the modules your professor does not assign. Some will touch you personally, others may give you something to think about, and some you may not agree with at all. Writing your answers to the "Your response…" questions should help you think about yourself as a student. Write your answers in the boxes provided.

Please read the *next* tip and the *last* one right now. Tip 2 is the simplest, and yet the most important. Tip 25 says more about the underlying theme of all these Effective Student Tips.

Your response…

Do you consider yourself an effective person? In what ways "yes" and in what ways "no"? *[Write answer here.]*

Learning Objectives

1. Understand the aims and contents of psychology as a distinct field of study within the social sciences.
2. Learn the *six approaches to understanding behavior* as the fundamental structure of this field and know them well enough to apply them to the particular facts and ideas in psychology.
3. Explain how psychology as a scientific study has developed in the modern world.
4. Appreciate how psychology has reflected the prejudices and discrimination in our culture and how professional psychology has worked to overcome them.
5. Learn what research in psychology suggests about the best strategy for taking class notes.
6. Consider the career opportunities and research areas in psychology in relation to your own interests and possible career choices.
7. Apply psychology to your immediate learning task of mastering the material in this module and to the broader goal of planning for success in the course.

Key Terms

Forget how big the textbook seems. You are not starting at square one in psychology. So much of psychology is becoming general knowledge these days that you already know quite a bit about it. Rod Plotnik and Haig Kouyoumdjian defined 26 terms in this module they thought were especially important to know. How many of the following terms mean something to you right now, even without intensive study of the module?

---

approaches to understanding behavior
autism
behavioral approach
biological approach
biological psychology (psychobiology)
clinical and counseling psychology
clinical psychologist
cognitive approach
cognitive neuroscience
cognitive psychology
cross-cultural approach
developmental psychology
eclectic approach
evolutionary approach
experimental psychology
functionalism
Gestalt approach
humanistic approach
industrial/organizational psychology
introspection
procrastination
psychiatrist
psychoanalytic approach
psychologist
psychology
psychometrics
social psychology
structuralism
test anxiety

The "PowerStudy 4.5 for Introduction to Psychology" CD-ROM includes a complete set of interactive learning activities for this module: quizzes, summary test, key terms, web site connections, critical thinking exercise, module outline, and more.

Outline

Reminder: This topic outline closely follows the textbook, with key terms in boldface. The outline is most useful for learning and review when you add your own notes and definitions. Try my questions, too (indicated by a checkbox □).

- *Introduction*

□ Why do you think Plotnik and Kouyoumdjian begin with one very rare and one quite common example?

1. Growing up in a strange world (Donna Williams' **autism**)
2. **Test anxiety** (students like you!)

A. Definition & Goals

1. Definition of **psychology**
2. Goals of psychology
    a. Describe
    b. Explain
    c. Predict
    d. Control

B. Modern Approaches

□ Can you learn the six major **approaches to understanding behavior**? Well enough to understand and remember them all through the course? If so, you will possess a master plan into which almost everything in psychology will fit.

1. **Biological approach**
    a. Autism (Donna Williams and Tito Mukhopadhyay)
    b. Test anxiety
2. **Cognitive approach**
    a. Autism (Donna Williams and Tito Mukhopadhyay)
    b. **Cognitive neuroscience**
    c. Test anxiety
3. **Behavioral approach**
    a. Autism (Donna Williams)
    b. B. F. Skinner (strict behaviorism) and Albert Bandura (social cognitive approach)
    c. Test anxiety and self-management
4. **Psychoanalytic approach**
    a. Autism (Donna Williams' childhood)
    b. Sigmund Freud's ideas
    c. Test anxiety: example of **procrastination**
5. **Humanistic approach**
    a. Autism (Donna Williams' achievements)
    b. Abraham Maslow: dissatisfaction with both psychoanalysis and behaviorism
    c. Test anxiety and human potential

6. **Cross-cultural approach**
    a. How is autism diagnosed in other cultures?
    b. Test anxiety in different cultures
        (1) United States
        (2) South Korea
7. Modern trends: **evolutionary approach** and **eclectic approach**

C. Historical Approaches

☐ Have you noticed that there is some overlap between the modern approaches (above) and the historical approaches (below)? Do you see how it's all part of the same story?

1. **Structuralism**: elements of the mind
    a. Wilhelm Wundt
    b. **Introspection**
2. **Functionalism**: functions of the mind
    a. William James
    b. Purpose of mental activity
3. **Gestalt approach**: sensations versus perceptions
    a. Max Wertheimer, Wolfgang Köhler, Kurt Koffka
    b. Perception as more than the sum of its parts
    c. Apparent motion (phi phenomenon)
4. **Behavioral approach**: observable behaviors
    a. John B. Watson ["Give me a dozen healthy infants… and my own special world to bring them up in…"]
    b. Objective, scientific analysis of observable behaviors
    c. B. F. Skinner and modern behaviorism
5. Survival of approaches

D. Cultural Diversity: Early Discrimination

1. Women in psychology
    a. Mary Calkins and Margaret Washburn
    b. Gains by women in psychology
2. Minorities in psychology
    a. Inez Prosser and George Sanchez
    b. Continuing under representation of ethnic minorities in psychology
3. Righting the wrongs: APA efforts to help minority students

E. Research Focus: Taking Class Notes

1. What's the best strategy for taking class notes?
2. A research study of three techniques (which also illustrates the four goals of psychology)

☐ Which technique worked best? Can you figure out why it was superior?

F. *Careers in Psychology*

1. Psychologist versus psychiatrist
   a. **Psychologist**
   b. **Clinical psychologist**
   c. **Psychiatrist**
2. Many career settings

G. *Research Areas*

1. Areas of specialization
   a. **Clinical and counseling psychology**
   b. **Social psychology**
   c. **Developmental psychology**
   d. **Experimental psychology**
   e. **Biological psychology** (psychobiology)
   f. **Cognitive psychology**
   g. **Psychometrics**
   h. **Industrial/organizational psychology**
2. Making decisions

H. *Application: Study Skills*

1. Improving study habits
   a. Common complaint
   b. Poor judges
   c. Reducing distractions
   d. Time management
2. Setting goals
   a. Time goal
   b. General goal
   c. Specific performance goal
3. Rewarding yourself (self-reinforcement)
4. Taking notes
   a. In your own words
   b. Outline format [like this one]
   c. Associate new material with old

☐ Check the Concept Review (p. 15) and Summary Test (pp. 22-23) in the textbook. Notice that Plotnik and Kouyoumdjian repeat the same illustrations they used in the text pages. Why is this a good learning strategy?

   d. Ask yourself questions as you study
5. Stopping procrastination
   a. Stop thinking or worrying about final goal
   b. Break overall task down into smaller goals
   c. Write down a realistic schedule

How English Works

Introduction to the Language Sections

English is a rich and complicated language. You know this already, although you might not know why our language has evolved to the form it has today. In this study guide, we'll see how and why his has happened, and, more importantly, how to make it work for you.

There's a very good chance that English isn't the language you spoke as a child. If so, there are special sections throughout this Study Guide designed for English as a Second Language (ESL) speakers and titled **ESL Tip**. These tips are presented in such a way as to be helpful to all students, whether native speakers or ESL students. In addition, there are **Vocabulary** sections in each module, as well as a variety of **Sentence Structure** review sections. Each module begins with definitions of **Words in the Textbook**. Reviewing each list will give you a quick check on your skills in English.

The reason for working your way through these review sections is a simple one:

Just as English helps us understand psychology,
so does psychology help us understand English.

Think, for example of the upcoming chapters where Plotnik and Kouyoumdjian explain how infants begin to learn language, from their first, noise-making stages to their mastery of full-blown sentences and paragraphs. You'll also study the debate over whether or not humans are born with a built-in structure that enables them to master their birth language, a common brain structure that works equally well for whatever language their birth has dealt them. With such an inborn mechanism, a person could have learned Danish, Basque, Urdu, ancient Babylonian, or American English as a baby, and, if necessary, have switched to a new tongue.

Likewise, the language you are using in this course (English) helps you to understand psychology, and that's why we're here. The sentences, concepts, terminology, and deepest meanings require an ability to use English as your key to unlocking the riches of psychology and all its countless variations. Psychology is a subject that relies on clear statements about ideas that might not be so clear. There are continuing debates and disagreements among psychologists, and it's important for you to have the language skills to appreciate these debates. This is a subject that relies on clear definitions of clear terminology.

As with any challenging thing worth knowing, you will have to use the rules and customs set up by experts in the field. You will find yourself thinking the way psychologists think and using English the way they use it.

So, tell yourself that the correct and creative use of English has a very productive payoff: As you study psychology, you will learn how psychologists think, speak, and explain themselves, and you will find yourself doing the very same things.

I am indebted to my colleague Professor Roger Conner for sharing the expertise he developed over many years of teaching ESL students at Harold Washington College.

Words in the Textbook

p. 3 involuntarily **anesthetized** = without feeling or sensations

10 times more **prevalent** = widespread

such as **grave** problems in developing spoken language = serious

figuring out the day of the week = identifying

getting through an ordinary day = completing the work of

p. 4 if they were **reared** by parents who were cold = raised

if they were reared by parents who were **cold** = without showing caring or love

prevent **potential** abuse = possible in the future

p. 5 **rigid corpselike stance** = standing like a dead body, unmoving

p. 6 **process** human faces = organize information into clear identification

stressful thoughts **trigger** the emotional component = stimulate, start

p. 7 students who **channeled** their worry into studying = directed, redirected

negative feedback = unwanted reaction from others

p. 9 Psychologists know that **ingrained** personality characteristics = deeply rooted

ESL Tip: How English Got That Way — Spelling

Why is English spelling so inconsistent and difficult? If you grew up speaking a different language — Spanish, for instance — you've found that learning to spell correctly in English can be very challenging. There's an old joke about how the English word ***fish*** could be spelled ***ghoti***: you take the ***gh*** from lau***gh***, add the ***o*** from w***o***men, end it with the ***ti*** from mo***ti***on, and you get something that should sound like ***fish***. Try it.

But seriously, English spelling is a confusing mess. In Spanish, if you know how a word is pronounced, you're pretty sure of how it should be spelled. Not so with English. To understand this, it will help to explore some of our language's history.

Back in 1066, English spelling was much simpler, but, of course, most people didn't worry about spelling because they could neither read nor write. That year the French army sailed across the English Channel, conquered the English, and set themselves up as rulers of the land. The language spoken at court in England for centuries to come would be French, while out on the English streets the conquered people spoke a language that we would recognize as English.

As time passed, the French rulers tried to learn their subjects' language, and the locals tried to learn what their new rulers were saying. When either side tried to spell what they heard, the result was a rich stew of bad pronunciations, translated into a bad choice of letters. Thus, we have inherited a collection of words that is very rich and flexible, but one that contains a tradition of haphazard spelling. Even Shakespeare spelled his own name several different ways. If you try to analyze and to reason your way toward the spelling of a modern English word, you will often find yourself up against this loose, confusing tradition.

As if this mix of French (which grew out of Latin, along with Spanish) and English were not enough, add in the fact that, from its earliest days, our language has eagerly borrowed and added words from many other languages.

So, how do you deal with this interesting composite? You get help wherever you can, and you start by making friends with your dictionary, whether it's contained in a book or your computer. You rely on your computer's spell checker, but with caution because it can tell you only that a word is spelled correctly, not whether you have chosen the right word or context. You look in your college's writing lab for the computerized programs and software that will train you to become a better speller.

It won't be easy, but if you can deal with this challenge and steadily increase your vocabulary, you will have one of the world's "power languages" as your own.

The Big Picture

Which statement below offers the best summary of the larger significance of this module?

A Building on a long history that goes back to the ancient world, psychology today offers respect, honor, and financial security to those few who can complete medical school and post-doctoral training.

B There is no single "true" psychology because it is still a young and hotly debated science. At this stage in its growth, six major theoretical approaches offer quite different but still valuable answers to life's complex problems.

C Psychology has not yet achieved the respect of the scientific community because there are so many answers and so many different specialties competing for our attention.

D A civil war has raged within psychology for more than a century, but the Freudian system is gradually emerging as the most convincing overall answer.

E How many psychologists does it take to change a light bulb, you ask? The answer is three: one to hold the ladder, one to change the bulb, and one to share the experience.

True-False

_____ 1. Psychologists now believe that the increase in childhood autism is due to childhood vaccinations.

_____ 2. The goals of psychology are to explain, describe, predict, and control behavior.

_____ 3. The psychoanalytic approach to psychology is based on the belief that childhood experiences greatly influence the development of later personality traits and psychological problems.

_____ 4. Abraham Maslow wanted humanistic psychology to be a new way of perceiving and thinking about the individual's capacity, freedom, and potential for growth.

_____ 5. It is best to pick one of the general approaches to psychology and organize your thinking and work around it exclusively.

_____ 6. Wilhelm Wundt attempted to accurately measure the conscious elements of the mind with his method of introspection.

_____ 7. The Gestalt approach emphasized that perception is more than the sum of its parts and studied how sensations are assembled into meaningful perceptual experiences.

_____ 8. There has been discrimination against ethnic minorities in psychology, but at least women have always been equally represented.

_____ 9. There are only a few career choices in psychology — but whichever one you choose, you are almost certain to make big bucks!

_____ 10. There is no special program for overcoming procrastination: just get off your duff and get to work.

Flashcards 1

_____	1. autism	a. The systematic scientific study of behaviors and mental processes
_____	2. behavioral approach	b. rare problem with severe impairments in communication, motor systems, and socialization
_____	3. biological approach	c. studies the influence of cultural and ethnic similarities and differences on functioning
_____	4. cognitive approach	d. studies how ideas such as adaptation and natural selection explain human behaviors and mental processes
_____	5. cross-cultural approach	e. emphasizes individual freedom, capacity for personal growth, and potential for self-fulfillment
_____	6. eclectic approach	f. interested in how we process, store, and use information; how information influences us
_____	7. evolutionary approach	g. psychologists using different approaches to study the same behavior
_____	8. humanistic approach	h. focuses on influence of unconscious fears, desires, and motivations on thoughts, and behavior
_____	9. psychoanalytic approach	i. examines how genes, hormones, and the nervous system interact with environments
_____	10. psychology	j. analyzes how organisms learn new behaviors through reward, punishment from environment

Flashcards 2

_____	1. clinical psychologist	a. study of the most basic elements, primarily sensations and perceptions, that make up our conscious mental processes
_____	2. cognitive neuroscience	b. emphasized that perception is more than sum of its parts; how sensation becomes perception
_____	3. developmental psychology	c. has completed four to five years of postgraduate education; has obtained Ph.D. in psychology (or Ed.D. or PsyD.)
_____	4. experimental psychology	d. includes areas of sensation, perception, learning, human performance, motivation, and emotion
_____	5. functionalism	e. study of the function rather than the structure of consciousness; how mind adapts to changing environment
_____	6. Gestalt approach	f. taking pictures and identifying structures and functions of the living brain during performance of mental processes
_____	7. introspection	g. medical doctor (M.D.) with additional years of clinical training in diagnosis and treatment; can prescribe drugs
_____	8. psychiatrist	h. has Ph.D. plus specialization in clinical psychology and supervised work in therapy
_____	9. psychologist	i. method of exploring conscious mental processes by asking subjects to look inward and report sensations, perceptions
_____	10. structuralism	j. examines moral, social, emotional, and cognitive development throughout a person's entire life

Multiple Choice

_____ 1. Plotnik and Kouyoumdjian tell the story of Donna's struggle with autism in order to make the point that psychology is
   a. the one science that has all the answers
   b. a rather grim science that involves lots of pain and suffering
   c. helpless when confronted with really severe human problems
   d. dedicated to answering questions about complex behaviors

_____ 2. One thing that was different about Donna in school was that
   a. when she made a friend, she tried to avoid getting a friendly hug
   b. when the teacher asked a question, she always had her hand up first
   c. when a student seemed sad, she was sympathetic and understanding
   d. when the school day ended, she always found a friend to walk home with

_____ 3. A small percentage of autistics are called "savants" because they
   a. believe they have been "saved" by religion
   b. have incredible artistic or memory skills
   c. probably will have to work in low-paying jobs like being servants
   d. are extremely smooth-talking with other people

_____ 4. Which one of the following is *not* one of the four goals of psychology?
   a. explain the causes of behavior
   b. predict behavior
   c. judge behavior
   d. control behavior

_____ 5. The biological approach to psychology focuses on
   a. the workings of our genes, hormones, and nervous system
   b. conscious processes like perception and memory
   c. the effects of reward and punishment on behavior
   d. unconscious processes

_____ 6. One of the most powerful new techniques in the biological approach is
   a. testing how people process, store, and use information
   b. discovering how individuals learn new behaviors or modify existing ones
   c. taking computerized photos of the activity of living brains
   d. studying how the first five years affect later personality development

_____ 7. The cognitive approach to psychology studies how we
   a. are motivated by unconscious processes
   b. are motivated by the need for self-fulfillment
   c. process, store, and use information
   d. program our behavior by seeking rewards and avoiding punishments

_____ 8. The major contributor to the behavioral approach to psychology was
   a. Sigmund Freud
   b. B. F. Skinner
   c. William James
   d. Abraham Maslow

_____ 9. Some behaviorists, such as Albert Bandura, disagree with strict behaviorism because
a. there are mysteries in psychology we will never understand
b. animals pressing levers are not the same as real people dealing with life
c. our behaviors are also influenced by observation, imitation, and thought processes
d. most psychologists like to take a position different from everyone else

_____ 10. The great importance of the unconscious is stressed in the _________ approach
a. psychoanalytic
b. cognitive
c. behavioral
d. biological

_____ 11. The psychoanalytic approach to understanding procrastination as a component of test anxiety would
a. emphasize the role of habitual modes of thinking and problem solving
b. study brain scans of procrastinators while they think about schoolwork
c. compare school strategies used by students in different cultures
d. look beneath the obvious reasons and try to identify unconscious personality problems

_____ 12. __________ was one of the major figures of the humanistic approach to psychology
a. Sigmund Freud
b. Abraham Maslow
c. B. F. Skinner
d. Donna Williams

_____ 13. Followers of the __________ approach would be interested in Donna's striving to reach her potential, her achievements, and her creativity in the arts
a. humanistic
b. psychoanalytic
c. biological
d. cross-cultural

_____ 14. The _________ approach is a new trend in psychology that emphasizes the role of adaptation and natural selection in behavior
a. psychoanalytic
b. humanistic
c. cognitive
d. evolutionary

_____ 15. The cross-cultural approach to psychology studies the influence of _________ on psychological functioning
a. brain chemistry
b. information processing
c. cultural and ethnic similarities and differences
d. automatic behaviors and deeply ingrained habits

_____ 16. Psychologists who use the eclectic approach
a. decide which of the six major approaches is best and stick to that choice
b. combine and use information from all six approaches
c. rely on electric shock therapy
d. probably don't understand the differences between the six major approaches

_____ 17. The difference between "structuralism" and "functionalism" in the early years of psychology concerned a choice between
  a. British or American psychology
  b. Abraham Maslow or John B. Watson
  c. studying the brain or the cultural setting of behavior
  d. studying narrow sensations or general adaptations to our changing environment

_____ 18. The first textbook in psychology (1890) was written by
  a. William James
  b. John B. Watson
  c. Max Wertheimer
  d. Wilhelm Wundt

_____ 19. By explaining perceptual phenomena like the phi phenomenon [apparent motion], Gestalt researchers gave psychology the idea that
  a. the whole is more than the sum of its parts
  b. research results could be profitable when applied to advertising
  c. Wundt and the structuralists had been right about the importance of the individual parts
  d. individual parts are more significant than resulting wholes

_____ 20. The pioneering psychologist who offered the famous guarantee about being able to shape a baby into any type of specialist you might want was
  a. William James
  b. John B. Watson
  c. Max Wertheimer
  d. Wilhelm Wundt

_____ 21. The early behaviorist John B. Watson wanted psychology to be a/n
  a. introspective investigation of how people understood the workings of their minds
  b. objective, scientific study of observable behavior
  c. philosophical study of the continuous flow of mental activity
  d. religious program for "building" moral children

_____ 22. Despite an earlier history of discrimination, today women in psychology
  a. earn more money than men
  b. are still stuck in teaching jobs at women's colleges
  c. are still barred from the elite university training programs
  d. earn more Ph.D. degrees than men

_____ 23. As measured by membership in the American Psychological Association, the numbers of ethnic minorities in psychology
  a. are still low compared to other Americans
  b. are about the same as their proportion of the general population
  c. will soon exceed white Americans
  d. may have lagged earlier, but have now almost caught up

_____ 24. After reading the material on careers and research areas, it would be reasonable to conclude that psychology
  a. requires so much education that few students should consider it
  b. will have fewer job opportunities in coming years
  c. offers a great variety of intellectual challenges and kinds of work
  d. is one of the best-paid professions today

_____ 25. Which one of the following is *not* a good strategy for overcoming procrastination?
a. stop thinking or worrying about the final goal
b. break the final assignment down into a number of smaller goals
c. write down a realistic schedule for reaching each of your smaller goals
d. only begin working when you are completely confident that you will succeed

Short Essay

All Short Essay questions are designed for answers of about 75 words.

1. Of the six approaches to understanding behavior, perhaps the *biological* and *cross-cultural* differ the most from each other. Explain, describing the key ideas and focus of study of each approach.
2. What point was John B. Watson making when he claimed that he could make a child into any kind of specialist if he could control the child's environment?
3. Summarize the history of discrimination against women and minorities in psychology.
4. How do the training and responsibilities of psychologists and psychiatrists differ?
5. What advice does psychology have to offer a student suffering from procrastination?

For Psych Majors Only…

Contributors to Psychology: A matching exercise based on important people in psychology.

_____	1. Albert Bandura	a. humanistic psychology movement
_____	2. Mary Calkins	b. authors of your psychology textbook
_____	3. Inez Prosser	c. denied a doctorate in psychology by Harvard
_____	4. William James	d. social learning theory
_____	5. Abraham Maslow	e. founded Gestalt psychology movement
_____	6. Rod Plotnik & Haig Kouyoumdjian	f. strict behaviorism
_____	7. B. F. Skinner	g. studied function of conscious activity
_____	8. John B. Watson	h. first laboratory for psychological research
_____	9. Max Wertheimer, Wolfgang Kohler, and Kurt Koffka	i. "Give me a dozen healthy infants… and my own special world to bring them up in…"
_____	10. Willhelm Wundt	j. First African American woman Ph.D. in psych

Answers to "Contributors to Psychology" quiz

1 d 2 c 3 j 4 g 5 a 6 b 7 f 8 i 9 e 10 h

Answers for Module 1

The Big Picture (explanations provided for incorrect choices)

A Neither medical school nor post-doctoral training is necessary for a career in psychology.
B *Correct! You see the "big picture" for this Module.*
C Science does not demand a single approach; there is controversy in all scientific fields.
D Just the opposite is true (Freud's theory is in decline today).
E It's just a joke!

True-False (explanations provided for False choices; page numbers given for all choices)

1	F	3	Childhood vaccinations have not been proven to be a cause of autism.
2	T	3	
3	T	9	
4	T	10	
5	F	11	Each of the six approaches can be a valuable source of information.
6	T	12	
7	T	13	
8	F	14	There has been discrimination against women as well as minority groups.
9	F	17	Psychology is a varied field with many career choices, but no guarantee of making "big bucks".
10	F	21	There are three specific steps you can take to overcome procrastination.

Flashcards 1

1 b 2 j 3 i 4 f 5 c 6 g 7 d 8 e 9 h 10 a

Flashcards 2

1 h 2 f 3 j 4 d 5 e 6 b 7 i 8 g 9 c 10 a

Multiple Choice (explanations provided for incorrect choices)

1 a Psychology does not claim to have all the answers.
b Psychology studies all human behavior, not just painful events.
c Like other sciences, psychology *in theory* can answer any question stated in operational terms.
d *Correct! See page 3.*

2 ***a*** *Correct! See page 3.*
b Autistics do not easily engage in social activities.
c Empathy does not come easily to autistics.
d Autistics would tend to avoid social situations.

3 a "Savant" refers to knowledge, not religion.
b *Correct! See page 3.*
c "Savant" refers to knowledge, not service.
d This would not fit the typical autistic.

4 a Understanding and explaining behavior is one of the four goals of psychology.
b Predicting behavior is one of the four goals of psychology.
c *Correct! See page 4.*
d Controlling behavior is one of the four goals of psychology.

5 ***a*** *Correct! See page 6.*
b This would be true for the cognitive approach.
c This would be true for the behavioral approach.
d This would be true for the psychoanalytic approach.

6 a This would be true for the cognitive approach.
b This would be true for the behavioral approach.
c *Correct! See page 6.*
d This would be true for the psychoanalytic approach.

7 a The psychoanalytic approach studies unconscious processes.
b The humanistic approach studies the need for self-fulfillment.
c *Correct! See page 7.*
d The behavioral approach studies reward and punishment.

8 a Sigmund Freud was the major contributor to the psychoanalytic approach.
b *Correct! See page 8.*
c William James was a major contributor to the cognitive approach.
d Abraham Maslow was a major contributor to the humanistic approach.

9 a Most scientists would not rule out any aspect of human behavior from eventual explanation.
b Behaviorists believe animals and humans follow the same basic laws of behavior.
c *Correct! See page 8.*
d For any good scientist, finding the truth is more important than individual fame.

10 ***a*** *Correct! See page 9.*
b The cognitive approach stresses conscious mental activity.
c The behavioral approach stresses learning through reinforcement.
d The biological approach stresses brain functioning and heredity.

11 a This would be truer of the behavioral approach.
b This would be truer of the biological approach.
c This would be truer of the cross-cultural approach.
d *Correct! See page 9.*

12 a Sigmund Freud was a major figure in the psychoanalytic approach.
b *Correct! See page 10.*
c B. F. Skinner was a major figure in the behavioral approach.
d Donna Williams is the autistic woman described in the textbook.

13 ***a*** *Correct! See page 10.*
b The psychoanalytic approach would be more interested in her inner life
c The biolgical approach would be more interested in her genetic and medical history
d The cross-cultural approach would be more interested in her social and cultural environment

14 a The psychoanalytic approach is a century old.
b The humanistic approach dates to the 1960s.
c The cognitive approach dates to the 1970s.
d *Correct! See page 10.*

15 a Brain anatomy and chemistry are studied by the biological approach.
b Information processing and thinking are studied by the cognitive approach.
c *Correct! See page 11.*
d Automatic behaviors and deeply ingrained habits are studied by the behavioral approach.

16 a Just the opposite is true.
b *Correct! See page 11.*
c That's "eclectic," not "electric!" Look it up.
d They know exactly what they are doing.

17 a The debate was not about national rivalry for leadership.
b Neither Maslow nor Watson was involved in the earlier debate between structuralism and functionalism.
c The debate was over specific or general mental activity, not brain or culture.
d *Correct! See page 12.*

18 ***a*** *Correct! See page 12.*
b Watson was the first behavioral psychologist.
c Wertheimer argued that the whole is more than the sum of its parts.
d Wundt established the first laboratory in psychology.

19 ***a*** *Correct! See page 13.*
b The Gestalt psychologists were motivated by science, not profit (too bad for them!).
c Just the opposite is true.
d Just the opposite is true.

20 a James wrote the famous *Principles of Psychology*.
b *Correct! See page 13.*
c Wertheimer was a pioneer of Gestalt, not behaviorist, psychology.
d Wundt established the first laboratory in psychology.

21 a Watson argued against introspection and in favor of an objective psychology.
b *Correct! See page 13.*
c This would be true for William James and cognitive psychology.
d This is a misreading of Watson's famous statement about shaping behavior.

22 a Women in psychology do not earn more than men.
b That was true earlier, but not now.
c That was true earlier, but not now.
d *Correct! See page 14.*

23 ***a*** *Correct! See page 14.*
b That is the goal, but psychology is still far from it.
c A wild exaggeration.
d That should be happening, but is not yet.

24 a Most desirable professions today require significant investment in education.
b Job opportunities in fields related to psychology are increasing.
c *Correct! See page 19.*
d Only a few specialties in psychology are especially well paid.

25 a Focusing on more immediate goals is a good way to overcome procrastination.
b Breaking the task down into smaller goals is a good way to overcome procrastination.
c Making a realistic schedule for reaching goals is a good way to overcome procrastination.
d *Correct! See page 21.*

Short Essay (sample answers)

1. The biological and cross-cultural approaches to understanding behavior differ more than any other pair. The biological approach is based on physical characteristics like genes, hormones, and the nervous system. The cross-cultural approach, in contrast, is based on cultural and ethnic similarities and differences on psychological and social functioning. The differences between the two approaches involve biology versus sociology, brain functions versus human interaction, and a focus on individuals versus a focus on groups.

2. Watson meant that the environment a person grows up in is more important than his or her inborn characteristics. He imagined that if he could control a child's environment he could shape that child into almost any kind of adult one might specify. Watson wanted psychology to be an objective, scientific analysis of observable behaviors. He believed that this approach, and only this approach, would provide the ability to predict and control behavior.

3. Psychology, as the scientific study of human behavior, should have rejected prejudice and discrimination from the beginning. But psychologists are also members of their culture, and they have reflected the prejudices and discriminatory practices of American society. Women and members of minority groups suffered the same discrimination in psychology as in the wider society. Today, psychology is trying hard to overcome this heritage, but women and minorities still lag significantly behind white males in the field.

4. Both psychologists and psychiatrists help people with mental health problems, although they differ in training and special focus. Psychologists usually have a Ph.D. in psychology, while psychiatrists have an M.D. and clinical training in psychiatry. Psychologists generally offer counseling and insight therapy, sometimes called "talk therapy," while psychiatrists consider physical and neurological causes of abnormal behavior and may prescribe drug therapy in addition to counseling.

5. Instead of panicking and freezing up, as overburdened students often do, psychology applies scientific analysis and an objective approach to the problem of procrastination. Three steps can help: (1) stop focusing on the final goal, (2) break the assignment down into smaller, easier to accomplish steps, and (3) write down a realistic schedule for reaching each of the smaller goals. Finally, use self-reinforcements or rewards to keep on schedule and accomplish the specific goals.

Module 2

Psychology & Science

Science and the Scientific Method

When we think of science, we imagine a person in a white lab coat working some kind of magic we can't understand. But that's not science. Science is a method of asking and answering questions about nature, including human nature. Science is only one of many ways of solving problems by answering questions through the analysis of gathered information. There are older and more widely used methods, such as reliance on tradition, custom, or authority. For much of our work, however, science is the most powerful intellectual tool yet invented.

Science offers a methodical procedure for the analysis of objective events. It is not simply the discoveries scientists make, or the techniques they use, or the beliefs that many scientists may hold. Instead, science is a way of approaching the task of gathering information and creating knowledge. It is a *method* of analysis.

Rules of Procedure and Basic Assumptions about Reality

Science consists of two related features: (1) a set of characteristics or rules of procedure, and (2) a set of basic assumptions about reality. The first feature constitutes the rules of the game that scientists follow in the laboratory. These rules require objectivity, freedom from bias, objective data collection, public procedures, precise definitions, careful measurements, logical reasoning, rigorous control of variables, systematic examination of relationships, and self-criticism. Through replication, scientists aim to create theories that allow prediction and control.

The second feature constitutes the starting point of science, what all scientists agree on about how nature works. These assumptions are that all events are naturally determined, that nature is orderly and regular, that truth is relative, and that knowledge is gained through empiricism, rationalism, and replication. Of course these basic assumptions about reality are assumptions rather than proven facts. Consequently, it is not necessary to believe that these assumptions are universally 'true' in order to use the scientific method.

Together these two features of the scientific method also serve as a checklist for the researcher. Any violation of or deviation from the rules of procedure or the basic assumptions about reality puts an investigation outside the realm of science and renders its results untrustworthy.

I hope you will write to me — not only about possible errors you found — but also about anything in my Study Guide you would like to discuss. <profenos@mac.com>

Effective Student Tip 2

Attend Every Class

I shudder when I hear about college teachers who advise, “Come to class if it helps, but attendance isn’t required.” That’s such poor psychology and such destructive advice. Students should attend *every* class, even the dull ones, because regular attendance leads directly to involvement and commitment, the basic ingredients of effective college work.

We aren’t talking morals here, we’re talking the psychology of effectiveness. Here’s why attendance is the basis of successful college work: (1) Good attendance makes you feel more confident, purposeful, and in control. (2) Attendance is the one feature of college that is completely under your control. (3) The reason for an absence usually reveals some area in which you feel ineffective. (4) Whether they make a big deal of it or not, your professors want and need your good attendance. What if no one came? (5) There is more to a class than the lecture. Other good things happen when you attend class regularly. Your professor gets to know you. You become better acquainted with your classmates. You learn from them and you learn by helping them. (6) Most students can achieve perfect attendance if they try, and their professors will admire them for it. You can help make a good class a great one.

Your response…

What is your attendance history? Do you have an attendance goal for this class?

Learning Objectives

1. Understand psychology as the scientific pursuit of knowledge about human behavior.

2. Know the main strengths and weaknesses of each of the three main methods of scientific research — the survey, the case study, and the experiment — and when each should be used.

3. Appreciate the concepts of bias, error, testimonials, correlation, and causation and explain why it is so important for educated people to understand them.

4. Apply the concept of a placebo to both research method and everyday human behavior.

5. Explain the logic of the scientific experiment, the seven rules it requires, and why only an experiment can reveal causation.

6. Appreciate how scientific research is attempting to resolve important controversies over ADHD.

7. Be aware of the controversies about science in psychology: the ethics of research, the role of deception, and problems with using both human and animal subjects.

Key Terms

The vocabulary of science has become essential for any educated person. How many of these key terms did you know something about already, even before you read the textbook?

---

animal model
attention-deficit/hyper-activity disorder (ADHD)
case study
control group
correlation
correlation coefficient
debriefing
dependent variable
double-blind procedure
experiment
experimental group
hypothesis
independent variable
interview
laboratory experiment
laboratory setting
naturalistic setting
placebo
placebo effect
questionnaire
random selection
scientific method
self-fulfilling prophecy
standardized test
statistical procedures
survey
testimonial

The "PowerStudy 4.5 for Introduction to Psychology" CD-ROM for this module is a "Super Module." In addition to the regular PowerStudy features (quizzes, summary test, key terms, web site connections, critical thinking exercise, module outline, and more), Super Modules also include self-paced, step-by-step multimedia presentations with animations and narration.

Outline

- *Introduction*

  1. **Attention-deficit/hyperactivity disorder (ADHD)** (Blake Taylor)
  2. Belief in centipedes and cough medicine

A. Answering Questions

1. Why the controversies about ADHD?
2. Three research methods
   a. **Survey**
   b. **Case study**
   c. **Experiment**

B. Surveys

1. Kind of information: examples of surveys
2. Disadvantages
   a. How questions are worded
   b. Who asks the questions
3. Advantages

☐ What are the main advantages and disadvantages of the survey method?

C. Case Study

1. Kind of information in a **case study**
2. Personal case study: **testimonial**

☐ What are the main advantages and disadvantages of a testimonial?

3. Error and bias in testimonials
   a. Personal beliefs
   b. **Self-fulfilling prophecy**

D. Cultural Diversity: Use of Placebos

1. Examples of mind over body
   a. **Placebo**
   b. **Placebo effect**
2. Common worldwide placebos
   a. Rhino horn
   b. Centipedes
   c. Tiger bones
   d. Cough medication

☐ What beliefs and practices in the United States might be thought of as our own "rhino horn"?

3. Conclusion: testimonials and placebos

E. Correlation

1. Definition
    a. **Correlation**
    b. **Correlation coefficient**
2. Correlation coefficients
    a. Perfect positive correlation coefficient (+1.00)
    b. Positive correlation coefficient (+0.01 to +0.99)
    c. Zero correlation (0.00)
    d. Negative correlation coefficient (-0.01 to -0.99)
    e. Perfect negative correlation coefficient (-1.00)
3. Correlation versus causation
4. Correlations as clues
5. Correlation and predictions

F. Decisions about Doing Research

1. Choosing research techniques
    a. **Questionnaires** and **interviews**
    b. **Standardized test**
    c. **Laboratory experiment**
    d. **Animal model**
2. Choosing research settings

☐ What are the main advantages and disadvantages of each setting?

   a. **Naturalistic setting** (case study)
   b. **Laboratory setting**

G. Scientific Method: Experiment

1. Advantages of scientific method
    a. **Scientific method**
    b. **Experiment**
2. Conducting an experiment: seven rules
    a. Rule 1: Ask (**hypothesis**)
    b. Rule 2: Identify variables
        (1) **Independent variable** (treatment)
        (2) **Dependent variable** (resulting behavior)
    c. Rule 3: Choose subjects (**random selection**)
    d. Rule 4: Assign subjects randomly
        (1) **Experimental group**
        (2) **Control group**

☐ Why is a control group needed in a scientific experiment?

e. Rule 5: Manipulate independent variable

(1) Administer treatment

(2) **Double-blind procedure**

☐ What makes the double-blind procedure superior to the typical experiment?

f. Rule 6: Measure resulting behavior (dependent variable)

g. Rule 7: Analyze data

(1) Sample

(2) **Statistical procedures** (see Appendix in textbook)

H. Research Focus: ADHD Controversies

☐ Do you know a hyperactive child? What is he or she like?

1. Controversy: diagnosis
2. Controversy: treatment
   a. Non-drug, behavioral treatment
   b. Combined drug and behavioral treatment
3. Controversy: long-term effects

☐ Do you have an opinion concerning the controversies surrounding ADHD?

I. Application: Research Concerns

1. Concerns about being a subject

☐ Would you volunteer to be a subject in a psychological experiment?

2. Code of ethics
   a. American Psychological Association ethical guidelines
   b. **Debriefing**
3. Role of deception
4. Ethics of animal research

☐ Do you believe that animals should be used in research?

a. How many animals are used in research?

b. Are research animals mistreated?

c. Is the use of animals justified?

d. Who checks on the use of animals in research?

e. How do we strike a balance?

How English Works

Words in the Textbook

p. 27 describes him as "off the wall" = not normal, too active

such as **fidgeting** = nervous moving

maladaptive development = growing in the wrong direction

children who are **rambunctious** = lively, full of energy

p. 28 a family **copes with** a child = manages problems of

my sons ate green **frosting** = sweet covering for cake

p. 30 observer has **preconceived notions** = ideas about something before it happens

p. 31 **poachers** had reduced the number of rhinos = illegal hunters

increase **flagging** libidos = decreasing, tired

increase flagging **libidos** *[lih-BEE-dohz]* = sexual drive or energy

p. 35 children **throw tantrums** = same as **throwing a fit** (see above)

p. 36 information can suggest but not **pinpoint** = identify precisely

p. 40 no **lingering** psychological worries = continuing

p. 41 may have seen a **disturbing** photo = makes you feel uncomfortable

isolated cases of **malpractice** = done in an unprofessional manner

I go through a **soul-searching** = thinking deeply about your values and beliefs

especially true **in light of** recent rules = considering

ESL Tip: Clauses / Adjective Clauses

First a brief grammar review. Words are grouped in ways that make sense and have a meaning. If a group of words contains a subject and a complete verb (not just a participle or –ing word, e.g., walk**ing**), it's called a **clause**. If the words in the group belong together but do not contain both a subject and complete verb, they form a **phrase**.

In the following example, the first four words make up a clause and the last three are a phrase:

I wear a hat / on my head

Also note that a clause can stand by itself as a complete sentence (I wear a hat) or as a clause that depends on another clause to make complete, grammatical sense (when it rains). The words "I wear a hat" make up an **independent clause**, and the words "when it rains" make up a **dependent** (or **subordinate**) clause.

Look at these examples: This is the football. It is ragged (two sentences, also two independent clauses). This is the ragged football (one sentence/clause). This is the football that the dog chewed (one sentence, two clauses. The second clause acts like an adjective and describes the football. It is called an **adjective clause**.)

These examples are fairly simple. However, if an adjective clause is put in the wrong place, a sentence can be easily ruined. For example: This football belongs to my daughter that the dog chewed. (Poor construction; who/what did the dog chew?) This football, which the dog chewed, belongs to my daughter. (Much better)

As you can probably tell, it's important to put the adjective clause directly after the word or words it describes.

Now take a look at this one. ESL students may have trouble with adjective clauses like the following: This is the restaurant. I told you about it. (two sentences) This is the restaurant that I told you about it. (One sentence/two clauses; the second one is an adjective clause describing the restaurant, but note carefully that the word **it** should be omitted.)

The sentence should read like this: This is the restaurant that I told you about. Not: This is the restaurant that I told you about **it**.

Vocabulary: "Affect" and "Effect"

Affect? Effect? Native speakers of English often confuse these words. **Affect** means to change or influence. (Heat and cold **affect** water in different ways.) **Effect** means a result or to cause something. (Steam is one **effect** of heating water.) Remember that only **effect** is used as a noun.

A bad grade can **affect** a student in different ways.

If the teacher can **effect** a change in Syed's attitude, he may do better.

Hard work will have a positive **effect** on his grade.

Each student's own personality will **affect** his or her own reaction.

Other variables, such as family problems, money problems, and physical health, can also __________ the student's response.

Parents worry about the __________ of violent movies on young children.

Drinking coffee can __________ both mind and body. Increased energy is one good __________, but trouble going to sleep is a bad __________.

Tip: Try substituting with the word "change." If it sounds correct, then use **affect**.

Test Yourself

Read the following passage and choose the <u>three</u> best words to fill the blanks.

affect / effect / bias / biased

Why did the dinosaurs disappear? One hypothesis is that a giant meteor hit the Earth. What sort of __________ would such an event have on animal life? Certainly the disaster would __________ the weather and the food sources for all animals, possibly leading to widespread death. Of course, these critics want to push their own theories, so their arguments could be __________.

Answers

Other variables, such as family problems, money problems, and physical health, can also **<u>affect</u>** the student's response.

Parents worry about the **<u>effect</u>** of violent movies on young children.

Drinking coffee can **<u>affect</u>** both mind and body. Increased energy is one good **<u>effect</u>**, but trouble going to sleep is a bad **<u>effect</u>**.

Why did the dinosaurs disappear? One hypothesis is that a giant meteor hit the Earth. What sort of **<u>effect</u>** would such an event have on animal life? Certainly the disaster would **<u>affect</u>** the weather and the food sources for all animals, possibly leading to widespread death. Of course, these critics want to push their own theories, so their arguments could be **<u>biased</u>**.

The Big Picture

Which statement below offers the best summary of the larger significance of this module?

A The essence of scientific research in psychology necessarily is deception. Therefore, it probably would be wise not to volunteer to be a subject in a psychological experiment.

B Psychology, because it sometimes uses the case study method and the survey method, is only partly a science. To be a true science, psychology would have to rely on the laboratory experiment alone.

C When psychology at last becomes completely scientific, it will be able to answer any question we might have about the truth of our beliefs, the rightness of our behaviors, and the meanings of our lives.

D Psychology uses several different research strategies and techniques. What makes psychology scientific, however, is that all of them have in common a devotion to *objectivity* (knowledge sought through the five senses).

E On the other hand, some people would argue that it only takes one psychologist to change a light bulb — if the light bulb *really wants to change*.

True-False

_____ 1. Plotnik and Kouyoumdjian's definition of psychology (in Module 1) as the "scientific study of behaviors and mental processes" means that psychology is strongly linked to the power of the scientific method.

_____ 2. The research technique with the *lowest* potential for error and bias is the survey method.

_____ 3. The main disadvantage of gathering information through surveys is that it takes so long and is so hard to do.

_____ 4. Testimonials have a high potential for error and bias.

_____ 5. If it turns out that there is a *negative* correlation between studying the textbook and getting good grades, you just wasted a big chunk of money.

_____ 6. If you can establish a significant correlation between two variables, you have also determined the causal relationship between them.

_____ 7. Research in naturalistic settings has greater reality, but research in the laboratory has greater control.

_____ 8. What the experimenter manipulates is called the dependent variable; how the subjects react is called the independent variable.

_____ 9. Random selection is crucial in choosing subjects because you want them to accurately represent the larger population you are studying.

_____ 10. There is no way to justify doing research using animals.

Flashcards 1

____	1. case study	a.	method for identifying cause-and-effect relationships by following a set of rules that minimize error, bias, chance
____	2. control group	b.	composed of subjects who receive the experimental treatment
____	3. correlation	c.	composed of subjects who undergo all the same procedures but who do not receive the treatment
____	4. dependent variable	d.	an in-depth analysis of the thoughts, feelings, beliefs, experiences, behaviors, or problems of a single person
____	5. experiment	e.	used to determine whether differences in dependent variables are due to independent variables or error, chance
____	6. experimental group	f.	a treatment or something that the researcher controls or manipulates
____	7. independent variable	g.	one or more of the subjects' behaviors that are used to measure the potential effects of the treatment
____	8. random selection	h.	a way to obtain information by asking many individuals to answer a fixed set of questions
____	9. statistical procedures	i.	each subject in a sample population has an equal chance of being selected to participate in the experiment
____	10. survey	j.	an association or relationship between the occurrence of two or more events

Flashcards 2

____	1. correlation coefficient	a.	a relatively normal environment in which researchers observe behavior but don't change or control it
____	2. debriefing	b.	neither the subjects nor the researchers know which group is receiving which treatment
____	3. double-blind procedure	c.	some intervention (pill, injection) that resembles medical therapy but has no actual medical effects
____	4. hypothesis	d.	a statement in support of a particular viewpoint based on observations of our personal experiences
____	5. laboratory setting	e.	studying individuals under systematic and controlled conditions, with real-world influences eliminated
____	6. naturalistic setting	f.	a technique for obtaining information by asking subjects to check answers on a list of questions
____	7. placebo	g.	having a strong belief or making a statement about a future behavior, then acting to carry out the behavior
____	8. questionnaire	h.	explaining the purpose and method of the experiment to subjects, helping them deal with doubts or guilt
____	9. self-fulfilling prophecy	i.	an educated guess about some phenomenon stated in precise, concrete language to rule out confusion
____	10. testimonial	j.	a number that indicates the strength of a relationship between two or more events

Multiple Choice

_____ 1. Plotnik and Kouyoumdjian begin this module with the example of Blake Taylor, a hyperactive seven-year-old, to show that
   a. often psychology must yield to medical science
   b. psychology needs accurate answers to highly complex problems
   c. science must recognize the problems for which it cannot find answers
   d. hyperactivity can be controlled by high doses of vitamin C

_____ 2. Like many other hyperactive children, Blake is treated with a drug called
   a. ADHD
   b. Calmatin
   c. Ritalin
   d. Stimulantin

_____ 3. About 4 to 12 percent of children in the United States are diagnosed with ADHD; we know this and other information about ADHD from
   a. survey research
   b. blood tests required for admission to school
   c. articles and books written by veteran teachers
   d. laboratory experiments on schoolchildren

_____ 4. Among the disadvantages of the survey method is that
   a. many people won't go to the trouble of filling out the survey
   b. responses can be affected by how the questions are worded and who asks them
   c. it is difficult to survey enough subjects to make the results valid
   d. it takes so long to conduct a survey that the method is impractical for most purposes

_____ 5. When you encounter a testimonial, you know that it is
   a. true, if enough other people also report it
   b. false, because it is only a personal belief
   c. true, if the person conveying it has a good reputation for honesty
   d. possibly true, but not proven by science

_____ 6. According to the __________, if we strongly believe that something is going to happen, we may unknowingly behave in such a way as to make it happen
   a. wish-fulfillment theory
   b. testimonial effect
   c. personal-belief problem
   d. self-fulfilling prophecy

_____ 7. A good example of a self-fulfilling prophecy is the belief that
   a. there's no use studying for multiple-choice exams because the questions are tricky
   b. psychology requires more study than literature
   c. if you do all your studying the night before the exam you'll do better
   d. you don't have to take notes in class if you listen carefully

_____ 8. Can a placebo administered in an experiment really cause change in a subject?
   a. no, because chemically the placebo is only a harmless sugar pill
   b. no, because subjects are aware that some of them are receiving placebos
   c. yes, because a few particles of the real drug often get on the placebo
   d. yes, but only if the subject believes a drug has been administered

_____ 9. A "correlation" is defined as
a. an association or relationship between the occurrence of two or more events
b. the connection between a cause and an effect
c. the association of family members into the extended family
d. an occurrence that can only be explained as random

_____ 10. You probably hope the correlation coefficient between using this Study Guide and getting an A in the course is
a. +1.00
b. -1.00
c. 0.00
d. +0.00

_____ 11. When she wears her lucky socks, Gail wins three golf matches out of four, a __________ correlation between wearing the socks and winning
a. perfect negative
b. negative
c. positive
d. perfect positive

_____ 12. Does this prove that the socks are the cause of Gail's winning?
a. yes, because it cannot be just coincidence
b. no, because correlation is not causation
c. it would if she won *every* time she wore the socks
d. by themselves, the socks Gail wears cannot affect the outcome of her matches

_____ 13. Whether to do research in a naturalistic or laboratory setting involves the issue of
a. comprehensiveness versus cost
b. testimonial versus science
c. realism versus control
d. objectivity versus subjectivity

_____ 14. Which one of the following research strategies has the *lowest* potential for error or bias?
a. case study
b. survey
c. experiment
d. testimonial

_____ 15. The scientific method is defined as
a. an approach to answering questions that minimizes errors and bias
b. a faith that precise equipment will produce accurate information
c. all of the findings of science in the modern era
d. a set of guidelines published by the American Academy of Science

_____ 16. The special treatment given to the subjects in the experimental group is called the
a. hypothesis
b. independent variable
c. dependent variable
d. control variable

_____ 17. The reason why researchers choose their subjects by random selection is that
a. in random selection, there is a positive correlation between subjects
b. it is a tradition that goes back to the days of Wilhelm Wundt's psychology lab
c. this method guarantees that the more motivated subjects will be selected
d. only this method guarantees an equal chance of being selected for the experiment

_____ 18. Which one of the following is an example of random selection?
a. winning numbers in the lottery
b. National Football League player draft
c. numbers people play in the lottery
d. Miss America contest

_____ 19. The purpose of having a control group in an experiment is to
a. show what results the opposite treatment would produce
b. show how a different group would react to the treatment
c. identify and rule out the behavior that results from simply participating in the experiment
d. provide backup subjects in case any members of the experimental group drop out

_____ 20. A double-blind procedure means that
a. the subjects are not informed that they are participating in an experiment
b. the subjects are not allowed to interact with each other
c. neither participants nor researchers know which group is receiving which treatment
d. neither drug companies nor doctors know that research is going on

_____ 21. One of the main controversies about ADHD is
a. how to find the precise dosage of Ritalin that works best
b. whether behavioral treatment or drug treatment is most effective
c. why girls are more likely than boys to exhibit ADHD
d. whether it is worse at school or in the home

_____ 22. Should you volunteer to be a subject in a psychological experiment?
a. no, because you are completely at the mercy of the researcher
b. yes, because ethical guidelines protect subjects from danger or undue deception
c. no, because they'll never tell you what the experiment was really about
d. yes, because occasionally looking dumb or foolish makes us more humble

_____ 23. We know that Dr. Frankenstein's ghoulish research did not have American Psychological Association approval, because he
a. did not submit a proposal for it to a university or federal research committee
b. was only interested in building a body, not a brain
c. did not plan what would happen to the monster after he threw the switch
d. was stopped by an angry mob of torch-carrying psychologists

_____ 24. The basic justification for using animals in biomedical research is that
a. it has not been proven that animals are harmed in research
b. animals do not feel pain and suffering like humans do
c. most religions place humans above animals in importance
d. the potential human benefits outweigh the harm done to the animal subjects

_____ 25. The attitude of most psychologists toward the use of animals in research is that
a. scientists must have complete freedom to conduct research however they see fit
b. ethical concerns are involved in research on humans but not on animals
c. animals have no rights
d. the issue is complicated and calls for a balance between animal rights and research needs

Short Essay

1. What is attention-deficit/hyperactivity disorder (ADHD) and why is it controversial?

2. Describe the placebo effect and give examples of its power in everyday life.

3. Why is public confusion about correlation and causation a problem?

4. Why is the experiment the most powerful method for identifying cause-and-effect relationships?

5. Explain your own position on the controversy over animal research.

Wanted!

(As I wrote in the "Introduction" to this Study Guide...)

On the first day of class, I pass out a corny "Wanted" poster urging my students to look for any errors I make in writing (factual, spelling, grammar, formatting). I offer a payoff to students who find an error.

Some students enjoy this challenge, and I thought you might, too. *Can you find any mistakes in this Study Guide?* I can't ask your instructor to pay off (it's my mistake, after all), but I will send you an e-mail you can show your teacher. Might make a good impression!

Please e-mail me if you find a mistake — any mistake, no matter how small! Write to me at <**profenos@mac.com**>.

Answers for Module 2

The Big Picture (explanations provided for incorrect choices)

A Scientific research in psychology is governed by rules of ethics designed to protect subjects.
B Both the case study method and the survey method can be scientific.
C Science can only answer questions that can be stated in operational terms, not beliefs.
D Correct! You see the "big picture" for this Module.
E It's just a joke!

True-False (explanations provided for False choices; page numbers given for all choices)

1	T	28	
2	F	28	The controlled laboratory experiment has the lowest potential for error and bias.
3	F	29	Surveys based on random sampling and objective methods are scientific.
4	T	30	
5	T	32	
6	F	33	The fact that two variables are related does not mean that one causes the other.
7	T	35	
8	F	36	Just the opposite is true.
9	T	36	
10	F	41	There are good arguments both for and against using animals in research.

Flashcards 1

1 d 2 c 3 j 4 g 5 a 6 b 7 f 8 i 9 e 10 h

Flashcards 2

1 j 2 h 3 b 4 i 5 e 6 a 7 c 8 f 9 g 10 d

Multiple Choice (explanations provided for incorrect choices)

1 a Plotnik and Kouyoumdjian do not make this point.
b Correct! See page 27.
c Science is an appropriate strategy for any problem that can be stated in objective terms.
d This is not one of the proposed treatments of hyperactivity.

2 a This is the name of the disorder, not the drug.
b There is no drug by this name.
c Correct! See page 27.
d There is no drug by this name.

3 *a Correct! See page 29.*
b There is no blood test for ADHD.
c Such individual writings could not reveal current and precise statistical data.
d How would a laboratory experiment reveal overall statistical data?

4 a Enough subjects complete surveys to make the results useful.
b Correct! See page 29.
c An advantage of the survey method is that it can be given to a large number of subjects.
d An advantage of the survey method is that it is quick.

5 a Testimonials are individual statements, not demonstrated facts.
b Testimonials, while not scientifically demonstrated facts, may be true.
c Testimonials are individual statements, not demonstrated facts.
d Correct! See page 30.

6 a This theory belongs to the psychoanalytic approach.
b This is a fictitious term.
c This is a fictitious term.
d Correct! See page 30.

7 ***a*** *Correct! See page 30.*
b Ask yourself, "Does believing this cause it to come true?"
c Ask yourself, "Does believing this cause it to come true?" (Actually, just the opposite).
d Ask yourself, "Does believing this cause it to come true?" (Actually, just the opposite).

8 a The point is that change results from beliefs, not chemical elements.
b How would this prevent change?
c Not true.
d *Correct! See page 31.*

9 ***a*** *Correct! See page 32.*
b Correlation different from causation.
c Correlation is a statistical, not a sociological, term.
d Just the opposite is true.

10 ***a*** *Correct! See page 32.*
b That would mean the more you use the Study Guide the worse your grade (I hope not!).
c That would mean using the Study Guide has no effect on your grade.
d Zero correlation is expressed as 0.00 (+0.00 is meaningless).

11 a A perfect negative correlation would be losing every time she wears the socks.
b A negative correlation would be losing most of the times she wears the socks.
c *Correct! See page 32.*
d A perfect positive correlation would be winning every time she wears the socks.

12 a Remember… *correlation is not causation!*
b *Correct! See page 33.*
c Remember… *correlation is not causation!*
d There might be a slight chance it could affect her state of mind, but remember… *correlation is not causation!*

13 a Either setting could be comprehensive or not, costly or not.
b Neither setting would rely on testimonials.
c *Correct! See page 35.*
d Scientists would strive for objectivity in either setting.

14 a The case study, with few controls, has high potential for error and bias.
b The survey has some controls, but also some potential for error and bias.
c *Correct! See page 36.*
d The testimonial is not a scientific research strategy.

15 ***a*** *Correct! See page 36.*
b Faith is not a value in science.
c Do not confuse the method of science with the discoveries of science.
d The scientific method is much more than a set of guidelines.

16 a The hypothesis is the presumed cause-and-effect relationship under investigation.
b *Correct! See page 36.*
c The dependent variable is how the subjects in the experiment respond.
d Control refers to elements in an experiment that are held constant.

17 a Just the opposite is true.
b Wundt pioneered the laboratory experiment, not the survey.
c Just the opposite is true.
d *Correct! See page 36.*

18 ***a*** *Correct! See page 36.*
b The NFL draft deliberately selects highly rated players, not all players.
c Lottery numbers that people play are affected by many non-random factors.
d Miss America isn't just any woman, but the most beautiful and talented woman in the country (right?).

19 a The control group does not get any special experimental treatment.
b The control group does not get the special experimental treatment.
c *Correct! See page 37.*
d Members of the control group stay in the control group.

20 a All subjects must give informed consent to participate in research.
b Even if true in a given case, this is not what is "blind" in the experiment.
c *Correct! See page 37.*
d The two parties that are "blind" are the researchers and the participants.

21 a The dosage itself is not controversial.
b *Correct! See page 39.*
c Just the opposite is true.
d The setting of the problem is not the basis of the controversy.

22 a Not true — there are ethical constraints on researchers and you always retain your freedom.
b *Correct! See page 40.*
c Research subjects must be debriefed after the experiment.
d It's just a joke!

23 ***a*** *Correct! See page 40.*
b Dr. Frankenstein was trying to create the whole package — body and brain.
c He may not have planned exactly, but that wouldn't have mattered to the APA.
d The participants in the angry mob carried torches, but were not members of the APA.

24 a Sadly, often animals are harmed, even killed.
b Science now knows what any pet owner could have told them — animals do feel pain and suffering.
c Some may, but few scientists would offer this as a justification for animal research.
d *Correct! See page 41.*

25 a Scientists work under many ethical and supervisory restraints.
b Ethical concerns of research apply to animals as well as to human subjects.
c More and more scientists believe animals do have rights.
d *Correct! See page 41.*

Short Essay (sample answers)

1. Attention-deficit/hyperactivity disorder (ADHD) is diagnosed in children who are inattentive, make careless mistakes in schoolwork, don't follow instructions, and are easily distracted. These children are also hyperactive, fidget, don't stay in their seats, run about, and talk excessively. A powerful stimulant called Ritalin is often prescribed. Diagnosis and treatment of ADHD are controversial because there are no objective tests to determine ADHD, and how Ritalin works and its safety are not fully understood.

2. The placebo effect is a change in the patient's illness that is attributable to an imagined treatment rather than to a medical treatment. In medical research, the placebo is often a sugar pill, not an actual medicine. In everyday life, the psychology of the placebo effect shows the power of the mind to affect the body. In other cultures, rhino horn, bear gallbladders, and tiger bones supposedly have curative effects. Magnets worn to cure pain may be an example from our own society.

3. The biggest mistake people make about correlations is assuming that they show cause and effect. When two things seem to go together it is difficult to resist the temptation to believe that one is causing the other. But instead of a causal linkage, all we have in correlation is systematic change. When one thing changes, the other does, too: the change itself does not indicate what causes it. This common mistake can have serious consequences — just ask a rhinoceros or endangered tiger.

4. The superior ability of the laboratory experiment to identify cause-and-effect relationships comes from using the seven rules that reduce error and bias and from the ironclad logic of experimental procedure. If the subjects have been randomly selected and all variables are controlled, only the difference in treatment between the experimental group and the control group can explain any resulting differences in behavior between the two groups (everything else was held constant).

5. There is no one “right” answer to this question. You could argue in favor of animal research, against it, or take some position in between. But your answer should deal with the facts that animal research has contributed to significant medical advances, and is likely to aid in conquering more diseases, but also that there are some cases of animal mistreatment and even death. Many scientists try to strike the right balance between animal rights and research needs, but is such a balance really possible, and how?

Module 3

Brain's Building Blocks

Psychology as a Spectrum of Approaches

In the first module we got acquainted with psychology and learned some of its history. In the second module we saw how psychologists pursue knowledge. It is all interesting and important, yet you could say that psychology itself really begins in Module 3.

Remember the six major approaches to psychology (and two new trends) discussed in the first module? I find it useful to think of them as forming a spectrum, a rainbow of ideas. At one end there is the biological approach — the brain and nervous system Plotnik and Kouyoumdjian describe in this module and the next. At the other end is the cross-cultural approach — the social interactions they cover in the last module, which examines social psychology.

I put the brain and nervous system at the beginning of the spectrum because the brain seems like the most obvious, most elemental starting point in psychology. You could just as well put social interaction first, however, because we become experts about other people long before we know anything about the brain. It doesn't really matter; the point is that the biological and cross-cultural approaches are polar opposites in how we think about psychology.

The other four approaches (psychoanalytic, cognitive, behavioral, and humanistic) fall somewhere within the spectrum. How you arrange them only reveals your biases about their relative importance. (Which process, for example, do you consider more dominant — thinking or feeling?)

Our Starting Point, Deep in the Fields of Biology and Chemistry

At the far extreme we are studying now, psychology is almost pure biology and chemistry. But when Plotnik and Kouyoumdjian discuss social psychology in the last module, or whenever they bring in the cross-cultural approach during one of their Cultural Diversity explorations, you will see just how deeply psychology also reaches into the fields of anthropology and sociology.

Now you can appreciate why this module is not an easy one to master (and probably wasn't an easy one to write, either). It involves a mini-course in biology. You could easily get lost just trying to remember the key terms. My advice is to concentrate on the *processes* involved. Try to appreciate how the brain and nervous system stand between us and the rest of the world, helping us understand it and make the best use of it. I suppose loyal Trekkers could compare the brain to the starship Enterprise, going bravely where no man has gone before, in the name of peace and the orderly regulation of our affairs.

Effective Student Tip 3

Meet Your New Friend, the Professor

Last semester it was Jason. Somewhat brash, but immediately likable, Jason came up to my desk after the first class and announced, "I'm getting an 'A' in your class!"

I like it when students make such pronouncements. For one thing, I learn their names right away. For another, we have the beginnings of a relationship. But most importantly, we have established a basis for working together. Now that I know Jason really wants an "A," I've got to pay attention to him and try to keep him on track. For his part, Jason has to make a genuine effort, unless he wants me to think he is just a blowhard. Some students may not have much of an investment in the class, but Jason and I know what we are doing. We're serious.

Meanwhile, that girl in the back who frowned all through the first lecture…, that guy who didn't take any notes…, and others who are just faces in the crowd for the first few weeks…, all these students could learn something useful from Jason.

Say hello to your professor right away. Let him or her get to know you. You need a friend in this new class, and what better person than the professor?

Your response…

What kind of relationship do you usually have with your teachers? Friendly? Formal? None at all?

Learning Objectives

1. Understand the brain as the electrical and chemical organ that initiates, organizes, and directs all thought, feeling, and behavior.
2. Learn the basic structures and functions of the parts of the brain.
3. Appreciate the differences between neurons and nerves and how they affect recovery from injuries.
4. Explain how the brain functions as an information system involving nerve impulses and neurotransmitters.
5. Explore the controversies and research surrounding the phenomenon of phantom limb pain in order to gain insight into the workings of the brain.
6. Appreciate the cultural differences in human attempts to affect brain functions and consciousness with different plants and drugs.
7. Consider your position on important controversies such as the philosophical debate over brain versus mind and the ethical problem of stem cell research.

Key Terms

Perhaps you know some of these terms from biology. Which will require the most study?

action potential
afferent (sensory) neurons
alcohol
all-or-none law
Alzheimer's disease
axon
axon membrane
basal ganglia
cell body
central nervous system
curare
dendrites
efferent (motor) neurons
end (terminal) bulbs
genes
glial cell
interneuron
ions
mescaline
mind-body question
multiple sclerosis
myelin sheath
nerve impulse
nerves
neuron
neurotransmitters
Parkinson's disease
peripheral nervous system
phantom limb
reflex
resting state
reuptake
sodium pump
stem cells
stereotaxic procedure
synapse
transmitter

The "PowerStudy 4.5 for Introduction to Psychology" CD-ROM for this module is a "Super Module." In addition to the regular PowerStudy features (quizzes, summary test, key terms, web site connections, critical thinking exercise, module outline, and more), Super Modules also include self-paced, step-by-step multimedia presentations with animations and narration.

Outline

- *Introduction*

  1. Losing one's mind: **Alzheimer's disease** (Charles Schneider)
  2. Diagnosis and causes (recent research)

  ☐ How does Alzheimer's disease illustrate the importance of the brain's building blocks?

A. *Overview: Human Brain*

1. Development of the brain
   a. **Genes**
   b. Developmental stages
2. Structure of the brain
   a. **Glial cell**
   b. **Neuron**
3. Growth of new neurons
   a. Canary songs
   b. Primate brains
   c. Repairing the brain
4. Brain versus mind
   a. **Mind-body question**
   b. How brain and mind influence each other

B. *Neurons: Structure & Function*

1. Three basic structures of the neuron
   a. **Cell body**
   b. **Dendrites**
   c. **Axon**
      (1) **Myelin sheath**
      (2) **End (terminal) bulbs**
      (3) **Synapse**
2. Alzheimer's disease and neurons

C. *Neurons Versus Nerves*

1. Reattaching limbs (John Thompson)
2. Transplanting a face (Isabelle)
3. **Peripheral nervous system**
   a. **Nerves**
   b. Ability to regrow nerves

4. **Central nervous system**

☐ How do the hopes for recovery of accident victim John Thompson and disease victim Montel Williams illustrate a key difference between nerves and neurons?

   a. Limited capacity of neurons for repair or regrowth

   b. **Multiple sclerosis** (Montel Williams)

D. *Sending Information*

1. Sequence: action potential
   a. Feeling a sharp object
   b. **Axon membrane**: chemical gates
   c. **Ions**: charged particles
   d. **Resting state**: charged battery
      (1) Chemical batteries in the brain
      (2) **Sodium pump**
   e. **Action potential**: sending information
2. Sequence: nerve impulse
   a. Sending information: **nerve impulse**
   b. **All-or-none law**
   c. Nerve impulse
      (1) Once begun, goes to end of the axon
      (2) Breaks in myelin sheath
   d. End bulbs and neurotransmitters

E. *Transmitters*

1. Excitatory and inhibitory
   a. **Transmitter**
   b. Chemical keys and chemical locks
   c. Excitatory transmitters and inhibitory transmitters
2. Neurotransmitters
   a. **Neurotransmitters**
   b. Chemical keys and chemical locks
   c. Excitatory neurotransmitters and inhibitory neurotransmitters
3. **Alcohol**
   a. GABA neurons
   b. GABA keys
4. New transmitters
   a. Endorphins
   b. Anandamide
   c. Nitric oxide
   d. Orexin (hypocretin)

F. Reflex Responses

1. Definition and sequence of a **reflex**
2. Sequence for how a reflex occurs
    a. Sensors
    b. **Afferent (sensory) neurons**
    c. **Interneuron**
    d. **Efferent (motor) neurons**
3. Functions of a reflex

G. Research Focus: What Is a Phantom Limb?

1. Case study (Sgt. Christian Bagge)
2. Definition and data
    (1) **Phantom limb** (amputated)
    (2) Pain is real
3. Answers and treatment

H. Cultural Diversity: Plants and Drugs

☐ If it is true that all human societies seem to discover or invent psychoactive drugs, what does this say about our species? Is there a lesson for psychology?

1. Cocaine: blocking **reuptake**
2. **Curare**: blocking receptors
3. **Mescaline**: mimicking a neurotransmitter

I. Application: Experimental Treatments

1. **Parkinson's disease** (Michael J. Fox)
    a. Symptoms and treatment (L-dopa)
    b. **Basal ganglia**
2. Issues involving transplants
    a. Human cells
    b. **Stem cells**
3. Experimental treatments
    a. Placing tissue in the brain (**stereotaxic procedure)**
    b. Removing parts of the brain
    c. Brain stimulation (DBS)

How English Works

Words in the Textbook

p. 47 prepare a full dinner **from scratch** = from the beginning

her **late** husband = not living now

the number of patients is **projected** to rise = predicted, expected

the worst is **yet to come** = coming in the future

with these new **leads** = clues

p. 49 **breeding** song = making babies

p. 50 myelin **sheath** = covering, protection

p. 51 stringlike **bundles** = groups

By **suppressing** his or her own immune system = to hold back

p. 52 by using the **analogy** of a battery = comparison

segment by segment = part by part, piece by piece

p. 54 your heart **pounding** = beating

A transmitter is a chemical messenger that **transmits** information = carries

p. 55 alcohol has **been around** for 3,000 years = existed, been available

more likely to **pick a fight** = to start a fight

p. 56 after eating **tainted** food = bad, full of harmful substances

p. 58 What is a **phantom** limb? = can't be seen, like a ghost

the brain **pieces together** a complete body image = organizes

virtual reality = unreal but perceived as real

p. 59 feelings of **euphoria** = great happiness

mimicking = acting the same as

p. 60 in which **fetal** brain tissue = from an unborn baby

young onset Parkinson's = beginning early in life

ESL Tip: How English Got That Way — Word Order versus Inflection

As Plotnik and Kouyoumdjian show in Module 14, scholars generally agree that the human brain has a built-in capacity for learning language. This inborn set of structures is amazing when you consider the major differences that exist among the world's 6,900 languages.

The majority of these languages fall roughly into two major categories: **inflected** and **word-order**. In fact, languages can even shift gradually from one of these groups to the other. To see this evolution we can look no further than English, which has been changing over the years from the first kind to the second.

Here's an example of exactly the same concept (woman sees dog)as expressed in each kind of language.

First, Latin, a highly **inflected** language: ***Mulier vidit canem.***

Then in English, a **word-order** language: **The woman sees the dog.**

Now, watch what happens to both sentences when the word order is reversed:

> ***Canem vidit mulier*** still means the same as it did in the original example, but **The dog sees the woman** does not. It means the opposite of the original. In fact, you could even say ***Mulier canem vidit***, putting the word for "sees" at the end of the sentence, and still keep the original meaning in a perfectly good Latin way, but **The Woman the dog sees** doesn't sound right. What's going on here?

This flexibility of word order works for Latin because of that ***–em*** ending on ***can-em;*** it's an **inflection** and it signals that the noun attached to it is having something done to it — it's being seen. If you wanted to have the dog see the woman, you'd do it this way: ***Canis vidit mulierem***. See the difference? Now an ***-em inflection*** is attached to the word for woman.

English used to be much more like this, with many, many inflected words and a looser word order. Over the years we've lost most of these inflections. Think of biblical or Shakespearean writing with words like did***st***, do***st***, and do***th***. Now we get along fine with do and do***es***. If we had kept our inflections in everyday language, we'd be saying, "Thou shalt not covet thy neighbor's iPod."

Losing many of our inflections has made the ones we've kept very important. For example, the **–s** inflection that turns singulars (cat) into plurals (cats) is essential. So is that **–ed** that changes a regular present tense verb (walk) into the past tense (walk**ed**) in the case of regular verbs.

However, the more we've given up our wealth of inflections, the more we've had to rely on exact word order. Note the difference:

> He said he **almost** liked her. He **almost** said he liked her.

Shift the order of one little word (almost), and it makes a big difference. This shift from dependence on inflections to dependence on strict word order will most likely continue in English. For example, your grandchildren will almost never see that inflected -m on the end of who (whom), except, maybe, in "to whom it may concern."

If your first or native language isn't English, ask yourself whether it falls, more or less, into one of these two major groups.

Vocabulary: "Bias" and "Biased"

Bias: (noun) means prejudice, a judgment distorted by personal feelings.

> Job applicants for the police department are tested for **bias** against particular races or groups. The chief of police has stated that racial **bias** and religious **bias** have no place in police work.
>
> Max's years of eating in school cafeterias developed his **bias** against macaroni-and-cheese.
>
> While guarding against error and **bias.**

Biased: (adjective) means distorted by personal feelings, influenced by bias

> Hyun loves hiking in the woods, so she is **biased in favor of** strong controls to protect the environment.
>
> Alvaro complains that his parents are **biased against** rap music because they won't even listen to the songs.
>
> Surveys may be **biased.**

Bias: (verb) means to influence or distort based on personal feelings.

The Big Picture

Which statement below offers the best summary of the larger significance of this module?

A No matter how much we discover about the structure and function of the brain, the workings of the mind will forever remain a mystery. Psychology should recognize that it must often yield to philosophy and religion.

B The widespread human craving for alcohol and drugs shows that while the brain may be essential to human survival, it can also be our biggest enemy. The brain is an ancient evolutionary left-over, but we are stuck with it.

C The brain could be described as an incredibly precise chemical and electrical information system. It is conceivable that brain science eventually will be able to decipher the composition and location of any single thought or idea.

D Alzheimer's disease and phantom limb pain illustrate the fragile nature of the brain and its tendency to malfunction and wear down. The conclusion is simply that we have to hope for the best.

E Having trouble learning all the terms in this module? Two words: brain transplant!

True-False

_____ 1. Many people are worried about the effects of drug use on the brain — as well they should, in light of the fact that damaged neurons are not regrown or replaced.

_____ 2. Science has determined that the mind is a separate entity from the brain.

_____ 3. Most neurons have a cell body, dendrites, and an axon.

_____ 4. Nerves are located in the central nervous system; neurons are in the peripheral nervous system.

_____ 5. The "all-or-none law" refers to the fact that ions are either positively or negatively charged.

_____ 6. Neurotransmitters are the keys that unlock the receptors of dendrites, cell bodies, muscles, and organs.

_____ 7. Alcohol is a psychoactive drug that depresses the activity of the central nervous system.

_____ 8. A reflex is an action you have learned to execute so fast you don't think about it.

_____ 9. Drugs like cocaine and mescaline achieve their effects by interfering with the normal workings of neurotransmitters.

_____ 10. The stereotaxic procedure is the treatment of Parkinson's disease with a drug called L-dopa.

Flashcards 1

____	1. action potential	a. brain cell with specialized extensions for receiving and transmitting electrical signals
____	2. all-or-none law	b. chemical keys with a particular shape that only fits a similarly shaped chemical lock or receptor
____	3. glial cells	c. series of separate action potentials that take place segment by segment down the length of the axon
____	4. ions	d. brain cells that provide scaffolding, insulation, chemicals to protect and support neuron growth
____	5. mind-body question	e. an unlearned, involuntary reaction to some stimulus; prewired by genetic instructions
____	6. nerve impulse	f. if an action potential starts at the beginning of an axon, it will continue to the very end of the axon
____	7. neuron	g. asks how complex mental activities can be generated by physical properties of the brain
____	8. neurotransmitters	h. chemical particles that have electrical charges; opposite charges attract and like charges repel
____	9. phantom limb	i. vivid experience of sensations and feelings coming from a limb that has been amputated
____	10. reflex	j. tiny electrical current that is generated when positive sodium ions rush inside the axon

Flashcards 2

____	1. Alzheimer's disease	a. a disease that attacks the myelin sheaths, which wrap around and insulate cells in the central nervous system
____	2. curare	b. incurable, fatal disease involving brain damage, with memory loss, deterioration of personality
____	3. dendrites	c. miniature containers at extreme ends of axon branches; store chemicals called neurotransmitters
____	4. end bulbs	d. a drug that enters the bloodstream and blocks receptors on muscles, causing paralysis
____	5. mescaline	e. includes symptoms of tremors and shakes in the limbs, slowing of voluntary movements, feelings of depression
____	6. multiple sclerosis	f. fixing a patient's head in a holder and drilling a small hole through the skull; syringe guided to a brain area
____	7. Parkinson's disease	g. process of removing neurotransmitters from synapse by reabsorbtion into terminal buttons
____	8. reuptake	h. branchlike extensions that arise from cell body and receive and pass signals to cell body
____	9. stereotaxic procedure	i. a drug that causes arousal, visual hallucinations; acts like neurotransmitter norepinephrine
____	10. synapse	j. very small space between terminal button and adjacent dendrite, muscle fiber, or body organ

Multiple Choice

_____ 1. Plotnik and Kouyoumdjian begin with the example of Alzheimer's disease to illustrate the
a. sad fact that the brain inevitably wears out
b. hope offered by a new operation for those afflicted with the disease
c. type of disease that could be prevented if people would take care of themselves
d. key importance of the building blocks that make up the brain's informational network

_____ 2. The initial symptoms of Alzheimer's disease are
a. profound memory loss
b. deterioration in personality
c. problems with memory, getting lost, and being mildly confused
d. emotional outbursts

_____ 3. Believe it or not, your brain contains about __________ cells (neurons plus glial cells)
a. one thousand
b. 100 thousand
c. 1 trillion
d. a gad-zillion

_____ 4. The __________ contain chemical instructions that program the development of the body and brain
a. glial cells
b. neurons
c. fertilized eggs
d. genes

_____ 5. A neuron is a brain cell that
a. determines the sex of the individual
b. receives and transmits electrical signals
c. looks like a small wrinkled melon
d. coats and protects the brain

_____ 6. Unlike nerves, neurons
a. are not replaced or regrown
b. have the ability to regrow or reattach
c. are located outside the brain and spinal cord
d. have no dendrites or axons

_____ 7. Recent research on animals suggests that the human brain
a. is less evolved than most bird brains
b. can develop new neurons each spring, as the canary does
c. continues to grow and develop neurons all through life
d. has only a limited capacity to repair or rewire itself after damage

_____ 8. Is the mind the same as the brain? Plotnik and Kouyoumdjian say that the
a. mind must be separate — otherwise there would be no soul
b. brain and mind are closely linked, and researchers are studying these links
c. physical brain is the only thing — there is no actual "mind"
d. questions like this are best left to philosophers

_____ 9. The __________ is a single threadlike structure that extends from, and carries signals away from, the cell body to neighboring neurons, organs, or muscles

a. axon
b. dendrite
c. myelin sheath
d. synapse

_____ 10. The purpose of the myelin sheath is to

a. receive signals from neurons, muscles, or sense organs
b. wrap around and insulate an axon
c. protect the nucleus of the cell body
d. drain dangerous electricity away from the brain

_____ 11. John Thompson's arms could be reattached because

a. neurons have the ability to regrow, regenerate, or reattach
b. neurons are part of the central nervous system
c. nerves have the ability to regrow, regenerate, or reattach
d. nerves are part of the peripheral nervous system

_____ 12. As a result of __________, Montel Williams has suffered from intense pain in his feet and legs for many years

a. Alzheimer's disease
b. multiple sclerosis
c. phantom limb
d. Parkinson's disease

_____ 13. The purpose of the ions in the axon's membrane is to

a. generate a miniature electrical current
b. plug up the tiny holes in the membrane's semipermeable skin
c. pump excess sodium out of the neuron
d. dry up the watery fluid that collects in the membrane

_____ 14. The __________ says that if an action potential starts at the beginning of an axon, the action potential will continue at the same speed, segment by segment, to the very end of the axon

a. unlocked-chemical-gate phenomenon
b. nerve impulse principle
c. all-or-none law
d. opposite charges law

_____ 15. The "all-or-none law" explains what happens when

a. positively and negatively charged ions meet
b. an impulse starts at the beginning of an axon
c. electrical impulses spread throughout the body
d. your brain gets the idea of a six-pack

_____ 16. The effect of a neurotransmitter on an adjacent neuron, muscle, or organ is

a. excitatory
b. inhibitory
c. either excitatory or inhibitory
d. determined by the all-or-none law

_____ 17. If receptors in muscle fibers are thought of as locks, the keys are
a. the action potential of the axon
b. synapses
c. the resting state of the axon
d. neurotransmitters

_____ 18. On many nights you hear the cry "Let's party!" Odd, because actually alcohol
a. increases tension and anxiety
b. sharpens social judgment, therefore heightening inhibitions and self-doubt
c. depresses activity of the central nervous system, dulling alertness
d. improves memory, creating the ideal time to study

_____ 19. The brain produces a neurotransmitter called __________ to decrease the effects of pain during great bodily stress, such as an accident
a. endorphin
b. anandamide
c. nitric oxide
d. happy dust

_____ 20. An unlearned, involuntary reaction to a stimulus is called a/n
a. explosion
b. electrical burst
c. conditioned reflex
d. reflex

_____ 21. Sgt. Christian Bagge, who was hit by two roadside bombs in Iraq and suffered amputations in both legs, now suffers from phantom limb pain. Researchers suspect that his pain comes from
a. cut nerves in the stump
b. a body image stored in the brain
c. his belief that his legs are still there even if he can't see them
d. terrifying memories of the horrible ordeal

_____ 22. The use of cocaine, curare, and mescaline in different parts of the world shows that humans
a. will use plants that imitate or affect actions of the brain
b. will get high one way or another
c. will never figure out how the brain really works
d. do not pay sufficient attention to the effects of some plants

_____ 23. One hope for sufferers of Parkinson's disease is to treat damaged cells with
a. a new drug called L-dopa
b. massive injections of dopamine
c. genetically engineered cells grown in the laboratory
d. transplanted human fetal brain tissue

_____ 24. The use of stem cells to treat Parkinson's disease is ethically and politically controversial because
a. human embryos are destroyed when the stem cells are removed
b. federal funding for stem cell research is limited
c. long-term use of L-dopa drug therapy is effective and safe
d. stem cells can change into and become any one of the 220 cells that make up a human body

_____ 25. The stereotaxic procedure for treating Parkinson's disease involves
a. deceiving the patient and relying on the placebo effect
b. playing loud music into the patient's ear to block out symptoms
c. removing the patient's adult brain and replacing it with a fetal brain
d. fixing a patient's head in a holder and drilling a small hole through the skull

Short Essay

1. Why is Alzheimer's disease a good example to use in this module?

2. Describe the "mind-body question" in psychology and offer your own answer to the problem.

3. Describe the central role of neurotransmitters in making your brain work.

4. What is the problem for scientists in explaining "phantom limb"?

5. Actor Michael J. Fox is battling Parkinson's disease. Explain why part of his battle involves ethical and political issues.

The "How English Works" Sections

Have you tried these special sections? John Thissen wrote this material especially for students new to English, but also for anyone who wants to use English more effectively.

I went through all of his exercises myself and found that they helped me understand English more fully, even when I already "knew" the right answers. John explains the construction of English grammar so clearly that you can't help but gain a better understanding of our wonderful language, even if you're good at it to begin with. That's why I am urging you to try John's lessons.

Please write and tell me how you like the
"How English Works" sections!

<profenos@mac.com>

Answers for Module 3

The Big Picture (explanations provided for incorrect choices)

A Many psychologists believe that mind and brain are actually the same thing.
B The brain is not our enemy; our evolution is largely the evolution of the human brain.
C Correct! You see the "big picture" for this Module.
D If the brain is exercised and the body is in good health, excellent brain function can be lifelong.
E It's just a joke!

True-False (explanations provided for False choices; page numbers given for all choices)

1	F	49	Mind (thinking) is one aspect of the brain.
2	T	49	
3	T	50	
4	F	51	Nerves are located throughout the body (except in the brain and spinal cord); neurons are brain cells.
5	F	52	The all-or-none law refers to the firing of a nerve impulse through the axon.
6	T	54	
7	T	55	
8	F	56	A reflex is an unlearned, involuntary reaction to some stimulus.
9	T	59	
10	F	61	The stereotaxic procedure refers to surgically implanting fetal brain tissue.

Flashcards 1

1 j 2 f 3 d 4 h 5 g 6 c 7 a 8 b 9 i 10 e

Flashcards 2

1 b 2 d 3 h 4 c 5 i 6 a 7 e 8 g 9 f 10 j

Multiple Choice (explanations provided for incorrect choices)

1 a The brain does not wear out.
b There is no operation for Alzheimer's disease.
c The potential for Alzheimer's disease is inherited.
d Correct! See page 47.

2 a That comes later.
b That comes later.
c Correct! See page 47.
d That may happen, but later in the course of the disease.

3 a If you think it is this few, re-read page 48.
b If you think it is only this many, re-read page 48.
c Correct! See page 48.
d Just how much *is* a "gad-zillion" anyway?

4 a Glial cells guide the growth of neurons and insulate them from other electrical signals.
b Neurons are brain cells that receive and transmit electrical signals.
c Fertilized eggs are containers for the genes, which do the work.
d Correct! See page 48.

5 a That would be a chromosome.
b Correct! See page 48.
c That is a description of the cortex.
d There is no single coating that protects the brain.

6 *a Correct! See page 49.*
b This is true of nerves, but not neurons.
c This is true of nerves, but not neurons.
d Neurons do have dendrites and axons.

7 a The human brain is *more* evolved (notice how you react when someone calls you a "birdbrain").
b Canaries may, but humans don't.
c This is true of nerves, but not neurons.
d *Correct! See page 49.*

8 a Plotnik and Kouyoumdjian do not refer to the soul in this discussion.
b *Correct! See page 49.*
c Plotnik and Kouyoumdjian point out that some researchers, but not all, take this position.
d Plotnik and Kouyoumdjian say that this is an important question for psychology to debate.

9 ***a*** *Correct! See page 50.*
b Dendrites receive and pass on signals.
c The myelin sheath protects the axon.
d A synapse is an infinitely small space between an end bulb and its adjacent body organ, muscle, or cell body.

10 a This is the function of the dendrites.
b *Correct! See page 50.*
c The cell body keeps the nucleus in working order.
d Electricity is a key element in brain functioning.

11 a Neurons cannot be regrown, regenerated, or reattached.
b True, but this feature of neurons is not related to the ability in question.
c *Correct! See page 51.*
d True, but this feature of nerves is not related to the ability in question.

12 a Alzheimer's disease causes progressive memory problems and eventual death.
b *Correct! See page 51.*
c Phantom limb pain sometimes results from loss of limbs.
d Parkinson's disease causes tremors and shakes and often results in depression.

13 ***a*** *Correct! See page 52.*
b For the axon to work, the membrane must be semipermeable.
c Sodium is essential in the working of the axon.
d Fluid is essential in the working of the axon.

14 a This is a fictitious term.
b This is a fictitious term.
c *Correct! See page 52.*
d This is a fictitious term.

15 a This creates the action potential (the all-or-none law comes next).
b *Correct! See page 52.*
c The all-or-none law applies only to the axon.
d It's just a joke!

16 a True, but this is only half the story.
b True, but this is only half the story.
c *Correct! See page 54.*
d The all-or-none law applies to electrical current before it reaches a neurotransmitter.

17 a The action potential refers to the beginnings of an electrical current.
b Synapses separate neurons.
c In the resting state, the axon is ready but is not yet generating an electrical signal.
d *Correct! See page 54.*

18 a Alcohol is a depressant.
b Alcohol causes loss of inhibitions and decreased self-control.
c *Correct! See page 55.*
d Alcohol decreases neural activity.

19 ***a*** *Correct! See page 55.*
b Close, since anandamide may help relieve stress, but endorphins are more related to bodily pain.
c Nitric oxide is a gas that functions like a neurotransmitter in the regulation of emotions.
d It's just a joke!

20 a This is not a correct technical term in brain physiology.
b This is not a correct technical term in brain physiology.
c A conditioned reflex is a learned response to a stimulus.
d *Correct! See page 56.*

21 a This early theory of phantom limb pain has been disproved.
b *Correct! See page 58.*
c He knows his legs are gone.
d The pain is not due entirely to psychological sources.

22 ***a*** *Correct! See page 59.*
b This may be true, but the point is *how* that effect is achieved.
c This is contradicted by abundant recent research.
d The trouble is that humans *do* pay attention to the effects.

23 a L-dopa controls but does not cure the symptoms of Parkinson's disease.
b This is not a treatment for Parkinson's disease.
c This is not a treatment for Parkinson's disease.
d *Correct! See page 60.*

24 ***a*** *Correct! See page 60.*
b Availability of funds is not the issue.
c Just the opposite is true.
d The power of stem cells is not the issue.

25 a The placebo effect is not involved.
b That is not the treatment used in the stereotaxic procedure.
c Just think about this for a minute!
d *Correct! See page 61.*

Short Essay (sample answers)

1. The gradual deterioration and eventual death caused by Alzheimer's disease dramatically illustrates the central role of the brain in our physical, mental, and emotional functioning. Alzheimer's disease slowly destroys the building blocks that form the brain's informational network. The deterioration of brain cells and the inability of the chemical message system to start and stop information result in loss of the very processes on which life depends.

2. Is the mind separate from the brain? Or is "mind" simply an abstraction for explaining the workings of the brain? The question of how complex mental activities, such as feeling, thinking, and learning, can be explained by the physical, chemical, and electrical activities of the brain has challenged philosophers and scientists throughout the modern age, and is still a matter of serious debate. As yet, neither side can completely answer or refute the arguments of the other position. (What is your own answer?)

3. Neurotransmitters are at the heart of the brain's informational system. Comprised of about a dozen different chemicals (more are being discovered), neurotransmitters cross the infinitely small space between end bulbs and dendrites, carrying messages from one neuron to another. These messages command the physical and mental activities of life. Communication between the billions of neurons does not get mixed up because the neurotransmitters act as chemical keys that fit only into specific chemical locks.

4. The problem is that it can't be! How could sensations of pain come from a limb that (because of amputation) is no longer there? Researchers have generated several different theories in the attempt to answer the question. It was once thought that the sensations came from the nerves in the stump, or from the spinal cord, but research has discredited these answers. Today it is thought that the sensations come from the brain itself, perhaps from a mental body image that continues to function even when a body part is gone.

5. Michael J. Fox had to interrupt his acting career when the tremors caused by Parkinson's disease became too severe. His fight to overcome the disease has become embroiled in ethical and political controversy because one promising treatment, fetal tissue transplants, involves the use of human embryonic stem cells, which, at present, involves destroying the embryos when the stem cells are removed. This procedure has been strongly opposed by anti-abortion spokespersons. Fox has been attacked and sharply criticized.

Module 4

Incredible Nervous System

A Golden Age of Biology

A researcher commenting on a startling and provocative new idea about human functioning observed that we are living in "a Golden Age of biology." Hardly a week goes by without the media reporting a new breakthrough in genetics, evolutionary science, or human health. When early 19th-century scientists discovered the Rosetta stone, they suddenly had a blueprint that unlocked the secrets of ancient Egypt. Today's scientists are mapping the genes and discovering the blueprint for how we humans are constructed.

Progress in psychology has been no less dramatic. Neuroscientists, who study the brain and nervous system, are coming closer and closer to explaining human consciousness, perhaps the greatest mystery of all.

In the previous module, Plotnik and Kouyoumdjian posed the question: are mind and brain two different things, or the same thing? This is an old argument in psychology and philosophy. Plotnik and Kouyoumdjian gave you some of the reasoning on both sides. The debate is rapidly changing, however. It is becoming less the province of philosophy and more the property of neuroscience. Philosophers continue to attempt to use logic and reason to find an answer, but for the first time neuroscientists are able to look into the functioning brain (Plotnik and Kouyoumdjian tell how) and conduct laboratory experiments on thinking in action.

The Biological Approach to Psychology

In the first module, Plotnik and Kouyoumdjian carefully laid out six major approaches to psychology. It is hard to overstress the importance of becoming familiar with these six approaches. If you can learn them, and begin to see their reflections in all the facts and ideas you encounter in the textbook, you will be well on your way to having an overall view of the structure of the field of psychology and a real grasp of its organization.

The previous module, on the workings of the brain, and this one, on the functioning of the nervous system, contain the heart of the biological approach to psychology. Understand that the six major approaches are not simply matters of the personal interests of researchers and practicing psychologists. They are bold claims to explain *everything* in psychology, and to have the best answers to our needs for specific health and therapeutic applications. Right now, the biological approach seems to be winning the debate, but an intriguing new version of the biological approach called evolutionary psychology is challenging traditional thinking. Another trend, called eclectic psychology, urges using the best features of each approach. We live in exciting times.

Effective Student Tip 4

Why You Must Be Effective in College

Effectiveness comes into play in all our endeavors, from the most trivial to the most crucial. Consider a systems analyst, triumphant in the solution of a tricky problem (effectiveness confirmed), who then wheels around and fires a paper ball in a perfect jump shot into the wastebasket across the room (effective again). The urge behind each effort was effectiveness, but realistically it's more important that our systems analyst solve the problem than make the imaginary buzzer-beating shot.

If we were only dealing with office wastebasketball, we could afford to ignore the psychological factor of effectiveness. The stakes aren't very high. College is a different matter — probably the highest stakes in your life so far.

College is an essential rite of passage in our society, a critical bridge over which you cross into adulthood. College is more important today than ever, with at least two outcomes of great consequence: (1) college may determine whether you gain admittance to a technologically sophisticated world of commerce, industry, and the professions, and (2) college helps shape your self-esteem and psychological health.

That's why you must handle your college experience effectively. Your future depends on it.

Your response…

Realistically, and aside from your "official" goals, what do you hope to get out of going to college?

Learning Objectives

1. Understand the nervous system as an incredibly sophisticated integrated mechanism for building and maintaining a human being.

2. Learn the basic organization and functions of the brain, limbic system, and endocrine system and how they have evolved to serve us by helping us adapt, and also how they sometimes fail us.

3. Explain how the brain, limbic system, and endocrine system function as an incredibly adaptive and powerful information system.

4. Understand the powerful influence of the limbic system on our emotions and the evolutionary significance of the "old brain."

5. Consider the research on possible sex differences in the brain and what practical significance such differences may have.

6. Examine a dark chapter in the history of psychology: the "research" into brain size and the accompanying racial myths.

7. Understand the debate over the importance of the two hemispheres of the brain and their influence on human behavior.

Key Terms

Psychology is becoming an increasingly biological discipline, and many of the Key Terms in this module are straight out of a course in biology. If you have studied biology, good for you. If not, well....

adrenal glands
amygdala
anencephaly
anterior pituitary
auditory association area
autonomic nervous system
Broca's area & Broca's aphasia
central nervous system
cerebellum
chromosome
cortex
dominant gene
endocrine system
evolutionary approach
fight-flight response
forebrain
fragile X syndrome
frontal lobe
frontal lobotomy
gene
genetic mutation
genetic testing
gonads
hippocampus
homeostasis
hypothalamus
limbic system
medulla
midbrain
motor cortex
MRI scan (magnetic resonance imaging) & fMRI scan (*functional* magnetic resonance imaging)
natural selection
neglect syndrome
occipital lobe
pancreas
parasympathetic division
parietal lobe
peripheral nervous system
PET scan (positron emission tomography)
pituitary gland
polymorphic gene
pons
posterior pituitary
primary auditory cortex
primary visual cortex
recessive gene
sex (gender) differences [brain]
somatic nervous system
somatosensory cortex
split-brain operation
sympathetic division
temporal lobe
thalamus
theory of evolution
thyroid
visual agnosia
visual association area
Wernicke's area & Wernicke's aphasia
zygote

Outline

- *Introduction*

  ☐ What do Plotnik and Kouyoumdjian's wildly different examples of four unusual brains tell us about the development and functioning of our own brains?

  1. Identical twins: genetic differences (Hassan and Abbas O.)
  2. Ming's brain: wrong instructions (genetic defect)
  3. Phillipa's brain: cruel fate (brain damage)
  4. Baby Theresa's brain: fatal flaw (birth defect)

A. *Genes & Evolution*

1. Genetic instructions
   a. Fertilization
   b. **Zygote**
   c. **Chromosome**
   d. Chemical alphabet (DNA)
   e. **Genes** and proteins
   f. **Polymorphic genes**
   g. **Dominant genes** and **recessive genes**
   h. Genome
2. Errors in genetic instructions
   a. **Fragile X syndrome**
   b. **Down syndrome**
3. **Genetic testing**
4. Evolution of the human brain
   a. **Theory of evolution**
   b. **Genetic mutations**
   c. **Natural selection**
   d. **Evolutionary approach**

B. *Studying the Living Brain*

1. Brain scans
2. Brain scans: MRI and fMRI
   a. **MRI scan (magnetic resonance imaging)**
   b. **fMRI scan (*functional* magnetic resonance imaging)**
3. Brain scans and cognitive neuroscience
   a. **PET scan (positron emission tomography)**
   b. Pictures of thinking
4. Faces versus bodies (face and body recognition)

C. Organization of the Brain

1. Divisions of the nervous system
   a. **Central nervous system** (CNS)
   b. **Peripheral nervous system** (PNS)
2. Subdivisions of the PNS
   a. **Somatic nervous system**
      (1) Afferent (sensory) fibers
      (2) Efferent (motor) fibers
   b. **Autonomic nervous system** (ANS)
3. Subdivisions of the ANS
   a. **Sympathetic division**
   b. **Parasympathetic division**
4. Major parts of the brain
   a. **Forebrain**
   b. **Midbrain**
   c. Hindbrain
      (1) **Pons**
      (2) **Medulla**
      (3) **Cerebellum**

D. Control Centers: Four Lobes

1. Overall view of the cortex

☐ What is the anatomical problem for which the wrinkled cortex is a clever solution?

   a. Wrinkled **cortex**
   b. Four lobes: frontal, parietal, occipital, and temporal
   c. Baby Theresa's brain: a fatal defect (**anencephaly**)

☐ Why did baby Theresa live only nine days?

2. **Frontal lobe**: functions of the largest lobe
   a. A terrible accident (story of Phineas Gage)
   b. **Frontal lobotomy**
   c. Results of lobotomies
3. Organization of the frontal lobe
   a. Location of **motor cortex**
   b. Organization and function of motor cortex (motor homunculus)
   c. Other functions of frontal lobe: executive function, aging
4. **Parietal lobe**: functions
   a. Location of **somatosensory cortex**
   b. Organization of somatosensory cortex
   c. Other functions of parietal lobe: sensory integration, spatial orientation, and language abilities

5. **Temporal lobe**: functions
    a. **Primary auditory cortex** and **auditory association area**
    b. **Broca's area** and **Broca's aphasia**
    c. **Wernicke's area** and **Wernicke's aphasia**
6. **Occipital lobe**: functions
    a. **Primary visual cortex** and **visual association area**
    b. **Visual agnosia**
    c. **Neglect syndrome**

E. Limbic System: Old Brain

1. Structures and functions of **limbic system**

☐ Why is the limbic system sometimes called our "old brain" or our "animal brain"?
☐ What is the function of each of its four parts?

    a. **Hypothalamus**
    b. **Amygdala**
    c. **Thalamus**
    d. **Hippocampus**
2. Autonomic nervous system
    a. Sympathetic nervous system
        (1) **Sympathetic division**
        (2) Increases physiological arousal
        (3) **Fight-flight response**
    b. Parasympathetic nervous system
        (1) **Parasympathetic division**
        (2) Decreases physiological arousal
    c. **Homeostasis** (balance)

F. Endocrine System

1. Hormonal system for sending information: **endocrine system**

☐ In what way is the endocrine system similar to the nervous system?

2. Endocrine system's glands and possible dysfunctions
    a. **Hypothalamus** (control center)
    b. **Pituitary gland**
    c. **Posterior pituitary**
    d. **Anterior pituitary**
    e. **Pancreas**
    f. **Thyroid**
    g. **Adrenal glands**
    h. **Gonads**

G. *Research Focus: Sex Differences in the Brain?*

1. Science and politics: **sex (gender) differences**
2. Differences in solving problems

☐ What factors might explain the existence of sex differences in the brain?

3. Differences between female and male brains
    a. Problem solving
    b. Emotional memories
    c. Movement and coordination
    d. Depression

☐ How important do you think these differences are in everyday life?

H. *Cultural Diversity: Brain Size & Racial Myths*

1. Skull size and intelligence
    a. Results (Samuel George Morton)
    b. Reanalyzed (Stephen Jay Gould)
2. Brain size and intelligence
    a. Female brains
    b. Correlations

I. *Application: Split Brain*

1. **Split-brain operation** (Victoria)
    a. Seizures
    b. Major breakthrough (Michael S. Gazzaniga)
    c. Testing a patient

☐ What does the split-brain operation reveal about how the brain works?

2. Behaviors following split brain
3. Different functions of hemispheres
    a. Left hemisphere
        (1) Verbal
        (2) Mathematical
        (3) Analytical
        (4) Recognizing self
    b. Right hemisphere
        (1) Nonverbal
        (2) Spatial
        (3) Holistic
        (4) Recognizing others
4. Left- or right-brained?
    a. Am I primarily "left-brained" or "right-brained"?
    b. How is my brain organized?

How English Works

Words in the Textbook

p. 67 that **chance** alone cannot possibly explain = luck

This **scenario** occurred = an imagined sequence of possible events

his developmental **milestones** = a significant or important event

The **press** called her Baby Theresa = newspapers and TV news

most dangerous **malformation** of the brain = abnormality in the structure of something

p. 68 Each **rung** of the DNA ladder = step

as well as mild to **profound** levels = noticeable

p. 69 a **three-fold** increase = multiplied three times

three major **milestones** = important events

p. 75 he did no controlled or **follow-up** studies = later, to check results

p. 76 emotional **swings** = changes, from very happy to very unhappy

p. 77 you can easily **tell** a key from a nickel = feel the difference

digests information = takes in

p. 80 many kinds of **fleeting** memories = quickly disappearing

p. 85 had unknowingly **swayed** his scientific judgment = bias

Vocabulary

You have read about the nervous system and encountered a series of words connected with the nervous system. The word beginnings **neuro** or **neur** relate to nerves or the nervous system. Here are some examples of the prefix (word beginning) of **neuro**. Try to guess the meaning.

For example: maximum **neural** activity occurred in an area of the brain.

Neural means relating to the nervous system.

Now you try it:

A relatively new area, called cognitive **neuro**science

What is this a study of?

Egas Moniz, a Portuguese **neuro**logist, used an untested surgical treatment.

What was Egas Moniz's job?

Imagine many billions of **neurons** laid on a sheet of paper.

What are **neurons**?

What's the difference between these two similar looking words?

Keep the body's arousal at an **optimum** level

Returns to a state of **optimal** functioning

It's a trick question. They both have the same meaning — the most favorable or the highest level possible. **Optimum** is most often used when writing about the highest level and, unlike **optimal**, can be used as a noun.

Vocabulary: "Relatively"

You have encountered the word **relatively** several times in Module 4.

> The above study is an example of a **relatively** new area.
>
> A larger body part indicates **relatively** more area on the motor cortex.
>
> All primates have a **relatively** poor sense of smell.
>
> The left hemisphere would recognize a face by analyzing it piece by piece… a **relatively** slow process.

Relatively means in comparison. As an example, let's describe the weather in Chicago.

> Compared to Arizona, the weather in Chicago is cold. Compared to the North Pole, the weather in Chicago is not so cold. So, we can say: The weather in Chicago is **relatively cold.** This means it is fairly cold, in relation to other places.

Let's try it:

> The textbook is over 500 pages long. That's fairly long, but not as long as an encyclopedia. So, the textbook book is __________.
>
> A mouse looks small next to an elephant. Still, a mouse is not as small as a spider. So, a mouse is __________.
>
> It's fairly expensive to buy a computer. Compared to buying a car, a computer is not so expensive, but compared to buying a radio, a computer is quite expensive. So, a computer is __________.
>
> Most nurses earn less money than most doctors. Nurses earn less than many lawyers and engineers, too. Of course, nurses earn more than dishwashers.
>
> Therefore, nurses earn __________ money than other professionals.

Answers

What is this a study of? A study of the nervous system.
What was Egas Moniz's job? A doctor who specializes in problems of nervous system.
What are **neurons?** They are cells in the nervous system.

So, the textbook is **relatively long.**
So, a mouse is **relatively small.**
So, a computer is **relatively expensive.**
Therefore, nurses earn **relatively less** money than other professionals.

The Big Picture

Which statement below offers the best summary of the larger significance of this module?

A The "nervous system" is the name that is commonly given to a number of quite separate biological functions. It really should not be called a "system" at all.

B The nervous system (including the brain) is an incredible regulatory arrangement that governs all the necessary functions and processes of human life. The nervous system makes us the most adaptable species on Earth.

C The finding that there are significant sex or gender differences in the brain suggests that there must be equally significant biological differences separating the various races and ethnic groups around the world.

D The nervous system and the brain make up the two halves of the story of human biology: the brain gives the orders and the nervous system carries them out. We could live without a nervous system, but not without a brain.

E The "nervous system" is the method by which psych students get ready for an exam.

True-False

_____ 1. The evolutionary approach studies how evolutionary ideas, such as adaptation and natural selection, explain human behaviors and mental processes.

_____ 2. The right and left hemispheres of the brain make up the peripheral nervous system.

_____ 3. More than any other part, it is the operation of the hindbrain that makes you a person.

_____ 4. When Igor hands Dr. Frankenstein a fresh brain, what we see quivering in his hands is the cortex.

_____ 5. As human society evolves, the limbic system incorporates newly developed cooperative and positive tendencies and feelings into the brain.

_____ 6. The general tendency of the autonomic nervous system is homeostasis.

_____ 7. In the endocrine system, glands secrete hormones that affect many important bodily processes.

_____ 8. Psychologists now know that human intelligence is determined by brain size.

_____ 9. The need to perform split-brain operations for medical purposes gives scientists a rare look at the degree of specialization in the brain's two hemispheres.

_____ 10. Science has finally explained why people are so different: each human being is either left-brained or right-brained.

Flashcards 1

_____	1. autonomic nervous system	a.	measuring a radioactive solution absorbed by brain cells; shows the activity of various neurons
_____	2. central nervous system	b.	regulates heart rate, breathing, blood pressure, and other mainly involuntary movements
_____	3. cortex	c.	a thin layer of cells covering the entire surface of the forebrain; folds over on itself to form a large area
_____	4. forebrain	d.	passing nonharmful radio frequencies through the brain and measuring how signals interact with brain cells
_____	5. gene	e.	a network of nerves that connect either to sensory receptors or to muscles you can move voluntarily
_____	6. midbrain	f.	the largest part of the brain; has right and left sides (hemispheres) responsible for many functions
_____	7. MRI scan (magnetic resonance imaging)	g.	made up of the brain and spinal cord; carries information back and forth between brain and body
_____	8. peripheral nervous system	h.	has a reward or pleasure center; has areas for visual and auditory reflexes; contains the reticular formation
_____	9. PET scan (positron emission tomography)	i.	a specific segment on the strand of DNA that contains instructions for building the brain and body
_____	10. somatic nervous system	j.	all nerves that extend from the spinal cord and carry messages to and from muscles, glands, and sense organs

Flashcards 2

_____	1. amygdala	a.	involved in processing visual information, which includes seeing colors and recognizing objects
_____	2. cerebellum	b.	keeps the body's level of arousal in balance for optimum functioning
_____	3. fight-flight response	c.	involved in hearing, speaking coherently, and understanding verbal and written material
_____	4. frontal lobe	d.	core of the forebrain; involved in many motivational behaviors and with organizing emotional behaviors
_____	5. gonads	e.	located directly behind the frontal lobe; its functions include the sense of touch, temperature, and pain
_____	6. homeostasis	f.	a relatively large cortical area at the front part of the brain; involved in many functions; works like an executive
_____	7. limbic system	g.	glands (ovaries in females, testes in males) that regulate sexual development and reproduction
_____	8. occipital lobe	h.	involved in forming, recognizing, and remembering emotional experiences and facial expressions
_____	9. parietal lobe	i.	a state of increased physiological arousal that helps the body cope with and survive threatening situations
_____	10. temporal lobe	j.	located at back of brain; involved in coordinating motor movements

Multiple Choice

_____ 1. Plotnik and Kouyoumdjian introduce us to identical twins Hassan and Abbas O., troubled Ming, mugger victim Phillipa, and baby Theresa, in order to show that
   a. one side of the brain controls most human behavior
   b. brain damage can strike almost anyone at any time
   c. humans have evolved an incredibly complex nervous system
   d. the brain will never be fully understood

_____ 2. The behavioral problems plaguing Ming, the child who had inherited fragile X syndrome, illustrate the role of __________ in human development
   a. evolution
   b. genetic instructions
   c. fertilization
   d. skull size

_____ 3. According to the theory of evolution, present-day humans descended from
   a. one branch of the modern apes (it is not known which one)
   b. no other primate — they occupy a family tree of their own
   c. a creature that split off from apes millions of years ago
   d. chimpanzees, with whom we share almost 99 percent of their DNA

_____ 4. The new techniques of brain scans have a great advantage:
   a. the information they yield is more than worth the harm they do
   b. they permit a look inside the living, functioning brain
   c. it is no longer necessary to perform frontal lobotomies in mental hospitals
   d. it's so hard to find volunteers for experimental brain surgery

_____ 5. MRI scans of brain damage, such as that suffered by mugger victim Phillipa, help us understand
   a. relationships between parts of the brain and specific behaviors and mental processes
   b. relationships between the protective skull and the fragile brain
   c. why X-rays, although useful, also cause damage to the brain
   d. why crime victims tend to avoid the places where they were attacked

_____ 6. Today, through the use of __________ scans, neuroscientists are able to obtain "pictures" of cognitive activities
   a. fPET
   b. POS
   c. MRI
   d. PET

_____ 7. The major divisions of the nervous system are the
   a. somatic and autonomic nervous systems
   b. fight or flight responses
   c. central and peripheral nervous systems
   d. sympathetic and parasympathetic divisions

_____ 8. Which one of the following is *not* one of the three main parts of the human brain?
   a. forebrain
   b. midbrain
   c. hindbrain
   d. topbrain

_____ 9. The cerebellum is an important part of the hindbrain that
a. initiates voluntary movements
b. influences social-emotional behavior
c. coordinates motor movements
d. makes humans distinct from all other animals

_____ 10. The cortex is all folded and crinkled up because the human brain
a. grows so fast during the first three years of life
b. is divided into four separate lobes
c. is protected by the skull
d. evolved faster than the human skull that holds it

_____ 11. Baby Theresa suffered from anencephaly, the condition of
a. surgical removal of the frontal lobe of the brain
b. the cortex being all wrinkled up
c. being born with almost no brain
d. having a metal rod blasted through the skull

_____ 12. The incredible story of Phineas Gage's accident shows that
a. the frontal lobe receives sensory information from the body
b. a person lives at best in a vegetative state after a frontal lobotomy
c. the frontal lobe is wired to the opposite side of the body
d. the frontal lobe is critical to personality

_____ 13. The __________ was a controversial surgical procedure once used to treat severe emotional problems
a. split-brain operation
b. phantom limb removal
c. left-brain/right-brain difference
d. frontal lobotomy

_____ 14. The function of the somatosensory cortex is to process
a. visual information from the eyes
b. sensory information from individual body parts
c. auditory information from the ears
d. secret information from the unconscious

_____ 15. Wernicke's aphasia and Broca's aphasia are evidence that
a. language abilities are more inherited than acquired
b. special areas of the lobes of the cortex control language abilities
c. if one area is damaged, the other takes over for it
d. human language is so complex that a number of things can go wrong with it

_____ 16. The failure of a patient to see objects or parts of the body on the side opposite the brain damage is called
a. the neglect syndrome
b. visual agnosia
c. hysterical blindness
d. visual association

_____ 17. When you understand the limbic system, you begin to see why
a. modern humans are so far advanced over their prehistoric ancestors
b. a human can do so much more than an alligator
c. modern society is still plagued by so many primitive behaviors
d. the social life of human beings is so much more complex than that of alligators

_____ 18. The limbic structure most involved in emotion is the
a. amygdala
b. hypothalamus
c. hippocampus
d. thalamus

_____ 19. If you see a snake crawling out from under your car, what happens next is an example of the
a. arouse-or-die response
b. homeostatic reaction
c. parasympathetic push
d. fight-flight response

_____ 20. The endocrine system and the nervous system are basically
a. similar — they are both chemical systems
b. similar — they both send information throughout the body
c. different — the nervous system affects the brain and the endocrine system affects the body
d. different — the nervous system causes positive functioning and the endocrine system causes dysfunctions

_____ 21. Me Tarzan, you Jane. Therefore, according to research on sex differences in the brain,
a. me spatial, you verbal
b. me verbal, you spatial
c. me emotional, you logical
d. me lusty, you cold

_____ 22. The sad history of research on the relationship between intelligence and skull and brain size shows that
a. when a Nobel Prize is involved, some scientists will fudge their data
b. science can be influenced by personal biases and the prejudices of the times
c. science is not always the best way to answer a question about human behavior
d. sloppy measurement can undercut a sound hypothesis

_____ 23. Results of the split-brain operation demonstrate that
a. there is intense communication between the two hemispheres of the brain
b. we would be better off with only the analytic left brain
c. we miss a lot by neglecting the holistic right brain
d. the body-piercing movement has gotten *way* out of hand

_____ 24. Which one of the following is *not* true about hemispheric specializations?
a. left hemisphere – verbal
b. right hemisphere – holistic
c. left hemisphere – mathematical
d. right hemisphere – analytic

_____ 25. Are you left-brained or right-brained? The best answer is that you are probably
a. left-brained, since you are a college student
b. constantly using both hemispheres
c. right-brained if you are female and left-brained if you are male
d. left-brained, since most people are

Short Essay

1. The module begins with Lucy, Baby Theresa, Steve, and Scott. How do their stories illustrate the basic forces that create the nervous system?
2. How do scientists study the brain?
3. What are the social implications of the evolution and function of the limbic system?
4. What is your take on the existence and importance of sex differences in the brain?
5. Do you consider yourself primarily left-brained or right-brained and why?

For Psych Majors Only…

The Brain and Nervous System: Match each system or structure to its main components or functions.

_____	1. central nervous system	a. sympathetic and parasympathetic divisions
_____	2. peripheral nervous system	b. verbal, mathematical, analytical
_____	3. somatic nervous system	c. motor cortex (motor behaviors)
_____	4. autonomic nervous system	d. brain and spinal cord
_____	5. frontal lobe	e. primary auditory cortex (hearing and speaking)
_____	6. parietal lobe	f. primary visual cortex (visual information)
_____	7. temporal lobe	g. somatic and autonomic nervous systems
_____	8. occipital lobe	h. afferent (sensory) and efferent (motor) fibers
_____	9. left hemisphere (of brain)	i. nonverbal, spatial, holistic
_____	10. right hemisphere (of brain)	j. somatosensory cortex (sensory information)

Answers to "The Brain and Nervous System" quiz

1 d 2 g 3 h 4 a 5 c 6 j 7 e 8 f 9 b 10 i

Answers for Module 4

The Big Picture (explanations provided for incorrect choices)

A The great strength of the nervous system is how beautifully all the parts work together
B Correct! You see the "big picture" for this Module.
C Sex and gender differences in the brain are not highly significant and do not point to this idea.
D We could not live without either one; the brain is part of the nervous system.
E It's just a joke!

True-False (explanations provided for False choices; page numbers given for all choices)

1	T	69	
2	F	72	The peripheral nervous system includes all the nerves in the body outside the brain and spinal cord.
3	F	73	It's the forebrain, not the hindbrain, which is most closely related to higher functions.
4	T	74	
5	F	80	The limbic system remains our older, more animalistic brain.
6	T	81	
7	T	82	
8	F	85	There is some correlation between brain size and intelligence, but it has little practical application.
9	T	86	
10	F	87	Humans probably use both sides of the brain almost equally.

Flashcards 1

1 b 2 g 3 c 4 f 5 i 6 h 7 d 8 j 9 a 10 e

Flashcards 2

1 h 2 j 3 i 4 f 5 g 6 b 7 d 8 a 9 e 10 c

Multiple Choice (explanations provided for incorrect choices)

1 a This is not true about brain functioning.
b Brain damage is rare and need not be feared.
c Correct! See page 67.
d Great progress is being made in understanding the brain.

2 a This disease is not specifically related to evolution.
b Correct! See page 69.
c This disease is not related to fertilization.
d This disease is not related to skull size.

3 a Humans and apes are both descended from an earlier ancestor.
b Some religions suggest this, but the theory of evolution does not.
c Correct! See page 69.
d Chimpanzees and humans are both descended from an earlier ancestor.

4 a These scans are relatively safe, but not 100 percent harmless.
b Correct! See page 70.
c Brain scans are unrelated to frontal lobotomies.
d It's just a joke!

5 *a Correct! See page 70.*
b It would not take a brain scan to demonstrate the function of the skull.
c The miracle of brain scans is that they do not cause great damage
d That is a function of learning, not brain structure

6 a There is no fPET scan.
b There is no POS scan.
c MRI scans show static views of the structure of the brain.
d Correct! See page 71.

7 a The somatic and autonomic nervous systems are parts of the peripheral nervous system.
b The fight-flight response is a function of the sympathetic nervous system.
c *Correct! See page 72.*
d The sympathetic and parasympathetic divisions are parts of the autonomic nervous system.

8 a The forebrain is one of the divisions of the human brain.
b The midbrain is one of the divisions of the human brain.
c The hindbrain is one of the divisions of the human brain.
d *Correct! See page 73.*

9 a The cerebellum does not initiate voluntary movement.
b This is true of the frontal lobe, not the cerebellum.
c *Correct! See page 73.*
d Other animals also possess these faculties.

10 a True, but this does not explain why the cortex is folded.
b True, but this does not explain why the cortex is folded.
c True, but this does not explain why the cortex is folded.
d *Correct! See page 74.*

11 a That would be the discredited frontal lobotomy operation.
b That is an evolutionary adaptation to our small skull size.
c *Correct! See page 74.*
d That refers to Phineas Gage's accident.

12 a The parietal lobe receives sensory information from the body.
b Phineas Gage was not in a vegetative state.
c Phineas Gage's accident did not reveal the special wiring of each hemisphere to the opposite side of the body.
d *Correct! See page 75.*

13 a The split-brain operation is used to combat seizures.
b There is no phantom limb removal operation (the limb is gone but the victim still feels pain).
c The left-brain/right-brain difference refers to abilities that may be particular to each hemisphere.
d *Correct! See page 75.*

14 a The primary visual cortex processes visual information.
b *Correct! See page 77.*
c The primary auditory cortex processes auditory information.
d "Secret unconscious" information, if there is such information, would be a form of thinking.

15 a Learned factors in language abilities are at least as important as inherited factors.
b *Correct! See page 78.*
c Wernicke's area and Broca's area each control different language functions.
d The two types of aphasia are relatively rare disorders.

16 ***a*** *Correct! See page 79.*
b Visual agnosia is the failure to recognize the whole object even though the parts are recognized.
c Hysterical blindness is a psychological problem not discussed in this module.
d Not a real term for a visual problem.

17 a The limbic system reveals our similarities to our prehistoric ancestors.
b It is not the limbic system that gives humans a cognitive advantage.
c *Correct! See page 80.*
d Other parts of the brain explain our greater social complexity.

18 ***a*** *Correct! See page 80.*
b The hypothalamus is more involved in regulating many motivational behaviors.
c The hippocampus is more involved in saving many kinds of fleeting memories.
d The thalamus is more involved in receiving sensory information.

19 a This is not a correct technical term.
b This is not a correct technical term.
c This is not a correct technical term.
d *Correct! See page 81.*

20 a The endocrine system is basically chemical but the nervous system is basically electrical
b *Correct! See page 82.*
c Both systems affect the brain and the body.
d Both promote positive functioning, but both can also have dysfunctions.

21 ***a*** *Correct! See page 84.*
b On some tests, men do better on spatial tasks and women better on verbal.
c This is the reverse of a commonly held opinion.
d It's just a joke! [And if you chose this answer, perhaps you should take some Women's Studies courses.]

22 a The Nobel Prize was not involved in this history.
b *Correct! See page 85.*
c Sometimes misused, science is still our most powerful method for answering questions about human behavior.
d In this case, the hypothesis was wrong because it was based on personal bias.

23 ***a*** *Correct! See page 86.*
b Would you want to live a life without feelings? Could you?
c True enough, but the split brain operation does not negate the right hemisphere.
d It's just a joke!

24 a The left hemisphere is thought to be more verbal than nonverbal.
b The right hemisphere is thought to be more holistic than analytical.
c The left hemisphere is thought to be more mathematical than spatial.
d *Correct! See page 87.*

25 a It is doubtful that any groups, or even many individuals, are truly "left-brained" or "right-brained."
b *Correct! See page 87.*
c It is doubtful that any groups, or even many individuals, are truly "left-brained" or "right-brained."
d It is doubtful that any groups, or even many individuals, are truly "left-brained" or "right-brained."

Short Essay (sample answers)

1. Each of these four people demonstrates an important aspect of the nervous system. Lucy shows the role evolution has played in developing modern humans. Baby Theresa shows that different parts of the brain control different aspects of life. Steve shows how brain damage both robs a person of basic functions and also points to specific links between parts of the brain and behavior. Scott shows how a complicated system of essential and interlocking genetic instructions underlies development.

2. Today scientists have powerful new tools with which to study the brain. MRI (magnetic resonance imaging) scans, in which radio waves are passed through the brain, reveal detailed images of the brain. The recently developed fMRI (functional magnetic resonance imaging) measures the activity of specific neurons that function during cognitive tasks, showing the brain in action. PET (positron emission tomography), based on radiation in brain cells, shows where thoughts and feelings occur during mental activity.

3. The limbic system is involved in motivational behaviors, emotional behaviors, and storing memories. The limbic system in humans is similar to that of animals like alligators and represents a primitive stage in our evolution. If our most basic motivational and emotional systems are no more evolved than those of the alligator, no wonder we have so much trouble living peacefully and cooperatively with our fellow humans. The questions for psychology are how accurate this picture is, and how much control the limbic system has.

4. Are there structural or functional differences in cognitive, behavioral, or brain processes that arise from being male or female? You could argue at one extreme that research has established fundamental differences. At the other extreme, you could argue that "differences" shown by cognitive tasks and brain scans are either inaccurate (like the skull size research) or unimportant (like hair color). In either case, you should offer your opinion on the possible social implications and practical consequences of such differences.

5. If you believe you are primarily left-brained, you should describe the verbal, mathematical, and analytic abilities you see as your main characteristics. If you believe you are primarily right-brained, you should describe the nonverbal, spatial, and holistic abilities you see as your main characteristics. In either case, you should acknowledge the opinion of experts that the whole left-brained/right-brained dichotomy is wrong. Is it possible that — in varying degrees — you possess all of these abilities?

Module 5

Sensation

What Is Real?

Back in the happy days before I studied psychology, I simply "knew" that there was a real world out there and that it came straight into my mind (I never thought to wonder what the "mind" was or how it worked). When you study sensation (Module 5), perception (Module 6), and consciousness (Module 7), however, it gets confusing. If you don't watch out, you could find yourself in the predicament of poor Descartes, whose search for a proof of existence had him doubting his own existence, until he decided that just thinking about the problem must prove he was there to do it.

The story begins in this module, with the mechanisms of the sense organs (eye, ear, nose, tongue, and skin) and the processes by which they receive stimuli (light and sound waves, chemicals, and pressures) from the environment. But be prepared for a disappointment: it doesn't mean a thing.

How We Relate to the World

Suppose that right in the middle of writing a great paper your computer suddenly crashed and all you could recover was a data dump of everything it "knew" about your paper. You would experience a similar disappointment. All you would see on the printout would be a long succession of ones and zeros, the binary code in which computers work. It wouldn't mean a thing.

The processes of perception transform meaningless sensations into useful information. It's sort of like the word-processing software that turns those ones and zeros in your paper into (hopefully) great prose. Now the raw sensations begin to take on meaning, as the perceptual processes involved interpret them.

Are we finally in contact with the real world? In a way, but notice that we are also one step removed from that world, apprehending it second-hand through the possibly distorted mechanisms of perception. Even then, exactly *what* do the perceptions mean? The researchers in neuroscience we mentioned in the previous module are trying to find out. We could guess that the answer will involve a complex interaction of cognition and emotion, each enriching the information and making it more useful to us.

We could say that at last we have the real world, but now it is at least three steps removed, as we experience it in our conscious (and unconscious?) mind. How real is it anymore? Perhaps psychology must leave the question of reality to philosophers and theologians. I still believe it's out there, but now I know that what's in my mind is constructed, not real.

Effective Student Tip 5

Go Ahead, Ask Me

I am always astounded when I review my class lists early in the new semester. There are more than a few students who have not yet said a word in class.

For some, it is politeness. Heaven knows, I am flying, and they hesitate to interrupt. For others, it is modesty. Maybe the point they would make isn't all that brilliant. For still others it is excruciating shyness. If they did speak up, they just know the class would turn as one and sneer, "You idiot!"

For each of these students, an effective strategy would be to ask a simple question. A good question can be just the thing to begin your involvement in the class.

As you prepare for the next class, find something in the textbook or your lecture notes that really interests you. What more would you like to know? Think how you could ask about it in a short, clear question. Pick a moment when your question is relevant, and then ask away. (If you feel you can't do it, ask your first question either before or after class. It's a start.)

What do you get out of it? Aside from the information you wanted, you have made contact with the professor and your fellow students. You have demonstrated to yourself that you can talk in class, and now the class is more fun.

Your response…

How comfortable do you feel in class? Do you talk? Is speaking in class something you enjoy, or dread?

Learning Objectives

1. Understand sensation as a process by which raw physical stimuli sent to the brain are changed into potentially useful experiences.

2. Learn the basic mechanisms of vision, audition, balance, taste and smell, touch, and pain.

3. Explain how each of the basic sensations (vision, audition, balance, taste, olfaction, and touch) involves the interaction of stimuli, sensors, and the brain.

4. Appreciate the considerable impact of cultural differences on a simple experience like tasting a common food thats considered good in some cultures but disgusting in others.

5. Consider the implications of placebos and the placebo effect for human psychology.

6. Understand the complicated dimensions of pain — not as simple as you might think.

7. Learn about exciting new applications of artificial senses to correct age-old problems of vision and audition.

Key Terms

There are many key terms in this module because it covers all of the senses. The terms may be easier to learn if you organize them by the senses they help explain. See the Outline for help.

acupuncture
adaptation
afterimage
auditory association area
auditory canal
auditory nerve
basilar membrane
cochlea
cochlear implant
color blindness
conduction deafness
cones
cornea
decibel
dichromats
direction of a sound
disgust
double-blind procedure
endorphins
external ear
farsightedness
flavor
frequency theory
gate control theory of pain
hair cells
iris
lens
loudness
Meniere's disease
middle ear
monochromats
motion sickness
nearsightedness
neural deafness
olfaction
olfactory cells
opponent-process theory
ossicles
outer ear
pain
perceptions
pitch
place theory
placebo
placebo effect
primary auditory cortex
pupil
retina
rods
semicircular canals
sensations
somatosensory cortex
sound waves
taste
taste buds
touch
transduction
trichromatic theory
tympanic membrane
vertigo
vestibular system
visible spectrum

Outline

- *Introduction*

1. Artificial eye: life-changing results (Terry Byland)
2. Three definitions of all senses (processes)

☐ Can you explain how the three processes of all senses produce the experiences of seeing, hearing, smelling, touching, tasting, and position?

   a. **Transduction**
   b. **Adaptation**
   c. **Sensations** into **perceptions**

A. Eye: Vision

1. Stimulus: light waves
   a. Invisible – too short
   b. Visible – just right (**visible spectrum**)
   c. Invisible – too long

☐ What is the visible spectrum and what makes it visible?

2. Structure and function

☐ What happens when you look at something? Can you explain the process of looking?

   a. Image reversed
   b. Light waves
   c. **Cornea**
   d. **Pupil**
   e. **Iris**
   f. **Lens**
   g. **Retina**
   h. Eyeball's shape and laser eye surgery
      (1) Normal vision
      (2) **Nearsightedness**
      (3) **Farsightedness**
      (4) Eye surgery

3. **Retina**: a miniature camera-computer
   a. Photoreceptors
   b. **Rods**
   c. **Cones**
   d. Transduction
   e. Nerve impulses, optic nerve, and blind spot

4. Visual pathways: eye to brain
    a. Optic nerve
    b. Primary visual cortex
        (1) Specialized cells
        (2) Stimulation or blindness
    c. Visual association areas
    d. Brain scan reveals visual activity
5. Color vision
    a. Making colors from wavelengths
    b. **Trichromatic theory**
    c. **Opponent-process theory**
        (1) **Afterimage**
        (2) Excited or inhibited
    d. Theories combined
    e. **Color blindness**
        (1) **Monochromats**
        (2) **Dichromats**

B. Ear: Audition

1. Stimulus: **sound waves**
    a. Amplitude and **loudness**
    b. Frequency and **pitch**
2. Measuring sound waves
    a. **Decibel**
    b. Decibels and deafness
3. Outer, middle, and inner ear
    a. **Outer ear**
        (1) **External ear**
        (2) **Auditory canal**
        (3) **Tympanic membrane** (eardrum)
    b. **Middle ear**
        (1) **Ossicles**
        (2) Hammer, anvil, and stirrup
        (3) Oval window
    c. Inner ear
        (1) **Cochlea**
        (2) **Hair cells** and **basilar membrane**
        (3) **Auditory nerve**

d. Auditory brain areas

(1) **Primary auditory cortex**

(2) **Auditory association area**

4. Auditory cues

a. Calculating **direction of a sound**

b. Calculating pitch

(1) **Frequency theory**

(2) **Place theory**

c. Calculating **loudness**

C. Vestibular System: Balance

1. Position and balance: **vestibular system**

a. **Semicircular canals**

b. Sensing position of head, keeping head upright, maintaining balance

2. **Motion sickness**

3. **Meniere's disease** and **vertigo**

D. Chemical Senses

1. **Taste**

a. Tongue: five basic tastes

(1) Sweet, salty, sour, bitter

(2) Plus a possible new one, *umami*

b. Surface of the tongue

c. **Taste buds**

d. All tongues are not the same

e. **Flavor**: taste and smell

2. Smell, or **olfaction**

a. Stimulus

b. **Olfactory cells**

c. Sensations and memories

d. Functions of olfaction

☐ What is a recently discovered function of olfaction?

E. Touch

1. Sense of **touch**

2. Receptors in the skin

a. Skin

b. Hair receptors

c. Free nerve endings

d. Pacinian corpuscle

3. Brain areas: **somatosensory cortex**

F. Cultural Diversity: Disgust

1. Psychological factors

☐ Although most foods cause delight, some otherwise edible substances cause disgust. What explains this phenomenon and why is it automatically translated into a facial expression?

   a. **Disgust** and universal facial expressions

   b. Cultural influence on foods

2. Cultural factors: plump grubs, fish eyes and whale fat, milk and blood

3. Cultural influences on disgust

G. Research Focus: Mind over Body?

1. Definitions

   a. **Placebo**

   b. **Placebo effect**

   c. Research methods: **double-blind procedure**

2. Power of pricing

☐ How can it be that an expensive pill works better than a cheaper one? Especially if both are placebos!

3. Conclusion: mind over body!

H. Pain

1. **Pain** sensations

   a. Tissue damage

   b. Social, psychological, and emotional factors

2. **Gate control theory of pain**

   a. Competing messages to the brain

   b. Pain: physical and psychological

3. **Endorphins**

4. Dread and waiting for pain

5. **Acupuncture**

   a. Ancient Chinese versus modern Western techniques

   b. Possible explanations

I. Application: Artificial Senses

1. Artificial visual system

   a. Artificial photoreceptors

   b. Artificial eye and brain implant

   c. Functional vision

2. Kinds of deafness

   a. **Conduction deafness**

   b. **Neural deafness**

3. **Cochlear implant**

How English Works

Words in the Textbook

p. 97 the ability to **tell** night from day = see the difference

p. 100 pitch is our **subjective** experience of a sound = personal

a **cheerleader's** yell = a person who guides others in supportive messages to a team

p. 101 **jackhammer** = noisy machine to break rocks and cement

firecracker = an exploding noise maker

threshold of hearing = point where effect begins

p. 102 auditory canal may become **clogged** = to be completely filled

p. 105 you rarely forget to **duck** (head) = move head to avoid danger

a sensory **mismatch** = wrong combination

malfunctioning of the vestibular system = wrong operation

feel a little **queasy** *[KWEE-zee]* = sick to the stomach

p. 106 an **innate** preference for sweet and salt = natural, inborn

such as a **brownie** = chocolate cake squares

p. 107 or if a **blow** to the head = a strong hit

that **elicit** pleasant memories = bring about

p. 112 this competition creates a **bottleneck** = obstacle, like a traffic jam

p. 113 scientists trained in the **rigorous** methods of the West = extremely careful

p. 114 **navigate** the subway = successfully travel

p. 115 the signals **trigger** impulses = activate, cause a series of actions or effects

ESL Tip: Articles and Determiners

Although some languages work fine without the use of **articles**, English has some strict rules for their use. These rules will become second nature to you as you continue to read.

Every noun (person, place, thing) that refers to an individual or to something that can be counted must have an **article** (a/an, the) or a **determiner** that identifies it. Here are some examples:

a bowl of chili (a, article in front of a consonant)

an elephant (an, article in front of a vowel)

the vice president (the, article)

Susie's baby (Susie's, determiner)

their opponent (their, determiner)

Most plural nouns and all nouns that refer to **things that can't be counted** do not have articles. Here are some examples:

Life is worth living (not "the" life is worth living).

He teaches mathematics (not the mathematics).

The team's company's success required teamwork (not "the" teamwork).

Vocabulary: Changing the Meaning

When you see **over-** at the beginning of a word, it usually means "too much." Look at these examples from the text and see if you can guess the meanings:

Overstimulation caused Donna to stare

A tremendous sensory **over**load that makes her freeze up

the use of Ritalin concerns whether it is being **over**prescribed

Words that begin with **mis-** mean something is wrong. For example:

eyewitnesses made **mis**takes = identifying the **wrong** person

subjects **mis**remembered what they saw = remember **wrong**ly

people may believe **mis**information = **wrong** information

the questions were deliberately **mis**leading = questions leading in the **wrong** direction

source **mis**attribution = giving credit to the **wrong** cause

So, **mis-** means __________.

Test Yourself

Here are some more words that begin with **mis-**. On the right side of the page are definitions of these words, but they're **mis**ordered. Draw a line connecting each word to its correct definition.

misclassify	identify illness wrongly
miscount	send in the wrong direction
misdiagnose	put in the wrong category
misfit	write 223 when the answer is 227
misguide	person who is in the wrong group
mishandle	give the wrong name
misidentify	apply talent for criminal (wrong) purpose
misinform	use resources in the wrong way
mismanage	treat in the wrong way
misuse	give the wrong fact

Answers

misclassify	=	put in the wrong category
miscount	=	write 223 when the answer is 227
misdiagnose	=	identify illness wrongly
misfit	=	person who is in the wrong group
misguide	=	send in the wrong direction
mishandle	=	treat in the wrong way
misidentify	=	give the wrong name
misinform	=	give the wrong fact
mismanage	=	apply talent for criminal (wrong) purpose
misuse	=	use resources in the wrong way

The Big Picture

Which statement below offers the best summary of the larger significance of this module?

A Sensation is the process by which the raw data we need for understanding the world around us comes into our brain. Perception is the process by which the brain makes the raw data meaningful.

B Study of the eye, ear, nose, tongue, and skin are traditional subjects in psychology. Today, however, it is becoming clear that these biological functions do not have much to do with psychology.

C Sensation is the collection of processes by which we understand what is happening in our world. For example, through vision we "make sense" out of what we see.

D Perception is how we gather data about the world. Sensation is how we make sense of that data. Therefore, in human psychology, sensation is more important than perception.

E Sensation is the excitement we feel when we see something really great, as in, "I saw a sensational babe at the beach today."

True-False

_____ 1. All of the senses share three characteristics: transduction, adaptation, and sensations experienced as perceptions.

_____ 2. The reason you can "see" a giraffe is that the animal emits light waves that humans can detect.

_____ 3. The retina is a round opening at the front of your eye that allows light waves to pass into the eye's interior.

_____ 4. The images you "see" are created by the primary visual cortex and related association area of the brain.

_____ 5. Sound waves vary in amplitude and frequency.

_____ 6. The vestibular system provides feedback on your body's position in space by interpreting sound waves from your environment.

_____ 7. The tongue has receptors for four or five basic tastes.

_____ 8. Humans won't eat just anything — we have biologically determined preferences for some foods and feelings of disgust at the thought of others.

_____ 9. When two medications address the same problem, most people will choose to buy the less expensive pill rather than the more expensive one.

_____ 10. Acupuncture often produces pain relief — perhaps by causing secretion of endorphins in the brain.

Flashcards 1

_____	1.	adaptation	a.	says rate at which nerve impulses reach brain determine how low a sound is
_____	2.	frequency theory	b.	meaningful sensory experiences that result after the brain combines hundreds of sensations
_____	3.	perceptions	c.	a sense organ that changes physical energy into electrical signals that in turn become neural impulses
_____	4.	place theory	d.	location of basilar membrane vibrations determines medium and higher sounds
_____	5.	sensations	e.	relatively meaningless bits of information that result when the brain processes electrical signals
_____	6.	sound waves	f.	stimuli for audition; resemble ripples on pond; have height (amplitude) and speed (frequency)
_____	7.	transduction	g.	three semicircular canals in inner ear that determine our sense of balance and position
_____	8.	trichromatic theory	h.	one particular segment of electromagnetic energy whose waves can be seen by human eye
_____	9.	vestibular system	i.	says color vision is due to three kinds of cones in retina sensitive to blue, green, or red
_____	10.	visible spectrum	j.	prolonged or continuous stimulation that results in a decreased response by the sense organs

Flashcards 2

_____	1.	acupuncture	a.	smell receptors located in nasal passages; use mucus into which volatile molecules dissolve
_____	2.	disgust	b.	dizziness and nausea resulting from malfunction of semicircular canals of vestibular system
_____	3.	endorphins	c.	includes pressure, temperature, and pain; from miniature sensors beneath outer layer of skin
_____	4.	gate control theory of pain	d.	a universal facial expression (eyes closed, lips curled downward) indicating rejection of foods
_____	5.	nearsightedness	e.	chemicals produced by the brain and secreted in response to injury or stress that cause reduced pain
_____	6.	olfactory cells	f.	may result when eyeball is too long; result is that near objects are clear but distant are blurry
_____	7.	placebo effect	g.	thin film with three layers of cells located at back of eyeball; includes photoreceptor cells
_____	8.	retina	h.	inserting thin needles into various points on the body's surface and twirling them to relieve pain
_____	9.	touch	i.	says rubbing an injured area or becoming involved in other activities blocks pain impulses
_____	10.	vertigo	j.	change in patient's illness attributable to an imagined treatment rather than to a medical one

Multiple Choice

_____ 1. Plotnik and Kouyoumdjian say the experience of Terry Byland, a blind man who had a microchip with 16 electrodes implanted into his eye, suggests the question

a. are some cases of blindness actually hysterical?
b. can blind people regain their sight through intense practice?
c. do you see with your eyes or with your brain?
d. can science go too far in tampering with human capabilities?

_____ 2. The process by which a sense organ changes physical stimuli into impulses is termed

a. adaptation
b. experiencing
c. sensing
d. transduction

_____ 3. A decline in responding with prolonged or continuous stimulation is called

a. transduction
b. adaptation
c. sensing
d. experiencing

_____ 4. When you get that new road rocket for graduation, you may want a radar detector, too, because those things

a. see the pulses of light that radar guns use
b. hear the faint vibrations of radar guns
c. see long wave lengths you can't
d. make your car look cool

_____ 5. The function of the cornea is to

a. add color to light waves entering the eye
b. screen out irrelevant light waves
c. prevent convergence from occurring too soon
d. bend and focus light waves into a narrower beam of light

_____ 6. If you see close objects clearly but distant objects appear blurry, you are

a. nearsighted
b. farsighted
c. normal
d. abnormal

_____ 7. The work of the retina is to

a. add sharp focus to what you see
b. transform light waves into electrical signals
c. turn the inverted image we see right side up
d. change impulses into light waves we can see

_____ 8. In the visual process of transduction, rods allow us to see __________ and cones to see __________.

a. bright colors / pastel colors
b. dangerous objects / safe objects
c. large objects / small objects
d. in dim light / color and fine details

_____ 9. According to the trichromatic theory, our color vision is based on
a. three primary colors, which are mixed to produce all colors
b. two opposite pairs of colors, red-green and blue-yellow
c. an afterimage created by a bright original light stimulus
d. a combination of the monochromat and dichromat theories

_____ 10. If a tree falls in an uninhabited forest, does it make any sound?
a. obviously, it does
b. not if there is no human there to "hear" it
c. it depends on whether we define "sound" as the waves of air or the subjective experience of hearing
d. I thought this was a class in psychology, not philosophy

_____ 11. How loud a sound seems is determined by the __________ of the sound waves
a. frequency
b. amplitude
c. pitch
d. cycle

_____ 12. The noise level near the speakers at a rock concert measures about
a. 30 decibels, which is very loud
b. 80 decibels, about the same as an iPod
c. 120 decibels, which can produce hearing loss
d. 1,000 decibels, the loudest humans can hear

_____ 13. The tympanic membrane is the scientific name for what is commonly called the
a. outer ear
b. inner ear
c. auditory canal
d. eardrum

_____ 14. The function of the cochlea is to
a. transform vibrations into nerve impulses
b. move fluid forward toward the oval window
c. house the hammer, anvil, and stirrup
d. house the band of fibers called the auditory nerve

_____ 15. Our sense of movement and position in space is determined by the
a. faint echoes from surrounding objects that the brain can decode
b. movement of fluid in the three semicircular canals of the vestibular system
c. primary visual cortex and related association areas
d. movement of fluid in the eardrum

_____ 16. Motion sickness is probably caused by
a. a sensory mismatch between the information from the vestibular system and the eyes
b. the violent bouncing around of the head during a rough stretch of road
c. individual personality factors
d. drug use

_____ 17. Which one of the following is *not* one of the four or five basic tastes?

a. sweet
b. sharp
c. salty
d. sour

_____ 18. Our experience of "flavor" results when we

a. overcome our sense of smell
b. ignore the taste buds
c. learn the taste called "umami"
d. combine the sensations of taste and smell

_____ 19. Our sense of touch comes from

a. a half-dozen miniature sensors located in the skin
b. millions of tiny nerves on the surface of the skin
c. special glands for pressure, temperature, and pain
d. stimulation of the tiny hairs that cover the body

_____ 20. The experience of the sense of touch is produced by the

a. auditory association area
b. vestibular system
c. somatosensory cortex
d. visual association area

_____ 21. Why do some edible substances produce a feeling of disgust?

a. our culture has taught us that these substances are not food
b. our taste buds warn us that some substances are harmful
c. the taste may be tolerable, but the smell is disgusting
d. some foods simply have no flavor

_____ 22. In the double-blind procedure,

a. there are blinds (screens) separating the researchers from the subjects
b. both researchers and subjects wear blindfolds in order to guarantee privacy
c. subjects first receive the treatment, then later receive a placebo
d. neither the researchers nor the subjects know who is receiving what treatment

_____ 23. "Let momma kiss it and make it better," is an example of a wise mother applying

a. her understanding of endorphins
b. her knowledge that TLC is always more effective than medicine
c. the gate control theory of pain
d. the unspoken threat of using acupuncture

_____ 24. Can the ancient Asian procedure called acupuncture actually relieve pain? Modern science says

a. yes, because there are some mysteries Western science is not equipped to explain
b. yes, but it comes from the power of people's belief in acupuncture, not the whirling needles
c. no, because there cannot be a relationship between twirling needles in the skin and pain caused by the nervous system
d. no, because there is no research to date that supports acupuncture

_____ 25. Cochlear implants are effective
a. in only a few rare cases, limiting their use to only a handful people worldwide
b. in conduction deafness, but not in neural deafness
c. because they are surgically planted deep inside the brain
d. because a mechanical device does the work of damaged auditory receptors

Short Essay

1. Why is the process of transduction essential to human functioning?

2. Explain the basic workings of the sensation called vision.

3. Yes, there is a "sixth" sense, but it is not some form of intuition. What is the sixth sense and how does it work?

4. What does the feeling of disgust suggest about the interaction of psychology and culture?

5. Why is the double-blind procedure necessary in scientific research?

The Beauty of Linguistics

A subtle advantage of reading these "How English Works" sections by John Thissen is that while you are learning how the English language works, you are also learning much more. In a way, you are learning how *all* languages work. That's the subject of the exciting field called linguistics, which explores the foundations of our human ability to communicate. John Thissen, the author of the materials, has taught English composition at several levels in his college courses. He has also taught English to students from other countries. You can learn a lot from him.

The "PowerStudy 4.5 for Introduction to Psychology" CD-ROM includes a complete set of interactive learning activities for this module: quizzes, summary test, key terms, web site connections, critical thinking exercise, module outline, and more.

Answers for Module 5

The Big Picture (explanations provided for incorrect choices)

A *Correct! You see the "big picture" for this Module.*
B The biological functions of sensation are the foundation of all psychological activity.
C This is a definition of "perception" and a misunderstanding of the term "sensation."
D This statement reverses the meanings of sensation and perception; both are necessary.
E It's just a joke!

True-False (explanations provided for False choices; page numbers given for all choices)

1	T	93	
2	F	94	The animal does not emit light waves, it reflects them.
3	F	95	This is a description of the pupil.
4	T	97	
5	T	100	
6	F	105	The vestibular system relies on fluid in the inner ear, not on sound.
7	T	106	
8	F	110	Food preferences and dislikes are determined more by culture than biology.
9	F	111	In an experiment, the more expensive pill was rated as more effective, although both were placebos.
10	T	113	

Flashcards 1

1 j 2 a 3 b 4 d 5 e 6 f 7 c 8 i 9 g 10 h

Flashcards 2

1 h 2 d 3 e 4 i 5 f 6 a 7 j 8 g 9 c 10 b

Multiple Choice (explanations provided for incorrect choices)

1 a Plotnik and Kouyoumdjian do not suggest this rare possibility.
b Do you really think this is a possibility?
c Correct! See page 93.
d Plotnik and Kouyoumdjian do not raise this concern.

2 a Adaptation is not the technical term for the process.
c Sensing is not the technical term for the process.
b Experiencing is not the technical term for the process.
d Correct! See page 93.

3 a Transduction refers to the process of changing physical stimuli into impulses.
b Correct! See page 93.
c Sensing is not the technical term for the process.
d Experiencing is not the technical term for the process.

4 a Radar is not based on pulses of light.
b Radar does not cause vibrations.
c Correct! See page 94.
d It's just a joke!

5 a Color is not created in the cornea.
b No light waves are irrelevant in and of themselves.
c Convergence explains the operation of the rods and cones, not the cornea.
d Correct! See page 95.

6 *a Correct! See page 95.*
b The opposite is true in farsightedness.
c Both near and far objects are clear in normal vision.
d This is a normal vision problem experienced by many people.

7 a Focus is controlled by the shape of the eyeball.
b *Correct! See page 96.*
c This is a function of the primary visual cortex in the brain.
d The retina changes light waves into impulses.

8 a Cones allow us to see color.
b The process of transduction does not tell us what is dangerous or safe.
c Both rods and cones are involved in seeing objects, large or small.
d *Correct! See page 96.*

9 ***a*** *Correct! See page 98.*
b This is the opponent-process theory.
c An afterimage is a visual sensation that continues after the original stimulus is removed.
d These are not theories, but two kinds of color blindness.

10 a How would we know if we aren't there to hear it?
b What if a tape recorder had been placed there?
c *Correct! See page 100.*
d Here we see that a philosophical question has a psychological answer.

11 a The frequency of sound waves determines the pitch of what we hear.
b *Correct! See page 100.*
c Pitch is related to frequency of sound waves.
d Cycles are a measure of the frequency of sound waves.

12 a 30 decibels is whisper quiet.
b This is going to be really bad news for Apple Computer!
c *Correct! See page 101.*
d 140 decibels is the upper threshold for human hearing.

13 a It's at the inner end of the outer ear (see diagram).
b It's just before the middle ear (see diagram).
c The auditory canal comes just before the tympanic membrane (see diagram).
d *Correct! See page 102.*

14 ***a*** *Correct! See page 102.*
b The cochlea is further in than the oval window.
c The hammer, anvil, and stirrup are housed in the middle ear.
d The auditory nerves are further in than the cochlea.

15 a True . . . for bats.
b *Correct! See page 105.*
c It is determined more by the ear than by the eye.
d Movement of fluid yes, but not in the eardrum.

16 ***a*** *Correct! See page 105.*
b It is not the bouncing but the mismatch with other information.
c Individual personality factors do not appear to cause motion sickness.
d Drug use does not appear to cause motion sickness.

17 a Sweet is one of the basic tastes.
b *Correct! See page 106.*
c Salty is one of the basic tastes.
d Sour is one of the basic tastes.

18 a Smell is an important part of flavor.
b Taste is an important part of flavor.
c Umami is one of the five tastes.
d *Correct! See page 106.*

19 ***a*** *Correct! See page 108.*
b Nerves do not reside on the surface of the skin.
c Pressure, temperature, and pain are features of the sense of touch.
d What about the smooth, hairless skin where you also experience the sense of touch?

20 a The auditory association area is involved in hearing.
b The vestibular system is involved in balance.
c *Correct! See page 108.*
d The visual association area is involved in vision.

21 ***a*** *Correct! See page 110.*
b But that experience is not the same as disgust.
c But what would make the smell "disgusting"?
d Flavor is the result of smell plus taste.

22 a In research, blind means not knowing the true nature of the treatment.
b Isn't this kind of silly?
c In research, subjects receive either the treatment or a placebo, not both.
d *Correct! See page 111.*

23 a Endorphins might be involved, but not because of the mother's attention.
b If this is true, you better reconsider applying to med school.
c *Correct! See page 112.*
d It's just a joke!

24 a Science does not accept the idea that there are mysteries it cannot explore.
b *Correct! See page 113.*
c What if it is not the twirling needles themselves but rather a byproduct of the needle stimulation?
d There is some evidence that acupuncture does relieve pain. The real question is how it works.

25 a About 100,000 cochlear implants have been done worldwide.
b Just the opposite is true.
c They are implanted in the ear, not in the brain.
d *Correct! See page 115.*

Short Essay (sample answers)

1. We are constantly bombarded by physical sensations gathered by the five basic senses. But in the form of physical energy this information is useless to us. It must be transformed into electrical signals that become neural impulses. In this form it can be sent to the brain for processing. This transformation is the process of transduction. Without transduction, the brain would be incapable of changing raw sensations into signals that can be used to interpret and understand the world that bombards us with its energy.

2. Vision begins with light waves of varying wavelength. In humans, the visible spectrum is the segment of electromagnetic energy we can see. The light waves enter the cornea, pass through the pupil in amounts controlled by the iris, are bent and focused by the lens, and absorbed by the retina. Rods and cones add detail and color and create nerve impulses that begin the process of transduction. The important quality of color is probably explained by a combination of the trichromatic theory and the opponent-process theory.

3. The "sixth" sense is balance, which is a product of the vestibular system of the inner ear. Three semicircular canals set at different angles contain fluid that moves in response to movements of your head. Tiny hair cells in the canals convey information about balance to the brain. If there is a mismatch between the information from the vestibular system and the eyes, you may experience motion sickness. Less well understood, and much more disturbing, are vertigo and Meniere's disease.

4. As any anthropologist or survivalist knows, we *could* eat many products of nature that normally we try hard to avoid. The physical products themselves are nourishing, and probably eaten by some peoples around the world. Yet our immediate reaction to them is disgust. Our faces register this emotion in a universally recognized expression that has survival value as a warning. Obviously this reaction is learned from our culture. No edible food is inherently disgusting. *Hey guys, "Fear Factor" is on!*

5. The laboratory experiment is the most powerful tool we have for determining cause-and-effect relationships in nature. If all other variables are held constant, any differences between control group and experimental group behavior should be due to the experimental treatment. But there is still a danger of bias from the knowledge of subjects and researchers. In the double-blind procedure, both subjects and researchers are "blind" to which group gets which, thus eliminating expectations about subject behaviors.

Module 6

Perception

How to Ruin a Professor's Day

When I took experimental psychology, years ago, our professor enjoyed bedeviling us with the same classic perceptual illusions that Plotnik and Kouyoumdjian discuss in Module 6. The one that really got us was the famous Müller-Lyer illusion. It is so powerful that it fooled us every time, even after we already knew the lines were the same length. One day a troublemaker in the back row asked, "But *why* does it work?" Our professor hung his head and had to admit, "I don't know."

Today, cognitive psychology has an intriguing answer (it's in Module 6). Besides the fascination of discovering how sensing and perceiving work, understanding these processes can be personally liberating. Here's why.

The Task of Self-Management

Step on a rattlesnake and it whirls and strikes. Step on a human and... a hundred different things could happen. Instinct governs much of the snake's behavior, but almost none of the human's. That's why we humans constantly face the task of self-management, or self-regulation. We also face parallel tasks of managing physical objects and other people, but self-management is the most difficult because it's so subjective. As you will see in the modules on mental disorders, it's easy for things to get out of whack. Normally, the activity of self-management goes on so automatically it seems unconscious, but we are constantly working at it.

That's what I like about the module on perception. It helps us appreciate the incredibly complex processes of apprehending and interpreting reality, and in so doing can help us be more realistic about ourselves. There are many things in life to worry about and to fear. An important part of self-management is deciding which stimuli represent real threats and which do not. The disadvantage of our limitless freedom to create wonderful new things is our equally great ability to create fears where they are not appropriate (and also to ignore fears when they could help us). When we get a better handle on our processes of self-management, however, we begin to appreciate that some apparent perceptions are really glitches in the self-managing process, and we realize that we are scaring ourselves needlessly.

There is a sense in which the key task of life is to live realistically. The modules on sensation and perception remind us that we are constantly creating our own reality. Just as illusions can fool us, we can torment ourselves with worries and fears about dangers that are illusory, not real.

Effective Student Tip 6

When You Participate, You Practice

My heart goes out to students who say "I would rather listen than talk…." They are invariably the quiet, supportive type of person the world needs a whole lot more of. (For a teacher, Hell would be a perpetual talk show, with everyone shouting at each other for all eternity and no one listening!) Yet I know that only listening is not really good for them.

Taking part in class discussion binds us to the group, satisfies deep social needs, and increases our sense of effectiveness. But it has a purely academic payoff as well. When you participate, you practice the facts and ideas of the course.

In class, you may have the strong feeling that you understand a point better than the student who is talking, maybe even better than the professor. When it's your turn to talk, you find out just how well you do understand it. As you struggle to put your ideas into words, you come to appreciate both what you have right and what you don't. The reactions of your professor and classmates further inform you how well you have grasped the material. Next time, you reword it, rework it, and begin to master it. The facts and ideas of the course are becoming more personal and more real. You aren't just sitting there waiting for the end of the period. You're really learning.

Your response…

Are you a talker or a listener in your classes? Is class discussion valuable or mostly a waste of time?

Learning Objectives

1. Understand perception as the psychological process of transforming physical stimuli into meaningful representations of reality.
2. Learn the basic differences between sensation and perception and how sensations are changed into perceptions.
3. Explain how the rules of organization, perceptual constancies, depth perception, and illusions work to create our perceptions.
4. Understand the research on subliminal perception, the controversy that led to that research, and the hopes and fears that the possibility of subliminal perception arouses.
5. Appreciate the influence of cultural diversity on the processes of perception and what that influence implies about the power of cultural learning.
6. Consider your position on the reality of extrasensory perception (ESP) and understand the arguments both for and against ESP.
7. Understand the procedures by which many perceptions can be created artificially.

Key Terms

These key terms open up a whole new world. You'll never see things quite the same way after you learn the principles they explain. This module can be fun!

absolute threshold
Ames room
apparent motion
atmospheric perspective
binocular depth cues
brightness constancy
closure rule
color constancy
continuity rule
convergence
cultural influences
depth perception
extrasensory perception (ESP)
figure-ground rule
Ganzfeld procedure
Gestalt psychologists
illusion
impossible figure
interposition
just noticeable difference (JND)
light and shadow
linear perspective
monocular depth cues
motion parallax
perception
perceptual constancy
perceptual sets
phi movement
proximity rule
psi
real motion
relative size
retinal disparity
rules of organization
self-fulfilling prophecies
sensation
shape constancy
similarity rule
simplicity rule
size constancy
structuralists
subliminal messages
subliminal stimulus
texture gradient
threshold
virtual reality
Weber's law

I hope you'll write to me — not only about possible errors you found, but also about anything in my Study Guide you would like to discuss. <profenos@mac.com>

Outline

- *Introduction*

1. Silent messages (Maria's self-esteem CD)
2. Nice dog, mean dog (Gabrielle's dog bite)
3. White spot (Maria's mammogram)
4. Perceiving things (three questions)

☐ What are the three basic questions about perception that Plotnik and Kouyoumdjian say psychology tries to answer?

A. *Perceptual Thresholds*

1. Becoming aware of a stimulus
   a. **Threshold** (Gustav Fechner)
   b. **Absolute threshold**
   c. **Subliminal stimulus**
   d. Accuracy problems
2. Weber's law
   a. **Just noticeable difference (JND)** (E. H. Weber)
   b. **Weber's law**
3. Just noticeable difference (JND) and soft towels

B. *Sensation versus Perception*

1. Basic differences
   a. **Sensation**
   b. **Perception**
2. Changing sensations into perceptions
   a. Stimulus
   b. Transduction
   c. Brain: primary areas
   d. Brain: association areas
   e. Personalized perceptions

C. *Rules of Organization*

1. Structuralists versus Gestalt psychologists
   a. **Structuralists**
   b. **Gestalt psychologists**
   c. Evidence for rules: who won the debate?
2. **Rules of organization**
   a. **Figure-ground rule**
   b. **Similarity rule**

c. **Closure rule**

d. **Proximity rule**

e. **Simplicity rule**

f. **Continuity rule**

D. Perceptual Constancy

1. Size, shape, brightness, and color constancy
2. **Perceptual constancy** in a potentially chaotic world

☐ How does perceptual constancy make our world understandable?

a. **Size constancy**

b. **Shape constancy**

c. **Brightness constancy** and **color constancy**

E. Depth Perception

1. Binocular (two eyes) depth cues

a. **Depth perception**

b. **Binocular depth cues**

2. **Convergence**
3. **Retinal disparity**
4. **Monocular depth cues**: organizational rules

a. **Linear perspective**

b. **Relative size**

c. **Interposition**

d. **Light and shadow**

e. **Texture gradient**

f. **Atmospheric perspective**

g. **Motion parallax**

F. Illusions

1. Strange perceptions

a. **Illusion**

b. Moon illusion

c. **Ames room**

d. Ponzo illusion

e. Müller-Lyer illusion

2. Learning from illusions

☐ How can an illusion help us understand the process of perception?

G. Research Focus: Subliminal Perception

1. Can "unsensed messages" change behavior (popcorn controversy)?

2. Changing specific behaviors (experiment)
   a. **Subliminal messages**
   b. **Self-fulfilling prophecies**
3. Influencing perceptions (experiment)

H. Cultural Diversity: Influence on Perceptions

1. What do **cultural influences** do?
2. Perception of faces (focus on eyes and mouth or nose)
3. Perception of images (analytical versus holistic thinking)
4. Perception of motion (Western cultural influences)
5. Perception of three dimensions (effect of formal education on an **impossible figure**)
6. Perception of beauty (cultural values)
7. **Perceptual sets** (learned expectations)

I. ESP: Extrasensory Perception

1. Definition and controversy
   a. **Extrasensory perception (ESP)**
      (1) **Telepathy**
      (2) **Precognition**
      (3) **Clairvoyance**
      (4) **Psychokinesis**
   b. **Psi**: believing in ESP
   c. Testimonials as evidence
2. Trickery and magic (the Amazing Randi)
3. ESP experiment: **Ganzfeld procedure**
4. Status of ESP and television psychics (importance of replication)

J. Application: Creating Perceptions

1. Creating movement: **phi movement** (Max Wertheimer)
2. Creating movies
   a. **Real motion**
   b. **Apparent motion**
3. Creating **virtual reality**
   a. Remote and robotic surgery
   b. Psychotherapy
4. Creating first impressions

How English Works

Words in the Textbook

p. 122 **absolute** value = basic, unquestioned

white spots that usually **stand out** = look distinct

lack of **expertise** = special knowledge

p. 124 we'll **take the liberty of** calling = risk, take a chance

p. 125 a series of **discrete** steps = completely separate

p. 126 a **heated** debate = full of strong emotions

a set of **innate** rules = contained within, inseparable

p. 128 **chaotic** world = not organized

p. 133 a **fixed** peephole = unmoving

p. 135 take **legislative** action = creating new laws

a self-fulfilling prophecy = a prediction that makes itself happen

impacting the way = affecting

p. 136 Americans are much more likely to **zero in on** = immediately see

That's **where the money is** = the center of interest

p. 138 55% believe in **psychics** = people who claim psychic powers

the **scrutiny** of scientific investigation = close examination

p. 139 an **acoustically isolated** room = closed to outside sounds

to **rule out** the potential for trickery = eliminate, prevent

questions from **perfect strangers** = complete strangers

self-proclaimed psychics = self-called (not approved by experts)

p. 140 **mind-blowing** three-dimensional world = amazing

p. 141 a **debilitating** fear of spiders = weakening

Sentence Structure: Commas

Commas are found in many languages, but how they are used can be quite different even by speakers of that same language.

One place where we find commas is when we have a series of three or more different nouns, verbs, or adjectives.

Eye, ear, tongue, nose, and skin

The continuous stimulation of glasses, jewelry, or clothes on your skin

Notice how the words "and" and "or" are used before the last word in the series.

Notice how a comma is used between each word. The comma before "and" and "or" is used commonly in American written English. This comma is not used in British written English.

Try this: Many people don't realize that we use commas when we speak. A comma is like a pause in speaking. Read the following sentences out loud, and see where you take a little break between words:

> Running as fast as possible the mouse ran into its hole.
>
> From beginning to end the movie was very funny.
>
> As a result of his broken leg Tom could not play football for months.

You probably put in a little breath after the words "possible," "end," and "leg." Now, if you put in a pause when you are reading the sentence aloud, you will probably need to put in a comma when you write the sentence. The pause helps the listener make sense of the sentence. In the same way, a comma helps the reader understand the meaning.

Commas as signposts: Commas let the reader know what is important and what is not important. In any sentence, the most important action comes from the main subject and verb.

So, any information that we put *before* the main subject and verb needs to be separated by a comma. Look at the following sentences from the text:

> Although your sense organs look so very different, they all share the three characteristics defined next.
>
> In the second step, the brain quickly changes sensations.
>
> After passing through the cornea and pupil, light waves reach the lens.
>
> Unlike rods, cones are wired individually to neighboring cells.
>
> Because rods are extremely light sensitive, they allow us to see in dim light.

In all these sentences, the comma tells us that the first part is *not* the main action of the sentence. When we see the comma, it tells us that the *next* words are the real action of the sentence.

So, the comma divides the introductory information from the main subject and verb. Try it yourself: read the following sentences. Each needs a comma, so you decide where to put it:

> Next to an elephant a mouse looks very small.
>
> When she didn't see her mother the baby started crying.
>
> After the war ended the soldiers all returned home.
>
> With no warning at all to the students the teacher began to sing.

Now, what happens if we reverse these sentences? Do we still need to use commas? What do you think?

> A mouse looks very small next to an elephant.
>
> The baby started crying when she didn't see her mother.
>
> The soldiers all returned home after the war ended.
>
> The teacher began to sing with no warning at all to the students.

All these sentences are correct. In all of them, the important action — the main subject and verb — comes at the beginning of the sentence. This action is clear, so when the extra information comes at the end, we don't need to separate it with a comma.

Answers

Next to an elephant, a mouse looks very small.
When she didn't see her mother, the baby started crying.
After the war ended, the soldiers all returned home.
With no warning at all to the students, the teacher began to sing.

The Big Picture

Which statement below offers the best summary of the larger significance of this module?

A Perception is the constant bombardment of sensory data on several specialized areas of the brain.

B Both sensation and perception are inborn biological processes — once again demonstrating that psychology is basically just biology.

C Through the several processes of perception, the mind creates the reality we take for granted. In a way, what is real is the picture of the world we create in our minds.

D Considering how illusions and the various perceptual rules work, we can only conclude that there is no real world, and that psychology is little more than guesswork and shots taken in the dark.

E The next time a teacher marks one of your answers "Wrong," just point out that, according to psychology, "it's all in how you look at it!"

True-False

_____ 1. A threshold is a point above which we are aware of a stimulus.

_____ 2. A biologist calls it "sensation" and a psychologist calls it "perception," but they are both talking about the same thing.

_____ 3. The brain follows a number of perceptual rules in order to make sense out of the mass of visual stimuli it receives.

_____ 4. If it were not for perceptual constancies, the world would seem ever-changing and chaotic.

_____ 5. In the Müller-Lyer illusion, one boy looks like a giant and the other like a midget.

_____ 6. Illusions are amusing, but can't teach us anything because they aren't real.

_____ 7. Anthropologists have discovered that how you see things depends at least in part on the culture in which you were raised.

_____ 8. A perceptual set is a kind of stubbornness that makes subjects stick to the first answer they give even if they realize they were wrong.

_____ 9. There is a large body of accepted scientific evidence that supports the existence of ESP.

_____ 10. Horses at the track, real motion; movie replay of the race, apparent motion.

Flashcards 1

_____	1. closure rule	a.	a point above which a stimulus is perceived and below which it is not perceived
_____	2. continuity rule	b.	our tendency to organize stimuli in the simplest way possible
_____	3. figure-ground rule	c.	found rules that specify how individual elements are organized into meaningful patterns or perceptions
_____	4. Gestalt psychologists	d.	tendency to perceive an object as remaining the same size even when its image on the retina grows or shrinks
_____	5. illusion	e.	our tendency to favor smooth or continuous paths when interpreting a series of points or lines
_____	6. impossible figure	f.	a perceptual experience of perceiving a strange object as being so distorted that it could not really exist
_____	7. shape constancy	g.	tendency to see an object as keeping its same form in spite of viewing it from different angles
_____	8. simplicity rule	h.	perceptual experience in which a drawing seems to defy basic geometric laws
_____	9. size constancy	i.	our tendency to automatically identify an element of more detail, which then stands out from the rest
_____	10. threshold	j.	our tendency to fill in any missing parts of a figure in order to see the figure as complete

Flashcards 2

_____	1. Ames room	a.	binocular cues for depth that depend on signals from muscles as they move both eyes inward to focus
_____	2. apparent motion	b.	computer simulated experience of being inside an object or environment or action
_____	3. convergence	c.	having strong beliefs about changing some behavior and then acting, unknowingly, to change the behavior
_____	4. extrasensory perception (ESP)	d.	a controlled method for eliminating trickery, error, and bias while testing telepathic communication
_____	5. Ganzfeld procedure	e.	illusion that closely positioned stationary lights flashing at regular intervals seem to be moving
_____	6. perceptual sets	f.	a group of presumed psychic experiences that lie outside the normal sensory processes or channels
_____	7. phi movement	g.	learned expectations that are based on our personal, social, or cultural experiences and change perceptions
_____	8. self-fulfilling prophecies	h.	a demonstration that our perception of size can be distorted by changing depth cues
_____	9. subliminal messages	i.	brief auditory or visual messages that are presented below the absolute threshold
_____	10. virtual reality	j.	illusion that a stimulus or object is moving in space when, in fact, the stimulus or object is stationary

Multiple Choice

_____ 1. An absolute threshold is the intensity level that you can
- a. detect every time it is presented
- b. guess is there, even if you can't quite detect it
- c. just barely detect
- d. detect 50 percent of the time

_____ 2. A subliminal stimulus has an intensity that gives a person __________ of detecting it
- a. a less than a 50 percent chance
- b. a more than a 50 percent chance
- c. no chance at all
- d. a 100 percent chance

_____ 3. Weber's law of the just noticeable difference explains why
- a. you study better if you have the radio on
- b. your parents don't believe you really turned your stereo down
- c. kids like heavy metal and their parents like lite rock
- d. contestants on American Idol try not to be too different

_____ 4. Sensation is to perception as __________ is to __________
- a. grownup / child
- b. complete / unfinished
- c. word / story
- d. movie / reality

_____ 5. Which *one* of the following is the correct sequence in perception?
- a. stimulus – sensation – perception – meaning
- b. meaning – stimulus – sensation – perception
- c. sensation – stimulus – perception – meaning
- d. perception – stimulus – meaning – sensation

_____ 6. Gestalt psychologists differed from structuralists in believing that
- a. you add together hundreds of basic elements to form complex perceptions
- b. perceptions result from our brain's ability to organize sensations according to a set of rules
- c. "the whole is equal to the sum of its parts"
- d. "the parts are more real than the whole"

_____ 7. The perceptual rule that makes important things stand out is called
- a. closure
- b. proximity
- c. figure dominance
- d. figure-ground

_____ 8. The perceptual rule that we tend to favor smooth or continuous paths when interpreting a series of points or lines is called
- a. shortest distance
- b. continuity
- c. closure
- d. simplicity

_____ 9. Which one of the following is *not* a perceptual constancy
a. shape constancy
b. size constancy
c. motion constancy
d. color constancy

_____ 10. Thank goodness for size constancy — without it you would
a. never know for sure how big or small anything really was
b. immediately get bigger after a single large meal
c. see things change in size whenever the light changed in brightness
d. think your sweetheart is getting smaller and smaller while walking away from you

_____ 11. The visual advantage to the human species of having two eyes is
a. figure-ground discrimination
b. monocular cues
c. retinal disparity
d. eyeglasses balance on the nose better

_____ 12. Which one of the following is *not* a monocular depth cue?
a. retinal disparity
b. linear perspective
c. relative size
d. motion parallax

_____ 13. The reason people seem to change size as they change sides in the Ames room is that
a. the room is not actually rectangular
b. hidden mirrors distort the images you see as you look in
c. a lens in the peephole forces you to view them upside down
d. the subtle coloring of the walls creates a hypnotic trance in the viewer

_____ 14. One explanation why the Müller-Lyer illusion lines don't appear to be the same length is that
a. our previous experience with arrows tells us they *aren't* all the same
b. they really aren't quite the same — there is a tiny difference in length
c. your experience with the corners of rooms makes you see the arrows differently
d. the famous illusion is still unexplained (even Professors Müller and Lyer couldn't explain it)

_____ 15. Should you scrap this Study Guide and buy a subliminal message tape? Research suggests that any improvement you get with those tapes is probably due to
a. the effects of extra practice
b. turning the volume up too high
c. the Ponzo illusion
d. a self-fulfilling prophecy

_____ 16. The reason you couldn't figure out the two-pronged/three-pronged impossible figure in the textbook is that
a. seeing it in a textbook aroused test anxiety and that threw you off
b. you were attempting to see it as an object in the real world
c. Westerners aren't as good at this kind of puzzle as Africans are
d. it was just a joke

_____ 17. The many brass coils worn by Burmese girls in the past are an example of how
a. culture influences the concept of beauty
b. Western cultural values influence concepts of beauty
c. formal education affects perception
d. analytical thinking affects perception

_____ 18. Because of a/n __________, you probably saw the body builder in the textbook as a big guy
a. impossible figure
b. perceptual set
c. formal education
d. holistic thinking approach

_____ 19. Which one of the following is *not* an ESP experience?
a. replication
b. telepathy
c. clairvoyance
d. psychokinesis

_____ 20. Tops on the list of people *not* to invite to an ESP demonstration:
a. Gustav Fechner
b. E. H. Weber
c. Max Wertheimer
d. Amazing Randi

_____ 21. Many people believe in it, but convincing evidence of ESP has been undercut by the
a. hocus-pocus that surrounds ESP demonstrations
b. refusal of psychologists to investigate it seriously
c. inability to repeat positive results
d. fact that some people have it and others don't

_____ 22. The purpose of the Ganzfeld procedure is to
a. win the challenge posed by James Randi
b. separate the effects of real motion from those of apparent motion
c. eliminate trickery, error, and bias during experiments testing ESP
d. investigate the powers of TV psychics like Miss Cleo

_____ 23. When John Wayne grabs the reins on the stagecoach, we "see" the horses as really flying because our brains
a. apply the principle of closure and fill in the blanks between frames of the movie
b. "suspend doubt" as we get more and more involved in the movie
c. accept the data coming in from the retina and optic nerve
d. know that the horses in the movie really were moving as they were being filmed

_____ 24. A perceptual revolution called virtual reality is now being used in psychotherapy to
a. help clients with feelings of guilt to become more virtuous in their real lives
b. allow clients to dial up famous psychologists on their home computers
c. see television programs of robots performing surgeries the clients dread
d. expose clients with phobias to feared stimuli in a realistic three-dimensional environment

_____ 25. The textbook showed you "photos" of a white family and a black family — actually the same family with different makeup — to demonstrate the point that

a. situations presented on television shows like *Black, White* do not happen in real life
b. first impressions are dramatically influenced by race
c. younger people, such as students, are not affected by racial stereotypes
d. all Americans should be forced to wear the same makeup

Short Essay

1. Describe the relationship between sensation and perception and explain its importance in psychology.

2. Why would we be helpless without the operation of the perceptual rules of organization, constancies, and depth perception?

3. Perceptual illusions are fun, but what do they have to teach us about psychology?

4. Describe the impact of culture on perception. Illustrate your answer with examples.

5. What is your opinion on the reality of ESP?

Do You Believe in ESP?

Tell the truth — do you believe that at least a few people possess the special power of perception we call ESP?

If you answered "yes," doesn't that create a problem with psychology as a science? Can a science of behavior be valid if some human abilities may sometimes fall outside its scope?

If you believe in ESP, how can you believe that psychology is a science? (That's okay; lots of people don't think psychology is completely scientific.)

If you believe that psychology can be, should be, must be a science, how can you believe in ESP?

The "PowerStudy 4.5 for Introduction to Psychology" CD-ROM for this module is a "Super Module." In addition to the regular PowerStudy features (quizzes, summary test, key terms, web site connections, critical thinking exercise, module outline, and more), Super Modules also include self-paced, step-by-step multimedia presentations with animations and narration.

Answers for Module 6

The Big Picture

A This is more like sensation, and not at all what perception is or how it works.
B Both sensation and perception are influenced by culture and learning.
C *Correct! You see the "big picture" for this Module.*
D This philosophical idea is too extreme. We have every reason to assume there is a real world we can understand.
E It's just a joke!

True-False (explanations provided for False choices; page numbers given for all choices)

1	T	122	
2	F	124	Perception creates meaningful experience out of sensory input.
3	T	126	
4	T	128	
5	F	133	That happens in the Ames room; the Müller-Lyer illusion compares two lines.
6	F	133	We learn from illusions that perception is an active process.
7	T	136	
8	F	137	A perceptual set is a learned tendency to see things only one way.
9	F	138	There is little scientific evidence (some would say "none") supporting ESP.
10	T	140	

Flashcards 1

1 j 2 e 3 i 4 c 5 f 6 h 7 g 8 b 9 d 10 a

Flashcards 2

1 h 2 j 3 a 4 f 5 d 6 g 7 e 8 c 9 i 10 b

Multiple Choice (explanations provided for incorrect choices)

1 a Remember that "threshold" means where you cross over.
b But how would you know it is there?
c This is more like a subliminal stimulus.
d *Correct! See page 122.*

2 ***a*** *Correct! See page 122.*
b Then it would hardly be subliminal.
c There is some chance, but how much?
d Then what would "sub" mean?

3 a Distraction, not volume, probably explains why you like the radio on.
b *Correct! See page 123.*
c Kids don't really like louder noises (they just think they do).
d Even if true, this would not be an example of the JND.

4 a The relationship between raw material and finished product explains sensation and perception.
b The relationship between raw material and finished product explains sensation and perception.
c *Correct! See page 124.*
d The relationship between raw material and finished product explains sensation and perception.

5 ***a*** *Correct! See page 124.*
b How could meaning come first?
c How could the sensation come before the stimulus?
d Sensation creates the raw materials for the perception.

6 a That would be truer of the structuralists.
b *Correct! See page 126.*
c The famous quote is "more than" the sum of the parts.
d This has the famous quote backwards.

7 a Closure refers to the tendency to see figures as complete.
b Proximity refers to the tendency to group objects that are close together.
c Figure dominance is not the correct technical term for this perceptual principle.
d *Correct! See page 127.*

8 a This is not a correct term in psychology.
b *Correct! See page 127.*
c Closure refers to the tendency to complete figures.
d Simplicity refers to the preference for simple figures.

9 a Shape constancy is one of the perceptual constancies.
b Size constancy is one of the perceptual constancies.
c *Correct! See page 128.*
d Color constancy is one of the perceptual constancies.

10 a Figure ground organization is not directly related to size constancy.
b Size constancy refers to perceived size, not real size.
c Light cues are not directly involved in size constancy.
d *Correct! See page 128.*

11 a Figure-ground discrimination can be achieved with one eye.
b It has to do with binocular cues.
c *Correct! See page 129.*
d It's just a joke!

12 ***a*** *Correct! See page 130.*
b Linear perspective is a monocular depth cue.
c Relative size is a monocular depth cue.
d Motion parallax is a monocular depth cue.

13 ***a*** *Correct! See page 133.*
b The Ames room is clever, but it's not done with mirrors.
c There is no lens in the peephole.
d The Ames room does not depend on a hypnotic trance.

14 a This illusion does not depend on our experience with arrows.
b The lines are exactly the same length, all right.
c *Correct! See page 133.*
d The good professors couldn't explain it, but modern cognitive psychologists have an answer.

15 a These tapes do not require practice (which is one reason why they don't work).
b High volume would only wake you up!
c The Ponzo illusion involves visual cues.
d *Correct! See page 135.*

16 a Test anxiety was not involved in your perception of the gadget.
b *Correct! See page 132.*
c This answer refers to an explanation of the Müller-Lyer illusion.
d It was not a joke, but this answer is!

17 ***a*** *Correct! See page 137.*
b Burmese society in the past was not exposed to Western concepts of beauty.
c Traditional Burmese did not have widespread formal education.
d It is not analytical thinking but cultural influence.

18 a He had an unusual (not impossible) figure, but why didn't we see that he was short?
b *Correct! See page 137.*
c Formal education is not involved.
d Holistic thinking is not involved.

19 ***a*** *Correct! See page 138.*
b Telepathy is the supposed ability to transfer one's thoughts to another or read the thoughts of others.
c Clairvoyance is the supposed ability to see objects that are out of view.
d Psychokinesis is the supposed ability to move objects by thoughts.

20 a Gustave Fechner defined the absolute threshold — he's O.K.
b E. H. Weber discovered "Weber's law" — he's O.K.
c Max Wertheimer discovered phi movement — he's O.K.
d *Correct! See page 138.*

21 a The hocus-pocus makes ESP look bad, but by itself does not disprove ESP.
b There has been considerable scientific research aimed at proving ESP.
c *Correct! See page 139.*
d If some people really do have it, then ESP must be a fact.

22 a The Ganzfeld procedure is designed to dispute ESP, not support it.
b The Ganzfeld procedure is about ESP, not motion.
c *Correct! See page 139.*
d The Ganzfeld procedure is designed to dispute ESP results, not psychic predictions.

23 ***a*** *Correct! See page 140.*
b Since movies are a visual experience, the answer must involve a principle of perception.
c Since movies are a visual experience, the answer must involve a principle of perception.
d Since movies are a visual experience, the answer must involve a principle of perception.

24 a Virtual reality is way better than 3-D.
b We already have computer simulation programs for psychology.
c Most research casts doubt on so-called "subliminal perception."
d *Correct! See page 141.*

25 a The point is the power of prejudice to influence perception, not the shortcomings of television shows.
b *Correct! See page 141.*
c Sad to say, this isn't true.
d Hey... now there's a solution to our racial problems!

Short Essay

1. The goal of psychology is to explain, predict, and control human behavior. One problem psychology must solve is how physical energy, like light waves, is transformed into thoughts and actions. Perception is the final step in that process. Through a series of perceptual rules, the brain almost instantly and almost automatically changes nerve impulses into recognizable and usable images. This completes the process of transduction and sets the stage for all human thought, feeling, and action.

2. If the perceptual rules of organization, constancies, and depth perception were suddenly abolished, our worlds would lose all stability, recognizability, and meaning. They would become like a cruel and terrifying form of insanity. Nothing would have meaning for us. Objects would continually change their size, shape, and color. People would seem larger or smaller as they came and went. In fact, we wouldn't recognize them as people at all, but perhaps oozing blobs of changing material. Thank goodness for perception!

3. Perceptual illusions, such as the two-pronged/three-pronged impossible figure in the textbook, make us realize how hard we work to change electrical signals into meaningful messages. In this case, our brain is presented with an impossible problem. An artist has cleverly created a two-dimensional drawing that we can't turn into a three-dimensional object in the real world. We keep trying, going back and forth from the two-pronged to the three-pronged end. Our struggle lets us actually experience the process.

4. One of the strengths of the textbook is that it takes full account of the impact of culture on psychological processes. The process of transduction is also affected by learning. There are numerous examples of the effect of culture on perception. Africans with no formal education did not see the two-pronged/three-pronged illusion. Traditional Burmese women were considered more beautiful with their necks stretched by brass coils. We see a small body builder as taller and heavier than he actually is. Culture is powerful!

5. You may believe in ESP or not (in surveys, most people say they do). In your answer, you should consider the opposing evidence of testimonials claiming ESP versus the scant scientific evidence for it. Your answer should include discussion of the rigorous Ganzfeld procedure (you might describe the experiment with Zener cards) and the scientific requirement of replication. By the way, for those who believe in ESP, James Randi still has $10,000 waiting for you!

Module 7

Sleep & Dreams

Do Dreams Have Meaning?

Freud is dead… Freud is dead… Freud is dead…. Keep repeating it long enough, and maybe Sigmund Freud will go away. He has a way of coming back, though, no matter how often psychology pronounces him dead wrong.

One of Freud's most provocative ideas is the notion that all dreams have meaning. He thought it was his most important discovery, and wrote, "Insight such as this falls to one's lot but once in a lifetime." Dreams were important to Freud because they allowed the best look into the workings of the unconscious. When you learn more about Freud's theory of personality (in Module 19) and his technique of psychoanalysis (in Module 24), you will see that he thought of dreaming, with unconscious meanings hidden behind innocent sounding or bizarre surface stories, as a model for all human psychic life. (See the box on p. 123 titled "How to Construct a Dream" for more on Freud's theory of dreams.)

The newer theories of dreaming discussed in Module 7 discount or reject Freud's theory, perhaps partly because — you knew this was coming — Freud says dreams represent sexual wishes. Building on laboratory research into sleep and brain biology, however, the new theories are filling in blanks Freud could only guess at.

Turn Your Bed into a Research Laboratory

The deciding evidence in the battle over the meaningfulness of dreams may be your own dreams. Why not use them as a research project? Many people find it useful to keep a dream journal, which helps them get down more details than we normally remember and also serves as a record that can be reviewed from time to time. The cares and worries of the day quickly chase dream details away, so try waking up slowly and peacefully. If you sense that you had a dream, keep your eyes closed and stay with it. Tell it to yourself a few times. Then get up (or grab your bedside pencil and pad if it's still night) and write down as much as you remember.

The hard part, of course, is trying to interpret the dream. Here's how. Review the story of the dream, then ask how it connects to your life. This is a process of indirection and confusion, and you have to go where the dream leads, no matter how apparently meaningless it seems. The *crucial clues* will be what Freudians call your *associations* to the dream, the things that come to mind as you think about each element of the dream. What feelings does it arouse? What thoughts (none sexual, of course) pop into your mind? How do the feelings and thoughts associated with the dream relate to issues in your psychological life? Is it possible that your dream does have meaning?

Effective Student Tip 7

Stay Focused

Everyone tells you how great it is that you are in college, but sometimes it seems like they don't really understand what you are up against. You may be away from home for the first time, trying to get along with your roommates, cheering on your college team, and worrying about how to get a date. Your parents and friends back home expect letters and phone calls. If you are a returning student, your children miss you, your spouse resents getting less attention, and your boss still asks you to stay late to finish that big project. In any case, you are discovering how easy it is to become distracted from your basic purpose for being in college.

No matter how important a party, your friend's need to talk all night, or extra work at the office may seem at the time, learning and succeeding are what college is really all about. The most important features of college are what happens in your classrooms and at your desk when it's time to study.

Keep your emotional radar attuned to incoming distractions. When all you hear is the beep, beep, beep of threats to learning and succeeding, it's time to defend yourself. Remind yourself why you are in college, and then make the necessary adjustments to get back to the work you came here to do.

Your response…

Think about a typical day in your college life. What distractions are you likely to face?

Learning Objectives

1. Understand consciousness as a *continuum* of awareness of one's thoughts and feelings, from full alertness to unconsciousness, in which sleep and dreaming are complex and fascinating components.
2. Learn the basic biology of sleeping and waking and the biological clocks and circadian rhythms that control them.
3. Explain the interplay of stages and types of sleep that together take up one-third of our lives.
4. Learn what research says about your personal style as a morning person or a night person.
5. Appreciate the winter depression called seasonal affective disorder (SAD) as an example of cultural differences in psychology.
6. Consider the competing theories of dreaming and dream interpretation and how they relate to larger theories of psychology.
7. Understand common sleep problems and their treatment, and apply your new understanding to your own life.

Key Terms

Everyone is fascinated by the topics in this module, especially sleep and dreaming. Learn these terms and you will be able to explain everything your friends want to know (well, enough to keep them listening).

activation-synthesis theory of dreams
adaptive theory
alpha stage
altered states of consciousness
automatic processes
benzodiazepines and non-benzodiazepines
biological clocks
circadian rhythm
consciousness
continuum of consciousness
controlled processes
daydreaming
dreaming
evening persons
extensions of waking life theory of dreams
food-entrainable (midnight snack) circadian clock
Freud's theory of dreams
implicit (nondeclarative) memory
insomnia
interval timing clock
jet lag
light therapy
melatonin
morning persons
narcolepsy
night terrors
nightmares
non-REM sleep
questionnaire
REM behavior disorder
REM rebound
REM sleep
repair theory
reticular formation
seasonal affective disorder (SAD)
sleep
sleep apnea
sleepwalking
stage 1 sleep
stage 2 sleep
stage 4 sleep
stages of sleep
suprachiasmatic nucleus
threat simulation theory of dreams
unconscious (Freud)
unconsciousness (physical)
VPN (ventrolateral preoptic nucleus)

Outline

- *Introduction*
  1. Living in a cave (Stefania)
  2. Chance discovery (REM sleep)

A. Continuum of Consciousness

1. Different states
   a. **Consciousness**
   b. **Continuum of consciousness**
      (1) **Controlled processes**
      (2) **Automatic processes**
      (3) **Daydreaming**
      (4) **Altered states of consciousness**
      (5) **Sleep** and **dreaming**
      (6) **Unconscious** (Sigmund Freud's theory) and **implicit (nondeclarative) memory**
      (7) **Unconsciousness** [physical]
2. Several kinds (why is consciousness so mysterious?)

B. Rhythms of Sleeping & Waking

1. Biological clocks
   a. **Biological clocks**
   b. **Circadian rhythm**
   b. Length of day
2. Location of biological clocks
   a. **Suprachiasmatic nucleus**
   b. **Interval timing clock**
   c. **Food-entrainable (midnight snack) circadian clock**
3. Circadian problems and treatments
   a. Shift workers
   b. **Jet lag**
   c. Resetting clock: **light therapy**
   d. **Melatonin**

C. World of Sleep

1. **Stages of sleep: alpha stage**
2. **Non-REM sleep**
   a. **Stage 1 sleep**
   b. **Stage 2 sleep**
   c. Stage 3 and **Stage 4 sleep** (slow wave or delta)

3. **REM sleep**
   a. Characteristics of REM sleep (**REM behavior disorder**)
   b. REM — dreaming (**REM rebound**) and remembering
4. Awake and alert
5. Sequence of stages (rollercoaster ride)
   a. Stage 1
   b. Stage 2
   c. Stage 4
   d. REM

D. Research Focus: Circadian Preference

1. Research: are you a morning person or an evening person?
   a. **Questionnaire**
   b. **Morning persons**
   c. **Evening persons**

☐ Are you a morning person or an evening person?

2. Body temperature differences
3. Brain differences
4. Behavioral and cognitive differences

E. Questions about Sleep

1. How much sleep do I need?
   a. Infancy and childhood
   b. Adolescence and adulthood
   c. Old age

☐ How much sleep do you personally seem to need?

2. Why do I sleep?
   a. **Repair theory**
   b. **Adaptive theory**
3. What if I miss sleep?

☐ What happens to you when you miss sleep?

   a. Effects on the body
   b. Effects on the brain
4. What causes sleep?
   a. Master sleep switch: **VPN (ventrolateral preoptic nucleus)**
   b. **Reticular formation**
   c. Going to sleep

F. Cultural Diversity: Incidence of SAD

1. Problem and treatment of **seasonal affective disorder (SAD)**
2. Occurrence of SAD (Florida, New Hampshire, and Iceland)
3. Cultural differences (explaining Iceland)

G. World of Dreams

1. Theories of dream interpretation
   a. **Freud's theory of dreams** (Sigmund Freud's *The Interpretation of Dreams*, 1900)
   b. **Extension of waking life theory of dreams** (Rosalind Cartwright)
   c. **Activation-synthesis theory of dreams** (J. Alan Hobson)
   d. **Threat simulation theory of dreams** (from evolutionary psychology approach)
2. Typical dreams

H. Application: Sleep Problems & Treatments

1. Occurrence

☐ Have you experienced a sleep problem? What was it like? What did you do about it?

2. **Insomnia**
   a. Psychological causes
   b. Physiological causes
3. Non-drug treatment
   a. Cognitive-behavioral: establishing an optimal sleep pattern
   b. Eight steps for more regular and efficient sleep
4. Drug treatment for insomnia (**benzodiazepines** and **non-benzodiazepines**)
5. **Sleep apnea**
6. **Narcolepsy**
7. Sleep disturbances
   a. **Night terrors** in children
   b. **Nightmares**
   c. **Sleepwalking**

Keep a Dream Journal

Many self-observing people have benefited from keeping dream journals. Keep a notepad and pen on your nightstand. When you have a dream (see other material in this Study Guide module on catching and interpreting dreams), jot down the essential points. Later, write a fuller version in your Dream Journal. It is fascinating to re-read these dreams after you have accumulated a number of them. Patterns may emerge. Common themes will be revealed. You will learn more about yourself.

How English Works

Words in the Textbook

p. 147 a **hardy** subject = strong, not easily tired

seemed to **come and go** = move from strong to weak

a publicity **stunt** = unusual act to get attention

p. 148 **evasive** action = avoiding

all external **restraints** = controls

p. 151 in a **lousy** mood = irritable, bad mood

to win **patents** = legal protection for inventions

(problems) that **plague** shift workers = disturb again and again

p. 153 which **goes by** the initials REM = uses

p. 156 activities during the day **deplete** key factors = use until empty

that are **replenished** = refilled

theories are not really **at odds** = conflicting, at war

p. 157 they **lapse into** (coma) = fall into

p. 160 she says something about her **acne** = skin problem

swamis = religious person, especially in traditions of India

Insights such as this **fall to one's lot** = are experienced

p. 161 **sighted** people = people who can see

repeatedly **simulating** events = mimicking or imitating something

p. 163 has **fleeting** urges to sleep throughout the day = brief, passing or fading quickly

Sentence Structure: Noun Clauses

Why do you sleep? is a question. **Why you sleep** is <u>not</u> a question. It's a clause that does the same job as a noun. We call this a noun clause.

Like a noun, you can use it as the <u>subject of a sentence</u>:

Why you sleep is an important topic.

Like a noun, you can use it as the <u>object of a sentence</u>:

Scientists are studying **why you sleep.**

Like a noun, you can use it as the <u>object of a preposition</u>:

Experts have different explanations of **why you sleep.**

How much sleep do you need? is a question. **How much sleep you need** is a noun clause.

How __________ depends on your age.

Where will we begin? is a question. **Where** __________ is a noun clause.

The first page of the first chapter is **where** __________.

How does a baby learn? is a question.

How __________ is a noun clause.

How __________ seems to be the same in all cultures.

When did Freud die? is a question.

When __________ is a noun clause.

The year 1939 is **when** __________.

Vocabulary: "Deprive"

Deprive (verb)

To **deprive** someone or something means to take away something important:

The baby cried when the mother deprived him of __________.

Losing her job will deprive Lydia of __________.

The heavy clouds today are depriving everyone of __________.

Deprived (adjective)

people or animals who are sleep **deprived**

The house plants died because they were __________ deprived.

Poor people are __________ deprived.

The people who weren't allowed to vote were __________ deprived.

Deprivation (noun)

The record for sleep **deprivation**

Feelings of hunger are the result of __________ deprivation.

Depression can be caused by deprivation of __________.

Deprivation of __________ in childhood can lead to weakness in bones in adults.

Answers

How much sleep you need depends on your age.
Where we'll begin is a noun clause.
The first page of the first chapter is **where we'll begin**.
How a baby learns is a noun clause.
How a baby learns seems to be the same in all cultures.
When Freud died is a noun clause.
The year 1939 is **when Freud died.**
The baby cried when the mother deprived him of **(his bottle) (his toy).**
Losing her job will deprive Lydia of **(her income) (money).**
The heavy clouds today are depriving everyone of **(sunlight).**
The house plants died because they were **(light)(water)** deprived.
Poor people are **(economically)** deprived.
The people who weren't allowed to vote were **(politically)** deprived.
Feelings of hunger are the result of **(food)** deprivation.
Depression can be caused by deprivation of **(love) (light).**
Deprivation of **(milk) (vitamins)** in childhood can lead to weakness in bones in adults.

The Big Picture

Which statement below offers the best summary of the larger significance of this module?

A In everyday life, we seem to live in two states: awake and asleep. In actuality, there are many subtle degrees of consciousness that psychology is only beginning to explore and understand.

B A new spirit of common sense is coming into the psychological study of consciousness. We are either conscious or unconscious, dreams mean very little, and sleep disturbances are minor problems.

C This module raises disturbing questions about just how scientific the study of psychology really is. Most of what is presented comes from personal experience and insight, and very little from empirical research.

D The puzzling experience of living in a cave and the existence of morning people and evening people cast doubt on the existence of biological clocks and biological regulation. Humans are controlled by culture and learning.

E If we were all meant to be "A" students, the Almighty would not have given us a need for sleep.

True-False

_____ 1. Human beings are always in one of two distinct states: awake and conscious or asleep and unconscious.

_____ 2. One adjustment problem faced by humans is that the circadian rhythm of our biological clocks is set not for 24 hours but for about 24 hours and 18 minutes.

_____ 3. Getting extra hours of sleep in a dark room is a fast way to reset our biological clocks.

_____ 4. Researchers study sleep by measuring brain waves.

_____ 5. Once you sink into true sleep, your bodily activity remains constant until you awake in the morning.

_____ 6. The existence of the REM rebound effect suggests that dreaming must have some special importance to humans.

_____ 7. Research on sleep deprivation and performance proves that the "repair theory" of sleep is correct.

_____ 8. Everyone dreams.

_____ 9. As with everything else in his theories, Freud's explanation of dreams has a sexual twist.

_____ 10. The activation-synthesis theory of dreams places great importance on getting to the underlying meaning of each dream.

Flashcards 1

_____	1. activation-synthesis theory of dreams	a. says dreaming represents the random and meaningless activity of nerve cells in the brain
_____	2. adaptive theory	b. says sleep replenishes key factors in brain and body depleted by activities during day; sleep as restorative
_____	3. circadian rhythm	c. says we dream about threatening life events and use these dreams to rehearse the skills needed for survival
_____	4. continuum of consciousness	d. wide range of experiences from being aware and alert to being unaware and unresponsive
_____	5. extensions of waking life theory of dreams	e. an increased percentage of time spent in REM sleep when we are deprived of REM sleep on previous night
_____	6. Freud's theory of dreams	f. sleep during which eyes move rapidly back and forth behind closed eyelids; associated with dreaming
_____	7. REM rebound	g. says sleep evolved to prevent energy waste and exposure to dangers of nocturnal predators
_____	8. REM sleep	h. a biological clock that is genetically programmed to regulate physiological responses in a 24+ hour day
_____	9. repair theory	i. says dreams are wish fulfillments, satisfaction of unconscious sexual or aggressive desires
_____	10. threat simulation theory of dreams	j. says our dreams reflect the same thoughts, fears, concerns, and problems as are present when awake

Flashcards 2

_____	1. altered states of consciousness	a. using meditation, drugs, or hypnosis to produce an awareness that differs from normal state
_____	2. automatic processes	b. repeated periods during sleep when a person stops breathing for ten seconds or longer; tiredness results
_____	3. controlled processes	c. a mental place sealed off from voluntary recall where we place threatening wishes or desires
_____	4. jet lag	d. when one's internal circadian rhythm is out of step with external clock time; fatigue, disorientation
_____	5. light therapy	e. in children, frightening sleep experiences starting with a scream, followed by sudden waking in a fearful state
_____	6. narcolepsy	f. a chronic disorder marked by sleep attacks or short lapses of sleep throughout the day; muscle paralysis
_____	7. night terrors	g. a pattern of depressive symptoms beginning in fall and winter and going away in spring
_____	8. seasonal affective disorder (SAD)	h. use of bright artificial light to reset circadian rhythms and to combat insomnia and drowsiness from jet lag
_____	9. sleep apnea	i. activities that require full awareness, alertness, and concentration to reach some goal; focused attention
_____	10. unconscious (Freud)	j. activities that require little awareness, take minimal attention, and do not interfere with other activities

Multiple Choice

_____ 1. Plotnik and Kouyoumdjian open the module on consciousness with the story of Stefania's four-month stay in a cave to illustrate the fact that
   a. body time runs slower than celestial time
   b. without sunlight, humans begin to lose their grip on reality
   c. without sunlight, Stefania's night vision became very acute
   d. we would all be much more cheerful if there were no clocks around

_____ 2. We naturally think in terms of the two states called "conscious" and "unconscious," but actually there is (are)
   a. three states, including the "high" from drugs
   b. four states: conscious, drowsy, dreaming, and unconscious
   c. a continuum of consciousness
   d. no measurable difference between consciousness and unconsciousness

_____ 3. Psychologists call activities that require full awareness, alertness, and concentration
   a. automatic processes
   b. altered states
   c. comas
   d. controlled processes

_____ 4. Activities that require little awareness, take minimal attention, and do not interfere with other ongoing activities are called
   a. implicit activities
   b. altered states of consciousness
   c. automatic processes
   d. unconsciousness

_____ 5. Have you noticed that you often wake up just before the alarm clock goes off? Credit it to the fact that we humans have a built-in
   a. aversion to jangling noise, which we try to avoid
   b. biological clock
   c. sense of responsibility
   d. brain mechanism that always monitors the external environment, even during sleep

_____ 6. If human beings were deprived of all mechanical means of telling time (like clocks), they would
   a. still value schedules and punctuality, thanks to their biological clocks
   b. follow a natural clock with a day about 30 hours long
   c. not stick to strict schedules the way we do now
   d. lose all sense of when things should be done

_____ 7. The brain structure that regulates many circadian rhythms is called the
   a. internal timing clock
   b. suprachiasmatic nucleus
   c. resetting clock center
   d. biological stopwatch

_____ 8. Once you begin to understand the biology of sleeping and waking, you realize that
a. we should allow people to sleep whenever and as long as they want to
b. most people waste hours in non-productive sleep they could do without
c. humans are evolving into a species that only needs a couple of hours of sleep a day
d. there is a disconnect between human biology and modern culture

_____ 9. The food-entrainable circadian clock
a. makes it easy to train subjects when food is used as a reward
b. explains the extra 18 minutes in the body's circadian clock
c. explains the importance of having breakfast every day
d. regulates eating patterns in people and animals

_____ 10. The most promising new treatment for jet lag appears to be
a. periods of bright light
b. avoidance of food for 24 hours before a long flight
c. surgical resetting of the biological clock
d. drugs that induce sleep in the new time zone

_____ 11. Sleep can be divided into __________ sleep and __________ sleep
a. alpha / beta
b. REM / non-REM
c. REM / pre-REM
d. stage 1 / stage 2

_____ 12. Dreams are most likely to occur during
a. stage 1 (theta waves)
b. EEG sleep
c. non-REM sleep
d. REM sleep

_____ 13. REM behavior disorder is a condition in which
a. you appear to be looking around even though obviously you can't see anything
b. you have dreams, but they don't make any sense
c. voluntary muscles are not paralyzed and sleepers can and do act out their dreams
d. voluntary muscles are paralyzed and you can't move no matter how hard you try

_____ 14. Evidence that dreaming is a necessary biological process is provided by
a. REM behavior disorder
b. REM rebound
c. stage 4 sleep
d. alpha stage sleep

_____ 15. In the textbook, Plotnik and Kouyoumdjian compare a night's sleep to
a. riding a roller-coaster
b. boating on a calm lake
c. wading in deep water
d. driving a luxury automobile

_____ 16. Research shows that sleep deprivation
  a. is a serious medical problem
  b. only occurs after 11 days without sleep
  c. is a minor problem, mostly affecting high school and college students
  d. isn't a problem, because the body will go to sleep when necessary

_____ 17. The VPN (ventrolateral preoptic nucleus) acts as a
  a. clue that makes it possible to tell if a sleeper is dreaming
  b. master on-off switch for sleep
  c. censor that disguises sexual and aggressive wishes in dreams
  d. light enhancer that combats feelings of depression during the winter months

_____ 18. Research in both Iceland and New Hampshire showed that seasonal affective disorder (SAD) is caused by
  a. an above average number of days of bright light
  b. a combination of diminished light and low temperature
  c. personal tragedy and family problems
  d. cultural factors as well as the amount of sunlight

_____ 19. According to Freud's famous theory, at the heart of every dream is a
  a. clue to the future
  b. disguised wish
  c. hate-filled thought
  d. shameful sexual memory

_____ 20. Rosalind Cartwright points out that dreams are difficult to understand because
  a. people don't remember their dreams very well
  b. most people don't remember their dreams at all
  c. dreams have very little to do with everyday life
  d. most dreams are dull, like typical everyday life

_____ 21. The activation-synthesis theory says that dreams result from
  a. a biological need to pull together and make sense of the day's activities
  b. "batch processing" of all the information gathered during the day
  c. random and meaningless chemical and neural activity in the brain
  d. the need to express hidden sexual and aggressive impulses

_____ 22. The threat simulation theory from evolutionary psychology says we dream in order to
  a. rehearse the skills needed for survival in dangerous life events
  b. diminish the role of natural selection in our lives
  c. simulate situations in which we threaten other people
  d. struggle against over stimulation of our sexual drives

_____ 23. The best advice for combating insomnia is to
  a. get in bed at the same time every night and stay there no matter what happens
  b. get out of bed, go to another room, and do something relaxing if you can't fall asleep
  c. review the problems of the day as you lie in bed trying to go to sleep
  d. try sleeping in another room, or on the couch, if you can't fall asleep in your bed

_____ 24. Which one of the following is *not* a sleep problem?
a. narcolepsy
b. night terrors
c. oversleeping
d. sleepwalking

_____ 25. The sleep problem that involves repeated stopping of breathing is called
a. benzodiazepine deficiency
b. narcolepsy
c. night terror
d. sleep apnea

Short Essay

1. Describe the idea and components of the continuum of consciousness.

2. What are biological clocks and why do we have them?

3. Describe the stages of sleep and what occurs in them.

4. Explain which theory of dreaming seems most persuasive to you and how your personal experience supports that theory.

5. Describe a sleep problem or disturbance you have experienced (whether mild or serious) and relate how you tried to deal with it.

How to Construct a Dream (Sigmund Freud)

If every dream represents a secret wish disguised as a jumbled, apparently meaningless story, how is the disguise constructed? Freud describes the "dream work" as four processes:

1. **Condensation** is the compression of several thoughts into a single element, which has the effect of making the dream seem *incoherent.*

2. **Displacement** is the transfer of psychical intensity from the actual dream thoughts to other ideas, which has the effect of making the dream seem *meaningless.*

3. **Symbolism** is the transformation of the dream thoughts into apparently unconnected pictorial arrangements or scenes, which has the effect of making the dream seem *illogical.*

4. **Secondary elaboration** is the interpretative revision of the hallucination content or scenes into stories, however absurd, which has the effect of making the dream seem *strange*, perhaps ridiculous or frightening, but *not connected to the dreamer.*

Freud said that the purpose of the disguise is to hide the disturbing wish from the dreamer, and thus to allow the dreamer to continue sleeping in relative peace. To learn about the unconscious wish, it is necessary to see through the disguise.

The next time you remember a dream fairly clearly, try using these ideas to take it apart. It's not easy, but you may gain insight into the meaning of your dreams, and also into the provocative genius of Sigmund Freud.

Answers for Module 7

The Big Picture

A *Correct! You see the "big picture" for this Module.*
B Each part of this statement is false, as is the statement as a whole.
C The psychology of consciousness, sleep, and dreams rests on highly scientific research findings.
D Just the opposite is true; the examples support the idea of biological regulation.
E It's just a joke!

True-False (explanations provided for False choices; page numbers given for all choices)

1	F	148	There is a continuum of consciousness.
2	T	150	
3	F	151	Exposure to bright light is a fast way to reset our biological clocks.
4	T	152	
5	F	152	There are four stages of sleep that alternate during the night.
6	T	153	
7	F	156	However logical it sounds, the repair theory of sleep is not supported by research.
8	T	160	
9	T	160	
10	F	161	Finding the underlying meaning of dreams is emphasized in the Freudian theory.

Flashcards 1

1 a 2 g 3 h 4 d 5 j 6 i 7 e 8 f 9 b 10 c

Flashcards 2

1 a 2 j 3 i 4 d 5 h 6 f 7 e 8 g 9 b 10 c

Multiple Choice (explanations provided for incorrect choices)

1 ***a*** *Correct! See page 147.*
b Stefania's mental health remained good.
c Night vision was not a factor in this experiment.
d Maybe true, but cheerfulness was not a factor in this experiment.

2 a There are more than three states of consciousness.
b There are more than four states of consciousness.
c *Correct! See page 148.*
d Consciousness and unconsciousness are distinct and different states.

3 a Automatic processes require little awareness.
b In altered states of consciousness, awareness and alertness are diminished.
c A coma is just the opposite.
d *Correct! See page 148.*

4 a This is not a correct term in psychology.
b Altered states of consciousness, such as meditation or psychoactive drugs, do interfere.
c *Correct! See page 148.*
d Unconsciousness absolutely prohibits other activities.

5 a Perhaps, but how would we know when to wake up and turn it off?
b *Correct! See page 150.*
c Ha! ha! ha! ha!
d There is no such brain mechanism.

6 a Belief in the value of schedules and punctuality is a cultural phenomenon.
b A day, according to our natural circadian rhythm, is about 24-25 hours long.
c *Correct! See page 150.*
d In preindustrial societies, humans followed many environmental and bodily cues in coordinating their activities.

7 a This is not a correct term in psychology.
b *Correct! See page 150.*
c This is not a correct term in psychology.
d This is not a correct term in psychology.

8 a How could modern society function under such circumstances?
b Most people get less sleep than is good for them.
c There is nothing to suggest that humans need less sleep than they did earlier in their evolution.
d *Correct! See page 150.*

9 a Subjects are learning a pattern of eating.
b It is not connected to the extra 18 minutes.
c This circadian clock does not make breakfast important, but it explains how we may come to feel a need for it.
d *Correct! See page 150.*

10 *a* *Correct! See page 151.*
b Food is not the issue in jet lag.
c Surgery after every trip? [Test-taking tip: be wary of statements that defy all common sense.]
d What if the problem is to stay awake?

11 a The alpha stage is just as you are going to sleep; there is no beta stage.
b *Correct! See page 152.*
c Half correct; there is no "pre-REM" sleep.
d There are four stages of sleep but two categories.

12 a Dreams begin to occur after stage 2 sleep.
b This is not a correct technical term in sleep research.
c Read page 165 on the difference between REM and non-REM sleep.
d *Correct! See page 153.*

13 a This is a description of REM sleep.
b Dreams typically do not make much sense.
c *Correct! See page 153.*
d During dreaming, the normal condition is for your body to lose muscle tension.

14 a This hints at it, but REM rebound suggests that our body demands dreaming.
b *Correct! See page 153.*
c Dreaming does not occur in stage 4 sleep.
d Dreaming does not occur in the alpha stage.

15 *a* *Correct! See page 154.*
b It is far from a calm, steady process.
c This analogy would make sleeping too difficult and troubling.
d If only!

16 *a* *Correct! See page 157.*
b As far as we know, only one person ever went 11 days without sleep.
c Sleep deprivation is a serious and widespread problem in modern society.
d As shown by the record of 11 days, with exertion sleep can be postponed for a long time.

17 a That would be REM sleep.
b *Correct! See page 157.*
c The VNP is not a psychological mechanism.
d That would be melatonin.

18 a Just the opposite is true.
b Temperature is not a factor in SAD.
c Personal tragedy and family problems are not primary factors in SAD.
d *Correct! See page 159.*

19 a Freud did not believe that dreams foretell the future.
b *Correct! See page 160.*
c Freud did not believe that dreams are primarily sadistic.
d Freud linked dreaming to sex, but not necessarily to shame.

20 ***a*** *Correct! See page 160.*
b A few people can't remember their dreams, but most remember some of them.
c Her theory of extensions of waking life says just the opposite.
d Dreams reflect everyday life, but they can be dramatic, exciting, scary, etc.

21 a No such biological need has been discovered.
b This would be true of an information processing theory of dreams.
c *Correct! See page 161.*
d This is true of Freud's theory of dreams.

22 ***a*** *Correct! See page 161.*
b If this alternative makes any sense at all, it is just the opposite of the correct answer.
c This answer misuses the terms "simulation" and "threat."
d Sounds more like a Freudian theory of dreams.

23 a This advice only makes insomnia worse.
b *Correct! See page 162.*
c This advice will only make it harder to fall asleep.
d This advice will make it difficult to form good sleep habits.

24 a Narcolepsy is a relatively rare sleep problem.
b Night terrors are a common childhood sleep problem.
c *Correct! See page 163.*
d Sleepwalking is a relatively rare sleep problem.

25 a This is not a correct term in psychology.
b Narcolepsy is falling asleep many times during the day.
c Night terrors are frightening experiences in which children wake up screaming with fear.
d *Correct! See page 163.*

Short Essay

1. Most people assume that we are either conscious (awake) or unconscious (asleep). Modern psychology knows that there is actually a continuum of consciousness consisting of at least seven different experiences. From most to least conscious, these experiences are: controlled processes, automatic processes, daydreaming, altered states, sleep and dreaming, the unconscious mind (Freud) or implicit (declarative) memory, and physical unconsciousness. Understanding the range helps us understand each part better.

2. Biological clocks are internal timing devices that are genetically set to regulate various physiological responses for different periods of time. These clocks are governed by the suprachiasmatic nucleus in the brain. Earlier in evolution, biological clocks and circadian rhythms helped humans stay in tune with nature. Even now, biological clocks keep us from straying too far from the basic tasks (eating, sleeping, and reproducing) that keep the species going.

3. Sleep is far from an unbroken, steady state. Based on studies of changes in brain waves, physiological arousal, and dreaming, sleep is more like a roller-coaster ride. In the alpha stage, you become drowsy and drift into stage 1, which lasts 1–7 minutes. Stage 2 is the first stage of real sleep. About 30–45 minutes after falling asleep, you go through stages 3 and 4, the latter being deep sleep. REM sleep, during which dreams occur, can happen 5–6 times over stages 2–4. These stages are depths, rather than sequences, of sleep.

4. You may be persuaded either by Freud's theory of dreams, the extensions of waking life theory, the activation-synthesis theory, or the new theory from evolutionary psychology called the threat simulation theory. You might favor some combination of these theories. However you argue, you should take account of a theory's strengths, weaknesses, and main competitors. Try to capture the essence of the theory you favor and why it best fits your own ideas about psychology and your own experience of dreaming.

5. I hope you have not experienced any of the serious sleep problems described in the textbook. If you have, you know all too well what to write about (be sure to tell what seems to help you). But it would be a rare student who has not at least struggled with periods of insomnia. If that fits you, describe the circumstances and what you tried to do about it. Comment on the program that Plotnik and Kouyoumdjian offer in the textbook for establishing an optimal sleep pattern. Would the program, or parts of it, work for you?

Module 8

Hypnosis & Drugs

We'll Have Ours Straight

Nature lovers have a kind of warped view of life. In general, we prefer it undiluted. When we're outdoors, we don't wear headsets because we would rather hear the birds, waves, and wind. When we're having fun, we would rather have all our senses set on normal, neither excited nor dulled by psychoactive agents, legal or otherwise.

For most humans, however, and apparently for most of human history, normal consciousness isn't quite satisfying. Sometimes we want it heightened, sometimes we need it muted, hence the long history of human attempts to alter consciousness and mood through self-medication. Almost all of us have found some technique, or some substance, that adjusts our consciousness and mood to the point where it feels just right — or at least less painful.

This module discusses two methods of altering consciousness. Hypnosis is either a state of great suggestibility or an alternate route to deeper truths about ourselves. Plotnik and Kouyoumdjian discuss the debate over what hypnosis is, how it works, and what it can do. But regardless of your position in this debate, hypnosis is different from ordinary consciousness. Psychoactive drugs are a mind-altering power of a different sort.

Why Do We Use Drugs?

In textbook after textbook I've seen, the section on drugs reads like something you would get in pharmacy school. Good, solid technical information on psychoactive drugs, including the most recent illegal drugs to hit the streets, but nothing on the really important issue — why we use psychoactive drugs at all, let alone to such excess.

Plotnik and Kouyoumdjian raise that question, and suggest provocative answers. They offer a balanced, dispassionate survey of contemporary drug use and abuse. Rather than succumbing to hysteria or personal beliefs, the common failing of so many politicians and public spokespersons, they carefully review the biological facts, the cultural connections, and the historical record of drug use and society's attempts to curtail it. If you read their discussion closely, you may discover that some of the things you always knew were 'true' about drugs may not be true after all.

Personally, I'm dead set against any use of psychoactive drugs […says he, after gulping down a can of caffeine-laced diet cola!], but I don't think it does any good to tell you that. Plotnik and Kouyoumdjian have it right. Instead of moralizing (as I am doing here), let's investigate the psychological processes by which almost all of us "self-medicate" in our continual attempt to control and manage our thoughts, feelings, and behavior.

Effective Student Tip 8

People Power

One of my arguments for setting a goal of perfect attendance is that when you go to class every day the group takes over. It's not that you feel like a captive, but more like a member of a family that is determined not to let you fail. In a good class, I often notice that the regulars kind of take an informal attendance, not satisfied until all the other regulars have arrived, or pointedly worrying about the one who hasn't.

These friendships become the basis for study groups, which prove invaluable for struggling students and even more valuable for the students helping them. (Here's a paradox of instruction: the teacher always learns more than the student, because in order to teach something to someone else you first have to really understand it yourself.) Study groups give their members ten times more opportunities to ask questions and talk than class time allows. This adds up to lots more practice.

Another reason to get acquainted with your classmates is the opportunity to make new friends and expand your cultural horizons. Most colleges attract students from every part of the city and from all over the world. Finally, there is the fact that we humans may be the most social species on Earth. Biologically speaking, other people replace our missing instincts. Practically speaking, friends make life fun.

Your response…

Do you talk to your classmates? How easily do you make new friends? Do you ever feel lonely?

Learning Objectives

1. Understand both hypnosis and drug use as altered states of consciousness — a prelude to the study of normal conscious processes that is coming in the next several modules.

2. Learn the basic facts about hypnosis and the essence of the controversy about what hypnosis is and how it works.

3. Appreciate the underlying reasons for drug use, the similarities of drug use in brain chemistry, and the social lessons in the history of drug abuse and control.

4. Learn the relationship of stimulants, opiates, and hallucinogens and the properties of the major drugs in each category.

5. Consider the significance of cultural risk factors as determinants of national differences in alcoholism rates.

6. Consider the implications of research on a popular drug prevention program (DARE).

7. Learn the essential ingredients of good treatment programs for drug abuse.

Key Terms

Most of these key terms are as timely as today's news, where you are likely to find them. All you need to do is sharpen up your definitions.

addiction
age regression
alcohol
alcoholism
altered state theory of hypnosis
caffeine
cocaine
DARE (Drug Abuse Resistance Education)
dependency
designer drugs
hallucinogens
hypnosis
hypnotic analgesia
hypnotic induction
imagined perception
LSD
marijuana
MDMA (ecstasy)
mescaline
methamphetamine
nicotine
opiates
posthypnotic amnesia
posthypnotic suggestion
psilocybin
psychoactive drugs
sociocognitive theory of hypnosis
stimulants
substance abuse
tolerance
withdrawal symptoms

The "PowerStudy 4.5 for Introduction to Psychology" CD-ROM for this module is a "Super Module." In addition to the regular PowerStudy features (quizzes, summary test, key terms, web site connections, critical thinking exercise, module outline, and more), Super Modules also include self-paced, step-by-step multimedia presentations with animations and narration.

Outline

- *Introduction*

☐ How are hypnosis and drug use somewhat alike?

1. Hypnosis (Rod and Paul at the nightclub)
2. Drugs (Albert Hoffman's bad trip)

A. Hypnosis

1. Definition of **hypnosis**
2. Three questions often asked about hypnosis
   a. Who can be hypnotized?
   b. Who is susceptible?
   c. How is someone hypnotized?
      (1) **Hypnotic induction**
      (2) Method to induce hypnosis
3. Theories of hypnosis
   a. **Altered state theory of hypnosis**
      (1) Explanation: altered or disconnected state
      (2) Hypnotic induction
   b. **Sociocognitive theory of hypnosis**
      (1) Explanation: special abilities and social pressures
      (2) Imaginative suggestibility
4. Behaviors
   a. **Hypnotic analgesia**
   b. **Posthypnotic suggestion**
   c. **Posthypnotic amnesia**
   d. **Age regression**
   e. **Imagined perception**
5. Medical and therapeutic applications
   a. Medical and dental uses
      (1) Brain scans
      (2) Thoughts or expectations
   b. Therapeutic and behavioral uses

B. Drugs: Overview

1. Reasons for use (**psychoactive drugs**)
2. Definition of terms

☐ Why is it significant that Freud had a problem? What does it say about drugs? About psychology?

   a. **Addiction**

b. **Tolerance**

c. **Dependency**

d. **Withdrawal symptoms**

3. Use of drugs

4. Effects on nervous system

a. Drugs affect neurotransmitters

(1) Mimicking neurotransmitters

(2) Blocking reuptake

b. Drugs affect the brain's reward/pleasure center

(1) Activating the brain's reward/pleasure center

(2) Addiction/dependency

C. *Stimulants*

1. **Stimulants**

☐ Plotnik and Kouyoumdjian quote a great marketing slogan used to sell amphetamines in Sweden in the 1940s. When we look back on our own times, what ad campaigns may seem equally irresponsible?

2. Amphetamines

a. Drug: **methamphetamine**

b. Nervous system

c. Dangers

3. Cocaine

a. Drug: **cocaine**

b. Nervous system

c. Dangers

4. Caffeine

a. Drug: **caffeine**

b. Nervous system

c. Dangers

5. Nicotine

a. Drug: **nicotine**

b. Nervous system

c. Dangers

D. *Opiates*

1. Opium, morphine, heroin

a. Drug: **opiates**

b. Nervous system

c. Dangers

2. Treatment

E. Hallucinogens

1. Definition: **hallucinogens**
2. LSD
   a. Drug: **LSD**
   b. Nervous system
   c. Dangers
3. Psilocybin ("magic mushrooms")
   a. Drug: **psilocybin**
   b. Nervous system
   c. Dangers
3. Mescaline (peyote cactus)
   a. Drug: **mescaline**
   b. Nervous system
   c. Dangers
4. **Designer drugs**
   a. Drug: **MDMA (ecstasy)**
   b. Nervous system
   c. Dangers

F. Alcohol

1. History and use
2. Definition and effects

☐ Are you curious about how alcohol works in your brain and nervous system? If so, you might want to review Module 3, page 55 in the textbook.

   a. Drug: **alcohol**
   b. Nervous system
   c. Dangers
3. Risk factors
   a. Psychological risk factors
   b. Genetic risk factors
4. Problems with alcohol

G. Cultural Diversity: Alcoholism Rates

1. **Alcoholism**
2. Cultural influences
   a. Genetic risk factors (facial flushing)
   b. Cultural risk factors
   c. Across cultures

H. Marijuana

1. Use and effects
   a. Medical marijuana
   b. Gateway effect
2. Marijuana
   a. Drug: **marijuana**
   b. Nervous system
   c. Dangers

I. Research Focus: Drug Prevention

1. Effectiveness of **DARE (Drug Abuse Resistance Education)**
2. Research on effectiveness of DARE program
   a. Method and procedure
   b. Results and discussion
   b. Conclusion

J. Application: Treatment for Drug Abuse

1. Developing a problem: a case history (Martin)
2. **Substance abuse**
3. Treatment
   a. Step 1: admit the problem
   b. Step 2: enter a program (four goals)
   c. Step 3: get therapy (three therapies)
   d. Step 4: stay sober (relapse prevention)

Multiple Choice Questions

Most multiple-choice questions have a stem and four alternatives. The first trick in handling multiple-choice questions is to know what the question is asking. One way to think about this is to ask yourself, "Which alternative turns the stem into a true statement?"

How English Works

Words Used in the Textbook

p. 169 we all **filed out** = walked out

pieces of furniture assumed **grotesque** [forms] = strange, ugly

p. 170 **compliance** = agreeing to follow other people's decisions

p. 172 [Clients] had **undergone** hypnosis = experienced

After an **exhaustive** review = complete, with every detail

Try to **swat** that fly = hit

not merely **faking** their responses = pretending false action

p. 173 the world's leading **practitioner** = user, person who practices method

p. 174 [Freud] tried to **cut down** = reduce his usage

it was beyond his human power to **bear** = tolerate

p. 176 **stiffer** penalties = stronger

available on **the black market** = illegal, hidden economy

authorities **raided** [laboratories] = attacked

its chemical **makeup** = composition, organization

a **crackdown** on amphetamines = strong action by police

p. 177 go through **a vicious circle** = series of actions where each solution makes a new problem

p. 180 the **net** effect is increased stimulation = final

frightening **flashbacks** = surprise return of drug effects

p. 181 use peyote as a **sacrament** = an important religious practice

p. 183 **manslaughter** convictions = killing

college women said they had **binged** = uncontrolled eating or drinking

college freshmen who **drop out** = leave school

p. 186 researchers identified and **synthesized** THC = artificially produced

joints of marijuana = cigarette-like shape

p. 187 politicians gave **glowing** testimonials = full of praise

mock courtroom exercise = artificial, imitation

p. 188 Martin's **knack** for learning helped him = ability

alcohol reduced his feelings of **self-loathing** = self-hating

his wife **could stand** his drinking no longer = tolerate, live with

Martin sat home with his **booze** = liquor

treatment to **get straightened out** = stop harmful behavior

it represents a **hurdle** = obstacle, problem

Sentence Structure: Commas as Interrupters

Previously, you read about the use of commas to show where the introductory material ended and the important action, the main subject and verb, began. But wait! Did you notice three commas in the sentence you just read?

Of course, the first comma is used to let us know that "you read" is the important action in the sentence. But what are those commas before and after "the main subject and verb" doing? These last two commas are work together to tell us that "the important action" means "main subject and verb." Look at this example from the text.

> Although it seemed like an ordinary week, Maria and her 7-year-old daughter, Gabrielle, would be involved in three relatively normal events that could change their lives forever.

Notice the commas before and after "Gabrielle." This extra information about the 7-year-old daughter's name is helpful, so the writer includes it in the sentence. The commas let us know that it is extra information. We can remove all the information between the two commas and the sentence doesn't change its meaning. We call these pairs of commas "interrupters."

> For higher-intensity stimuli, such as heavy weights, a much larger difference in intensity was required.

> One group, called the structuralists, strongly believed that we added together thousands of sensations to form a perception.

Writers use interrupters to give examples or specific names that will help the reader understand the sentence.

Although we most often see interrupters in the middle of sentences, an interrupter can also appear at the end of a sentence. In this case, we don't need a comma at the end because we are using a period to identify the end of the sentence. From the textbook:

> Weber's law has many practical applications, such as how to detect a difference in the softness of towels.

Vocabulary: "Clear"

Are you **clear** on the many meanings of the word **clear**? Glass can be **clear** or **opaque**.

> The windshield of a car should be __________. A bathroom window should be __________.

An explanation can be **clear** or **confusing**.

> The textbook uses examples that are __________. Learning many theories can be __________.

Air can be **clear** or **hazy**.

> The view from the mountaintop is __________. Air pollution makes everything look __________.

An action can look **clear** or **blurry**.

> A good camera takes pictures that are __________. But if you move, the photo looks __________.

Answers

clear / opaque
clear / confusing
clear / hazy
clear / blurry

The Big Picture

Which statement below offers the best summary of the larger significance of this module?

A This module comes right out and says it: the War on Drugs not only is a waste of time, but it may be contrary to human health. We need the pleasures that drugs provide and we can tolerate a few victimless crimes.

B The material on hypnosis is a stage-setter for the message of this module. If we have so little control over our behavior, we cannot allow even the smallest existence of a drug culture. Zero tolerance is our only hope.

C When we crack down on one psychoactive drug, people who are weak just find some other mood-altering substance. That's why the module concludes that government regulation of the drug trade is the only sensible answer.

D As much as we might not like to admit it, drug use may be almost "natural." We seem driven to alter our consciousness, perhaps to make life more bearable, and history suggests that almost nothing will stop us.

E Say something about this module? Well, it's like, totally awesome… you know what I mean?… like, you know?… whatever… oh man, I'm really wasted!

True-False

____ 1. Stage hypnotism really isn't so remarkable, since anyone can be hypnotized.

____ 2. According to the altered state theory, during hypnosis a person enters a special state of consciousness that is different from the normal waking state.

____ 3. The debate in psychology about hypnosis concerns whether entertainers should be allowed to exploit hypnosis for profit.

____ 4. One good use for hypnosis is to reduce pain during medical or dental procedures.

____ 5. Hypnosis is more effective than any other technique in helping people quit smoking.

____ 6. History shows that if our government would follow a consistent policy, one by one all illegal drugs could be eradicated.

____ 7. Psychoactive drugs create effects on behavior by interfering with the normal activity of neurotransmitters.

____ 8. Illegal drugs are scary, but legal drugs like alcohol and nicotine do, by far, the greatest harm.

____ 9. Your risk for becoming an alcoholic rises significantly if members of your family were alcoholics.

____ 10. Research proves that in DARE (Drug Abuse Resistance Education) we finally have a program that works — if only we had the resolve to use it in every school in the nation.

Flashcards 1

_____	1. age regression	a.	says hypnosis is a state during which a person experiences different sensations and feelings
_____	2. altered state theory of hypnosis	b.	experiencing sensations, perceiving stimuli, or performing behaviors from one's imagination
_____	3. hypnosis	c.	giving hypnotized subjects an idea about performing a particular behavior upon coming out of hypnosis
_____	4. hypnotic analgesia	d.	not remembering what happened during hypnosis if hypnotist told you that you wouldn't
_____	5. hypnotic induction	e.	various methods to induce hypnosis, including asking subjects to close their eyes, go to sleep
_____	6. imagined perception	f.	reduction in pain after hypnosis, suggestions that reduce anxiety and promote relaxation
_____	7. posthypnotic amnesia	g.	procedure for experiencing changes in sensations, perceptions, thoughts, feelings, or behaviors
_____	8. posthypnotic suggestion	h.	says hypnosis is state of powerful social or personal influences and pressures to conform to suggestions
_____	9. psychoactive drugs	i.	drugs that increase the activity of the nervous system and result in heightened alertness and arousal
_____	10. sociocognitive theory of hypnosis	j.	subjects under hypnosis being asked to return or regress to an earlier period, such as early childhood

Flashcards 2

_____	1. addiction	a.	change in nervous system so a person needs to take the drug to prevent painful withdrawal symptoms
_____	2. caffeine	b.	a behavioral pattern marked by overwhelming and compulsive desire to use a drug; tendency to relapse
_____	3. dependency	c.	manufactured or synthetic illegal drugs designed to produce psychoactive effects
_____	4. designer drugs	d.	a mild stimulant that produces moderate physiological arousal; alertness, decreased fatigue
_____	5. hallucinogens	e.	drugs that increase activity of nervous system and result in heightened alertness, arousal, and euphoria
_____	6. nicotine	f.	drugs that produce strange and unreal perceptual, sensory, and cognitive experiences
_____	7. opiates	g.	addictive drugs that come from the opium poppy, such as opium, morphine, heroin; highly addictive
_____	8. stimulants	h.	dangerously addictive drug that triggers brain's reward /pleasure center to produce good feelings [hint: it's legal!]
_____	9. tolerance	i.	original dose of drug no longer produces the desired effect, so person must take increasingly larger doses
_____	10. withdrawal symptoms	j.	painful physical and psychological symptoms that occur after drug-dependent person stops using drug

Multiple Choice

____ 1. Rod Plotnik tells the story about attending a stage hypnotist's act to illustrate the point that
   a. a trained psychologist cannot be hypnotized
   b. hypnotism produces remarkable effects, but there is debate about what it really is
   c. hypnotism is an art that many have attempted to learn, but only a rare few have mastered
   d. entertainment pays better than psychology

____ 2. Which one of the following is *not* a necessary part of hypnotic induction?
   a. swing a watch (and it must be a pocket watch) slowly back and forth until the subject's eyes glaze over
   b. create a sense of trust
   c. suggest that the subject concentrate on something
   d. suggest what the subject will experience during hypnosis

____ 3. The main issue in the psychological debate over hypnosis is
   a. not whether it exists, but how it is induced
   b. why subjects tend to play along with the hypnotist
   c. whether hidden observers really can spot stage hypnotist's tricks
   d. whether it is a special state of consciousness

____ 4. The sociocognitive theory of hypnosis says that hypnosis is based on a/n
   a. special ability of responding to imaginative suggestions and social pressures
   b. altered state of consciousness
   c. good-natured desire to go along with what people want
   d. extreme tendency to give in to authority

____ 5. Which one of the following is *not* an effect claimed for hypnosis?
   a. age regression
   b. imagined perception
   c. hypnotic analgesia
   d. superhuman acts of strength

____ 6. The hypnotist tells Janet, "When you wake up, you won't remember what you did on stage tonight." This instruction produces
   a. posthypnotic amnesia
   b. prehypnotic suggestion
   c. posthypnotic ordering
   d. hypnotic analgesia

____ 7. Research into the use of hypnosis to change problem behaviors suggests that hypnosis
   a. is a miracle treatment in changing behavior
   b. does not help in attempts to change behavior
   c. can be useful in combination with other treatments
   d. is useful in helping people quit smoking, but not in weight loss

____ 8. Why do people use drugs? The answer involves
   a. personality factors — there are as many reasons as there are drug users
   b. pharmacological, psychological, and cultural factors
   c. the power of chemistry, which creates a "one try and you're hooked" result
   d. the pressures of modern society (ancient cultures didn't have drugs)

_____ 9. Many students are shocked to learn that the great psychologist Sigmund Freud had a serious drug problem with

a. cocaine
b. nicotine
c. alcohol
d. marijuana

_____ 10. "Tolerance" for a drug means that the brain and the body

a. adjust to the drug and use it with no ill effects
b. no longer get any effect from using the drug
c. shut out the drug, which passes harmlessly through the system
d. require increasingly larger doses of the drug to achieve the same effect

_____ 11. Basically, all drugs work by interfering with the normal operation of

a. neurotransmitters in the brain
b. glucose in the blood
c. DNA in the genes
d. sensory receptors in the eyes, ears, nose, tongue, and skin

_____ 12. Only 60 years ago, a now-illegal drug was marketed in Sweden under the slogan

a. "Things go better with caffeine!"
b. "Two pills beat a month's vacation."
c. "I'd walk a mile for a Camel."
d. "Hey dude, where's my joint?"

_____ 13. Specifically, drugs cause addiction and dependency by

a. destroying brain centers that control will power
b. activating the brain's pain center
c. interfering with the normal levels of dopamine in the brain
d. making sexual behavior impossible without drugs

_____ 14. All of the following are stimulants *except*

a. cocaine
b. caffeine
c. alcohol
d. nicotine

_____ 15. One sad lesson from the history of amphetamine, cocaine, and methamphetamine use is that

a. cracking down on one illegal drug leads to an increase in use of another illegal drug
b. the more dangerous the illegal drug, the harder it is to suppress it
c. the most dangerous drugs are the depressants
d. there is a certain class of people who must — and will — have drugs

_____ 16. The main reason it is so tough to quit smoking is that

a. tolerance for nicotine takes a long time to develop
b. physical addiction can continue for years after quitting
c. withdrawal symptoms are so painful
d. psychological dependency is deepened by the fact that smoking solves problems

_____ 17. The three main effects of __________ are pain reduction, euphoria, and constipation
a. opiates
b. stimulants
c. hallucinogens
d. designer drugs

_____ 18. In its effects, which one of the following does *not* belong with the others?
a. peyote
b. LSD
c. psilocybin
d. heroin

_____ 19. The clear lesson of the history of prohibition (1920 to 1933) is that
a. it may be impossible to ban a drug that is so popular and widely used
b. we must abandon our on-again/off-again enforcement strategies and declare an all-out war on drugs
c. eventually people get tired of any drug
d. legalization would reduce the problem to manageable dimensions

_____ 20. Despite all the drug abuse horror stories we hear, the truth is that the two most costly and deadly drugs in our society are
a. heroin and cocaine
b. marijuana and ecstasy
c. psilocybin and mescaline
d. alcohol and tobacco

_____ 21. Studies of national rates of alcoholism around the world suggest that alcoholism is a/n
a. individual problem, relatively unaffected by where the individual lives
b. partly genetic and partly cultural problem
c. genetic problem, independent of national origins
d. family problem, passed down through the generations

_____ 22. One reason offered for enforcing tough penalties against marijuana use is the
a. lack of evidence that marijuana has any medical value
b. medical abuse of marijuana caused by liberal doctors
c. theory of the gateway effect
d. success of the DARE program

_____ 23. After years of studying the harmfulness of marijuana, scientists have concluded that it
a. eventually causes brain damage
b. often leads to mental illness
c. typically leads to the use of hard drugs
d. may or may not be dangerous in the long run — the research is not yet definitive

_____ 24. The story of "Martin," the high school drinker who became a drug-abusing doctor, suggests that
a. environmental causes like poverty don't help explain substance abuse
b. instead of blaming addicts, we should offer them treatment
c. if alcohol had been illegal, Martin never would have gotten into hard drugs
d. Martin should have been left alone, unless he actually harmed a patient

_____ 25. Good news/bad news — an eight-year study of three therapies for alcoholism showed that
a. psychoanalytic therapy is the most effective, but the costs are prohibitively high
b. the programs had initial success, but in four months all the subjects were drinking again
c. the programs were equally effective, but the overall success rate was only 30 to 45 percent
d. all three therapies have some strengths, but nothing beats individual will power

Short Essay

1. What are the arguments that hypnosis is or is not a special state of consciousness?

2. Explain the brain chemistry of drug use, addiction, and dependency (non-technical terms are okay).

3. How do stimulants, opiates, and hallucinogens differ? Illustrate your explanation with examples of each.

4. Consider the fact that humans have used drugs for thousands of years. What does that say about how we should approach the social and personal problems of drug use?

5. *Don't write this answer out!* Consider your own involvement in drug use, or your rejection of it. What have you tried, what were the effects, and what do you think about it now? If you don't use drugs, what keeps you from it? Suppose the president called and asked you what to do about drug use. What advice would you give?

For Hip Students Only...

A Special Quiz on Psychoactive Drugs: Sorry, but suspicious results may be sent home to your parents!

_____	1. alcohol	a. America's number one cash crop
_____	2. caffeine	b. creates vicious circle of highs, depression, intense craving for more
_____	3. cocaine	c. most widely used drug in the world, relatively harmless
_____	4. ecstasy	d. very clear and vivid visual hallucinations
_____	5. heroin	e. responsible for the most drug deaths
_____	6. LSD	f. designer drug
_____	7. marijuana	g. oldest drug made by humans; still society's most serious drug problem
_____	8. mescaline	h. speed, crank, crystal, ice
_____	9. nicotine	i. opium poppy
_____	10. methamphetamine	j. severe bad trips could lead to psychotic reactions

Scoring:

1 to 3 correct	*You've been living in a monastery, right?*
4 to 6 correct	*I'm new on campus, myself!*
7 to 9 correct	*This seems very suspicious.*
all 10 correct	*Report to Student Health immediately — you know too much!*

Answers to "A Special Quiz on Psychoactive Drugs"

1 g 2 c 3 b 4 f 5 i 6 j 7 a 8 d 9 e 10 h

Answers for Module 8

The Big Picture (explanations provided for incorrect choices)

A Plotnik raises questions, but he does not make any of these extreme statements.
B Hypnosis does not destroy self-control, nor does zero tolerance seem to work very well.
C The module offers no such conclusion.
D *Correct! You see the "big picture" for this Module.*
E It's just a joke!

True-False (explanations provided for False choices; page numbers given for all choices)

1	F	170	Not everyone can be hypnotized.
2	T	171	
3	F	171	The debate concerns whether hypnosis is a special state of consciousness.
4	T	172	
5	F	173	Research suggests that hypnosis is no more effective than other treatments.
6	F	175	History suggests swings in drug popularity that are not the result of legal action.
7	T	175	
8	T	175	
9	T	185	
10	F	187	DARE is an admirable program, but research has not proven its effectiveness.

Flashcards 1

1 j 2 a 3 g 4 f 5 e 6 b 7 d 8 c 9 i 10 h

Flashcards 2

1 b 2 d 3 a 4 c 5 f 6 h 7 g 8 e 9 i 10 j

Multiple Choice (explanations provided for incorrect choices)

1 a Of course they can. That's what Rod Plotnik was worried about!
b *Correct! See page 169.*
c With adequate training, almost anyone can learn hypnotism.
d Why would Plotnik want to make this point, even if it were true?

2 *a* *Correct! See page 170.*
b Trust is essential to hypnotism.
c Suggestion is the key feature of hypnotism.
d Suggestion is the key feature of hypnotism. Here, the subject believes the behavior is caused by hypnosis.

3 a There is considerable debate over how real hypnosis is.
b It is well established that hypnotized subjects are highly suggestible.
c This is a misstatement of the "hidden observer" phenomenon. See page 171.
d *Correct! See page 171.*

4 *a* *Correct! See page 171.*
b Just the opposite is true.
c It is based on responsiveness and social pressure, but not on being good-natured.
d It is based on responsiveness and social pressure, but not on giving in to authority.

5 a Age regression refers to asking hypnotized subjects to re-experience an earlier age.
b Imagined perception refers to asking hypnotized subjects to experience something that does not exist.
c Hypnotic analgesia refers to suggesting that a hypnotized subject will not experience pain.
d *Correct! See page 172.*

6 *a* *Correct! See page 172.*
b This is not a correct technical term in hypnosis.
c This is not a correct technical term in hypnosis.
d Hypnotic analgesia refers to suggesting that a hypnotized subject will not experience pain.

7 a Then we assume you are going to a psychology tutor who uses hypnosis?
b Some people have reported success in changing behaviors with hypnosis.
c *Correct! See page 173.*
d If it were good for one problem, it would be good for related problems.

8 a If this were true there would be no way to understand and treat drug abuse.
b *Correct! See page 174.*
c Most drugs are not nearly this powerful.
d Drugs have been used for at least 6,000 years.

9 a Freud experimented with cocaine, but that isn't the drug that eventually killed him.
b *Correct! See page 174.*
c This was not a problem for Freud.
d This was not a problem for Freud.

10 a This is only partly true — the drug isn't giving the same high, but it still hurts the body.
b This is partly true — there is less of the desired effect.
c Harm continues to be done.
d *Correct! See page 174.*

11 ***a*** *Correct! See page 175.*
b Possible side effects of illegal drugs on blood glucose do not explain how these drugs work.
c Illegal drugs have no significant effect on DNA in the genes.
d Illegal drugs affect the brain, not sensory receptors.

12 a An American slogan for soda implies this.
b *Correct! See page 176.*
c This was a famous slogan for cigarettes.
d It's just a joke!

13 a We do not know of brain centers that control "will power."
b There is no pain center in the brain.
c *Correct! See page 175.*
d Other than relaxing inhibitions, drug use tends to interfere with normal sexual response.

14 a Cocaine is a stimulant.
b Caffeine is a stimulant (the student's friend!).
c *Correct! See page 176.*
d Nicotine is a stimulant.

15 ***a*** *Correct! See page 177.*
b As shown by efforts to ban alcohol and marijuana, it is harder to suppress less dangerous drugs.
c Stimulants like amphetamines and cocaine are more dangerous.
d This prejudice is a stereotype that is contradicted by every survey of drug use.

16 a This would not explain why it is so tough to quit smoking.
b Fortunately, this is untrue. The physical addiction ends quickly.
c *Correct! See page 178.*
d Other than providing a brief, calming break from stressful activities, smoking does not solve problems.

17 ***a*** *Correct! See page 179.*
b Stimulants cause heightened alertness, arousal, euphoria, and decreased appetite and fatigue.
c Hallucinogens produce strange and unusual perceptual, sensory, and cognitive experiences.
d Designer drugs mimic the psychoactive effects of already existing illegal drugs.

18 a Peyote is a hallucinogen; heroin is an opiate.
b LSD is a hallucinogen; heroin is an opiate.
c Psilocybin is a hallucinogen; heroin is an opiate.
d *Correct! See page 180.*

19 ***a*** *Correct! See page 182.*
b Like Prohibition? History says it won't work.
c Rather than disinterest, people continually shift their drug usage seeking the optimal ratio of costs to benefits.
d There is no clear evidence that legalization would work any better than prohibition.

20 a Bad as these are, two others do far more damage in our society.
b Bad as these are, two others do far more damage in our society.
c Bad as these are, two others do far more damage in our society.
d *Correct! See page 183.*

21 a Just the opposite is true.
b *Correct! See page 185.*
c This is not suggested by rates of alcoholism around the world.
d This is not suggested by rates of alcoholism around the world.

22 a There is evidence that marijuana has some medical value.
b There may be some unethical doctors, but this is a small part of the problem.
c *Correct! See page 186.*
d Research throws the effectiveness of the DARE program into serious doubt.

23 a There is no firm evidence for this claim.
b There is no firm evidence for this claim.
c Sometimes, but not inevitably.
d *Correct! See page 186.*

24 a Martin may not fit, but abundant evidence connects drug abuse and environmental conditions.
b *Correct! See page 188.*
c Prohibition didn't work before, and Martin's psychological problems still would have been there.
d Society could not allow Martin to write illegal prescriptions, which could eventually have harmed others.

25 a Psychoanalysis was not one of the three therapies evaluated.
b Some subjects, from 30 to 45 percent, stayed sober for a year.
c *Correct! See page 189.*
d Individual will power, which would be difficult to define and measure, was not a variable in this study.

Short Essay (sample answers)

1. "Hypnotized" subjects show remarkable degrees of compliance with requests, no matter how outlandish, and many people believe they have received medical or therapeutic help through hypnosis. The question is why? The altered state theory says hypnosis is a special state of consciousness that disconnects subjects from reality. The sociocultural theory says that hypnosis results from having the special ability of responding to imaginative suggestions and social pressures. Research continues.

2. All drugs work by mimicking, or even changing, the chemistry of the brain's information system. Neurotransmitters carry information back and forth. Some drugs mimic how neurotransmitters work, removing neurotransmitters by blocking their normal reuptake. Some drugs directly activate the brain's reward/pleasure center by increasing dopamine levels. Other drugs become substitutes for dopamine. When the user's reward/pleasure center becomes dependent on outside drugs, addiction occurs.

3. Stimulants, opiates, and hallucinogens all change brain chemistry and alter consciousness, but do it in different ways. Stimulants (methamphetamine, cocaine, caffeine, and nicotine) increase the activity of the CNS and heighten arousal and alertness. Opiates (opium, morphine, and heroin) reduce pain and produce a pleasurable state between waking and sleeping. Hallucinogens (LSD, psilocybin, and mescaline) produce strange and unusual perceptual, sensory, and cognitive experiences. But all these effects have a high cost.

4. The 6,000-year history of drug use provides ample, if worrisome, evidence that using drugs to alter consciousness may be a permanent feature of the human experience. Attempts to outlaw drugs have been unsuccessful (alcohol) or uneven (caffeine and nicotine remain legal). Like most psychologists, Plotnik and Kouyoumdjian seem to favor treatment over punishment. But even when treatment is available the success rates are meager, perhaps only 35 percent, — and many drug users and abusers resist treatment.

5. I may have been kidding when I said, *"Don't write this answer out!"* but this question has a serious purpose. A course in psychology is an obvious opportunity to examine an aspect of your life that may be disturbing to you, or which may be under attack from classmates, the media, and other social pressures. Better self-understanding can only help you change, if you use, or strengthen your resolve, if you don't. Think about it, privately or with a trusted friend or teacher or counselor, but think about it honestly.

Module 9

Classical Conditioning

The Paradox of Behaviorist Psychology

Most students begin reading about the psychology of learning with good intentions, but soon give up. It's just too darn complicated. They have run smack into The Paradox.

In truth, the basic principles of learning discovered by Pavlov, Skinner, and others (described in Modules 9 and 10) are elegantly simple, wonderfully powerful, and among the most useful products of psychology. Once you do understand them you'll say, "Makes sense…, I sort of knew that already." The problem is the language they come wrapped in.

Ivan Pavlov was a pure scientist, a Nobel prize winner. Naturally, he used the precise, mathematical language of the laboratory. The psychologists who followed Pavlov, the ones we call behaviorists, also prided themselves on being laboratory scientists. One of the strongest points in favor of the behaviorist approach is its insistence that psychology stick to observable, measurable phenomena (no murky, mentalistic concepts like Freud's unconscious). We teachers can appreciate this approach, because we studied it thoroughly in graduate school. But when undergraduate students encounter behaviorism, they don't have much time to learn the technical language. Yet we expect them to gulp it all down in a couple of weeks. Most gag instead.

These poor beleaguered psychology students have a point. Reform in our terminology is long overdue. The first term we could do without is "conditioning." We're really talking about *learning*. Classical conditioning and operant conditioning are also learning, each by a different route, but learning all the same. Even the terms "stimulus" and "response" say more about Pavlov's fame than about how human life really works.

Overcoming the Language Barrier

Your instructor will tell you which terms to learn, but as you study you can make some mental translations. Keep in mind that we're always talking about *learning*. When you read "classical conditioning," remind yourself that you are reading about Pavlov's kind of learning, where a dog's natural reflex to drool at meat got connected to something else (a bell). When you bump into a technical term like Skinner's "positive reinforcement," make up an everyday-life story that illustrates the term: "If my little brother cleans up his room and my parents reward him with extra allowance money, he will be more likely to clean up his room again next week."

Don't let yourself be cheated out of what might be the most useful ideas in psychology, just because the terminology is difficult. Use stories to illustrate concepts. Translate technical terms into more common words and phrases.

Effective Student Tip 9

Adopt a Strategy of Effectiveness

You're probably getting more advice about how to be successful in college than you know what to do with. By itself, any specific piece of advice tends to get lost in the crowd. You need a way to pull the really good advice together and put it to regular use. You need a *strategy* of success.

An overall strategy is important because it gives you a way of evaluating any particular suggestion and of adjusting to whatever conditions arise. It is more than a single game plan, because it is both more comprehensive and more flexible. If your game plan for the next test is to work like the devil, what do you do if hard work doesn't seem to be enough?

Any plan is better than no plan, but I suggest a special kind of strategy, a strategy of effectiveness. The strategy of effectiveness is simply this: (1) You recognize that you have a basic need to be effective in everything you do, especially your college work, since that's your most important task right now. (2) You measure everything you do in college by asking, "Is this procedure getting the job done?" (In other words, is it effective?) (3) Whenever a method isn't working, instead of continuing to do the same ineffective things, you experiment with new procedures, ones that work.

Your response…

Do you have an overall strategy for earning a college degree? [Most students don't.]

Learning Objectives

1. Understand classical conditioning, first described by Ivan Pavlov, as one of three powerful theories of learning that behaviorists have argued govern all human action.
2. Learn the basic mechanisms of classical conditioning as illustrated by Pavlov's famous salivating dog experiment.
3. Explain the classical conditioning concepts of generalization, discrimination, extinction, and spontaneous recovery.
4. Explain the role adaptive value plays in taste aversion learning and conditioned emotional responses.
5. Consider the differences in the three basic explanations of how and why conditioning occurs.
6. Appreciate how conditioning can affect emotional responses, as illustrated by John B. Watson's famous experiment with "Little Albert."
7. Describe how the behavioral therapy called systematic desensitization works to eliminate a conditioned fear.

Key Terms

Make difficult technical terms easier to understand. Translate each of them into everyday language about learning. Invent a little story that describes and explains what each term means.

adaptive value
anticipatory nausea
classical conditioning
cognitive learning
cognitive perspective
conditioned emotional response
conditioned response (CR)
conditioned stimulus (CS)
contiguity theory
discrimination
extinction
generalization
law of effect
learning
neutral stimulus
operant conditioning
preparedness
spontaneous recovery
stimulus substitution
systematic desensitization
taste-aversion learning
unconditioned response (UCR)
unconditioned stimulus (UCS)

The "PowerStudy 4.5 for Introduction to Psychology" CD-ROM for this module is a "Super Module." In addition to the regular PowerStudy features (quizzes, summary test, key terms, web site connections, critical thinking exercise, module outline, and more), Super Modules also include self-paced, step-by-step multimedia presentations with animations and narration.

Outline

- *Introduction*

☐ "Learning" is one of those everyday terms about which we say, "Of course I know what it means…" until we try to put it into words. How would you define learning? Seriously… give it a try.

1. It's only aftershave (Carla's perfume phobia)
2. It's only a needle (Rod's needle fear)
3. It's only dish soap (Michelle's conditioned nausea)
   a. Conditioning
   b. **Learning**

A. *Three Kinds Of Learning*

1. **Classical conditioning**
   a. Ivan Pavlov's famous experiment
   b. Conditioned reflex
   c. Learning through pairing stimuli
2. **Operant conditioning**
   a. **Law of effect** (E. L. Thorndike)
   b. Consequences and learning (B. F. Skinner)
   c. Learning through effects or consequences of actions
3. **Cognitive learning**
   a. Mental processes
   b. Observation and imitation (Albert Bandura)
   c. Learning through observing and thinking

B. *Procedure: Classical Conditioning*

1. Pavlov's experiment

☐ There is a beautiful logic to the way Pavlov worked out conditioning in his famous experiment with the drooling dog. Can you tell the story?

   a. Step 1: Choosing stimulus and response
      (1) **Neutral stimulus**
      (2) **Unconditioned stimulus (UCS)**
      (3) **Unconditioned response (UCR)**
   b. Step 2: Establishing classical conditioning
      (1) Neutral stimulus
      (2) Unconditioned stimulus (UCS)
      (3) Unconditioned response (UCR)
   c. Step 3: Testing for conditioning
      (1) **Conditioned stimulus (CS)**
      (2) **Conditioned response (CR)**

2. Terms in classical conditioning

☐ See if you can apply Pavlov's logic to the example of poor Carla. Use the three steps below.
   Step 1: Choosing stimulus and response
   Step 2: Establishing classical conditioning
   Step 3: Testing for conditioning

C. *Other Conditioning Concepts*

1. **Generalization**
2. **Discrimination**
3. **Extinction**
4. **Spontaneous recovery**

D. *Adaptive Value & Uses*

1. **Adaptive value**
2. **Taste aversion learning**
3. Explanation: **preparedness**
4. Classical conditioning and adaptive value
   a. Bluejays and monarch butterflies
   b. Hot fudge sundaes
5. Classical conditioning and emotions: **conditioned emotional response**
6. Classical conditioning in the brain

E. *Three Explanations*

1. Theories of classical conditioning
2. Stimulus substitution and contiguity theory
   a. **Stimulus substitution** (Pavlov)
   b. **Contiguity theory**
3. **Cognitive perspective** (Robert Rescorla)
   a. Predictable relationship
   b. Backward conditioning

F. *Research Focus: Conditioning Little Albert*

1. Can emotional responses be conditioned?
   a. John Watson and Rosalie Rayner (1920)
   b. "Little Albert"
2. Method: identify terms
3. Procedure: establish and test for classical conditioning
4. Results and conclusions

G. *Cultural Diversity: Conditioning Dental Fears*

1. In the dentist's chair
2. Cultural practices
3. Origins
4. Effects of fear

H. *Application: Conditioned Fear & Nausea*

1. Examples of classical conditioning
   a. Conditioned emotional response
   b. **Anticipatory nausea**
   c. Conditioning anticipatory nausea
2. **Systematic desensitization** (Joseph Wolpe)
   a. Systematic desensitization procedure: three steps
      (1) Learning to relax
      (2) Making an anxiety hierarchy
      (3) Imagining and relaxing
   b. Effectiveness of systematic desensitization

How Behaviorism Revolutionized Psychology

Living in an age of scientific psychology, it is hard for us to comprehend how profoundly behaviorism revolutionized psychology. William James, the "father" of American psychology, was more a philosopher than a psychologist. He and others in the new field relied on the method of introspection, rather than on laboratory research, to figure out how the mind worked.

Watson, extending Pavlov's scientific method to the study of human behavior, urged the following rule: "Given the stimulus, predict the response; given the response, find the stimulus; given a change in response, find a change in the stimulus."

My mother took a psychology course when she attended the University of Wisconsin in the early 1920s. Psychology was only a small part of the philosophy department back then, but the air was charged with Watson's crusade for a psychology based on objective science rather than philosophical speculation. She still remembers her young professor, no doubt following Watson, challenging his students: *"Stimulus and response, stimulus and response — learn to think in terms of stimulus and response!"*

How English Works

Words in the Textbook

p. 195 I **assured** Carla = said it was true or possible

One [side effect] is severe **nausea** = sick feeling in stomach

its odor made her **salivate** = produce liquid in mouth (saliva)

p. 198 behaviors that are **associated** with = connect one thing with another in the mind

p. 199 these **phenomena** = facts or occurrences that can be observed

p. 200 Rat **exterminators** = workers who destroy [rats]

bait poison = material used to catch or trap

They baited **grazing** areas = open areas of grass where animals eat

sheep flesh **laced** with a chemical = combined with

p. 201 For example, blue jays **feast on** butterflies = eat with pleasure

One purpose of salivation is to **lubricate** your mouth = make slippery

p. 202 a pizza [becomes] **bonded** = connected

p. 204 was described as healthy, **stolid** = without emotion

which made a loud noise and elicited **startle** = surprise

Watson's demonstration **laid the groundwork** = formed the basis

p. 206 conditioned nausea is especially **troublesome** = extremely difficult, presenting a problem

p. 207 try a **nonmedical** treatment = one that works on the mind instead of the body

this **intentional** relaxation = done on purpose, not by accident

it's **evident** that = easy or clear to see or understand

ESL Tip: Conditional and Time Clauses

Another common problem for ESL students occurs in sentences that discuss **something that is likely to happen or could happen.**

If the plane takes off, I will get to Cleveland.

I will pay you when you install the new sink.

In these two examples the main/independent clause is in the **future** tense, and the subordinate/dependent clause is in the **present** tense.

Another common use for conditional/time clauses is to express an unlikely possibility, for instance:

If the Cubs won the World Series, Chicago would go crazy.

Corporations could hire more if taxes went down.

I could do it better if only I wanted to.

In sentences like these last two, the main clause uses the conditional tense of "will" or "can" ("would" or "should") and the subordinate clause usually uses the past tense.

Vocabulary: "Anticipate" and "Extinguish"

Anticipate = expect, plan ahead

Pavlov's dog **anticipated** food when it heard the bell.

No one can **anticipate** all the surprises that life might bring.

In anticipation of = expecting, before

The dog's mouth began to salivate **in anticipation of** the food.

Marta cleaned her house completely **in anticipation of** her mother's visit.

Anticipatory = planned, before something happens

Pavlov considered this sort of **anticipatory** salivation to be a bothersome problem.

Dinner wasn't ready yet, but Toshio enjoyed the smells in the kitchen with **anticipatory** pleasure.

Note the differences between these two words:

Extinguish (verb) means to bring to a complete end

Marco blew hard **to extinguish** the candle.

The smell of the aftershave had been **extinguished.**

Extinction (noun) means the process of ending, erasing a conditioned response

Carla worked with a therapist on **the extinction of** her reaction to the aftershave.

The extinction of this conditioned response was a goal of her therapy.

Test Yourself

Read the following passage and choose the best word to fill the blank:

anticipate / in anticipation of / anticipatory

Mrs. Billings knew that she was pregnant, but she was surprised when the doctor told her to __________ the birth of twins. In the months before she had the babies, her husband made some __________ changes to their house; in fact, he built a new bedroom for the newcomers. Mrs. Billings kept a suitcase ready, with a nightgown and personal items, __________ of a sudden trip to the hospital.

Answers

Mrs. Billings knew that she was pregnant, but she was surprised when the doctor told her to **anticipate** the birth of twins. In the months before she had the babies, her husband made some **anticipatory** changes to their house; in fact, he built a new bedroom for the newcomers. Mrs. Billings kept a suitcase ready, with a nightgown and personal items, **in anticipation of** a sudden trip to the hospital.

The Big Picture

Which statement below offers the best summary of the larger significance of this module?

A Beginning with Ivan Pavlov's famous experiment with the salivating dog, behaviorists have performed remarkable feats of animal training. Almost all of their attempts to bring about such learning in humans, however, have failed.

B Conditioning offers a powerful explanation of learning to fear things like rats, poisons, chemotherapy, etc. All that is lacking for a complete psychology of learning is a way to condition people to *like* things.

C By demonstrating learning through "classical conditioning," Pavlov pioneered an objective laboratory psychology. When Watson showed conditioning in humans, the stage was set for a scientific psychology of human behavior.

D Although the behaviorists did demonstrate how simple behaviors can be taught and learned, behaviorist concepts cannot begin to explain the rich complexity of human behavior. Behaviorism is a very limited theory.

E You think drooling to a bell was amazing? Wait 'til you hear what *my* dog did to my homework!

True-False

_____ 1. Learning is a relatively permanent change in behavior as a result of experience.

_____ 2. Ivan Pavlov's famous explanation of learning was so persuasive that no other theory has challenged it since.

_____ 3. The key to Pavlov's experiment was finding a reward that would make the dog salivate.

_____ 4. At first, UCS □ UCR, but after the conditioning procedure, CS □ CR.

_____ 5. Once conditioning has taken place, *generalization* may cause similar stimuli to elicit the response, but *discrimination* should work to establish control by the specified stimuli.

_____ 6. Blue jays avoid eating monarch butterflies because of taste-aversion learning.

_____ 7. The cognitive perspective explains classical conditioning as the result of a neutral stimulus (bell) becoming a substitute for the food.

_____ 8. In John Watson's classic experiment, Little Albert gradually learned to like a previously feared white rat when he was given candy for petting it.

_____ 9. If you are like most people, the sound of the dentist's drill has become an unconditioned stimulus.

_____ 10. The goal of systematic desensitization is to *uncondition* (unlearn) conditioned stimuli and make them neutral again.

Flashcards 1

_____	1. adaptive value	a. tendency for the conditioned (learned) response to reappear after being extinguished
_____	2. conditioned response (CR)	b. a formerly neutral stimulus that has acquired the ability to elicit the same response as the unconditioned stimulus
_____	3. conditioned stimulus (CS)	c. learning to make a particular response to some stimuli but not to others
_____	4. discrimination	d. usefulness of certain evolved abilities or traits in animals and humans that tend to increase their chances of survival
_____	5. extinction	e. an unlearned, innate, involuntary physiological reflex that is elicited by the unconditioned stimulus
_____	6. generalization	f. failure of a conditioned stimulus to elicit a response when repeatedly presented without the UCS
_____	7. neutral stimulus	g. new response elicited by a conditioned stimulus; similar to the unconditioned response
_____	8. spontaneous recovery	h. some stimulus that triggers or elicits a physiological reflex, such as salivation or eye blink
_____	9. unconditioned response (UCR)	i. tendency for a stimulus that is similar to the original conditioned stimulus to elicit the same response
_____	10. unconditioned stimulus (UCS)	j. some stimulus that produces a response, but does not produce the reflex being tested

Flashcards 2

_____	1. anticipatory nausea	a. procedure in which a person eliminates anxiety-evoking stimuli by relaxation; counterconditioning
_____	2. classical conditioning	b. a relatively enduring or permanent change in behavior that results from experience with stimuli
_____	3. cognitive learning	c. feeling fear or pleasure when experiencing a stimulus that initially accompanied a painful or pleasant event
_____	4. conditioned emotional response	d. learning in which a neutral stimulus acquires the ability to produce a response (Ivan Pavlov)
_____	5. contiguity theory	e. feelings of sickness elicited by stimuli that are associated with receiving chemotherapy treatments
_____	6. law of effect	f. if actions are followed by a pleasurable consequence or reward, they tend to be repeated (E. L. Thorndike)
_____	7. learning	g. explains classical conditioning as occurring because two stimuli are paired closely together in time
_____	8. preparedness	h. associating a sensory cue (smell, taste, sound, or sight) with getting sick, then avoiding that cue in the future
_____	9. systematic desensitization	i. a kind of learning that involves mental processes alone; may not require rewards or overt behavior
_____	10. taste-aversion learning	j. biological readiness to associate some combinations of conditioned and unconditioned stimuli

Multiple Choice

_____ 1. Plotnik and Kouyoumdjian begin this module with the story of Carla and the dentist's aftershave to show how
   a. learning often occurs when we least expect it
   b. learning is more likely to occur in some environments than in others
   c. we can learn a response simply because it occurs along with some other response
   d. we can like something very much, then turn against it for no clear reason

_____ 2. Plotnik also tells about a bad medical experience of his own, in order to show how
   a. thoughtless doctors can poison your mind toward medicine in general
   b. strong fear can become attached to simple events
   c. not long ago, a simple medical procedure like getting a shot was extremely painful
   d. when going to the dentist also means getting a shot, it can be more than a child can bear

_____ 3. An early theory of learning that became part of operant conditioning was
   a. Bandura's cognitive learning
   b. Freud's unconscious thinking
   c. Plotnik's fear conditioning
   d. Thorndike's law of effect

_____ 4. Operant conditioning differs from classical conditioning in placing the emphasis on
   a. consequences that follow some behavior
   b. pairing a neutral stimulus with an unconditioned response
   c. waiting until the subject accidentally performs the right behavior
   d. allowing subjects to watch others perform some behavior

_____ 5. Albert Bandura found that he could get children to play aggressively (punching a doll) by
   a. offering them a reward (candy) for hitting the doll
   b. showing them a film of adults happily punching the doll
   c. giving them a learning session in which they practiced punching the doll
   d. sternly forbidding them to punch the doll

_____ 6. All of the following plain language translations work *except*
   a. unconditioned stimulus = behavior that occurs naturally
   b. unconditioned response = response that occurs naturally
   c. conditioned stimulus = behavior that only occurs in certain conditions
   d. conditioned response = new behavior

_____ 7. In the language of classical conditioning a stimulus S elicits a response R, so since S □ R, then obviously UCS □ UCR, and naturally CS □
   a. UCS
   b. UCR
   c. CR
   d. neutral stimulus

_____ 8. In Pavlov's experiment, the actual *learning* took place when the
   a. neutral stimulus was paired with the neutral response
   b. conditioned reflex was presented again and again
   c. unconditioned stimulus (food) was paired with the conditioned stimulus (tone)
   d. paired unconditioned stimulus (food) and neutral stimulus (tone) were presented together in several trials

_____ 9. Now even the smell of her own shampoo can make Carla anxious: this is an example of
   a. generalization
   b. extinction
   c. discrimination
   d. spontaneous recovery

_____ 10. But the smell of her nail polish does *not* make Carla feel anxious; this is an example of
   a. generalization
   b. extinction
   c. spontaneous recovery
   d. discrimination

_____ 11. When a conditioned stimulus (like a tone) is repeatedly presented by itself, *without* the unconditioned stimulus (like food), eventually __________ will occur
   a. generalization
   b. discrimination
   c. extinction
   d. spontaneous recovery

_____ 12. We seem to be biologically ready to associate some combinations of conditioned and unconditioned stimuli in as little as a single trial, a phenomenon called
   a. conditioned nausea
   b. phobia
   c. taste-aversion learning
   d. preparedness

_____ 13. Blue jays love most butterflies, but they won't eat monarch butterflies because
   a. taste aversion learning teaches them to avoid the distinctive coloring pattern
   b. an inborn hatred of black and orange makes them avoid monarchs
   c. one bite of a monarch brings instant death to a bluejay
   d. monarchs have an evasive flight pattern that makes them almost impossible to catch

_____ 14. From the point of view of a behavioral psychologist, Rod Plotnik's fear of needles is a/n
   a. expression of an unconscious conflict
   b. representation of a hidden wish
   c. conditioned emotional response
   d. unconditioned response

_____ 15. Rod Plotnik understands his needle phobia — but how often have you thought about some behavior of your own and wondered, "Why do I do that?" The answer is probably that
   a. much human behavior is simply unexplainable
   b. you inherited it from your parents
   c. without realizing it, you acquired a conditioned emotional response
   d. learning a little psychology can be dangerous!

_____ 16. Which one of the following is *not* a theory about why conditioning occurs?
   a. all stimuli (neutral, unconditioned, and conditioned) occur randomly
   b. after repeated pairing, the neutral stimulus substitutes for the unconditioned stimulus
   c. two stimuli are contiguous (paired close together in time)
   d. we learn that the neutral stimulus predicts the occurrence of the unconditioned stimulus

_____ 17. The contiguity theory says that classical conditioning occurs because
a. whichever stimulus is remembered better comes to predominate
b. a new stimulus comes to substitute for an earlier one
c. one stimulus predicts the occurrence of another
d. two stimuli are paired close together in time

_____ 18. According to Robert Rescorla's cognitive explanation of Pavlov's experiment, the conditioned reflex gets established because
a. the dog wants to do what Pavlov seems to want it to do
b. the dog learns that the tone predicts the presentation of the food
c. Pavlov unwittingly tips off the dog by looking at the food tray
d. Pavlov simply waits until the dog makes the right response

_____ 19. John Watson was excited by Pavlov's discovery of the conditioned reflex because it
a. provided the first look inside the thinking mind
b. explained the operation of cognitive factors in learning
c. explained learning in terms of observable behaviors, not unobservable mental events
d. showed that canine and human brains work in much the same way

_____ 20. To the early behaviorists, Watson's Little Albert experiment showed that
a. human learning is very different from animal learning
b. humans have an inborn fear of rats
c. even infants can learn
d. observable behaviors explain human psychology better than inner conflicts or thoughts

_____ 21. The reason for Little Albert's fame in psychology is the fact that
a. Watson showed that emotional responses could be classically conditioned in humans
b. Pavlov was unable to replicate his salivation procedure with Little Albert
c. Rescorla used the Little Albert experiment to disprove Pavlov
d. Carla learned not to fear the dentist through the example of this brave little boy

_____ 22. Cultural differences affecting conditioning are revealed by
a. American children's fear of getting shots
b. varying national rates of dental fears in children
c. the fact that dental procedures in every country are painful
d. the common tendency around the world to avoid dental treatment if at all possible

_____ 23. American children show more dental fear than Scandinavian children because
a. American dentists are not as well trained
b. American children have seen many scary movies about cruel dentists
c. health care systems in the two societies are different
d. Scandinavian dentists give their patients lots of candy for not crying

_____ 24. A classically conditioned response often observed in patients receiving chemotherapy is
a. anticipatory nausea
b. pleasure
c. taste-aversion learning
d. preparedness

_____ 25. Which one of the following is *not* necessary to the systematic desensitization procedure
a. learning to relax
b. identifying unconscious conflicts
c. making an anxiety hierarchy
d. imagining and relaxing while moving up and down the anxiety hierarchy

Short Essay

1. Recount Pavlov's famous salivating dog experiment and explain why it was such a bombshell in psychology.

2. How does classical conditioning occur in the brain and why does it have adaptive value?

3. How has psychology tried to explain why conditioning occurs? Explain stimulus substitution, contiguity theory, and the cognitive perspective.

4. Describe John B. Watson's famous conditioning experiment with "Little Albert" and explain why Watson thought it would revolutionize psychology.

5. Remember what happened to little Rod Plotnik in the doctor's office? Describe an exaggerated emotional response of your own, and speculate on how it was conditioned and how it might be unconditioned by a behavioral therapy like systematic desensitization.

Test-Taking Tips

You don't have to remember *everything* in order to get the question right. Often, carefully reading the question, plus relying on your own knowledge and intelligence, will reveal the correct answer.

- Be wary of answers stated in extreme terms like "always," "never," or "100 percent."
- Be wary of answers that defy all common sense.

Answers for Module 9

The Big Picture (explanations provided for incorrect choices)

A There is a wealth of research showing conditioning in humans.
B We are conditioned to like things all the time; it's called advertising!
C *Correct! You see the "big picture" for this Module.*
D Anti-behaviorists make this argument, but behaviorists have explanations for almost all human behavior.
E It's just a joke!

True-False (explanations provided for False choices; page numbers given for all choices)

1	T	195	
2	F	196	Many different theories of learning have been advanced since Pavlov.
3	F	197	Reward relates to Skinner; Pavlov used pairing.
4	T	197	
5	T	199	
6	T	201	
7	F	202	That is stimulus substitution; the cognitive perspective says a stimulus predicts a reinforcement.
8	F	204	"Little Albert" left the hospital before Watson could "uncondition" the fear.
9	F	205	The sound of the drill is a conditioned (not natural) stimulus.
10	T	207	

Flashcards 1

1 d 2 g 3 b 4 c 5 f 6 i 7 j 8 a 9 e 10 h

Flashcards 2

1 e 2 d 3 i 4 c 5 g 6 f 7 b 8 j 9 a 10 h

Multiple Choice (explanations provided for incorrect choices)

1 a Sometimes true, but why would Plotnik and Kouyoumdjian want to emphasize that?
b Learning can occur in any environment.
c *Correct! See page 195*
d Scientific psychology assumes that for every effect there must be a cause.

2 a There was nothing wrong with Rod's doctor.
b *Correct! See page 195.*
c Not true.
d It did not happen at the dentist's office.

3 a Cognitive learning came after operant conditioning and in some ways is a challenge to it.
b Operant conditioning does not draw on Freudian ideas.
c Plotnik described his fear, but did not offer a new theory.
d *Correct! See page 196.*

4 ***a*** *Correct! See page 196.*
b This is classical conditioning.
c This is Thorndike's experimental procedure.
d This is Bandura's cognitive learning.

5 a That's the point — no external reward was necessary.
b *Correct! See page 196.*
c That's the point — no teaching was necessary.
d Because children are contrary? But they were not forbidden to punch the doll.

6 a An unconditioned stimulus is a cause that occurs naturally (not learned).
b An unconditioned response is a behavior that occurs naturally (not learned).
c *Correct! See page 196.*
d A conditioned response is a new, learned, behavior.

7 a Substitute words for letters, "causes" for the arrow, and you get the answer in Pavlov's laboratory language.
b Substitute words for letters, "causes" for the arrow, and you get the answer in Pavlov's laboratory language.
c *Correct! See page 197.*
d Substitute words for letters, "causes" for the arrow, and you get the answer in Pavlov's laboratory language.

8 a There is no "neutral" response — every response is linked to some stimulus.
b The conditioned reflex is the end result (what was learned).
c The conditioned stimulus does not exist until the learning has taken place.
d *Correct! See page 197.*

9 ***a*** *Correct! See page 199.*
b Extinction occurs when there is no stimulus over a period of time.
c In discrimination, learning is narrowed to a specific appropriate response.
d Spontaneous recovery occurs after extinction.

10 a In generalization, learning spreads to similar objects and situations.
b Extinction occurs when there is no stimulus over a period of time.
c Spontaneous recovery occurs after extinction.
d *Correct! See page 199.*

11 a In generalization, learning spreads to similar objects and situations.
b In discrimination, learning is narrowed to a specific appropriate response.
c *Correct! See page 199.*
d Spontaneous recovery occurs after extinction.

12 a This is an effect of learning, not a cause of learning.
b This is an effect of learning, not a cause of learning.
c This is an effect of learning, not a cause of learning.
d *Correct! See page 200.*

13 ***a*** *Correct! See page 201.*
b That's the point — it's not inborn.
c Not true.
d Not true (just ask any lepidopterist).

14 a This would be true of a psychoanalytic psychologist.
b This would be true of a psychoanalytic psychologist.
c *Correct! See page 201.*
d That would mean fears are inborn, not learned.

15 a As a science, psychology believes all behavior is potentially explainable.
b Humans inherit very little specific behavior — almost all human behavior is learned.
c Correct! See page 201.
d It's just a joke!

16 ***a*** *Correct! See page 202.*
b This is the stimulus substitution theory of conditioning.
c This is the contiguity theory of conditioning.
d This is the cognitive theory of conditioning.

17 a Although it sounds cognitive, this is not a theory of conditioning.
b This is the stimulus substitution theory of conditioning.
c This is the cognitive theory of conditioning.
d *Correct! See page 202.*

18 a This statement does not fit the facts in Pavlov's experiment.
b *Correct! See page 202.*
c This statement does not fit the facts in Pavlov's experiment.
d This statement does not fit the facts in Pavlov's experiment.

19 a Pavlov studied outside behavior, not inside thinking.
b Watson and the behaviorists were interested in learned behavior, not cognition.
c *Correct! See page 204.*
d Pavlov was not studying the brain.

20 a Behaviorists believe just the opposite.
b Little Albert was not afraid of the white rat.
c That fact was generally accepted.
d *Correct! See page 204.*

21 ***a*** *Correct! See page 204.*
b Pavlov was not involved with Little Albert.
c Rescorla was not involved with Little Albert.
d Carla was not involved with Little Albert.

22 a Perhaps true, but this would not explain varying national rates.
b *Correct! See page 205.*
c Not true of modern dentistry.
d That wouldn't explain dental fears.

23 a This is not true.
b This is not true.
c *Correct! See page 205.*
d This is not true.

24 ***a*** *Correct! See page 206.*
b Have you known a person undergoing chemotherapy?
c Taste is not the crucial element.
d Preparedness is a tendency to learn, not a response.

25 a Relaxation is of key importance to the systematic desensitization procedure.
b *Correct! See page 207.*
c A hierarchy of feared situations is essential to the systematic desensitization procedure.
d Moving through the hierarchy is part of the systematic desensitization procedure.

Short Essay (sample answers)

1. Pavlov showed that dogs naturally salivate when food is presented (easier to swallow). Next, he presented a sound. Naturally, the dog did not salivate. Now, just before presenting the food, Pavlov presented the sound. The dog salivated because of the food. But here was the surprise. After a few such trials, the dog salivated to the sound alone. A neutral stimulus had acquired the power of an unconditioned stimulus. Pavlov called this learned behavior a conditioned response. No reference to the mind or thinking was necessary.

2. Both motor responses, such as the eye blink reflex, and emotional responses, such as fear of needles and injections, are susceptible to classical conditioning. Motor response conditioning is dependent on the cerebellum, and emotional response conditioning is dependent on the amygdala. Such conditioning occurs rapidly and automatically. This smooth learning process, while sometimes causing problems (like phobias) in modern society, helps us adapt and survive. We don't have time to think about everything!

3. Psychologists knew Pavlov was not a magician. Something had to explain why conditioning occurred. At first, it was thought that the new stimulus took the place of the natural stimulus. Problem was, the substitution was not perfect. Next it was proposed that the learning took place because the old and new stimuli were associated in time (contiguous). The newest explanation, a cognitive one, suggests that the subject learns that the new stimulus predicts the occurrence of the old, unconditioned stimulus.

4. Watson first showed that little Albert showed no fear of a white lab rat and other animals. Then Watson made a loud noise in the presence of the rat and Albert cried and showed fear. Two months later, Albert was shown the rat again and again cried and showed fear. Watson announced that the child had acquired a new emotional response from a simple experience. Now psychology would not need to consider thinking and inner conflicts, only observable behavior. At last, said Watson, psychology could become a real science.

5. Is there something you are "phobic" about? (One of my students was afraid of statues in the park!) Can you trace the fear back to its first occurrence? Can you explain why the experience may have been especially powerful, beyond what it normally would have been? Finally, can you imagine a way by which you might "unlearn" the fear? What would you have to do? You might explore how a behavioral therapy like systematic desensitization could help you.

Module 10

Operant & Cognitive Approaches

B. F. Skinner and the Behavioral Approach

Which psychologist has had the greatest impact? The only obvious alternative to B. F. Skinner is Sigmund Freud himself. Even then, many would give Skinner the award for discovering actual laws of behavior and their practical applications. Skinner made psychology a science and discovered a series of principles that have become a permanent part of the field.

As a scientist, Skinner spent his career pursuing principles of behavior that could be demonstrated in the laboratory, but he was equally concerned with what psychology is *not*. Often criticized for a mechanistic approach to psychology, Skinner once protested, "I have feelings!" The point he was trying to make was that no matter how real and important feelings are, they are difficult to study objectively. Skinner refused to speculate about any psychological phenomena that could not be subjected to rigorous laboratory investigation. Plotnik and Kouyoumdjian tell a fascinating story about how Skinner stuck to his scientific guns to the end of his life, even at the cost of offending members of a lecture audience who were there to honor him.

Is "Cognitive Learning" a Contradiction in Terms?

For Skinner and the "radical" behaviorists, as they came to be called, learning meant the principles of acquiring and modifying behavior as explained *without* reference to any nonobservable phenomena like cognition or mind. "Cognitive" learning, which Plotnik and Kouyoumdjian cover in this module, brings in what Skinner called nonobservable, and hence nonscientific, mental activity.

For most psychologists, even many of Skinner's young disciples like Albert Bandura, this uncompromising stand seemed to require a deliberate turning away from factors that were obvious and suggestive of further insights about learning. They were unwilling to leave so much out. So, without rejecting Skinner's classic discoveries, they entered the forbidden territory of the mind anyway. The result has been a very fruitful combining of behavioral principles and cognitive processes. Because psychologists using a combined cognitive-behavioral approach have been willing to speculate about mental processes, they have developed many innovative and effective therapeutic applications. When the Skinnerians were at the peak of their influence, they assumed that since they understood the laws of behavior it would be a simple matter to apply those laws to curing human psychological suffering. Since real life is so much more complicated than the laboratory, it didn't work out that way, and many of Skinner's frustrated followers drifted into the cognitive camp.

Effective Student Tip 10

Build Effective Routines

Anyone who loves computers also values orderly procedures. To get the most out of your computer, you must learn procedures and follow them.

Why not apply the same tactic to your college studies? When it comes to advice about how to do better in college, there are tons of useful techniques, hints, tips, tricks, and shortcuts out there. Become a consumer of useful procedures. Adapt them to your needs. Invent your own. Gather advice about how to be successful in school, but do it with a difference.

First, take a *procedural* point of view. Pay less attention to advice that is mainly sloganeering ("You've just got to work harder!") and more to specific procedures (see Tip 19, "Three Secrets of Effective Writing," for example).

Second, gather all these useful procedures under the umbrella of *effectiveness*. Judge every procedure by whether it makes you a better student. If it works, keep it in your arsenal of useful procedures. If it doesn't, drop it. I once had a friend who decided to make himself lean and strong by eating *nothing but apples*. Excited about his new plan, for several days we never saw him without his bag of apples. P.S. It didn't work.

Your response…

What advice about college have you gotten that wasn't really very helpful? What was wrong with the advice?

Learning Objectives

1. Understand operant conditioning, B. F. Skinner's theory of learning, as the linchpin of the behavioral theory, itself one of the six major approaches to psychology.
2. Learn the basic principles and procedures of operant conditioning, and how these and other conditioning concepts differ from those of classical conditioning (discussed in the previous module).
3. Explain how the idea of consequences lies at the heart of reinforcement and punishment.
4. Understand the four basic schedules of reinforcement, how they are measured, and how they explain much (most?) behavior in humans and other animals.
5. Explain how the power of operant conditioning is modified by both the cognitive learning principles of observational learning and insight learning as well as the biological principles of imprinting and prepared learning.
6. Learn how the very effective Suzuki method of learning to play a musical instrument matches Bandura's social learning principles.
7. Consider your position on using punishment in therapy (autism) in particular and child rearing (spanking) in general.

Key Terms

Oh, oh! More language problems! Module 9 offers a good introduction; here, we have additional technical laboratory language, but each key term is still about how we learn stuff. Try to make up a little story for each one. Two hints to make it easier: (1) many of these terms are already in the vocabulary of educated people, so you may already understand them; and (2) if you studied Module 9, "Classical Conditioning," you will notice that we have already covered several of the key terms below.

---

autism
behavior modification
biofeedback
biological factors
cognitive learning
cognitive map
continuous reinforcement
critical (sensitive) period
cumulative record
discrimination
discriminative stimulus
ethologists
extinction
fixed-interval schedule
fixed-ratio schedule
generalization
imprinting
insight
law of effect
learning-performance distinction
negative punishment
negative reinforcement
noncompliance
operant conditioning
operant response
partial reinforcement
pica
positive punishment
positive reinforcement
positive reinforcer
preparedness (prepared learning)
primary reinforcer
punishment
reinforcement
schedule of reinforcement
secondary reinforcer
shaping
social cognitive learning
social cognitive theory
spontaneous recovery
superstitious behavior
time-out
variable-interval schedule
variable-ratio schedule

Outline

- *Introduction*
  1. Learning 45 commands (Bart the bear): **operant conditioning**
  2. Learning to skateboard (Tony Hawk): cognitive learning through observation and imitation

A. Operant Conditioning

1. Background: Thorndike and Skinner
   a. Thorndike's law of effect
      (1) **Law of effect**
      (2) Effects strengthen or weaken behavior
   b. Skinner's operant conditioning
      (1) **Operant response**
      (2) Voluntary behavior and consequences
2. Principles and procedures

☐ You could almost say that the process of shaping is at the heart of operant conditioning. Why?

   a. **Shaping**
      (1) Shaping: facing the bar
      (2) Shaping: touching the bar
      (3) Shaping: pressing the bar
   b. Immediate reinforcement: **superstitious behavior**
3. Examples of operant conditioning
   a. Toilet training
      (1) Target behavior
      (2) Preparation
      (3) Reinforcers
      (4) Shaping
   b. Food refusal
      (1) Target behavior
      (2) Preparation
      (3) Reinforcers
      (4) Shaping
4. Operant versus classical conditioning

☐ How do classical conditioning and operant conditioning differ? What do they have in common?

   a. Operant conditioning
      (1) Goal
      (2) Voluntary response
      (3) Emitted response

(4) Contingent on behavior

(5) Consequences

b. Classical conditioning

(1) Goal

(2) Involuntary response

(3) Elicited response

(4) Conditioned response

(5) Expectancy

B. Reinforcers (the explanations in brackets are intended to help clarify Skinner's terms)

1. Consequences [Understanding *consequences* is the key to understanding Skinner's theory]

a. **Reinforcement** [*increases* behavior]

b. **Punishment** [*decreases* behavior]

c. **Pica**

d. Changing the consequences

2. Reinforcement [*increases* behavior]

a. **Positive reinforcement** and **positive reinforcer** [*increase* behavior by giving reward]

b. **Negative reinforcement** [*increases* behavior by not giving pain]

3. Reinforcers

a. **Primary reinforcer** [*innate*, not learned]

b. **Secondary reinforcer** [*learned*]

4. Punishment [*decreases* behavior] (I used quotes below because these two terms are so awkward and unnatural; IMHO they should be banned)

a. **"Positive" punishment** [*decrease* behavior by giving pain]

b. **"Negative" punishment** [*decrease* behavior by not giving reward]

(1) **Noncompliance**

(2) **Time-out**

C. Schedules of Reinforcement

1. Skinner's contributions: **schedule of reinforcement**

2. Measuring ongoing behavior: **cumulative record**

3. Schedules of reinforcement

a. **Continuous reinforcement**

b. **Partial reinforcement**

4. Partial reinforcement schedules

☐ Can you think of an example from everyday life for each of the four schedules of reinforcement?

a. **Fixed-ratio schedule**

b. **Fixed-interval schedule**

c. **Variable-ratio schedule**

d. **Variable-interval schedule**

5. Applying Skinner's principles
    a. Mine detection
    b. Dolphins

D. *Other Conditioning Concepts*

1. **Generalization**
2. **Discrimination** and **discriminative stimulus**
3. **Extinction** and **spontaneous recovery**

E. *Cognitive Learning*

1. Three viewpoints of **cognitive learning**
    a. Against: B. F. Skinner
    b. In favor: Edward Tolman (**cognitive map**)
    c. In favor: Albert Bandura (**social cognitive learning**)
2. Observational learning

☐ Some psychologists say Bandura's classic Bobo doll experiment disproves Skinner. How so?

    a. Bobo doll experiment
        (1) Procedure
        (2) Results
        (3) Conclusion
    b. Learning versus performance (**learning-performance distinction**)
3. Bandura's **social cognitive theory**
    a. Social cognitive learning: four processes
        (1) Attention
        (2) Memory
        (3) Imitation
        (4) Motivation
    b. Social cognitive learning applied to fear of snakes
        (1) Background
        (2) Treatment
        (3) Results and conclusion
4. Insight learning
    a. **Insight** (Wolfgang Köhler)
    b. Insight in animals (how Sultan got the banana)
    c. Insight in humans (the "ah ha" experience)

F. *Biological Factors*

1. Definition: **biological factors**
2. Imprinting
    a. **Ethologists**

b. **Imprinting** (Konrad Lorenz)

(1) **Critical (sensitive) period**

(2) Irreversible

3. Prepared learning

a. Incredible memory (birds): **preparedness (prepared learning)**

b. Incredible sounds (human infants)

G. Research Focus: Viewing Aggression

1. Relational and physical aggression in the media

2. Study: effects of viewing physical and relational aggression in the media

a. Results

b. Conclusion

H. Cultural Diversity: East Meets West

1. Suzuki method (teaching violin) and Bandura's social cognitive learning

2. Different cultures but similar learning principles: teacher Suzuki and researcher Bandura

a. Attention

b. Memory

c. Imitation

d. Motivation

I. Application: Behavior Modification

1. Definitions

a. **Behavior modification**

b. **Autism**

2. Behavior modification and autism

a. Program (Ivar Lovaas)

b. Results

c. Follow-up

3. **Biofeedback**

4. Pros and cons of punishment

☐ Do you believe in spanking? Were you spanked as a child? Do you spank your own children?

a. Spanking: "positive" punishment

b. Time-out: "negative" punishment

How to Trade Bad Habits for Good

The central idea of behaviorism is that almost all human behavior is learned, the result of reinforcement through consequences. Your bad habits are not intrinsic parts of you; they are the result of learning. If that is true, then you can unlearn them, too, or crowd them out by learning new and better habits.

How can you accomplish this? By keeping the focus on behavior, understanding behavior as a transaction with the environment, and constructing better environments that support better habits. Of course this is easier said than done, because you have a long and largely forgotten learning history, and also because social environments are complicated structures.

Have you noticed that nothing has been said about faults and weaknesses, blame or guilt? They have no place in behavior analysis. That's why the title of this box is not strictly accurate — habits are neither "good" nor "bad" in and of themselves. Behavior is simply behavior. How well any given behavior serves our purposes, however, leads to value judgments that can become guides to action.

Test-Taking Tips

Carefully reading the question, plus your own general knowledge and intelligence, often reveals the correct answer. Some hints:

- Be wary of answers that appear to be way off the point.
- Be wary of answers that contain nonsense statements or that don't make sense.

The "PowerStudy 4.5 for Introduction to Psychology" CD-ROM for this module is a "Super Module." In addition to the regular PowerStudy features (quizzes, summary test, key terms, web site connections, critical thinking exercise, module outline, and more), Super Modules also include self-paced, step-by-step multimedia presentations with animations and narration.

How English Works

Words in the Textbook

p. 215 a naïve rat does not usually **waltz over** = go directly

p. 216 give flowers to your **honey** = boyfriend or girlfriend

baseline = basic behavior, before attempts to change it

p. 218 **playing hookey** from school = being absent

p. 219 **coupon** [COO-pahn] = a ticket that promises payment

the driver could **get rolling** = start driving

spanking = hitting child on backside as punishment

a child's **allowance** = weekly money given by parents to child

p. 220 **slot machine** = gambling machine

the pen moves up a **notch** = step, unit of measurement

p. 223 caused many in the audience to **gasp** = make sound of surprise

p. 226 **vainly** grasp at the out-of-reach banana = unsuccessfully

he seemed to **hit on** the solution = find

p. .229 **phenomenal** memories = extraordinary

humans' vocal **apparatus** = equipment

p. 230 **carry out** a request = perform

temper tantrums = child's outbursts marked by losing control

Vocabulary: Subjective / Objective

A simple but useful way to measure reasoning in a more **objective** way:

A **subjective** statement focuses on the **subject** — the person making the statement. It is **subjective** because it expresses personal opinions, feelings, and biases. "This hamburger tastes good" is a **subjective** statement. You believe it, but someone else might not.

An **objective** statement focuses on the **object** — the thing or action that is observed. It is **objective** because it reports only facts that can be measured or proved. "This hamburger weighs 10.6 ounces" is an **objective** statement. Everyone who weighs it will agree.

Subjective statements often contain words of judgment, like should" or "better." Objective statements often contain words of description or measurement.

Now you try it: Think about each of the statements below. If you think the statement is **Subjective,** write **S** in the blank. If you think the statement is **Objective,** write **O** in the blank.

____ "Textbooks cost too much."

____ "Apples have more vitamins than potatoes."

____ "Everyone should eat an apple every day."

____ "Most children like chocolate."

____ "It is better to be clean than dirty."

____ "American football is a more violent game than soccer."

Vocabulary: Suffixes

The endings of words, called suffixes, can tell us just how the word is used. By knowing these word endings, you'll be able to identify the word families that you meet. Let's look at some common suffixes from the textbook:

In which a person imagines or visualizes fearful or anxiety-evoking stimuli.

The **-ize** ending makes the adjective **visual** into a verb.

Visual = able to see. **Visualize** = to be able to see.

So if **general** means not specific, **generalize** would mean _________.

By adding **-ation**, the verb becomes a noun.

Visualize = to be able to see. **Visualization** = the action of being able to see.

Generalize = _________. **Generalization** = the action of being not specific.

Sensitize = to make full of feeling. **Sensitization** = _________.

Sentence Structure: Making Connections

When you are reading, it's vitally important to understand all the logical help that writers give you. Certain words will help you by showing you the connection between one sentence and the next one.

Is the next sentence about *more* of the same? The writer should tell you with words like:

moreover / furthermore / in addition

Jack liked to watch golf on television. Moreover, he loved to pretend to play golf.

After watching the model, children kicked and hit the Bobo doll. Furthermore, they yelled, "Hit him! Kick him!"

Tolman showed that rats learned the layout of a maze. In addition, the rats formed a cognitive map.

Practicing this kind of thinking will help you understand what you read more quickly and more deeply. Let's try more, but remember that there is no one right answer:

Faysal never eats meat. **Moreover,** _________.

It rained all night. **Furthermore,** _________.

Bogdana works hard during the week. **In addition,** _________.

Answers

Subjective: "Textbooks cost too much." = "too much" is an opinion.
Objective: "Apples have more vitamins than potatoes." = this can be proven.
Subjective: "Everyone should eat an apple every day." = "should" is an opinion.
Objective: "Most children like chocolate." = this can be proven with statistics.
Subjective: "It is better to be clean than dirty." = most people share this opinion, but it is still an opinion.
Subjective: "American football is a more violent game than soccer." = what is or is not "violent" is an opinion, although it is possible to count the number of violent acts and compare them.
Faysal never eats meat. **Moreover,** he (never eats eggs)(wears a cloth belt) (does not wear leather).
It rained all night. **Furthermore,** (it is still raining now) (it might rain later).
Bogdana works hard during the week. **In addition,** she (has a weekend job) (goes to school on Saturdays).

The Big Picture

Which statement below offers the best summary of the larger significance of this module?

A If B. F. Skinner is correct, most human behaviors are learned through the reinforcing powers of consequences. Because learning can be studied objectively and experimentally, psychology can become a real science of behavior.

B Skinner and the behaviorists reduced psychology to a study of rats and pigeons. They lost sight of the fact that humans are unique, individual, and not reducible to a set of laws organized around reinforcement.

C Skinner thought his "operant conditioning" would replace Pavlov's "classical conditioning" as the fullest description of human behavior. Today we know that most human behavior is based on reflexes, and so Pavlov wins.

D The behaviorists launched a revolution that led to a wealth of research in psychology. By the time he died, however, Skinner had turned to a belief in the importance of biological and cognitive factors to explain behavior.

E True story: I know a psychotherapist whose client gave him a button reading, "Before therapy, I was a raging [jerk], but I'm comfortable with that now." (Substitute something much more vulgar for "jerk!")

True-False

_____ 1. Classical conditioning concerns involuntary (reflex) behavior, while operant conditioning concerns voluntary behavior.

_____ 2. The secret of successful shaping is waiting until the animal emits the desired final target behavior, then immediately applying reinforcement.

_____ 3. The key to operant conditioning is making consequences contingent on behavior.

_____ 4. Positive reinforcement makes behavior more likely to occur again; negative reinforcement makes it less likely to occur again.

_____ 5. If you want effective learning, you must use primary reinforcers instead of secondary reinforcers.

_____ 6. Schedules of reinforcement are the specific times of the day when animals in learning experiments must receive their reinforcement.

_____ 7. Social cognitive learning shows how there is a difference between learning a behavior and performing that behavior.

_____ 8. Social cognitive learning, unlike operant conditioning, does not depend on external reinforcement.

_____ 9. A good example of operant conditioning was when Sultan piled up several boxes so he could reach the banana.

_____ 10. Operant conditioning is powerful, but not all powerful — in some cases, it's limited by biological factors.

Flashcards 1

_____	1. continuous reinforcement	a.	the presentation of a stimulus that increases the probability of a behavior occurring again
_____	2. "negative" punishment	b.	a rule that determines how and when the occurrence of a response will be followed by a reinforcer
_____	3. negative reinforcement	c.	a consequence that occurs after behavior and decreases chance of that behavior occurring again
_____	4. partial reinforcement	d.	a situation in which responding is reinforced only some of the time
_____	5. pica	e.	a procedure of successive reinforcement of behaviors that lead up to or approximate the desired behavior
_____	6. "positive" punishment	f.	a behavioral disorder, often seen in mental retardation, that involves eating inedible objects or unhealthy substances
_____	7. positive reinforcement	g.	removing a reinforcing stimulus (allowance) after response; decreases chances of response recurring
_____	8. punishment	h.	presenting an aversive stimulus (spanking) after a response; decreases chances of response recurring
_____	9. schedule of reinforcement	i.	every occurrence of the operant response results in delivery of the reinforcer
_____	10. shaping	j.	an aversive stimulus whose removal increases the likelihood of the preceding response occurring again

Flashcards 2

_____	1. behavior modification	a.	inherited tendencies or responses that are displayed by newborn animals encountering certain stimuli
_____	2. cognitive map	b.	a treatment or therapy that modifies problems by using principles of learning and conditioning
_____	3. fixed-interval schedule	c.	a reinforcer occurs only after a fixed number of responses are made by the subject
_____	4. fixed-ratio schedule	d.	an innate or biological tendency of animals to recognize and attend to certain cues and stimuli
_____	5. imprinting	e.	a mental representation in the brain of the layout of an environment and its features
_____	6. insight	f.	a reinforcer occurs following the first response that occurs after a fixed interval of time
_____	7. preparedness (prepared learning)	g.	a reinforcer occurs following the first correct response after an average amount of time has passed
_____	8. superstitious behavior	h.	a mental process marked by the sudden solution to a problem; the "ah ha" phenomenon
_____	9. variable-interval schedule	i.	a reinforcer is delivered after an average number of correct responses has occurred
_____	10. variable-ratio schedule	j.	behavior that increases in frequency because its occurrence is accidentally paired with the delivery of a reinforcer

Multiple Choice

_____ 1. Plotnik and Kouyoumdjian tell us about the starring performance of 1,800-pound Bart in *The Bear* to make the point that
   a. although most animals do not have the capacity for learning, a few do quite well
   b. the key to learning (and teaching) is perseverance: keep working
   c. you shouldn't believe that what you see in the movies reflects actual behavior in the wild
   d. operant conditioning procedures are powerful (no other technique could have produced Bart's learning)

_____ 2. But Plotnik and Kouyoumdjian's other example, the skateboarding star Tony Hawk, raises a different possibility — that
   a. learning can also occur just by observation, without external rewards
   b. human learning differs greatly from animal learning
   c. rewards actually interfere with learning
   d. what Bart the bear did was just trickery, but Jack was really learning

_____ 3. Skinner gets the credit for operant conditioning instead of Thorndike because
   a. Skinner realized that there are biological limits on learning
   c. Thorndike's law of effect was essentially a restatement of Pavlov's conditioned reflex
   b. Skinner studied rats, pigeons, and other animals instead of limiting himself to cats
   d. Thorndike stated a general principle; Skinner developed and expanded on it

_____ 4. The basic principle of operant conditioning is that
   b. conditioned stimuli produce conditioned responses
   a. the performance of undesired behaviors brings swift consequences
   c. consequences are contingent on behavior
   d. consequences are less important than feelings of guilt

_____ 5. The shaping procedure succeeds or fails depending on
   a. how long you are willing to wait for the target behavior to occur
   b. exactly which behaviors of the subject you choose to reinforce
   c. how many times you reinforce the target behavior
   d. selecting the best one of several reinforcers

_____ 6. During shaping, the behaviors that must be reinforced are those that
   a. lead step-by-step to the target behavior
   b. cause the subject to move around in some direction
   c. occur precisely every ten seconds, not more and not less
   d. demonstrate that the subject is truly motivated to work

_____ 7. In shaping, it is very important that the reinforcer come
   a. immediately before the desired behavior
   b. immediately after the desired behavior
   c. only after the subject has had time to appreciate what's happening
   d. at the same time that the target behavior is occurring

_____ 8. Superstitious behavior is any behavior that increases in frequency because
   a. somehow you just know that it will happen again
   b. the belief system of the subject contains elements of superstition
   c. it appears to happen by accident, with no understandable cause
   d. its occurrence is accidentally paired with the delivery of a reinforcer

_____ 9. You could argue that Skinner's discoveries are more important than Pavlov's in that
   a. beginning a quarter of a century later, Skinner could build on Pavlov's discoveries
   b. American science offers more freedom than Russian science
   c. almost all important human behavior is voluntary (not reflex) behavior
   d. the conditioned reflex isn't fully explained until you bring in the concepts of both positive and negative reinforcement

_____ 10. Which one of the following pairs is *not* a difference between *operant* and *classical* conditioning?
   a. consequences of behavior / conditioned reflex
   b. voluntary behavior / physiological reflex
   c. emitted response / elicited response
   d. decreases rate of behavior / increases rate of behavior

_____ 11. The main difference between reinforcement and punishment is that
   a. reinforcement increases rates of behavior, but punishment decreases them
   b. reinforcement is very effective, but punishment rarely is
   c. reinforcement leads to good behavior, but punishment often creates pica
   d. people obviously dislike punishment, but they don't really like reinforcement much more

_____ 12. The student on probation who finally buckles down and begins studying in earnest is under the control of an operant conditioning procedure called
   a. positive reinforcement
   b. negative reinforcement
   c. punishment
   d. extinction

_____ 13. The little child who gets a good hard spanking for running out into the street is experiencing an operant conditioning procedure called
   a. positive reinforcement
   b. negative reinforcement
   c. positive punishment
   d. extinction

_____ 14. When your date shakes your hand and says, "Thanks for a wonderful evening," you reply, "Gee, I was kind of hoping for a __________"
   a. token of your affection
   b. partial reinforcement
   c. secondary reinforcer
   d. primary reinforcer

_____ 15. "Positive punishment" is an awkward term (psychology be cursed!) to express the idea of
   a. punishment strong enough to really work
   b. punishment based on taking something pleasant away from you
   c. punishment based on "giving" you something unpleasant
   d. a positive rather than a negative approach to discipline

_____ 16. "Poor fool," you think to yourself when your friend tells you she lost on the lottery again, "another helpless victim of the __________ schedule of reinforcement"
   a. fixed-ratio
   b. variable-ratio
   c. fixed-interval
   d. variable-interval

_____ 17. Skinner opposed cognitive theories of learning to the end of his life because
a. it is difficult to admit that the work of a lifetime was misguided
b. they are based on philosophical speculation rather than on laboratory research
c. they bring in the "mind," which he said couldn't be observed or measured directly
d. you can't teach an old dog new tricks

_____ 18. Although you haven't made a conscious effort to memorize the campus area, you probably can get to any point on it relatively easily; Edward Tolman would say you
a. exhibited attention, memory, imitation, and motivation
b. learned through observation as you moved around campus
c. can call on the power of insight when necessary
d. automatically had developed a cognitive map of the campus

_____ 19. Albert Bandura's famous Bobo doll experiment showed all of the following outcomes *except*
a. the children did not imitate the adult model until they were given a reward
b. the children learned even though they did not receive tangible rewards
c. the children learned even though they were not engaging in any overt behavior
d. some subjects did not imitate the model (proving learning had occurred) until they were reinforced for doing so

_____ 20. Which one of the following is *not* a factor in Bandura's theory of social cognitive learning?
a. attention
b. memory
c. rehearsal
d. motivation

_____ 21. According to the learning-performance distinction,
a. learning may occur but not be immediately evident in behavior
b. learning may not occur in situations calling for immediate performance
c. girls probably learn better than boys but may not perform as well on tests
d. girls are naturally aggressive but hide aggressive performance better

_____ 22. The important thing about the solution Sultan came up with for the out-of-reach banana problem was
a. how an old conditioned reflex spontaneously recovered
b. how he used trial and error
c. how he built on previously reinforced behavior
d. what was *missing* in his solution — namely, all the factors above

_____ 23. Limitations on the power of operant conditioning to explain behavior were discovered by
a. ethnologists studying pica in baby ducks during the insensitive period
b. ethologists studying imprinting during the critical period for learning
c. ethicists studying the virtue of punishing self-injurious behaviors of autistic children
d. ethanologists studying the power of biological products to get us around

_____ 24. Which one of the following was *not* a finding of a study on viewing physical and relational aggression in the media?
a. although seeing physical aggression (*Kill Bill*) is harmful to children, seeing relational aggression (*Mean Girls*) has little effect
b. watching violent movies made subjects act aggressively to a rude researcher
c. watching one form of aggression can influence the occurrence of other forms of aggression
d. relational aggression and physical aggression in the media can both harm children

_____ 25. The Suzuki method of teaching violin to children closely resembles the processes of
a. Pavlov's classical conditioning
b. Bandura's social cognitive learning
c. Skinner's operant conditioning
d. Kohler's insight learning

Short Essay

1. Sketch the history of behaviorism, using the names Ivan Pavlov, John Watson, B. F. Skinner, and Albert Bandura.
2. How does operant conditioning differ from classical conditioning?
3. It could be argued that Skinner's crowning achievement is his exploration and definition of schedules of reinforcement. Explain.
4. How does biology affect learning? Describe the biological limitations on conditioning.
5. Do you believe that research on rats and pigeons in the laboratory can help us understand how human beings operate in the real world?

The One Most Important Thing

If you were to ask me for one suggestion — *but only one* — for how to become a more successful student, I wouldn't hesitate. My answer would be to *read, read, read!*

Reading is the core activity, the essential skill, and the necessary passion on which academic success is built. There's a trick to this: what you read must be interesting to you. It must pull you along. When you "can't put it down," you're on the right track. So start with interesting stuff, even if it's not all that serious. Popular magazines, romance novels, even the comics. But *read!* Once it becomes a habit, it won't be long before academic material is interesting, too.

I hope you will write to me — not only about possible errors you found — but also about anything in my Study Guide you would like to discuss. <profenos@mac.com>

Answers for Module 10

The Big Picture (explanations provided for incorrect choices)

A *Correct! You see the "big picture" for this Module.*
B For Skinner, behavior is consistent across species; schedules of reinforcement work in both pigeons and people.
C Most human behavior is voluntary, not reflexive, so this conclusion is wrong.
D Skinner stuck to his guns on behavioral psychology versus cognitive explanations to the end.
E It's just a joke!

True-False (explanations provided for False choices; page numbers given for all choices)

1	T	213	
2	F	215	The secret is to reinforce a behavior that is a little closer to the target behavior.
3	T	217	
4	F	218	Negative reinforcement also makes behavior more likely to occur again.
5	F	219	Both primary and secondary reinforcers motivate behavior.
6	F	220	Schedules of reinforcement are payoff rules (not specific times) for different patterns of performance.
7	T	223	
8	T	223	
9	F	226	Sultan's behavior demonstrated insight learning.
10	T	228	

Flashcards 1

1 i 2 g 3 j 4 d 5 f 6 h 7 a 8 c 9 b 10 e

Flashcards 2

1 b 2 e 3 f 4 c 5 a 6 h 7 d 8 j 9 g 10 i

Multiple Choice (explanations provided for incorrect choices)

1
a Almost all animals can learn, but how is it accomplished?
b Perseverance is involved, but it is by no means the main story.
c This movie, although not a documentary, did attempt to present natural animal behavior.
d *Correct! See page 213.*

2
a *Correct! See page 213.*
b Skinner and the behaviorists believed just the opposite.
c Some cognitive learning proponents say this, but most behaviorists disagree.
d It was sort of a trick, but Bart *learned* how to do it.

3
a This is far from Skinner's main idea.
b Skinner believed that the laws of learning applied to all animals, including humans.
c Thorndike's explanation of learning was very different from Pavlov's.
d *Correct! See page 214.*

4
a Not unless the situation has been set up that way.
b This is true in classical conditioning.
c *Correct! See page 214.*
d The concept of guilt feelings belongs to psychoanalysis.

5
a In shaping, you don't wait for the target behavior to occur.
b *Correct! See page 215.*
c By the time you have the target behavior, shaping is complete.
d Any reinforcer that works can be used in shaping.

6
a *Correct! See page 215.*
b Then the subject would end up spinning around and getting nowhere!
c Then the subject would learn to do something different every 10 seconds!
d How would you know which behaviors show motivation and which don't?

7 a How would this reinforce the desired behavior? More likely, the previous behavior.
b *Correct! See page 215.*
c How would we know when (or whether) the subject appreciated what was happening?
d The target behavior is the desired final behavior; first we have to reinforce the behaviors that lead up to it.

8 a Too mystical. Behaviorism explains you not by your ideas, but by your behavior.
b It's not what the subject believes, but what happens just before a rewarding event occurs.
c There is an understandable cause, if you analyze what the subject was doing before the rewarding event.
d *Correct! See page 215.*

9 a Somewhat true, but Skinner's work is very different from Pavlov's.
b Skinner believed that the laws of learning applied to all animals, including humans.
c *Correct! See page 214.*
d The conditioned reflex and positive and negative reinforcement are essentially different concepts.

10 a Consequences operant, conditioned reflex classical. This is a valid difference.
b Voluntary operant, reflex classical. This is a valid difference.
c Emitted operant, elicited classical. This is a valid difference.
d *Correct! See page 217.*

11 *a* *Correct! See page 218.*
b Punishment can be very effective, maybe even more effective than reinforcement.
c Not true. Pica is a disorder involving eating inedible objects or unhealthy substances.
d Only half true (they may not like *negative* reinforcement).

12 a Positive reinforcement is the strengthening of behavior by applying a desired consequence.
b *Correct! See page 218.*
c Punishment is the suppression of behavior through unpleasant consequences.
d Extinction is the gradual elimination of behavior through the removal of a consequence.

13 a Positive reinforcement is the strengthening of behavior by applying a desired consequence.
b Negative reinforcement is the strengthening of behavior through threats.
c *Correct! See page 218.*
d Extinction is the gradual elimination of behavior through the removal of a consequence.

14 a That would be your date giving you a poker chip you could trade in later.
b That would be your date reinforcing you some times and not others.
c What you got *was* a secondary reinforcer!
d *Correct! See page 219.*

15 a It's not the strength of the punishment, but how it operates.
b That would be "negative punishment" (another awkward term).
c *Correct! See page 219.*
d Sadly, any punishment is a negative approach to discipline.

16 a Fixed-ratio would be winning every X number of times she bought a ticket.
b *Correct! See page 221.*
c Fixed-interval would be winning every week regardless of how many tickets she bought.
d Variable-interval would be winning every now and then regardless of how many tickets she bought.

17 a There was no reason for Skinner to doubt the value of his life's work.
b Skinner knew cognitive theories of learning were based on laboratory research (but he was critical of it).
c *Correct! See page 223.*
d It's just a joke!

18 a These variables apply to Albert Bandura's theory of observational learning.
b This idea applies to Albert Bandura's theory of observational learning.
c This idea applies to Wolfgang Köhler's theory of insight learning.
d *Correct! See page 223.*

19 *a* *Correct! See page 224.*
b The absence of tangible reinforcement is of key importance to this experiment.
c The absence of overt behavior is important in this experiment.
d The later exhibition of the learning is important in this experiment.

20 a Attention is one of the four processes necessary for observational learning.
b Memory is one of the four processes necessary for observational learning.
c *Correct! See page 225.*
d Motivation is one of the four processes necessary for observational learning.

21 ***a*** *Correct! See page 224.*
b Bandura's experiment did not suggest this conclusion.
c Bandura's experiment did not suggest this conclusion.
d Bandura's experiment did not suggest this conclusion.

22 a No, because this was a completely new problem for Sultan.
b No, because Sultan solved the problem suddenly.
c No, because no deliberate previous learning led up to Sultan's solution.
d *Correct! See page 226.*

23 a Ethnologists study cultural differences. Review the meaning of pica. There is no insensitive period.
b *Correct! See page 228.*
c Behavior modification may raise ethical questions, but it does work.
d It's just a joke! (Ethanol in gas — get it?)

24 ***a*** *Correct! See page 230.*
b This was a finding of the study described.
c This was a finding of the study described.
d This was a finding of the study described.

25 a Classical conditioning is reflex learning.
b *Correct! See page 231.*
c Operant conditioning does not emphasize cognitive learning.
d Insight learning is sudden rather than the result of practice.

Short Essay (sample answers)

1. Ivan Pavlov's discovery of the conditioned reflex changed the course of modern psychology and led to the behaviorist movement. John B. Watson showed that emotional responses could be classically conditioned in humans. B. F. Skinner shifted the emphasis from reflexes to consequences, and developed the laws of operant conditioning. Skinner described the schedules of reinforcement that govern behavior. Albert Bandura explored learning by observation and imitation, adding a cognitive element to behaviorism.

2. Skinner's operant conditioning of voluntary behavior greatly expanded the scope of Pavlov's classical conditioning of reflexes. Classical conditioning limits learning to pairing a new behavior with an existing reflex. Operant conditioning says all organisms constantly emit behavior, which in turn is reinforced or punished by the consequences that follow. Since almost all human behavior is voluntary, Skinner was able to explore learning fully, establishing the laws of reinforcement and describing schedules of reinforcement.

3. Skinner realized that continuous reinforcement is not necessary to maintain behavior: partial reinforcement works as well or better. In humans, few activities are continuously reinforced. So Skinner set out to describe the various relationships between behavior and reinforcement. Through research, he established the very precise rules that govern these relationships and went on to apply them to the great majority of behaviors engaged in by humans and other animals. Few "laws" of behavior have such precision and applicability.

4. At first, behaviorists thought they could explain any behavior through the laws of reinforcement. But there are biological factors in behavior and learning. Ethologists like Konrad Lorenz, who observed that ducklings automatically follow anything near them, explored critical or sensitive periods in learning. Preparedness (prepared learning) explains why animals may pay special attention to certain cues. A human infant's brain, for example, is wired so the child is prepared to learn all the sounds that make up any human language.

5. One of the strongest and most persistent criticisms of behaviorism is that laboratory research on animals cannot explain the most important features of human behavior in the real world. But behaviorists like Skinner seemed to show in their laboratories that human behavior, although perhaps more complicated, is governed by the same laws of behavior as other creatures. Where do you come down on this essential dispute? What do you think of modern behaviorism? What evidence supports your conclusion?

Module 11

Types of Memory

Nothing in This Module Is True

The biological and cognitive approaches to psychology have made great strides in the last two decades. One of the results is a much clearer picture of how memory works. Even so, there is a sense in which none of it is true.

The answers we want are buried at least two layers down. First, how does the physical brain work? We are learning more about the brain every day, yet for all their discoveries neuroscientists have barely scratched the surface. The need to understand elusive electrical activity, not just gray matter, complicates the task. Second, how does the mind work? If the mind is an abstraction, a concept (unless you say "mind" and "brain" are the same thing), we cannot apprehend it directly, making it even more difficult to understand.

Today, we are fond of comparing the mind to a computer, simply because the computer is the most powerful mechanical thinking device we know, and therefore makes a good comparison. Yet when we develop a *new* generation of thinking machines, perhaps based on liquid instead of silicone chips, we will stop comparing the mind to a computer and compare it to this new device instead, since the new device will seem much more like the human mind. The mind is not really a computer; the computer merely makes a good model for understanding the mind, at least today.

The Beauty of a Good Model

No wonder that dress looks so beautiful on the model sashaying down the runway in the fashion show. She isn't an actual human being — obviously, no one could be that tall, that thin, that perfect! Consequently, when draped around this abstraction of a human, we can see much more clearly how the clothing itself really looks.

A model helps us understand the real world because it's an ideal against which we can compare specific phenomena. When we try to understand the workings of the mind, all we see are awkward elbows and knees. We need a model to help us visualize what it must really be like.

What we are struggling to understand is how the process of grasping the world and putting parts of it in our heads must work. Many of the formulations Plotnik and Kouyoumdjian present in Module 11 are models of what this process may be like. Because this is not yet certain knowledge, several theories, or models, compete for our acceptance. I think you can learn these theories better if you keep in mind the idea that they are, in fact, just models, not reality.

Effective Student Tip 11

High Grades Count Most

Here is a hard truth. It's unfair, maybe, but true. Anyone who looks at your transcript, whether for admission to another school or for employment, is going to be looking for the *high* grades. It's difficult for them to tell exactly what "C" means. In some schools, "C" may mean little more than that you attended class. The grade "B" begins to say more about your abilities and character, but it it's the "A" that is really convincing. No matter in what course or at what school, an "A" says you did everything asked of you and did it well. That's a quality that admissions people and personnel officers look for.

High grades have other rewards, too. You get on the school's honors list. You can join honors societies. You qualify for scholarships. With every "A," your sense of effectiveness goes up a notch. You are more confident and enjoy greater self-esteem. (Keeps mom and dad happy, too!)

Tailor your work toward earning high grades. Take fewer courses, stay up later studying, write papers over, and ruthlessly cut fun out of your life (just kidding).

Earning high grades in a few courses beats getting average grades in many courses. The fastest route toward your goal is a conservative selection of courses in which you do well, resulting in a good record and confidence in your effectiveness as a student.

Your response…

Can you remember a time when you thought you had an "A," then didn't get it? What went wrong?

Learning Objectives

1. Understand memory and memory processes as models — inferred explanations of brain functions for which we do not as yet have the tools to investigate directly at the physiological level.

2. Learn the three basic types of memory and how they work together as an integrated process to help us retain and use the information we need as thinking (not just reacting) animals.

3. Know the component parts, functions, and steps in the three types of memory.

4. Understand the processes of encoding and the implications of different memory strategies for students attempting to master complex materials.

5. Consider your position on the repressed memory controversy and how accusations of child abuse should be handled.

6. Appreciate cultural differences in memory processes through cross-cultural research in memory.

7. Learn how the unusual abilities of photographic memory, eidetic imagery, and flashbulb memory suggest the great potential power of human memory.

Key Terms

Many of these terms are based on a model of the mind. Learn the model and it will be easier to learn the terms.

automatic encoding
chunking
declarative memory
echoic memory
effortful encoding
elaborative rehearsal
encoding
episodic memory
flashbulb memories
iconic memory
interference
levels-of-processing theory
long-term memory
maintenance rehearsal
memory
photographic memory
primacy effect
primacy-recency effect
procedural (nondeclarative) memory
recency effect
repression
retrieving
semantic memory
sensory memory
short-term (working) memory
storing

The "PowerStudy 4.5 for Introduction to Psychology" CD-ROM for this module is a "Super Module." In addition to the regular PowerStudy features (quizzes, summary test, key terms, web site connections, critical thinking exercise, module outline, and more), Super Modules also include self-paced, step-by-step multimedia presentations with animations and narration.

Outline

- *Introduction*
  1. Incredible memory (Daniel Tammet)
  2. Memory problem (Clive Wearing)
  3. Definitions
     a. **Memory**
     b. Three memory processes
        (1) **Encoding**
        (2) **Storing**
        (3) **Retrieving**

A. Three Types of Memory

1. Three types of memory
   a. **Sensory memory**
   b. **Short-term (working) memory**
   c. **Long-term memory**
2. Memory processes

B. Sensory Memory: Recording

1. **Iconic memory** (visual information)
2. **Echoic memory** (auditory information)

☐ How do iconic and echoic memory work? What is their purpose?

3. Functions of sensory memory
   a. Prevents being overwhelmed
   b. Gives decision time
   c. Provides stability, playback, and recognition

C. Short-Term Memory: Working

1. Definition: **short-term (working) memory**
2. Two features
   a. Limited duration
      (1) From two to 30 seconds
      (2) **Maintenance rehearsal**
   b. Limited capacity
      (1) About seven items or bits (George Miller)
      (2) Memory span test
      (3) **Interference**
3. **Chunking**

4. Functions of short-term memory
    a. Attending
    b. Rehearsing
    c. Storing

D. Long-Term Memory: Storing

1. Putting information into long-term memory
    a. Sensory memory
    b. Attention
    c. Short-term memory
    d. **Encoding**
    e. **Long-term memory**
    f. **Retrieving**
2. Features of long-term memory
    a. Capacity and permanence
    b. Chances of retrieval
    c. Accuracy of long-term memory
3. Separate memory systems

☐ Can you work out the logic of the memory processes involved in these concepts?

    a. Primacy versus recency
        (1) **Primacy effect** (first four, five items)
        (2) **Recency effect** (last four, five items)
        (3) **Primacy-recency effect** (beginning and end of list)
    b. Short-term versus long-term memory
4. Declarative versus procedural or nondeclarative
    a. **Declarative memory**
        (1) **Semantic memory**
        (2) **Episodic memory**
    b. **Procedural (nondeclarative) memory**
        (1) Memories for motor skills, some cognitive skills, and conditioned emotional behaviors
        (2) Cannot be recalled or retrieved

E. Research Focus: Do Emotions Affect Memories?

1. Hormones and memories (James McGaugh)
2. Memories of emotional events
    a. Procedure
    b. Hypothesis
    c. Results and conclusion

F. Encoding: Transferring

1. Two kinds of **encoding**
    a. **Automatic encoding**
    b. **Effortful encoding**
2. Rehearsing and encoding
    a. **Maintenance rehearsal** (repeating)
    b. **Elaborative rehearsal** (meaningful associations)
3. **Levels-of-processing theory**

G. Repressed Memories

1. Recovered memories
2. Definition of repressed memories: **repression** (Sigmund Freud)
3. Therapist's role in recovered memories (Elizabeth Loftus)
4. Implanting false memories
5. Accuracy of recovered memories

H. Cultural Diversity: Oral versus Written

1. United States versus Africa
2. Remembering spoken information

I. Application: Unusual Memories

1. **Photographic memory** (adults)
    a. Extraordinary episodic memory
    b. Super memory for faces
2. **Flashbulb memories**
    a. Impact and accuracy
    b. Most remembered events
    c. Remote historical events
    d. Brains and hormones
    e. Pictures versus impressions

Test-Taking Tips

More hints:

- Be wary of answers that seem way out there for the subject involved.
- Be wary of answers that don't fit in with everything else you know about the subject.

How English Works

Words in the Textbook

p. 239 before the **packed** house = crowded with people

He did not **err** = make a mistake

such **gargantuan** memory powers = huge, great

p. 240 you are **bombarded** = attacked

a lone guitarist playing for **spare change** = extra money

p. 241 you are **absorbed in** reading a novel = completely interested

p. 243 a **unique visual image** = picture that is different from all others

become **intertwined** = linked together

p. 245 brain damage can **wipe out** long-term memory = destroy

while completely **sparing** short-term memory = not affecting, protecting

p. 247 highly **charged** emotional situations = full of feeling

seeing a series of **slides** = a type of photograph

his feet were **severed** = cut off

McGaugh and his **colleagues** = co-workers, fellow researchers

lay the basis for similar studies = prepare, form

p. 248 **avid** sports fans = very enthusiastic

p. 250 **allegedly** molesting her = claimed but not yet proven

Katrina's memories first **surfaced** = came to conscious level

so-called repressed memories = popularly known as

p. 251 found **corroborating** evidence = evidence that supports or confirms something

reason for some **skepticism** = tendency to doubt what others are saying

p. 254 able to recall (notes) **verbatim** = perfectly, every word

Sentence Structure: Connecting Ideas

It's vitally important to understand all the logical help that writers give you. Certain words will help you by showing you the connection between one sentence and the next one.

If the second sentence shows a result of the first sentence, certain words will tell you this: **consequently, as a result, thus, for this reason**

The first sentence provides the reason, while the second sentence gives the result.

Reason = Eric had an important job interview on Tuesday morning.

Result = **For this reason**, he ironed his shirt on Monday night.

Reason = It was snowing heavily in Ohio that evening.

Result = **As a result**, airplanes could not land at the Cleveland airport.

Reason = Nina had to watch the children.

Result = **Consequently**, she was not able to come to class.

Let's look at an example from the text:

> Fortunately, there are also many examples of therapists who have helped clients recover and deal with terrible repressed memories. **Thus**, therapists are in the difficult position of trying to distinguish accurate accounts of repressed memories from those that may have been shaped or reinforced by suggestions or expectations of the therapist.

The reason = therapists help their clients recover and deal with the repressed memories.

The result = therapists have to distinguish between the accurate accounts and their own expectations.

Now you try it. In the sentence below, how do you think the story will continue? Esmeralda just signed a contract to play in a movie. **As a result,** __________.

There is no one right answer. You could have written any of the following:

As a result, she is excited.

As a result, she is planning to move to Hollywood.

As a result, she might become rich and famous.

Practicing this kind of thinking will help you understand what you read more quickly and more deeply. Let's try more:

Faysal never eats meat. **Consequently,** __________.

It rained all night. **Thus,** __________.

The movie is almost four hours long. **For this reason,** __________.

Bogdana works hard during the week. **As a result,** __________.

Now, let's see what difference it makes if we reverse the order. In many cases, you'll have a completely different story:

__________. **Consequently,** Faysal never eats meat.

__________. **Thus,** it rained all night.

__________. **For this reason,** the movie is four hours long.

__________. **As a result,** Bogdana works hard during the week.

Answers

Faysal never eats meat. **Consequently,** he (is thin) (eats a lot of rice) (saves money).

It rained all night. **Thus,** (the streets are wet) (the roads are flooded).

The movie is almost four hours long. **For this reason,** (no one wants to see it) (you should buy lots of popcorn) (go to the bathroom before).

Bogdana works hard during the week. **As a result,** she (is tired by Friday) (has a lot of money) (has no extra time).

(He loves animals) (He thinks vegetarianism is healthy). **Consequently,** Faysal never eats meat.

(A storm began) (It's the rainy season). **Thus,** it rained all night.

(It's a long story) (The film covers 100 years). **For this reason,** the movie is four hours long.

(She needs money for her education) (She's saving to buy a car) (She has bills to pay). **As a result,** Bogdana works hard during the week.

The Big Picture

Which statement below offers the best summary of the larger significance of this module?

A The study of memory shows that humans are destined to disappointment in their endeavors to learn. The best we can achieve is a fragmentary and temporary grasp of facts and ideas that are of importance to us.

B The human brain is like a vast container, which we fill with facts and ideas from birth to death. Every time we attend to something in our environment, it goes into the box to be saved for later use.

C In the future, psychology will use electrical and chemical examination to locate and identify every specific memory in the brain. Until then, we really can't say anything definitive about what memory is or how it works.

D Although we are just beginning to find the precise mechanisms of memory in the brain, several theories (models) of memory illustrate the processes that seem to be occurring as we perceive, learn, and remember.

E Types of memory: long-term, short-term, and examination (real-short-term).

True-False

_____ 1. Memory involves three basic processes: encoding, storing, and retrieving.

_____ 2. There are four basic kinds of memory: flashbulb snapshots, temporary, impermanent, and permanent.

_____ 3. Without the stage called sensory memory, we would drown in a sea of incoming visual, auditory, and other sensations.

_____ 4. Short-term memory is capable of holding several dozen bits of information for several minutes.

_____ 5. When you attempt to remember a list of animals, the recency effect takes precedence over the primacy effect.

_____ 6. Encoding is transferring information from short-term to long-term memory.

_____ 7. If you are studying for the next psych exam, elaborative rehearsal will be a more effective strategy than maintenance rehearsal.

_____ 8. The best way to get information into long-term memory is to repeat it over and over again.

_____ 9. A good strategy for remembering something is to associate it with some distinctive visual image.

_____ 10. When you find someone who has unusual powers of memory, you can be fairly certain that the person possesses a photographic memory.

Flashcards 1

_____ 1.	declarative memory	a.	a form of sensory memory that holds auditory information for one or two seconds
_____ 2.	echoic memory	b.	process that can hold only a limited amount of information (average of seven items) for only a short period (2 to 30 sec)
_____ 3.	encoding	c.	memories for performing motor tasks, habits, conditioning; not conscious or retrievable
_____ 4.	iconic memory	d.	a type of declarative memory; involves knowledge of facts, concepts, words, definitions, and language rules
_____ 5.	long-term memory	e.	a form of sensory memory that holds visual information for about a quarter of a second
_____ 6.	procedural memory	f.	the process of getting or recalling information that has been placed into short-term or long-term storage
_____ 7.	retrieving	g.	the process of placing encoded information into relatively permanent mental storage for later recall
_____ 8.	semantic memory	h.	memories for facts or events (scenes, stories, faces, etc.); conscious and retrievable
_____ 9.	short-term (working) memory	i.	the process of storing almost unlimited amounts of information over long periods of time
_____ 10.	storing	j.	making mental representations of information so that it can be placed or put into our memories

Flashcards 2

_____ 1.	chunking	a.	the ability to form sharp, detailed visual images of a page, then to recall the entire image at a later date
_____ 2.	effortful encoding	b.	better recall of information presented at the beginning and at the end of a task
_____ 3.	elaborative rehearsal	c.	vivid recollections, usually in great detail, of dramatic or emotionally charged incidents of great interest
_____ 4.	episodic memory	d.	process of pushing memories of threat or trauma into the unconscious, from which it cannot be retrieved
_____ 5.	flashbulb memories	e.	transfer of information from short-term into long-term memory by working hard to do so
_____ 6.	interference	f.	results when new information enters short-term memory and overwrites information already there
_____ 7.	maintenance rehearsal	g.	making meaningful associations between information to be learned and information already stored
_____ 8.	photographic memory	h.	simply repeating or rehearsing the information rather than forming any new associations
_____ 9.	primacy-recency effect	i.	a type of declarative memory involving knowledge of specific events, personal experiences, or activities
_____ 10.	repression	j.	combining separate items of information into a larger unit, then remembering the unit as a whole

Multiple Choice

____ 1. Plotnik and Kouyoumdjian discuss Daniel Temmet, who memorized more than 22,500 digits of pi, because Daniel's rare abilities

a. show that extreme concentration of mental ability in one area is usually accompanied by significant mental deficiencies in other areas
b. are possessed only by people who are otherwise retarded or autistic
c. could be duplicated by any of us… if we put our minds to it
d. offer an extreme example of the memory processes we all use

____ 2. Plotnik and Kouyoumdjian also tell the story of Clive Wearing, who suffers severe memory impairment, to illustrate the idea that

a. without memories, we would live in a never-ending present
b. our memories can cause pain and suffering
c. memories are inconsistent — some things you can remember, some you can't
d. we remember bad things more often than good things

____ 3. Which one of the following is *not* one of the three processes of memory?

a. encoding
b. storing
c. deciphering
d. retrieving

____ 4. The function of sensory memory is to

a. hold information in its raw form for a brief period of time
b. make quick associations between new data and things you already know
c. weed out what is irrelevant in incoming information
d. burn sensations into long-term memory for later retrieval and inspection

____ 5. Short-term memory can hold information for about

a. 1 to 2 minutes
b. one-tenth of a second
c. 2 to 30 seconds
d. 10 minutes

____ 6. __________ memory holds visual information for about a quarter of a second

a. Chunk
b. Iconic
c. Pictorial
d. Echoic

____ 7. Thanks to __________ memory, incoming speech sounds linger just long enough so we can recognize the sounds as words

a. chunking
b. iconic
c. verbal
d. echoic

_____ 8. Which statement below best describes what short-term (working) memory is?
   a. your perceptual processes react to it
   b. you freeze it briefly in order to pay attention to it
   c. you work with it to accomplish some immediate task
   d. you retrieve it later when you need it again

_____ 9. Out of change at the pay phone, you frantically repeat the 10-digit number you just got from Information over and over again; that's called
   a. chunking
   b. maintenance rehearsal
   c. memory span stretching
   d. duration enhancement

_____ 10. A classic study by George Miller showed that short-term memory can hold
   a. one item or bit of information at a time
   b. an unlimited amount of information
   c. about a dozen items or bits
   d. about seven items or bits

_____ 11. Why doesn't information in short-term memory simply become permanent? One reason is
   a. limited storage space in the brain
   b. fascination with the new and different
   c. incompatibility with previously processed information
   d. interference caused by newly arriving information

_____ 12. Using the process of __________, Daniel Temmet memorized more than 22,500 digits of pi
   a. chunking
   b. maintenance rehearsal
   c. memory span stretching
   d. duration enhancement

_____ 13. Short-term memory is also called *working* memory, in order to emphasize that it is
   a. hard work, which most of us like to avoid
   b. an active process involving attending, rehearsing, and storing
   c. a fragile process that often breaks down (explaining why we forget things)
   d. something you can't do indefinitely without a period of rest

_____ 14. Plotnik and Kouyoumdjian advise you to think of long-term memory as a
   a. process of storing almost unlimited amounts of information
   b. process of storing information, but only a limited amount of what we learn
   c. place where information is deposited for possible future use
   d. place where important information is kept and unimportant information is discarded

_____ 15. If you attempt to remember a list of animal names, you will be more likely to remember
   a. the first few names
   b. the last few names
   c. both the first and last few names
   d. neither the first or last few names, but the ones occurring in the middle of the list

_____ 16. The memory function described in the previous question is called the
a. paradoxical memory effect
b. primacy effect
c. recency effect
d. primacy-recency effect

_____ 17. Remembering how you did on your last psych test involves __________ memory
a. episodic
b. semantic
c. consequential
d. procedural

_____ 18. The actual knowledge required for that test involves __________ memory
a. episodic
b. semantic
c. consequential
d. procedural

_____ 19. Your manual ability to write out the answers on the test involves __________ memory
a. episodic
b. semantic
c. consequential
d. procedural

_____ 20. Of the four memory concepts below, the one most important to you as a student is
a. automatic encoding
b. elaborative rehearsal
c. maintenance rehearsal
d. power-of-will encoding (willpower)

_____ 21. Plotnik and Kouyoumdjian put psychology to good use in their textbook by providing __________ to help you encode the material you must learn
a. distinctive visual associations
b. flashbulb memories
c. maintenance rehearsal drills
d. chunking strategies

_____ 22. The main problem with repressed memories of childhood abuse is that
a. very few people can remember that far back
b. we now know that the "unconscious" does not exist
c. therapists may unwittingly help patients form memories that seem to explain their key problems
d. so far, all the claimed cases of abuse in childhood have been proven to be lies

_____ 23. Students in Ghana remembered a story better than students in New York because of the
a. lower intelligence of Ghanaian students due to poverty and a poor diet
b. long oral tradition of their culture versus the written tradition of New York culture
c. fact that the story was from their culture, which was foreign to New Yorkers
d. cultural tradition of cynical New Yorkers not to believe *any* story

_____ 24. Now in her 40s, Jill Price can remember almost everything that has happened to her every day since the age of 14, an amazing example of __________ memory

a. flashbulb
b. echoic
c. episodic
d. photographic

_____ 25. Research shows that flashbulb memories are

a. impressive and vivid, but not necessarily accurate
b. blinding images that are impossible to forget
c. always associated with tragedies, like where you were when September 11 happened
d. frightening memories that you can't quite bring into clear detail

Short Essay

1. Summarize how three types of memory processes transform potentially useful information into available memories.
2. Contrast the two types of long-term memory by describing how they work.
3. What did you learn from this module that could help you become a more effective student?
4. What are the basic arguments for and against the existence of repressed memories of sexual abuse?
5. Describe the research Plotnik and Kouyoumdjian offered in support of the idea that cultural influences affect memory processes.

Gloomy Psychology

Here is a gloomy, possibly discouraging thought (considering how much you paid for your textbook): perhaps *nothing* in psychology is really true. Perhaps everything you are slaving so hard to learn is simply the best understanding we have now, eventually to be replaced by better ways of grasping how psychology works.

I suggested that the computer is merely a temporary model for understanding the mind. Let's go further and suggest that *all* the wonderful theories you study in psychology are models, none ultimately "true." There is no "unconscious" region of the mind, no pure "schedule of reinforcement," and no ethereal "self." They are all fictions — fictions we need in order to make sense of the facts.

There is one happy possibility in this dismal thought. Think how eagerly psychology is waiting for the better model *you* might construct one day. Keep working on your favorite theories.

Answers for Module 11

The Big Picture (explanations provided for incorrect choices)

A Far too pessimistic! Human memory is powerful and effective in guiding our lives.
B Far too simplistic! Selection of what to remember and method of organizing it in the mind are complex processes.
C This may be true in the future, but until then we still have useful theories about how memory works.
D *Correct! You see the "big picture" for this Module.*
E It's just a joke!

True-False (explanations provided for False choices; page numbers given for all choices)

1	T	239	
2	F	240	The three basic kinds of memory are sensory, short-term, and long-term.
3	T	241	
4	F	242	Short-term memory is limited to about seven bits of information.
5	F	245	Both the recency effect and the primacy effect are in operation.
6	T	248	
7	T	249	
8	F	249	Associating information with other information is the best way.
9	T	249	
10	F	254	Unusual memory powers are explained by association rather than the rare photographic memory.

Flashcards 1

1 h 2 a 3 j 4 e 5 i 6 c 7 f 8 d 9 b 10 g

Flashcards 2

1 j 2 e 3 g 4 i 5 c 6 f 7 h 8 a 9 b 10 d

Multiple Choice (explanations provided for incorrect choices)

1 a Daniel Temmet has a few quirks, but is fairly normal in most respects.
b This statement is untrue.
c Only a half-dozen people in the world posses such gargantuan memory powers.
d *Correct! See page 239.*

2 ***a*** *Correct! See page 239.*
b True, but not illustrated by Clive Wearing's problem.
c Perhaps, but not illustrated by Clive Wearing's problem.
d Maybe true, but not illustrated by Clive Wearing's problem.

3 a Encoding is one of the three memory processes.
b Storing is one of the three memory processes.
c *Correct! See page 239.*
d Retrieving is one of the three memory processes.

4 ***a*** *Correct! See page 240.*
b This is a function of long-term memory.
c This is a function of short-term memory.
d This is not how information is stored in long-term memory.

5 a At this length of time, we would be overwhelmed by new information.
b This would hardly be enough time to consider the information.
c *Correct! See page 240.*
d Could you think of only one thing and nothing else going on around you for 10 minutes?

6 a Chunking refers to grouping bits of information into larger units.
b *Correct! See page 241.*
c This is not a correct technical term in the psychology of memory.
d Echoic memory refers to holding auditory information for one or two seconds.

7 a Chunking refers to grouping bits of information into larger units.
b Iconic memory refers to holding visual information for about a quarter of a second.
c This is not a correct technical term in the psychology of memory.
d *Correct! See page 241.*

8 a Perceptual processes come before memory.
b Short-term memory is an active process.
c *Correct! See page 242.*
d This statement refers to long-term memory.

9 a Chunking refers to grouping bits of information into larger units.
b *Correct! See page 242.*
c This is not a correct technical term in the psychology of memory.
d This is not a correct technical term in the psychology of memory.

10 a If true, how could we follow directions or remember a phone number?
b This may be true of long-term memory.
c Close, but no cigar.
d *Correct! See page 242.*

11 a No limits on storage space in the brain have been established.
b If this were the explanation, how would anything enter long-term memory?
c If this were the explanation, how would we learn anything truly new?
d *Correct! See page 242.*

12 ***a*** *Correct! See page 243.*
b Maintenance rehearsal refers to intentionally repeating information so it remains longer in short-term memory.
c This is not a correct technical term in the psychology of memory.
d This is not a correct technical term in the psychology of memory.

13 a Working is used in the sense of a process.
b *Correct! See page 243.*
c It operates as long as we are conscious.
d You couldn't take a break from it if you wanted to.

14 ***a*** *Correct! See page 244.*
b It can store almost unlimited amounts of information.
c That's the point — it's a process, not a place.
d That's the point — it's a process, not a place.

15 a This answer is only partly true.
b This answer is only partly true.
c *Correct! See page 245.*
d The names in the middle of the list are the most poorly remembered.

16 a This is not a correct term in psychology.
b Half correct; see definitions.
c Half correct; see definitions.
d *Correct! See page 245.*

17 ***a*** *Correct! See page 246.*
b Semantic information refers to general knowledge, book learning, facts, and definitions of words.
c This is not a correct technical term in the psychology of memory.
d Procedural information refers to knowledge about motor skills and conditioned reflexes.

18 a Episodic information refers to knowledge about one's personal experiences.
b *Correct! See page 246.*
c This is not a correct technical term in the psychology of memory.
d Procedural information refers to knowledge about motor skills and conditioned reflexes.

19 a Episodic information refers to knowledge about one's personal experiences.
b Semantic information refers to general knowledge, book learning, facts, and definitions of words.
c This is not a correct technical term in the psychology of memory.
d *Correct! See page 246.*

20 a Automatic encoding refers to easily remembering interesting, personal, but not academic information.
b *Correct! See page 249.*
c Maintenance rehearsal refers to keeping information in short-term memory.
d This is not a correct term in psychology.

21 ***a*** *Correct! See page 249.*
b Think about why the marvelous pictures in the text are repeated in concept reviews and summary tests.
c Think about why the marvelous pictures in the text are repeated in concept reviews and summary tests.
d Think about why the marvelous pictures in the text are repeated in concept reviews and summary tests.

22 a Most people remember many events from age four or five onward.
b Many psychologists continue to use the concept of the unconscious.
c *Correct! See page 250.*
d Sadly, most claims of child abuse may be true.

23 a Intelligence was not a variable in this research.
b *Correct! See page 253.*
c The story was not from either culture.
d They may be worldly wise, and maybe cynical, but they love stories as much as anyone.

24 a Flashbulb memories are rare, vivid recollections of dramatic or emotionally charged incidents.
b This term refers to auditory memory.
c *Correct! See page 254.*
d Photographic memory refers to a camera-like ability to remember a page seen only for a short time.

25 ***a*** *Correct! See page 255.*
b Flashbulb memories may last, but also may be forgotten.
c Not always, because some concern happy events like graduations or senior proms.
d Not all are frightening, but all flashbulb memories are clear and vivid.

Short Essay (sample answers)

1. Sensory memory receives and holds incoming environmental information in its raw form for an instant to several seconds while you consider what to do with it. Short-term (working) memory holds information you are paying attention to for a brief time, from two to 30 seconds, while you rehearse the information you want to keep. Finally, that information is encoded for storage in long-term memory on a relatively permanent basis. The best way to encode and recall new information is to associate it with old information.

2. The two types of long-term memory are declarative and procedural — facts versus actions. Declarative memory involves memory for fact or events, such as scenes, stories, words, conversations, faces, or daily events. These memories can be semantic, basically factual, or episodic, more personal. Procedural (nondeclarative) memory involves memories for motor skills, cognitive skills, and emotional behavior like fears learned through classical conditioning. Name of your old bike (declarative); how to ride it (procedural).

3. Your professor probably assigns a module of the textbook a week. How can you master the many terms and concepts? In your answer, you should talk about effortful encoding and elaborative rehearsal. Both involve working hard to repeat or rehearse information and actively making meaningful associations between new information you wish to remember and old or familiar information you've already stored in long-term memory.

4. Sigmund Freud brought the concept of repression into psychology. According to that idea, memories of painful traumatic events can be buried in the unconscious. Therapy, which is a kind of exploration of the unconscious mind, might bring such memories into consciousness. But Elizabeth Loftus and other researchers have demonstrated not only that some "recovered" memories are false, but also that false "memories" can be implanted in suggestible minds. The law correctly demands irrefutable evidence.

5. Does culture influence memory? Researchers read a dramatic (but neutral) story twice to both English-speaking college students in Ghana and college students in New York. Sixteen days later, and without having been forewarned, both groups of students were asked to write down as much as they could remember of the story. The Ghanaians, who grew up in a culture with a strong oral tradition, remembered significantly more than the New Yorkers, whose education emphasized a written tradition.

Module 12

Remembering & Forgetting

What If You Could Remember Nothing?

Can you imagine how terrifying it must be to suffer from amnesia? In one form of amnesia, you can't remember back before a certain point. In a less common form, you can't construct new memories. In either case, you are rootless, adrift in a world with no clear sense of past, present, and future. You wouldn't really know who you are, why you exist, or what will happen to you.

What if you could *forget* nothing? Happily, there is no such psychiatric condition (although you could use such powers, along about now, with mid-term exams coming up). If you were incapable of ever forgetting anything you would be immobilized in a sea of indistinguishable bits and pieces of information, incapable of ever making a decision or taking action because the necessary review of past information and action would be never-ending.

The processes of remembering and forgetting are so immediate and so crucial that we take them for granted. But science, of course, takes nothing for granted. Plotnik and Kouyoumdjian show us what the science of psychology has learned about these vital memory processes.

Forget About It

When something is too painful to endure, a common psychiatric reaction is to forget it, in part or completely. Often victims of auto accidents experience temporary amnesia for the immediate events of the crash. All of us "forget" bad grades and other humiliating defeats.

As we have learned more about child abuse, we have come to realize how its victims often repress their trauma, in order to go on living. Uncovering these repressed memories has become an important part of psychotherapy. Many therapists are convinced that the suffering child cannot become well again unless the painful memories are dug out and worked through.

But memory is ever so much more complicated. Now we are also learning that it is quite possible to "remember" things that never happened. Plotnik and Kouyoumdjian reveal the interesting and disturbing dangers of false memories, both those of eyewitness testimony in court cases and childhood memories in psychotherapy. Is it really possible that an eyewitness to a crime could make the wrong identification, or that a child could be wrong about having been sexually abused? Must we not believe what children and good people say when they testify in court? Forget about it!

Effective Student Tip 12

Manage Your Grade

True, we professors set the course standards and assign the final grades. Since most professors stick to their rules once they are established, however, *you* have almost total control over what that grade will be. But wishing doesn't make it so: you have to know how to make it happen. The trick is to take a management attitude toward your grades.

Taking charge and managing your grade involves six steps: (1) understand your inner motivation concerning grades, to guard against self-sabotage; (2) understand the details and logic of your professor's grading system; (3) keep accurate records of your scores and grades (all of them, including any assignments or quizzes you missed); (4) project your final grade from your current performance; (5) determine what immediate steps you must take; and (6) make whatever adjustments seem necessary for effective pursuit of your goal.

Don't underestimate the importance of grades to your mental health. Rightly or wrongly, we interpret grades, like earnings, as powerful messages about our effectiveness.

You can passively allow your grades to happen to you, as many students do, or you can take charge and make them what you want.

Your response…

How important are grades to you? How much control do you seem to have over the grades you get?

Learning Objectives

1. Understand remembering and forgetting as related processes that are indispensable in navigating our way through the barrage of information and complexity of tasks we face, literally, from moment to moment.

2. Learn the basic theories, mechanisms, and research methods in the field of remembering and forgetting.

3. Learn how neuroscience is investigating the biology of memory in the brain and bringing psychology closer to a physical explanation of how the processes of remembering and forgetting work.

4. Improve your learning strategies and techniques by applying the lessons of remembering and forgetting, such as encoding, the reasons for forgetting, and combating forgetting with mnemonics.

5. Appreciate the power of cultural differences, even in something as fundamental as memory, through an example of Aborigine and white Australian learning and memory abilities.

6. Consider the legal and social implications of recent research on false memories and how they can be created and implanted.

7. Reconsider the reputation of eyewitness testimony in light of research on the accuracy of eyewitnesses and how they can be mislead by factors such as how questions are worded.

Key Terms

These key terms touch on an area of psychology that researchers are just beginning to understand. But what could be more important than the way we orient ourselves to time and place?

amnesia
cognitive interview
eyewitness testimony
forgetting
forgetting curve
interference
long-term potentiation (LTP)
method of loci
mnemonic methods
network hierarchy
network theory
neural assemblies
nodes
peg method
proactive interference
recall
recognition
repression
retrieval cues
retroactive interference
source misattribution
state-dependent learning
tip-of-the-tongue phenomenon

The "PowerStudy 4.5 for Introduction to Psychology" CD-ROM for this module is a "Super Module." In addition to the regular PowerStudy features (quizzes, summary test, key terms, web site connections, critical thinking exercise, module outline, and more), Super Modules also include self-paced, step-by-step multimedia presentations with animations and narration.

Outline

- *Introduction*
  1. Watching a crime (mugged!)

☐ Were you surprised when you tried Plotnik and Kouyoumdjian's quiz about the assault?

  2. **Recall** versus **recognition** (remembering)

☐ Can you see how essay exams and multiple-choice exams require different study techniques?

  3. Eyewitness testimony (Lineup)

A. Organization of Memories

1. Filing and organizing 87,967 memories: **network theory**
2. Network theory of memory organization: searching for a memory
   a. Nodes
   b. Associations
   c. Network
3. Organization of network hierarchy
   a. **Nodes**
   b. **Network hierarchy**
   c. Searching nodes
4. Categories in the brain

B. Forgetting Curves

1. Early memories
2. Unfamiliar and uninteresting
   a. **Forgetting curve** (Hermann Ebbinghaus)
   b. Nonsense syllables
3. Familiar and interesting

C. Reasons for Forgetting

1. Overview: **forgetting**
   a. **Repression** (Freud)
   b. Poor **retrieval cues**/poor encoding
   c. **Interference**
   d. **Amnesia**
   e. Distortion
2. **Interference**
   a. **Proactive interference**
   b. **Retroactive interference**
   c. Why did viewers forget the mugger's face?

3. **Retrieval cues**
    a. Forming effective retrieval cues
    b. **Tip-of-the-tongue phenomenon**
4. **State-dependent learning**

D. Biological Bases of Memory

1. Location of memories in the brain
    a. Cortex: short-term memories
    b. Cortex: long-term memories
    c. Amygdala: emotional memories
    d. Hippocampus: transferring memories
    e. Brain: memory model
2. Making a short-term memory: **neural assemblies**
3. Making a long-term memory: **long-term potentiation (LTP)**
4. Forgetting unwanted long-term memories (see Critical Thinking on p. 278)

E. Mnemonics: Memorization Methods

1. Improving your memory: **mnemonic methods**
2. **Method of loci**
3. **Peg method**
4. Effectiveness of methods

F. Cultural Diversity: Aborigines versus White Australians

1. Retrieval cues
2. Visual versus verbal memory
    a. Using visual cues
    b. Performance
    c. Culture and retrieval cues

G. Research Focus: Memory Accuracy

1. How accurate are students' memories?
2. Research method to evaluate memory accuracy
    a. Procedure
    b. Results
    c. Conclusion

H. Application: Eyewitness Testimony

1. How accurate is **eyewitness testimony**?
2. Can an eyewitness be misled?
3. Can questions change the answers? (Elizabeth Loftus)
4. Is what you say, what you believe? (**source misattribution**)
5. Which interview technique works best? (**cognitive interview**)

How English Works

Words in the Textbook

p. 261 tried to **ward off** the oncoming threat = push away

with a **menacing** gesture = threatening

the **mugger's** jacket = attacking thief's

p. 262 Norman's **train of thought** = direction of thinking

p. 264 He **got around** the fact = avoided the problem

the ticking of a **metronome** = (for a picture of a metronome, see p. 12)

He used only **rote** memory = mechanical, routine

p. 265 **prominent** memory researchers = well-known

if you study primarily by **cramming** = studying the night before the exam

While **showing off** her new pair of skates = attract attention

p. 268 have **long assumed** = for a long time have taken for granted

p. 269 how people **cope** = deal successfully with a difficult problem

after **traumatic** experiences = extremely distressing or frightening

p. 271 **at my fingertips** = easily available (in memory)

p. 272 harsh, endless, **barren** desert = with no trees or other plants growing

p. 274 the **damning** evidence = proving that somebody is guilty

implicated another man = showed that somebody played a part in a crime

a series of **armed** robberies = using guns

The police had few **leads** = clues, information

After being **prompted** to look = encouraged

wearing a **clerical** collar = for priests or religious leaders

p. 275 a **hit-and-run** accident = driver escapes, does not stop to help

police **interrogation** = questioning

ESL Tip: Idioms

Learning a new language is fairly basic at first. You find out how simple ideas are expressed (My name is Molly.), and you practice them. The real challenges come when you run into **idioms**. You often can't explain them except by admitting, "Well, that's just the way we say it in this language." The use of some verbs can be very idiomatic. For example, look at this form of the verb **run:**

I am **running** in the Boston Marathon.

I am **running** for the train.

I am **running** for the senate.

I am **running** down this list of players.

I am **running** down your reputation.

I am **running** around in a state of panic.

I am **running** up a large bill at the supermarket.

I am **running** through all the money my aunt left me.

It will not be easy to understand how English speakers use *running* in these idiomatic expressions, but with exposure to repeated examples and large doses of patience, it will happen. Here are some more examples, this time idiomatic uses of the verb **get**:

Let's **get** down to business.

Let's **get** going.

Come on, Pierre, **get** with it.

How do I **get** this across to you?

I'm trying to **get** through to my students.

Be patient with yourself. Idiomatic expressions are the most difficult, but often the richest, uses of English you will encounter. They are well worth the effort it takes to master them.

Vocabulary: "While"

Look at these two sentences and see if you can find the difference in the meaning of **while**: **While** showing off her new pair of skates, my sister fell down. Aborigines used visual retrieval cues, **while** the white Australians used verbal retrieval cues. The **while** in the first sentence tells the reader that it is happening at the same time. The **while** in the second sentence is used to show a difference. The most common use of **while** is to show that two things are occurring at the same time:

Romeo washed the dishes **while** Juliet dried them.

While Bob was studying Module 12, he was watching a kung fu film.

Notice how there is a comma when the sentence starts with **while** because it is not the main subject and verb, but no commas if **while** comes after the main subject and verb. The comma is used differently when **while** shows a difference:

His father is a smoker, **while** Luis is not.

The sentence above shows a difference with *exactly* the same meaning as <u>but</u> and <u>although</u> sentences. So, we have three ways to show a difference:

His father is a smoker, **while** Luis is not.

His father is a smoker, **but** Luis is not.

Although his father is a smoker, Luis is not.

We can also use this form of **while** at the beginning of the sentence:

While Yang Li can speak Chinese, she is unable to read it.

The sentence above shows a difference in the same way as <u>but</u> and <u>although</u> sentences. Try it:

While Yang Li can speak Chinese, she is unable to read it. __________, **but** she is unable to read it. **Although** Yang Li can speak Chinese, __________.

Answers

Yang Li can speak Chinese, but she is unable to read it. Although Yang Li can speak Chinese, **she is unable to read it.**

The Big Picture

Which statement below offers the best summary of the larger significance of this module?

A Research has demonstrated that eyewitness testimony is not very reliable and that false memories can be implanted. These discoveries throw our whole understanding of memory up for grabs.

B We may be stuck with the cognitive models that now describe remembering and forgetting, since a biological understanding of the neural basis of memory appears to be beyond the reach of neuroscience.

C The subtle operations of acquiring (and then sometimes losing) memories suggest that remembering and forgetting work together in a reciprocal balance to meet the changing demands of our environments.

D The fact that Aborigines remember in a different way than white Australians suggests that the mechanisms of memory are mainly cultural, and have little common biological or evolutionary basis.

E Would a psych instructor *dare* expect us to remember all this complicated stuff for an exam? We think not!

True-False

_____ 1. Of the two ways to remember, recall is easier than recognition.

_____ 2. According to network theory, memory is organized like a gigantic map on which roads connect cities of related information.

_____ 3. Forgetting curves measure the length of time that pieces of information will remain in long-term memory.

_____ 4. Rod Plotnik uses the story of his sister's memory loss after her fall on the ice to illustrate Freud's theory of repression — something very embarrassing happened!

_____ 5. Amnesia is the loss of memory that may occur following drug use, damage to the brain, or after severe psychological trauma.

_____ 6. Proactive interference occurs when you are trying too hard to remember new information.

_____ 7. Although it is the brain that does the "thinking," the spinal cord stores the actual memories.

_____ 8. Both the method of loci and the peg method are mnemonic strategies.

_____ 9. It turns out that people *are* different in mental ability — Aborigines, for example, score lower than white Australians on intelligence tests.

_____ 10. Psychologists have discovered that introducing misleading information during questioning can distort eyewitness testimony.

Flashcards 1

_____	1. amnesia	a. memory files that contain related information organized around a specific topic or category
_____	2. forgetting	b. mental reminders we create by forming vivid mental images or creating associations between bits of information
_____	3. interference	c. identifying previously learned information with the help of more external cues
_____	4. long-term potentiation (LTP)	d. a common reason for forgetting; recall of a particular memory is blocked by other related memories
_____	5. network theory	e. says we store related ideas in separate categories or files called nodes, all linked together in a network
_____	6. nodes	f. the inability to retrieve, recall, or recognize information that was stored in long-term memory
_____	7. recall	g. loss of memory caused by a blow or damage to the brain or by drug use, or by severe psychological stress
_____	8. recognition	h. a neuron becoming more sensitive to stimulation after it has been repeatedly stimulated
_____	9. repression	i. retrieving previously learned information without the aid of (or with very few) external cues
_____	10. retrieval cues	j. a Freudian mental process that automatically hides emotionally threatening information in the unconscious

Flashcards 2

_____	1. cognitive interview	a. when new information (learned later) blocks the retrieval of related old information (learned earlier)
_____	2. forgetting curve	b. encoding technique that creates visual associations between memorized places and items to memorize
_____	3. method of loci	c. a technique for questioning eyewitnesses by having them imagine and reconstruct details of an event fully
_____	4. network hierarchy	d. encoding technique that creates associations between number-word rhymes and items to be memorized
_____	5. peg method	e. when old information (learned earlier) blocks the remembering of new information (learned later)
_____	6. proactive interference	f. despite great effort, temporary inability to recall information we absolutely know is in our memory
_____	7. retroactive interference	g. easier to recall information when in same emotional or physiological state or setting as when first learned
_____	8. source misattribution	h. a memory error that results when a person has difficulty in deciding where a memory came from
_____	9. state-dependent learning	i. measures amount of previously learned information that subjects can recall or recognize across time
_____	10. tip-of-the-tongue phenomenon	j. arranging nodes so concrete information is at bottom of hierarchy, with abstract ideas at top level

Multiple Choice

_____ 1. Plotnik and Kouyoumdjian begin this module with a scene from a campus mugging. Their point is to show that
   a. crime is so scary that we are likely to remember every detail
   b. crime is a special situation, in which the everyday rules of memory do not apply
   c. remembering and forgetting are automatic in dramatic situations like this one
   d. remembering and forgetting are not as simple as most people think

_____ 2. Your brow beading with perspiration, you struggle to answer this multiple-choice question, desperately summoning your best powers of
   a. recall
   b. reflection
   c. recognition
   d. recollection

_____ 3. If you only glanced through the module, pray that the pop quiz will be
   a. essay
   b. multiple-choice
   c. short essay
   d. oral

_____ 4. According to network theory, memory is organized by
   a. nodes, associations, and links among pieces of information
   b. most important to least important information
   c. chronological order, according to when information was acquired
   d. "programs" of information, similar to a TV "network"

_____ 5. Memory files containing related information organized around a specific topic are called
   a. network hierarchies
   b. nodes
   c. network theories
   d. modules

_____ 6. Recent brain scan research shows that the brain comes with
   a. prewired categories for processing information
   b. specific, tiny locations for each individual bit of information you remember
   c. hundreds, or even thousands, of different nodes for filing information
   d. identifiable networks that are like well-traveled highways connecting nodes

_____ 7. Which of the following groups of items would provide the best material for scientific research on memory over time?
   a. names and faces of childhood friends
   b. commonly studied facts, such as state capitals
   c. foreign language vocabulary
   d. nonsense syllables

_____ 8. Analysis of the data yielded by such research (above) would yield
   a. rates of retention
   b. memory percentages
   c. forgetting curves
   d. cognitive charts

_____ 9. A friend says you did something terribly embarrassing at the party, but you can't remember it — this is an example of
   a. repression
   b. poor retrieval cues
   c. amnesia
   d. interference

_____ 10. You were introduced to your friend's professor recently, but there was no time to chat, and now you can't recall the professor's name — this is an example of
   a. repression
   b. poor retrieval cues
   c. amnesia
   d. interference

_____ 11. Amnesia is usually caused by
   a. forcing a painful memory out of consciousness
   b. being blocked or prevented by other related memories
   c. a blow or damage to the brain
   d. failing to create vivid mental images or associations

_____ 12. Sometimes we misremember something (like our grades!) due to memory distortions caused by
   a. low intelligence
   b. sleep deprivation
   c. recreational drug use
   d. bias or suggestibility

_____ 13. Proactive interference is when
   a. information learned later now disrupts retrieval of information learned earlier
   b. learning positive information interferes with the retrieval of negative information
   c. information learned earlier now disrupts retrieval of information learned later
   d. retrospective thinking interferes with potential learning

_____ 14. Retroactive interference is when
   a. information learned later now disrupts retrieval of information learned earlier
   b. learning positive information interferes with the retrieval of negative information
   c. information learned earlier now disrupts retrieval of information learned later
   d. retrospective thinking interferes with potential learning

_____ 15. Darn! I know it as well as I know my own name, but I just can't remember it right now — sounds like a case of
   a. false memory
   b. source misattribution
   c. state-dependent learning
   d. tip-of-the-tongue phenomenon

_____ 16. An example of state-dependent learning would be when you
   a. become so emotional you can't remember something you are sure you know
   b. get angry at someone and suddenly recall related past annoyances
   c. become so emotional you completely forget something painful
   d. get better grades in psychology after transferring to a school in another state

_____ 17. Brain scans are advancing our knowledge of remembering and forgetting by identifying the
a. struggle of the cortex to control the amygdala and hippocampus
b. neural assemblies that form long-term memories
c. brain areas involved in processing and storing different thoughts and memories
d. precise synapses where new memories are formed

_____ 18. The process in which a neuron becomes more sensitive to stimulation after it has been repeatedly stimulated is called
a. long-term potentiation (LTP)
b. state-dependent learning
c. neural assembly formation
d. interference

_____ 19. Long-term potentiation (LTP) works by
a. stimulating the amygdala
b. changing the structure and function of neurons
c. adding short-term memories together
d. not repeating new information too many times

_____ 20. Both the method of loci and the peg method work by
a. causing learning to be strengthened through repeated practice
b. creating strong associations that will serve as effective retrieval cues
c. connecting material to be learned to the purpose it will be used for
d. considering material to be memorized as easy and pleasant to learn

_____ 21. Bulletin from the research front on memory-enhancing products:
a. the popular herbal supplement ginkgo does not help
b. concentrating on encoding techniques such as making good associations does not help
c. listening to an audiocassette program on photographic memory does help
d. using marijuana in sufficient quantities does help

_____ 22. Aborigine children performed significantly better than white Australian children on memory tasks when
a. only Aborigine objects were used
b. the task involved auditory cues
c. testing was done outdoors in a natural setting
d. the task involved visual cues

_____ 23. Recent research on false memories of abuse in young children has shown that
a. children can be coached to lie about trivial matters, but not about sexual abuse
b. false memories can be created through repeated suggestions
c. children make things up because they really can't remember very well at that age
d. children tend to lie about most things if they can get something out of it

_____ 24. When evaluating eyewitness testimony, pay close attention to
a. whether the eyewitness has anything to gain or lose by testifying
b. how confident the eyewitness appears to be
c. how the questions to the eyewitness are worded
d. whether the eyewitness seems biased in favor of or against the defendant

_____ 25. Because of research on eyewitness testimony, police now use a technique called the
a. cognitive interview
b. good cop/bad cop strategy
c. bait-and-switch method
d. skeptical questioning interview

Short Essay

1. Summarize the current psychological explanation for how memory works.

2. What are the main reasons for forgetting and how do they work?

3. What is the main lesson of this module for you as a college student?

4. Why did Aborigines do better than white Australians on a memory test?

5. What are the implications of research on false memories for the legal system and for psychotherapy?

Test-Taking Tips

More hints:

- Be on the lookout for any *part* of an answer that makes the *whole* answer untrue.
- When you find an answer that sounds correct, you must also check the others — to make sure there isn't another answer that is even *more* true.

Answers for Module 12

The Big Picture (explanations provided for incorrect choices)

A Actually these discoveries reinforce the model of the mind as constructive and flexible.
B A biological understanding of the neural basis of memory is rapidly approaching.
C *Correct! You see the "big picture" for this Module.*
D An unwarranted deduction. The example shows that our common biology can be influenced by cultural factors.
E It's just a joke!

True-False (explanations provided for False choices; page numbers given for all choices)

1	F	261	Recognition is easier than recall because cues are available.
2	T	262	
3	T	264	
4	F	265	Her memory loss was due to amnesia from hitting her head on the ice, not to repression.
5	T	265	
6	F	266	Proactive interference occurs when old information interferes with learning new information.
7	F	268	The brain controls both thinking and memory.
8	T	271	
9	F	272	In tasks involving visual retrieval cues, Aborigine children did better than white Australian children.
10	T	274	

Flashcards 1

1 g 2 f 3 d 4 h 5 e 6 a 7 i 8 c 9 j 10 b

Flashcards 2

1 c 2 i 3 b 4 j 5 d 6 e 7 a 8 h 9 g 10 f

Multiple Choice (explanations provided for incorrect choices)

1 a Well, how did you do on the quiz?
b The rules have to apply to crime, too, or they cannot be considered rules.
c More likely it is just the opposite.
d *Correct! See page 261.*

2 a Recall refers to retrieving previously learned material without the aid of any external cues.
b Reflection is not a correct technical term in the psychology of memory.
c *Correct! See page 261.*
d Recollection is not a correct technical term in the psychology of memory.

3 a Think about which is easier — recall or recognition?
b *Correct! See page 261.*
c Think about which is easier — recall or recognition?
d Think about which is easier — recall or recognition?

4 ***a*** *Correct! See page 262.*
b How would "importance" be determined?
c Then we would always have to remember *when* we acquired the information.
d This analogy misunderstands the meaning of "network."

5 a Network hierarchies are arrangements of nodes into a certain order, like blue jay – bird – animal.
b *Correct! See page 263.*
c Network theory is a larger idea built on the concepts of nodes and hierarchies.
d Plotnik uses the term modules for the sections of his textbook.

6 ***a*** *Correct! See page 263.*
b Sounds logical, but brain scans can't show that much yet.
c Even if brain scans could identify nodes, the number of them would be vastly greater than thousands.
d Even if brain scans could identify networks, they would be more like associations than highways.

7 a Memory of these items would be influenced by a subject's life history.
b Memory of these items would be influenced by a subject's general knowledge.
c Memory of these items would be influenced by what language a subject speaks.
d *Correct! See page 264.*

8 a This is not a correct technical term in the psychology of memory.
b This is not a correct technical term in the psychology of memory.
c *Correct! See page 264.*
d This is not a correct technical term in the psychology of memory.

9 ***a*** *Correct! See page 265.*
b No, because you didn't make a special effort to remember it.
c No, because you remember other things about the party.
d No, because no related memories interfered.

10 a No, because there was nothing threatening about the name or the professor.
b *Correct! See page 265.*
c No, because you didn't receive a blow or damage to the brain.
d No, because related memories did not interfere with remembering the professor's name.

11 a That would be repression.
b That would be interference.
c *Correct! See page 265.*
d That would be poor retrieval cues.

12 a Intelligence was not a variable in this research.
b Forgetting perhaps, but not *mis*-remembering.
c Forgetting perhaps, but not *mis*-remembering.
d *Correct! See page 265.*

13 a This is retroactive interference.
b There is no evidence that this occurs in memory.
c *Correct! See page 266.*
d This is a nonsense statement.

14 ***a*** *Correct! See page 266.*
b There is no evidence that this occurs in memory.
c This is proactive interference.
d This is a nonsense statement.

15 a False memories refer to things you never knew.
b Source misattribution refers to a memory error.
c State-dependent learning refers to a situation that aids remembering.
d *Correct! See page 267.*

16 a Sounds more like tip-of-the-tongue phenomenon.
b *Correct! See page 267.*
c Sounds more like Freud's repression.
d It's just a joke! (Kind of lame, I admit!)

17 a All three of these areas of the brain are involved in forming long-term memories.
b Neural assemblies are involved in the work of short-term memory.
c *Correct! See page 268.*
d Brain scans, valuable as they are, can't begin to approach such precision.

18 ***a*** *Correct! See page 269.*
b State-dependent learning refers to a situation that aids remembering. See page 267.
c Neural assemblies refer to short-term memory processes.
d Interference refers to situations that make remembering more difficult. See page 265.

19 a The amygdala is involved in emotional memories.
b *Correct! See page 269.*
c LTP involves long-term, not short-term, memory.
d Just the opposite is true.

20 a Practice alone, as in rote learning, is slow and difficult.
b *Correct! See page 271.*
c This is a possible learning strategy, but not the same as the methods in question.
d This is a possible motivational approach, but not the same as the methods in question.

21 ***a*** *Correct! See page 271.*
b On the contrary, it's the only thing that does help.
c Research says it doesn't.
d You wish!

22 a Non-Aborigine objects were also used.
b It is the type of cue that is important, but the cues weren't auditory.
c The testing was not done outdoors.
d *Correct! See page 272.*

23 a There is no such research finding.
b *Correct! See page 273.*
c There is no such research finding.
d There is no such research finding.

24 a What about eyewitnesses with nothing to gain or lose?
b An eyewitness can be completely confident . . . and also mistaken.
c *Correct! See page 274.*
d What about eyewitnesses with no apparent biases either way?

25 ***a*** *Correct! See page 275.*
b On TV shows they still use it!
c That is a deceptive sales technique in business.
d This is not an actual term in psychology.

Short Essay (sample answers)

1. Network theory is currently the most popular model for how we file and organize memories. According to this theory, we store related ideas in separate categories or memory files called nodes. Through associations, we link thousands of nodes into a gigantic interconnected network. We can navigate through the network because the nodes are organized in hierarchies around specific topics or categories. We work our way up or down through the appropriate network hierarchy, from concrete to more specific to abstract information.

2. There are four main reasons for forgetting. Repression is Freud's idea that emotionally threatening or anxiety-producing information is buried in the unconscious. Poor retrieval cues are failures to make useful associations during encoding. Interference is caused by related information blocking recall. Amnesia is the temporary or permanent loss of memories caused by a blow or brain damage. A fifth possible reason for forgetting is distortion caused by bias or suggestibility, which interferes with the accuracy of remembering.

3. Becoming aware of memory dynamics, like why we remember and forget, and learning mnemonic strategies, like the method of loci and the peg method, may be of some help in becoming a more successful student. But the main lesson is that better long-term memory is made up of good encoding through powerful retrieval cues. Forming vivid mental images or creating associations between new information and information we already know sets the stage for effective retrieval of information when it is needed.

4. The test involved remembering where objects had been placed on a board divided into 20 squares. Aborigine adolescents did better than white Australian adolescents. The task capitalized on traditional Aborigine culture and learning, which emphasizes reliance on visual retrieval cues for survival in a harsh desert environment. On the other hand, the white adolescents, raised in an industrial culture, did better on tests that emphasized verbal learning cues.

5. Research shows that, through repeated suggestions, obviously false memories (getting one's hand caught in a mousetrap and having to go to the hospital to have it removed!) can be implanted in children's minds. Apparently, both district attorneys and psychotherapists were convinced of the accuracy of such wildly false memories, with harmful consequences to those involved. Legal authorities must be aware that children can become convinced that false memories are true; psychotherapists must be careful not to encourage them.

Module 13

Intelligence

The Social Psychology of Psychology

Perhaps no single topic reveals the interconnectedness of psychology and society more clearly than the complicated issue of intelligence. Delineating the nature and quality of human thought, captured in the concept of intelligence, has always been a primary goal of psychology. Yet few other subjects have entangled the science of psychology more controversially in the needs and passions of society.

Few would argue the importance of addressing the special needs of the super bright and the severely retarded. It seems obvious that something real is going on in both cases. But what about the rest of us, the great majority? How real are the differences among us that psychology measures with such precision, and, until recently, with such confidence? Questions like these evoke the central question of the social sciences.

The Nature-Nurture Question in the Social Sciences

Heredity or environment? Personality or experience? Are we best explained by reference to our nature (what is built in) or to our nurture (how we are raised)? This is the essence of the nature-nurture question, an old argument over basic assumptions that continues to rage in the social sciences. Two controversies illustrate the nature-nurture question: (1) How important is what we inherit (genetics) compared to what we experience (learning)? (2) To what extent can we control our thoughts, feelings, and actions (free will) compared to control over us by outside forces (determinism).

You will find echoes of the nature-nurture question in almost everything you read about psychological research and theory. Your basic orientation toward nature or nurture will influence which major theories in psychology you find most convincing, which giants of psychology you like or dislike, what research you believe or doubt, and even what "facts" you accept or reject. Whenever you come across an idea in psychology that arouses your strong interest, whether positive or negative, try examining the idea from the perspective of the nature-nurture debate. Odds are, the idea strongly supports or challenges your basic assumptions about life.

In the long run, thoughtful study of psychology will drive us more and more toward a middle position, an "interactionist" point of view that sees humans as products of the interplay of heredity and environment, individual uniqueness and group pressure, and rational choice and force of habit. Still, I'm willing to bet that most of us will continue to feel the pull of our basic adherence either to the argument of nature or the argument of nurture.

Effective Student Tip 13

Risk a New Idea

You didn't come to college to stay the same. You intend to be a better and more fully developed person when you leave. You hope to grow in many ways, and one of the most important is cognitive. Intellectual growth requires a spirit of openness to change, of willingness to risk new ideas.

If you don't try out a new idea in college, you probably never will. As time goes on, work, family, and responsibility all conspire to make most of us more cautious and more conservative. Never again will you encounter as many new and different ideas as in college. In one sense, the very mission of colleges and universities is to hit us with new ideas. If everything was dandy just the way it is now, we really wouldn't need colleges and universities.

When a professor or student throws out a challenging idea, seriously consider whether it might be true. If true, how would it change what you believe? If false, how do your own ideas offer a better explanation?

Accepting intellectual challenges will strengthen your ideas and your ability to defend them. You might even solve a problem you have been puzzling over. Most of the time, however, you will augment and improve your understanding of the world and yourself only slightly. This is a great victory. We call it growth.

Your response…

What startling new idea have you encountered recently? What was your reaction to that idea?

Learning Objectives

1. Understand intelligence as an awesome set of skills and abilities, a potential that could serve to unite all humans but that has often divided and alienated us.

2. Learn how different definitions of intelligence have led to three different theories of what it is and how it affects our lives.

3. Explain how intelligence has been measured, how intelligence tests were developed, and how IQ scores are distributed and used.

4. Appreciate the individual and social problems inherent in attempts to measure intelligence and use IQ scores in everything from education to employment.

5. Consider the fundamental importance of the nature-nurture question in psychology and the social sciences, and attempt to determine where you stand on this issue.

6. Appreciate the subject of intelligence as an example of the complex interaction between science and culture, as illustrated by the social history of IQ tests and immigration.

7. Learn what psychological research suggests about the value of intervention programs like Head Start and whether such programs should be continued.

Key Terms

Understanding the controversies over intelligence will make these key terms easier to learn.

Binet-Simon Intelligence Scale
cultural bias
cultural-familial retardation
fraternal twins
Gardner's multiple-intelligence theory
gifted
heritability
identical twins
intelligence quotient
intervention program
mental age
mental retardation
nature-nurture question
non-intellectual factors
normal distribution
organic retardation
psychometric approach
psychometrics
reaction range
reliability
Sternberg's triarchic theory
two-factor theory (Spearman)
validity
Wechsler Adult Intelligence Scale (WAIS-III)
Wechsler Intelligence Scale for Children (WISC-IV)

The "PowerStudy 4.5 for Introduction to Psychology" CD-ROM includes a complete set of interactive learning activities for this module: quizzes, summary test, key terms, web site connections, critical thinking exercise, module outline, and more.

Outline

- *Introduction*
  1. Mirror, mirror, on the wall, who's the most intelligent of them all? (five winners)
     a. How would you rank these five unusual people on intelligence?
     b. What were the reasons for your rankings?
  2. **Psychometrics** (most intelligent?)

A. Defining Intelligence

1. Problem: definition

☐ Consider both the advantages and disadvantages of the following definitions of intelligence. Which theory makes the most sense to you?

2. Two-factor theory (Charles Spearman)
   a. **Psychometric approach**
   b. **Two-factor theory**
   c. Advantages and disadvantages
3. Multiple-intelligence theory (Howard Gardner)
   a. **Gardner's multiple-intelligence theory**
   b. Advantages and disadvantages
4. Triarchic theory (Robert Sternberg)
   a. **Sternberg's triarchic theory**
   b. Advantages and disadvantages
5. Current status

B. Measuring Intelligence

1. Earlier attempts to measure intelligence
   a. Head size and intelligence (Francis Galton)
   b. Brain size and intelligence (Paul Broca)
   c. Brain size and achievement
   d. Brain size, sex differences, and intelligence
   e. Measuring intelligence
2. Binet's breakthrough (Albert Binet)
   a. **Binet-Simon Intelligence Scale**
   b. **Mental age**: measure of intelligence
3. Formula for IQ (Lewis Terman)

☐ What is the essential difference between Binet's and Terman's approach to intelligence?

   a. **Intelligence quotient**
   b. Ratio IQ replaced by deviation IQ

4. Is IQ the same as intelligence? (examples of IQ tests)
    a. **Wechsler Adult Intelligence Scale (WAIS-III)**
    b. **Wechsler Intelligence Scale for Children (WISC-IV)**
5. Two characteristics of tests

☐ The two terms below are absolutely essential to an understanding of science, and therefore to an appreciation of the basis of psychology. Can you define each term? Give an example of each?

    a. **Validity**
    b. **Reliability**

C. *Distribution & Use of IQ Scores*

1. **Normal distribution** of IQ scores
2. **Mental retardation**: IQ scores
    a. Mild mental retardation
    b. Moderate mental retardation
    c. Severely/profound mental retardation
    d. Causes
        (1) **Organic retardation**
        (2) **Cultural-familial retardation**
3. Vast majority: IQ scores
    a. Do IQ scores predict academic achievement?
    b. Do IQ scores predict job performance?
4. Gifted: IQ scores
    a. **Gifted**
    b. How do gifted individuals turn out? (Lewis Terman)

D. *Potential Problems of IQ Testing*

1. Binet's two warnings
    a. Intelligence tests do not measure innate abilities or natural intelligence
    b. Intelligence tests, by themselves, should not be used to label people
2. Racial discrimination
    a. Definition of mental retardation
    b. Educational decisions
3. **Cultural bias**
4. Other cultures
5. **Non-intellectual factors**

E. *Nature-Nurture Question*

1. Definitions: the **nature-nurture question**

2. Twin studies
   a. **Fraternal twins** and **identical twins**
   b. Genetic factors
   c. Definition of intelligence
   d. Interaction of nature and nurture
   e. Interaction
3. Adoption studies
4. Interaction: nature and nurture
   a. **Heritability**
   b. **Reaction range**
5. Racial controversy (*The Bell Curve,* by Richard Herrnstein and Charles Murray)
   a. Difference between IQ scores
   b. Cause of IQ differences
      (1) Group differences
      (2) Differences in skin color

F. *Cultural Diversity: Races, IQs, & Immigration*

1. Misuse of IQ tests
   a. Innate intelligence (Lewis Terman)
   b. Classifying races (Robert Yerkes)
2. Immigration laws
   a. Immigration Law of 1924
   b. Mismeasurement examined (Stephen Jay Gould)

G. *Research Focus: New Approaches*

1. Can genius be found in the brain?
2. How does a prodigy's brain develop?
   a. Method
   b. Results
   c. Conclusions

H. *Application: Intervention Programs*

1. Definition of **intervention program**
   a. Parent training
   b. Head Start
2. Raising IQ scores
3. Need for intervention programs

How English Works

Words in the Textbook

p. 281 she **made a big stir** = caused excitement

in **classical music circles** = an informal group of people in the same profession

p. 283 **spatial** intelligence = ability to perceive differences in terms of space

p. 284 Efforts to measure intelligence began in **earnest** = with serious work

Galton **switched gears** = changed methods

p. 285 Binet was very **pessimistic** = doubtful

By a strange **twist of fate** = unexpected result

p. 286 on a **one-to-one basis** = one examiner with one student (not group)

from a **deprived** environment = without such things as money, home, food, etc.

rule out other cultural or educational problems = exclude

p. 287 this characteristic **makes or breaks** a test = decides the success of

p. 288 a greatly **impoverished** environment = very limited, without necessities

p. 289 labeled as **nerds** and **geeks** = unfashionable people, often working with computers

2% actually **flunked out** = left school because of bad grades

p. 290 considered a **dead end** = hopeless, with no hope of success

a **class action suit** = lawsuit with group of people suing one company

on behalf of = for the benefit of

people **of color** = non-white

p. 292 **written in stone** = cannot be changed, permanent

p. 296 a **meager** 13 years = very small number

unconstrained breeding = uncontrolled, unlimited

feebleminded = with weak mental ability

The **fair** peoples = with blond hair and light skin

congressmen **sought** a way = looked for (were seeking)

Yerkes's data were so **riddled** with errors = overloaded

p. 299 below the **poverty line** = standard of income that classifies people as poor or not-poor

Sentence Structure: Making Connections

We can use **which** to connect two sentences that have the same word in common:

Americans like to eat fast food. Fast food can be unhealthy.

Americans like to eat fast food, which can be unhealthy.

In the same way, we can use which to connect and to measure with words like **some**, **all**, **many**, or any number.

Marcella has a lot of work tonight. Some of the work is important.

Marcella has a lot of work tonight, some of which is important.

In this example, we replaced the subject of the second sentence, some of the work, with **some of which**. Notice how it is used in the text:

> Along with using IQ scores to label individuals came racial and cultural discrimination, **some of which** continue to the present.

As the reader, we know that **some of which** in this sentence means that some racial and cultural discrimination still continues. Try to connect the following sentences:

> Sharella bought a dozen eggs. Three of them were cracked.
>
> Sharella __________.
>
> The library has 85,000 books. Most of them are about technical subjects.
>
> The library __________.

Did you remember to put in the comma after the first sentence? You need the comma to show that the two are connected, not joined into one. Try some more:

> Mr. and Mrs. Smith have a lot of problems. Ninety percent of them can be solved.
>
> Mr. and Mrs. Smith __________.
>
> Chang-Woo had ten math problems to solve. All 10 of them required a calculator.
>
> Chang-Woo __________.

Now look at the following example:

> Marcella has a lot of work tonight. She has finished some of the work.
>
> Marcella has a lot of work tonight, **some of which** she has finished.

In this example, some of the work is the object of the sentence, but we can still replace it with **some of which**. The difference is that we have to move the word that connects to the first sentence (some of the work) to the beginning of the second sentence we are connecting. Try to connect the following sentences:

> Jenny has a lot of research to do. The professor wants all of it tomorrow.
>
> Jenny __________.
>
> Ernie wrote a 27-page paper. His dog ate half of it.
>
> Ernie __________.
>
> Marco read 135 pages of the textbook. He remembered none of it the next morning.
>
> Marco __________.

Answers

Sharella bought a dozen eggs, **three of which** were cracked.
The library has 85,000 books, **most of which** are about technical subjects.
Mr. and Mrs. Smith have a lot of problems, **90 percent of which** can be solved.
Chang-Woo had 10 math problems to solve, **all ten of which** required a calculator.
Jenny has a lot of research to do, **all of which** the professor wants tomorrow.
Ernie wrote a 27-page paper, **half of which** his dog ate.
Marco read 135 pages of the textbook, **none of which** he remembered the next morning.

The Big Picture

Which statement below offers the best summary of the larger significance of this module?

A Intelligence is a real dimension along which people do vary, but it must be measured and used with great sensitivity because we do not know with certainty how it is formed and how it influences a person's life.

B From Binet to the present, psychology has refined the measurement of intelligence to a degree of precision where IQ scores can and should be used in a wide variety of personal and social decisions.

C Psychology has wasted great energy and resources pursuing the nature-nurture question, when it should have been obvious all along that we get our smarts from an irreversible throw of the genetic dice.

D The measurement of intelligence has been so riddled with bias and discrimination that most psychologists are ready to abandon the concept of intelligence altogether.

E My psych instructor must think I'm real stoopid. She just handed out a page of questions and thought I wouldn't notice there are no answers on it!

True-False

_____ 1. The key issue in defining intelligence is whether it is essentially cognitive abilities or a combination of cognitive abilities and other skills.

_____ 2. It is generally true that the larger the brain the more intelligent the person.

_____ 3. Alfred Binet gave us the concept of an intelligence quotient (IQ).

_____ 4. Lewis Terman's formula for determining IQ was mental age divided by chronological age times 100.

_____ 5. If you use a precise doctor's scale in an attempt to measure your intelligence, your results will be reliable, but not valid.

_____ 6. As a result of protest movements, the major intelligence tests are now independent of culture.

_____ 7. Twin studies suggest that we inherit only a small percentage of our intelligence.

_____ 8. Adoption studies suggest that environment plays a significant role in determining intelligence.

_____ 9. Measurements of intelligence have been used to support racial and ethnic discrimination.

_____ 10. Research shows that intervention programs like Head Start, while well meaning, have few long-term benefits.

Flashcards 1

____	1. Binet-Simon Intelligence Scale	a. says intelligence is three skills — analytical thinking, problem solving, and practical thinking
____	2. Gardner's multiple-intelligence theory	b. says there can be at least seven different kinds of intelligence: verbal, musical, logical, spatial, body…
____	3. intelligence quotient	c. Binet; estimates intellectual progress by comparing child's score on an IQ test to average children of same age
____	4. mental age	d. Terman; computed by dividing a child's mental age (MA) by the child's chronological age (CA) then times 100
____	5. nature-nurture question	e. degree to which a test measures what it is supposed to measure
____	6. psychometrics	f. says that intelligence is based on a general mental abilities factor (g) plus specific mental abilities (s)
____	7. reliability	g. asks how hereditary or genetic factors interact with environmental factors in development (e.g., intelligence)
____	8. Sternberg's triarchic theory	h. area of psychology concerned with developing tests that assess abilities, skills, beliefs, and traits
____	9. two-factor theory	i. consistency; a person's test score on a test at one time should be similar to the score on a similar test later
____	10. validity	j. first intelligence test; items of increasing difficulty measured vocabulary, memory, common knowledge

Flashcards 2

____	1. cultural bias	a. substantial limitation in functioning characterized by sub-average intellectual functioning, other limits
____	2. gifted	b. question wording and background experiences more familiar to some social groups than to others
____	3. heritability	c. measures or quantifies cognitive abilities or factors that are thought to be involved in intellectual performance
____	4. intervention program	d. extent to which traits, abilities, or IQ scores increase or decrease as result of interaction with environment
____	5. mental retardation	e. a statistical arrangement of scores so that they resemble the shape of a bell; the bell-shaped curve
____	6. non-intellectual factors	f. amount or proportion of some ability, characteristic, or trait that can be attributed to genetic factors
____	7. psychometric approach	g. impressive cognitive abilities; moderate defined by IQ scores of 130 to 150, profoundly by 180 and above
____	8. normal distribution	h. factors such as attitude, experience, and emotional functioning that may help or hinder performance on tests
____	9. organic retardation	i. creates environment that offers more opportunities for intellectual, social, and personal development
____	10. reaction range	j. mental deficits resulting from genetic problems or brain damage

Multiple Choice

_____ 1. Plotnik and Kouyoumdjian challenged you to rank five unusual people according to intelligence to show that

a. although Bill Gates dropped out of Harvard, he is clearly the smartest of the group
b. intelligence is related to gender, race, and social class
c. although they were all high achievers, only Alia Sabur had an IQ score "off the charts"
d. intelligence could be defined in several different ways

_____ 2. Solving scientific puzzles like the one above is the goal of a branch of psychology called

a. genetics
b. psychometrics
c. twin studies
d. psychodynamics

_____ 3. Charles Spearman's two-factor theory says that intelligence is a

a. general factor (g) plus specific mental abilities (s)
b. group of separate and equally important mental abilities
c. set of processes for solving problems
d. combination of biological functions of the brain and nervous system

_____ 4. An advantage of both Howard Gardner's multiple-intelligence theory and Robert Sternberg's triarchic theory is that they

a. yield a single score that is useful for predicting academic performance
b. measure each of the five known areas of intelligence
c. take into account abilities not covered by standard IQ tests
d. define intelligence in a way that is completely free of cultural influence

_____ 5. Which theory would best take into account both Halle Berry's acting skills and Jay Greenberg's accomplishments in music?

a. Spearman's two-factor theory of intelligence
b. Gardner's multiple-intelligence theory of intelligence
c. Sternberg's triarchic theory of intelligence
d. Gates' "wealth rules" theory of intelligence

_____ 6. At one time, each of the following *except* __________ size has been proposed as an indication of intelligence

a. head
b. skull
c. brain
d. neuron

_____ 7. The first intelligence test was devised by

a. Charles Spearman
b. Louis Terman
c. Alfred Binet
d. Howard Gardner

_____ 8. The original purpose of Binet's Intelligence Scale was to
a. differentiate children of normal intelligence from those who needed special help
b. identify specially gifted children who could benefit from government scholarships
c. isolate those children who were so slow nothing would help them
d. replace the much criticized SAT in college admissions

_____ 9. The formula for computing IQ (developed by Lewis Terman) is
a. level of schooling divided by actual age
b. mental age divided by chronological age times 100
c. test score divided by grade in school plus 100
d. chronological age divided by mental age

_____ 10. The most widely used intelligence test for adults is the
a. Wechsler Adult Intelligence Scale (WAIS-III)
b. Binet-Simon Intelligence Scale
c. Gardner Multiple Tasks Scale
d. Sternberg Triarchic Scale

_____ 11. Ten times your sister jumps on the scale, and ten times it reads 115 pounds. "Wow," she exclaims, "I'm taller than the average American woman!" Her results are
a. both reliable and valid
b. neither reliable nor valid
c. reliable, but not valid
d. valid, but not reliable

_____ 12. If you measured the intelligence of everyone in the United States, a distribution of all the scores would look like a
a. curve sloping gently upward to the right
b. bell-shaped curve
c. flat horizon line with a skyscraper in the middle
d. curve that rises and falls at regular intervals

_____ 13. Research suggests that gifted children, like those in Terman's famous study, grow up to be
a. not as greatly different from other children as high intelligence might predict
b. plagued by the mental instability that goes with high intelligence
c. much lonelier, sadder, and more eccentric than average
d. far more healthy, happy, and successful than children of average intelligence

_____ 14. One serious problem with IQ tests is that they are
a. completely free of cultural bias
b. seldom used to get children into the right classes in school
c. sometimes used to label people and discriminate against them
d. unable to predict how well a child will do in school

_____ 15. In intelligence testing, cultural bias refers to
a. whether tests are both valid and reliable
b. intellectual factors like honors classes and high IQ
c. distrust of non-Western cultures
d. how questions are worded and what experiences they are based on

_____ 16. Attitudes, experience, and emotions that may help or hinder performance on tests are called
a. cognitive factors
b. invalidating variables
c. nonintellectual factors
d. racial variables

_____ 17. In the matter of intelligence, the answer to the nature-nurture question is that
a. twin studies prove the predominance of nurture
b. adoption studies prove the predominance of nature
c. intervention programs show that intelligence is fixed at birth
d. both nature and nurture contribute about equally to the formation of intelligence

_____ 18. Twin studies suggest that intelligence is
a. about 90 percent inherited
b. only slightly influenced by heredity
c. about 50 percent determined by genetics
d. a random phenomenon unaffected by heredity

_____ 19. Adoption studies suggest that intelligence
a. can be positively affected by improved environmental conditions
b. is essentially fixed at birth by heredity
c. is lessened by the loss of one's biological parents
d. does not change much, regardless of family environment

_____ 20. The _________ indicates the extent to which traits, abilities, or IQ scores may increase or decrease as a result of interaction with environmental factors
a. nurture rating
b. genetic research index
c. heritability factor
d. reaction range

_____ 21. One problem with the racial conclusions drawn by the authors of *The Bell Curve* is that
a. blacks and whites consistently score the same on intelligence tests
b. the APA prohibits collecting data about race in research on intelligence
c. research shows that the 15-point IQ difference is narrowing
d. Herrnstein and Murray did not say IQ differences were genetic

_____ 22. The story of IQ tests and immigration shows that
a. good research can be used for bad purposes
b. scientific research often reflects the prejudices of the times
c. good research can be used to right injustice
d. scientific research is politically neutral

_____ 23. Recent research examining intelligence and brain development in children found that child prodigies
a. have no brain differences from average children
b. have thinner and more permeable cortexes
c. develop thicker cortexes than average children
d. are exceptional because they have *four* hemispheres in their brains

_____ 24. Studies of the effectiveness of intervention programs like Head Start suggest that
a. however well-intentioned, intervention programs don't work
b. there are many social needs and benefits that justify continuing these programs
c. the short-term benefits fail to justify the high costs of these programs
d. the main benefits of these programs go to the middle-class professionals they employ

_____ 25. When you look back at how you rated the intelligence of the five unusual people described on the first page of this module, you might well conclude that intelligence is
a. a topic that can offend, but people should just get over it
b. like politics and religion, a subject that is beyond scientific discussion
c. a topic psychology would be better off to drop
d. one of the most complicated and controversial topics in psychology

Short Essay

1. Why is "intelligence" so difficult to define and measure?

2. Describe the main theories of intelligence and how they differ.

3. Why have IQ scores been criticized as a faulty invention of psychology?

4. Why are psychologists who investigate intelligence so interested in studying twins and adopted children?

5. Intervention programs, like Head Start, are well intentioned, but also costly and of limited effectiveness in raising IQ scores. Should such programs be ended, or continued and even expanded?

College Study

The longer you are in college, the more you will appreciate the great overlap in all fields of study. The way we have them neatly arranged in the college catalog is artificial. Therefore, whether you are a business major or English major, congratulate yourself on having had the wisdom to enroll in psychology. You'll find that there are many connections and tie-ins between psychology and other fields of study.

Test-Taking Tips

More hints:

- Trust your common knowledge and don't choose an answer that is obviously not the way the world really works.

- Often the question itself contains a strong hint about the right answer.

Answers for Module 13

The Big Picture (explanations provided for incorrect choices)

A	*Correct! You see the "big picture" for this Module.*
B	Applying IQ scores to practical decisions is not easy. Psychologists do not yet agree on what IQ is or how to use it.
C	Think about all the research on how environmental conditions can affect IQ.
D	Not true. Most psychologists believe the concept is valid, but must be defined more carefully.
E	It's just a joke!

True-False (explanations provided for False choices; page numbers given for all choices)

1	T	282	
2	F	284	Brain size has no practical relation to intelligence.
3	F	285	The mathematical intelligence quotient was devised by Lewis Terman.
4	T	285	
5	T	287	
6	F	291	Every intelligence test is affected by culture, although most are now free of obvious cultural bias.
7	F	292	Twin studies suggest that we inherit up to 50 percent of our intelligence.
8	T	293	
9	T	296	
10	F	298	Research finds long-term benefits, although perhaps not as many as program advocates hoped for.

Flashcards 1

1 j 2 b 3 d 4 c 5 g 6 h 7 i 8 a 9 f 10 e

Flashcards 2

1 b 2 g 3 f 4 i 5 a 6 h 7 c 8 e 9 j 10 d

Multiple Choice (explanations provided for incorrect choices)

1	a	He's fabulously wealthy, but does that prove he's the most intelligent?
	b	These five accomplished people would seem to disprove that notion.
	c	She has an incredibly high measured IQ, but does that prove she's "smarter" than the others?
	d	*Correct! See page 281.*
2	a	Genetics refers to the biology of inheritance.
	b	*Correct! See page 281.*
	c	Twin studies are a specific strategy for studying intelligence.
	d	Psychodynamics refers to the psychoanalytic method pioneered by Sigmund Freud.
3	***a***	*Correct! See page 282.*
	b	Check the name of Spearman's theory again.
	c	Check the name of Spearman's theory again.
	d	Psychometricians study how intelligence works more than its biological components.
4	a	Both theories see intelligence as several abilities.
	b	Psychologists do not agree that there are exactly five areas of intelligence.
	c	*Correct! See page 283.*
	d	Since all measures of intelligence are based on language and experience, none is independent of culture.
5	a	Spearman's theory emphasizes mental abilities.
	b	*Correct! See page 283.*
	c	Sternberg's theory emphasizes three different kinds of reasoning processes.
	d	This connection of wealth and intelligence isn't really serious, but we often act like it is.
6	a	There is no significant relationship between head size and intelligence.
	b	There is no significant relationship between skull size and intelligence.
	c	There is no significant relationship between brain size and intelligence.
	d	*Correct! See page 284.*

7 a Spearman is known for his definition of intelligence.
b Terman invented the concept of the intelligence quotient (IQ).
c *Correct! See page 285.*
d Gardner is a contemporary psychologist with a new theory of intelligence.

8 ***a*** *Correct! See page 285.*
b That's the point — giftedness wasn't an original focus of intelligence testing.
c That's the point — discrimination wasn't an original focus of intelligence testing.
d Hint: think early 20th-century France!

9 a This is close to Binet's formula for mental age.
b *Correct! See page 285.*
c This is a nonsense formula.
d Then lower numbers would indicate higher intelligence.

10 ***a*** *Correct! See page 286.*
b This was the original intelligence test, now replaced by the Stanford-Binet test.
c Gardner has not developed a generally accepted overall intelligence test.
d Sternberg has not been able to develop a test that works according to his theory.

11 a This is half right (check the definition of valid).
b This is half right (check the definition of reliable).
c *Correct! See page 287.*
d A valid test measures what it is supposed to measure.

12 a Would that mean most people have very high intelligence?
b *Correct! See page 288.*
c Would this mean almost everyone has the same intelligence?
d Such a curve would show changes over time, not absolute amounts.

13 ***a*** *Correct! See page 289.*
b Mental instability does not go with high intelligence.
c If anything, it tends to be the opposite.
d Sounds logical, but the differences are not great.

14 a Even if true, how would that be a problem?
b They are often used for this purpose (but how fairly does it work?)
c *Correct! See page 290.*
d IQ tests do predict school success to some extent.

15 a Validity might be indirectly involved, but not reliability.
b *Non*-intellectual factors can be involved, but not these intellectual factors.
c It is not distrust, but failure to take account of cultural differences that is a problem.
d *Correct! See page 291.*

16 a *Non*-cognitive factors might have been somewhat correct.
b This is not an actual term in psychology.
c *Correct! See page 291.*
d Some of these factors may involve race, but most do not.

17 a Twin studies have strengthened the nature side, but they have not ended the debate.
b Adoption studies have strengthened the nurture side, but they have not ended the debate.
c Intervention programs strengthen the nurture side, but they haven't ended the debate.
d *Correct! See page 292.*

18 a If this were true, many of our democratic ideas might have to change.
b Twin studies suggest just the opposite.
c *Correct! See page 292.*
d Twin studies suggest just the opposite.

19 ***a*** *Correct! See page 293.*
b Adoption studies suggest just the opposite.
c Adopted children do not suffer drops in intelligence.
d Adoption studies do show changes in intelligence.

20 a Sounds right, but this is not a correct term in psychology.
b It wouldn't be genetic research as much as environmental research.
c Heritability is the amount of some ability, characteristic, or trait that can be attributed to genetic factors.
d *Correct! See page 293.*

21 a There are racial differences in IQ scores — the question is why.
b It does not.
c *Correct! See page 294.*
d That is exactly what they said.

22 a In this case, neither the research nor the purpose was good.
b *Correct! See page 296.*
c In this case, research contributed to injustice.
d This research had a definite, and deplorable, political purpose.

23 a New research shows that the brain develops differently in highly intelligent children.
b Just the opposite is true.
c *Correct! See page 297.*
d Not true (hint: "hemi" means one half).

24 a Definite benefits have been identified — the question is cost and long-range effectiveness.
b *Correct! See page 298.*
c The short-term benefits probably do justify the costs.
d This cynical view is not supported by the research.

25 a No one needs to accept being offended, and psychology should take care not to do so.
b No subject should be beyond careful and sensitive scientific investigation.
c As a science, psychology must pursue the truth wherever it leads.
d *Correct! See page 281.*

Short Essay (sample answers)

1. We were introduced to five unusual people, each of whom is accomplished, but in different ways. Could we devise a single test that would show just how they differ from others? Wouldn't a test that showed any of them as "average" be untrue to their special abilities? How could their different talents be reduced to a single score that would correctly place them in a hierarchy of all people? Finally, how would we take account of both the inherited characteristics and unique experiences that went into making them who they are?

2. There are three main theories of intelligence. The traditional definition, entirely cognitive, is Charles Spearman's two-factor theory, in which there is a general mental ability factor (g) plus many specific mental abilities. A broader idea of intelligence is Howard Gardner's multiple-intelligence theory, in which there are at least seven different kinds of intelligence, not all cognitive. Finally, Robert Sternberg's triarchic theory bases intelligence on analytical thinking skills, problem-solving skills, and practical thinking skills.

3. IQ scores can be harmful. Alfred Binet sought to identify children who needed special help, but when Lewis Terman invented a numerical score to summarize intelligence, IQ scores became labels with the power to glorify or stigmatize individuals and whole groups. Examples of the misuse of IQ scores range from the Immigration Act of 1924 to the misplacement of minority children in remedial classes. Intelligence tests themselves have been shown to contain cultural bias in their wording or the experiences they reflect.

4. Intelligence may be the best example of the nature-nurture question. How much comes from heredity and how much from environmental experience? It is very difficult to separate out these variables in individual cases, but the experiences of twins, exactly (identical) or strongly (fraternal) alike in heredity, and children adopted into different circumstances, offer natural experiments on the effects of nature and nurture. Twins can be compared to each other and adopted children can be compared to their siblings and natural parents.

5. The aim of the original intervention program was to give disadvantaged children a "head start" by providing early IQ-raising experiences that would help them later in school. However, initial increases in IQ didn't last after children left the program. Still, follow-up research shows other long-term benefits. Take account of these facts in your answer about ending or extending these programs. You might also refer to the current social and economic needs of many people, as well as budget constraints faced by governmental agencies.

Module 14

Thought & Language

Can We Study Ourselves Scientifically?

Historians of science have pointed out that the accumulation of human knowledge seems backwards. We understood the far-away phenomena of astronomy centuries ago, gradually grasped the principles of physics and biology in modern times, but only now are beginning to penetrate the mysteries of the brain and the mind. The closer we are to something, the harder it is to study it objectively. Add to this difficulty an even greater one — we *are* the very thing we want to study. Natural scientists say this problem alone dooms the social sciences to be inherently subjective and therefore not really scientific. Social scientists disagree, of course, but they admit that being objective about ourselves presents enormous challenges.

Processes that Make Us Human

As an animal lover, I welcome every discovery of animals engaging in behavior (like tool-using) previously thought to be the exclusive property of *Homo sapiens.* Those of us who observe animals in the wild know they communicate very effectively. New research shows that elephants communicate at a decibel level we can't even hear. Still, is it really language? (See Plotnik and Kouyoumdjian's fascinating review of whether apes can acquire language.)

In our efforts to win greater respect for the rights and inherent value of other animals, some of us argue that we humans aren't so different and shouldn't consider ourselves morally superior. Nevertheless, we have to admit that humans have strikingly unique skills and abilities in three areas that perhaps define our species. We have unmatched intellectual potential, unrivaled flexibility in exploiting that potential, and a system of communication that preserves and extends those mental powers. In this module, Plotnik and Kouyoumdjian continue the story of these quintessential human properties, helping us appreciate how interrelated they are.

Science is never easy, however. We all know what thought and language are, yet how do we describe and explain them? Our own subjective experience seems to get in the way of objective understanding. We have to fight for every piece of knowledge. Further complicating matters is the sad fact that science is not always neutral. In the previous module, Plotnik and Kouyoumdjian described times in our history when racial prejudice distorted the measurement of intelligence. After weighing all the evidence on whether other primates can acquire language, most psychologists have concluded that, however remarkable, the linguistic abilities of apes are not true language. So says science. Or is it our human prejudice?

Effective Student Tip 14

What Can You Do?

Some students freeze up when they get an assignment, fearing that, unless they instantly know what to do and how to do it, they're dead. The solution, if only they realized it, is right at hand. One of the best ways to tackle a new challenge is to draw on what you already do well. Step away from the course for a moment. What can you do competently right now?

Perhaps your work relates to the course (a business student at a bank, or a psychology student in a day-care center). Your experiences and observations would make great examples to use in class discussion or in written reports. Most professors delight in having students relate the subject matter of the course to the realities of the working world. If you prepare presentations or reports at work, you can use those same techniques to prepare papers so beautiful they'll knock your professor's socks off. If you are an athlete, can you use your knowledge of effective training techniques to work out a schedule for gradually building up your academic skills?

You only start from square one once, and that was years ago. By now you have acquired many competencies, some quite special. Use them to enhance your college work.

Your response…

What are you really good at? Could that skill be used in your schoolwork? (Don't say "no" too quickly!)

Learning Objectives

1. Understand thought and language as related achievements that make humans the most adaptive and accomplished species on Earth.
2. Learn the basic mechanisms of concept formation, problem solving, and creativity.
3. Learn the four basic rules that define language and the four basic stages in acquiring language.
4. Explain how thought and language are united in the cognitive approach to psychology.
5. Understand dyslexia as an illustration of the difficult skill of reading.
6. Consider your position on the role of cultural and gender influences on thinking.
7. Review the research on the controversy over whether animals have language.

Key Terms

Another tough set of key terms (some you may know from other courses). This module covers two areas of psychology, thought and language, which are related but also separate and complete fields of study in their own right. Both are complicated and offer some highly technical facts and concepts (that's one of the terms). Buckle down!

algorithms
analogy
availability heuristic
babbling
basic rules of grammar
Chomsky's theory of language
cognitive approach
communication
concept
convergent thinking
creative individual
creative thinking
critical language period
deep structure
divergent thinking
dyslexia
environmental language factors
exemplar model
functional fixedness
grammar
heuristics
innate language factors
insight
language
language stages
morpheme
morphology
overgeneralization
parentese (motherese)
phonemes
phonology
problem solving
prototype theory
savants [autistic]
semantics
sentences
single words
social cognitive learning
subgoals
surface structure
syntax (grammar)
telegraphic speech
theory of linguistic relativity
thinking
transformational rules
two-word combinations
word

The "PowerStudy 4.5 for Introduction to Psychology" CD-ROM includes a complete set of interactive learning activities for this module: quizzes, summary test, key terms, web site connections, critical thinking exercise, module outline, and more.

Outline

- *Introduction*
  1. Concepts (four-year-old Jeff)
  2. Creativity (rap artist Jay-Z)
  3. **Cognitive approach**
     a. **Thinking** (reasoning)
     b. **Language**

A. *Forming Concepts*

1. **Concept**

☐ "Concept" is another of those deceptively simple common terms. Can you define it formally?

2. **Exemplar model** (problems)
   a. Too many features
   b. Too many exceptions
3. **Prototype theory** (advantages)
   a. Average features
   b. Quick recognition
4. Early formation
5. Categories in the brain
6. Functions of concepts
   a. Organize information
   b. Avoid relearning

B. *Solving Problems*

1. **Problem solving**
2. Different ways of thinking
   a. **Algorithms**
   b. **Heuristics** and the **availability heuristic**
   c. Artificial intelligence
3. Three strategies for solving problems
   a. Changing one's mental set
      (1) **Functional fixedness**
      (2) **Insight**
   b. Using an **analogy**
   c. Forming **subgoals**

C. *Thinking Creatively*

1. How is creativity defined?

☐ Do you consider yourself a creative person? How do you express your creativity?

   a. **Creative thinking**
   b. **Creative individual**
   c. Psychometric approach
      (1) **Convergent thinking**
      (2) **Divergent thinking**
   d. Case study approach
   e. Cognitive approach
2. Is IQ related to creativity? (autistic **savants**)
3. How do creative people think and behave?
   a. Focus
   b. Cognition
   c. Personality
   d. Motivation
4. Is creativity related to mental disorders?

D. Language: Basic Rules

1. **Language**
   a. **Word**
   b. **Grammar**
2. Four rules of language
   a. **Phonology** and **phonemes**
   b. **Morphology** and **morpheme**
   c. **Syntax (grammar)**
   d. **Semantics**
3. Understanding language (Noam Chomsky)
   a. Mental grammar
   b. Innate brain program
4. Different structure, same meaning
   a. **Surface structure**
   b. **Deep structure**
   c. **Transformational rules**
   d. **Chomsky's theory of language**

E. Acquiring Language

1. Four stages in acquiring language (**language stages**)
   a. **Babbling**
   b. **Single words** and **parentese (motherese)**
   c. **Two-word combinations**
   d. **Sentences**

d. **Sentences**

(1) **Telegraphic speech**

(2) **Basic rules of grammar**

(3) **Overgeneralization**

e. Going through the stages

2. Learning a particular language

a. What are *innate* factors?

(1) **Innate language factors**

(2) **Critical language period**

b. What are *environmental* factors?

(1) **Environmental language factors**

(2) **Social cognitive learning**

F. Decisions, Thought & Language

1. Decisions

a. Gambling decisions

b. Political decisions

2. Words and thoughts: **theory of linguistic relativity** (Benjamin Whorf)

a. Inuit versus American words for snow

b. Thinking in two languages

G. Research Focus: Dyslexia

1. What kind of problem is **dyslexia**?

2. Cognitive approach plus physiological approach

a. What's involved in reading?

(1) Phoneme (sound) producer

(2) Word analyzer

(3) Automatic detector

b. Why can't dyslexics read?

c. Can training help?

H. Cultural Diversity: Influences on Thinking

1. Differences in thinking

2. Male-female differences

a. Men and women use language differently (Deborah Tannen)

b. Brains process words differently

3. Difference in language, similarity in thought

I. Application: Do Animals Have Language?

☐ What is the difference between *communication* and *language*?

1. Criteria for **language**: going beyond **communication**

☐ Humans can meet the following four criteria for language — can any other animal do all four?

a. Learning a set of abstract symbols

b. Using abstract symbols to express thoughts

c. Learning complex rules of grammar

d. Generate an endless number of meaningful sentences

2. Dolphins (Louis Herman)

3. Gorilla and chimpanzee

   a. Koko (Francine Patterson)

   b. Washoe (Beatrice and Allan Gardner)

   c. Criticisms (Herbert Terrace)

4. Bonobo chimp: star pupil

   a. Kanzi (Sue Savage-Rumbaugh)

   b. Early humans developed a "language" gene (FOXP2)

Wanted!

(As I wrote in the "Introduction" to this Study Guide...)

On the first day of class, I pass out a corny "Wanted" poster urging my students to look for any errors I make in writing (factual, spelling, grammar, and formatting). I offer a payoff to students who find an error.

Some students enjoy this challenge, and I thought you might, too. *Can you find any mistakes in this Study Guide?* I can't ask your instructor to pay off (it's my mistake, after all), but I will send you an e-mail you can show your teacher. Might make a good impression!

Please e-mail me if you find a mistake — any mistake, no matter how small! Write to me at <**profenos@mac.com**>.

How English Works

Words in the Textbook

p. 305 No one thought Carter would **amount to much** = be successful

exploring the hip-hop **scene** = characteristic situation in which an activity is carried out

one of the most successful **entrepreneurs** = sets up and finances new businesses

passionately describes = expressed with intense emotion

p. 306 would **tax** the best of memories = be difficult for

p. 308 **novices** become too focused = newcomers

Heuristics are **rules of thumb** = quick rules

p. 309 the sudden **grasp** of a solution = understanding

p. 310 perhaps, most **notably** = extremely or remarkably

this **intriguing** story = makes us greatly interested or curious

p. 311 **unconventional** = outside ordinary behavior

their creative **fires are fueled** = energies are powered, stimulated

achieved creative **breakthroughs** = new solutions

p. 312 as of this **writing** = at the time when this was written

A word is an **arbitrary** pairing = random, without a reason

p. 313 the brain's **innate** program for learning = something you are born with

p. 314 **facilitate** language development = make it easy or easier to do

p. 315 shows **warmth** = friendly, loving quality

p. 316 father **strapped** her to a potty chair = tied

period of social deprivation **left its mark** = had long-lasting effects

p. 319 Whorf's story **lives on** = continues (is not forgotten)

very **temperamental** = moody, sensitive, unpredictable

p. 322 the answer **hinges on** the difference = depends on

to **probe** the sea = explore, investigate

Frisbee = plastic disk used in game

Sentence Structure: Active and Passive Sentences

As Plotnik and Kouyoumdjian explain on p. 313, most of us can see the difference between **active** sentences ("You picked up a caterpillar") and **passive** sentences ("A caterpillar was picked up by you"). But how can we choose which one to use? It depends on the focus of your sentence, the main subject.

Most sentences are active: someone does/did something. For example:

Darwin wrote the first book about evolution.

So, if your focus is Darwin, his many actions and achievements, then you will want to keep Darwin **active** in your sentence, so you will have the person writing.

On the other hand, sometimes you will want to write about an object. For example:

The first book about evolution was written by Darwin.

If your focus is evolution, the development and importance of the idea, then you will want to make your reader think about evolution and the first book about it. In this case, you will probably choose to keep Darwin **passive** in your sentence.

Another reason to use a passive sentence is when the writer wants to hide the active part. To avoid trouble, it is better to say, "The copy machine is broken," than "I broke the copy machine."

Look at how the textbook uses a passive sentence in this way to introduce their next topic:

The exemplar model has generally been replaced by a different theory of how we form concepts: the prototype theory.

Tip: When you see the word **by** in a sentence, there is a good chance it's a **passive** sentence. Moreover, the word after **by** is probably the doer of the action in the sentence. If the word after **by** can do the action in the verb, you have a passive sentence.

Sometimes, in an active sentence, the person or force performing the action is obvious or not important, so we choose to use a passive sentence. So, instead of writing **People often use heuristics in daily life**, Plotnik and Kouyoumdjian write **Heuristics are often used in daily life**.

Look at these sentences from the text and decide if they are active or passive sentences. Think about the verb in the sentence. Is the subject doing the action in the verb (active), or is someone or something else doing the action to the subject (passive)?

1) Researchers have studied creative individuals.

2) They are driven by internal values or personal goals.

3) Their creative fires are fueled by psychological or mental problems.

4) A commonly used heuristic is called the availability heuristic.

5) Studies show that savants lack verbal intelligence.

Vocabulary: Opposites

Draw a line connecting each word with its opposite meaning:

implicit	subjective
optimistic	progress
objective	pessimistic
passive	explicit
regress	active

Answers

1) Researchers have studied creative individuals. *Active:* The researchers study.
2) They are driven by internal values or personal goals. *Passive:* The values and goals drive them.
3) Their creative fires are fueled by psychological or mental problems. *Passive:* The problems fuel the fires.
4) A commonly used heuristic is called the availability heuristic. *Passive:* People call the commonly used heuristic the availability heuristic.
5) Studies show that savants lack verbal intelligence. *Active:* The studies show

implicit	=	explicit
optimistic	=	pessimistic
objective	=	subjective
passive	=	active
regress	=	progress

The Big Picture

Which statement below offers the best summary of the larger significance of this module?

A There you go again, Plotnik and Kouyoumdjian! You didn't have enough space in your textbook, so you crammed two subjects into this module even though they don't have much in common.

B Both subjects are interesting, but the material on thought is essentially philosophical while the material on language is truly psychological. Therefore, the section on thought could have been omitted from a textbook in general psychology.

C Thought and language, while technically separate topics in psychology, are intimately connected. In their sophisticated human form, each would be impossible without the other. It is likely that they developed together.

D Plotnik and Kouyoumdjian included material on both language and thought in the same module because *language* is learned in childhood and *thought* explains adult psychology. Together, they show precisely how childhood and adulthood are connected.

E What do I think about this module? Gee, I don't know… I can't put it into words.

True-False

_____ 1. According to prototype theory, we form a concept by constructing a complete list of all the properties that define an object, event, or characteristic.

_____ 2. Because they employ such powerful heuristics, today computer programs can beat all but the very best human chess players.

_____ 3. Good thinking: insight, analogy, subgoals. Bad thinking: functional fixedness.

_____ 4. Divergent thinking is a popular psychometric measure of creativity.

_____ 5. There is no scientific data to back up the common belief that creativity is related to an increased risk of mental instability.

_____ 6. Noam Chomsky bases his theory of language on the premise that humans have inborn language capabilities.

_____ 7. Children complete the essential tasks of learning language during the three-word stage.

_____ 8. It is easier to learn a foreign language in grade school than in college.

_____ 9. Inuit people (Eskimos) probably think differently about snow because they have so many more words for it than other people do.

_____ 10. Despite the fascinating research on communication in dolphins, gorillas, and chimpanzees, so far it appears that only humans clearly meet the four criteria for true language.

Flashcards 1

_____	1. algorithms	a. says you form a concept by creating a mental image based on the average characteristics of an object
_____	2. analogy	b. flexibility in thinking plus reorganization of thought to produce innovative ideas and solutions
_____	3. concept	c. a mental set characterized by inability to see an object having a function different from its usual one
_____	4. convergent thinking	d. beginning with a problem and coming up with a single correct solution
_____	5. creative thinking	e. a fixed set of rules that, if followed correctly, will eventually lead to a solution
_____	6. divergent thinking	f. rules of thumb or clever short-cuts that reduce the number of operations needed to solve a problem
_____	7. exemplar model	g. beginning with a problem and coming up with many different solutions
_____	8. functional fixedness	h. a way to group objects, events, etc., on the basis of some characteristics they all share in common
_____	9. heuristics	i. says you form a concept of an object or event by making a mental list of its essential characteristics
_____	10. prototype theory	j. a strategy for finding a similarity between the new situation and an old, familiar situation

Flashcards 2

_____	1. critical language period	a. the smallest meaningful combination of sounds in a language
_____	2. dyslexia	b. applying a grammatical rule to cases where it should not be used ("I goed to store")
_____	3. morpheme	c. a way adults speak to young children; slower, higher than normal voice, simple sentences, repeated words
_____	4. overgeneralization	d. procedures for converting our ideas from surface structures into deep structures and back again
_____	5. parentese (motherese)	e. the basic sounds of consonants and vowels (any word can be broken down into these units)
_____	6. phonemes	f. a distinctive pattern of speaking in which the child omits articles, prepositions, and parts of verbs
_____	7. semantics	g. specifies the meaning of words or phrases when they appear in various sentences or contexts
_____	8. telegraphic speech	h. reading, spelling, and writing difficulties that may include reversing or skipping letters and numbers
_____	9. theory of linguistic relativity	i. states that the differences among languages result in similar differences in how people think and perceive world
_____	10. transformational rules	j. the time from infancy to adolescence when language is easier to learn; more difficult to learn after this period

Multiple Choice

_____ 1. For Plotnik and Kouyoumdjian, this module illustrates the importance of the _________ approach to psychology
   a. behavioral
   b. cognitive
   c. humanistic
   d. psychodynamic

_____ 2. Concepts are crucial to effective thinking because without concepts we would
   a. not know the rules for logical thought
   b. forget most of what we learn
   c. be overwhelmed by apparently unrelated pieces of information
   d. lose our motivation to think

_____ 3. Most psychologists favor the _________ explanation of concept formation because it _________
   a. exemplar model / is based on good, sound definitions
   b. exemplar model / accounts for the exceptions to the rule
   c. prototype theory / is based on complete listings of essential properties
   d. prototype theory / accounts for more objects using fewer features

_____ 4. Children quickly form and develop concepts because the human brain
   a. is set up to store different categories in different areas
   b. is made up of a sponge-like material that easily sops up new information
   c. operates at the conscious level
   d. places each new bit of information in a separate category

_____ 5. A computer program finally has defeated a top human chess player, primarily because
   a. increasingly more powerful algorithms finally won
   b. good heuristics finally won
   c. computers don't have to take breaks for food and drink
   d. there is an element of luck in any game

_____ 6. When your friend remarks pessimistically that crime is increasing ("Did you see that gruesome murder on the news last night?"), you recognize the operation of the
   a. accuracy algorithm
   b. availability heuristic
   c. prototype theory
   d. subgoal strategy

_____ 7. If you were not able to solve the nine-dot problem, it probably was because of
   a. functional fixedness
   b. lack of insight
   c. using poor analogies
   d. failure to establish subgoals

_____ 8. Remember how Sultan figured out how to get a banana that was out of reach (Module 10)? That was a classic example of solving problems by using
   a. subgoals
   b. analogies
   c. insight
   d. functional fixedness

_____ 9. One of the best ways to finish your assignment on time is to
   a. have the problem in the back of your mind, and wait for a sudden flash of insight
   b. use the analogy of other, similar assignments you have done before
   c. fix your thoughts on the function that is involved in the assignment
   d. break the assignment down into subtasks and subgoals

_____ 10. A serious problem with too many college courses is that they place all the emphasis on __________ thinking
   a. creative
   b. convergent
   c. divergent
   d. brainstorm

_____ 11. The existence of autistic savants shows that the link between creativity and intelligence is
   a. strong, because autistic savants always have high IQ scores
   b. moderate, because autistic savants typically have normal IQ scores
   c. nonexistent, because autistic savants seldom show creativity
   d. weak, because autistic savants usually have low IQ scores

_____ 12. From most *particular* to most *general* in the rules of language, the correct order is
   a. morpheme – phoneme – syntax – semantics
   b. syntax – phoneme – semantics – morpheme
   c. phoneme – morpheme – syntax – semantics
   d. semantics – syntax – morpheme – phoneme

_____ 13. According to Noam Chomsky, language operates at two levels:
   a. spoken words and censored words
   b. surface structure and deep structure
   c. obvious meaning and implied meaning
   d. sentences and telegraphic speech

_____ 14. Chomsky's theory of language says that children
   a. learn those words and phrases that are reinforced by the environment
   b. learn those sentences that are spoken by their parents
   c. inherit a special ability to understand the language spoken by their parents
   d. inherit a mental program for learning a universal grammar

_____ 15. Which is the correct sequence of stages in children's acquisition of language?
   a. crying, begging, asking, reasoning
   b. senseless noises, listening, imitation, original productions
   c. babbling, one-word, two-word, three-word, four-word, etc.
   d. babbling, single word, two-word combinations, sentences

_____ 16. "I goed to store" is an example of
   a. babbling
   b. parentese
   c. overgeneralization
   d. telegraphic speech

_____ 17. The debate over how we acquire language concerns _________ versus _________
a. innate language abilities / environmental language factors
b. universal abilities / different skills from one cultural group to another
c. superficial / deep-seated
d. individual / common to the group

_____ 18. Bad news if you are planning to study a foreign language in college: the existence of
a. transformational rules
b. telegraphic speech
c. the critical language period
d. parentese

_____ 19. New research on making decisions is revealing the fact that
a. the more important the decision, the more logical and rational we become
b. emotions can influence or bias our decisions
c. gambling decisions are based mostly on logic
d. political decisions are based mainly on careful analysis of the candidates

_____ 20. Benjamin Whorf's theory of linguistic relativity might be proved by the observation that Inuit people (Eskimos) have many more words for snow… except for the fact that
a. they also have fewer words for rain
b. snow is obviously such a crucial factor in their lives
c. there is no relationship between language and thought
d. the claim turned out to be untrue

_____ 21. Which one of the following is *not* a brain area involved in learning to read?
a. dyslexic arranger
b. phoneme (sound) producer
c. word analyzer
d. automatic detector

_____ 22. When American and Japanese students looked at an underwater scene, cultural differences in thinking were revealed by
a. Americans seeing the fish as food and Japanese seeing them as works of art
b. American analytical thinking versus Japanese holistic thinking
c. Japanese studious observation versus American casual observation
d. Japanese interest in the large fish and American interest in the background

_____ 23. Male-female differences in using language may be explained by new research showing that
a. men and women are raised according to different rules and standards
b. men have developed a better style of speaking
c. women prefer to attack problems while men prefer to listen, give support, or be sympathetic
d. male and female brains process language differently

_____ 24. When Rod Plotnik says he talks to his dog "Bear," his point is that
a. Bear can communicate, but only Rod has language
b. Bear has learned hundreds of words and can understand sentences
c. Bear has learned the dog version of language, but he isn't really communicating
d. Bear has mastered the four criteria for communication

_____ 25. The bottom line in the debate over whether animals can acquire true language seems to be that
a. dolphins may possess a system of communication far superior to human language
b. pygmy chimps are the only animals able to learn true language
c. only humans clearly meet the four criteria for true language
d. several of the higher primates can acquire the language skills of five-year-old children

Short Essay

1. How do the topics of thought and language illustrate the importance and power of the cognitive approach to psychology?

2. Describe the prototype theory of concept formation, and explain why it is considered superior to the exemplar model of concept formation.

3. In what ways did Noam Chomsky change the way we understand language abilities and language acquisition?

4. Are male-female differences in thinking real, or mainly stereotypes? What evidence supports your position?

5. Do animals have language?

Test-Taking Tips

More hints:

- Use everything you know. Even if you can't recall the specific information needed, think about what you *do* remember concerning the subject.
- Don't jump to the conclusion that an answer is correct just because it uses the right word. The entire statement must be true.

Answers for Module 14

The Big Picture (explanations provided for incorrect choices)

A There are powerful connections between thought and language. Think about what I am saying!
B The study of thought is highly philosophical, but what is closer to the essence of humanness?
C Correct! You see the "big picture" for this Module.
D Close, since language is an essential part of child psychology, but thought applies to both children and adults.
E It's just a joke!

True-False (explanations provided for False choices; page numbers given for all choices)

1	F	306	Concept formation relies on relationships between ideas.
2	F	308	Computer programs play chess by comparing thousands of rules or algorithms.
3	T	309	
4	T	310	
5	F	311	Some evidence exists, but it is possible that mood disorders may be sources of artistic inspiration.
6	T	313	
7	F	315	There is no "three-word" stage.
8	T	316	
9	F	319	New research finds that Inuit people (Eskimos) *do not* have more words for snow.
10	T	322	

Flashcards 1

1 e 2 j 3 h 4 d 5 b 6 g 7 i 8 c 9 f 10 a

Flashcards 2

1 j 2 h 3 a 4 b 5 c 6 e 7 g 8 f 9 i 10 d

Multiple Choice (explanations provided for incorrect choices)

1
a The behavioral approach stresses the power of the environment in conditioning.
b Correct! See page 305.
c The humanistic approach stresses self-concept and human potential.
d The psychodynamic approach stresses unconscious processes and conflicts.

2
a Concepts are not the same as rules.
b Concepts are not the main factor in memory.
c Correct! See page 306.
d Why should concepts and motivation to think be linked? This is a nonsense statement.

3
a Wrong theory.
b Wrong theory.
c Right theory, but specification of advantages goes with the other theory.
d Correct! See page 306.

4
a Correct! See page 307.
b The brain does not operate like a sponge (more like an electrical signaling system).
c The processes involved in concept formation go on at an unconscious level.
d If that were true, the brain would be overwhelmed by separate bits of unrelated information.

5
a Correct! See page 308.
b Humans employ heuristics better than computers can.
c True, but human needs did not explain the loss.
d Wake up! You aren't paying attention!

6
a This is not a correct technical term in the psychology of problem solving.
b Correct! See page 308.
c Prototype theory refers to concept formation rather than perception.
d The strategy of using subgoals refers to problem solving.

7 ***a*** *Correct! See page 309.*
b The question is, what prevented insight from occurring?
c Analogies would not be of much help in this problem.
d Subgoals would not be of much help in this problem.

8 a Sultan did not break the task down into separate parts.
b Sultan did not relate the new situation to an old, familiar situation.
c *Correct! See page 309.*
d Functional fixedness hinders, not aids, problem solving.

9 a Waiting is the worst thing to do.
b Sounds good, but that wouldn't be the strongest strategy.
c This is a nonsense statement that alludes to the term functional fixedness.
d *Correct! See page 309.*

10 a That will be the day!
b *Correct! See page 310.*
c Divergent thinking refers to coming up with many possible answers.
d Brainstorming refers to a group "thinking out loud" together.

11 a Savants usually have low IQ scores.
b Savants usually have low IQ scores.
c Savants often show remarkable creativity.
d *Correct! See page 311.*

12 a Ask yourself, which is the smallest unit of speech?
b Ask yourself, which is the smallest unit of speech?
c *Correct! See page 312.*
d Ask yourself, which is the smallest unit of speech?

13 a The concept of censoring is not part of Chomsky's theory.
b *Correct! See page 313.*
c The concepts of obvious and implied meaning are not part of Chomsky's theory.
d Correct terms, but not what Chomsky meant.

14 a Chomsky's theory downplays the importance of the environment.
b That would not explain why children can produce sentences they have never heard before.
c That would not explain how children adopted from other countries learn language.
d *Correct! See page 313.*

15 a These are not the technical terms used in psychology.
b These are not the technical terms used in psychology.
c Close, but there is no three-word (or more) stage.
d *Correct! See page 314.*

16 a Babbling refers to the sounds six-month-old infants make.
b Parentese refers to how adults talk to children who are learning to speak.
c *Correct! See page 315.*
d Telegraphic speech refers to the first sentences, from which parts are left out.

17 ***a*** *Correct! See page 316.*
b The debate is not over the effects of culture.
c Both sides agree that language abilities are profoundly important.
d The debate is not over individual or group factors.

18 a This is Chomsky's term for procedures of converting ideas from surface structure to deep structure.
b Telegraphic speech is a childhood pattern of speech in which elements are left out.
c *Correct! See page 316.*
d Hopefully, your parents stopped talking to you like that after infancy.

19 a Decisions are often based on emotion rather than intellect.
b *Correct! See page 318.*
c Emotions have a very strong influence on gambling decisions.
d Emotions have a very strong influence on political decisions.

20 a They do not have fewer words for rain.
b This fact tends to support the linguistic relativity theory.
c This statement is obviously untrue.
d *Correct! See page 319.*

21 ***a*** *Correct! See page 320.*
b This brain function is the first step in reading.
c This brain function is the second step in reading.
d This brain function is the third step in reading.

22 a This was not a difference between the two groups.
b *Correct! See page 321.*
c This was not a difference between the two groups.
d Just the opposite was true.

23 a Language differences may be rooted more in physiology than in culture.
b Deborah Tannen says male and female styles are different, but not necessarily better or worse.
c Wouldn't that be wonderful!
d *Correct! See page 321.*

24 ***a*** *Correct! See page 322.*
b Bear understands what Rod is communicating, but he does not know words or understand sentences.
c Oh, he's communicating all right (just look at the cute picture)!
d The four criteria relate to language, which is a special form of communication.

25 a Fascinating theory, but can they acquire what we consider language?
b Do pygmy chimps meet the four criteria for true language?
c *Correct! See page 322.*
d None even comes close.

Short Essay (sample answers)

1. The cognitive approach to psychology emphasizes processing, storing, and using information, and studies the effect of information on human abilities and activities. Thinking, or reasoning, involves forming concepts, solving problems, and engaging in creative activities. Language, a special form of communication, involves complex rules to form and manipulate symbols and generate meaningful sentences. These mental activities, the heart of the cognitive approach, are the processes that differentiate humans from other animals.

2. Nothing is more important to thinking than concepts, but how do we form them? According to the exemplar model, we build up lists of essential characteristics of things. But there are too many characteristics to remember and too many exceptions to the lists. According to prototype theory, we create mental images based on the average characteristics of things. It is easier to match new things to existing prototypes than to long lists of characteristics. Prototype theory is a better explanation of our power to form new concepts.

3. Noam Chomsky changed the way we think about language. Rather than emphasizing experience, Chomsky proposed that the human brain is already wired to learn language. A mental grammar allows language production and an innate brain program guides language learning. Below the surface structure of language (the wording of a sentence) lies the deep structure (the underlying meaning of the sentence). All languages share a common universal grammar, and children inherit a mental program to learn this universal grammar.

4. The idea that men and women think differently is popular, but are such supposed differences real or mainly stereotypes? If there are differences, are they inherent? And are they important? However you argue in your answer, you should consider Deborah Tannen's research and the recent findings from brain scans that, on the same language tasks, men and women use different areas of their brains. Even if you agree that there are differences, are they important? As Tannen says, different does not necessarily mean better.

5. There's a fascinating history of attempts to prove that at least some animals have language. Louis Herman's dolphins learned 50 hand signals, Francine Patterson's Koko has a vocabulary of 800 signs, and Sue Savage-Rumbaugh's Kanzi uses symbols and knows 200 spoken English words. Are these impressive accomplishments language, or imitation? So far, no animal has met the four criteria for true language: learning and using abstract symbols, learning rules of grammar, and constructing meaningful sentences.

Module 15

Motivation

Does Learning Move You?

Studying psychology offers a wonderful extra payoff: learning how to become a more effective student. Sometimes Plotnik and Kouyoumdjian give you an outright suggestion and sometimes you have to make the connection yourself, but each module contains a fact or an insight you can apply to becoming more effective in your college work. One of the most important ideas concerns motivation.

Module 15 introduces the idea of intrinsic motivation, the kind of motivation that goes beyond working for a specific, immediate, tangible payoff. Not that there's anything wrong with motivation through overt rewards. That's what gets us to work and makes us meet specific goals. In the long run, however, sustained pursuit of complex goals requires that extrinsic reinforcement be supplemented by intrinsic motivation. That's why you get smiley faces on your papers in grade school, but not in college.

It is important to understand your motivation for attending college. If the real reason you enrolled was to please your parents or because all your friends went, you may have a difficult time mustering the energy and finding the time that college work demands. If you find the activity of learning itself interesting, however, your college studies should be exciting and fun.

Our Motivation to Be Effective

I believe that the most significant of all motivations is the universal need to be effective. Oh sure, thirst, hunger, and sex are more immediate and can be insanely demanding, but what is it that we want all the time? We want to be effective in our dealings with the world, in our interactions with other people, and in managing our personal lives. Some call this a sense of mastery or control, but I like the word "effectiveness" to convey our broad need to do things that work.

The idea comes from pioneering psychologist Robert W. White, who wrote persuasively about "competence motivation" 50 years ago. Unfortunately, his idea of competence has become so deeply woven into the fabric of modern psychology that it tends to be taken for granted, and its deeper meaning overlooked. I believe effectiveness is such a significant need that it deserves explicit recognition.

With effectiveness in mind, perhaps you see why it is so important to do well in college. Success in college is the crucial measure of effectiveness at this point in your life. Examine your thoughts, feelings, and behavior. Doing something well — being effective — makes you pleased and happy, but when you're ineffective, you feel awful. Everything in your psychological makeup says you want to be effective in college.

Effective Student Tip 15

The One Day You Must Not Miss Class

The day the term paper is due? The day a surprise quiz is likely? The big exam? All these are important days to attend, but there is one day when you absolutely must not miss class. That's the day you don't have the assigned paper ready or aren't prepared for the test.

Of course, this is exactly the day you are most tempted to cut. The embarrassment! The humiliation! Yet that's the very day when you can profit most from attending.

What you dread probably won't happen. Turns out you weren't the only one who goofed, and no one is taken out and shot. Not planning to read the papers until the weekend anyway, the professor may take yours later. Some professors will reassign a tough paper, reschedule an exam, or even allow a retake.

One especially good thing can happen when you attend on that agonizing day: you learn more about yourself. Why did you procrastinate? Why did you trip yourself up by not leaving enough time? What are your true feelings about the teacher, and how did they come into play? If you go to class and discuss it, all of this becomes clearer, your relationship becomes more honest, and you take an important step toward becoming a more effective student. If you stay in bed, everything just gets worse.

Your response…

Have you ever avoided a class when there was a problem? What happened?

Learning Objectives

1. Understand motivation as the force (or forces) driving those actions that make us human and keep us alive and emotionally vibrant.

2. Learn the basic theories that have been proposed in an effort to explain our biological and social needs.

3. Understand the biology and psychology of hunger and the special problems we face in contemporary society as we attempt to regulate this absolutely essential motivating force.

4. Understand the biology and psychology of sexual behavior and the special problems we face in contemporary society as we attempt to understand this essential yet complex motivating force.

5. Consider your position on the clash of cultures over the tradition of genital cutting.

6. Appreciate achievement as a unique human need that is revealed in striving for success, fear of failure, and the remarkable accomplishments of immigrant children.

7. Apply the findings and ideas of psychology to one of the most pressing issues of the day: eating problems and treatment.

Key Terms

There are lots of key terms in this module because Plotnik and Kouyoumdjian discuss several major areas of motivation, like hunger, sex, and aggression. Read through the list below. I think you'll find that many of these terms are already part of your general knowledge.

achievement need
AIDS (Acquired Immune Deficiency Syndrome)
anorexia nervosa
biological hunger factors
biological needs
biological sex factors
biosocial theory
bulimia nervosa
central cues
cognitive factors in motivation
double standard for sexual behavior
evolutionary theory
extrinsic motivation
fat cells
fear of failure
female hypothalamus
fixed action pattern
gender identity
gender identity disorder
gender roles
genetic hunger factors
genetic sex factors
genital cutting
high need for achievement
HIV positive
incentives
inhibited female orgasm
instincts
interactive model of sexual orientation
intrinsic motivation
male hypothalamus
Maslow's hierarchy of needs
metabolic rate
motivation
obesity
optimal (ideal) weight
organic factors
overweight
paraphilias
peripheral cues
premature (rapid) ejaculation
psychological factors
psychological sex factors
psychosocial hunger factors
reward/pleasure center
self-handicapping
set point
sex chromosome
sex hormones
sexual dysfunctions
sexual orientation (preference): homosexual, bisexual, heterosexual
social needs
Thematic Apperception Test (TAT)
underachievers
weight-regulating genes

Outline

- *Introduction*
  1. **Motivation** (Erik Weihenmayer)
  2. Achievement (Victor)

- ☐ What was the hardest thing you have ever done? The greatest victory you have ever achieved? How do you explain your behavior in these extreme situations?

A. *Theories of Motivation*

1. Instinct (William McDougall)
   a. **Instincts**
   b. **Fixed action pattern**
2. Brain: **reward/pleasure center**
3. **Incentives**
4. Cognitive factors
   a. **Extrinsic motivation**
   b. **Intrinsic motivation**
5. Explaining human motivation
   a. Reward/pleasure center of the brain, incentives, and cognitive or intrinsic factors (this Module)
   b. Emotional and personality factors (Modules 16, 19, and 20)

B. *Biological & Social Needs*

1. **Biological needs**
   a. When genes are defective
   b. When psychological factors interfere
2. **Social needs**
3. Satisfying needs: **Maslow's hierarchy of needs** (Abraham Maslow)
4. Maslow's hierarchy of needs (arranged as a pyramid)
   a. Level 5: self-actualization
   b. Level 4: esteem needs
   c. Level 3: love and belonging needs
   d. Level 2: safety needs
   e. Level 1: physiological needs

C. *Hunger*

1. Optimal weight
   a. **Optimal (ideal) weight**
   b. Natural regulation
2. Overweight
   a. **Overweight**
   b. **Obesity**

3. Three hunger factors
    a. **Biological hunger factors**
    b. **Psychosocial hunger factors**
    c. **Genetic hunger factors**
4. Biological hunger factors
    a. **Peripheral cues**
    b. **Central cues**
5. **Genetic hunger factors**
    a. **Fat cells**
    b. **Metabolic rate**
    c. **Set point**
    d. **Weight-regulating genes**
6. **Psychosocial hunger factors**
    a. Learned associations
    b. Socio-cultural influences
    c. Personality and mood factors

D. Sexual Behavior

☐ Does sex, which Freud claimed was central to human psychology, cause any particular concerns or problems in your life? Good…, I thought not!

1. Three factors
    a. **Genetic sex factors**
    b. **Biological sex factors**
    c. **Psychological sex factors**
2. Genetic influences on sexual behavior
    a. **Sex chromosome**
    b. Differentiation
    c. Male sex organ and male brain
    d. Female sex organs and female brain
    e. Importance of testosterone
3. Biological influences
    a. **Sex hormones**
    b. **Male hypothalamus**
    c. **Female hypothalamus**
    d. Sexual motivation
4. Psychological influences: **psychological sex factors**
    a. 1st step: gender identity
        (1) **Gender identity**
        (2) **Gender identity disorder**

b. 2nd step: gender roles

(1) **Gender roles**

(2) Stereotypic or traditional expectations

c. 3rd step: **sexual orientation (preference)**

(1) **Homosexual orientation, bisexual orientation,** and **heterosexual orientation**

(2) **Interactive model of sexual orientation**

5. Male-female sex differences

☐ Is the "double standard" still operating among the people you know?

a. **Double standard for sexual behavior**

b. **Biosocial theory**

c. **Evolutionary theory**

6. Homosexuality

a. Genetic/biological factors

b. Psychological factors

7. Sexual response, problems, and treatments

a. **Paraphilias**

b. **Sexual dysfunctions**

c. **Organic factors**

d. **Psychological factors**

e. Four-stage model of sexual response (William Masters and Virginia Johnson)

(1) Excitement

(2) Plateau

(3) Orgasm

(4) Resolution

f. **Premature (rapid) ejaculation**

g. **Inhibited female orgasm**

8. AIDS: Acquired Immune Deficiency Syndrome

a. **HIV positive**

b. **AIDS (Acquired Immune Deficiency Syndrome)**

(1) Risk for AIDS

(2) Progression of disease

(3) Treatment

E. Cultural Diversity: Genital Cutting

1. Good tradition or cruel mutilation?

☐ If you value the ideal of cultural diversity, can you still condemn the practice of genital cutting in those cultures that believe it is an important part of becoming a woman?

2. Issues involved in **genital cutting**
   a. What is its purpose?
   b. Are there complications?
   c. Is there a solution?

F. Achievement

1. Kinds of achievement

☐ Do you feel a strong need for achievement? How does achievement influence your life?

   a. **Social needs**
   b. **Achievement need** (David McClelland and John Atkinson)
   c. How is the need for achievement measured? **Thematic Apperception Test (TAT)**
   d. What is **high need for achievement**?
2. **Fear of failure: self-handicapping**
3. Underachievement
   a. **Underachievers**
   b. Characteristics
4. Three components of success
5. Cognitive influences
   a. **Cognitive factors in motivation**
   b. **Intrinsic motivation**
   c. **Extrinsic motivation**
6. Intrinsic motivation

G. Research Focus: Overcoming Educational Disadvantages

1. Why did poor and minority students do well?
2. A study of academic performance
   a. Procedure and results (KIPP schools)
   b. Conclusions

H. Application: Eating Problems & Treatment

1. Dieting: problems, concerns, and benefits

☐ Why are eating problems so common?

   a. Overweight and dieting (Oprah Winfrey)
   b. Diet program/life style
      (1) Low-fat or low-carbohydrate diet?
      (2) Food addiction
2. Serious eating disorders: risk factors and treatment
   a. **Anorexia nervosa**
   b. **Bulimia nervosa**

How English Works

Words in the Textbook

p. 332 biological needs to **run amok** = to be out of control

p. 333 we face **roadblocks** = setbacks, obstacles

p. 336 after birth and **reared** in adopted family = raised

p. 337 Examples may be **cited** = given as proof

p. 339 you are **destined** to be = forced

p. 340 **exerts** a powerful influence = presents, gives off

mannerisms of the other sex = ways of moving and speaking

rough and tumble play = not polite, with possible violence

p. 342 **extramarital affairs** = sex outside the marriage relationship

offspring of low quality = children

p. 344 using a **vibrator** = device used to stimulate sexual feeling

p. 345 through **casual** contact = common, ordinary (not close)

1,000 times more **infectious** = able to spread disease

walking **time bomb** = scheduled to explode

p. 346 men want to marry **virgins** = women who have never had sex

ancient **rite of passage** = custom to mark new stage of life

Muslim **clerics** = religious leaders

serves no **hygienic** purpose = health, cleanliness

amputation of the male's penis = removal, cutting off

bleeding, and even **hemorrhaging** = losing large amounts of blood

cysts = abnormal growths on the body

maintain female **chastity** = pure??? state (without sexual experience)

organizations have **endorsed** anti-circumcision laws = approved

p. 348 people in **ambiguous** situations = without clear meaning

p. 349 The **paradox** of underachievement = puzzle, contradiction

p. 350 very little **charitable work** = unpaid volunteer helping poor

p. 351 **nod** = move head up and down

ESL Tip: Direct / Indirect Quotations

English as a Second Language students — and others — will understand the difference between direct and indirect quotations by imagining that the person who is quoted had been electronically recorded, or not. In a recording, for example, you would hear Sheila's voice saying, "I am going to walk the dog." Her words go inside quotation marks. However, if I report this situation to you, I might say this: Sheila said that she was going to walk the dog. Now Sheila's words are quoted indirectly, and no quotation marks are used.

There are two possible differences to be aware of — sometimes there is a difference in pronoun use between direct and indirect quotations:

Direct: Gregor said, "***I*** will meet you at school."

Indirect: Gregor said ***he*** would meet me at school.

Sometimes there is a difference in tense between a direct and indirect quotation:

Direct: LaShaun said, "I **will be** on the 5:00 train."

Indirect: LaShaun said she **would** be on the 5:00 train.

Just remember that a direct quotation (*with* quotation marks) uses only the exact, word-for-word expression of the person who speaks it. Otherwise, it's an indirect quote (*without* quotation marks).

Vocabulary: "Abstain"

Abstain (verb)

To **abstain** is to decide to not do something.

To take personal responsibility to **abstain from** drinking.

Librarians always ask people to **abstain from** talking in the library.

The doctor advised Halina to **abstain from** food for 24 hours before her operation.

Abstinent (adjective)

How many clients remain **abstinent.**

Abstinent guests are popular at parties because they can safely drive other people home.

It's hard to stay **abstinent** when everyone around is eating and drinking.

Abstinence (noun)

That total **abstinence** is the only solution.

The war was a time of **abstinence** for everyone.

In the month of Ramadan, Muslims practice **abstinence from** eating and drinking during daylight hours.

Test Yourself

Read the following passage and choose the best word to fill the blank. You will need to use one word more than once.

abstain / abstinent / abstinence

Darryl is very lazy; he __________ from exercise as much as possible. But he is not at all __________ when it's time for dinner. He prefers __________ from exercise, not from hamburgers. However, his friends __________ from criticizing him.

Answers

Darryl is very lazy; he **abstains** from exercise as much as possible. But he is not at all **abstinent** when it's time for dinner. He prefers **abstinence** from exercise, not from hamburgers. However, his friends **abstain** from criticizing him.

The Big Picture

Which statement below offers the best summary of the larger significance of this module?

A One day we may have a single explanation of human motivation, but for now there seem to be several useful ways of looking at it. These different approaches to motivation parallel the general approaches to psychology.

B Plotnik and Kouyoumdjian give us several different areas of motivation (hunger, sex, achievement) to show that each area of human behavior has its own particular kind of motivation. There is no overall theory of motivation.

C In areas like hunger, sex, and achievement, human motivation is radically different from animal motivation. Thus the study of motivation shows that humans are far above the lower animals, a fact psychology should recognize.

D After years of exploring the reasons how and why humans pursue their goals, it seems to come down to "mind over matter." Once again, cognitive psychology is shown to be superior to the other approaches.

E Oh sure, I *could* learn all the stuff in this module. But why bother?

True-False

_____ 1. The strong biological commands called instincts in animals are called fixed action patterns in humans.

_____ 2. The concept of homeostasis supports the drive reduction theory.

_____ 3. The concept of intrinsic motivation rests on a recognition of the importance of external factors.

_____ 4. Maslow's hierarchy of needs nicely brings together both biological and social needs.

_____ 5. Humans are the only animal for whom learned cues to eating are more powerful than biological cues.

_____ 6. As one might expect, the male lion gets sex whenever he wants it.

_____ 7. The percentage of people who are homosexual is rising rapidly.

_____ 8. A sexual attraction to particular articles of clothing, such as shoes, is classified as a paraphilia.

_____ 9. Researchers believe they will find a cure for AIDS in the next year or two.

_____ 10. The dull truth is that the only realistic solution to weight problems is a combination of better eating habits and exercise.

Flashcards 1

_____	1. achievement need	a. innate tendencies or biological forces that determine behavior
_____	2. extrinsic motivation	b. goals that can be either objects or thoughts, which we learn to value and which we are motivated to obtain
_____	3. fear of failure	c. engaging in certain behaviors because the behaviors themselves are personally rewarding or fulfill our beliefs
_____	4. fixed action pattern	d. a motivation to avoid failure by choosing easy, nonchallenging tasks where failure is unlikely
_____	5. incentives	e. individuals who score relatively high on tests of ability but perform more poorly than scores predict
_____	6. instincts	f. an ascending order in which biological needs are placed at the bottom and social needs at the top
_____	7. intrinsic motivation	g. engaging in certain behaviors that either reduce biological needs or help us obtain external rewards
_____	8. Maslow's hierarchy of needs	h. an innate biological predisposition toward a specific behavior in a specific environmental condition
_____	9. self-handicapping	i. a tendency to do things that contribute to failure and then to use these things as excuses for failure
_____	10. underachievers	j. your desire to set challenging goals and to persist in pursuing those goals in the face of obstacles

Flashcards 2

_____	1. anorexia nervosa	a. problems of sexual arousal or orgasm that interfere with adequate functioning during sexual behavior
_____	2. bulimia nervosa	b. traditional or stereotypic behaviors, attitudes, and personality traits designated masculine or feminine
_____	3. double standard for sexual behavior	c. beliefs, values, or expectations that subtly encourage sexual activity in men but discourage same behavior in women
_____	4. gender identity	d. a certain level of body fat that our body strives to maintain constant throughout our lives
_____	5. gender roles	e. characterized by binge-eating and purging and an excessive concern about body shape and weight
_____	6. genital cutting	f. a serious eating disorder characterized by refusing to eat, an intense fear of fat, and a distorted body image
_____	7. inhibited female orgasm	g. sexual deviations characterized by repetitive or preferred sexual fantasies about nonhuman objects
_____	8. paraphilias	h. a persistent delay or absence of orgasm after becoming aroused and excited
_____	9. set point	i. the individual's subjective experience and feelings of being either a male or a female
_____	10. sexual dysfunctions	j. practice in some traditional African cultures of cutting away the female's external genitalia

Multiple Choice

_____ 1. Plotnik and Kouyoumdjian tell the story of Erik Weilhenmayer's achievements in mountain climbing and racing — although he's blind! — to illustrate the idea that
   a. you can do anything you really put your mind to
   b. you should take risks in life, but also have strong ropes!
   c. the causes of human actions are complex, yet important to understand
   d. there must be a mysterious single source of motivation, as yet undiscovered

_____ 2. Early in this century, most psychologists believed that motivation was explained by
   a. will power
   b. instincts
   c. environmental incentives
   d. beliefs and expectations

_____ 3. What were once called instincts are now called
   a. fixed action patterns
   b. incentives
   c. rewards
   d. energizers

_____ 4. Brain scans have revealed a new source of motivation, the
   a. instinct
   b. fixed action pattern
   c. reward/pleasure center
   d. incentive

_____ 5. The newest theory of motivation places greatest emphasis on
   a. will power
   b. instincts
   c. environmental incentives
   d. beliefs and expectations

_____ 6. The key idea of Maslow's hierarchy of needs is that
   a. unless social needs like esteem are satisfied, one cannot deal effectively with biological needs like safety
   b. basic biological needs must be satisfied before higher social needs can be dealt with
   c. unless you achieve level five, you are a defective person
   d. the higher needs are essential; the lower needs are incidental

_____ 7. The highest level need (at the top of the pyramid) in Maslow's hierarchy is
   a. safety needs
   b. love and belonging needs
   c. esteem needs
   d. self-actualization

_____ 8. Which one of the following is *not* a biological cue for hunger?
   a. glucose in the blood
   b. the hypothalamus
   c. learned associations
   d. the walls of the stomach

_____ 9. Which one of the following is *not* a genetic factor that influences body weight?
a. fat cells
b. metabolic rate
c. set point
d. responsiveness to food cues

_____ 10. The best explanation of the common tendency of dieters to regain the weight they lose is the
a. fat cell
b. metabolic rate
c. set point
d. weight-regulating gene

_____ 11. All of the following are examples of psychosocial hunger factors *except*
a. striving to maintain a constant level of body fat
b. large portions and tasty junk foods high in calories
c. mass media images of the ideal woman as thin
d. depression, anxiety, markedly low self-esteem, and being overly sensitive to rejection

_____ 12. Lions never go on talk shows; their sexual behavior is kept in line by the fact that
a. females do most of the hunting
b. hormones and pheromones prevail
c. social roles and rules predominate
d. a lioness' bite can be fatal

_____ 13. Gender identity disorder is commonly referred to as
a. bisexuality
b. homosexuality
c. sexual disorientation
d. transsexualism

_____ 14. The term "double standard" means the
a. social expectation that men will be more sexually active than women
b. biological fact that women want one man but men want more than one woman
c. added burden modern women face of both working and caring for their families
d. new idea that a woman can ask a man out and still expect him to pick up the check

_____ 15. What makes a person homosexual? Much of the new evidence points to
a. social factors like having homosexual teachers
b. biological factors like genetic and hormonal influences
c. family factors like overbearing mothers
d. intellectual factors like fascination with art

_____ 16. Which *one* of the following is the correct order of the four-stage human sexual response model?
a. excitement – plateau – orgasm – resolution
b. plateau – excitement – orgasm – resolution
c. excitement – orgasm – plateau – resolution
d. orgasm – excitement – resolution – plateau

_____ 17. The most effective treatment for AIDS is to
   a. take a drug "cocktail" daily until the symptoms are gone
   b. take a drug "cocktail" daily for the rest of one's life
   c. cease all sexual activity for an indefinite period
   d. cease all intravenous drug use immediately

_____ 18. The influence of culture in sexuality is clearly seen in the debate over
   a. celibacy
   b. paraphilias
   c. genital cutting
   d. sexual dysfunctions

_____ 19. In the story of Victor, whose buddies taunted him as a "white boy," we see a
   a. determination to have white friends even if his schoolmates disapproved
   b. triumph of the achievement need over peer pressure not to succeed in school
   c. refusal to be ashamed of being white in a mostly black school
   d. fear of failure causing him to take only easy, unchallenging courses

_____ 20. The best motivation for superior academic performance is having a
   a. high need for achievement
   b. high fear of failure
   c. very efficient self-handicapping strategy
   d. reasonable excuse for occasional failure

_____ 21. Which of the following is the best example of self-handicapping?
   a. choosing easy, nonchallenging tasks where failure is unlikely
   b. performing more poorly on an exam than IQ scores would predict
   c. getting plenty of sleep before the exam, but doing poorly anyway
   d. having a hangover during the exam, then blaming drug use for poor results

_____ 22. Which pair below illustrates the difference between *extrinsic* and *intrinsic* motivation?
   a. smiley face on child's homework / name on honor roll
   b. paycheck at work / pride in doing a good job
   c. voting in national election / picking up litter in public park
   d. male lion getting sex / male lion not getting sex

_____ 22. KIPP (Knowledge is Power Program) schools owe their success with poor and minority children to emphasis on
   a. personality and behavioral factors
   b. ancient Greece and Rome, the origins of Western civilization
   c. strict requirements for school uniforms
   d. long periods of silent study and meditation

_____ 24. Oprah Winfrey, who has fought being overweight for years, now realizes that she
   a. suffers from an unconscious tendency toward bulimia nervosa
   b. needs to cut back on her daily running because it only causes greater hunger
   c. needs a maintenance program that involves eating less and exercising more
   d. suffers from a serious lack of will power

_____ 25. Girls with anorexia nervosa and those with bulimia nervosa have in common
- a. upper-class family backgrounds
- b. regularly engaging in vomiting or use of laxatives
- c. histories of sexual abuse in childhood
- d. distorted thinking about body image and weight

Short Essay

1. Describe the three hunger factors that control eating behavior and regulate weight.
2. Is the double standard for sexual behavior still in operation? Illustrate your answer with examples from your own experience.
3. What are the issues in the controversy over genital cutting?
4. Is intrinsic motivation superior to extrinsic motivation?
5. Whether you are overweight, underweight, or just right, what did you learn about hunger motivation in this module that you can apply to your own life?

Our Need for Effectiveness

Please go back to page 250 and re-read what I wrote about effectiveness. I really think I have an important message here, although perhaps I could have explained it better. Can you see what I am getting at? Could the key to a happier and more successful life begin with recognition of our universal need to be effective?

The "PowerStudy 4.5 for Introduction to Psychology" CD-ROM includes a complete set of interactive learning activities for this module: quizzes, summary test, key terms, web site connections, critical thinking exercise, module outline, and more.

Answers for Module 15

The Big Picture (explanations provided for incorrect choices)

A *Correct! You see the "big picture" for this Module.*
B There are several overall theories of motivation, each seeking to explain all areas of behavior.
C There are too many similarities between animal and human motivation to justify the statement.
D The idea of "mind over matter" is not supported by most psychological theories.
E It's just a joke!

True-False (explanations provided for False choices; page numbers given for all choices)

1	F	330	Instincts and fixed action patterns are the same; humans have few of them.
2	T	330	
3	F	331	Intrinsic motivation refers to internal factors in motivation.
4	T	333	
5	T	334	
6	F	338	The male lion gets sex only when the female lion is receptive and interested.
7	F	343	The small percentage of people who are homosexual remains constant.
8	T	344	
9	F	345	Sadly, there is no cure for AIDS in sight.
10	T	352	

Flashcards 1

1 j 2 g 3 d 4 h 5 b 6 a 7 c 8 f 9 i 10 e

Flashcards 2

1 f 2 e 3 c 4 i 5 b 6 j 7 h 8 g 9 d 10 a

Multiple Choice (explanations provided for incorrect choices)

1 a An inspiring slogan, but as psychologists, Plotnik and Kouyoumdjian cannot be satisfied with slogans.
b This answer, which does not show much understanding of Erik Weilhenmayer, is at best funny, at worst silly.
c *Correct! See page 329.*
d A mysterious single source of motivation would mean there is no scientific way to explain it.

2 a Will power is not a widely accepted concept in psychology.
b *Correct! See page 330.*
c Environmental incentives refers to a modern behavioral explanation of motivation.
d Beliefs and expectations refers to a relatively recent cognitive explanation of motivation.

3 ***a*** *Correct! See page 330.*
b Incentives are learned goals; instincts are inborn.
c Rewards are learned goals; instincts are inborn.
d This is not a correct term in psychology.

4 a Instincts cannot be precisely located in the brain.
b Fixed action patterns cannot be precisely located in the brain.
c *Correct! See page 330.*
d Incentives cannot be precisely located in the brain.

5 a Will power is not a widely accepted concept in psychology.
b Instincts refers to the original biological theory of motivation.
c Environmental incentives refers to a modern behavioral explanation of motivation.
d *Correct! See page 331.*

6 a Maslow's theory says exactly the opposite.
b *Correct! See page 332.*
c Maslow doubts that many people in contemporary society can achieve the highest need level.
d Maslow says almost the opposite (although he does value the higher needs).

7 a Safety needs are at level two (of five).
b Love and belonging needs are at level three (of five).
c Esteem needs are at level four (of five).
d *Correct! See page 333.*

8 a Glucose is a peripheral biological cue for hunger.
b The hypothalamus is a central biological cue for hunger.
c *Correct! See page 334.*
d The stomach walls are peripheral biological cues for hunger.

9 a Fat cells are genetically influenced.
b Metabolic rates are genetically influenced.
c The set point probably is genetically influenced.
d *Correct! See page 336.*

10 a This genetic factor would not explain regaining the weight lost.
b This genetic factor would not explain regaining the weight lost.
c *Correct! See page 336.*
d This factor, by itself, would suggest a continual weight gain.

11 ***a*** *Correct! See page 337.*
b These are examples of learned associations to foods.
c These are examples of socio-cultural influences on eating.
d These are examples of personality traits associated with eating problems.

12 a What would that have to do with sexual behavior?
b *Correct! See page 338.*
c Felines are not highly social animals — other factors control their sexual behavior.
d It's just a joke!

13 a Bisexuality refers to a pattern of sexual arousal by persons of both sexes.
b Homosexuality refers to a pattern of sexual arousal by persons of the same sex.
c This is not a correct term in psychology.
d *Correct! See page 340.*

14 ***a*** *Correct! See page 342.*
b This commonly believed statement (not the definition) is probably untrue.
c The term refers to sexual attitudes and behavior.
d Sounds like this answer (not the definition) was written by a man!

15 a There is no evidence that children are influenced to be homosexual by role models.
b *Correct! See page 341.*
c This is an old idea that never had much research support.
d This idea reflects a common and unsupported prejudice.

16 ***a*** *Correct! See page 344.*
b Ask yourself, which one obviously comes first?
c Would orgasm come immediately after excitement?
d Ask yourself, which one obviously comes first?

17 a No drugs we have today kill the virus.
b *Correct! See page 345.*
c That wouldn't affect the disease that already exists.
d That wouldn't affect the disease that already exists.

18 a Culture does not play a large part in the American debate over celibacy.
b There is no real debate over paraphilias.
c *Correct! See page 346.*
d There is no real debate over sexual dysfunctions.

19 a The story of Victor was not about having white friends.
b *Correct! See page 348.*
c The story of Victor was not about a white student.
d The story of Victor was not about fear of failure (just the opposite).

20 ***a*** *Correct! See page 348.*
b Positive motives are stronger than negative motives.
c Self-handicapping strategy refers to making up excuses for failure.
d Excuses are never as useful as realistic appraisals.

21 a This could be fear of failure.
b This would be underachievement.
c Being rested is a good strategy, not an example of self-handicapping.
d *Correct! See page 349.*

22 a Both are examples of extrinsic motivation.
b *Correct! See page 350.*
c Both are examples of intrinsic motivation.
d Both are examples of biologically determined behaviors.

23 ***a*** *Correct! See page 351.*
b KIPP schools do not place special emphasis on the classics of Western civilization.
c Wearing uniforms is not key to the educational success of KIPP schools.
d Students in KIPP classrooms are quite active and vocal.

24 a Oprah did not say she had been bulimic.
b Oprah has a good exercise program that includes daily runs.
c *Correct! See page 352.*
d Will power is not a useful concept in weight management.

25 a They can come from any social class.
b This applies mainly to bulimics.
c A few do, but most do not.
d *Correct! See page 353.*

Short Essay (sample answers)

1. Three factors interact to influence weight. Biological hunger factors come from physiological changes in blood chemistry and signals from digestive organs that provide feedback to the brain. Psychosocial hunger factors come from learned associations between food and other stimuli. Genetic hunger factors come from inherited instructions found in our genes. Together, these three factors influence the brain to ask for more calories or fewer, and to expend energy that burns more calories or less.

2. The double standard for sexual behavior refers to a set of beliefs, values, and expectations that subtly encourages sexual activity in males but discourages the same behavior in females. He's a lover; she's a slut! Is this double standard still in force? Or has your generation risen above such outdated beliefs? Support your answer with evidence from your observations of society at large as well as from the interactions you personally see among your acquaintances and fellow students.

3. Genital cutting involves cutting away the female's external genitalia and sewing together the remaining edges. This ancient rite of passage, practiced in traditional cultures in parts of Africa and the Arabian Peninsula, is extremely painful and inhibits later sexual satisfaction. Does the acceptance of this practice in traditional cultures justify its continuation? Are Westerners justified in condemning the practices of other cultures? The United Nations opposes the practice, but has had only limited success in eliminating it.

4. Are people more likely to give blood to obtain a material reward or to enjoy the satisfaction of helping others? Research suggested that offering money actually decreased volunteering. This finding supported the idea that intrinsic motivation is superior to extrinsic motivation. But later research showed the issue to be more complex, emphasizing how people perceive rewards. Phony praise for doing little work actually discourages students. Perhaps the distinction between kinds of motivation is not entirely useful.

5. Most animals in nature maintain an optimal weight in favorable conditions, but we humans enjoy few natural constraints on eating behavior. It is so easy to eat too much, or too little, and so difficult to eat just right. Even for those of you whose weight is optimal, good health is constantly threatened by social (TV ads and shows) and political (price supports for sugar) considerations, and you won't be young forever. What did you learn from the wealth of information in the textbook about hunger that could help you live better?

Module 16

Emotion

A Gift of Nature

If visitors from outer space dropped in for a visit, what would impress them the most about us? Not our powers of logic and reason (theirs would be superior). Perhaps our emotions, which add the vitality to our life experience, would impress them as truly marvelous. "What a wonderful gift nature has given you," they might tell us. We would be surprised, because feelings seem to create such problems for us.

In this module, Plotnik and Kouyoumdjian carefully unravel the most important theories about what emotion is and how it works. All the theories keep coming back to two problems: (1) Does the body's reaction to a stimulus cause an emotion, or does an emotion trigger a physiological response? (2) Does a thought cause an emotion, or does an emotion trigger a thought? Plotnik and Kouyoumdjian show us the competing answers psychology has offered.

Still, something seems to be missing. No one of these classic theories of emotion has triumphed, and none seems fully satisfying, no matter how intriguing the research findings are. What if the *answers* are correct, but the *questions* are wrong? What if emotion is not separate from thinking, but an integral part of it? We know from our own lives that emotion is enormously important, but the current theories of emotion do not seem to capture our experience.

A Different View of Emotion

New discoveries in neuroscience are beginning to suggest that sensory data doesn't really become thought until it is charged by the force of emotion. A dual mental system both transforms sensory experience to tell us what's out there and also uses emotion to tell us how important it is. In guiding our behavior, feelings and thoughts are inseparable.

The new discoveries fit nicely with a different view of emotion, discovered by psychotherapist and writer Kenneth Isaacs. In *Uses of Emotion: Nature's Vital Gift* (Praeger: 1998), Isaacs says feelings are always benign and potentially useful parts of mental activity. Emotion comes and goes almost instantaneously, and therefore cannot build up in us. We may remember a feeling, but the actual emotion is already gone and cannot possibly harm us. The mistaken idea that feelings are dangerous entities that must be "gotten out," or at least controlled and regulated, robs many people of a rich emotional life and cripples others with extreme fear of emotion expressed in a wide variety of symptoms. The real dangers are our misunderstanding and fear of emotion, and, for many people, a constant and pervasive discomfort with their emotions.

Instead of fighting to control emotion, says Isaacs, we should welcome feelings as useful sources of information. We couldn't get along without our emotions any more than we could do without other information. If Kenneth Isaacs is correct, many ideas in psychology will have to be reconsidered.

Effective Student Tip 16

How to Beat Test Anxiety

In a famous experiment, dogs that received shocks in a closed box didn't even try to escape when given shocks in an open box. The experimenter called it "learned helplessness." If we could ask them, the dogs might tell us that 'test anxiety' made them fail to jump over to the safe side.

Sometimes school can be like the shock box. Too many painful defeats, and you learn to accept failure as a normal part of life. You don't like it, but you have no experience of escaping it. So don't be too quick to say you are no good at tests. You may have learned to think so, but you can't really know until you take a test *for which you have prepared effectively.*

Scratch the surface of most test anxiety and you find ineffective techniques. The first thing to do is stop blaming yourself. Next, discard the idea that you simply have to try harder. Finally, dissect your weaknesses in note taking, studying, and test-taking and replace them with better techniques.

You will begin to feel effective when you begin to be effective. As your sense of effectiveness increases, your ability to work out winning strategies will also increase. You may still experience some jitters (phobic effects linger), but who cares? Test anxiety will no longer rule your life.

Your response…

If you were brutally honest with yourself, what steps could you take to improve your test preparation?

Learning Objectives

1. Understand emotion as a vital force that, through the intensity and variety of feelings, helps us interpret the world around us and make decisions on everything from simple daily activities to significant delights or dangers.
2. Learn the basic theories that psychology has devised in attempting to explain emotion.
3. Learn how the brain produces feelings and uses them to promote our welfare.
4. Appreciate the significance of universal facial expressions of emotions and the functions of emotions like happiness.
5. Learn how cultural rules governing the display of emotions differ around the world.
6. Consider what research says about the new concept of emotional intelligence.
7. Understand the strengths and weaknesses of lie detectors.

Key Terms

Try to understand the battle of psychological theories of emotion that is reflected in many of these key terms.

adaptation level theory
affective neuroscience approach
amygdala
cognitive appraisal theory of emotions
cognitive appraisal theory
Control Question Technique
display rules
emotion
emotional intelligence
evolutionary theory of emotions
facial expressions
facial feedback theory
galvanic skin response
happiness
happiness set point
James-Lange theory
lie detector (polygraph) tests
peripheral theory of emotions
reward/pleasure center
universal emotional expressions
Yerkes-Dodson law

The "PowerStudy 4.5 for Introduction to Psychology" CD-ROM includes a complete set of interactive learning activities for this module: quizzes, summary test, key terms, web site connections, critical thinking exercise, module outline, and more.

Outline

- *Introduction*

☐ You will see that psychologists do not agree on how emotion works. What is *your* understanding of emotion?

1. Emotional experience: **emotion** (Surfer Bethany)
   a. Interpret or appraise the stimulus
   b. Subjective experience or feeling
   c. Physiological responses
   d. Overt or observable behaviors
2. Staying happy (Lottery winners)

A. Peripheral Theories

1. Studying emotions
   a. **Peripheral theory of emotions**
   b. **Cognitive appraisal theory of emotions**
   3. **Affective neuroscience approach**

☐ In both of the two famous peripheral theories of emotion (below), the key is the sequence. Be sure to work it out for each theory. What do modern research findings say about each of the two theories?

2. **James-Lange theory**
   a. Sequence for emotional components
   b. Criticisms
3. **Facial feedback theory**
   a. Sequence for emotional components
   b. Criticisms

B. Cognitive Appraisal Theory

1. Thoughts and emotions
2. Schachter-Singer experiment
   a. Procedure
   b. Sequence for emotional components
3. **Cognitive appraisal theory**

☐ Can you work out the sequence for emotions in this theory?

   a. Thought then emotion
   b. Emotion without conscious thought

C. Affective Neuroscience Approach

1. Four qualities of emotion
   a. Felt and expressed in stereotypic facial expressions and accompanied by distinctive physiological responses
   b. Less controllable, may not respond to reason

c. Influence many cognitive processes

d. Hard-wired in the brain

e. Study of emotions: **affective neuroscience approach** (neural circuits)

2. Emotional detector and memorizer

a. Detecting stimuli

b. Emotional detector: **amygdala**

c. Emotional memorizer

3. Brain circuits for emotions (in fearful stimulus situation)

a. Slower circuit: visual cortex and amygdala involved

b. Faster circuit: without awareness or conscious thought

c. Prefrontal cortex: rational control over emotions

4. Fear and the amygdala

a. Social phobias

b. Why our anxieties often control our thoughts

D. Universal Facial Expressions

□ What does it mean when someone says, "I can read you like a book"?

1. Definition

a. **Universal emotional expressions** (Charles Darwin)

b. Number of expressions (seven)

2. Cross-cultural evidence

□ Why are some emotions universal? Why doesn't each culture have its own unique emotions?

3. Genetic evidence (smiling)

E. Functions of Emotions

1. Social signals: **facial expressions**

2. Survival, attention, and memory: **evolutionary theory of emotions**

a. Attention

b. Memory

3. Arousal and motivation: **Yerkes-Dodson law**

F. Happiness

1. Positive emotions

a. **Happiness**

b. **Reward/pleasure center**

2. Long-term happiness

a. **Adaptation level theory**

b. Genetic differences in happiness: **happiness set point**

G. Cultural Diversity: Emotions across Cultures

1. Showing emotions
   a. **Display rules**
   b. Cultural difference in display rules
2. Perceiving emotions
   a. Display rules about intensity
   b. Power of culture

H. Research Focus: Emotional Intelligence

1. What is **emotional intelligence**? (Daniel Goleman)
2. How important is emotional intelligence?
   a. Influence of emotions
   b. Preliminary findings about emotional intelligence
3. How do we perceive emotional expressions?
   a. Perceiving emotions in others
   b. Mirror neurons

I. Application: Lie Detection

1. What is the theory?
   a. **Lie detector (polygraph) tests**
   b. **Galvanic skin response**
2. What is a lie detector test?

☐ Have you ever taken a lie detector test? Would you do so willingly if asked?

   a. **Control Question Technique** (neutral questions and critical questions)
   b. Assessing galvanic skin responses
3. How accurate are lie detector tests?
   a. Innocent or faking
   b. Restrictions
   c. New tests

How English Works

Words in the Textbook

p. 359 **appraise** some stimulus = judge, estimate the effect

frantic swimming = very nervous, out of control

playing **poker** = card game

the emotional **high** = experience of pleasure

such an enormous **windfall** = unexpected good fortune

p. 364 innate or **genetically programmed** = built into the genes, not learned

p. 365 **written in stone** = as permanent as a sign chipped into a marble marker

p. 366 **holding down** two jobs = working

p. 369 continue to be **in development** = not yet finished, still being worked on

findings are considered **preliminary** = occurring before and leading up to something

being more **empathetic** = able to understand another person's feelings or problems

p. 370 Ames **pleaded** guilty = answered in court

espionage = spying

skin **conductance** = ability to transmit

They had a **warrant** and arrested him = court order, permission to arrest

the **prosecutor** offered = lawyer responsible for starting lawsuit

Floyd **jumped at the chance** = eagerly agreed to cooperate

several years **behind bars** = in prison

his lawyer **tracked down** the real robbers = found

p. 371 associated **neural** activity = relating to or located in the nervous system

Vocabulary: Making Connections

Earlier we looked at connecting sentences with a preposition and whom, but the word whom can only be used with people. We can use the same principle with all other things by using **which** as follows:

> Abraham Lincoln was born in a house. The house no longer exists.
>
> The house in which Abraham Lincoln was born no longer exists.

Notice how **in which** comes right after the house, the word that they had in common. Notice the order of the rest of the sentence. This is somewhat different from speaking. We would probably say:

> The house where Abraham Lincoln was born no longer exists.

This sentence is easier to make, but students have to practice the more formal **in which** sentence because this is the language of textbooks and professional work. Did you notice the following sentence in this textbook?

> Thousands of people train for months to run grueling 26-mile-long marathons, **in which** only the top two or three receive any prize money.

This is really two sentences. The first sentence is:

> Thousands of people train for months to run grueling 26-mile-long **marathons**.

The second one is:

> **In these marathons** only the top two or three receive any prize money.

Notice that the word **marathons** is repeated. We don't want to repeat the same word, so we replace the second **marathons** with **which**. We can join two sentences with any preposition and **which** in combinations like **with which, at which, for which, to which, from which,** and many others.

Now you try it. See if you can put together sentences in the same way. Read the following sentences, and then use the preposition + **which** form to make one sentence, as in the following:

> The strength surprised me. The child shook my hand with strength.
>
> The strength **with which the child shook my hand** surprised me.

Don't bother with commas here. You're joining these two sentences together and not interrupting the main idea. Try some now. If you're not sure of your answers, you can always check the Answers at the bottom of the page.

1) The temperature is zero degrees centigrade. Water freezes below this temperature.

   The __________.

2) The factory is closed for repairs. Miguel's father works at the factory.

   The __________.

3) The letter never arrived. Anya was waiting for the letter.

   The __________.

4) The company went out of business. We bought our computers from the company.

   The __________.

5) The land lies in an earthquake zone. The nuclear power plant is built on the land.

   The __________.

Now let's work backwards. See if you can take the sentence below and turn it into two sentences.

> These data come from less realistic laboratory settings that use simple tasks, such as identifying some object **about which** the subject — often a college student — has been told to lie.

Answers

1) The temperature **below which water freezes** is zero degrees centigrade.
2) The factory **at which Miguel's father works** is closed for repairs.
3) The letter **for which** Anya was waiting never arrived.
4) The company **from which we bought our computers** went out of business.
5) The land **on which the nuclear power plant is built** lies in an earthquake zone.

"These data come from less realistic laboratory settings that use simple tasks, such as identifying some object."
"The subject — often a college student — has been told to lie about it (identifying some object, a simple task)."

The Big Picture

Which statement below offers the best summary of the larger significance of this module?

A There is a reason why Plotnik and Kouyoumdjian talk about sharks, primitive peoples, and greed in this module: emotion almost seems to be left over from an earlier period in our evolution, something we would be better off without.

B Nothing is more basic to our common psychological experience than emotional processes, yet science has not yet agreed on how to explain emotion. In science, that which is closest to us is often the last to be understood.

C Emotions provide startling evidence for the cultural and environmental side of the nature-nurture debate. All over the world people treat emotions very differently, with little evidence of commonality.

D Emotions are not terribly important in human affairs, but they add a much-needed drama and spice to life. The best way to handle emotions is to not pay too much attention to them.

E Sheesh! This $&!# module really ticks me off! All those %!$# theories to learn! Why is emotion important, anyhow?

True-False

_____ 1. Psychologists now agree that the James-Lange theory provides the best explanation of how emotions work.

_____ 2. The amygdala monitors and evaluates whether stimuli have positive or negative emotional significance for our well-being and survival.

_____ 3. People all over the world recognize the expression of a few universal emotions.

_____ 4. The evolutionary theory of emotions says one function of emotions is to help us evaluate objects, people, and situations in terms of how good or bad they are for our well-being and survival.

_____ 5. Emotions are essential to our survival.

_____ 6. Human emotions, like the human appendix, are left over from our primitive past and are not really needed today.

_____ 7. The reason the joy of winning the lottery doesn't last is that taxes soon take most of the winnings.

_____ 8. Display rules are cultural expectations that govern the presentation and control of emotional expression in specific situations.

_____ 9. People all over the world rate happiness as the most intense emotion.

_____ 10. Lie detector tests determine whether a statement is true or false.

Flashcards 1

_____	1. affective neuroscience approach	a.	has four components: (1) appraisal (2) subjective feeling (3) physiological responses, and (4) overt behaviors
_____	2. cognitive appraisal theory of emotions	b.	based on theory that a person telling a lie feels guilt or fear and exhibits involuntary physical responses
_____	3. emotion	c.	feeling a positive emotion, being satisfied with one's life, and not experiencing negative emotions
_____	4. emotional intelligence	d.	emphasizes how your interpretations or appraisals of situations result in emotional feelings
_____	5. evolutionary theory of emotions	e.	emphasizes how physiological changes in the body give rise to emotional feelings
_____	6. facial feedback theory	f.	says sensations from movement of facial muscles and skin are interpreted by the brain as different feelings
_____	7. happiness	g.	a number of specific inherited facial patterns or expressions that signal specific feelings
_____	8. lie detector (polygraph) tests	h.	ability to perceive emotions accurately, to take feelings into account, and to understand and manage emotions
_____	9. peripheral theory of emotions	i.	studies the underlying neural bases of mood and emotion by focusing on the brain's neural circuits for emotion
_____	10. universal emotional expressions	j.	says we evolved basic emotional patterns to adapt and solve problems important for our survival

Flashcards 2

_____	1. adaptation level theory	a.	communicate state of your personal feelings and provide different social signals to others around you
_____	2. amygdala	b.	specific cultural norms that regulate how, when, and where we should express emotion (and how much)
_____	3. cognitive appraisal theory	c.	changes in sweating of fingers (or palms) that accompany emotional experiences and are independent of perspiration
_____	4. Control Question Technique	d.	says performance on a task is an interaction between the level of arousal and the difficulty of the task
_____	5. display rules	e.	monitors and evaluates whether stimuli have positive or negative emotional significance for our well-being
_____	6. facial expressions	f.	each individual has a genetically determined level for experiencing happiness, some more and some less
_____	7. galvanic skin response	g.	says we quickly become accustomed to receiving some good fortune (winning lottery), so the initial joy fades
_____	8. James-Lange theory	h.	says your interpretation of situation, object, or event can contribute to experiencing different feelings
_____	9. happiness set point	i.	says the brain interprets specific physiological changes as feelings or emotions (see bear – run – feel fear)
_____	10. Yerkes-Dodson law	j.	lie detection procedure that utilizes both neutral questions and critical (emotional) questions

Multiple Choice

_____ 1. Plotnik and Kouyoumdjian tell us about the surfer who was attacked by a shark to show that
   a. sometimes you can feel all the emotions at once
   b. emotions play a major role in our lives
   c. sometimes survival depends on having no emotions
   d. emotions (like the joy of surfing) can get in the way of common sense

_____ 2. Which one of the following is *not* a component of an emotion?
   a. appraising a stimulus
   b. physiological responses
   c. overt behaviors
   d. genetic variation

_____ 3. Plotnik and Kouyoumdjian suggest that instant lottery millionaires make a good case study of the
   a. emotional foundations of risk taking
   b. gender differences in joy over winning
   c. duration of happiness over time
   d. feelings of guilt that accompany winning while others are losing

_____ 4. The __________ theory says emotions result from specific physiological changes in the body
   a. shark bite
   b. James-Lange
   c. facial feedback
   d. cognitive appraisal

_____ 5. The __________ theory says emotions result from our brain's interpretation of muscle and skin movements that occur when we express an emotion
   a. Schacter-Singer
   b. James-Lange
   c. facial feedback
   d. cognitive appraisal

_____ 6. The __________ theory says that your interpretation of a situation, object, or event can contribute to, or result in, your experiencing different emotional states
   a. Plotnik-Kouyoumdjian
   b. James-Lange
   c. facial feedback
   d. cognitive appraisal

_____ 7. The most recent explanation of emotions is the
   a. affective neuroscience approach
   b. cognitive appraisal theory
   c. facial feedback theory
   d. James-Lange theory

_____ 8. Among the main functions of the amygdala are
   a. suppressing feelings of fear and covering over memories of fear
   b. maintaining calm and promoting a meditative state
   c. sensing feelings of hunger and maintaining a set weight
   d. detecting threats and storing memories with emotional content

_____ 9. The affective neuroscience approach to understanding fear studies all of the following *except* the
a. thalamus
b. visual cortex
c. amygdala
d. prefrontal cortex

_____ 10. Evidence for the universality of emotional expression comes from the fact that people all over the world
a. consider happiness to be the most intense emotion
b. follow the same rules about how to show emotions
c. recognize facial expressions of certain basic emotions
d. make up rules about how to show emotions

_____ 11. Which one of the following is *not* a universally recognized emotion?
a. indecision
b. happiness
c. surprise
d. anger

_____ 12. The fact that blind infants begin to smile around four to six weeks shows that
a. they are socially delayed, because sighted infants smile almost immediately
b. blind children can learn anything sighted children can
c. some facial expressions are biologically programmed
d. at least in the beginning, humans have a cheerful disposition

_____ 13. Which one of the following is *not* something emotions do for us?
a. help us attain well-being and survival
b. help us answer questions of fact
c. motivate and arouse us
d. help us send social signals

_____ 14. The relationship between emotional arousal and performance on a task is explained by the
a. Yerkes-Dodson law
b. James-Lange theory
c. Schacter-Singer law
d. Darwinian law of survival

_____ 15. At the most basic level, the feeling of happiness is best explained by the
a. realization that we possess more than others
b. speed with which we adapt to good fortune
c. facial muscles that produce smiles
d. reward/pleasure center in the brain

_____ 16. Adaptation level theory explains why people who win big in the lottery
a. don't come forward to claim their prizes right away
b. often spend lavishly until they are right back where they started
c. don't feel much happier than anyone else after a while
d. often report that winning permanently changed them from being discontented to happy

_____ 17. Can money buy happiness? Psychology suggests that the answer is
- a. yes, because once a person climbs above the poverty level worries tend to disappear
- b. no, because humans appear to have a genetically determined happiness set point
- c. yes, money raises us above the adaptation level
- d. no, but it sure finances the illusion

_____ 18. Cultural rules that govern emotional expression in specific situations are called
- a. display rules
- b. feelings guides
- c. emotion set points
- d. intensity rules

_____ 19. Cross-cultural research reveals that the most intense emotion is
- a. happiness
- b. disgust
- c. anger
- d. (it differs from culture to culture)

_____ 20. The new concept called emotional intelligence includes all of the following *except*
- a. excluding emotions when making crucial decisions
- b. perceiving emotions accurately
- c. taking feelings into account when reasoning
- d. managing emotions in oneself and others

_____ 21. Results from programs attempting to teach and improve emotional intelligence suggest that the concept may be
- a. the breakthrough in teaching that education has been waiting for
- b. confirmed by the many new tests developed to measure it
- c. the answer to the problem of test anxiety
- d. more hype than substance

_____ 22. Lie detector tests measure
- a. whether a statement is true or false
- b. how much physiological arousal the subject feels
- c. whether the subject is basically honest or dishonest
- d. how much character a person has

_____ 23. The purpose of the Control Question Technique is to
- a. eventually eliminate the need for trial by jury
- b. control for the effect of the polygraph
- c. eliminate the contaminating effect of the galvanic skin response
- d. compare responses to neutral questions and critical questions

_____ 24. In most courtrooms, lie detector test results are
- a. admissible, because they give scientifically derived evidence
- b. admissible, because the jury must hear any evidence available
- c. inadmissible, because of their potential for error
- d. inadmissible, because they would put lawyers out of work

_____ 25. [*For Trekkers only*] The subject matter of this module helps us understand why, in a perverse way, we find the character of __________ so fascinating

a. Spock
b. Uhura
c. Kirk
d. Scotty

Short Essay

1. Summarize the three different explanations through which psychology has tried to understand emotion.
2. Why are universal facial expressions of emotion recognized around the world?
3. What are the functions of emotions?
4. What are display rules for the expression of emotion and what do they tell us about emotion in general?
5. If you were accused of committing a crime, would you be willing to take a lie detector test?

For Psych Majors Only…

Emotion — Myths and Actualities: Which statements about emotion are true and which are false? Don't worry about your score, because these statements are more the foundation of a theory than a quiz. When you check the 'answers,' see if you can understand the theory (it was described in my module introduction).

_____ 1. Emotions can be dangerous.

_____ 2. Emotions have no constructive function.

_____ 3. Emotions, once evoked, remain in a kind of pressured storage until discharged.

_____ 4. Emotions, while in storage, become a source of damage to the person.

_____ 5. Discharging emotions must be done very carefully so as to cause the least amount of damage.

_____ 6. Emotions are vital aspects of human functioning.

_____ 7. Emotions are automatic subjective responses to internal and external events.

_____ 8. Emotions serve the vital function of informing us of qualities of internal and external events.

_____ 9. Emotions are fleeting and in their initial reactive form are impossible to store or accrue.

_____ 10. Because emotions are fleeting, their discharge is not mandatory and their expression is optional.

Answers to "Emotion — Myths and Actualities" Quiz

The first five items (all false) represent what Kenneth Isaacs calls *myths* about feelings, false beliefs that cause us to misunderstand emotion. The second five items (all true) represent what Isaacs sees as *actualities* of emotion, truths that could make us healthier and happier.

Answers for Module 16

The Big Picture (explanations provided for incorrect choices)

A Emotion is vital to human adaptation and functioning. We need emotion to live.
B Correct! You see the "big picture" for this Module.
C Just the opposite is true. Read the material on universal emotions.
D Just the opposite is true. Most psychologists agree that emotions provide vital clues to our inner life and motivation.
E It's just a joke!

True-False (explanations provided for False choices; page numbers given for all choices)

1	F	360	Psychologists do not agree on which theory of emotions is correct.
2	T	362	
3	T	364	
4	T	365	
5	T	365	
6	F	365	Emotion is crucial to human functioning and survival.
7	F	366	The joy doesn't last, because even winners get used to their new advantages.
8	T	367	
9	F	367	Different cultures vary in which emotion they see as most intense.
10	F	370	Lie detector tests measure physiological arousal, not lying.

Flashcards 1

1 i 2 d 3 a 4 h 5 j 6 f 7 c 8 b 9 e 10 g

Flashcards 2

1 g 2 e 3 h 4 j 5 b 6 a 7 c 8 i 9 f 10 d

Multiple Choice (explanations provided for incorrect choices)

1 a This statement is untrue.
b Correct! See page 359.
c Emotions are very important to survival.
d It's just a joke!

2 a Conscious experience is one of the three components of emotion.
b Physiological arousal is one of the three components of emotion.
c Overt behavior is one of the three components of emotion.
d Correct! See page 359.

3 a Risk taking is not the research interest here.
b Gender differences were not involved in happiness over winning.
c Correct! See page 359.
d Guilt feelings are not the research interest here.

4 a Stop worrying! There is no shark bite theory of emotions.
b Correct! See page 360.
c The facial feedback theory says emotions result from how our brain interprets movement of facial muscles.
d This theory says emotions result from appraising situations as having positive or negative impact on our lives.

5 a This famous experiment supports the cognitive appraisal theory.
b The James-Lange theory says emotions result from specific physiological changes in the body.
c Correct! See page 361.
d This theory says emotions result from appraising situations as having positive or negative impact on our lives.

6 a Plotnik and Kouyoumdjian are the authors of the psych textbook you are using.
b The James-Lange theory says emotions result from specific physiological changes in the body.
c The facial feedback theory says emotions result from how our brain interprets movement of facial muscles.
d Correct! See page 362.

7 *a* *Correct! See page 362.*
b The cognitive appraisal theory goes back to the Schacter-Singer experiment in 1962.
c The facial feedback theory is several decades old.
d The James-Lange theory dates back to the late 1800s.

8 a Just the opposite is true.
b Just the opposite is true.
c Hunger and eating are controlled by the hypothalamus, not the amygdala.
d *Correct! See page 362.*

9 a The thalamus is involved in gathering information about a threat.
b *Correct! See page 363.*
c The amygdala is involved in identifying and warning about a threat.
d The prefrontal cortex is involved in analyzing and remembering a threat.

10 a There are cultural variations in ranking the intensity of emotions.
b There are cultural variations in rules about showing emotions.
c *Correct! See page 364.*
d True, but this would not be evidence of the universality of emotions.

11 *a* *Correct! See page 364.*
b Happiness is one of the basic emotions.
c Surprise is one of the basic emotions.
d Fear is one of the basic emotions.

12 a Sighted infants also begin to smile at four to six weeks.
b Smiling is not learned, the potential to smile is built in.
c *Correct! See page 364.*
d Early smiling is more about social bonding than disposition.

13 a Emotions do help us adapt and survive.
b *Correct! See page 365.*
c Emotions do motivate and arouse us.
d Emotions do express social signals.

14 *a* *Correct! See page 365.*
b The James-Lange theory says body changes lead to emotional feelings.
c The Schacter-Singer experiment (not law) supports the cognitive appraisal theory of emotion.
d Darwin was the first to propose the existence of universal emotions.

15 a Shame on you! (OK, that's a small part of it, but it's not the main explanation for happiness.)
b Wouldn't that be an explanation for the decline of feelings of happiness?
c That's what the facial feedback theory implies, but facial muscles can't be more basic than brain functions.
d *Correct! See page 366.*

16 a Some do, some don't (they see their lawyers first).
b Most use their winnings wisely.
c *Correct! See page 366.*
d The point is that this rarely happens . . . but why not?

17 a Don't quit school, but people experience unhappiness at every income level.
b *Correct! See page 366.*
c This answer is a confusion of the meaning of the adaptation level theory.
d It's just a joke!

18 *a* *Correct! See page 367.*
b This is not a correct technical term in psychology.
c This is not a correct technical term in psychology.
d This is not a correct technical term in psychology.

19 a There are cultural variations in ranking the intensity of emotions.
b There are cultural variations in ranking the intensity of emotions.
c There are cultural variations in ranking the intensity of emotions.
d *Correct! See page 367.*

20 ***a*** *Correct! See page 369.*
b This is one of the components of the definition of emotional intelligence.
c This is one of the components of the definition of emotional intelligence.
d This is one of the components of the definition of emotional intelligence.

21 a Emotional intelligence relates to education, but is not a teaching method.
b There is not yet an established test to measure emotional intelligence.
c Test anxiety is not the main focus of the concept of emotional intelligence.
d *Correct! See page 369.*

22 a Lie detector tests do not actually measure truth or falsity.
b *Correct! See page 370.*
c Lie detector tests do not actually measure truth or falsity.
d Character is an intangible factor no machine could measure easily.

23 a What about the constitutional guarantee of trial by a jury of your peers?
b The polygraph is the lie detector machine.
c The galvanic skin response is what is measured and compared.
d *Correct! See page 371.*

24 a Because lie detector tests measure arousal rather than lying, they can be unreliable.
b Because lie detector tests measure arousal rather than lying, they can be unreliable.
c *Correct! See page 371.*
d It's just a joke!

25 ***a*** *Correct! See page 359.*
b Uhura shows the full range of emotional responses, but Spock exhibits little emotion.
c Kirk shows the full range of emotional responses, but Spock exhibits little emotion
d Scotty shows the full range of emotional responses, but Spock exhibits little emotion

Short Essay (sample answers)

1. Does emotion come from bodily changes, thoughts and evaluations, or brain processes? Peripheral theories say that changes in the body, like running or smiling, cause changes in emotion. The cognitive appraisal theory says that changes in thoughts or evaluation of situations cause changes in emotion. More recently, the affective neuroscience approach says that the brain's neural circuits, especially the amygdala, evaluate stimuli and produce or contribute to experiencing different emotional states. Bet on brain processes!

2. Seven facial expressions for emotion (anger, happiness, fear, surprise, disgust, sadness, and contempt) that are universally recognized across cultures. They probably evolved because they served adaptive and survival functions for our ancestors. All infants develop facial expressions in a predictable order, even blind infants who aren't copying adults. These universal facial expressions, present from infancy, suggest that emotion is natural, ever-present, and beneficial. We should welcome it and use it.

3. Emotions have three basic functions. First, through signals conveyed by facial expressions, emotions send powerful social signals about our feelings or needs. Second, the evolutionary theory of emotions says they help us adapt and survive by evaluating objects, people, and situations in terms of how good or bad they are for our well-being. Emotions also focus our attention and increase memory and recall. Third, emotions arouse and motivate many behaviors that prepare the body for some action.

4. We're learning in this textbook that culture has a powerful effect on psychology. Display rules are a good example. Although there are universal emotions and universal facial expressions that accompany them, each culture works out rules for how these emotions are displayed. American culture encourages public display of emotion, such as open-mouth laughing, but Japanese culture discourages showing much emotion in public, so the mouth is often covered when laughing in public. Emotion is universal; display is particular.

5. It is often suggested that if you "have nothing to hide" you should agree to take a lie-detector test to exonerate yourself. But lie-detector tests exonerated the spy Aldrich Ames, and researchers estimate that the polygraph is wrong anywhere from 25–75 percent of the time! The problem is that the polygraph measures galvanic skin responses (physiological changes), not "lies." Until lie detection methods are improved, perhaps with brain scans of neural activity, the courts will be right to not admit polygraph results.

Module 17

Infancy & Childhood

The Competent Child

One of the most striking changes in psychological thinking about child development in recent years has been the emerging view of the child as a competent person, right from the beginning. It had been thought that human infants were essentially helpless, completely dependent on the care of adults. Plotnik and Kouyoumdjian show how current research on newborns' abilities and better understanding of how children interact with adult caregivers has given us a fresh picture of childhood. We now see children as incredibly active, responsive people who spend much of their day "working" at building relationships and creating environments most conducive to growth. If the little rug rats could talk, they would probably even claim that *they* are in charge, not us.

The Importance of Childhood in Psychology

One of psychology's most important contributions to modern knowledge is the idea of childhood as a separate, special phase of human life, with processes of development crucial for the rest of life. That idea seems obvious today, but not long ago most people thought of children simply as small adults, not really different in any special way, or as happy innocents enjoying a carefree period of freedom before the onset of adult concerns.

Once psychology recognized the importance of childhood, every comprehensive theory had to attempt to explain it. Not surprisingly, most of the "big" theories in psychology are also theories of childhood. Sigmund Freud argued that in the first five years children struggle through a series of conflicts that essentially shape personality. Erik Erikson placed the most fundamental developmental tasks in the early years and showed how they affected all later growth. Jean Piaget claimed that mature thinking evolves just as obviously as the physical body, and illustrated the many ways in which children think differently than adults. Albert Bandura demonstrated that children learn even from the simple act of observing, and have a powerful tendency to imitate what they see around them. If you can master this module, with its heavy involvement of psychology's most famous names, you can congratulate yourself on appreciating the major theories of modern psychology.

Thinking about childhood inevitably leads to ideas about psychology in general. In order to explain what children are like, it is necessary to say what humans are like. In no time at all, we are back debating the nature-nurture question. One more thing — if we find a strong urge in children to be competent, doesn't that mean the need to be effective is a basic human drive?

Effective Student Tip 17

Overstudy!

My favorite myth about tests is the often-heard lament, "I studied too hard!" The idea seems to be that what you learn has only a fragile and temporary residence in your head, and studying too much disorganizes it or knocks it right back out again. A sadder myth is the belief so many students have that they are "no good at tests," when the truth is that, for whatever reasons, they have not yet *done* well. No less misguided is the teeth-clenching determination to "do better next time," with no idea of what specific steps to take to bring that about.

A closer look would reveal that each of these misguided students is making the same mistake: not studying hard enough, or effectively enough. When I am able to persuade students to read the assigned chapters three or four times (they thought once was enough), the results amaze them. Almost invariably, their test grades go from "D" or "C" to "B" or "A." Why? Because with more study, and better study, they are really mastering the material.

Determine how much studying you think will be enough for the next test. Then do more. Lots more. The single best way to improve your test scores is to overstudy the material.

Your response…

Have you ever studied much harder for a test than seemed necessary? What happened?

Learning Objectives

1. Understand infancy and childhood as closely related periods in a sequence of development that leads to adolescence and adulthood.
2. Appreciate the crucial importance of the nature-nurture question in psychology and social science through investigation of genetic and environmental influences on infancy and childhood.
3. Learn the basic biology of prenatal influences, the prenatal period, newborn's abilities, and the principles of sensory and motor development.
4. Understand emotional development in infancy and childhood through the psychology of temperament, emotions, and attachment.
5. Learn the classic theories of cognitive and social development: Piaget's cognitive development, Freud's psychosexual stages, Erikson's psychosocial stages, and Bandura's social cognitive theory.
6. Consider your position on the origin, meaning, and significance of gender differences and gender roles.
7. Explore the problem of child abuse — its causes, treatment, and prevention.

Key Terms

The inclusion of four major psychological theories in this module brings in many key terms. Group the terms by the famous psychologists who used them to build their theories.

accommodation
amniocentesis
anal stage
assimilation
attachment
cephalocaudal principle
child abuse and neglect
cognitive development
cognitive developmental theory
conception (fertilization)
concrete operations stage
conservation
cross-sectional method
developmental norms
developmental psychologists
Down syndrome
egocentric thinking
embryonic stage
emotional development
evolutionary theory
fetal alcohol syndrome (FAS)
fetal stage
formal operations stage
gender identity
gender roles
gender schemas
genital stage
germinal stage
inhibited/fearful children
insecure attachment
latency stage
longitudinal method
maturation
motor development
nature-nurture question
object permanence
oral stage
ovulation
phallic stage
Piaget's cognitive stages
placenta
prenatal period
preoperational stage
principle of bidirectionality
prodigy
proximodistal principle
psychosexual stages
psychosocial stages
reactive attachment disorder
resiliency
secure attachment
sensorimotor stage
separation anxiety
social cognitive theory
social development
social role theory
temperament
teratogen
visual cliff
vulnerability

Outline

- *Introduction*

  ☐ The nature-nurture question may be the most fundamental issue in the social sciences. It comes up again and again in psychology. Do you understand the basic issues?

  1. **Reactive attachment disorder** (Alex, an adopted Romanian child)
  2. **Nature-nurture question**
  3. **Developmental psychologists**

A. *Prenatal Influences*

1. Nature and nurture
   a. **Prodigy**
   b. Nature-nurture interaction
2. Genetic and environmental factors
   a. Parents, daughters, and son
   b. Interaction
3. **Prenatal period**: three stages
   a. **Germinal stage**
      (1) **Ovulation**
      (2) **Conception (fertilization)**
   b. **Embryonic stage**
   c. **Fetal stage**
      (1) Placenta and teratogens
         (a) **Placenta**
         (b) **Teratogen**
      (2) Birth defects and amniocentesis
         (a) **Amniocentesis**
         (b) **Down syndrome**
4. Drugs and prenatal development
   a. Drug use and exposure to chemicals
      (1) Cocaine plus other drugs
      (2) Smoking and nicotine
      (3) Lead
      (4) Air pollutants
   b. Alcohol
      (1) Heavy drinking: **fetal alcohol syndrome (FAS)**
      (2) Moderate drinking: fetal alcohol effects (FAE)

B. Newborn's Abilities

1. Genetic developmental program
    a. Genetic program
    b. Brain growth
2. Sensory development
    a. Faces
    b. Hearing
    c. Touch
    d. Smell and taste
    e. Depth perception: **visual cliff**
3. **Motor development**
    a. **Proximodistal principle**
    b. **Cephalocaudal principle**
    c. **Maturation**
    d. **Developmental norms**
    e. Neural connections: interaction of genetic program and environmental stimulation

C. Emotional Development

1. Definition: **emotional development**
2. **Temperament** and emotions
    a. Study of infant temperament (Thomas and Chess)
        (1) Easy babies (40%)
        (2) Slow-to-warm-up babies (15%)
        (3) Difficult babies (10%)
        (4) No-single-category babies (35%)
    b. Genetic influence and environmental influence
3. **Attachment** (John Bowlby)
    a. How does attachment occur? **separation anxiety** (Mary Ainsworth)
    b. Are there different kinds of attachment?
        (1) **Secure attachment**
        (2) **Insecure attachment**
    c. What are the effects of attachment?

D. Research Focus: Temperament

1. Are some infants born fearful?
    a. **Longitudinal method**: disadvantages and advantages
    b. **Cross-sectional method**: advantage and disadvantage

2. Research methods for studying developmental changes (Jerome Kagan)
   a. Procedure: **inhibited/fearful children**
   b. Results
      (1) How many were fearful/inhibited?
      (2) How many changed temperaments?
      (3) What happens in the brain?
   c. Conclusions: how to help fearful children?

E. Cognitive Development

☐ When you're with young children, does their thinking seem like yours, except less developed, or does it seem quite different from adult thought?

1. Piaget's theory: **cognitive development**
   a. **Assimilation**
   b. **Accommodation**
2. **Piaget's cognitive stages**
   a. **Sensorimotor stage**
      (1) Hidden objects
      (2) **Object permanence**
   b. **Preoperational stage**
      (1) Symbols
      (2) **Conservation**
      (3) **Egocentric thinking**
   c. **Concrete operations stage**
      (1) Conservation
      (2) Classification
      (3) New abilities
   d. **Formal operations stage**
      (1) Adult thinking and reasoning
      (2) Abstract ideas and hypothetical constructs
      (3) Return of egocentric thinking
         (a) Imaginary audience
         (b) Personal fable
   e. Piaget's key ideas (about children and cognitive development)
      (1) Gradually develop reasoning through assimilation and accommodation
      (2) Naturally curious, intrinsically motivated to explore, develop cognitive skills
      (3) Acquire different kinds of thinking and reasoning abilities through different stages
3. Evaluation of Piaget's theory
   a. Impact and criticisms
      (1) Impact of Piaget's theory

(2) Criticisms

(3) Current status

b. New information

(1) Genetic factors

(2) Brain development

F. Social Development

1. **Social development**
2. Freud's **psychosexual stages** (and potential conflicts)

☐ The heart of Sigmund Freud's theory is the sexual conflict at each stage. Do you buy his descriptions?

a. **Oral stage**

b. **Anal stage**

c. **Phallic stage**

d. **Latency stage**

e. **Genital stage**

3. Erikson's **psychosocial stages** (and potential problems) [Stages 1–5 here and 6–8 in Module 18.]

☐ The heart of Erik Erikson's theory is the potential social problem at each stage. Do his ideas make sense?

a. Stage 1: trust versus mistrust

b. Stage 2: autonomy versus shame and doubt

c. Stage 3: initiative versus guilt

d. Stage 4: industry versus inferiority

e. Stage 5: identity versus role confusion

f. Evaluation of Erikson's and Freud's theories

4. Bandura's **social cognitive theory**

☐ Albert Bandura, originally a behaviorist, wanted to bring thinking into learning (see Module 10). Can you see why his theory is called both "social" and "cognitive"?

5. Resiliency

a. **Vulnerability**

b. **Resiliency**

6. Gender differences

a. Social development

(1) **Gender identity**

(2) **Gender roles**

b. **Social role theory**

c. **Cognitive developmental theory** and **gender schemas**

7. Differences in gender traits

a. Social role theory: outside pressures

b. Cognitive developmental theory: inside pressures

8. Male and female differences

☐ What position do you take in the debate over gender differences?

   a. Career choices

   b. Aggression

   c. Different brains

9. Review: the Big Picture

☐ Here's another of those excellent Plotnik and Kouyoumdjian summaries: worth studying carefully.

   a. Newborn's abilities

   b. Motor development

   c. Emotional development

   d. Cognitive development

   e. Social development

   f. Importance of childhood

G. Cultural Diversity: Gender Roles

1. Identifying gender roles
2. Gender roles across cultures
3. Two answers
   a. **Social role theory**
   b. **Evolutionary theory**

H. Application: Child Abuse

1. Teri Hatcher's terrible secret
2. Kinds of abuse: **child abuse and neglect**
3. What problems do abused children have?
4. Who abuses children? **principle of bidirectionality**
5. How are abusive parents helped?

A Day in the Nursery

You know that little brat who gets in the way and makes it difficult for you to study? Instead of muttering "rug rat" under your breath, think "research subject" instead! The theories you are studying are somewhat abstract when presented in a textbook, but you've got the real article right in front of you. Put on your mental lab coat and look at this child coolly and dispassionately (i.e., scientifically). Does the behavior you observe support or contradict the theories you are studying? All right! Now psychology is getting real.

P.S. Wouldn't this make a good topic for a psych paper? Just sayin'....

How English Works

Words in the Textbook

p. 377 courts have **sided with** biological parents = agree with

they have **a good bond** in the home = a strong relationship

the **age-old** question = long-time

p. 378 He **walks on the waves** = he makes miracles

p. 379 the ovum is **sloughed off** = separated, removed

when most **miscarriages** occur = death of fetus inside mother

p. 381 short **stature** = height

gets a **pat on the backside** = slap from the doctor at birth to stimulate breathing

ready **to take on the world** = for the future

p. 382 very **keen** hearing = good, well-developed

p. 383 they can control their **trunks** = bodies (from shoulders to hips)

p. 387 **fretting** = worrying behavior

p. 388 an infant is soon ready to **creep** = move on the floor

p. 390 computer **hackers** = users who break into private information

if **going steady** is a good idea = dating only one person exclusively

p. 392 being very neat, **stingy** = unwilling to share or spend money

p. 396 not **mutually exclusive** = unable to exist together

armed forces = soldiers, army

society rewards boys for **acting out** = expressing their impulses

p. 400 all the **trappings** of being perfect = outward signs

a **pillar** of the Denver community = leader

ESL Tip: Non-Count Nouns

You have probably discovered that some nouns in English are **non-count**, which means that we cannot count them directly. Many ESL students are surprised that we cannot count the following words in English because these words can be counted in their languages.

research / advice / equipment / information / knowledge / evidence

We can *never* use "a" or "an" with any of these words.

Also, we can *never* add an "s" to make a plural with any of the words above.

But isn't there some way to count research? Yes, but we need to use another word: It's possible to say **a piece of research** or **a research project**. We can also add other words: the professor assigned **some research** or **a lot of research** or **too much research** or **several pieces of research** or **three research projects**.

If you think that you are hearing people say "researches," you are right. But they are not counting their research. Instead, they are reporting an action: What does she do? <u>She researches</u> the influence of alcohol on fetal development.

To practice these non-count nouns, read the following sentences. Choose the correct form of the underlined word and circle it. The answers provide possible replacement nouns that can be counted.

Grandpa enjoys giving advice / advices to young people.

Maryam is spending hours in the library on her research / researches.

Willard stopped at the Tourist Office to get some information / informations.

The failed business sold all its equipment / equipments to pay its bills.

The team of lawyers presented surprising evidence / evidences about the crime.

A lot of knowledge / knowledges disappeared when the library burned down.

Vocabulary: Irregular Plurals

Check out this sentence:

In most cases, only a single **ovum** is released during ovulation, but sometimes two **ova** are released.

Notice the ending of the word **ovum** is quite different in the plural form **ova**. Here are some other words you may have encountered recently with unusual plural forms

one **crisis**, two **crises**

one **criterion**, several **criteria**

Try to test yourself with the correct form below and then check the answers:

The president has had to solve many public **cris**____ , but the problem of global warming may be the most difficult **cris**____.

Cost and convenience are two of the **criteri**____ used by most students when they are choosing a college, yet a more important **criteri**____ should be the program of studies.

One of the world's most expensive foods is caviar, which is actually the **ov**____ from a large fish called a sturgeon. Each **ov**____ is so small that a spoon can hold 50 or more.

Answers

Grandpa enjoys giving advice to young people. (You could say "recommendations" or "suggestions.")

Maryam is spending hours in the library on her research. (You could say "projects.")

Willard stopped at the Tourist Office to get some information. (You could say "facts.")

The failed business sold all its equipment to pay its bills. (You could say "machines.")

The team of lawyers presented surprising evidence about the crime. (You could say "facts.")

A lot of knowledge disappeared when the library burned down. (You could say "facts" or "ideas.")

The president has had to solve many public **crises** , but the problem of global warming may be the most difficult **crisis.**

Cost and convenience are two of the **criteria** used by most students when they are choosing a college, yet a more important **criterion** should be the program of studies.

One of the world's most expensive foods is caviar, which is actually the **ova** from a large fish called a sturgeon. Each **ovum** is so small that a spoon can hold 50 or more.

The Big Picture

Which statement below offers the best summary of the larger significance of this module?

A It is in areas like infancy and childhood that psychology risks losing the respect of the general public. If we present theories as outrageous as Freud's and as strange as Piaget's, how can we expect to be taken seriously?

B The fact that this module ends with a section on child abuse is sad testimony to the state of childhood today. If you read it carefully, you realize that this module is mostly about the injuries and misfortunes suffered by children.

C In the ongoing argument over nature and nurture, the pendulum is clearly swinging toward nurture. All the major theories (Freud, Erikson, Piaget) say that our personalities are shaped mainly by our environment.

D The processes of development that take place during infancy and childhood reveal the complex and subtle interaction of the forces of nature and nurture, suggesting that this interplay probably continues throughout life.

E This theory of Freud's about an oral stage is really a crock! Say, get me another brewski, would you?

True-False

_____ 1. The nature-nurture question asks how much development owes to inheritance and how much to learning and experience.

_____ 2. The "visual cliff" is the distance beyond which infants cannot see clearly.

_____ 3. The cephalocaudal principle of motor development says that the parts closer to the head develop before the parts closer to the feet.

_____ 4. The concept of maturation is closer to "nurture" than to "nature."

_____ 5. Attachment is the close emotional bond that develops between infant and parent.

_____ 6. In Piaget's first stage of cognitive development, the child relates sensory experiences to motor actions.

_____ 7. When Piaget used the word "operations," he meant physical behaviors such as walking and talking that accomplish important tasks for the child.

_____ 8. In Erikson's scheme, each stage of life contains a "test" that, if failed, prevents you from entering the next stage.

_____ 9. Studies of "resilient" children tend to support Erikson's idea that later positive experiences can compensate for early traumas.

_____ 10. Ninety percent of abusive parents were themselves abused children.

Flashcards 1

_____	1. anal stage	a. Freud's 1st stage; age 0-18 months; infant's pleasure seeking is centered on the mouth
_____	2. concrete operations stage	b. Freud's 2nd stage, age 1–3 years; infant's pleasure seeking centered on anus and its functions of elimination
_____	3. formal operations stage	c. Freud's 3rd stage, age 3–6 years; child's pleasure seeking is centered on the genitals
_____	4. genital stage	d. Piaget's 4th stage, from age 12; adolescents develop ability to think about and solve abstract problems
_____	5. latency stage	e. Piaget's 2nd stage, age 2–7 years; children learn to use symbols like words to think about things not present
_____	6. nature-nurture question	f. Piaget's 3rd stage, age 7–11 years; children perform logical mental operations on physically present objects
_____	7. oral stage	g. Freud's 4th stage, age 6–puberty; child represses sexual thoughts and engages in nonsexual activities
_____	8. phallic stage	h. Freud's 5th stage; after puberty; individual has renewed sexual desires fulfilled through relationships
_____	9. preoperational stage	i. asks how much genetic factors and environmental factors each contribute to a person's development
_____	10. sensorimotor stage	j. Piaget's 1st stage, birth–age 2 years; infant interacts with environment by sensory experience and motor action

Flashcards 2

_____	1. attachment	a. any environmental agent (such as a disease, drug, or chemical) that can harm a developing fetus
_____	2. cephalocaudal principle	b. personality, family, and other factors that compensate for increased life stresses to prevent expected problems
_____	3. gender schemas	c. states that parts closer to center of infant's body develop before parts farther away
_____	4. maturation	d. an infant's distress (loud protests, crying, and agitation) whenever the infant's parents temporarily leave
_____	5. proximodistal principle	e. a close fundamental emotional bond that develops between the infant and a parent or caregiver
_____	6. resiliency	f. developmental changes that are genetically or biologically programmed rather than learned
_____	7. separation anxiety	g. states that parts of the body closer to the infant's head develop before parts closer to the feet
_____	8. temperament	h. stable behavioral and emotional reactions that appear early and are influenced largely by genetics
_____	9. teratogen	i. a glass tabletop with checkerboard and clear glass surfaces to create the illusion of a drop to the floor
_____	10. visual cliff	j. sets of information and rules organized around how either a male or a female should think and behave

Multiple Choice

_____ 1. Plotnik and Kouyoumdjian begin the module with the story of Alex, who spent the first three years of his life in a bleak Romanian orphanage, to illustrate the
  a. sad truth that adoptive parents cannot love children as much as birth parents
  b. long-term effects of physical abuse in childhood
  c. devastating effects of years of malnutrition
  d. nature-nurture question in the actual life of a child

_____ 2. Applying the nature-nurture question to Yehudi Menuhin, the child violin prodigy, we would ask whether his special abilities
  a. are a gift of God or an accident of nature
  b. are inborn or the product of learning and experience
  c. will stay with him or fade as he gets older
  d. are genuine or the result of good publicity

_____ 3. The briefest period of prenatal development is the
  a. germinal stage
  b. embryonic stage
  c. fetal stage
  d. baby-making stage (just kidding!)

_____ 4. The medical test called __________ is performed to indicate genetic problems like __________
  a. teratogen identification / lead poisoning
  b. placentosis / fetal alcohol syndrome (FAS)
  c. fetal stage assessment / brain damage
  d. amniocentesis / Down syndrome

_____ 5. If you believe what the textbook says about teratogens, you would tell pregnant women to
  a. watch their weight gain very carefully
  b. get plenty of rest — even more as they approach delivery
  c. avoid alcohol entirely
  d. avoid becoming overly stressed

_____ 6. Infants first use their more developed arms, and then their fingers, whose control develops later — this is the
  a. cephalocaudal principle
  b. proximodistal principle
  c. principle of maturation
  d. principle of normal development

_____ 7. The term "temperament" refers to
  a. contrary behavior that is typical of the "terrible twos"
  b. emotional characteristics that are largely influenced by environmental factors
  c. relatively stable individual differences in mood and emotional behavior
  d. the formal name in psychology for childhood temper tantrums

_____ 8. A longitudinal study of infant temperament found that
  a. infants develop a distinct temperament in the first two to three months
  b. infants' temperaments tend to mirror their parents' temperaments
  c. temperament is determined by the emotional state of the mother during pregnancy
  d. temperament fluctuates widely during infancy

_____ 9. The research on infant temperament tends to support the
   a. prenatal influences theory
   b. nature side of the nature-nurture question
   c. concept of gradual maturation
   d. nurture position in child development

_____ 10. Research suggests that the fearful or inhibited temperament is caused by
   a. a more active amygdala in the brain
   b. overprotective parental care
   c. nutritional deficiencies in infancy
   d. an unacceptably high number of frightening experiences during infancy

_____ 11. For Jean Piaget, children deal with and adjust to the world through twin processes he called
   a. conservation and revisionism
   b. motor learning and cognitive learning
   c. egocentric thinking and magical thinking
   d. assimilation and accommodation

_____ 12. The essence of Piaget's theory of cognitive development is that
   a. through thousands and thousands of mistakes, the child gradually builds a factual picture of the world
   b. the child's picture of the world is slowly but steadily shaped by the accumulation of learning experiences
   c. each stage is characterized by a distinctly different way of understanding the world
   d. the child's mind is the same as that of an adult — there just isn't as much information in it

_____ 13. The concept of object permanence develops during the _________ stage
   a. sensorimotor
   b. preoperational
   c. concrete operations
   d. formal operations

_____ 14. Watching juice poured from a short, wide glass into a tall, narrow glass, the child cries, "I want (the tall) glass!" thus illustrating the problem of
   a. object permanence
   b. egocentric thinking
   c. classification
   d. conservation

_____ 15. Piaget said adult thinking is finally achieved in the _________ stage
   a. preoperational
   b. sensorimotor
   c. formal operations
   d. concrete operations

_____ 16. If there is a single idea that Erik Erikson's theory clearly modifies, it is
   a. Freud's emphasis on the critical importance of the first five years
   b. the idea that childhood development takes place in stages
   c. Piaget's emphasis on how children see the world
   d. Bandura's idea that children learn through social interaction

_____ 17. All of the following are positive outcomes in Erikson's first four stages, but which list is in the correct chronological order?
a. trust – autonomy – industry – initiative
b. trust – initiative – industry – autonomy
c. trust – autonomy – initiative – industry
d. autonomy – initiative – industry – trust

_____ 18. Perhaps the most attractive aspect of Erikson's theory is that he sees development as
a. packed into the formative years, so a happy child almost automatically becomes a happy adult
b. biologically predetermined in a positive direction, so only extreme trauma results in negative personality traits
c. arising from a foundation of essential human goodness and positiveness
d. continuing throughout life, with many opportunities for reworking and rebuilding personality traits

_____ 19. Albert Bandura's social cognitive theory emphasizes the importance of
a. thinking about the social interaction going on around you
b. extrinsic motivation over intrinsic motivation
c. learning through observation
d. performing observable behaviors and receiving external rewards

_____ 20. Which one of the following is *not* an essential ingredient of resiliency?
a. a positive temperament
b. parents free from mental and financial problems
c. a substitute caregiver
d. social support from peers

_____ 21. When do you know whether you're a girl or a boy? The answer is
a. between the ages of five and seven
b. between the ages of two and three
c. when you first observe other kids (as in bathing) and notice the obvious anatomical differences
d. as soon as you learn what girls do and what boys do

_____ 22. New research suggests that girls and women may develop traits of being concerned, sensitive, and nurturing because
a. as victims of discrimination, they know hurt and suffering intimately
b. generations of women have found that sticking together is a good strategy
c. their brains are wired for processing, coding, and remembering emotional experiences
d. their smaller size and lesser strength means they have to rely on other abilities

_____ 23. Why are gender roles similar across cultures? Social role theory points to __________, while evolutionary theory emphasizes __________
a. women's natural friendliness / men's natural shyness
b. developing from different divisions of labor / continuations of early survival mechanisms
c. differences in size and strength / differences in nurturance and sociability
d. competition over access to mates / assigning different work to males and females

_____ 24. Do children who suffer abuse grow up to be child abusers themselves?
a. about 30 percent do, but there are compensatory factors that can prevent this from happening
b. a few do, but for reasons other than the abuse they suffered as children
c. about 85 percent do, which means we can identify the future abusers
d. almost none do — the abuse–abuser link is a popular myth

_____ 25. Treatment for child abuse involves at least two goals:
a. arresting the abusing parent and removing the child from the home
b. placing the child in a temporary foster home and enrolling the parent in counseling
c. teaching the parent not to hit so hard and telling the child to "toughen up"
d. overcoming the parent's personal problems and changing parent–child interactions

Short Essay

1. Describe the two sides of the nature-nurture question, and explain why this debate is so important in psychology and social science.
2. What is attachment and how is it crucial to emotional development in infancy and childhood?
3. Summarize Piaget's four stages of cognitive development.
4. How are Freud's and Erikson's theories of development similar and how do they differ?
5. What is your answer to the question of differences in gender traits and gender roles, and the social significance of such differences?

The "PowerStudy 4.5 for Introduction to Psychology" CD-ROM for this module is a "Super Module." In addition to the regular PowerStudy features (quizzes, summary test, key terms, web site connections, critical thinking exercise, module outline, and more), Super Modules also include self-paced, step-by-step multimedia presentations with animations and narration.

I hope you'll write to me — not only about possible errors you found, but also about anything in my Study Guide you would like to discuss. <profenos@mac.com>

Answers for Module 17

The Big Picture (explanations provided for incorrect choices)

A At very least, theories like Freud's and Piaget's provoke us to think about human behavior in new ways.
B The module also offers many ideas about the resiliency and strengths of childhood.
C The pendulum is swinging back toward the nature. The theories cited place more emphasis on nature than nurture.
D Correct! You see the "big picture" for this Module.
E It's just a joke!

True-False (explanations provided for False choices; page numbers given for all choices)

1	T	377	
2	F	382	The visual cliff is an experimental device to test depth perception.
3	T	383	
4	F	383	Maturation refers to changes that are genetically or biologically programmed — that's "nature."
5	T	385	
6	T	389	
7	F	390	For Piaget, "operations" are mental manipulations of information.
8	F	393	It's not pass or fail; each stage presents a problem each person solves in a slightly different way.
9	T	394	
10	F	401	Some abused children (about 30 percent) grow up to become abusive parents, but most do not.

Flashcards 1

1 b	2 f	3 d	4 h	5 g	6 i	7 a	8 c	9 e	10 j

Flashcards 2

1 e	2 g	3 j	4 f	5 c	6 b	7 d	8 h	9 a	10 i

Multiple Choice (explanations provided for incorrect choices)

1 a Alex was fully loved by his adoptive American parents.
b Alex was not physically abused.
c Alex was adequately fed in the orphanage.
d Correct! See page 377.

2 a This is a misstatement of the nature-nurture question.
b Correct! See page 378.
c This is a misstatement of the nature-nurture question.
d This is a misstatement of the nature-nurture question.

3 *a Correct! See page 379.*
b The embryonic period spans the two to eight weeks after conception.
c The fetal period covers most of the nine months after conception.
d It's just a [bad] joke!

4 a Not a correct term / not a genetic problem.
b Not a correct term / not a genetic problem.
c Not a correct term / not a genetic problem.
d Correct! See page 380.

5 a Teratogens do not refer to weight.
b Teratogens do not refer to rest.
c Correct! See page 380.
d Teratogens do not refer to stress.

6 a The cephalocaudal principle says parts of the body closer to the head develop before parts closer to the feet.
b Correct! See page 383.
c Maturation refers to the pattern according to which development unfolds.
d This is not a correct technical term in developmental psychology.

7 a The term is much broader than the narrow meaning of "temper."
b Temperament is thought to be mainly influenced by genetic factors.
c *Correct! See page 384.*
d The term is much broader than the narrow meaning of "temper tantrums."

8 *a* *Correct! See page 384.*
b Each individual comes into the world with a unique temperament.
c Temperament is probably genetically influenced.
d Temperament is relatively constant.

9 a This is not a correct technical term in developmental psychology.
b *Correct! See page 384.*
c Temperament appears to be present at birth.
d Nurture refers to the influence of experience and the environment.

10 *a* *Correct! See page 387.*
b Research does not suggest overprotection as the cause.
c Research does not suggest nutritional deficiencies as the cause.
d Research does not suggest frightening experiences as the cause.

11 a Although they reflect some of Piaget's thinking, these are not his overall processes.
b Although they reflect some of Piaget's thinking, these are not his overall processes.
c Although they reflect some of Piaget's thinking, these are not his overall processes.
d *Correct! See page 388.*

12 a Piaget's theory is not based on trial and error learning.
b This would be truer of a behavioral approach to learning.
c *Correct! See page 388.*
d Piaget believed that children's and adults' minds are qualitatively different.

13 *a* *Correct! See page 389.*
b Remember that object permanence is the first cognitive achievement.
c Remember that object permanence is the first cognitive achievement.
d Remember that object permanence is the first cognitive achievement.

14 a Object permanence means understanding that objects still exist even if they can no longer be seen, etc.
b Egocentric thinking refers to seeing the world only from your own viewpoint.
c Classification refers to the ability to organize objects mentally according to some dimension.
d *Correct! See page 389.*

15 a This is the second stage.
b This is the first stage.
c *Correct! See page 390.*
d This is the third stage.

16 *a* *Correct! See page 393.*
b Erikson's theory is a stage theory.
c Erikson's theory doesn't emphasize cognitive development, but doesn't reject the importance of mental life.
d Erikson also emphasizes social interaction.

17 a This is almost right. Review *industry* and *initiative*.
b This is almost right. Review the importance of *autonomy*.
c *Correct! See page 393.*
d Is it reasonable that an infant would develop a sense of autonomy first?

18 a Erikson assumes that development continues throughout the life span.
b Erikson notes that many difficulties, large and small, occur in life.
c Erikson does not assume that humans are basically good.
d *Correct! See page 393.*

19 a No doubt important, but not what Bandura emphasized.
b Just the opposite is true.
c *Correct! See page 394.*
d Just the opposite is true.

20 a This is one of the three factors that characterize resilient children.
b Correct! See page 394.
c This is one of the three factors that characterize resilient children.
d This is one of the three factors that characterize resilient children.

21 a What an innocent and sweet view of childhood you have!
b Correct! See page 395.
c Knowledge of anatomical differences is not the same as understanding gender identity and gender roles.
d Gender roles are learned, but gender identity is a subjective experience and feeling of being female or male.

22 a Possible, but the new research comes from brain scans.
b Possible, but the new research comes from brain scans.
c Correct! See page 396.
d Possible, but the new research comes from brain scans.

23 a The distinction is neither true nor the basis of the differences in theories.
b Correct! See page 399.
c Just the opposite is true.
d Just the opposite is true.

24 *a Correct! See page 401.*
b Sadly, there is a strong link between being abused and abusing.
c It is nowhere near this automatic.
d Unfortunately, it is not a myth.

25 a These are extreme measures used in cases of imminent danger to the child.
b Such a recommendation would be costly and extreme.
c Such a recommendation would accept the idea that abuse would continue.
d Correct! See page 401.

Short Essay (sample answers)

1. The nature-nurture question asks how much genetic factors (nature) and environmental factors (nurture) contribute to a person's biological, emotional, cognitive, personal, and social development. This question is one of the most fundamental issues in understanding others and ourselves. It is involved in almost every problem in psychology, from intelligence to temperament to gender differences. As we saw in the story of Alex, from a Romanian orphanage, the nature-nurture question is often at the heart of real-life situations.

2. Attachment is a close, fundamental emotional bond that develops between an infant and his or her parents or caregiver. John Bowlby believed that attachment behavior evolved due to its adaptive value in our species. Mary Ainsworth discovered separation anxiety (when parents temporarily leave) and two kinds of attachment, secure (parents as a home base for exploration) and insecure (ambivalence or resistance toward parents). Secure attachment is the foundation for successful adult relationships.

3. Jean Piaget said that by means of the interaction of assimilation and accommodation children advance through four stages of cognitive development. (1) Sensorimotor: relate their sensory experiences to their motor actions, attain object permanence. (2) Preoperational: learn to use symbols to think about things that are not present, attain conservation. (3) Concrete operations: perform a number of logical mental operations on concrete objects. (4) Formal operations: think about and solve abstract problems in a logical manner.

4. Psychoanalysts Sigmund Freud and Erik Erikson saw development as the progression through a series of stages, each with a special conflict or problem. For Freud, each of five "psychosexual" stages, completed by age five, presented a sexual conflict to resolve. For Erikson, each of eight "psychosocial" stages, from birth to death, presented a social need to satisfy. These influential personality theories are complete philosophies of human nature, but are more descriptive than explanatory, and difficult to verify or test experimentally.

5. Psychology has always been fascinated (obsessed?) with gender differences, which have been noted again and again, most recently in differing brain activity. Children are not all alike, but are the differences sexual, or temperamental? Where there are apparent differences, such as in career choice or aggression, are the differences better explained by social role theory or evolutionary theory? Your answer should consider these factors, but should also take account of your own accumulating experience in the world of men and women.

Module 18

Adolescence & Adulthood

All about You

If there's one module in the textbook that clearly is about *you*, this is it. If you're in college, you've just been an adolescent and now you're an adult. Therefore, it will be the hardest module to learn.

Say what?

When studying something like the brain or memory or language, even though it's all right on top of our shoulders, it seems removed from our everyday knowledge. In a way, this makes it easier to objectify, and hence to learn.

The facts and theories of adolescence and adulthood, on the other hand, are so close to our everyday experience that it is difficult to obtain sufficient distance to allow getting a handle on them. As you read, you say "yes…," "yes…," yes…," but later it's hard to remember what ought to stand out as important to learn.

I suggest a three-step process in studying this material. First, give yourself credit for what you have learned from your own experience. Don't expect every idea in the module to be new to you. Second, recognize that many of the new ideas discussed in the module may be interesting, but have not yet been accepted as permanent contributions to knowledge. Find out from your professor what to master. Third, have one simple question in mind as you read and study: is this idea helpful? In other words, does what you are reading seem true about yourself, add to your knowledge, and deepen your understanding? Pay special attention to those facts and ideas that do.

The Elegance of Erik Erikson

In this module Plotnik and Kouyoumdjian conclude their review of Erik Erikson's fascinating theory of development across the lifespan. (Erikson, considered a "neo-Freudian," does appear again in their discussion of psychoanalytic personality theories in Module 19.)

To win a place in the educated public's understanding, a theory needs sharp edges and distinctive, even shocking, premises. We all remember Pavlov's confused dog, Freud's obsession with sex, Piaget's surprising ideas about how children think, and Skinner's untiring lever-pressing rats. Erik Erikson's elegant, almost poetic saga of human life lacks all that. Consequently, although psychologists respect Erikson highly, the educated public doesn't know his outlook very well. That's a shame, because it might be the most true-to-life theory of all.

Re-read Plotnik and Kouyoumdjian's thoughtful discussion of Erikson in Modules 17 and 18. Put Erikson on your list of giants of psychology to learn more about.

Effective Student Tip 18

What the Professor Wants

I remember a student who would walk me to class and offer an admiring comment on my shirt, or some such, but then fail to turn in the assignment. Professors love compliments and admiring students. We're human, after all. But this isn't what we really want, though.

Every professor wants to be an effective teacher. What your professor wants from you personally is that you really do *learn*. The best thing you can do for your professor is also the best thing you can do for yourself: learn, achieve your goals, and be successful.

Professors sometimes deceive themselves and each other by saying, "If I can help just one student, it's all worth while…," but they don't really believe it. Deep down, they wish *every one* of their students would learn and progress. Then, they would know what they're doing is right, which would satisfy their own urge to be effective.

Like you, your professor wants to be effective, but because the measure of that effectiveness is your learning, only you can bring it about. Does it occur to you that you and the professor really need each other? Both of you want to be effective in life, and you can help each other achieve that effectiveness. Don't underestimate your power. The professor's fate is in your hands!

Your response…

Of all the teachers you've known, which one meant the most to you? Explain why.

Learning Objectives

1. Understand adolescence and adulthood as the continuation and completion of the four-stage human life cycle: infancy, childhood, adolescence, and adulthood.

2. Learn the basic biology of puberty and sexual behavior in adolescent girls and boys, and the kinds of changes that come with aging later in adulthood.

3. Explore cognitive and emotional changes through examining Jean Piaget's theory of cognitive development, new discoveries in brain development, Lawrence Kohlberg's theory of moral reasoning, and studies of parenting styles.

4. Learn about personality and social changes through consideration of the psychology of self-esteem, Erik Erikson's adult psychosocial stages, and personality change in adulthood.

5. Understand gender roles and gender expectations, the different kinds of love, choosing a partner, and the success or failure of long-term relationships.

6. Explore the research on happy marriages, why marriages succeed or fail, and cultural differences in preferences for partners and reasons for marrying.

7. Refine your understanding of teenage suicide and explore the issue of doctor-assisted suicide in the elderly.

Key Terms

The key terms for this module show great variety. Some are crucial terms from famous theories, while others denote biological facts or interesting concepts from new research and thinking about adolescence and adulthood. You probably already know some of these terms, since they increasingly appear in newspaper and magazine articles about adolescence and adulthood, sex and love, and self-identity and aging.

adolescence
aging process
authoritarian parents
authoritative parents
BioPsychoSocial approach
cognitive development
companionate love
conventional level
estrogen
female secondary sexual characteristics
formal operations stage
gender roles
male secondary sexual characteristics
menarche
menopause
normal aging
passionate love
pathological aging
perceptual speed
permissive parents
personal (self-) identity
personality and social development
postconventional level
preconventional level
processing speed
puberty
reaction time
schema
self-esteem
testosterone
triangular theory of love

The "PowerStudy 4.5 for Introduction to Psychology" CD-ROM includes a complete set of interactive learning activities for this module: quizzes, summary test, key terms, web site connections, critical thinking exercise, module outline, and more.

Outline

- *Introduction*

1. **Adolescence** (ambitious teen Brandi)

☐ What was your own adolescence like? Was it the best of times or the worst of times?

2. Adulthood (troubled actor Charlie Sheen)

A. *Puberty & Sexual Behavior*

1. Definition: **puberty**

☐ Do you remember a time when you were confused or troubled by how your body was changing? What were your thoughts and feelings about it at the time?

2. Girls during puberty
   a. Physical growth
   b. Female sexual maturity: **menarche** and **estrogen**
   c. **Female secondary sexual characteristics**
   d. Early versus late maturing
3. Boys during puberty
   a. Physical growth
   b. Male sexual maturity: **testosterone**
   c. **Male secondary sexual characteristics**
   d. Early versus late maturing
4. Adolescents: sexually mature
   a. Conflicting answers
      (1) Advise
      (2) Approach: **BioPsychoSocial approach**
   b. Decisions about becoming sexually active
      (1) Abstinence
      (2) Problems

B. *Cognitive & Emotional Changes*

1. Definition: **cognitive development**
2. Piaget's cognitive stages: continued
   a. Stage 4: **Formal operations stage**
   b. Thinking abstractly
3. Brain development: reason and emotion
   a. Prefrontal cortex: executive functions
      (1) Vulnerability
      (2) Risk-taking behavior

- b. Limbic system: emotional behaviors
  - (1) Moody, emotional, and impulsive behaviors
  - (2) Conclusion

4. Kohlberg's theory of moral reasoning
   - a. Three levels of moral reasoning
     - (1) **Preconventional level**
     - (2) **Conventional level**
     - (3) **Postconventional level**
   - b. Evaluating Kohlberg's theory
     - (1) Stages
     - (2) Thinking versus behaving (Carol Gilligan)
     - (3) Brain or neural factors
5. Parenting styles and effects

☐ Which of Diana Baumrind's parenting styles describes your family?

   - a. Personal experiences
   - b. Different styles of parenting (Diana Baumrind)
     - (1) **Authoritarian parents**
     - (2) **Authoritative parents**
     - (3) **Permissive parents**
   - c. Effects of parenting styles
6. Adolescence: Big Picture
   - a. Girls during puberty
   - b. Boys during puberty
   - c. Sexual maturity
   - d. Piaget's stages (continued): **formal operations stage**
   - e. Brain development: reason and emotion
   - f. Kohlberg's theory of moral reasoning
7. Beyond adolescence
   - a. Changes in cognitive speed
     - (1) **Processing speed**
     - (2) **Perceptual speed**
     - (3) **Reaction time**
   - b. Changes in memory
     - (1) Memory differences
     - (2) Brain changes
     - (3) Memory-enhancing products
   - c. Resiliency
   - d. Emotions

C. *Personality & Social Changes*

1. Definition
   a. **Personality** and **social development**
   b. **Personal (self-) identity**
2. Development of **self-esteem**
   a. High self-esteem
   b. Low self-esteem
   c. Reversals
   d. Forces shaping self-esteem
   e. Development and importance of self-esteem
3. Adulthood: Erikson's psychosocial stages [Stages 1-5 were discussed in Module 17]

☐ Erikson finds a unique psychosocial conflict at each stage. Each stage presents a special problem that must be solved in order to achieve positive growth. Can you explain the challenge of each stage?

   a. Stage 5: Identity versus Role Confusion
   b. Stage 6: Intimacy versus Isolation
   c. Stage 7: Generativity versus Stagnation
   d. Stage 8: Integrity versus Despair
4. Personality change (Mick Jagger)

D. *Gender Roles, Love & Relationships*

1. Definition: **gender roles**
   a. Current gender roles: U.S. and worldwide
      (1) U.S. gender roles
      (2) Worldwide gender roles
      (3) Changes
   b. Gender roles: development and function
      (1) Evolutionary psychology theory
      (2) Social role theory
2. Expectations
3. Kinds of love
   a. **Passionate love**
   b. **Companionate love**
   c. **Triangular theory of love** (Robert Sternberg)

☐ Apply Sternberg's "love triangle" to your own most recent romance. Does it reveal anything you hadn't realized?

      (1) Passion
      (2) Intimacy
      (3) Commitment
   d. Brain in love (reward/pleasure center)

4. Choosing a partner: **schema**
5. Long-term relationship: success or failure? (John Gottman)
   a. Critical factors
   b. Happy relationships
   c. Happiness graph

E. Research Focus: Happy Marriages

1. Why do marriages succeed or fail?
2. "Love Lab" study (John Gottman)
   a. Method
      (1) Facial responses
      (2) Physiological responses
      (3) Longitudinal method
   b. Results and conclusions
      (1) Unsuccessful relationships
      (2) Successful relationships
      (3) Advice

F. Cultural Diversity: Preferences for Partners

1. Measuring cultural influences
2. Desirable traits
   a. What is considered desirable in a potential partner?
   b. How much is virginity valued around the world?
3. Reasons for marrying
   a. How much is love valued?
   b. How do women decide?
   c. How do men decide?

G. Physical Changes: Aging

1. Kinds of aging
   a. **Normal aging**
   b. **Pathological aging**
2. Aging and physiological changes
   a. **Aging process**
   b. Physiological changes through adulthood
3. Sexual changes with aging
   a. Sexual changes in women: **menopause**
      (1) Physical symptoms
      (2) Psychological symptoms
      (3) Sexual activities

b. Sexual changes in men

(1) Sexual responding

(2) Psychological problems

H. Application: Suicide

1. Teenage/young adult suicide

☐ If you're like most of us, you know someone who committed suicide (or tried to). What happened?

2. Problems related to suicide

a. Problems and symptoms

b. Precipitators

3. Preventing suicide

a. Identify risk factors

b. Psychiatric evaluation and psychosocial intervention

4. Suicide in the elderly

☐ Do you oppose or support doctor-assisted suicide? What are your reasons?

a. Risk factors

b. Assisted suicide

c. Opponents and proponents of doctor-assisted suicide

Flashcards for the fun of it…

A Special Rock 'n Roll Quiz on Adolescence: Teenagers have always been aware of living in an emotional pressure cooker, and the music they listen to reflects their concerns. Can you match these worries of adolescence with the "golden oldies" that expressed them so memorably? After you try this quiz, how about making up one of your own? Perhaps you could base it on current hits.

	Adolescent Concerns	Golden Oldies
_____	1. masculinity	a. "Why Do Fools Fall in Love?"
_____	2. femininity	b. "Fifty Ways to Leave Your Lover"
_____	3. self-esteem	c. "Walk Like a Man"
_____	4. vulnerability	d. "Get a Job"
_____	5. chastity	e. "Big Girls Don't Cry"
_____	6. intimacy	f. "Sweet Little Sixteen"
_____	7. romantic love	g. "Do Wah Diddy"
_____	8. career	h. "Where Did My Baby Go?"
_____	9. marriage	i. "Under the Boardwalk"
_____	10. commitment *(not!)*	j. "Going to the Chapel"

Answers to "A Special Rock 'n' Roll Quiz on Adolescence"

1 c 2 e 3 g 4 h 5 f 6 i 7 a 8 d 9 j 10 b

How English Works

Words in the Textbook

p. 407 **Stay in there** = keep trying

elected **prom** queen = yearly dance in high school

levelheaded person = with good judgment

cocky-type person = happy, risk-taking

she did not **figure on** a divorce = predict

p. 408 this growth **spurt** begins = sudden increase

p. 409 not using **contraceptives** = devices to prevent pregnancy

p. 410 I'm very **outspoken** = open, not afraid to give opinion

p. 411 getting a tongue pierced **on a dare** = because of a challenge from friend

p. 412 may involve **making bargains** = balancing good and bad effects

p. 413 I **get around** them = avoid the rules

I'm asking for **the world** = too much

My parents never **make** their punishments **stick** = enforce

I play right into it = I use their feelings to my advantage

different **costs** and benefits = disadvantages

p. 419 a friend **fixed me up with** Charlie = arranged a date with

p. 420 **stonewalling** = rejecting any discussion (like a stone wall)

p. 422 his claim is **nothing but** amazing = completely, totally

a known **sore point** = cause of disagreement

husbands who were **autocratic** = controlling

p. 423 simply **out of the question** = not considered

p. 425 results in **cessation** of ovulation = ending, stopping of a process

baby boomers = people born soon after World War II, from 1945 to 1960.

women experience **hot flashes** = sudden feeling of heat

a society that **glorifies** being young = honors, praises

p. 426 considered teenage **histrionics** = dramatic behavior

listen to **oldies** = old songs

I've finally **slipped over the edge** = moved into dangerous situation

gregarious = friendly, sociable

Sentence Structure: Making Connections

When you're reading, it's helpful to understand all the transition words that writers give you because they tell you what to expect next.

What do you expect when you see these transition words?

however / nevertheless / still / on the other hand / conversely / in contrast

These words tell you that the sentence that follows will be opposite from the previous sentence. Here are some examples:

I think English grammar is hard. **On the other hand**, "How English Works" makes it easy.

These transitions help the reader anticipate the next sentence. **However,** not all transitions are equal.

However is the most commonly used of these transitions because we can use it in any situation to warn the reader of a change from the first sentence. **On the other hand**, transitions like **conversely**, **in contrast,** and **on the other hand** can only be used to illustrate a direct opposite from the sentence before, so you couldn't use them in the second sentence.

Look at the examples from the text and notice the difference in how they are used.

Teenage girls report that sex and pregnancy are the number one issues they face today. **However**, curiosity, media coverage, and peer pressure play a large role in motivating sexual activity.

Happy marriages had husbands who were good at not immediately rejecting their wives' advice. **In contrast**, unhappy marriages had husbands who were autocratic.

How would you complete the following sentence with this transition?

Esmeralda just signed a contract to play in a movie.

Nevertheless, __________.

You probably wrote a sentence similar to one of these:

Nevertheless, she is not at all excited.

Nevertheless, she will probably not move to Hollywood.

Nevertheless, she is not giving up her job at the bank.

These are not directly opposite from the sentence before, but these sentences are opposite from what you would expect. **Nevertheless** and **Still** work best in these cases.

Practicing this kind of thinking will help you understand what you read more quickly and more deeply. Read the following sentences and fill in with what transitions would work best.

Faysal never eats meat. __________, he sometimes eats fish.

Bogdana works hard during the week. __________, she relaxes all weekend.

Arthur's father is a strict disciplinarian. __________, Arthur's mother is not.

She has no acting experience. __________, Esmeralda just signed a contract to play in a movie.

Some teenagers get their tongues pierced. __________, I think this is disgusting.

Answers

Faysal never eats meat. **Still / Nevertheless / However,** he sometimes eats fish.

Bogdana works hard during the week. **Conversely / On the other hand / In contrast / However,** she relaxes all weekend.

Arthur's father is a strict disciplinarian. **Conversely / On the other hand / In contrast / However,** Arthur's mother is not.

She has no acting experience. **Still / Nevertheless / However,** Esmeralda just signed a contract to play in a movie.

Some teenagers get their tongues pierced. **Still / Nevertheless / However,** I think this is disgusting.

The Big Picture

Which statement below offers the best summary of the larger significance of this module?

A There is at least one compensation for the physical, cognitive, and emotional upheaval of adolescence — it's followed by adulthood, a period of calm and psychological smooth sailing while waiting for the end.

B Although psychological theories of development tend to place great importance on infancy and childhood, we should remember that adolescence and adulthood are also periods of significant change.

C Plotnik and Kouyoumdjian want us to understand that Erikson's psychosocial stage theory of human development is the best, because it's the only one that takes into account adolescence, adulthood, and old age.

D Once again psychology challenges the popular notion that men and women are equal. Discoveries in every area — physical, cognitive, and personality — reveal significant differences between the way men and women function.

E Have you noticed that your parents are getting smarter as you get older?

True-False

_____ 1. Contrary to the traditional view, new research suggests that adolescence is not necessarily a period of great psychological turmoil and severe emotional stress.

_____ 2. Girls normally experience the physical changes of puberty about two years earlier than boys.

_____ 3. For obvious reasons, early maturing girls are more confident and outgoing than late maturing girls.

_____ 4. The good news (too late for you) is that the happiest, best-adjusted adolescents come from families using the permissive style of parenting.

_____ 5. Enjoy it while you can! The sad fact is that *all* cognitive abilities decline with age.

_____ 6. Erik Erikson saw the key developmental issue of adolescence as the acquisition of a positive sense of identity.

_____ 7. According to Erikson, the main task of young adulthood is to find intimacy by developing loving relationships.

_____ 8. Robert Sternberg's triangular theory of love explains why romantic love doesn't last — it has passion and intimacy, but it lacks commitment.

_____ 9. Regardless of culture, young adults all over the world ranked traits desirable in a potential mate in almost exactly the same way.

_____ 10. Most women report a kind of relief after menopause — at least they don't have to endure sex anymore.

Flashcards 1

_____	1. adolescence	a. the major male hormone; stimulates growth of genital organs and development of sexual characteristics
_____	2. estrogen	b. the first menstrual period; a signal that ovulation may have occurred; potential to conceive child
_____	3. formal operations stage	c. the last of Piaget's cognitive stages (age 12–adulthood), when adolescents develop the ability to think logically
_____	4. personal (self-) identity	d. how we describe ourselves; includes our values, goals, traits, interests, and motivations
_____	5. menarche	e. how much one likes oneself; includes feelings of self-worth, attractiveness, and social competence
_____	6. normal aging	f. may be caused by genetic defects, physiological problems, or diseases, all of which accelerate the aging process
_____	7. pathological aging	g. a developmental period (age 9–17) of significant biological changes resulting in secondary sexual characteristics
_____	8. puberty	h. a gradual and natural slowing of our physical and psychological processes from middle to late adulthood
_____	9. self-esteem	i. one of the major female hormones; at puberty, stimulates development of sexual characteristics
_____	10. testosterone	j. a developmental period (age 12–18) during which many characteristics change from childlike to adult-like

Flashcards 2

_____	1. authoritarian parents	a. traditional or stereotypic behaviors, attitudes, and personality traits adults expect of males and females
_____	2. authoritative parents	b. continuously thinking about loved one: accompanied by warm sexual feelings and powerful emotions
_____	3. companionate love	c. less controlling; nonpunishing and accepting attitude; make few demands on their children
_____	4. female secondary sexual characteristics	d. having trusting and tender feelings for someone whose life is closely bound up with one's own
_____	5. gender roles	e. attempt to control behavior of their children in accordance with an absolute standard of conduct
_____	6. male secondary sexual characteristics	f. increased secretion of estrogen, include growth of pubic hair, development of breasts, and widening of hips
_____	7. menopause	g. increased secretion of testosterone, include growth of pubic and facial hair, development of muscles, and deeper voice
_____	8. passionate love	h. gradual stoppage in secretion of estrogen, causing cessation of ovulation, menstrual cycle
_____	9. permissive parents	i. says love has three components: passion, intimacy, and commitment
_____	10. triangular theory of love	j. attempt to direct their children's activities in a rational way; supportive, loving; discuss their rules and policies

Multiple Choice

_____ 1. Plotnik and Kouyoumdjian introduce us to the ambitious teen Branndi and the troubled actor Charlie Sheen in order to show that
   a. teen Branndi lives a more turbulent life than adult Charlie Sheen
   b. Branndi's personality is all over the place, while Charlie Sheen is calmer and more stable
   c. adolescence and adulthood are both periods of great change, as was childhood
   d. most change occurs in childhood, less in adolescence, and even less in adulthood

_____ 2. Experts now believe that adolescence is *not* a period of
   a. great psychological turmoil
   b. considerable biological, cognitive, and social changes
   c. searching for personal identity
   d. dramatic positive or negative changes in self-esteem

_____ 3. When you compare the development of sexual maturity in girls and boys during puberty, you find that the changes are
   a. radically different in girls and boys
   b. gradual in girls but sudden in boys
   c. essentially the same, but occur about two years earlier in girls
   d. somewhat similar, except that the difference between a boy and a man is far greater than the difference between a girl and a woman

_____ 4. The __________ is likely to be better adjusted and have fewer psychological problems
   a. early maturing girl
   b. late maturing girl
   c. early maturing boy
   d. late maturing boy

_____ 5. For today's biology lesson, we'll be discussing adolescent
   a. estrogen in girls and testosterone in boys
   b. female secondary sexual characteristics and male primary sexual characteristics
   c. varying rates of menarche in girls and boys during puberty
   d. puberty results: female sexual maturity and male sexual immaturity

_____ 6. According to the BioPsychoSocial approach, problems of adolescent sexual behavior
   a. dominate adolescents' biology, their psychology, and their social lives
   b. cannot be discussed independently of hormonal, cognitive, personality, or emotional factors
   c. tend to be overrated, although they do have a minor effect on many parts of adolescents' lives
   d. (there is no "BioPsychoSocial" approach; this is a nonsense term)

_____ 7. The stage during which adolescents develop the ability to think about abstract or hypothetical concepts and solve problems in a logical way is
   a. Freud's Stage 3: the phallic stage
   b. Erikson's Stage 8: integrity versus despair
   c. Piaget's Stage 4: formal operations
   d. Kohlberg's Stage 2: conventional level

_____ 8. New research suggests that teenagers engage in irresponsible, risky behaviors because their
a. beliefs include an irrational confidence in their invulnerability
b. limbic systems are still at a primitive level of development
c. brains are often "rewired" by alcohol and drug use
d. brains have underdeveloped executive functions but a well-developed emotional center

_____ 9. Lawrence Kohlberg based his theory of moral development on research into the
a. behaviors that children of different ages listed as "good" or "bad"
b. stories children made up when asked to illustrate good and bad behavior
c. correlation between how children rated their own behavior and how their teachers rated it
d. reasoning children used to solve problems that posed moral dilemmas

_____ 10. One of the main criticisms of Kohlberg's theory of moral reasoning is that
a. his theory describes moral behavior more than moral thinking
b. Carol Gilligan showed that men and women think alike on moral questions
c. new findings show how brain and neural factors influence moral thinking
d. only Stage 6, the highest stage of moral reasoning, has firm research support

_____ 11. Your new friend seems to be competent, independent, and achievement oriented; thinking like Diana Baumrind, you guess that she had _________ parents
a. authoritarian
b. authoritative
c. permissive
d. protective

_____ 12. Which one of the following cognitive abilities does *not* decrease with aging?
a. processing speed
b. perceptual speed
c. reaction time
d. interpretation

_____ 13. Grandmother forgets a name and worries that she's "losing it" — you should reassure her that
a. some memory problems often occur in people 60 and over
b. her memory may be slipping, but her reaction time will speed up
c. if she lives long enough, it is likely she will get Alzheimer's disease
d. daily intake of the supplement ginkgo biloba should improve her memory

_____ 14. Probably the most disturbing finding about self-esteem during adolescence is that
a. boys' self-esteem plunges unless they are good at athletics
b. girls are more likely to show declining or low self-esteem
c. both boys' and girls' self-esteem rises rapidly, then falls during adulthood
d. once self-esteem declines, it almost never recovers or increases

_____ 15. In Erik Erikson's psychosocial stage theory, an adolescent who does not develop a positive sense of identity is likely to suffer from
a. role confusion
b. stagnation
c. a sense of inferiority
d. isolation

____ 16. According to Erik Erikson's Stage 8, what we need in late adulthood is
a. recognition, respect, and honor from our family and colleagues
b. a sense of pride in our acquisitions and our standing in the community
c. a sense of contentment about how we lived and what we accomplished
d. mainly good health — without it there is despair

____ 17. What is this thing called love? Robert Sternberg's triangular theory says love is a mix of
a. romantic love, respect, and companionship
b. romance, sharing, and loyalty
c. infatuated love plus companionate love
d. passion, intimacy, and commitment

____ 18. You feel euphoria and intense passion when you find your "one true love," probably because
a. your relationship has advanced from infatuated love to companionate love
b. you are experiencing what Sternberg calls "companionate love"
c. the reward/pleasure center of your brain is experiencing increased activity
d. (you can't explain it, because love is too mysterious for scientific study)

____ 19. John Gottman has identified four major problems between couples that often lead to divorce:
a. criticism, defensiveness, contempt, and stonewalling
b. poverty, impulsive spending, lack of savings, and unemployment
c. age differences, religious differences, political differences, and language differences
d. physical attractiveness, flirting, jealousy, and lack of inhibitions

____ 20. Which one of the following is *not* a procedure used in John Gottman's "Love Lab"?
a. recording each partner's facial expressions while they discuss marriage sore points
b. recording each partner's physiological responses during discussions of marriage problems
c. longitudinal methods (retesting the same couples regularly over 14 years)
d. learning better sexual performance, but in the lab with a professional sex surrogate

____ 21. Based on studies done in his "Love Lab," John Gottman's advice for couples is to
a. behave like good friends — respect, affection, empathy
b. add some spice occasionally — everyone secretly enjoys something kinky
c. work hard for financial success — the basis of all good relationships
d. avoid discussions of sex that are too honest or revealing

____ 22. Culture influences preferences for marriage partners — we know that because
a. women express more stringent standards in deciding whom to marry
b. the value placed on female virginity varies from country to country
c. the importance of love in choosing a spouse is about the same from country to country
d. women tend to marry younger men who are physically attractive

____ 23. The most significant gender difference in aging is that at about age 50
a. men lose the ability to have erections
b. men experience a sudden increase in sexual desire
c. women experience menopause
d. women lose all sexual desire

_____ 24. When a young person commits suicide, our typical reaction is an anguished "Why? Why?"… but the truth is that

a. nothing can stop a person who has decided to commit suicide
b. there probably were signs of psychological problems and behavioral symptoms long before
c. psychology has no answer to the riddle of why adolescents, with their whole lives before them, sometimes take their own lives
d. adolescents who are contemplating suicide go to great lengths to disguise their intentions

_____ 25. Perhaps the main reason why the debate over assisted suicide is intensifying is that

a. a doctor has invented a machine that makes it relatively easy
b. psychologists, as scientists, are unwilling to become involved in a moral question
c. morals in our country are breaking down
d. the population of the elderly will almost double in the next 35 years

Short Essay

1. Which of the three basic styles of parenting described by Diana Baumrind (authoritarian, authoritative, or permissive) best describes how your parents tried to raise you? How successful were their efforts? Give examples from your adolescence.

2. How does Erik Erikson describe the basic task or social problem of adolescence and the possible outcomes of attempts to resolve it?

3. What is Robert Sternberg's triangular theory of love, and why is it so useful?

4. What has psychology learned about why marriages succeed or fail?

5. What is your position on the controversial topic of doctor-assisted suicide?

More about My Mother

I love the story my mother recalled from her college days way back in the 1920s (see "How Behaviorism Revolutionized Psychology" on page 150 of this Study Guide). She's a remarkable person in many ways. Very much in the spirit of Erik Erikson's life span development theory, she and others like her are redefining our understanding of old age.

When she retired, my mother discovered the joys of running. She religiously went out every day and jogged two or three miles. Once a year, to celebrate her birthday, she ran five miles. As she got older, the runs became walks, and in the last few years, she has split the five-mile birthday walk between a morning and an afternoon outing.

In April, 2009, we celebrated her 104th birthday! And yes, she did her five miles! I hope that you, too, have the good fortune to continue learning wonderful lessons from your parents.

Answers for Module 18

The Big Picture (explanations provided for incorrect choices)

A Adolescence is neither so tumultuous nor adulthood so stagnant as this gloomy statement suggests.
B *Correct! You see the "big picture" for this Module.*
C That is a strength of Erikson's theory, but Plotnik does not advocate adherence in any one approach to psychology.
D Evolution seems to have created some gender differences, but how significant they are today remains debatable.
E It's just a joke!

True-False (explanations provided for False choices; page numbers given for all choices)

1	T	407	
2	T	408	
3	F	408	Early maturing girls tend to be less confident and outgoing. (Can you see why this might happen?)
4	F	413	Happiness and good adjustment are related to the authoritative style of parenting.
5	F	415	Not all cognitive abilities decline with aging (some even improve).
6	T	417	
7	T	417	
8	T	419	
9	F	420	There is considerable cultural variation in desirable characteristics of potential mates.
10	F	425	Menopause is a stressful life change for many women.

Flashcards 1

1 j 2 i 3 c 4 d 5 b 6 h 7 f 8 g 9 e 10 a

Flashcards 2

1 e 2 j 3 d 4 f 5 a 6 g 7 h 8 b 9 c 10 i

Multiple Choice (explanations provided for incorrect choices)

1 a Brandi may be more exuberant, but Charlie has experienced both peaks and lows in his life and career.
b Brandi has the energy of adolescence, but Charlie has experienced both the joys and pains of adulthood.
c *Correct! See page 407.*
d All three of these stages bring great change in a person's life.

2 ***a*** *Correct! See page 407.*
b These changes, especially the biological ones, are obvious.
c Searching for identity continues to be seen as a key factor in adolescence.
d Research points to the importance of changes in self-esteem in adolescence.

3 a Adolescent boys and girls go through the same developmental processes.
b The same things happen, but not at the same times.
c *Correct! See page 408.*
d Does this statement really make sense?

4 a It turns out they have problems. (Can you see why?)
b This situation is neither very good nor very bad.
c *Correct! See page 408.*
d It turns out they have problems. (Can you see why?)

5 ***a*** *Correct! See page 408.*
b Both girls and boys show development of secondary sexual characteristics in adolescence.
c Menarche only occurs in girls.
d Puberty results in sexual maturity in both females and males (although sometimes it doesn't seem like it!).

6 a Dominate is too strong, and not the focus of the BioPsychoSocial approach.
b *Correct! See page 409.*
c Problems like sexual behavior are real; the question is how best to understand them.
d Like it or not, there is such a term.

7 a Too young — this would refer to the kindergarten period.
b Too old — this would refer to old age.
c *Correct! See page 410.*
d Too young — this would be the middle stage of moral reasoning.

8 a The "invulnerability" explanation has been replaced by new findings about brain development.
b The limbic system is well developed; it is the executive functions that are still developing.
c Alcohol and drug use are dangerous, but do not rewire the brain.
d *Correct! See page 411.*

9 a Kohlberg did not use the survey method.
b Kohlberg used stories in his research, but the children did not make them up.
c Kohlberg did not use teachers in his research.
d *Correct! See page 412.*

10 a Kohlberg has been criticized for just the opposite emphasis.
b Gilligan attempted to show just the opposite.
c *Correct! See page 412.*
d Stage 6 has now been omitted because so few people reach it.

11 a Authoritarian parents tend to produce hostile boys and dependent girls.
b *Correct! See page 413.*
c Permissive parents tend to produce less assertive and less achievement-oriented children.
d This is not one of Diana Baumrind's three parenting styles.

12 a Research shows that processing speed declines with age.
b Research shows that perceptual speed declines with age.
c Research shows that reaction time declines with age.
d *Correct! See page 415.*

13 ***a*** *Correct! See page 415.*
b Reaction time also slows down beginning in the late 50s.
c So far, her memory loss seems natural and not the sign of worse to come.
d Researchers found that ginkgo biloba did not improve memory or concentration.

14 a Athletics are important for boys in our culture, but not all important.
b *Correct! See page 416.*
c There is no such predictable rise and fall in self-esteem.
d Fortunately, this is not true. It depends on circumstances like earned successes, or therapy.

15 ***a*** *Correct! See page 417.*
b Stagnation is an outcome of poor development in middle adulthood.
c A sense of inferiority is an outcome of poor development in middle and late childhood.
d Isolation (instead of intimacy) is an outcome of poor development in young adulthood.

16 a This answer assumes that we are mainly egotistical.
b This answer assumes that we are mainly vain.
c *Correct! See page 417.*
d Many people live satisfying lives even with health problems.

17 a Romantic love lacks one of Robert Sternberg's three components of love.
b These factors are not among Robert Sternberg's three components of love.
c Wouldn't a triangular theory require *three* elements?
d *Correct! See page 419.*

18 a That would involve a decline in euphoria and passion.
b Companionate love is a combination of intimacy and commitment without any sexual passion.
c *Correct! See page 419.*
d Tell that to Robert Sternberg, John Gottman, and various researchers in neuroscience!

19 ***a*** *Correct! See page 420.*
b These economic factors are less important than a couple's social interactions.
c These personal factors are less important than a couple's social interactions.
d These sexual factors are less important than a couple's social interactions.

20 a This was an important part of Gottman's "Love Lab" procedure.
b This was an important part of Gottman's "Love Lab" procedure.
c This was an important part of Gottman's "Love Lab" procedure.
d *Correct! See page 422.*

21 ***a*** *Correct! See page 422.*
b Gottman studied emotional responses and feelings over time, not sexual adjustment.
c Maybe true, but not the focus of Gottman's research.
d Maybe true, but not the focus of Gottman's research.

22 a Men express more stringent standards.
b *Correct! See page 423.*
c If true (it's not), this would refute the importance of cultural influences.
d This tendency is truer of men than of women.

23 a The ads you see on TV might make you think so, but in general it is not true.
b Some men might act like it, but there is no physiological basis for such a change.
c *Correct! See page 425.*
d Some women might act like it, but there is no physiological basis for such a change.

24 a If you believe this, you must learn more about suicide prevention. A friend may need your help one day.
b *Correct! See page 426.*
c Psychology does not have all the answers, but it does have some good advice and prevention techniques.
d Just the opposite is true — they usually give signals. (But are we sensitive enough to recognize them?)

25 a This fact gives the media something to focus on, but doesn't explain the debate.
b Even if true, why would that intensify the debate?
c This is too broad a generalization to prove anything.
d *Correct! See page 427.*

Short Essay (sample answers)

1. If you said *authoritarian*, you need examples of attempts to shape, control, and evaluate your behavior in accordance with a set standard of conduct that comes from religious or respected authorities. If you said *authoritative*, you need examples of attempts to direct your activities in a rational and intelligent way, being supportive, loving, and committed, and discussing rules. If you said *permissive*, you need examples of less controlling, nonpunishing, accepting attitudes, using reason, making few demands. How well did it work?

2. For Erikson, adolescents (ages 12–20) are going through Stage 5, "identity versus role confusion." They're leaving behind the carefree, irresponsible, and impulsive behaviors of childhood and developing the more purposeful, planned, and responsible behaviors of adulthood. If adolescents successfully resolve this problem, they will develop a healthy and confident sense of identity. If unsuccessful, they will experience role confusion, which results in having low self-esteem and becoming unstable or socially withdrawn.

3. It turns out love is *not* a many splendored thing! Sternberg says there's a love triangle with three sides, intimacy, passion, and commitment. You feel love in passion, share emotional and material love in intimacy, and form a serious relationship in commitment. The genius of Sternberg's theory is that the three sides can be arranged in different combinations, explaining passionate love and companionate love, and answering questions about love at first sight, quick marriage, love without sex, and why romantic love doesn't last.

4. There is a kind of contradiction in marriage right from the beginning. Couples are brought together by passionate feelings generated by the reward/pleasure center of the brain, but kept together by deeper social and personal satisfactions. In his "Love Lab" [note to professor: I'll volunteer!]. John Gottman has discovered four major problems in interaction that couples face: (1) giving too many criticisms, (2) becoming too defensive, (3) showing contempt of a partner, and (4) stonewalling on disagreements.

5. As the population of elderly people almost doubles over the next 35 years, the pros and cons of doctor-assisted suicide will only be argued more intensely. Whichever side you support, you should also take account of the opposite view. Opponents argue that allowing people to take their own lives opens the door to many abuses, from poor decisions by the mentally ill to abuses from the profit motive. Proponents argue that it would end unbearable suffering in incurable patients. Give examples from family or friend's experiences.

Module 19

Freudian & Humanistic Theories

Big Theories to Answer Big Questions

In Modules 19 and 20, Plotnik and Kouyoumdjian discuss personality theory, one of the most absorbing areas in all of psychology. Personality theories tackle the big questions, the ones we think about when we try to understand who we are and what meaning and purpose our lives have. We feel that we are unique individuals, but aren't we essentially like everyone else? We know we are growing and developing, but aren't we also somehow very much the same from year to year? We would like to change some things about ourselves, but why does that seem so difficult to do?

A theory of personality is necessarily comprehensive. The better it is, the more of our questions about ourselves it answers. As you study these two modules, pay attention to each theory's basic assumptions about human nature. Do you agree with them? To what extent can you see yourself in each theory? Does it describe you and explain your life?

But Do They Explain You?

I've said it before, but it's especially true for the two modules on personality: *challenge every new idea you meet*. Ask yourself, is this idea really true? Does that concept explain my own experience accurately? Does this theory capture how I feel about life and myself in general?

When Sigmund Freud says you have inborn sexual and aggressive tendencies, do you find them in yourself? When Abraham Maslow and Carl Rogers portray humans as fundamentally good, does that square with what you know about people? When Albert Bandura (next module) suggests that we are what we have learned to expect ourselves and the world to be, ask yourself if you are something more than a collection of past experiences. When Gordon Allport (also next module) paints your personality as a complex mosaic of tendencies to behave in certain ways, ask yourself if that captures everything that you are.

Finally, you might think about your own theory of personality. You do have one, even though you probably haven't tried to work it out in any detail. Anyone who studies psychology inevitably comes to have some sort of theory of personality — a global view of how all the facts and ideas in psychology fit together, and how they apply to everyday life. Reflecting on your own ideas about human nature will help you understand psychology's famous theories of personality.

Effective Student Tip 19

Three Secrets of Effective Writing

Too many students think the ability to write well is something you have to be born with. The truth is just the opposite. Any student can become a good writer. The *art* of writing requires curiosity and creativity, but we all have those qualities. The *craft* of writing is as learnable as cooking or carpentry. Three secrets of effective writing reveal how any serious student can get started on becoming a better writer.

Secret #1: Tell a *story* that's important to you. We organize our memory around stories. A well-told story is the most effective way to convey information.

Secret #2: Paint *word pictures*. We understand best what we can visualize. A beautifully worded description is the most effective way to create understanding in writing.

Secret #3: Think of writing as a *craft* (the artistry will come naturally, flowering as you work). One by one acquire the skills of good writing. Start by learning how to prepare an attractive, well-organized paper, the easiest procedure to learn and the one with the most immediate effect on your reader.

When you think of writing as a craft, you realize that the goal is progress, not perfection. It doesn't really matter how good your next paper is, as long as it's a little bit better than the last one. That's progress.

Your response…

What was the best paper you ever wrote? What made it so good?

Learning Objectives

1. Understand Freudian and humanistic theories, which emphasize our inner life, as the first half of four major approaches to personality (social cognitive and trait theories are covered in the next module).
2. Learn the basic concepts of the psychodynamic approach to the understanding of personality through mastering the basic concepts of Sigmund Freud.
3. Appreciate Freud's psychoanalytic theory, with its ideas of motivation, divisions of the mind, and developmental stages, as a comprehensive approach to human nature.
4. Learn the basic concepts of the humanistic approach to the understanding of personality through mastering the basic concepts of Abraham Maslow and Carl Rogers.
5. Appreciate the cultural factors that help account for the unexpected academic success of the Indo-Chinese boat people who fled to the United States after the Vietnam conflict.
6. Study shyness as an example of personality problems and how they're understood and treated.
7. Understand the most important projective tests as basic assessment tools in the study of personality.

Key Terms

Many of the key terms for this module have become part of the general vocabulary of the educated person.

ability tests
anal stage
anxiety
collective unconscious
conditional positive regard
conscious thoughts
defense mechanisms
deficiency needs
denial
displacement
dream interpretation
ego
fixation
free association
Freud's psychodynamic theory of personality
Freudian slips
genital stage
growth needs
holistic view
humanistic theories
id
ideal self
implicit (nondeclarative) memory
latency stage
Maslow's hierarchy of needs
Oedipus complex
oral stage
personality
personality tests
phallic stage
phenomenological perspective
pleasure principle
positive regard
projection
projective tests
psychological assessment
psychosexual stages
rationalization
reaction formation
real self
reality principle
reliability
repression
Rogers's self-actualizing tendency
Rorschach inkblot test
self (self-actualization) theory
self or self-concept
self-actualization
shyness
sublimation
superego
Thematic Apperception Test (TAT)
theory of personality
unconditional positive regard
unconscious forces
unconscious motivation
validity

Outline

- *Introduction*
    1. Personality (Ted Haggard)
        a. **Personality**
        b. **Theory of personality**
    2. Changing personality (Charles Dutton)

A. Freud's Psychodynamic Theory

1. Definition
    a. **Freud's psychodynamic theory of personality**
    b. Childhood
    c. A method of psychotherapy (Module 24) plus a theory of personality (this module)
2. Conscious versus unconscious forces
    a. **Conscious thoughts**
    b. **Unconscious forces**
    c. **Unconscious motivation**
3. Techniques to discover the unconscious
    a. **Free association**
    b. **Dream interpretation**
    c. **Freudian slips**

B. Divisions of the Mind

1. Id, ego, and superego

☐ How do Freud's twin concepts of the pleasure principle and the reality principle make conflict inevitable in his personality theory?

    a. **Id**: pleasure seeker (**pleasure principle**)
    b. **Ego**: executive negotiator between id and superego (**reality principle**)
    c. **Superego**: regulator (conscience)
2. **Anxiety**
3. **Defense mechanisms**

☐ Freud didn't mean that defense mechanisms are bad. Can you think of an everyday life example for each defense mechanism that also shows how it promotes our adaptation and survival?

    a. **Rationalization**
    b. **Denial**
    c. **Repression**
    d. **Projection**
    e. **Reaction formation**
    f. **Displacement**
    g. **Sublimation**

C. *Developmental Stages*

1. Development: dealing with conflicts
   a. **Psychosexual stages**
   b. Conflict
2. Fixation: potential personality problems
   a. **Fixation**
   b. Too little or too much gratification
3. Five psychosexual stages

☐ For this theory to make any sense, you must appreciate the conflict in each stage. Think about children you've known (including yourself!) and try to come up with examples for each stage.

   a. **Oral stage**
   b. **Anal stage**
   c. **Phallic stage** and the **Oedipus complex**
   d. **Latency stage**
   e. **Genital stage**

D. *Freud's Followers & Critics*

☐ Why did Freud's most creative followers eventually become critics?

1. Carl Jung (analytical psychology) and the **collective unconscious**
2. Alfred Adler (individual psychology) and social urges
3. Karen Horney (psychology of women) and social interaction
4. Neo-Freudians (Erik Erikson: psychosocial stages instead of psychosexual stages)
5. Freudian theory today
   a. How valid is Freud's theory?
      (1) Too comprehensive
      (2) Difficult to test
      (3) Must be updated
   b. How important are the first five years?
      (1) Resilient children
      (2) Longitudinal studies
   c. Are there unconscious forces?
      (1) **Implicit (nondeclarative) memory**
      (2) Cognitive-emotional explanations
   d. What was Freud's impact?

E. *Humanistic Theories*

1. Three characteristics of **humanistic theories**
   a. **Phenomenological perspective**
   b. **Holistic view**
   c. **Self-actualization**

2. Abraham Maslow: need hierarchy and self-actualization
   a. **Maslow's hierarchy of needs**
      (1) **Deficiency needs**
      (2) **Growth needs**
   b. **Self-actualization**: characteristics of self-actualized individuals
3. Carl Rogers: self theory
   a. **Self (self-actualization) theory**
      (1) **Rogers's self-actualizing tendency**
      (2) **Self (self-concept)**
   b. **Real self** versus **ideal self**
   c. **Positive regard**
   d. **Conditional positive regard** and **unconditional positive regard**
   e. Importance of self-actualization
4. Applying humanistic ideas: Erin Gruwell and the Freedom Writers
5. Evaluation of humanistic theories
   a. Impact
   b. Criticisms

F. Cultural Diversity: Unexpected High Achievement

1. Boat people: remarkable achievement
2. Values and motivation
3. Parental attitudes

G. Research Focus: Shyness

1. What is **shyness** and what causes it? (Philip Zimbardo)
2. Psychodynamic approach
3. Social cognitive theory

H. Application: Assessment — Projective Tests

1. Definition of projective tests
   a. **Psychological assessment**
   b. **Personality tests**
   c. **Ability tests**
2. Examples of **projective tests**
   a. **Rorschach inkblot test**
   b. **Thematic Apperception Test (TAT)**
3. Two characteristics of effective tests
   a. **Validity**
   b. **Reliability**
4. Usefulness of projective tests: advantages and disadvantages

How English Works

Words in the Textbook

p. 433 **reform schools** = semi-prison for troubled young people

punished with **solitary confinement** = imprisoned alone in cell

after his **parole** = release from prison

his inner **demons** = serious emotional problems (devils)

p. 436 **analogous** to an iceberg = similar to

p. 438 **lays the groundwork** for personality growth = prepared the basis

p. 439 fears of **castration** = removal of sexual organs

p. 441 difficult to **verify** = prove that something is true

p. 442 **#1 ranked** female golfer = wins more often than any other female golfer

becoming a **humanitarian** = committed to improving the lives of other people

p. 445 people need to feel **appreciated** = recognized and liked for one's qualities

grouchy = irritable

foster the development = encourage

p. 450 interpretation of **slips of the tongue** = accidentally speaking your true thoughts

Vocabulary: Concept / Principle / Theory

About now you might be a little uncertain about the difference between a **concept** and a **principle** and a **theory**. Yes, all three are kinds of thoughts, the result of thinking, but how are they different?

A <u>concept</u> is an idea: Before Darwin, few people believed that biology had a direction. Then Darwin produced **the concept of evolution**. In the same way, before Freud few people believed that our behavior might be influenced or controlled by hidden drives and feelings. Then Freud formulated his **concept of the unconscious**. These two contributions were new ideas, claims that such forces really exist.

A <u>principle</u> is a law: A principle says that some behavior always happens or usually happens. For example, Darwin took his concept of evolution and described how it works in nature. This resulted in the **principle of natural selection**: this law says that evolution works to preserve useful attributes and eliminates ones that aren't useful. Thus, when Darwin took his concept and showed how it works, he was describing a principle.

A <u>theory</u> is a system: A theory explains how principles work together in relation to each other in a bigger framework. So, Freud put together his concept of the unconscious and his belief that unresolved sexual conflicts are stored in the unconscious. Next, he added the idea that anxiety arises from such unexpressed conflicts. Finally, he claimed that psychoanalysis can be a useful way to resolve these problems. All of this interaction can be described as Freud's **theory of the unconscious.**

Be careful, though: different writers can use these words differently, and certain subject areas — like philosophy or physics — can give them special meanings.

Sentence Structure: Colons

Did you notice this heading in the text? Superego : Regulator.

The punctuation mark between the words is a **colon**. When you see a colon, you are seeing a kind of **equal sign**. It has the same meaning as Superego = Regulator.

The colon tells you that both sides — the words before the colon and the words after it — are the same. When you see the colon, the words that follow will **define or explain**. Look at the definition in the following example:

> Equally noteworthy was the children's overall performance in math: almost 50% of the children earned A's, while another 33% earned B's.

A colon also can introduce a **list**, as in the following examples:

> Maslow divided our needs into two general categories: deficiency and growth needs.
>
> We'll describe each of the three characteristics unique to humanistic theory: having a phenomenological perspective, a holistic view, and a goal of self-actualization.

Test Yourself

Read the following sentences. Each one needs a colon to make the meaning clear. Decide where the colon is needed and write it in. You can check yourself in the "answers":

> The airline offered three drink choices coffee, tea, and juice.
>
> To open a childproof bottle, you must do the following actions push down on the cap, align the arrows, and then turn the cap.
>
> The coach explained that there were only two ways to play the game his way and the wrong way.
>
> Anorexics have a disturbed body image they are thin but see themselves as fat.
>
> When asked if she was a person or an animal, Koko the gorilla used sign language to answer with three words "fine animal gorilla."
>
> Vietnamese culture values respect for elders a child should never show disrespect for adults.
>
> One symbol of America is now found throughout the world blue jeans.
>
> In her magazine, Oprah Winfrey started a new idea in publishing she puts her own picture on the cover of every issue.

Answers

The airline offered three drink choices: coffee, tea, and juice.

To open a childproof bottle, you must do the following actions: push down on the cap, align the arrows, and then turn the cap.

The coach explained that there were only two ways to play the game: his way and the wrong way.

Anorexics have a disturbed body image : they are thin but see themselves as fat.

When asked if she was a person or an animal, Koko the gorilla used sign language to answer with three words: "fine animal gorilla."

Vietnamese culture values respect for elders: a child should never show disrespect for adults.

One symbol of America is now found throughout the world: blue jeans.

In her magazine, Oprah Winfrey started a new idea in publishing: she puts her own picture on the cover of every issue.

The Big Picture

Which statement below offers the best summary of the larger significance of this module?

A The space problems of any textbook are evident in this module. Humanistic psychology has nothing in common with psychoanalytic psychology and belongs in a separate module. These theories are completely different.

B Behaviorists have always been skeptical about the concept of personality, and the two theories in this module show why. Many Freudian ideas are outlandish, and humanistic ideas often seem naive and idealistic.

C Psychoanalytic and humanistic personality theories are essentially the same. Freud talks about ego, Rogers about self. Freud's unconscious motivation is like Maslow's hierarchy of needs. Superego could be self-actualization, etc.

D Both psychodynamic and humanistic theories of personality describe processes that go on inside us. But where Freud finds childhood all important, Maslow and Rogers emphasize the challenges of the future.

E "I made an awful Freudian slip when I was having dinner at my mother's house the other day," one psychologist told another. "I meant to say, 'Please pass the butter,' " but what I actually said was, 'You [rhymes with witch], you ruined my life!' "

True-False

_____ 1. Freud's key concept is the idea of conscious processes — how we understand reality.

_____ 2. Free association is necessary because we cannot know the unconscious directly.

_____ 3. For Freud, most personality development takes place during the first five years of life.

_____ 4. Because almost all of Freud's main followers broke with him, today his ideas have little influence.

_____ 5. Freud's famous personality theory is provocative, but hard to test scientifically.

_____ 6. Maslow and Rogers are pessimistic about the degree to which personality can change.

_____ 7. The hierarchy of needs helps explain why children who come to school hungry don't learn well.

_____ 8. Self-actualization means honestly recognizing your actual faults and weaknesses.

_____ 9. Rogers warns that a child who receives only unconditional positive regard will grow up spoiled and unrealistic about life.

_____ 10. For a personality test to be scientifically useful, it must possess the twin characteristics of reliability and validity.

Flashcards 1

____	1. dream interpretation	a.	related to id: operates to satisfy drives, avoid pain, without concern for moral restrictions or society's regulations
____	2. ego	b.	the influence of repressed thoughts, desires, or impulses on our conscious thoughts and behaviors
____	3. fixation	c.	this term could serve as the heading for all the other terms in Flashcards 1 (they all relate to this one)
____	4. Freud's psychodynamic theory of personality	d.	being locked into an earlier psychosexual stage because wishes were overgratified or undergratified
____	5. id	e.	assumes that dreams contain underlying, hidden meanings and symbols that provide clues to unconscious thoughts
____	6. Oedipus complex	f.	contains biological drives of sex and aggression that are the source of all psychic or mental energy; goal is pleasure
____	7. pleasure principle	g.	develops from id; goal is to find safe, socially acceptable ways of satisfying id's desires and superego's prohibitions
____	8. reality principle	h.	develops from ego; goal is to apply the moral values and standards of parents and society in satisfying one's wishes
____	9. superego	i.	process where child competes with same-sex parent for affections and pleasures of opposite-sex parent
____	10. unconscious motivation	j.	related to ego; has a policy of satisfying a wish or desire only if there's a socially acceptable outlet available

Flashcards 2

____	1. conditional positive regard	a.	our inherent tendency to develop and reach our true potentials; fulfillment of one's unique human potential
____	2. holistic view	b.	according to Rogers, is based on our hopes and wishes and reflects how we would like to see ourselves
____	3. humanistic theories	c.	love, sympathy, warmth, acceptance, and respect, which we crave from family, friends, and people important to us
____	4. ideal self	d.	the warmth, acceptance, and love others could show you as a valued human being, even when you disappoint them
____	5. phenomenological perspective	e.	according to Rogers, is based on our actual experiences and represents how we really see ourselves
____	6. positive regard	f.	this term could serve as the heading for all the other terms in Flashcards 2 (they all relate to this one)
____	7. real self	g.	how we see or describe ourselves; made up of many self-perceptions, abilities, and personality characteristics
____	8. self (self-concept)	h.	personality is more than the sum of its parts; the individual parts form a unique and total entity that functions as a unit
____	9. self-actualization	i.	the positive regard we receive if we behave in certain, acceptable ways, such as meeting the standards of others
____	10. unconditional positive regard	j.	your perception or view of the world, whether or not it is accurate, becomes your reality

Multiple Choice

_____ 1. Plotnik and Kouyoumdjian tell the stories of preacher Ted Haggard and actor Charles Dutton to illustrate the life changing forces of __________ and __________

a. humiliation / punishment
b. deceit / crime
c. wasted lives / lucky breaks
d. hidden urges / personality change

_____ 2. In psychology, the term "personality" means

a. a fixed way of responding to other people that is based on our inherited emotional makeup
b. a combination of long-lasting and distinctive behaviors, thoughts, motives, and emotions that typify how we react to other people and situations
c. favorable and unfavorable personal characteristics
d. how interesting and attractive we are to other people

_____ 3. In Sigmund Freud's psychodynamic theory of personality, the unconscious contains

a. everything we're aware of at a given moment
b. feelings and thoughts we remember from long ago
c. material that can easily be brought to awareness
d. repressed wishes, desires, or thoughts

_____ 4. Saying whatever comes to mind, even if it seems senseless, painful, or embarrassing, is part of the Freudian technique known as

a. a defense mechanism
b. a Freudian slip
c. free association
d. projection

_____ 5. Which *one* of the following is an example of a Freudian slip?

a. you can't remember the name of a person you just met
b. you call your current sweetheart by the name of your ex
c. you call your boss "an old grouch" behind his back
d. you guess that your friend is taking chemistry but it's actually biology

_____ 6. Freud's three mental processes develop in the following order:

a. superego – id – ego
b. ego – id – superego
c. id – ego – superego
d. (all three are present at birth)

_____ 7. The ability to create feelings of guilt gives the __________ its power

a. superego
b. ego
c. id
d. unconscious

_____ 8. If you told Freud you were experiencing anxiety, he would suggest that you are suffering from

a. nervousness resulting from sleep deprivation due to studying
b. inner conflicts between the primitive desires of your id and the moral goals of your superego
c. a conscious dislike of the courses you're taking
d. open tension between the demands of your id and what you really want to do

_____ 9. A student who blames poor test performance on "tricky questions" — rather than admit to poor preparation — is using the defense mechanism of
a. compensation
b. denial
c. projection
d. rationalization

_____ 10. The defense mechanism in which unacceptable wishes are turned into their opposites is known as
a. projection
b. reaction-formation
c. compensation
d. rationalization

_____ 11. Which one of the following shows the correct order of Freud's psychosexual stages?
a. oral, anal, phallic, latency, genital
b. anal, latency, phallic, oral, genital
c. genital, phallic, oral, anal, latency
d. latency, anal, oral, phallic, genital

_____ 12. The concept of the collective unconscious was proposed by
a. Carl Jung
b. Alfred Adler
c. Karen Horney
d. B. F. Skinner

_____ 13. Cognitive neuroscientists have developed the concept of __________ to take the place of Freud's theory of repressed unconscious forces
a. conscious thoughts
b. the collective unconscious
c. implicit or nondeclarative memory
d. the phenomenological perspective

_____ 14. Unlike psychodynamic theories, humanistic theories of personality emphasize
a. the continual operation of contradictory forces buried deep in our unconscious minds
b. our capacity for personal growth, the development of our potential, and freedom to choose our destiny
c. how difficult it is — even with therapy — to change personality significantly
d. the importance of perceptions and beliefs

_____ 15. The key concept of the humanistic approach to personality is
a. self-actualization
b. the phenomenological perspective
c. the holistic view
d. deficiency needs

_____ 16. At the first level of Abraham Maslow's hierarchy, we find __________ needs
a. self-actualization
b. esteem
c. love and belongingness
d. physiological

_____ 17. By self-actualization, Maslow meant
a. fulfillment of our unique human potential
b. having our deficiency needs satisfied
c. being loved and loving someone in return
d. gaining recognition and status in society

_____ 18. Rogers's concept of our self-actualizing tendency is most clearly a rejection of
a. Maslow's growth needs and self-actualization
b. Freud's id and pleasure principle
c. Jung's collective unconscious
d. Dutton's humanistic theory

_____ 19. Why are so many people unhappy? Carl Rogers says it's because
a. happiness is only possible when we become self-actualized
b. happiness is only an illusion
c. we have both a real self and an ideal self, and often they are in conflict
d. we have a positive self and a negative self, and one always dominates

_____ 20. National appreciation days (like mother's day) and the popularity of pets (especially dogs) are both examples of Rogers's concept of
a. shyness
b. self theory
c. conditional positive regard
d. positive regard

_____ 21. The old warning, "Of course, mommy loves you… when you're good!" is an example of Rogers's concept of
a. self-actualization
b. self-esteem needs
c. conditional positive regard
d. unconditional positive regard

_____ 22. An evaluation of humanistic theories of personality would emphasize their
a. positive, hopeful philosophy of human nature rather than scientific explanation of personality development
b. rational, scientific assessment of the biological strengths and limitations of our species
c. addition to psychology of new research in personality from genetics and neuroscience
d. demonstration of how human personality is driven by unconscious irrational forces

_____ 23. The remarkable academic achievement of children of the Indo-Chinese boat people is best explained by the
a. political values of anti-communism they shared with their new neighbors
b. restrictive immigration policy that allowed in only well-educated families
c. high value Protestantism places on school achievement
d. personal and cultural values concerning education transmitted by their parents

_____ 24. Because they use __________, projective tests often bring out unconscious material
a. pictures of people
b. simple materials
c. ambiguous stimuli
d. computer analysis

____ 25. One of the *disadvantages* of projective tests like the Rorschach inkblot test is that
a. they're difficult to score because they use ambiguous stimuli with no right or wrong answers
b. they're difficult to fake because there are no correct or socially desirable answers
c. they assess a client's hidden and unrecognized unconscious thoughts and desires
d. you get ink all over your shirt when you try to make the inkblots

Short Essay

1. Describe Freud's divisions of the mind, showing how the three parts interact in governing our behavior.

2. Defense mechanisms are often presented as crutches or excuses, but they're also essential to our healthy functioning. Give examples that illustrate this point.

3. Describe Maslow's hierarchy of needs and explain how it helps us understand human personality.

4. Explain Rogers's twin ideas of conditional and unconditional positive regard.

5. Which concept of personality seems closer to the truth — Freud's psychoanalytic approach or the humanistic approach of Maslow and Rogers? Explain the reasons for your choice.

A Freudian Slip

I have heard (and made) some dandy Freudian slips, but I'm not going to tell them, not here! They can be so revealing. A Freudian slip is saying something you didn't mean to say, breaking something, losing something, etc. The trick is to interpret the hidden meaning lying beneath the actual mistake. Treat the slip as you would a dream: carefully examine the manifest content and try to decipher the latent content (see p. 411, the introductory page of Module 24 in this Study Guide). Start listening for the Freudian slips people make. Listen for your own, too! You may be amazed by what you discover!

The "PowerStudy 4.5 for Introduction to Psychology" CD-ROM includes a complete set of interactive learning activities for this module: quizzes, summary test, key terms, web site connections, critical thinking exercise, module outline, and more.

Answers for Module 19

The Big Picture (explanations provided for incorrect choices)

A Humanistic psychology borrows from psychoanalytic psychology, and both emphasize the importance of inner life.
B Both psychoanalytic and humanistic approaches are standing the test of time, with many followers and admirers.
C Humanistic and psychoanalytic theories differ significantly over motivation, childhood, past and future, change, etc.
D *Correct! You see the "big picture" for this Module.*
E It's just a joke!

True-False (explanations provided for False choices; page numbers given for all choices)

1	F	434	Freud's key concept is unconscious processes.
2	T	435	
3	T	439	
4	F	440	Freud's ideas continue to influence modern psychology.
5	T	441	
6	F	442	Maslow and Rogers are optimistic about human change.
7	T	443	
8	F	443	Self-actualization refers to fulfilling one's unique human potential.
9	F	445	Rogers believes the more unconditional positive regard the better.
10	T	451	

Flashcards 1

1 e 2 g 3 d 4 c 5 f 6 i 7 a 8 j 9 h 10 b

Flashcards 2

1 i 2 h 3 f 4 b 5 j 6 c 7 e 8 g 9 a 10 d

Multiple Choice (explanations provided for incorrect choices)

1 a Humiliation and punishment apply, but neither is the point the textbook wants to make about personality.
b Deceit and crime apply, but neither is the point the textbook wants to make about personality.
c Both lives were wasted at times, but "lucky breaks" does not apply to either Haggard or Dutton.
d *Correct! See page 433.*

2 a Personality is neither fixed nor totally inherited.
b *Correct! See page 433.*
c This is a common meaning of personality, not the psychological definition.
d This is a common meaning of personality, not the psychological definition.

3 a This statement fits Freud's idea of the conscious mind, not the unconscious.
b This statement fits Freud's idea of the conscious mind, not the unconscious.
c This statement fits Freud's idea of the conscious mind, not the unconscious.
d *Correct! See page 434.*

4 a Defense mechanisms are unconscious distortions of the truth that protect our favorable sense of self.
b A Freudian slip is saying something one did not intend to say.
c *Correct! See page 435.*
d Projection is a defense mechanism in which unacceptable thoughts are attributed to others.

5 a Instead of an unconscious mistake, this is a case of failing to memorize the name of the person you just met.
b *Correct! See page 435.*
c Instead of an unconscious mistake, this is a case of intentional but hidden hostility.
d Instead of an unconscious mistake, this is a case of simply not possessing the correct information.

6 a Which process is most basic? That would have to be first.
b Which process is most basic? That would have to be first.
c *Correct! See page 436.*
d Since they develop in a sequence, they can't all be present at birth.

7 ***a*** *Correct! See page 436.*
b The ego is based on mainly realistic appraisals of the world, not on guilt.
c The id represents basic biological urges, not feelings of guilt.
d The unconscious is a state of mind, in which feelings of guilt may reside.

8 a Freud would look for a mental, not physiological, cause for anxiety.
b *Correct! See page 437.*
c Anxiety must relate to unconscious thoughts and feelings.
d From the Freudian point of view, everything about this statement is backwards.

9 a Compensation is making up for deficiencies in one area by overemphasizing attainments in another.
b Denial is refusing to recognize some anxiety-provoking event or idea.
c Projection is attributing unacceptable thoughts to others rather than to oneself.
d *Correct! See page 437.*

10 a Projection is attributing unacceptable thoughts to others rather than to oneself.
b *Correct! See page 437.*
c Compensation is making up for deficiencies in one area by overemphasizing attainments in another.
d Rationalization is making up acceptable excuses for behaviors that make us feel anxious.

11 ***a*** *Correct! See page 439.*
b How does a baby deal with the world? That has to be the *first* stage.
c How does a baby deal with the world? That has to be the *first* stage.
d How does a baby deal with the world? That has to be the *first* stage.

12 ***a*** *Correct! See page 440.*
b Adler developed a theory called "individual psychology."
c Horney challenged Freud's concept of penis envy.
d Skinner was a behaviorist (and therefore doubted that the unconscious even exists).

13 a Cognitive neuroscientists are not denying unconscious activity, but changing its explanation.
b This is Carl Jung's theory of unconscious activity.
c *Correct! See page 441.*
d This is humanistic psychology's explanation of how we understand the world.

14 a This is the basic assumption of psychodynamic theories of personality.
b *Correct! See page 442.*
c Humanistic theories are optimistic about the possibility of change.
d This is the basic assumption of cognitive theories of personality.

15 ***a*** *Correct! See page 442.*
b Important, but by itself does not explain what drives personality.
c Important, but by itself does not explain what drives personality.
d Deficiency needs are the lower-level needs, like food and safety, in Maslow's hierarchy.

16 a Of the four choices, which is the one you absolutely could not live without?
b Of the four choices, which is the one you absolutely could not live without?
c Of the four choices, which is the one you absolutely could not live without?
d *Correct! See page 443.*

17 ***a*** *Correct! See page 443.*
b Self-actualization comes from satisfying growth needs, not deficiency needs.
c Love is important, but (this may come as a shock) not all-important.
d Recognition and status are temporary and shallow values.

18 a Maslow's and Rogers's ideas of self-actualization are similar.
b *Correct! See page 444.*
c Jung disagreed with Freud about the importance of the sex drive, as did later humanistic psychologists.
d Charles Dutton is an actor whom Plotnik and Kouyoumdjian use as an example of personality change.

19 a Self-actualization is a higher goal we should strive for, but happiness does not depend on achieving it.
b This statement is far too cynical for Rogers.
c *Correct! See page 444.*
d These are not the two selves Rogers described.

20 a Shyness is a personality problem addressed more clearly by psychodynamic than humanistic psychology.
b Self theory is partly correct, in that it includes positive regard, but it also refers to self-actualization.
c Unconditional positive regard would be closer to correct, but positive regard is more general.
d *Correct! See page 445.*

21 a What's mommy saying about her love for you?
b What's mommy saying about her love for you?
c *Correct! See page 445.*
d What's mommy saying about her love for you?

22 ***a*** *Correct! See page 446.*
b This would be truer of psychodynamic theories.
c Humanistic theories have not yet been much influenced by research in genetics and neuroscience.
d This would be true of psychodynamic theories.

23 a That feeling may have been there, but it does not explain the high academic achievement.
b There was no such policy; the boat people were a diverse group.
c Most boat people were not members of Protestant churches.
d *Correct! See page 448.*

24 a Think about the materials used in the Rorschach (a projective test).
b Think about the materials used in the Rorschach (a projective test).
c *Correct! See page 450.*
d Think about the materials used in the Rorschach (a projective test).

25 ***a*** *Correct! See page 451.*
b This is an *advantage* of projective tests.
c This is an *advantage* of projective tests.
d It's just a joke!

Short Essay (sample answers)

1. For Freud, human personality is a war between the desire for pleasure and the need to be realistic. At birth, the child is all id (pleasure principle), the biological drives of sex and aggression. As the demands of the real world intrude, part of the id becomes the ego (reality principle), attempting to satisfy id desires in safe and socially acceptable ways. Finally, through interaction with parents, part of the ego becomes the superego, a conscience that forces obedience to social and moral demands through the power of guilt feelings.

2. We usually think of defense mechanisms as excuses, like "rationalizing" poor test performance as caused by tricky questions. But our ability to be "rational" is also our greatest human achievement. In the same manner, "denial" can help us be courageous, "repression" can help us escape domination by unacceptable ideas, "projection" can help us understand threatening thoughts, "reaction formation" and "displacement" can help us focus on problems we can solve, and "sublimation" can help us avoid forbidden desires.

3. Every theory of personality must explain motivation, what makes us go. Maslow's hierarchy of needs has the strength of stressing higher needs while not underrating the importance of basic needs. Maslow's five levels are: (1) physiological needs, essential for life, followed by (2) safety needs, and (3) love and belonging needs. Higher needs are (4) esteem and achievement, and finally (5) self-actualization. The higher needs are most important for full development, but you can't get there unless the lower needs are met first.

4. When good old Spot happily greets you after the test, you understand why Rogers thinks positive regard is what we want and need. Trouble is, you need more than Spot: you need other people, and they are much less accepting than Spot. You rightly think you deserve unconditional positive regard: warmth, acceptance, and love simply because you are valued as a human being. But all too often, what you get is *conditional* positive regard: warmth, etc., when you behave as others expect. Only Spot loves you unconditionally.

5. This is a hard choice, so don't decide too quickly. The humanists seem so much nicer and more positive than the sour and negative Freudians. But when you actually evaluate other people and make decisions about them, are you a sunny humanist or a cynical Freudian? Today we know more about human nature and human behavior than the Freudians or humanists did. What does our accumulated scientific knowledge, as well as your own self-understanding and experience with others, suggest about which approach is truer?

Module 20

Social Cognitive & Trait Theories

The Story of a Cold-Blooded Killer

Did you know that you're reading the work of a cold-blooded killer? One who could take out a long-bladed knife and charge at an enemy, screaming "Kill! Kill!"? Of course, the enemy in this case was a sack of straw and the killer was a draftee whose only real concern, in a time when our country was totally at peace, was how to get out of KP duty. An ironic twist: when it began raining half-way through the exercise, the officer in charge blew his whistle, loaded us into our trucks, and took us back to our dry barracks. The last thing our commanding officer needed was a complaint from some concerned parents' congressperson about how he was treating their boy!

The point of my "war story" is that I wasn't a killer at all (far from it!) and the officer who let us off easy was actually a good soldier. But what if there had been a real war? Maybe I would have acted on my army training. Then what would I have been?

The Genius and Fault of Modern Psychology

In Module 20 Plotnik and Kouyoumdjian continue their survey of four dominant personality theories (psychoanalytic, humanistic, social cognitive, and trait) and raise one of the most fundamental questions in psychology: How stable is personality? (See their discussion of person-situation interaction.) If the concept of personality is real, people must show a certain degree of consistency over a wide range of situations. But if people exhibit significantly different behavior in varying situations, how real is the idea of personality?

The genius of modern psychology is to help us see inside. You might say that psychoanalytic theory reveals the dark side of human nature and humanistic the positive, but both place the truth inside. They assume that inner tendencies guide our behavior. On the other hand, social cognitive theories and trait theories assume that our experience in the external world guides our behavior. Experience leads to the development of expectancies and traits. This focus on the outside world introduces a dangerous question: could it be the other way around, with the situation determining the person?

The tendency to find the problem inside is also one of the main faults of modern psychology. We become so good at digging out the "real" reasons for psychological problems, as Sigmund Freud taught us to do, that we often overlook obvious situational causes like unemployment or discrimination or even environmental pollution. We learn to manage stress, discover dysfunctions, and blame ourselves. Sometimes we miss the real problem.

By the way, I fudged at that bayonet drill years ago. I was too embarrassed to actually scream "Kill! Kill!", so I just pretended to yell. Does that added detail ruin the point I was trying to make? Or does it remind us that psychology is a complicated and fascinating science?

Effective Student Tip 20

What Moves You?

When Delores scored her exam paper, she marked down how many questions she got right (32) and the corresponding letter grade ("D"). She handed me her answer sheet and fled. I began recording her score and grade, and then it hit me: by the grading standards I had written on the board, 32 was a "C", not a "D."

A classmate chased her down the hall and when I showed Delores her mistake and asked her why, she said, "I guess because I always get a 'D'."

Like many students, Delores never did quite as well as I thought she would. Was her "slip of the pen" an indication of mixed motivation? Many students aren't really sure why they're in school, why they've taken a certain class, or why they aren't doing as well as their abilities would suggest. All of these questions involve motivation, the basic forces that account for our actions.

Are you in college for your parents? Taking a course to "get it out of the way"? Cutting class without much idea why? These are common cases of mixed or poorly understood motivation. Don't let it happen to you. Try to discover your true motivation. Watch for clues that alert you to possible confusion. You'll become more successful, and do it more easily, when you get your motivations and your goals in line. Honesty is the best policy.

Your response…

Try making a totally honest [and private] list of the reasons why you are in college.

Learning Objectives

1. Understand social cognitive and trait theories, which emphasize environmental forces of experience and learning, as the other half of the four basic approaches to personality.

2. Learn the basic concepts of the social cognitive approach to understanding personality through exploring the work of Albert Bandura, Julian Rotter, and Walter Mischel.

3. Learn the basic concepts of the trait approach to understanding personality through exploring the work of Gordon Allport and research leading to the "Big Five" supertraits.

4. Appreciate the new contributions to personality theory from behavioral genetics and the concept of heritability.

5. Consider the effect of culture on personality through the example of suicide bombers.

6. Review the founders and key concepts of the four main personality theories presented in this and the previous modules.

7. Explore the role of objective tests in personality assessment and revisit the concepts of reliability and validity in scientific research.

Key Terms

The key terms from the personality theories discussed in this module are somewhat less commonly known than those in the previous module, but look how few of them there are to learn. Piece of cake!

Bandura's social cognitive theory
Barnum principle
behavioral genetics
cognitive factors
delay of gratification
environmental factors
factor analysis
five-factor model (OCEAN)
heritability
locus of control (internal/external)
longitudinal method
Minnesota Multiphasic Personality Inventory-2–RF (MMPI-2)
objective personality tests (self-report questionnaires)
person-situation interaction
personal factors
quantum personality change
reliability
self-efficacy
social cognitive theory
structured interviews
trait
trait theory
validity

The "PowerStudy 4.5 for Introduction to Psychology" CD-ROM includes a complete set of interactive learning activities for this module: quizzes, summary test, key terms, web site connections, critical thinking exercise, module outline, and more.

Outline

- *Introduction*

  1. Power of beliefs (Wangari Maathai, Nobel Peace Prize winner)
  2. Determination (Kiran Bedi, hero and role model for Indian women)

  □ How do these two examples illuminate the concept of personality and questions about it?

A. *Social Cognitive Theory*

1. Review and definition: **social cognitive theory**
2. Interaction of three factors
   a. Cognitive-personal factors
      (1) **Cognitive factors**
      (2) **Personal factors**
   b. Behaviors
   c. **Environmental factors**
3. **Bandura's social cognitive theory**
   a. Four cognitive factors
      (1) Language ability
      (2) Observational learning
      (3) Purposeful behavior
      (4) Self-analysis
   b. **Locus of control: internal/external** (Julian Rotter)
      (1) Internal locus of control
      (2) External locus of control
   c. **Delay of gratification**
      (1) Preferred rewards and delay
      (2) Important to delay gratification?
   d. **Self-efficacy** (Albert Bandura)
      (1) Sources of information
      (2) Influence of self-efficacy
4. Evaluation of social cognitive theory
   a. Comprehensive approach
   b. Experimentally based
   c. Programs for change
   d. Criticisms and conclusions

B. *Trait Theory*

1. Definition
   a. **Trait theory**
   b. **Trait**

2. Identifying traits
    a. How many traits can there be? (Gordon Allport)
        (1) Original list of 18,000 terms
        (2) Reduced to 4,500 traits
    b. Aren't some traits related?
        (1) **Factor analysis** (Raymond Cattell)
        (2) Reduced list to 35 traits
3. Finding traits: Big Five (supertraits)
    a. **Five-factor model** (OCEAN)
        (1) **O**penness
        (2) **C**onscientiousness
        (3) **E**xtraversion
        (4) **A**greeableness
        (5) **N**euroticism
    b. Importance of the Big Five
    c. Big Five in the real world
4. Person versus situation (Walter Mischel)
    a. Experiment: person-situation
        (1) Failure of traits to predict behaviors across different situations
        (2) **Person-situation interaction**
    b. Conclusions
        (1) Descriptions
        (2) Predictions
5. Stability versus change: **longitudinal method**

☐ What is your age, relative to the big three-oh? What does this suggest about your personality?

    a. 3 to 21 years old
    b. 22 to 80 years old

C. Genetic Influences on Traits

1. **Behavioral genetics**
2. Studying genetic influences: **heritability** (Thomas Bouchard)
3. Data from twin studies
4. Influences on personality
    a. Genetic factors (40 percent)
    b. Nonshared environmental factors (27 percent)
    c. Error (26 percent)
    d. Shared environmental factors (7 percent)

D. *Evaluation of Trait Theory*

1. How good is the list? (Big Five supertraits)
2. Can traits predict? (person-situation interaction)
3. What influences traits? (shared and nonshared factors)

E. *Research Focus: 180-Degree Change*

1. How much can people change in a day (**quantum personality change**)?
2. A study of personality change
   a. Method: **structured interviews**
   b. Results
   c. Conclusions

F. *Cultural Diversity: Suicide Bombers*

1. Story of a suicide bomber
2. Cultural and personal reasons
   a. What conditions lead to suicide attacks?
   b. What motivates a suicide bomber?
   c. Do suicide bombers share certain traits?
   d. What does the future hold?

G. *Four Theories of Personality*

☐ Plotnik and Kouyoumdjian give you a beautiful summary of the important but complex material of Modules 19 and 20. Take advantage of their chart (summarized on the next page). Use the chart as a study tool. Can you describe each theory and its key concepts? This would be a good exercise for a study group or for studying with a friend.

H. *Application: Assessment — Objective Tests*

1. Definition
   a. **Objective personality tests (self-report questionnaires)**
   b. Structured (specific questions and answers)
2. Examples of objective tests
   a. Integrity tests
   b. **Minnesota Multiphasic Personality Inventory-2-RF (MMPI-2)**
3. Reliability and validity
   a. **Barnum principle**
   b. **Validity**
   c. **Reliability**
4. Usefulness
   a. Disadvantages
   b. Advantages

Plotnik & Kouyoumdjian's Magic Personality Theory Chart (see pages 472–473 in the textbook)

1. Psychodynamic theory (Sigmund Freud)
   a. Unconscious motivation
      (1) Free association
      (2) Dream interpretation
      (3) Slips of the tongue
   b. Divisions of the mind
      (1) Id (pleasure principle)
      (2) Ego (reality principle)
      (3) Superego (conscience and sense of guilt)
   c. Psychosexual stages
      (1) Oral
      (2) Anal
      (3) Phallic (Oedipus and Electra complexes)
      (4) Latency
      (5) Genital
2. Humanistic theories (Abraham Maslow and Carl Rogers)
   a. Phenomenal perspective, holistic view, and self-actualization
   b. Abraham Maslow's humanistic theory
      (1) Capacity for growth
      (2) Hierarchy of needs
   c. Carl Rogers' self theory
      (1) Self-actualization tendency
      (2) Need for positive regard
3. Social cognitive theory (Albert Bandura)
   a. Cognitive factors
   b. Locus of control
   c. Delay of gratification
   d. Self-efficacy
4. Trait theory (Gordon Allport)
   a. Basic traits
   b. Five-factor model (Big Five supertraits or OCEAN)
      (1) Person-situation interaction
      (2) Changeable and stable
      (3) Genetic factors

How English Works

Words in the Textbook

p. 457 her **petite** stature = a small and delicate build

less likely to **trigger showdowns** = set off confrontations over conflicts or disputes

p. 462 **domestic abuse** = violent fighting within family

street **thugs** = criminals

this **elusive** list = hard to find

p. 464 The best-known, **right wing** talk-radio host = politically conservative

Our priorities are **out of whack** = not correct

whites are **getting away** with drug use = not penalized

send them up the river = send them to jail

caught in a drug **ring** = criminal group

you might very well **draw the line** = refuse to continue

you must **take into account** = consider, judge

p. 465 **thrill seekers** = people who value excitement and danger

p. 466 **chain-smoked** = smoked one cigarette after another without stopping

they were **flabbergasted** = shocked, very surprised

p. 468 should not be **blown out of proportion** = emphasized too much

p. 470 **Alcoholics Anonymous** = organization to help alcoholics stop drinking

the **battery** of personality tests = group, set

relieved of a mental **burden** = worry

p. 471 culture considers them to be **martyrs** = people who die for political or religious reasons

p. 472 **go after** one's dream = pursue, work to achieve

a socially acceptable **outlet** = way to release pressure

p. 474 has become **big business** = profitable, resulting in new companies

a **parole board** = official group who decide if a prisoner is ready for release

Sentence Structure: Who / Whom

Maybe your English teacher made you practice using **whom** in sentences like the following:

The rock star whom I interviewed has a new hit song.

This sentence is perfectly correct, but modern grammar experts agree that this way to use **whom** is dying. Why? Because it's hard to use it correctly, so it slows down our communication. Most grammar teachers now believe that it's perfectly acceptable to write:

The rock star who I interviewed has a new hit song.

Still, this doesn't mean that **whom** is completely dead! We still must use **whom** after a preposition like **of, for, with, to,** and **from**. This is a very useful way to join sentences together that have the same person in both sentences. For example, look at the following two sentences:

> The man works for the government. Ludmila is married **to him.**

Since **him** in the second sentence refers to the man, we can place the second sentence starting with the preposition and **whom** for **him** right after the word man to create the following single sentence:

> The man **to whom** Ludmila is married works for the government.

You probably wouldn't hear someone say this in everyday conversation. Instead, you would hear a shortened form like this:

> The man Ludmila is married to works for the government.

Although this sentence is easier, it's important to understand the use of the more formal **to whom** sentence because textbooks and professional work use this language, like this example from the text:

> After we have acquired a gender identity, gender role, and sexual orientation, there remain occasionally difficult decisions about when, where, and **with whom** sexual behavior is appropriate.

Now you try it. See if you can put together sentences in the same way. Read the following sentences, and then use the **preposition/whom** form to make one sentence:

> Example: The tourists spent a lot of money. Jin traveled with them to Korea.
>
> The tourists **with whom Jin traveled** to Korea spent a lot of money.

Don't bother with commas here; you're joining these two sentences together. Try some now. If you're not sure of your answers, you can always check the answers below.

The new nurse never smiles. All the patients are complaining about her.

The __________.

The fat man is called Santa Claus. Many children believe in him.

The __________.

The model will arrive in five minutes. The photographer is waiting for her.

The __________.

The grandmother comes from Norway. Claus inherited his blue eyes from her.

The __________.

The dancer injured her leg. The ballet cannot start without her.

The __________.

Answers

The new nurse about whom all the patients are complaining never smiles.
The fat man in whom many children believe is called Santa Claus.
The model for whom the photographer is waiting will arrive in five minutes.
The grandmother from whom Claus inherited his blue eyes comes from Norway.
The dancer without whom the ballet cannot start injured her leg.

The Big Picture

Which statement below offers the best summary of the larger significance of this module?

A Social cognitive and trait theories of personality are coming together in a single, persuasive description of human behavior. The central idea of this new, unified theory is well represented in the acronym OCEAN.

B For all the efforts of psychology to work out a convincing explanation of personality, the newly discovered phenomenon of quantum personality change (often happening in a single day) makes nonsense of any single theory of personality.

C The most important idea presented in this module is the "cultural diversity" discussion of collectivistic and individualistic cultures (Japan and the United States). The point is that the most important personality variables are cultural.

D This module must be read in conjunction with the previous one. Together these modules describe the four major theoretical approaches to our understanding of personality. The study of personality shows how we're all alike, yet individuals.

E So what if I have no will power. I don't like marshmallows anyway!

True-False

_____ 1. Social cognitive theory combines learning and behavior with ideas about how we think.

_____ 2. Gordon Allport and Raymond Cattell were early pioneers of social cognitive theory.

_____ 3. One of the key ideas of Albert Bandura's social cognitive theory is observational learning.

_____ 4. College students who think they "can't beat the system" ought to study the concept of locus of control.

_____ 5. The most important measure of self-efficacy is the ability to delay gratification.

_____ 6. A trait is a personal quirk — something that makes you different from everyone else in the world.

_____ 7. After a long search, researchers have now gotten the trait list down to 35 supertraits.

_____ 8. One problem with the concept of traits is that traits are not always consistent across situations.

_____ 9. Most changes in personality occur before the age of 30.

_____ 10. Genetic influences can determine physical factors like height, but not psychological factors like personality.

Flashcards 1

_____	1. behavioral genetics	a. a statistical measure that estimates how much of a trait is influenced by genetic factors
_____	2. delay of gratification	b. beliefs concerning how much control (internal or external) we have over situations or rewards
_____	3. factor analysis	c. your personal belief concerning how capable you are in controlling events and situations in your life
_____	4. five-factor model	d. voluntarily postponing an immediate reward to continue a task for the promise of a future reward
_____	5. heritability	e. says personality is shaped by environmental conditions, cognitive-personal factors, and behavior
_____	6. locus of control	f. a relatively stable and enduring tendency to behave in a particular way
_____	7. self-efficacy	g. a complicated statistical method; finds relationships among many diverse items and groups them
_____	8. social cognitive theory	h. **O**penness, **C**onscientiousness, **E**xtraversion, **A**greeable-ness, and **N**euroticism are key factors in personality
_____	9. trait	i. an approach for analyzing structure of personality by measuring, identifying, and classifying similarities
_____	10. trait theory	j. study of how inherited or genetic factors affect personality, intelligence, emotions, and behavior

Flashcards 2

_____	1. Barnum principle	a. asking each individual same set of focused questions so same information is obtained from everyone
_____	2. cognitive factors	b. consistency; a person's test score at one time should be similar to score on a similar test later
_____	3. longitudinal method	c. our behavior results from an interaction between our traits and the effects of being in a particular situation
_____	4. Minnesota Multiphasic Personality Inventory-2	d. those cognitive factors that include our beliefs, expectations, values, intentions, and social roles`
_____	5. objective personality test (self-report questionnaire)	e. sudden (in a single day) and radical or dramatic shift in one's personality, beliefs, or values
_____	6. person-situation interaction	f. studying the same group of individuals repeatedly at many different points in time
_____	7. quantum personality change	g. listing a number of traits in such a general way (like a horoscope) that every reader sees himself or herself in it
_____	8. reliability	h. degree to which a test actually does measure what it claims to measure
_____	9. structured interviews	i. true-false self-report questionnaire (567 items) describing normal and abnormal behaviors
_____	10. validity	j. specific written statements requiring subjects to respond ("true" or "false") about applicability

Multiple Choice

_____ 1. Plotnik and Kouyoumdjian tell the stories of Nobel Prize winner Wangari Maathai and pioneering policewoman Kiran Bedi to illustrate the
   a. beliefs and traits that motivate human personality
   b. powerful personalities that have been produced by the peoples of Africa and India
   c. key role of prisons and law enforcement in maintaining social stability
   d. unconscious forces that are the foundation of all personality

_____ 2. Which one of the following forces is *not* a component of social cognitive theory?
   a. environmental conditions (learning)
   b. cognitive-personal factors
   c. unconscious motivation
   d. behavior

_____ 3. One of the key concepts in Albert Bandura's social cognitive theory is
   a. need for social approval
   b. observational learning
   c. self-actualization
   d. unconscious conflict

_____ 4. The only statement below that shows *internal* locus of control is:
   a. exam questions are so often unrelated to course work that studying is useless
   b. no matter how hard you try, some people just don't like you
   c. it isn't always wise to plan too far ahead, because many things just turn out to be a matter of good or bad fortune
   d. when I make plans, I'm almost certain I can make them work

_____ 5. Children and marshmallows were used in a classic study of
   a. observational learning
   b. locus of control
   c. delay of gratification
   d. traits

_____ 6. When the four-year-olds in the delay of gratification experiment were retested 10 years later,
   a. high delay and low delay children were now about the same
   b. being good at delay was related to many other positive characteristics
   c. high delay children had become anxious, worrywart teens
   d. many had become Scouts, but, curiously, refused to make s'mores

_____ 7. Which one of the following is *not* included by Bandura in the keys to determining your sense of self-efficacy?
   a. previous experiences of success or failure on similar tasks
   b. comparing your capabilities with those of others
   c. listening to what others say about your capabilities
   d. the power of our conscience to make us feel guilty

_____ 8. One of the major contributions of social cognitive theory to understanding personality is
   a. going beyond symptoms to the deeper emotional or unconscious causes of problems
   b. the development of successful programs for changing behavior and personality
   c. explaining the emotional and genetic causes of behavior
   d. offering a complete theory of personality and human nature

_____ 9. Do women make better cops? Evidence suggests that the answer is
   a. yes, at least for now, because women have a greater determination to succeed
   b. no, because women in our society tend to have a lower sense of self-efficacy
   c. yes, because personality traits shared by many women are useful in police work
   d. no, because the performance of male and female officers is about the same

_____ 10. A trait is defined as a
   a. relatively stable and enduring tendency to behave in a particular way
   b. personal idiosyncrasy that distinguishes us from all others
   c. behavioral tendency that is genetically determined
   d. specific belief about the world that influences our personality

_____ 11. For years, research in personality has tried to identify the
   a. single trait that all humans share
   b. particular traits that make up a healthy personality
   c. most complete list of terms that deal with personality differences
   d. fewest number of traits that cover the largest range of human behaviors

_____ 12. The result of this effort (above) is the current belief that human personality is best described by
   a. five supertraits
   b. 35 basic traits
   c. 4,500 personality traits
   d. 18,000 descriptive terms

_____ 13. The five-factor model of personality gets its range and depth from the fact that
   a. if we know just five things about a person, we can produce a complete picture of him or her
   b. each of the factors is set by age five
   c. each of the factors is determined by the culture in which the person was raised
   d. each factor is actually a continuum, with many related traits at the hot and cold ends

_____ 14. One of the sharpest attacks on the concept of traits was
   a. Mischel's argument that behavior changes in different situations
   b. Bandura's theory that we learn by observing others
   c. Cattell's discovery that needs are arranged in a hierarchy
   d. Allport's list of 18,000 terms that deal with personality differences

_____ 15. In Walter Mischel's classic study of conscientious behavior by college students across different situations, the trait of conscientiousness
   a. governed student behavior with high consistency across different situations
   b. did not predict student behavior in either old or new situations
   c. failed to predict how students would behave in different situations
   d. correctly predicted student behavior in each of the five supertraits (OCEAN)

_____ 16. When are you most likely to make changes in your personality? Research says
   a. by age five
   b. before age 30
   c. after age 30
   d. when the end is near

_____ 17. The new area of psychology called behavioral genetics is providing evidence that
   a. twins are very different from single-birth children
   b. twins may appear outwardly similar, but in most respects they are quite different
   c. sharing a family environment is the major influence on personality
   d. inheritance sets a range of behaviors for many aspects of personality

_____ 18. The statistical measure called heritability is a significant scientific advance in the study of personality because it
   a. reveals that environmental factors have far more influence on personality than genetic factors
   b. uses research to estimate how much a trait is influenced by genetic factors
   c. eliminates the need for traditional personality tests and measures
   d. means that if we know a person's genetic code, we know his or her personality

_____ 19. It is now believed that __________ of the development of personality traits is explained by genetics
   a. about half
   b. about one-fifth
   c. almost all
   d. almost none

_____ 20. In evaluating trait theory, critics raise all of the following questions *except*
   a. how good is the Big Five list of traits?
   b. can traits predict behaviors?
   c. how much do genetic factors influence traits?
   d. how are traits learned?

_____ 21. Some people experience a very sudden (in a single day) and radical or dramatic shift in personality, beliefs, or values; psychology calls this a
   a. flash of insight, or "ah ha" experience
   b. born-again spiritual experience
   c. quantum personality change
   d. quantitative personality change

_____ 22. What motivates a suicide bomber like the young Palestinian woman described in the text?
   a. a cluster of distinct traits, such as being quick to anger
   b. a combination of personal reasons (like the death of a friend) and cultural influences (like power)
   c. most appear to have been motivated by an external locus of control
   d. they aren't really motivated (most don't know they have been wired with a live bomb)

_____ 23. A good example of a highly structured objective personality test is the
   a. Thematic Apperception Test (TAT)
   b. Rorschach inkblot test
   c. Minnesota Multiphasic Personality Inventory-2-R (MMPI)
   d. traditional psychological interview

_____ 24. According to the Barnum principle, horoscopes can "predict" your future because
   a. the traits listed are so general that they apply to almost everyone
   b. there is a specific astrological constellation for the date of your birth
   c. astrological signs have been worked out over many millennia
   d. life is a circus — who knows what will happen?

_____ 25. It's so important that it bears repeating: reliability = _________ and validity = _________
a. truth / consistency
b. being on target / being correct time after time
c. hucksterism (Barnum principle) / scientific truth
d. scores are consistent over time / measures what it claims to measure

Short Essay

1. How might the concept of locus of control help explain both successful and unsuccessful students?
2. Describe the experiment that tested the concept of delay of gratification.
3. Describe the "hot" and "cold" ends of the categories (OCEAN) in the Big Five trait theory of personality (okay, this is hard!).
4. In what ways are suicide bombers examples of cultural diversity?
5. Describe how the Barnum principle explains the popularity of horoscopes.

For Psych Majors Only...

Pioneers in Personality Theory: Psych majors should know the famous pioneers of personality theory discussed in Modules 19 and 20. Can you match these psychologists to the phrase that fits their work or ideas?

_____	1. Sigmund Freud	a. individual psychology
_____	2. Carl Jung	b. "penis envy" is nonsense
_____	3. Alfred Adler	c. hierarchy of needs
_____	4. Karen Horney	d. personality traits
_____	5. Abraham Maslow	e. delay of gratification
_____	6. Carl Rogers	f. locus of control
_____	7. Albert Bandura	g. collective unconscious
_____	8. Walter Mischel	h. unconditional positive regard
_____	9. Gordon Allport	i. observational learning
_____	10. Julian Rotter	j. unconscious motivation

Answers to "Pioneers in Personality Theory" Quiz

1 j 2 g 3 a 4 b 5 c 6 h 7 i 8 e 9 d 10 f

Answers for Module 20

The Big Picture (explanations provided for incorrect choices)

A There are significant differences between social cognitive and trait theories of personality.
B If quantum personality change holds up, each approach will have its own explanation of this kind of change.
C Although humans show wide cultural variations, in the most important ways we are more alike than different.
D Correct! You see the "big picture" for this Module.
E It's just a joke!

True-False (explanations provided for False choices; page numbers given for all choices)

1	T	458	
2	F	458	Allport and Cattell were pioneers of the trait approach to personality.
3	T	459	
4	T	459	
5	F	460	Self-efficacy refers to belief in one's ability to accomplish goals.
6	F	462	A trait is a tendency to act in a consistent manner (not a quirk).
7	F	463	Current research has reduced all traits to five supertraits.
8	T	464	
9	T	465	
10	F	466	Current research suggests that there is a significant genetic component in personality.

Flashcards 1

1 j 2 d 3 g 4 h 5 a 6 b 7 c 8 e 9 f 10 i

Flashcards 2

1 g 2 d 3 f 4 i 5 j 6 c 7 e 8 b 9 a 10 h

Multiple Choice (explanations provided for incorrect choices)

1 ***a*** *Correct! See page 457.*
b These two remarkable people are from Africa and India, but more general personality factors are the point.
c The main point of these twin stories concerns beliefs and determination, not social stability.
d Just the opposite is true for the personality theories in this module.

2 a This is one of the three forces that social cognitive theory says shape personality development.
b This is one of the three forces that social cognitive theory says shape personality development.
c *Correct! See page 458.*
d This is one of the three forces that social cognitive theory says shape personality development.

3 a This general idea is not a key concept in personality.
b *Correct! See page 459.*
c Self-actualization belongs to Abraham Maslow and Carl Rogers.
d Unconscious conflict belongs to Sigmund Freud.

4 a So there is nothing I can do to get a better grade.
b So my social skills count for nothing.
c So my individual efforts will not be effective.
d *Correct! See page 459.*

5 a Observational learning was studied by Albert Bandura.
b Locus of control was studied by Julian Rotter.
c *Correct! See page 460.*
d Traits were studied by Gordon Allport.

6 a High delay children continued to show better adjustment than low delay children.
b *Correct! See page 460.*
c High delay children showed many personality strengths 10 years later.
d It's just a joke!

7 a Would this influence how effective you believe you are?
b Would this influence how effective you believe you are?
c Would this influence how effective you believe you are?
d *Correct! See page 460.*

8 a This would fit psychodynamic theories.
b *Correct! See page 461.*
c No theory combines emotional and genetic factors to explain personality.
d This would fit Sigmund Freud's psychoanalytic theory of personality.

9 a Determination was not the factor indicated by research.
b Even if true, this idea did not apply to female cops.
c *Correct! See page 462.*
d Research indicated some performance differences. What were they?

10 *a* *Correct! See page 462.*
b This is a common definition of a trait, but not the psychological definition.
c Traits are not all genetically determined.
d Traits are not exclusively cognitive.

11 a Rather than a single trait, there probably are five basic traits.
b This may be a particular concern of some psychologists, but it is not the main research goal.
c Allport compiled such a list, but it was only a starting point in defining traits.
d *Correct! See page 462.*

12 *a* *Correct! See page 463.*
b This is the result of factor analysis of the 4,500 traits.
c This is what the 18,000 descriptive terms became when translated into traits.
d This is where Allport started.

13 a It is far more complicated than five things, because of the continuum each of the five factors represents.
b This would be truer of psychoanalytic theories; trait theories do not specify when traits appear.
c Research suggests that personality arises from a universal experience or biological basis rather than culture.
d *Correct! See page 463.*

14 *a* *Correct! See page 464.*
b Bandura's theory does not exclude the concept of traits.
c Maslow's theory does not exclude the concept of traits.
d Allport's list helped develop the concept of traits.

15 a That was the point of the experiment — just the opposite was true.
b The trait did predict behavior in old, similar situations.
c *Correct! See page 464.*
d Conscientiousness is itself one of the five supertraits.

16 a Then at what age is personality first formed?
b *Correct! See page 465.*
c The author of the Study Guide only wishes this was true!
d At death?

17 a Twins are studied not because they are different but because they are alike.
b Twins are studied not because they are different but because they are alike.
c Possibly true, but this is an environmental influence, not a genetic one.
d *Correct! See page 466.*

18 a Current thinking says that personality is about half genetic and half environmental.
b *Correct! See page 466.*
c Such tests and measures provide the data that genetic information is able to reinterpret.
d If this were true, it would mean that experience is irrelevant to personality development.

19 *a* *Correct! See page 467.*
b This idea considerably understates genetic influences.
c This statement is far too extreme.
d This statement is far too extreme.

20	a	This is one of the three major questions about traits.
	b	This is one of the three major questions about traits.
	c	This is one of the three major questions about traits.
	d	*Correct! See page 468.*
21	a	Insight refers to understanding more than to change.
	b	This is not a term in psychology.
	c	*Correct! See page 470.*
	d	Sounds right, but check the first word.
22	a	No specific personality profile or traits have been identified.
	b	*Correct! See page 471.*
	c	This has not been reported in studies of suicide bombers.
	d	They know what they are doing.
23	a	This is a projective test.
	b	This is a projective test.
	c	*Correct! See page 474.*
	d	An interview is the opposite of a psychological test.
24	***a***	*Correct! See page 475.*
	b	True, but what connection do they have with your future?
	c	True, but what connection do they have with your future?
	d	Barnum owned a circus, but this idea is not the Barnum principle.
25	a	If anything, just the opposite (but "truth" is too strong for science).
	b	"On target" could refer to validity, but "being correct" isn't right for either term.
	c	An interesting opposition, but not the meaning of reliability and validity.
	d	*Correct! See page 475.*

Short Essay (sample answers)

1. Julian Rotter's concept of locus of control refers to a continuum of beliefs about how much control we have over situations and rewards. Internal locus of control is the belief that we control our destiny, while external locus of control is the belief that events outside ourselves (fate) determine what happens. Students who believe graduation depends on motivation and determination show internal locus of control, while students who believe graduation depends on chance or things outside their control show external locus of control.

2. Young children were told they could have one marshmallow right now or two marshmallows if they waited until the experimenter returned. The children faced the dilemma of taking a less preferred single marshmallow immediately or delaying gratification but obtaining a more preferred reward by waiting. Delay was more difficult if they looked at the marshmallows. When examined 10 years later, the children who showed an ability to delay gratification now exhibited several desirable personality characteristics.

3. OCEAN stands for the following five supertraits, each representing a continuum. They should describe every person. <u>Openness</u>: from *open to novel experiences* to *has narrow interests*. <u>Conscientiousness</u>: from *responsible and dependable* to *impulsive and careless*. <u>Extraversion</u>: from *outgoing and decisive* to *retiring and withdrawn*. <u>Agreeableness</u>: from *warm and good-natured* to *unfriendly and cold*. <u>Neuroticism</u>: from *stable and not a worrier* to *nervous and emotionally unstable*. ("Correct" if you got the general idea.)

4. Do suicide bombers share certain traits? They have some traits in common, but only general traits that also apply to others who don't become suicide bombers. Instead of common traits, suicide bombers have in common personal reasons (the death of a loved one), and cultural influences (the conviction that the suicide bombing makes up for the powerlessness of their parents and the humiliations of their group). The extreme example of suicide bombers demonstrates that individual traits can be outweighed by cultural influences.

5. Loads of people (75 pecent) read horoscopes, and many believe they're so correct that they were written especially for them. But examination shows that horoscopes contain general traits, at least a few of which apply to almost everyone (like the horoscope Rod Plotnik wrote that fooled his students). Despite the fake astronomy, horoscopes are no more scientific than fortune cookies. In their failure to identify or predict traits for a particular person, horoscopes lack validity: they don't measure what they claim to measure.

Module 21

Health, Stress & Coping

This Module Could Save Your Life!

Okay, maybe I'm exaggerating, but then again, maybe not. As proof, see Plotnik and Kouyoumdjian's discussion of the relationship between illness and stress (in the section on psychosomatic symptoms), and also note how much illness doctors estimate is stress-related. The percentages are staggering.

It's becoming clear that stress is one of the greatest health hazards we face. We all feel it. Sometimes it seems that modern life is not only more stressful than "the good old days," but that the number of our daily stressors continues to increase.

Does it have to be this way?

Ironically, considering its prevalence, stress is the one health hazard that is not inevitable, at least not in theory. Old age, if nothing else, is going to get each of us. Accidents will happen. We won't eliminate all disease. You can't solve the problem of environmental pollution all by yourself. Yet you are not doomed to be ravaged by stress.

What can you do about it? First, you can adopt a positive attitude and a healthy lifestyle that will tend to protect you against stress. Second, you can learn how to manage the stress you can't escape. Module 21 explains how both of these safeguards work.

Never mind your grade on the test. Study this module and learn how to live a long and healthy life!

Should Stress Be Managed?

What about stress in *your* life? Do you enjoy a good balance between the demands of your environment and your mental and physical abilities to meet them? Or do you see signs in your behavior or your physical health that suggest too much stress in your life?

The suggestion of psychology often seems to be that, in order to avoid physical and psychological problems, we should learn how to "manage" the stress causes them. A different approach would be to think of stress factors as clues to aspects of life that aren't working effectively. While a heart attack certainly qualifies as a "clue," most stress clues are much more commonplace, and therefore are easy to overlook. Search for the small distortions in your everyday behavior (like swearing, irritation, speeding, and headaches) that could be evidence of stress. Look for feelings, thoughts, and actions that may betray problems in your life and suggest connections to pressures from your environment. Meditation and relaxation certainly are valuable, but changing your life and solving your problems, where possible, would be better.

Effective Student Tip 21

No One Is Lazy

All right, go ahead and call yourself "lazy," if it makes you feel better, but it isn't good psychology. First, it may be what cognitive psychologists call a self-handicapping strategy, where you excuse yourself in advance for poor performance. ("I probably won't pass the test…, I'm too lazy to study!") Well, at least they can't say you're dumb! Just lazy.

Second, I would argue that no one is lazy. Oh, sure, we humans like to lie around and we goof off a lot, but that probably has more to do with defending our freedom and autonomy against the regimentation of organized work. The natural tendency of all animals is activity. Watch children at play. Look at the time and energy we put into second jobs, hobbies, sports, and social activities. Normally, we prefer to be doing something, because only activity creates the opportunity to feed our constant hunger to be effective.

When we feel lazy, we really are feeling ineffective. The task before us seems too difficult, too unrewarding, or too lacking in novelty and challenge. When you feel "too lazy" to tackle your schoolwork, the real problem is that you haven't figured out how to handle it effectively, or how to make it deliver positive feedback attesting to your effectiveness.

Your response…

Many of my own students violently disagree with me on this Tip. What do you think?

Learning Objectives

1. Understand health, stress, and coping as immediate, important, personal applications of psychological science to your everyday wellbeing and long-term survival.
2. Learn our basic physiological responses to stress and how they have led to a new understanding of the connection between mind and body.
3. Learn the different kinds of stress and stressors, how we react to them, and how we attempt to deal with them.
4. Appreciate the connection between stress and both personality and social factors.
5. Understand different kinds of coping, choosing a coping strategy, and how people cope with severe trauma.
6. Appreciate how the meditation techniques of Tibetan monks turn Western science on its head, but in so doing, teach modern psychology a valuable lesson about the connections between mind and body.
7. Learn how to apply stress management programs and techniques to reducing stress in your daily life.

Key Terms

Many of these key terms are as immediate as the morning newspaper, where, in fact, you may find them. Others are psychological terms that take the discussion of stress and coping a bit deeper. All are relevant to your daily life and important to your health and welfare.

adjustment disorder
alarm stage
anxiety
anxiety (Freud)
approach-approach conflict
approach-avoidance conflict
autonomic nervous system
avoidance-avoidance conflict
biofeedback
burnout
case study
challenge appraisal
conditioned emotional response
conflict
emotion-focused coping
eustress
exhaustion stage
experiment
fight-flight response
frustration
galvanic skin response
general adaptation syndrome (GAS)
hardiness
harm/loss appraisal
hassles
immune system
locus of control
major life events
mind-body connection
mind-body therapy
observational learning
optimism
pessimism
panic attack
panic disorder
positive psychology
posttraumatic stress disorder (PTSD)
primary appraisal
problem-focused coping
progressive relaxation
psychoneuroimmunology
psychosomatic symptoms
resistance stage
secondary appraisal
social support
stress
stress management program
threat appraisal
transcendental meditation (TM)
Type A behavior
Type D behavior
uplifts
yoga

Outline

- *Introduction*
  1. **Stress** (Luisa's intense fears)
     a. **Panic disorder**
     b. **Panic attack**
  2. Coping (Brenda Combs' stresses and coping techniques)

A. *Appraisal*

1. **Primary appraisal**
2. Three ways to appraise a stressful situation
   a. **Harm/loss appraisal**
   b. **Threat appraisal**
   c. **Challenge appraisal**
3. Situations and primary appraisals
4. Appraisal and stress level
   a. **Galvanic skin response**
   b. Stress experiment
5. Same situation, different appraisals
6. Sequence: appraisal to arousal

B. *Physiological Responses*

☐ Can you explain why the fight-flight response was so valuable in our early evolution but has become such a problem in modern life? (See "It's a Jungle Out There" box on page 364.)

1. **Fight-flight response** (physical and psychological stimuli)
   a. Sequence for activation of the fight-flight response
      (1) Appraisal
      (2) Hypothalamus
      (3) Sympathetic division
      (4) Fight-flight response
   b. Fight-flight: physiological and hormonal responses
      (1) Stress appraisal
      (2) Respiration
      (3) Heart rate
      (4) Liver
      (5) Pupils
      (6) Hair
      (7) Adrenal glands
      (8) Muscle tension
      (9) Male-female difference (female "tend and befriend" instead of fight-flight response)

2. **Psychosomatic symptoms**

☐ Do you ever experience psychosomatic symptoms? (The truthful answer is "Yes!") Can you describe a typical symptom you sometimes have and relate it to stress in your life?

3. Development of symptoms
    a. Common psychosomatic symptoms
    b. Development of psychosomatic symptoms
4. **General adaptation syndrome (GAS)** (Hans Selye)
    a. **Alarm stage**
    b. **Resistance stage**
    c. **Exhaustion stage**
5. **Mind-body connection** and **mind-body therapy**
6. **Immune system**
    a. **Psychoneuroimmunology** (Ader and Cohen)
    b. Evidence for psychoneuroimmunology
    c. Conditioning the immune system
        (1) Classical conditioning experiment
        (2) History of psychoneuroimmunology

C. Stressful Experiences

1. Kinds of stressors
    a. **Hassles**
    b. **Uplifts**
    b. **Major life events**
        (1) Social Readjustment Rating Scale
        (2) **Adjustment disorder**
2. Situational stressors
    a. **Frustration**
    b. **Burnout**
    c. Violence: **post-traumatic stress disorder (PTSD)**
3. **Conflict** (having to make a choice can be stressful)
    a. Three common kinds of conflicts (choices)
        (1) **Approach-approach conflict**
        (2) **Avoidance-avoidance conflict**
        (3) **Approach-avoidance conflict**
    b. Five styles of dealing with conflict
        (1) Avoidance
        (2) Accommodation
        (3) Domination

(4) Compromise

(5) Integration

4. **Anxiety**

   a. Three ways of developing anxiety

      (1) Classical conditioning: **conditioned emotional response**

      (2) **Observational learning**

      (3) Unconscious conflict: **anxiety (Freud)**

   b. Positive stress: **eustress**

D. Personality & Social Factors

1. **Hardiness** (skateboarder Shaun White)

   a. The 3 Cs — control, commitment, and challenge

   b. Stressors as opportunities for growth

2. **Locus of control**

   a. External locus of control

   b. Internal locus of control

3. Optimism versus pessimism

   a. **Optimism** (optimists)

   b. **Pessimism** (pessimists)

   c. Personality factors (positive or negative emotions)

4. **Positive psychology** (Martin Seligman): three main concerns

   a. Positive emotions

   b. Positive individual traits

   c. Positive institutions

5. **Type A behavior** (Friedman and Rosenman)

   a. Personality and heart attacks

   b. Revised definition of Type A behavior over three decades

      (1) 1970s — impatient, hostile, workaholic

      (2) 1980s & 1990s — depressed, angry

6. (2000s) **Type D behavior**

   a. Chronic distress

   b. Negative affectivity

   c. Social inhibition

7. **Social support** (Roseto, Pennsylvania, study)

   a. Buffer against stress

   b. Social conflict (stressful social interactions)

E. Kinds of Coping

1. Appraisal: **secondary appraisal**

2. Kinds of coping
    a. **Problem-focused coping**
    b. **Emotion-focused coping**
3. Choosing a coping strategy

F. Research Focus: Treatment for Panic Disorder

1. How effective is treatment for panic disorder?
2. Research methods
    a. **Case study**
    b. **Experiment**
3. How can panic disorder be treated?
4. Which treatment is most effective?
5. Conclusions

G. Cultural Diversity: Tibetan Monks

1. Monks' amazing abilities

☐ Does Plotnik and Kouyoumdjian's example of Tibetan monks mean that modern science is flawed?

2. Voluntary control of **autonomic nervous system**
    a. Voluntary control — hand warming
    b. Explanation
    c. Studying the mind's abilities

H. Application: Stress Management Programs

1. Definition: **stress management program**

☐ Could you apply the basic principles of a stress management program to your own life?

2. Changing thoughts
    a. Use challenge appraisals
    b. Substitute positive self-statements
3. Changing behaviors
    a. Emotion-focused coping
    b. Problem-focused coping
4. Learning to relax
    a. **Biofeedback**
    b. **Progressive relaxation**
    c. Meditation
        (1) Two Eastern forms of meditation: **transcendental meditation (TM)** and **yoga**
        (2) Benefits of meditation
5. Stopping stress responses

It's a Jungle Out There!

Imagine two of your prehuman ancestors venturing away from the trees looking for food. Suddenly, they hear a low growling and see a huge cat with enormous fangs coming toward them. One is delighted with the new creature and decides to approach it for a closer look. The other, feeling sick but also all charged up, makes an instant decision to run for the nearest tree and climb like never before. The survivor, whose makeup contained a little more of what became our fight-flight response, lived to contribute genes to the next generation. The other one made a contribution to the genes of the saber-toothed tiger.

Fast forward to today at the office. Suddenly, the boss is standing over your desk saying something about a project that was supposed to be finished. Should you calmly explain that one of the reports you need hasn't arrived yet, or should you run for the nearest tree, like your ancestor did? Is it just another simple problem, or is it a real saber-toothed tiger? You get all charged up just trying to decide.

The situation in today's jungle of school, work, and relationships is much more complicated than it was for our ancestors. It's hard to tell the real emergencies, so we exhaust ourselves with constant false alerts. The fight-flight response was supposed to be for the rare enemy or tiger, not for the uncomplicated, solvable problems of daily life.

One Small Step

If this module got to you at all, now might be a good time to take a step toward modifying your lifestyle. Start by making one small change. Nothing big, just something that takes only a few minutes a day. Take a walk around the block. Spend a few minutes in silent contemplation. Munch veggies instead of chips.

What small, realistic change could you make that would be the first step toward a healthier and less stressful lifestyle?

How English Works

Words in the Textbook

p. 481 continue to **spiral downward** = move in a curved line going down; out of control

received a **wake-up call** = makes someone suddenly alert and paying attention

day was so **scorching** hot = extremely hot

an **inspirational role model** = stimulating people into greater efforts

p. 482 need to **mobilize** your physical energy = gather, activate

p. 483 not to **identify with** the injured = feel sympathy for

p. 484 stomach **knotting** = uncomfortable tight feeling

situations that are **novel** = new

p. 487 **coed** Joan = college student (female)

taking a toll on her stomach = hurting, causing harm

signaling stages of resistance = information communicated by an action or sign

p. 488 **coming down with something** = beginning to feel sick from illness

they **tackled** this question **head-on** = tried to solve it directly

p. 490 makes no **distinction** between = difference between two or more things or people

p. 492 individuals **go to any lengths** to win = do anything necessary, even bad actions

p. 493 had a **debilitating** fear of = reducing somebody's strength or energy

p. 494 gives them a real **edge** in dealing with = gives an advantage in doing something

p. 495 **focus** more on problems or weaknesses = concentrate attention on a particular thing

than on strengths or **virtues** = a particular quality that is good or admirable

p. 496 their **chronic** distress = always present, occurring over and over again

p. 497 their understanding **moved forward** = went further toward complete knowledge of

facilitates our maintaining good mental health = makes something easier to do

p. 503 **Eastern** forms of meditation = relating or belonging to the countries of Asia

ESL Tip: Compound Tenses

Compound tenses (requiring more than one-word verbs) in English can be difficult for ESL students, but the effort spent in mastering them will pay off in clear comprehension and clear writing. Here's how they work.

Simple Past Tense is used only for single actions that happened at a particular time, or for actions that happened during a specific period in the past. Examples: She went to the store yesterday. Lincoln lived during the Civil War.

But actions that happened at an indefinite time in the past — sometime before "now" — are put into **Present Perfect Tense**. Examples: I have seen that DVD. I have never liked Lima beans. I have given up on the Chicago Cubs.

Use the **Past Perfect Tense** for actions that happened before a specific time in the past — "before then." Examples: He *had eaten* before the rest of us started to eat. The phone *had* already *stopped* ringing before I could answer it.

Past Progressive Tense (or continuous tense) is more complicated. It is used only for actions that were in progress when they were interrupted by another (**Simple Past Tense**) action, or while another continuing action was going on. Examples: I *was watching* TV when the phone rang. My daughter *was looking* out the window while I was cooking.

Sentence Structure: Whom

Do you remember **some of which, all of which,** and **half of which**? These forms help us to count and measure objects.

We can join sentences that count and measure people in the same way with similar forms like **some of whom, all of whom,** and **half of whom.**

Look at the following pair of sentences:

The professor gave a surprise quiz to the students.

None of the students was expecting it.

We can join these sentences together using **none of whom**:

The professor gave a surprise quiz to the students, **none of whom** was expecting it.

We use a comma here because it provides extra information about the students. It isn't necessary for understanding *which* students.

Look at another example. This one is from the text:

They tackled this question head-on by giving the same amount of cold virus to 394 subjects, **all of whom** were quarantined for a week.

We can tell from this sentence that all 394 subjects were quarantined for a week.

Test Yourself

Join the sentences below by using **whom**:

The meeting was attended by all the employees. **Some of them** arrived late.

The meeting __________.

Emma invited 20 people to her birthday party. **All of them** brought gifts.

Emma __________.

The experiment used 324 college students. **Half of them** were given placebos.

The experiment __________.

The United States has elected 43 presidents. **Not one of them** was named "Bob."

The United States __________.

Answers

The meeting was attended by all the employees, **some of whom** arrived late.
Emma invited 20 people to her birthday party, **all of whom** brought gifts.
The experiment used 324 college students, **half of whom** were given placebos.
The United States has elected 43 presidents, **not one of whom** was named "Bob."

The Big Picture

Which statement below offers the best summary of the larger significance of this module?

A With the creation of the new field of psychoneuroimmunology, psychology has at last proved the truth of the old motto "mind over matter." We now know that using mental processes can solve any physical problem.

B Although Western science tends to treat mind and body as separate entities, obviously they are part of the same whole. This module brings together our current understanding of stress and the many new techniques for coping with it in our lives.

C The purpose of this module is to alert psychology students to the many misuses of science fostered by the holistic health movement and to warn them not to be fooled by stress management courses, Tibetan monks, meditation tapes, and other mind-body fakery.

D Psychology is learning how to build stress-resistant people. By using discoveries like hardiness, coping mechanisms, locus of control, Type A behavior, and the fight-flight syndrome, everyone can be free from stress.

E *Stress!? Stress!?* You want to fix *stress!?* Just cancel that %$&# exam!

True-False

_____ 1. Stress depends partly on how we evaluate a situation.

_____ 2. To "appraise" something means to feel very positive about it.

_____ 3. The fight-flight response goes back to the earliest days of the human species.

_____ 4. Research shows that small daily hassles are far more stressful than major life events.

_____ 5. The way we respond to frustration influences our levels of stress.

_____ 6. Conflict means the inevitable run-ins that occur when you have to work with someone else.

_____ 7. Your personality can influence how well you deal with stress.

_____ 8. One of the best prescriptions for successfully handling stress is to have many relationships that confer social support.

_____ 9. Some Tibetan monks have developed a type of yoga that allows them to levitate their bodies several inches off the ground.

_____ 10. Biofeedback is a technique for clearing your head of all thoughts, worrisome and otherwise.

Flashcards 1

_____	1. fight-flight response	a. body reacting to stressful situations by going through three stages: alarm, resistance, exhaustion
_____	2. general adaptation syndrome (GAS)	b. continuum of beliefs about the extent to which one is in control of one's own future
_____	3. locus of control	c. how your thoughts, beliefs, and emotions produce beneficial or detrimental physiological changes
_____	4. mind-body connection	d. anxious or threatening feeling of a situation being more than our resources can adequately handle
_____	5. post-traumatic stress disorder (PTSD)	e. real, often painful symptoms that are caused by psychological factors such as worry, tension, and stress
_____	6. primary appraisal	f. theory that traits of aggressive workaholism, anger, competition, and hostility can lead to a heart attack
_____	7. psychosomatic symptoms	g. directs great sources of energy to muscles and brain, creating preparation of body for action
_____	8. stress	h. result of direct personal experience of an event involving actual or threatened injury or death
_____	9. Type A behavior	i. an Eastern form of meditation that can be an effective method for relaxing and reducing stress
_____	10. yoga	j. initial, subjective evaluation of a situation in which you balance demands against your abilities

Flashcards 2

_____	1. burnout	a. combination of three personality traits (control, commitment, and challenge) that protect us from stress
_____	2. emotion-focused coping	b. moderation of stress by having groups, family, and friends who provide attachment and resources
_____	3. exhaustion stage	c. those small, irritating, frustrating events that we face daily and that we usually appraise or interpret as stressful
_____	4. hardiness	d. being physically overwhelmed and exhausted, finding the job/task unrewarding, cynical or detached about job/task
_____	5. hassles	e. breakdown in internal organs or weakening of immune system due to long-term, continuous stress
_____	6. major life events	f. primarily doing things to deal with emotional distress, such as seeking support, avoiding, or denying
_____	7. problem-focused coping	g. study of the relationship between central nervous system, endocrine system, and psychosocial factors
_____	8. psychoneuro-immunology	h. potentially disturbing or disruptive situations that we appraise as having significant impact on our lives
_____	9. social support	i. assuming a comfortable position, eyes closed, and repeating a sound to clear one's head of all thoughts
_____	10. transcendental meditation (TM)	j. solving a problem by seeking information, changing your behavior, or taking whatever action is necessary

Multiple Choice

____ 1. Plotnik and Kouyoumdjian use Luisa's sudden panic to show that
   a. how we interpret or appraise a situation determines the stress it causes
   b. a bad scare in childhood will stay with you for the rest of your life
   c. everyone experiences sudden, extreme fear of dying now and then
   d. stress can overcome a person for no apparent reason

____ 2. Luisa's initial, subjective evaluation of her sudden fear of dying is an example of a
   a. secondary appraisal
   b. challenge appraisal
   c. primary appraisal
   d. tertiary appraisal

____ 3. Which one of the following is *not* a type of primary appraisal?
   a. harm/loss
   b. threat
   c. challenge
   d. advantage/resource

____ 4. A good clue to whether a person is experiencing stress is the
   a. potential danger of the situation (like operating a chainsaw)
   b. amount of blood at the scene
   c. galvanic skin response
   d. "deer caught in the headlights" expression

____ 5. Rod Plotnik and Haig Kouyoumdjian list their students' reactions to a number of common stressors in order to illustrate the point that
   a. modern life has become almost unbearably stressful
   b. not everyone appraises these situations the same way
   c. there is a core of common experiences that everyone considers stressful
   d. the one thing everybody hates is waiting

____ 6. The reason why the fight-flight response can harm our health is that
   a. every time it is triggered our bodies go through an automatic process of arousal
   b. overuse is a kind of "crying wolf" that eventually results in letting our guard down
   c. biologically, humans were designed for quiet, peaceful lives
   d. psychologically, humans do not tolerate challenge very well

____ 7. The fact that the fight-flight response is also found in animals such as alligators suggests that
   a. except for a thin layer of civilization, humans are basically the same as reptiles
   b. evolution sometimes creates mechanisms that are harmful to the species (us)
   c. we may desire a peaceful existence, but our basic nature is aggressive and violent
   d. it must be an old and powerful evolutionary mechanism for survival

____ 8. Which one of the following is *not* a common psychosomatic symptom?
   a. intense cramping and nausea due to food poisoning
   b. muscle pain and tension in the neck, shoulders, and back
   c. having either tension or migraine headaches
   d. eating problems like feeling compelled to eat or having no appetite

_____ 9. Which one of the following is *not* a stage in the general adaptation syndrome?
   a. alarm
   b. attack
   c. resistance
   d. exhaustion

_____ 10. The mind-body connection and mind-body therapy are both based on the idea that
   a. thoughts and emotions come from changes in bodily activity
   b. thoughts and emotions can change physiological and immune responses
   c. when you have a strong feeling or powerful idea, you must express it through bodily action
   d. mind and body are two separate and independent areas of activity

_____ 11. "Psychoneuroimmunology" is the study of how
   a. physical factors often create psychological symptoms
   b. diet and exercise work to prevent mental illness
   c. psychological factors can influence the immune system
   d. (this is a trick question — that is a made-up word)

_____ 12. The total score on the Social Readjustment Rating Scale
   a. subtracts positive life events from negative life changes
   b. gives a precise cut-off point for becoming ill or staying well
   c. reflects how well you cope with stress
   d. reflects how many major life events you have experienced in the past year

_____ 13. Having feelings of doing poorly, physically wearing out, or becoming emotionally exhausted because of stress at work is called
   a. frustration
   b. burnout
   c. conflict
   d. stress

_____ 14. According to Freud's explanation, we try to reduce anxiety by employing
   a. problem-focused coping at the ego level
   b. defense mechanisms at the unconscious level
   c. approach/avoidance choices at the ego level
   d. "snap out of it" coping messages at the superego level

_____ 15. Which one of the following is *not* an ingredient of hardiness?
   a. control
   b. commitment
   c. contentment
   d. challenge

_____ 16. Positive psychology is a new direction that urges psychology to
   a. better understand the positive, adaptive, and fulfilling aspects of life
   b. steer patients away from focusing on painful memories
   c. abandon the scientific method in favor of the positive wisdom of the past
   d. try to find something good in everything that happens to people

_____ 17. The famous "Type A behavior" research attempted to relate certain personality traits to
a. hardy personality
b. locus of control
c. increased risk of cancer
d. increased risk of heart attack

_____ 18. People in Roseto, Pennsylvania, didn't follow healthy lifestyles, but they had lower rates of heart attacks, ulcers, and emotional problems — probably because
a. the steep Pennsylvania hills forced them to exercise whether they wanted to or not
b. being the home of the University of Pennsylvania, the town had superb medical facilities
c. years of intermarriage over many generations had built up a good genetic background
d. relationships with family and neighbors were extremely close and mutually supportive

_____ 19. Over the last 30 years, we've learned that _______________ is a key factor in the relationship between stress and physical health
a. social support
b. financial advantage
c. political influence in the community
d. eating a healthy diet

_____ 20. Solving a problem by seeking information, changing your own behavior, or taking whatever action is necessary is called
a. problem-focused coping
b. emotion-focused coping
c. primary appraisal
d. secondary appraisal

_____ 21. All of the following are sex differences in choosing coping strategies *except:*
a. women tend to use more coping strategies
b. men are more likely to withdraw or avoid problems
c. men are more likely to engage in emotion-focused coping in dealing with stressors
d. women are more likely to use emotion-focused coping to seek emotional support and advice

_____ 22. Our understanding of __________ makes it hard for us to explain the amazing abilities of Tibetan monks
a. cultural diversity
b. the autonomic nervous system
c. biofeedback training
d. the relaxation response

_____ 23. If Tibetan monks can raise their body temperature through meditation, then perhaps
a. Western medicine — not Asian — represents the real medical fakery
b. Western medicine should pay more attention to psychological factors
c. every culture has a form of medicine that is best for its own members
d. every culture develops some phenomena that can't be fully explained

_____ 24. A good way to prevent taking an exam from becoming more stressful is to
a. repeat over and over again that the exam can't be all that bad
b. use threat appraisals to scare yourself into taking the exam seriously
c. engage in biofeedback sessions to learn to control physiological responses
d. work at substituting positive self-statements for negative self-statements

_____ 25. __________ is a relaxation technique that involves learning to control physiological responses by recording and displaying them

a. The relaxation response
b. Progressive relaxation
c. Biofeedback
d. Transcendental meditation (TM)

Short Essay

1. Why was the fight-flight response good for early humans (and still is for alligators) but not so good for modern humans?

2. Are you aware of exhibiting any psychosomatic symptoms? Can you connect any of these symptoms to stresses in your life? Give one good example.

3. Isn't it maddening when you get sick *after* the semester is over, just as you are ready to kick back and have fun? Describe how the new science of psychoneuroimmunology explains this phenomenon.

4. Why is it better to be an optimist than a pessimist?

5. People in the small town of Roseto, Pennsylvania, had an awful diet and lifestyle, yet they suffered fewer heart attacks, had fewer ulcers, and fewer emotional problems than the national average. Why? Showoffs can also tell what happened when people moved to better homes in the countryside.

The "PowerStudy 4.5 for Introduction to Psychology" CD-ROM for this module is a "Super Module." In addition to the regular PowerStudy features (quizzes, summary test, key terms, web site connections, critical thinking exercise, module outline, and more), Super Modules also include self-paced, step-by-step multimedia presentations with animations and narration.

Answers for Module 21

The Big Picture (explanations provided for incorrect choices)

A This statement is too extreme. We now see the influence of mental factors, but not a dominance of them.
B *Correct! You see the "big picture" for this Module.*
C Too extreme. Use caution and common sense, but the new alternative health approaches do deserve consideration.
D Stress has a useful function in alerting us to unhealthy aspects of our environment. We can't be entirely stress-free.
E It's just a joke!

True-False (explanations provided for False choices; page numbers given for all choices)

1	T	482	
2	F	482	Appraisal refers to how we evaluate a person or situation.
3	T	484	
4	F	490	It isn't that hassles are more stressful, but that there are so many more of them.
5	T	491	
6	F	492	Conflict refers to situations in which there are competing possible solutions.
7	T	494	
8	T	497	
9	F	501	They're good . . . but not *that* good! (Read the statement again!)
10	F	503	Biofeedback is voluntarily learning to control physiological responses such as blood pressure.

Flashcards 1

1 g 2 a 3 b 4 c 5 h 6 j 7 e 8 d 9 f 10 i

Flashcards 2

1 d 2 f 3 e 4 a 5 c 6 h 7 j 8 g 9 b 10 i

Multiple Choice (explanations provided for incorrect choices)

1 ***a*** *Correct! See page 481.*
b Not necessarily — it depends on how you come to understand it later.
c They may worry about death, but few people experience the sudden, overwhelming fear of a panic attack.
d Stress can be predicted, understood, and handled without harmful effects.

2 a A secondary appraisal involves deciding how to deal with a potentially stressful situation.
b A challenge appraisal means you have the potential for gain or personal growth in a situation.
c *Correct! See page 482.*
d There is no tertiary appraisal.

3 a If we appraise a situation as causing us harm or loss, it is stressful.
b If we appraise a situation as threatening, it is stressful.
c If we appraise a situation as challenging, it demands resources, but is usually less stressful.
d *Correct! See page 482.*

4 a Many people would show caution, but not necessarily stress, around a chainsaw.
b Some of us would recoil at the sight of blood, but many would feel a desire to help.
c *Correct! See page 483.*
d That might show surprise, but not necessarily stress (besides, it's too inaccurate a measure).

5 a Could be true, but this is not Plotnik and Kouyoumdjian's point.
b *Correct! See page 483.*
c Just the opposite is true.
d Annoying as waiting is, only 65 percent (not everyone) rated it as stressful.

6 ***a*** *Correct! See page 484.*
b The body does not let down its guard — that's the point.
c Throughout evolution, humans have faced challenge and threat.
d Humans seem to thrive on change and actively seek it.

7 a That is far too extreme an implication; despite this mechanism, we are very different from reptiles.
b That is not the way evolution works; the fight-flight response must have helped our species survive.
c The fight-flight response is designed to help us in extreme situations, not to govern our general behavior.
d *Correct! See page 484.*

8 ***a*** *Correct! See page 486.*
b This is a common psychosomatic symptom.
c This is a common psychosomatic symptom.
d This is a common psychosomatic symptom.

9 a Alarm is one of the three stages of the general adaptation syndrome.
b *Correct! See page 487.*
c Resistance is one of the three stages of the general adaptation syndrome.
d Exhaustion is one of the three stages of the general adaptation syndrome.

10 a It is not true that ideas and feelings come mainly from changes in the body.
b *Correct! See page 487.*
c Ideas and feelings do not have to be expressed in physical behavior.
d The mind-body connection and mind-body therapy assume just the opposite.

11 a There might be some truth in this, but it is not the definition of psychoneuroimmunology.
b They might help somewhat, but this is not what psychoneuroimmunology is about.
c *Correct! See page 488.*
d It is a real word, and conveys an important new concept.

12 a This is not how the SRRS works.
b The SRRS gives a general indication, but not a precise cut-off point.
c The SRRS measures amounts of stress, but not how well you deal with it.
d *Correct! See page 490.*

13 a Frustration is the particular feeling that results when our attempts to reach some goal are blocked.
b *Correct! See page 491.*
c Conflict is the feeling we experience when we must decide between two or more incompatible choices.
d Stress is a more general feeling of a situation straining or overloading our psychological resources.

14 a This is a cognitive, not psychoanalytic, explanation.
b *Correct! See page 493.*
c This is a behavioral, not psychoanalytic, explanation.
d This is a nonsense statement.

15 a Control is one of the three personality traits that make up hardiness.
b Commitment is one of the three personality traits that make up hardiness.
c *Correct! See page 494.*
d Challenge is one of the three personality traits that make up hardiness.

16 ***a*** *Correct! See page 495.*
b Positive psychology does not deny or downplay the real problems people have.
c Positive psychology, like all good psychology, seeks knowledge through use of the scientific method.
d Positive psychology does not take this unrealistically encouraging view of life.

17 a The hardy personality is a different factor in stress management.
b Locus of control is a different factor in stress management.
c Close, but no cigar.
d *Correct! See page 496.*

18 a Sounds logical, but the facts stated are not true.
b Sounds logical, but the facts stated are not true.
c Sounds logical, but the facts stated are not true.
d *Correct! See page 497.*

19 ***a*** *Correct! See page 497.*
b The typical Type A personality is likely to be successful in business.
c Not everyone can wield political influence in their community.
d The people of Roseto, Pennsylvania, did not eat a particularly healthy diet

20 ***a*** *Correct! See page 499.*
b Emotion-focused coping does not involve taking direct action to change the problem situation.
c Primary appraisal does not refer to solving a problem.
d Secondary appraisal does not refer to solving a problem.

21 a Research shows that this is a sex difference in coping strategies.
b Research shows that this is a sex difference in coping strategies.
c *Correct! See page 499.*
d Research shows that this is a sex difference in coping strategies.

22 a Cultural diversity should make us more sensitive to the amazing abilities the monks possess.
b *Correct! See page 501.*
c Biofeedback training should help us understand how monks control involuntary responses.
d The relaxation response is not directly related to the monks' control of involuntary responses.

23 a Serious medical practices, regardless of culture, should not be regarded as fakery.
b *Correct! See page 501.*
c Effective medical treatment (if accepted) works regardless of culture.
d Science does not, *cannot*, place any physical phenomenon out of bounds for study.

24 a This will only make you less likely to prepare for the exam by studying.
b Using challenge appraisals might help, but not threat appraisals.
c This would work for lowering your blood pressure, but how would that help remove the stress of an exam?
d *Correct! See page 502.*

25 a The relaxation response is a method of inducing a relaxed state.
b Progressive relaxation is a method of inducing a relaxed state.
c *Correct! See page 503.*
d Transcendental meditation (TM) is a method of inducing a relaxed state.

Short Essay (sample answers)

1. Imagine conditions for early humans, who had to deal with dangers including larger, stronger, and faster animals. A threat wouldn't be constant, but it could be sudden and deadly. (Ditto for alligators.) Those who could make quick decisions on whether to fight or flee would survive (and pass their genes on to the next generation). The dangers of modern life aren't so clear, yet seem to come at us constantly. As we gear up for fight or flight again and again, our immune systems and our health suffer. Better appraisals could help.

2. *Psycho* (mind) *somatic* (body) symptoms are the real and sometimes painful physical symptoms that are caused by increased physiological arousal resulting from psychological factors, such as worry, stress, and anxiety. (Review the list on page 486.) Describe a psychosomatic symptom you are aware of in your own life and explain what stressful conditions seem to bring it about. If you can't come up with one from your own life, talk about a friend's problem — but be aware that you are very unusual, or not looking too deeply!

3. Psychoneuroimmunology is the relatively new science of the relationship between the central nervous system, the endocrine system, and psychosocial factors. During a long, difficult semester, many students go through a cycle of feeling stress, mobilizing strength to resist it, but then instead of resting and restoring bodily resources, go through the cycle all over again. About the time finals are over, your immune system is badly depleted. Wham-o! You get a cold, just when you thought you could relax and have fun.

4. The answer has to do with feeling positive or negative emotions, which are involved in increasing or decreasing stress levels and the chances of developing psychosomatic symptoms. Optimism leads to believing and expecting that good things will happen, and therefore to experiencing more positive emotions. Pessimism leads to believing and expecting that bad things will happen, and therefore to more negative emotions. Both are relatively stable personality traits, not easy to change, but worth working on.

5. The crucial difference in Roseto turned out to be that family relationships were extremely close and mutually supportive, and this wonderful social support system extended to neighbors and to the community as a whole. That the health benefits of social support came as a surprise in a profoundly social species is a telling commentary on modern psychology, with its relentless efforts to look inside. BTW, when prosperous former residents moved out into the countryside, the health benefits of close social support began to decline!

Module 22

Assessment & Anxiety Disorders

What Is Psychological Abnormality?

We can often recognize when a fellow human is psychologically "abnormal," but when we try to say exactly what makes the person abnormal, we find that it's not so easy.

Plotnik and Kouyoumdjian begin this module with a hard problem for psychology and psychiatry: how to understand and treat mental disorders. In their examples of infamous criminals and everyday problems, you'll see that psychological science has not yet attained the agreement and precision of medical science. All doctors will agree on the diagnosis of a broken arm, but what about a broken mind? Since psychology has such a long way to go before it can claim a comprehensive and satisfactory definition of abnormality, perhaps I can be forgiven for trying my own definition.

One Try at a Definition of Psychological Abnormality

Psychological abnormality is a typically temporary condition of dysfunction and distress caused by deficits or breakdowns in the universal need to be effective. Lack of effectiveness can occur in any one or more of six areas of human psychological functioning: biological, emotional, cognitive, behavioral, philosophical or spiritual, and social.

The most damaging results of the loss of effectiveness are the corresponding breakdowns in those processes of regulation and self-regulation that are so crucial to the welfare of human beings, who lack guidance by instincts or reflexes. It is the loss of regulation and self-regulation that seems "abnormal," and is so frightening, both to the troubled person and to others.

If we suffer from psychological abnormality, the best thing we can do is begin to take competent action. But this is not so easy. Intervention and treatment may be needed in any one or more of the six realms of psychological functioning. (1) We may need psychoactive drugs to restore the regulation of a biologically based mental function. (2) We may need to explore the past and learn to understand our basic psychological processes, especially emotion. (3) We may need to reverse a negative self-image and learn to think more realistically about others and ourselves. (4) We may need to modify old habits that no longer work and develop new skills and abilities. (5) We may need to project our values and hopes into the future, to discover our true aspirations and real selves. (6) We may need to rebuild and strengthen our ties to others, in order to gain the social support we need to resurrect old competencies and build new ones.

Notice that this proposed definition of psychological abnormality is organized around the central theme of our *need to be effective* in all six areas of psychological functioning. We tend to focus on the loss of regulation and self-regulation in troubled people, but beneath their disturbing symptoms we should look for fundamental losses of effectiveness.

My definition of psychological abnormality is quite densely packed. Please read it again.

Effective Student Tip 22

What "Boring" Really Means

Students often complain that they aren't doing well because their classes and schoolwork are boring. I could suggest that *they* are interesting people, and therefore have a duty to help make their classes interesting, but that wouldn't be fair. It would be more realistic to advise them to reconsider what boring really means.

Most students think certain people (not themselves!) or certain activities are boring, but that is incorrect. Psychologically, boredom means being trapped, not being able to engage in an activity that is good for you. The next time you feel bored, ask yourself if there is anything taking place that allows you to grow and to express what is uniquely you. I'll bet you'll discover that "boring" means not being able to exercise your urge to be effective.

Nothing is intrinsically boring. Every experienced teacher I've known had something worthwhile to say. Give me any example of activity or knowledge you might consider boring and I'll find someone, somewhere, whose great passion in life is pursuing exactly that activity or acquiring precisely that knowledge. Your schoolwork isn't boring, but perhaps you haven't yet found a way to connect it to the passions in *your* life.

Your response…

Think of something really boring. Now reconsider. Is there a way in which it might *not* be boring?

Learning Objectives

1. Understand *assessment* as a scientific procedure for determining psychological abnormalities and their treatment, and *anxiety disorders* as the more common, less crippling mental disorders (the more debilitating kind, mood disorders and schizophrenia, are treated in the next module).
2. Learn the causes of abnormal behavior and how it is defined and assessed.
3. Learn how mental disorders are diagnosed and understood with the American Psychiatric Association's *Diagnostic and Statistical Manual of Mental Disorders-IV-Text Revision* (DSM IV-TR).
4. Understand the roots and varieties of anxiety disorders and somatoform disorders.
5. Learn how culture affects mental disorders through the example of taijin kyofusho (TKS).
6. Explore the research on understanding and preventing teenage school shootings.
7. Learn how common phobias are understood and treated.

Key Terms

The key terms in this module ask you to be part lawyer, part historian, and part doctor. They will require more study than many other modules, but hard study will pay off. BTW, the next module is worse!

agoraphobia
case study
clinical assessment
clinical diagnosis
clinical interview
cognitive-behavioral therapy
cognitive-emotional-behavioral and environmental factors
conduct disorder
conversion disorder
Diagnostic and Statistical Manual of Mental Disorders-IV-Text Revision (DSM-IV-TR)
exposure therapy
generalized anxiety disorder (GAD)
genetic factors
insanity
labeling
maladaptive behavior approach
mass hysteria
mental disorder
obsessive-compulsive disorder (OCD)
panic attack
panic disorder
personality tests
phobia
posttraumatic stress disorder (PTSD)
social norms approach
social phobias
somatization disorder
somatoform disorders
specific phobias
statistical frequency approach
taijin kyofusho (TKS)

The "PowerStudy 4.5 for Introduction to Psychology" CD-ROM for this module is a "Super Module." In addition to the regular PowerStudy features (quizzes, summary test, key terms, web site connections, critical thinking exercise, module outline, and more), Super Modules also include self-paced, step-by-step multimedia presentations with animations and narration.

Outline

- *Introduction*

    1. Mental disorder (Dennis Rader, the BTK killer)
        a. **Insanity**
        b. **Mental disorder**
    2. **Phobia** (Kate Premo's aviophobia)

A. Factors in Mental Disorders

1. Causes of abnormal behavior
    a. Biological factors
        (1) **Genetic factors**
        (2) Neurological factors
    b. **Cognitive-emotional-behavioral and environmental factors**
2. Definitions of abnormal behavior
    a. **Statistical frequency approach**
    b. **Social norms approach**
    c. **Maladaptive behavior approach**

B. Assessing Mental Disorders

1. Definition of assessment
    a. Case of Susan Smith
    b. **Clinical assessment**
2. Three methods of assessment
    a. Neurological tests
    b. **Clinical interview**
    c. **Personality tests** (objective tests and projective tests)

C. Diagnosing Mental Disorders

1. Real-life assessment: Susan Smith
    a. Her past
    b. Her present
2. DSM-IV-TR
    a. **Clinical diagnosis**
    b. ***Diagnostic and Statistical Manual of Mental Disorders-IV-Text Revision* (DSM-IV-TR)**
3. Nine major problems: Axis I
    a. Disorders usually first diagnosed in infancy, childhood, or adolescence
    b. Organic mental disorders
    c. Substance-related disorders
    d. Schizophrenia and other psychotic disorders

e. Mood disorders (Susan Smith: diagnosis — mood disorder)

f. Anxiety disorders (Kate Premo: diagnosis — specific phobia)

g. Somatoform disorders

h. Dissociative disorders

i. Sexual and gender-identity disorders

4. Other problems and disorders: Axes II, III, IV, V

a. Axis II: personality disorders (Dennis Rader: diagnosis — antisocial personality disorder)

b. Axis III: general medical conditions

c. Axis IV: psychosocial and environmental problems

d. Axis V: global assessment of functioning scale

e. Using all five axes

f. Usefulness of DSM-IV-TR

5. Potential problems with using the DSM-IV-TR

a. **Labeling** mental disorders

b. Social and political implications

c. Frequency of mental disorders

D. Anxiety Disorders

1. **Generalized anxiety disorder (GAD)**

☐ Do you sometimes experience anxiety? How does it feel?

a. Symptoms

b. Treatment

2. **Panic disorder**

a. Symptoms (**panic attack**)

b. Treatment

3. **Phobia**

a. **Social phobias**

b. **Specific phobias**

c. **Agoraphobia**

4. **Obsessive-compulsive disorder (OCD)**

☐ No, you don't have the disorder, but what are some of your obsessive-compulsive behaviors?

a. Symptoms

b. Treatment

(1) **Exposure therapy**

(2) Antidepressant drugs

(3) Effectiveness

5. **Posttraumatic stress disorder (PTSD)**

a. Symptoms

b. Treatment

E. Somatoform Disorders

1. **Somatoform disorders**

☐ Do you worry about your body or your health? Are your worries realistic or exaggerated?

   a. **Somatization disorder**
   b. **Conversion disorder**

2. **Mass hysteria**

F. Cultural Diversity: An Asian Disorder

1. **Taijin kyofusho (TKS)**

☐ What is taijin kyofusho and what are its implications for psychiatry?

   a. Occurrence
   b. Cultural values

2. Social customs (cultural differences)

G. Research Focus: School Shootings

1. What drove teens to kill fellow students and teachers?
   a. **Conduct disorder**
   b. **Case study**
2. Case studies
3. Risks shared by adolescent school shooters
   a. Risk factors
   b. Neurological factors

H. Application: Treating Phobias

1. Specific phobia: flying (Kate Premo)

☐ Is there anything you are "phobic" about?

2. **Cognitive-behavioral therapy**
   a. Thoughts
   b. Behaviors
3. **Exposure therapy**
   a. Confronting feared situations
   b. Virtual reality therapy
4. Social phobia: public speaking
   a. Explain
   b. Learn and substitute
   c. Expose
   d. Practice
5. Drug treatment of phobias
   a. Tranquilizers and antidepressants
   b. Problems with drug treatments
   c. Which treatment to choose?

How English Works

Words in the Textbook

p. 509 **serial killers** = criminals who murder again and again in a pattern

p. 511 no **adverse** consequences to society = bad, negative

p. 513 the **defense** = lawyers who prove innocence

and **prosecution** = lawyers who prove criminality

refused to **press charges** = make formal complaint to police

scarred by her father's suicide = emotionally injured

a **heightened** emotional reaction = stronger than normal

p. 514 **enuresis** = bedwetting (associated with childish lack of control)

delirium = state of mental confusion, with possible hallucinations

dementia = madness, loss of all connection with reality

the **cardinal** feature = most important

p. 516 political and social **implications** = suggested as natural consequences of something else

p. 517 **fidgeting** in his chair = moving nervously

became so **nauseous** she almost vomited = sick with an unsettling feeling in the stomach

p. 518 a person **goes to great lengths** to avoid = tries unusually hard

characterized by irrational, **marked**, and continuous fears = strong, noticeable

caused **stark** terror = total, harsh

p. 519 **hoarding** = collecting and storing supplies (often hidden)

interfere with normal **functioning** = working the way something is supposed to work

p. 520 in the **soprano** section = people who sing in the highest voice

p. 522 result in **a loss of face** = dignity, respect in society

p. 523 he wanted to **get back at** a popular boy = take revenge on

immigrated to the U.S. = to enter a new country for the purpose of settling there

who are **picked on** and **bullied** = to be abused verbally and physically

p. 524 she was **groggy** for days = weak, unable to think clearly

p. 529 become a **full-blown** phobia = in its most complete, strongest, or developed form

Connecting Ideas: Semicolons

When you see a semi-colon, it is probably telling you that one complete independent clause has some connection with the next complete independent clause. Look at this example:

Jiang isn't Chinese ; he is Korean.

A common example seen in advertisements is as follows:

Buy now ; pay later.

Both sides of the semi-colon are strong independent clauses. Both can stand alone, but the semi-colon links them together. So, the semi-colon **separates**, like a period (full stop), because it ends a complete thought. But it also **connects**, like a colon, because it shows a relationship.

Did you notice the following examples in the text? Look at how the semi-colon connects the meanings of the two sentences in the following examples:

An estimated 25 million Americans have a similar irrational and intense fear of flying, which is called *aviophobia*; they refuse to get on a plane.

In comparison, making eye contact is very common in Western culture; if you did not make eye contact in social interactions, you would be judged as shy or lacking in social skills.

Often transitions are used after a semi-colon. These transitions can let the reader know that the next sentence continues with more information, such as **in addition** or **besides**; they can inform the reader that the next sentence is a result of the first with **as a result** and **consequently**; and they can even indicate that the next sentence is opposite from the first with transitions like **however, on the other hand**, and **nevertheless.**

Did you notice how many sentences were connected using semi-colons in the above sentence? Look at how three sentences are connected with semi-colons in the text:

Almost all of us 'people watch'; we observe parents, brothers, sisters, peers, friends, and teachers; by doing so, we learn a great deal.

Most (87%) said that, during the quantum experience, an important truth was revealed to them; 78% said that they were relieved of a mental burden; and 60% said that they felt completely loved.

Now you try it. Where do you think a semi-colon should go in the sentences below? Write in a semi-colon. You may need to change the punctuation in the sentences below:

Jack's dog doesn't bite in fact, his dog has no teeth.

The family was flying to Seattle their luggage was sent to Moscow.

Veronica applied for a job at Big National Bank in addition, she filled out applications at Dollars-R-Us Bank.

Pedro planned to have a nice, relaxing bike ride in reality Jacque's dog chased him everywhere he went.

Lily is a big fan of Leonardo Di Caprio for example, she has seen **Titanic** 37 times.

The following passage needs more than one semi-colon. Write them in where they are needed:

Arnold Schwarzenegger started as a body builder then he moved to Hollywood for a career in acting finally he changed to politics, becoming governor of California.

Answers

Jack's dog doesn't bite; in fact, his dog has no teeth.
The family was flying to Seattle; their luggage was sent to Moscow.
Veronica applied for a job at Big National Bank; in addition, she filled out applications at Dollars-R-Us Bank.
Pedro planned to have a nice, relaxing bike ride; in reality, Jacque's dog chased him everywhere he went.
Lily is a big fan of Leonardo Di Caprio**;** for example, she has seen **Titanic** thirty-37 times.

Arnold Schwarzenegger started as a body builder; then he moved to Hollywood for a career in acting**;** finally he changed to politics, becoming governor of California.

The Big Picture

Which statement below offers the best summary of the larger significance of this module?

A A major goal of modern psychology is to apply science to the tasks of understanding the causes of mental disorders, developing methods of assessment, and working out effective techniques of treatment.

B Psychology is more an art than a science. Lacking specific guidance, each clinical psychologist or psychiatrist must rely on experience, intuition, and sometimes guesswork in assessing and treating suffering people.

C It is in the area of psychological disorders that modern psychology has encountered its most stubborn difficulties. There are so many specific disorders that it is almost impossible to understand them scientifically.

D Now that psychology has the new, improved fourth edition of the Diagnostic and Statistical Manual of Mental Disorders (DSM-IV-TR), it has become simple to identify a person's problem and prescribe the correct treatment for it.

E When asked why he had placed 10-foot poles with a rope at the top all around his yard, the man responded, "To keep out the giraffes." "But there are no giraffes around here," his astonished neighbor replied. "Sure keeps them out, doesn't it!"

True-False

_____ 1. Because of his extreme abnormal behavior, Dennis Rader (the BTK killer) clearly was insane.

_____ 2. Clinical assessment revealed that Susan Smith, who drowned her own children, was a cold-blooded killer who finally got caught.

_____ 3. When psychiatrists need to make diagnoses, they turn to the *Diagnostic and Statistical Manual of Mental Disorders* (DSM).

_____ 4. About one in two people will develop a mental disorder sometime in their life.

_____ 5. Anxiety is a general problem that can result in many different disorders.

_____ 6. Panic disorder is more common among women than men.

_____ 7. Don't waste time worrying about your phobias — they usually disappear in a few months.

_____ 8. Experiences like going back inside to check that you turned off the oven show that obsessive-compulsive disorder is common and widespread in the general population.

_____ 9. Taijin kyofusho (TKS) is a social phobia characterized by a morbid fear of offending others.

_____ 10. Research has shown that drug treatment is superior to cognitive-behavior programs for getting rid of phobias.

Flashcards 1

_____	1. clinical interview	a. legal term meaning not knowing the difference between right and wrong
_____	2. cognitive-behavioral therapy	b. says a behavior is abnormal if it deviates greatly from accepted social standards, values, or norms
_____	3. *Diagnostic and Statistical Manual*... (DSM-IV-TR)	c. anxiety disorder with intense, irrational fear out of all proportion to possible danger of object or situation
_____	4. exposure therapy	d. one method of gathering information about a person's past and present behaviors, beliefs, emotions, and problems
_____	5. insanity	e. changing negative thoughts by substituting positive ones; changing limiting behaviors by learning new behaviors
_____	6. labeling	f. says a behavior is abnormal if it interferes with the individual's ability to function personally or in society
_____	7. maladaptive behavior approach	g. says a behavior is abnormal if it occurs rarely or infrequently relative to the general population
_____	8. phobia	h. gradually exposing a person to the real anxiety-producing situations or objects that the person is attempting to avoid
_____	9. social norms approach	i. identifying and naming differences among individuals; placing them in specific categories; negative associations
_____	10. statistical frequency approach	j. describes a uniform system for assessing specific symptoms and matching them to 300 disorders

Flashcards 2

_____	1. agoraphobia	a. characterized by marked and persistent fears that are unreasonable; fear of an object or situation
_____	2. generalized anxiety disorder	b. characterized by a terrible fear of offending others through awkward social or physical behavior
_____	3. mass hysteria	c. prolonged or recurring problem that interferes with ability to live a satisfying personal life or function in society
_____	4. mental disorder	d. characterized by recurrent and unexpected panic attacks; continued worry about having more attacks
_____	5. obsessive-compulsive disorder (OCD)	e. characterized by excessive, unrealistic worry about almost everything; feeling that something bad is about to happen
_____	6. panic disorder	f. results from experiencing an event that involves death or serious injury; causes disturbing memories and intense fear
_____	7. post-traumatic stress disorder (PTSD)	g. characterized by anxiety about being in places or situations from which escape might be difficult if panic occurs
_____	8. somatoform disorders	h. process in which a group of people develop similar fears, delusions, behaviors, or physical symptoms
_____	9. specific phobias	i. persistent, recurring irrational thoughts along with irresistible impulses to perform an act repeatedly
_____	10. taijin kyofusho (TKS)	j. complaints of a pattern of recurring, multiple, and significant bodily symptoms; no physical causes

Multiple Choice

_____ 1. The first issue in the BTK killer trial was whether Dennis Rader
   a. killed 10 people or actually many more
   b. killed when under the influence of drugs
   c. knew the difference between right and wrong when he killed
   d. really did hear voices commanding him to kill

_____ 2. The difference between the terms insanity and mental disorder is that
   a. insanity is more severe than a mental disorder
   b. insanity is a legal term while mental disorder is a medical term
   c. mental disorders are specific forms of insanity
   d. mental disorders don't qualify for insurance reimbursement

_____ 3. In the attempt to understand the causes of abnormal behavior, the newest area of interest is
   a. biological factors (genetic and neurological)
   b. unconscious factors (Oedipus and Electra complexes)
   c. environmental factors (poverty and deprivation)
   d. serial killers like Dennis Rader

_____ 4. Which one of the following is *not* a way of defining abnormal behavior?
   a. statistical frequency approach
   b. deviation from social norms approach
   c. maladaptive behavior approach
   d. slips of the tongue approach

_____ 5. The method most commonly used to assess abnormal behavior is the
   a. Rorschach inkblot test
   b. neurological examination
   c. personality test
   d. clinical interview

_____ 6. Plotnik and Kouyoumdjian tell the story of Susan Smith in great detail to make the point that
   a. clinical diagnosis is a complicated yet necessary process
   b. childhood sexual abuse almost always results in adult problems
   c. despite all we know about Susan Smith, we still can't understand why she did it
   d. her friends and neighbors should have seen the tragedy coming

_____ 7. The most widely used system of psychological classification is the
   a. *Freudian Psychoanalytic System (FPS)*
   b. *Diagnostic and Statistical Manual of Mental Disorders-IV-Text Revision* (DSM-IV-TR)
   c. *Disordered Mind Standards-III (DMS-III)*
   d. *Federal Uniform Psychopathology Code (UPC)*

_____ 8. One interesting and troubling fact about the official manual of diagnosis is that with each new edition
   a. the Freudian explanation of mental disorders has become more dominant
   b. research findings continue to be ignored in favor of clinical opinions
   c. new findings from genetics and neuroscience are used to identify causes of mental disorders
   d. the number of disorders has increased

_____ 9. When you first read about the DSM, it seems overly complicated (why not just a list?), but the purpose of having all the axes, syndromes, and problems is to
a. give all kinds of therapists (Freudian, humanistic, behavioral, etc.) the categories they need
b. give the many clinicians who use it lots of diagnoses to choose from
c. ensure that nothing important about a person's condition is overlooked
d. rule out any possible disagreement among clinicians

_____ 10. You're not like the nutcases described in the textbook, are you? *Now don't start cry babying about*
a. the DSM
b. labeling
c. the frequency of mental disorders
d. assessment

_____ 11. A recent large-scale study showed that __________ percent of all Americans had at least one mental disorder during their lifetime
a. only 15
b. almost 50
c. fully 80
d. almost 100

_____ 12. After substance abuse disorders, the most commonly reported mental disorders are
a. schizophrenic disorders
b. mood disorders
c. anxiety disorders
d. organic mental disorders

_____ 13. The anxiety disorder that causes the greatest terror and suffering is
a. panic disorder
b. simple phobia
c. generalized anxiety disorder
d. social phobia

_____ 14. Psychologically, the interesting thing about panic attacks is that
a. often people who are fearful in one situation are quite brave in others
b. realistically, the person suffering the attack is not in danger at all
c. people suffering these attacks have been shown to crave attention and sympathy
d. they are brief, relatively mild affairs that the person can laugh about later

_____ 15. Rose is so afraid of suffering a panic attack when out in public that she stays at home all the time now; she suffers from
a. a simple phobia
b. a social phobia
c. agoraphobia
d. claustrophobia

_____ 16. Remember the case of Shirley, who had to do everything precisely 17 times? The theory is that she was trying to
a. reduce or avoid anxiety associated with feeling dirty
b. obey inner voices that told her God loves cleanliness
c. cleanse her mind of confusing hallucinations
d. please her mother, who used to punish her severely whenever she got her clothes dirty while playing

_____ 17. Shirley's obsessive-compulsive disorder might be lessened by a new treatment called
a. depth therapy
b. hypnotherapy
c. stimulant drug therapy
d. exposure therapy

_____ 18. The key feature of somatoform disorders is
a. pretending to be sick to avoid school or work
b. real physical symptoms but no physical causes
c. imagining physical symptoms that aren't really there
d. psychological problems but no physical symptoms

_____ 19. Medical doctors need to know psychology, because some of their patients are likely to be suffering from
a. agoraphobia
b. antisocial personality disorder
c. somatization disorder
d. mass hysteria

_____ 20. When half of the 500 children gathered to perform in a concert suddenly became ill, the cause was determined to be
a. mass hysteria
b. mass delusion
c. somatoform disorder
d. somatization disorder

_____ 21. Of all the mental disorders we know, it's a good bet you don't have to worry about getting TKS, mainly because you
a. are in college, and therefore too old to get it
b. are in college, and therefore too intelligent to get it
c. got shots for it as a child
d. don't live in Japan

_____ 22. The community is always shocked, yet most teenage school shooters
a. gave warning signs of their violent intentions, which were not taken seriously
b. came from among the poorest families in the community
c. had fathers, uncles, or cousins who were members of extremist groups
d. were well known to the local police as habitual lawbreakers

_____ 23. A neurological risk factor for becoming a teenage school shooter is that the
a. limbic system has not yet learned to control violent behavior
b. prefrontal cortex in the adolescent brain is still immature
c. shooters have a history of aggression and discipline problems at school or home
d. prefrontal cortex is a primitive part of the brain that exhibits emotional and violent impulses

_____ 24. Kate Premo was helped to overcome her fear of flying by
a. engaging in a romantic relationship with a pilot she admired and looked up to
b. undergoing hypnosis and receiving the implanted the message, "You will not be afraid"
c. undergoing depth therapy to psychoanalyze the childhood roots of her fear of flying
d. receiving a combination of cognitive-behavioral therapy and exposure therapy

_____ 25. Which one of the following is *not* a technique for treating phobia?
a. gradually exposing a client to the feared situation
b. administering an antidepressant drug to the client
c. hospitalizing the client until his or her fears begin to diminish
d. teaching the client to become aware of thoughts about the feared situation

Short Essay

1. Lacking a simple test for abnormality, psychology has offered three different ways to define it. What are they?

2. Describe the scope and the advantages and disadvantages of the *Diagnostic and Statistical Manual of Mental Disorders-IV-Text Revision* (DSM-IV-TR).

3. What are somatoform disorders? Give some examples.

4. Describe the Asian mental disorder called taijin kyofusho (TKS) and what we can learn about mental illness from it.

5. How was Kate Premo helped to overcome her severe aviophobia?

Psychology at Its Most Real

Now, boys and girls, can you say "diathesis stress theory" and "dialectical behavior therapy"? You will by the time you're finished with this module and the next.

These two modules are tough, partly because the subject involves the technical terminology of medical science and the concept of the medical model of illness. You must learn to think and talk like a doctor. But the main reason is that the subject touches on the most difficult challenge faced by psychology: how to understand why things go wrong for troubled people and how to help them.

Have you noticed how frequently new discoveries about the causes and treatment of mental illnesses are in the news? The field of abnormal psychology is developing right before your eyes. Memorize what you must in these modules, but keep your eyes on the big picture, too.

Yes, these modules are tough, but they present psychology at its most real.

Answers for Module 22

The Big Picture (explanations provided for incorrect choices)

A *Correct! You see the "big picture" for this Module.*
B Clinical psychology rests on a considerable foundation of empirical support and shared professional experience.
C Debate over psychological disorders continues, but a great deal is known about them and research continues.
D Most psychotherapists see DSM-IV-TR as an advance, but diagnosis is not yet perfect. There is still much to learn.
E It's just a joke!

True-False (explanations provided for False choices; page numbers given for all choices)

1	F	509	However horribly abnormal his behavior was, Rader does not meet the legal criteria for insanity.
2	F	513	Susan Smith was a deeply troubled person who suffered from major depression.
3	T	514	
4	T	516	
5	T	517	
6	T	517	
7	F	518	Phobias tend to persist and may require therapy.
8	F	519	These everyday experiences don't interfere with normal functioning, and so are not a mental disorder.
9	T	522	
10	F	525	Psychotherapy is at least equally effective in combating phobias.

Flashcards 1

1 d 2 e 3 j 4 h 5 a 6 i 7 f 8 c 9 b 10 g

Flashcards 2

1 g 2 e 3 h 4 c 5 i 6 d 7 f 8 j 9 a 10 b

Multiple Choice (explanations provided for incorrect choices)

1 a It seems clear that Rader killed 10 people.
b Rader did not claim diminished capacity because of drug use.
c *Correct! See page 509.*
d Rader did not claim to hear voices commanding him to kill.

2 a These two terms describe the same condition, but from different perspectives.
b *Correct! See page 509.*
c These two terms describe the same condition, but from different perspectives.
d Mental disorders do qualify for insurance reimbursement.

3 *a* *Correct! See page 510.*
b While still important, these are not the newest areas of interest and discovery.
c While still important, these were emphasized in the 1960s.
d That is only one specific (and rare) aspect of abnormal behavior.

4 a Statistical frequency is a way to define abnormal behavior.
b Deviation from social norms is a way to define abnormal behavior.
c Maladaptive behavior is a way to define abnormal behavior.
d *Correct! See page 511.*

5 a Is this procedure administered to most mental patients?
b Is this procedure administered to most mental patients?
c Is this procedure administered to most mental patients?
d *Correct! See page 512.*

6 *a* *Correct! See page 512.*
b This statement might be true, but it is not Plotnik's point.
c Accurate diagnosis yields understanding of many apparently baffling cases.
d Susan Smith's problems were deep and well hidden from her friends and neighbors.

7 a This is a made-up title, not a real manual.
b *Correct! See page 514.*
c This is a made-up title, not a real manual.
d This is a made-up title, not a real manual.

8 a DSM III (1980) dropped the Freudian terminology and orientation in favor of specific symptoms and criteria.
b Just the opposite is true.
c Rather than a problem, this will be a strength of the next DSM (likely in 2010).
d *Correct! See page 513.*

9 a This is just the opposite of the aim of the DSM.
b This is just the opposite of the aim of the DSM.
c *Correct! See page 514.*
d There is still disagreement, as in the court battles over whether defendants are insane or not.

10 a That does not describe the slur contained in this question!
b *Correct! See page 516.*
c That does not describe the slur contained in this question!
d That does not describe the slur contained in this question!

11 a This figure is too small.
b *Correct! See page 516.*
c This figure is too large.
d Does this figure square with your own observations?

12 a These disorders affect less than 1 percent of people.
b These disorders affect about 20 percent of people.
c *Correct! See page 517.*
d These disorders affect only a small number of people.

13 *a* *Correct! See page 517.*
b Simple phobias, like a fear of snakes, can be handled relatively easily by avoiding the feared object.
c Generalized anxiety disorder is uncomfortable, but not a cause of terror.
d Social phobia cause fear and avoidance of groups, but not necessarily terror.

14 a The point is sudden, unexplained fear, not bravery in the face of real danger.
b *Correct! See page 517.*
c If anything, sufferers try to hide the fact that they have panic attacks.
d Nothing could be farther from the truth.

15 a Simple phobias, like a fear of snakes, can be handled relatively easily by avoiding the feared object.
b Social phobias are fears of social situations (not just public places).
c *Correct! See page 518.*
d Claustrophobia is fear of being in enclosed spaces.

16 *a* *Correct! See page 519.*
b Shirley did not hear voices (more common in schizophrenia).
c Shirley did not suffer from hallucinations (more common in schizophrenia).
d This was not part of Shirley's case history.

17 a Talk therapy has not been particularly successful in treating OCD.
b This therapy has not been particularly successful in treating OCD.
c Drug therapy is used for OCD, but the drugs are antidepressant, not stimulant.
d *Correct! See page 519.*

18 a Sufferers of somatoform disorders are not faking.
b *Correct! See page 520.*
c The physical symptoms are actually present.
d There are physical symptoms.

19 a This rare disorder (if the patient came to the office at all!) would be obvious to most doctors.
b This rare disorder would not disguise itself as a physical complaint.
c *Correct! See page 520.*
d You wouldn't see mass hysteria in a single, individual patient.

20 ***a*** *Correct! See page 520.*
b This is not a correct technical term in psychology.
c Somatoform disorder applies to single cases of having a symptom without a physical cause.
d Somatization disorder is having numerous symptoms with physical causes.

21 a It can strike college students. (But you will see that this is a misleading clue!)
b Intelligent people can get it. (But you will see that this is a misleading clue!)
c There are no shots for TKS.
d *Correct! See page 522.*

22 ***a*** *Correct! See page 513.*
b The "facts" stated here are not true.
c The "facts" stated here are not true.
d The "facts" stated here are not true.

23 a The executive prefrontal cortex must control the more primitive limbic system.
b *Correct! See page 523.*
c These are environmental, not neurological, risk factors.
d That would be true of the limbic system, not the prefrontal cortex.

24 a A supportive pilot helped, but that was not the key factor.
b Hypnotherapy was not used to treat Kate Premo.
c Depth therapy was not involved.
d *Correct! See page 524.*

25 a Gradual exposure is a treatment for phobias.
b Administering antidepressant drugs is a treatment for phobias.
c *Correct! See page 524.*
d Teaching clients to become aware of their thoughts is a treatment for phobias.

Short Essay (sample answers)

1. Psychology has nothing like a simple blood test that could immediately identify abnormality. Instead, practitioners in the field use three different definitions of abnormality. (1) The *statistical frequency approach* says behavior may be abnormal if it is rare or infrequent. (2) The *social norms approach* says behavior may be abnormal if it deviates greatly from accepted social standards. (3) The *maladaptive behavior approach* says behavior may be abnormal if it interferes with an individual's ability to function in personal life or society.

2. The DSM has grown to be a large book covering almost 300 mental disorders. It describes the symptoms of nine major clinical syndromes on Axis I, personality disorders on Axis II, and related conditions on three more axes. The advantages of the DSM are objective guidelines and scientific precision in communicating with other professionals, conducting research, and designing treatment programs. The disadvantages are continuing disagreements on diagnoses and potential social, political, and labeling problems.

3. Somatoform disorders are genuine (not faked) ailments consisting of bodily symptoms with no physical causes — the real causes are psychological and related to anxiety. Two kinds are somatization disorder and conversion disorder. Experienced medical practitioners know that many of the complaints their patients present are actually psychological problems disguised as bodily problems. The doctor's advice to "take two aspirins and call me in the morning" is actually not far from what is needed: sympathy and understanding.

4. Taijin kyofusho (TKS) is a kind of social phobia characterized by a terrible fear of offending others through awkward social or physical behavior, such as staring, blushing, giving off an offensive odor, having an unpleasant facial expression, or having trembling hands. The fact that TKS is common in Japan but unknown in the United States shows the power of cultural norms to shape the particular expression of a psychological problem — in this case, anxiety, the second most common mental disorder in both countries.

5. Kate Premo overcame a specific phobia (aviophobia, fear of flying) by combining two methods. First, cognitive-behavioral therapy, in which she changed negative or distorted thoughts ("That noise must mean trouble!") by substituting realistic ones ("It's just the landing gear going down."). Second, exposure therapy, in which she learned and practiced new skills by facing the anxiety-producing situation (actually flying), but in a supportive environment and after she had learned how to combat anxiety by relaxing and calming down.

Module 23

Mood Disorders & Schizophrenia

The Story of a Troubled Person

One of the most perplexing and controversial problems of psychology is how to understand and treat human anguish and suffering. The great danger is that we may classify, label, and prescribe, but without really understanding. Modern psychology has come a long way from the unthinking and often cruel "treatment" in use not so long ago, but we are still far from having a reliable science of diagnosis and therapy.

I want to suggest an exercise that may help you think about the great complexity of emotional disturbance, yet also show you that your own psychological sensitivity and insight into human suffering may be greater than you realize. The exercise is to write a brief paper about a troubled person you know. I think this would be a good paper to use for an assignment in psychology or English.

An Exercise in Understanding

Write about someone you know fairly well, such as a relative or friend, who seems unable to enjoy the normal human satisfactions of love and work (that was Freud's definition of emotional disturbance). The reasons for the troubled person's distress could be anything from the broad spectrum of mental problems: severe depression or schizophrenia, common problems of anxiety, panic, and phobia, or social problems like alcoholism and child abuse. What you already know about the person is enough for this exercise.

Work hard to draw a clear picture of your troubled person. Include a personality description, a brief life history, and look for significant turning points in the person's life. Bring in ideas from the relevant approaches to psychology and famous theories of personality and treatment.

Your conclusion should reinforce three points: (1) your theory about why the person became troubled, (2) how the person could be helped (what might work), and finally (3) what the story of this troubled person teaches us about human behavior in general — what lessons it has for our own lives.

You could use this exercise as an opportunity to think and write about your own life and problems, too. Even though you probably aren't a troubled person, you may have private doubts and worries or painful experiences you would benefit from exploring.

Effective Student Tip 23

Try, Try Again

I envied my brilliant classmates. I felt guilty when I read about the successes of others. "How did they do it?" I asked when I read about a new book or scientific breakthrough or business achievement. Taking nothing away from the few true geniuses among us, I now realize that most successful people just kept on trying.

Newly famous stars often ruefully acknowledge their "overnight success." They know they've waited tables and taken any part they could get for years before their big break. Perhaps they are uncomfortable with fame because they know it is illusory. The reality is the love for their craft that kept them working at it no matter how few the rewards.

Again and again, when you read about a new discovery or a great accomplishment, you find that a previously unheralded person, probably not much different from you or me, has been working at it for years. What these admirable people do have is persistence, a force psychology could do well to study in greater depth.

The moral is simply this: most great achievements result from a combination of an idea that won't let go of the person, sufficient time to work and rework the idea, and persistence in seeing it through. If at first you don't succeed…

Your response…

Looking back over your life, are there goals you wish you had pursued with greater determination?

Learning Objectives

1. Understand mood disorders and schizophrenia as the most serious and life-threatening psychological abnormalities we humans face.

2. Learn the basic kinds, causes, and treatments of mood disorders, including the last-resort treatment called electroconvulsive therapy (ECT).

3. Learn six kinds of personality disorders, including the uncommon but dangerous antisocial personality disorder.

4. Understand the types, symptoms, causes, and treatment of the devastating group of disorders called schizophrenia.

5. Understand the causes and startling symptoms of the rare dissociative disorders.

6. Appreciate how worldwide psychological abnormalities are interpreted differently by particular cultures.

7. Investigate research on the psychologically curative powers of exercise, and learn the steps you can take to deal with the common experience of mild depression.

Key Terms

You're in med school now, baby! You've really got to work to learn all these key terms, but if you can do it, you will gain a whole new world of understanding.

---

antidepressant drugs
antisocial personality disorder
atypical neuroleptic drugs
Beck's cognitive theory of depression
biological factors underlying depression
bipolar I disorder
borderline personality disorder
catatonic schizophrenia
culture-specific disorder
dependent personality disorder
dialectical behavior therapy
diathesis stress theory
disorganized schizophrenia
dissociative amnesia
dissociative disorder
dissociative fugue
dissociative identity disorder
dopamine theory
dysthymic disorder
electroconvulsive therapy (ECT)
genetic marker
hallucinations
histrionic personality disorder
major depressive disorder
mood disorder
negative symptoms of schizophrenia
neuroleptic (antipsychotic) drugs
obsessive-compulsive personality disorder
paranoid personality disorder
paranoid schizophrenia
personality disorder
positive symptoms of schizophrenia
psychosocial factors
schizophrenia
schizotypal personality disorder
tardive dyskinesia
transcranial magnetic stimulation (TMS)
Type I schizophrenia
Type II schizophrenia
typical neuroleptic drugs

Outline

- *Introduction*
  1. Mood disorder (Chuck Elliot)
  2. Schizophrenia (Michael McCabe)

☐ The introductory examples above differ from those in the last module in one major way. How?

A. *Mood Disorders*

1. Kinds of **mood disorder**

☐ Do you ever feel depressed? How does it affect you? How do you fight it?

   a. **Major depressive disorder** (Sheryl Crow, major depression)

   b. **Bipolar I disorder** (Chuck Elliot)

   c. **Dysthymic disorder**

2. Causes of mood disorders

   a. **Biological factors underlying depression**

      (1) Genetic factors

      (2) Neurological factors

      (3) Brain scans

   b. **Psychosocial factors**

      (1) Stressful life events

      (2) Negative cognitive style

      (3) Personality factors

      (4) Depressed mothers

3. Treatment of mood disorders

   a. Major depression and dysthymic disorder

      (1) **Antidepressant drugs**

      (2) Selective serotonin reuptake inhibitors (SSRIs)

      (3) Effectiveness of antidepressants

      (4) Psychotherapy

      (5) Relapse

   b. Bipolar I disorder

      (1) Treatment: lithium

      (2) Mania

      (3) Relapse

B. *Electroconvulsive Therapy*

1. Definition and usage

☐ Why is ECT, which seems to work, such a controversial form of therapy?

   a. **Electroconvulsive therapy (ECT)**

   b. Usage

2. Effectiveness of ECT
   a. Modern ECT
   b. Memory loss
   c. New treatment: **transcranial magnetic stimulation (TNS)**

C. Personality Disorders

1. Definition and types: **personality disorder**

☐ No, you're not sick, but which of these personality disorders is closest to your own personality?

   a. **Paranoid personality disorder**
   b. **Schizotypal personality disorder**
   c. **Histrionic personality disorder**
   d. **Obsessive-compulsive personality disorder**
   e. **Dependent personality disorder**
   f. **Borderline personality disorder**
   g. **Antisocial personality disorder**
2. Borderline personality disorder
   a. Causes
   b. Treatment (**dialectical behavior therapy**)
3. Antisocial personality disorder: continuum of symptoms from delinquent to serial killer
   a. Causes
      (1) Psychosocial factors
      (2) Biological factors
   b. Treatment

D. Schizophrenia

1. Definition and types of **schizophrenia** (Michael McCabe)
   a. Subcategories of schizophrenia
      (1) **Paranoid schizophrenia**
      (2) **Disorganized schizophrenia**
      (3) **Catatonic schizophrenia**
   b. Chance of recovery
      (1) **Type I schizophrenia** (positive symptoms)
      (2) **Type II schizophrenia** (negative symptoms)
2. Symptoms
   a. Disorders of thought
   b. Disorders of attention
   c. Disorders of perception: **hallucinations**
   d. Motor disorders
   e. Emotional (affective) disorders

3. Biological causes
   a. Genetic predisposition (the Genain quadruplets)
   b. **Genetic marker**
      (1) Breakthroughs
      (2) Infections
4. Neurological causes
   a. Ventricle size
   b. Frontal lobe: prefrontal cortex
5. Environmental causes
   a. Environmental risk factors
   b. **Diathesis stress theory** of schizophrenia
6. Treatment
   a. Symptoms
      (1) **Positive symptoms of schizophrenia**
      (2) **Negative symptoms of schizophrenia**
      (3) **Neuroleptic (antipsychotic) drugs**
   b. Typical neuroleptics
      (1) **Typical neuroleptic drugs**
      (2) **Dopamine theory**
   c. Atypical neuroleptics
      (1) **Atypical neuroleptic drugs**
      (2) Current treatment: newer atypical neuroleptics
7. Evaluation of neuroleptic drugs
   a. Typical neuroleptics
      (1) Side effects: **tardive dyskinesia**
      (2) Effectiveness
      (3) Relapse
   b. Atypical neuroleptics
      (1) Side effects
      (2) Effectiveness and relapse
      (3) Conclusions
      (4) New directions

E. Dissociative Disorders

1. Definition: **dissociative disorder**

☐ What features do all the dissociative disorders have in common? (And don't say you forgot!)

2. **Dissociative amnesia**
3. **Dissociative fugue**

4. **Dissociative identity disorder** [formerly called multiple personality disorder]
   a. Definition
   b. Occurrence and causes
      (1) Explanations
      (2) Treatment

F. Cultural Diversity: Interpreting Symptoms

1. Spirit possession
2. **Culture-specific disorder**
3. Gender differences in mental disorders

G. Research Focus: Exercise versus Drugs

1. Choices of therapy for depression: **major depressive disorder**
2. Exercise experiment: seven rules [of scientific experimentation]
   a. Method and results
   b. Relapse
   c. Conclusions

H. Application: Dealing with Mild Depression

1. Mild versus major depression
   a. Continuum
   b. College students
   c. Vulnerability
2. Beck's theory of depression
   a. **Beck's cognitive theory of depression**
   b. Specific negative, maladaptive thoughts (overgeneralization, selective attention)
3. Overcoming mild depression
   a. Improving social skills
      (1) Problem: poor social skills; program: positive steps
      (2) Problem: low self-esteem; program: thought substitution
   b. Eliminating negative thoughts
      (1) Problem: negative, maladaptive thoughts
      (2) Program: substituting positive thoughts
   c. Power of positive thinking
      (1) Brain scans
      (2) Altering brain functioning by talk therapy

How English Works

Words in the Textbook

p. 531 the boss fired him **on the spot** = immediately

no better off than he had been before = not improved at all

Marsha was **at her wit's end** = upset, desperate for a solution

p. 535 causing a **grand-mal seizure** = very strong attack, involving entire body

as if I've just **downed** a frozen margarita = drunk

No more **egregious** highs or lows = terrible

I'm clearheaded and **even-keeled** = balance

medication **keeps** my illness **in check** = controls

p. 536 **Don't judge a book by its cover** = Look more deeply, go below the surface

cold-blooded killers = with no sympathy or mercy for victims

p. 537 developed into **full-blown** psychopaths = with a complete range of symptoms

p. 538 I was so **high on life** = happy, optimistic

p. 539 How in the hell **were we dealt this hand**? = How did this happen to us?

associated with an increased risk = to connect one thing with another in the mind

p. 541 equally effective in **boosting** cognitive skills = to improve or strengthen something

p. 542 experience **intolerable** side effects = so bad, difficult, or painful that it cannot be endured

p. 548 **scrape up enough bucks** to pay my rent = find enough money

tired of my **moping around** = acting unhappy, not being active

I should just **get over him** = stop thinking about him

what do I do to get out of **my funk** = my feelings of depression

making a **blanket** judgment = too general

p. 549 we **get down in the dumps** = feel depressed

I've got a lot going for me = I have many advantages and possibilities

Sentence Structure: More about Commas as Interrupters

Earlier we learned that commas could be used to interrupt the main idea of the sentence with some extra information. Remember that this information has a comma at the beginning and a comma at the end, so that you can remove the information and it does not affect the sentence. There are many different reasons why a writer might want to use interrupters. Let's look at some of them.

Interrupters allow the writer to provide several **examples**:

> Stressful events, **such as having hostile parents, poor social relations, the death of a parent or loved one, and career or personal problems**, can contribute to the development and onset of schizophrenia.

They can allow the writer to **identify** a word within the sentence:

> Researchers found that a group of neurotransmitters, called the monoamines (**especially serotonin and norepinephrine**), are known to be involved in mood problems.

The interrupter can identify **time**:

> We discussed how, **after treatment for a mental disorder**, a certain percent of patients relapse or again return to having serious symptoms.

Interrupters can also help the writer **classify** a word:

> Unlike Sheryl Crow's problem, **which was major depressive disorder**, Chuck Elliot has bipolar 1 disorder, which means that he cycles between episodes of depression and mania.

If the writer really wants to draw attention to the extra information, he may use **dashes** (—) instead of **commas** (,). We find dashes more often in newspaper and magazine writing and less in academic writing. Look at the following two examples from the text. Notice how the sentence with the dashes draws your eyes more to the information inside the interrupter than the commas:

> The psychiatrist was pointing out three major factors — biological, neurological, and environmental — that interact in the development of schizophrenia.

> The psychiatrist was pointing out three major factors, such as biological, neurological, and environmental, that interact in the development of schizophrenia.

When you read your textbook, you'll notice the first sentence with the dashes more. Notice also that the writer would need to add a transitional word when using commas.

Now you try it. Underline the interrupter in this sentence and include the missing commas, all four of them.

> In other cases, mental disorders may involve a relatively common behavior or event that through some learning observation or other process has the power to elicit tremendous anxiety and becomes a phobia.

Sentence Structure: Active / Passive and Objective / Subjective

Read the following sentences and circle the best choice to describe the sentence.

> The psychodynamic theory of personality was developed by Sigmund Freud. Is this *Active* or *Passive*?

> Sigmund Freud is often called the "father of psychoanalysis." Is this *Active* or *Passive*?

> Freud wrote about people like little Hans and the Rat Man. Is this *Active* or *Passive*?

> This review is good practice. Is this *Objective* or *Subjective*?

> There are 25 modules in the textbook. Is this *Objective* or *Subjective*?

Answers

In other cases, mental disorders may involve a relatively common behavior or event that, **through some learning, observation, or other process,** has the power to elicit tremendous anxiety and becomes a phobia.

The psychodynamic theory of personality was developed by Sigmund Freud. *Passive*

Sigmund Freud is often called the "father of psychoanalysis." *Passive*

Freud wrote about people like little Hans and the Rat Man. *Active*

This review is good practice. *Subjective*

There are 25 modules in the textbook. *Objective*

The Big Picture

Which statement below offers the best summary of the larger significance of this module?

A When you see the wide variety of psychological illnesses affecting people, you are tempted to conclude that consciousness may be the fatal weakness of the human species. We think too much, and torture ourselves with fears.

B With every additional discovery in neuroscience, it becomes more obvious that "psychological" disorders are essentially biological. There is not much we can do to prevent or cure these disorders: you either have good genes or you don't.

C There is a class of psychological disorders that are characterized by their crippling effect on a person's ability to function in society. In their extreme forms, they may interfere with a person's contact with reality.

D Psychiatry has discovered a definite hierarchy of disorders. From *least* harmful to *most* harmful, they are: dissociative disorders, schizophrenia, personality disorders, and mood disorders.

E Every time the psychiatrist held up a new Rorschach ink blot card, the subject gave an interpretation that was more disgusting and more vulgar than the last. When the exasperated psychiatrist remarked on this, the subject protested, "But doc, you're the one showing the dirty pictures!"

True-False

____ 1. The most serious mood disorder is major depression.

____ 2. Dysthymic disorder is characterized by fluctuations between episodes of depression and mania.

____ 3. Sheryl Crow was famous and successful, so she was able to get over her depression fairly easily.

____ 4. The most common treatment for major depression is electroconvulsive therapy (ECT).

____ 5. People suffering from antisocial personality disorder are extremely shy and attempt to avoid other people.

____ 6. People suffering from Type I schizophrenia (more positive symptoms) have a better chance for recovery than those suffering from Type II schizophrenia (more negative symptoms).

____ 7. The importance of the Genain quadruplets is that they provided evidence for a genetic component in schizophrenia.

____ 8. Antipsychotic drugs are effective, but they also have serious side effects.

____ 9. Dissociative disorders work like this: dissociative amnesia, forget; dissociative fugue, flee; dissociative identity disorder, split off.

____ 10. Although many people experience occasional mild depression, there is not much they can do except tough it out.

Flashcards 1

_____	1. antisocial personality disorder	a.	being chronically but not continuously depressed for a period of two years; poor appetite, insomnia, and fatigue
_____	2. bipolar I disorder	b.	a pattern of disregarding or violating the rights of others without feeling guilt or remorse (usually male)
_____	3. catatonic schizophrenia	c.	characterized by excessive emotionality and attention seeking
_____	4. culture-specific disorder	d.	characterized by periods of wild excitement or periods of rigid, prolonged immobility; frozen posture
_____	5. dysthymic disorder	e.	a pattern of distrust and suspiciousness and perceiving others as having evil motives
_____	6. histrionic personality disorder	f.	continually being in a bad mood, having no interest in anything, and getting no pleasure from activities
_____	7. major depressive disorder	g.	an intense interest in being orderly, achieving perfection, and having control
_____	8. obsessive-compulsive personality disorder	h.	marked by fluctuations between episodes of depression and mania; two extreme moods
_____	9. paranoid personality disorder	i.	characterized by auditory hallucinations or delusions of being persecuted or delusions of grandeur
_____	10. paranoid schizophrenia	j.	*latah, bibloqtoq, susto, koro* — they are all genuine mental disorders, but what kind?

Flashcards 2

_____	1. diathesis stress theory	a.	suddenly and unexpectedly traveling away from home or place of work and being unable to recall one's past
_____	2. dissociative amnesia	b.	says dopamine neurotransmitter system is somehow overactive and causes schizophrenic symptoms
_____	3. dissociative fugue	c.	says that some people have a genetic predisposition interacting with life stressors to cause schizophrenia
_____	4. dissociative identity disorder	d.	characterized by inability to recall important personal information or events; associated with stress, trauma
_____	5. dopamine theory	e.	a noninvasive technique that activates neurons by sending doses of magnetic energy into the brain
_____	6. electroconvulsive therapy (ECT)	f.	presence of two or more distinct identities, each with its own pattern of thinking about, and relating to, the world
_____	7. genetic marker	g.	an identifiable gene, or genes, or a specific segment of chromosome directly linked to a trait or disease
_____	8. mood disorder	h.	serious mental disorder with symptoms of delusions, hallucinations, and disorganized speech and behavior
_____	9. schizophrenia	i.	administration of mild electrical current that passes through the brain and causes a seizure
_____	10. transcranial magnetic stimulation (TMS)	j.	prolonged and disturbed emotional state that affects almost all of a person's thoughts, feelings, and behaviors

Multiple Choice

_____ 1. Plotnik and Kouyoumdjian offer the examples of Chuck Elliot and Michael McCabe to show that
   a. people who have used illegal drugs are more likely to become mentally ill
   b. mood disorders and schizophrenia can be terrifying, crippling disorders
   c. anyone can become mentally ill at almost any time
   d. brilliant, creative people are more likely to become mentally ill

_____ 2. Which one of the following is *not* a mood disorder?
   a. major depression
   b. bipolar I disorder
   c. antisocial personality disorder
   d. dysthymic disorder

_____ 3. __________ disorder is marked by fluctuations between episodes of depression and mania
   a. Bipolar I
   b. Major depressive
   c. Dysthymic
   d. Minor depressive

_____ 4. New research points to __________ as a cause of depression
   a. food additives
   b. gender differences in mood
   c. old age
   d. faulty brain structure or function

_____ 5. Psychosocial factors putting a person at risk for depression include all of the following *except*
   a. stressful life events
   b. genetic inheritance
   c. negative cognitive style
   d. personality factors

_____ 6. Antidepressant drugs work by
   a. attacking and destroying depressive memory cells that cause depression
   b. creating feelings of peace and well-being similar to the effects of alcohol
   c. preventing neurons from being over stimulated
   d. increasing the levels of neurotransmitters involved in regulating emotions and moods

_____ 7. If you saw the movie *One Flew over the Cuckoo's Nest*, you may be surprised to learn that
   a. ECT does not in fact cause memory loss
   b. although some doctors use ECT today, it remains a dangerously unsafe treatment
   c. the use of ECT (as a last resort) has increased since 1980
   d. a new use has been found for ECT — the treatment of schizophrenia

_____ 8. ECT is a controversial treatment for depression because it
   a. has serious side effects, such as memory loss
   b. is based on the use of antidepressant drugs
   c. has no effect at all on many patients
   d. is prescribed by psychiatrists but not by clinical psychologists

_____ 9. Which one of the following is *not* a personality disorder?
a. paranoid personality disorder
b. histrionic personality disorder
c. obsessive-compulsive personality disorder
d. depressive personality disorder

_____ 10. Jeffrey Dahmer represented an extreme case of _________ personality disorder
a. histrionic
b. paranoid
c. antisocial
d. schizotypical

_____ 11. Psychotherapy has not proved very effective in treating psychopaths (like Dahmer) because
a. they are fundamentally dishonest and don't see themselves as ill
b. most therapists are afraid to work with psychopaths, knowing their violent ways
c. psychopaths result almost entirely from biological factors, which psychotherapy can't touch
d. this is a genetic, "bad seed" disease, against which talk therapy is helpless

_____ 12. The highest percentages of mental hospital inpatients are there because of
a. major depression
b. schizophrenia
c. antisocial personality disorder
d. dissociative amnesia

_____ 13. Chances for recovery from schizophrenia are best in patients with
a. symptoms of dulled emotions, little inclination to speak, and a loss of normal functions
b. Type II schizophrenia (negative symptoms)
c. Type I schizophrenia (positive symptoms)
d. (cases of recovery from schizophrenia are so rare as to be statistically insignificant)

_____ 14. Which one of the following problems is *not* a symptom of schizophrenia?
a. disorders of thought
b. disorders of attention
c. disorders of perception
d. disorders of moral character

_____ 15. Plotnik and Kouyoumdjian tell us about the famous Genain quadruplets to illustrate the fact that
a. there must be a genetic factor in schizophrenia
b. science is filled with amazing coincidences
c. children can "learn" to be schizophrenic from close contact with family members who are ill
d. schizophrenia strikes in a random, unpredictable fashion

_____ 16. New brain research using MRI and fMRI scans have revealed that schizophrenics show
a. overactivation of the prefrontal cortex, resulting in disordered thinking
b. overwired brains, with too many connections to permit rational thinking
c. excessive neuron development, accounting for the somewhat larger brains of schizophrenics
d. larger ventricles, fewer brain cells, and fewer connections among neurons

_____ 17. The diathesis-stress theory of schizophrenia says that some people have a/n

a. overactive dopamine neurotransmitter system
b. genetic predisposition that interacts with life stressors to cause the disease
c. atypical neuroleptic tendency in their brains
d. overactive diathesis in the prefrontal cortex

_____ 18. According to the __________ theory, schizophrenia is caused by the overactivity of neurotransmitters in the brain

a. dopamine
b. diathesis stress
c. genetic marker
d. tardive dyskinesia

_____ 19. Antipsychotic or neuroleptic drugs work by

a. increasing levels of the neurotransmitter dopamine
b. changing levels of neurotransmitters in the brain
c. increasing levels of the neurotransmitter serotonin
d. increasing positive symptoms of schizophrenia

_____ 20. What can we conclude about the battle against schizophrenia?

a. science is on the brink of new drug treatments that will wipe out this disease
b. drug treatment, considering the high rates of relapse and the dangerous side effects, must be considered a failure
c. it can be a life-long problem, with a high risk for relapse, needing drug treatment, psychotherapy, and social support
d. it remains too complicated to understand, and may never be conquered by science

_____ 21. The difference between dissociative amnesia and dissociative fugue is that

a. in the former, you stay in contact with reality; in the latter you become schizophrenic
b. in the former, you have memory gaps; in the latter you may wander away and assume a new identity
c. in the former, you forget more than in the latter
d. these are really two different terms for the same disorder

_____ 22. The case of Jeffrey Ingram, a missing Seattle man found wandering in Denver, illustrates

a. dissociative fugue
b. dissociative amnesia
c. dissociative identity disorder
d. multiple personality disorder

_____ 23. An underlying cause often reported in dissociative identity disorder is

a. physical trauma, such as a head injury
b. unstable parents who give their children mixed messages about what they expect
c. a flighty personality along with a tendency to overdramatize every situation
d. severe physical or sexual abuse during childhood

_____ 24. According to Aaron Beck's cognitive theory of depression, depressed people

a. learn depressive habits from other depressed people in their families
b. have many relatives who also are depressed, suggesting a genetic link
c. automatically and continually think negative thoughts that they rarely notice
d. suffer from repressed feelings of guilt and overactive superegos

_____ 25. Good advice if you are trying to overcome mild depression includes all of the following *except*
a. improve your social skills
b. improve your self-esteem
c. substitute positive thoughts for negative, maladaptive thoughts
d. learn to accept the fact that your life is really bad

Short Essay

1. Describe the two kinds of factors that cause mood disorders such as depression. If you wish, use Sheryl Crow's depression to illustrate your answer.

2. What progress is being made in understanding and treating schizophrenia?

3. Describe dissociative fugue. In your answer, you might use the case Plotnik and Kouyoumdjian cite (Jeffrey Ingram, found wandering the streets of Denver).

4. Tell the history of dissociative identity disorder and explain why the diagnosis has been controversial.

5. Why does this textbook of scientific psychology include a discussion of spirit possession? What does spirit possession suggest about how "scientific" our own mental health practices are?

Psychology Is Dead!

That's what my nephew Bruce, who has just earned his Ph.D. in psychopharmacology, said to his father, Larry, who is a psychotherapist. Bruce spends long days with lab animals while conducting research on the neuroscience of drug addiction and treatment. His challenge was meant to be provocative, but also a gentle tease on his father, whose treatment methods are eclectic but more traditional. The therapy Larry offers is something of an art, while Bruce strives to make his work pure science. For young Bruce, strictly speaking, the old psychology *is* dead — eventually to be replaced by a completely scientific biology of behavior.

Is this the future of psychotherapy? Actually, as Bruce told me recently, he believes the best treatment today is a combination of medication and supportive talk therapy. But sometimes it's fun to make your point by indulging in bold proclamations like, *"Psychology is dead!"*

Use College to Learn More about Yourself

In the "Introduction" to this module, I suggested writing a paper on understanding emotional illness. When I give this assignment in my classes, the best papers are often autobiographical. I remember a kindly and understanding English professor I had many years ago who allowed me to write about something painful in my own life. I learned from it, and gained a measure of peace as well. Write — and learn — about yourself.

Answers for Module 23

The Big Picture (explanations provided for incorrect choices)

A It sometimes seems that way, but consciousness also has allowed the triumph of our species.
B There is a genetic basis to many illnesses, but even these are preventable and curable.
C *Correct! You see the "big picture" for this Module.*
D This hierarchy does not make sense (see definitions), as well as the many disorders that this statement leaves out.
E It's just a joke!

True-False (explanations provided for False choices; page numbers given for all choices)

1	T	532	
2	F	532	That describes bipolar I disorder.
3	F	534	Major depression is serious — for anyone — and requires long and careful treatment.
4	F	535	ECT is a rarely used treatment of last resort for depression.
5	F	536	People with antisocial personality can be charming and popular with other people.
6	T	538	
7	T	539	
8	T	542	
9	T	544	
10	F	549	There are several steps people can take to combat mild depression.

Flashcards 1

1 b 2 h 3 d 4 j 5 a 6 c 7 f 8 g 9 e 10 i

Flashcards 2

1 c 2 d 3 a 4 f 5 b 6 i 7 g 8 j 9 h 10 e

Multiple Choice (explanations provided for incorrect choices)

1 a Illegal drugs are not the main issue here.
b *Correct! See page 531.*
c Be assured that this statement is untrue.
d The small amount of evidence for the connection does not support this popular belief.

2 a Major depression is a mood disorder.
b Bipolar disorder is a mood disorder.
c *Correct! See page 532.*
d Dysthymic disorder is a mood disorder.

3 ***a*** *Correct! See page 532.*
b Major depressive disorder does not feature episodes of mania.
c Dysthymic disorder does not feature episodes of mania.
d There is no disorder with this name.

4 a There is no significant evidence of this.
b This old idea has been discounted.
c Many older people are living fully and happily.
d *Correct! See page 533.*

5 a This is a psychosocial risk factor for depression.
b *Correct! See page 533.*
c This is a psychosocial risk factor for depression.
d This is a psychosocial risk factor for depression.

6 a These drugs do not cause memory loss.
b Alcohol is itself a depressant and does not help depressed people.
c This is more true of lithium (used for bipolar I disorder).
d *Correct! See page 534.*

7 a Memory loss is one of the side effects of ECT.
b ECT is safer today, and does not cause brain damage or turn people into vegetables.
c *Correct! See page 535.*
d ECT is still used to treat mood disorders.

8 ***a*** *Correct! See page 535.*
b ECT is not based on the use of antidepressant drugs.
c ECT has an immediate effect on almost all patients receiving it.
d This is not a cause of controversy.

9 a This is one of the personality disorders.
b This is one of the personality disorders.
c This is one of the personality disorders.
d *Correct! See page 536.*

10 a This personality disorder does not cause a person to harm others.
b This personality disorder does not cause a person to harm others.
c *Correct! See page 536.*
d This personality disorder does not cause a person to harm others.

11 ***a*** *Correct! See page 537.*
b This might be true in a few, extreme cases, but not for the majority of potential patients.
c Psychopaths are caused by both psychosocial and biological factors.
d There may be a genetic component, but it accounts for no more than 30 to 50 percent in an individual.

12 a Good guess, but another mental illness accounts for a full 30 percent of all inpatients.
b *Correct! See page 538.*
c Antisocial personality disorder is a rare problem.
d Dissociative amnesia does not require hospitalization.

13 a These are symptoms of Type II schizophrenia, in which chances of recovery are poor.
b The negative symptoms and loss of normal functions of Type II schizophrenia make recovery less likely.
c *Correct! See page 538.*
d Chances of recovery from schizophrenia are fairly good, especially if therapy and support are continued.

14 a Disorders of thought are important symptoms of schizophrenia.
b Disorders of attention are important symptoms of schizophrenia.
c Disorders of perception are important symptoms of schizophrenia.
d *Correct! See page 538.*

15 ***a*** *Correct! See page 539.*
b The fact that they were identical (quadruplets) rules out coincidence.
c This statement does not fit the case of the Genain quadruplets.
d This statement does not fit the case of the Genain quadruplets.

16 a Just the opposite is true.
b Just the opposite is true.
c Schizophrenics do not have either too many neurons or larger brains.
d *Correct! See page 540.*

17 a This is the dopamine theory of schizophrenia.
b *Correct! See page 540.*
c Atypical neuroleptics are antipsychotic drugs used to combat schizophrenia.
d Diathesis indicates a genetic predisposition, not a part of the brain.

18 ***a*** *Correct! See page 541.*
b The diathesis-stress theory involves both brain abnormalities and environmental stress.
c A genetic marker is an identifiable link to a trait or disease.
d Tardive dyskinesia is a serious side effect of antipsychotic drugs.

19 a They reduce, not increase, levels of dopamine.
b *Correct! See page 542.*
c They reduce, not increase, levels of serotonin.
d These symptoms must be decreased (back in the direction of normal functioning).

20 a Too optimistic — there is still vast suffering and no "magic bullet" seems to be on the horizon.
b On the contrary, drug treatment offers the best hope now and may well improve.
c *Correct! See page 542.*
d Too pessimistic — with medication, many sufferers can live productive and relatively normal lives.

21 a Loss of contact with reality does not occur in either disorder.
b *Correct! See page 544.*
c The truth is just the opposite.
d The two disorders are quite different.

22 ***a*** *Correct! See page 544.*
b Think about why he was missing from home.
c Dissociative identity disorder was formerly called multiple personality disorder.
d Did he manifest more than one personality?

23 a Head injury is not a factor in dissociative identity disorder.
b This is one explanation of schizophrenia.
c This is characteristic of certain personality disorders.
d *Correct! See page 545.*

24 a This would be a behaviorist explanation.
b Beck's theory is not based on genetics.
c *Correct! See page 548.*
d This would be a psychoanalytic explanation.

25 a Taking positive action to improve your social skills can help you overcome mild depression.
b Giving yourself credit can improve your self-esteem and help you overcome mild depression.
c Focusing on positive events can help you overcome mild depression.
d *Correct! See page 549.*

Short Essay (sample answers)

1. Popular singer-songwriter Sheryl Crow illustrates the causes of depression. First, biological risk factors emphasize underlying genetic (Sheryl's family has a history of depression), neurological, chemical or physiological components (Sheryl knew something was wrong). Second, psychosocial factors, such as personality traits, cognitive styles, social supports, and the ability to deal with stressors (like a world tour and struggling to get a new record contract) interact with predisposing biological factors to put one at risk.

2. Schizophrenia is the most devastating of the mental disorders, but progress is being made. Genetic markers identify people at risk. Brain scans reveal abnormalities that are involved in the disease. The diathesis stress theory shows how psychosocial stressors interact with biological risk factors. The main advance is the continuing development of antipsychotic (neuroleptic) drugs that change levels of neurotransmitters and therefore the way the brain works. Harmful side effects like tardive dyskinesia are being reduced.

3. Dissociative disorders are rare mental disorders in which there is a disruption or split in the normally integrated self, consciousness, memory, or sense of identity. In dissociative fugue, a person forgets who he is, travels away from home, and may assume a new identity. A confused man found wandering in Denver, unable to remember who he was, turned out to be a man from Seattle who had been on his way to Canada to visit his best friend, dying of cancer. Dissociative fugue is often related to stressful or traumatic life events.

4. An epidemic in the 1970s and 1980s of the previously rare "multiple personality disorder," in which two or more distinct identities or personality states take control of the individual's thoughts and behaviors at different times, led to controversy and revision in clinical psychology. The diagnosis, usually in women, was connected to claims of childhood sexual abuse. Some therapists were guilty of encouraging patients to play the roles. Still controversial but less commonly diagnosed, today it is called "dissociative identity disorder."

5. How would you diagnose a person who reports that sometimes a spirit takes possession of her body and mind and makes her do and say things she doesn't always remember? She would be called delusional and abnormal in the United States, but normal in the context of her culture in Northern Sudan. Before you say, "That's crazy!" think about all the disorders diagnosed more often in women in our country! Spirit possession is an example of how cultural factors determine whether symptoms are interpreted as normal or abnormal.

Module 24

Therapies

The Contribution of Psychodynamic Psychology to Therapy

Psychotherapy is one of the great inventions of modern times. Whether you consider it an art or a science, it is a young and constantly evolving process. Plotnik and Kouyoumdjian discuss four current approaches to psychotherapy, each with numerous varieties and special techniques.

At the heart of most forms of psychotherapy lie a basic assumption and a fundamental process that come from psychodynamic psychology and the work of a great pioneer, good old You-Know-Who. Both the assumption and the technique are inherent in his theory of dreams, about which you read way back in Module 7.

A Model for Understanding Psychotherapy... and Life

The key idea is the distinction between manifest (surface) content and latent (underlying) content. The manifest content of a dream is the story (however bizarre) we remember in the morning. The latent content is the disguised, unconscious wish hidden in the apparently meaningless story of the dream. The challenge to the dreamer, perhaps a patient in psychotherapy, is to gain insight into that latent content because it is a direct line [Our Hero called it the *via regia*, or royal road] to the unconscious. With a therapist's help, the patient examines thoughts and feelings connected to the dream in the expectation that these associations will suggest an underlying meaning, a meaning that provides insight into the patient's "dynamics," or psychological life.

This key idea has broad implications. Freud saw dreams and other unconscious acts (slips of the tongue, losing things, forgetting, accidents) as miniature neuroses, reflecting the larger neuroses of which we all have more than a few. Therefore, we can interpret *any* behavior like a dream. Here's the formula. First, examine the behavior (a comment, an act, even a thought) very carefully. Exactly what happened? That's the manifest content. Next, search the manifest content for clues about what the *latent* content might be. Why did you forget the assignment? Lose your keys? Call your sweetheart the wrong name? Bingo! Insight into how your unconscious mind works.

This fundamental idea of psychodynamic psychology underlies most forms of therapy, and can be used as a model for understanding almost anything in life, from the meaning of Shakespeare's plays to why your roommate is driving you crazy. Just answer two questions: What is the manifest content? What is the latent content?

Effective Student Tip 24

Take Teachers, Not Courses

Take at least a few courses far from your major area of study. Some advisors will urge you to take only courses that fit into your major, but that can be a mistake. One of the purposes of higher education is to broaden your horizons and show you worlds you scarcely know exist. When else will you have the opportunity to investigate ancient history, nutrition, figure drawing, astronomy, women's literature, and other fascinating subjects that aren't required for graduation?

Graduate students, who have been through it all and know all there is to know (just ask them), often say you should "take teachers, not courses." What they mean is that you should sign up for professors with reputations as especially stimulating teachers, without too much regard for how well the interesting courses fit into your official program.

You will come to know quite a bit about the faculty at your school. Some professors will begin to stand out as people you would like to study with and get to know. Try to give yourself at least a few of these experiences. You might learn more from an inspired, creative teacher in an unrelated course than from an average teacher in the course that fits so neatly into your major.

Your response…

If neither time nor money mattered, what courses would you like to take just for your own interest?

☐ *Even if Module 25 is not assigned in your course, please read* Effective Student Tip 25!

Learning Objectives

1. Understand therapies — putting psychology to work helping troubled people — as the ultimate reason and payoff for all the study and research poured into understanding psychology.
2. Appreciate the historical background of therapy as the groundwork for understanding and evaluating the different forms of treatment… and as a fascinating story in itself!
3. Learn the principles and procedures of the insight therapies of psychoanalysis, client-centered therapy, and cognitive therapy.
4. Learn the principles and procedures of behavior therapy and cognitive-behavior therapy.
5. Understand the basic questions about psychotherapy, including its assumptions, methods, techniques, effectiveness, and common factors.
6. Consider mental healing from a cultural perspective through an example from Bali and evaluate research on a new form of psychotherapy called EMDR.
7. Apply current cognitive-behavior techniques to possible problems you or others in your life may have.

Key Terms

Most of the key terms in this module are closely related to terms you have already learned in other modules.

behavior therapy (behavior modification)
client-centered therapy
clinical psychologists
cognitive therapy
cognitive-behavior therapy
common factors
community mental health centers
counseling psychologists
cybertherapy
deinstitutionalization
dream interpretation
eclectic approach
eye movement desensitization and reprocessing (EMDR)
free association
insight therapy
intrusive thoughts
medical therapy
meta-analysis
moral therapy
neuroses
phenothiazines
psychiatrists
psychoanalysis
psychotherapy
resistance
short-term dynamic psychotherapy
systematic desensitization
transference

The "PowerStudy 4.5 for Introduction to Psychology" CD-ROM includes a complete set of interactive learning activities for this module: quizzes, summary test, key terms, web site connections, critical thinking exercise, module outline, and more.

Outline

- *Introduction*

  ☐ What parts did Anna O and Little Albert play in the history of psychotherapy?

  1. Beginning of psychoanalysis (Anna O.)
  2. Beginning of behavior therapy (Little Albert)

A. *Historical Background*

1. Definition: **psychotherapy**
2. Early treatments
3. Reform movement: **moral therapy** (Dorothea Dix)
4. **Phenothiazines** and **deinstitutionalization**
   a. Discovery of drugs
   b. Homeless
5. **Community mental health centers**

B. *Questions about Psychotherapy*

1. Do I need professional help?
2. Are there different kinds of therapists?
   a. **Psychiatrists**
   b. **Clinical psychologists**
   c. **Counseling psychologists**
3. What are the different approaches?
   a. **Insight therapy**
   b. **Cognitive-behavior therapy**
   c. **Eclectic approach**
   d. **Medical therapy**
4. How effective is psychotherapy?
   a. **Meta-analysis**
   b. Major findings

C. *Insight Therapies*

☐ Plotnik and Kouyoumdjian quote from sessions illustrating the three insight therapies. Can you describe the different emphasis and style of each approach?

1. **Psychoanalysis** (Sigmund Freud)
   a. Three major assumptions
      (1) Unconscious conflicts
      (2) Techniques of free association, dream interpretation, and analysis of slips of the tongue
      (3) Transfer strong emotions onto therapist
   b. Therapy session

c. Role of analyst
   (1) Free association
   (2) Interpretation
   (3) Unconscious conflicts
d. Techniques to reveal the unconscious: **neuroses**
   (1) Rat Man: **free association**
   (2) Wolf-Man: **dream interpretation**
   (3) Case studies: Anna O., Rat Man, and Wolf-Man
e. Problems during therapy
   (1) Rat Man: **transference**
   (2) Wolf-Man: **resistance**
   (3) **Short-term dynamic psychotherapy**
f. Psychoanalysis: evaluation
   (1) Decline in popularity
      (a) Lack of research
      (b) Competing therapies
      (c) Psychoactive drugs
   (2) Current status
      (a) Freudian concepts
      (b) Conclusion

2. **Client-centered therapy** (Carl Rogers)
   a. Therapy session
   b. Client-centered approach
   c. Therapist's traits
      (1) Empathy
      (2) Positive regard
      (3) Genuineness
   d. Effectiveness
3. **Cognitive therapy** (Aaron Beck)
   a. Therapy session
   b. Cognitive approach
   c. Important factors
      (1) Overgeneralization
      (2) Polarized thinking
      (3) Selective attention
   d. Cognitive techniques
   e. Effectiveness

D. Behavior Therapy

1. Definition: **behavior therapy (behavior modification)**

☐ In what ways is behavior therapy radically different from the insight therapies?

   a. Therapy session

   b. Behavioral approach

   c. Two goals

2. **Systematic desensitization** (Joseph Wolpe)

   a. Relaxation

   b. Stimulus hierarchy

   c. Exposure

   d. Exposure: *imagined* or *in vivo* (real life)

3. **Cognitive-behavior therapy**

   a. Combining therapies

   b. Cognitive-behavior techniques

4. Kinds of problems

   a. Problem behaviors

   b. Effectiveness

E. Review: Evaluation of Approaches

☐ Another great Plotnik and Kouyoumdjian summary! Can you master the basic elements of each approach?

1. Background, assumptions, and techniques

   a. Psychoanalysis

      (1) Background

      (2) Basic assumption

      (3) Techniques

   b. Client-centered therapy

      (1) Background

      (2) Basic assumption

      (3) Techniques

   c. Cognitive therapy

      (1) Background

      (2) Basic assumption

      (3) Techniques

   d. Behavior therapy

      (1) Background

      (2) Basic assumption

      (3) Techniques

2. Effectiveness of psychotherapy

3. **Common factors**
4. **Cybertherapy**

F. Cultural Diversity: Different Healer

☐ Hmmm… If the balian usually obtains cures, what does that suggest about the success of Western therapy?

1. Case study: young woman (Bali)
    a. Western assumptions (depression)
    b. Local healer or balian (witchcraft)
2. Healer's diagnosis and treatment
3. Healers versus Western therapists

G. Research Focus: EMDR — New Therapy

1. Does EMDR stop traumatic memories?
    a. **Eye Movement Desensitization and Reprocessing (EMDR)**
    b. Francine Shapiro's discovery
2. Evidence from case studies
3. Evidence from experiments
    a. Does EMDR work?
    b. How does EMDR work?
    c. Why is EMDR controversial?

H. Application: Cognitive-Behavior Techniques

1. Thought problems
2. Thought-stopping program: **intrusive thoughts**
    a. Self-monitoring
    b. Thought stopping
    c. Thought substitution
3. Thought substitution
    a. Irrational thoughts
    b. Rational thoughts
4. Treatment for insomnia

How English Works

Words in the Textbook

p. 555 developed a terrible **squint** = habit of keeping eyes partly closed

a **gagging** feeling = choking

her **governess**'s dog = woman working as a tutor for a family

an **up-and-coming** behaviorist = young, becoming known

how psychotherapy **came about** = began

p. 556 until they **passed out** = fainted, lost consciousness

a relaxed and **decent** environment = sympathetic

funds became tight = money was hard to find

milled about in a large room = moved without direction or purpose

the **wretched** conditions = terrible, miserable

p. 557 **halfway houses** = rehabilitation centers (halfway between institutions and normal life)

p. 558 a psychiatric **residency** = medical training through working in hospital

an **applied clinical setting** = practical situation in real conditions

p. 559 the **classic** example = perfect as a standard of its kind

p. 560 **comprehensive** theory = complete, explaining everything

laypersons = non-professionals

an **appreciation** of what happens = understanding

Who are you that I should care = What makes you so important?

p. 561 made him **pledge** himself = promise, commit

the window opened **of its own accord** = by its own power

their ears **pricked** like dogs = standing up straight

p. 562 called Freud a **"filthy swine"** = dirty pig

the analyst must use **tact** = sensitive understanding

therapy can proceed and **stay on course** = move toward the goal

p. 563 such a question was **unheard of** = never spoken

p. 564 the old **vacuum** = empty feeling

develop a positive **working** relationship = not perfect, but good enough for the purpose

p. 565 **bouts** of depression = temporary or short-lived attacks of illness

p. 566 gave a real **jump-start** = stimulus, strong push

let people step all over me = allow others to control me

run through some of the situations here = practice

p. 571 less likely to be **credentialed** = have a certificate that qualifies somebody to do something

p. 572 periods of **fasting** = not eating food

a small **pulsation** = rhythmic beat or pulse that takes place in an artery

p. 573 to emotionally **distance** themselves from = increase space separating feelings for others

Vocabulary Exercises

Test your knowledge of opposites. Here are some words used in the last few modules. Draw a line from a word on the left to the word that means its opposite on the right:

downplay	moving
casual	dysfunctional
clear-cut	formal
fixed	extraverted
functional	ambiguous
introverted	emphasize

Try to complete these sentences using **once** to mean **after.**

Once summertime begins, the children __________.

Once __________, we washed the dishes.

Once you finish this module, you __________.

Once __________, the class could start.

Once her visit to the dentist was over, Lydia __________.

In the sentences below, write the appropriate form of the word. Example: The information you **perceive** is your *perception.*

An experience that **affects** many people has a great __________.

An individual who has a **bias** is a __________ person.

If you are **deprived** of sleep, you experience sleep __________.

A person who **abstains** from food is described as __________.

When something is **anticipatory,** it means that people __________ it.

Answers

downplay	=	emphasize
casual	=	formal
clear-cut	=	ambiguous
fixed	=	moving
functional	=	dysfunctional
introverted	=	extraverted

Once summertime begins, the children (will not be in school) (will be free to play).
Once (we finished dinner) (dinner ended), we washed the dishes.
Once you finish this module, you (will be almost finished) (can do the next module).
Once (the teacher arrived) (the students were quiet), the class could start.
Once her visit to the dentist was over, Lydia (felt happy) (received a bill).

An experience that **affects** many people has a great **effect.**
An individual who has a **bias** is a **biased** person.
If you are **deprived** of sleep, you experience sleep **deprivation.**
A person who **abstains** from food is described as **abstinent.**
When something is **anticipatory,** it means that people **anticipate** it.

For Psych Majors Only…

The Story of Psychotherapy: You met many famous and intriguing characters from the history of psychology in this module, people like Anna O., Rat Man, and Little Albert (almost sounds like a circus, doesn't it?). If you were to arrange these names in historical order (as I have done below) and add what each contributed, you could construct a capsule history of the development of modern psychotherapy.

Try it — match each name to the most appropriate phrase. As you do so, see if you can tell yourself the story of how the four strands of modern psychotherapy emerged, and how they differ from each other.

_____	1. Dorothea Dix	a. reduced hysterical symptoms by talking about them
_____	2. Anna O.	b. publicized the cruel treatment of "lunatics" in poorhouses
_____	3. Sigmund Freud	c. developed cognitive therapy for depressive thoughts
_____	4. Rat Man	d. developed a very positive client-centered therapy
_____	5. Wolf-Man	e. interpretation of his dreams revealed sexual fears
_____	6. John B. Watson	f. worked out a therapy called systematic desensitization
_____	7. Little Albert	g. believed emotional problems are conditioned (learned)
_____	8. Carl Rogers	h. conditioned to fear a rat in a famous experiment
_____	9. Joseph Wolpe	i. free association revealed his repressed childhood memories
_____	10. Aaron Beck	j. invented psychoanalysis — the first psychotherapy

Answers to "The Story of Psychotherapy" Quiz

1 b 2 a 3 j 4 i 5 e 6 g 7 h 8 d 9 f 10 c

Congratulations!

Here you are, finishing perhaps the last module you were assigned. You have completed a big textbook and a long study guide, which means you have done a ton of work this term, and I'm proud of you! Be sure to give yourself the praise you deserve — and a meaningful reward, too! You have earned it.

Now that it's over, I would love to know what you thought of your introductory psychology class. Are you glad you took psychology? Did it change you in any way? What was the most important thing you learned?

Please tell me by e-mail! **<profenos@mac.com>**

The Big Picture

Which statement below offers the best summary of the larger significance of this module?

A A painful truth: psychotherapy is the witchcraft of the modern Western world. Plotnik and Kouyoumdjian's fascinating discussion of a healer (the balian) in Bali shows why we shouldn't take psychotherapy too seriously. It's all based on belief and faith.

B That there are several competing theories of psychotherapy is not so much an embarrassment as a reflection of the youth and vigor of psychology. The competing psychotherapies reflect the different approaches to the field.

C The crowded field of psychotherapy is finally experiencing what economists call a shakeout. One by one, the old methods are being abandoned, as more and more psychotherapists adopt EMDR because of its greater effectiveness.

D Which method of psychotherapy is best? It is mainly a matter of individual preference. All therapies share the common assumption that problems lie buried in the unconscious, and must be exhumed and examined.

E As the famous movie producer Samuel Goldwyn once observed, "Anyone who goes to a psychiatrist should have his head examined!"

True-False

_____ 1. The history of therapeutic effort is a story of continued improvement in the humane treatment of the mentally ill.

_____ 2. Psychotherapists today are more likely to see themselves as eclectic than as adhering to one of the traditional approaches to psychotherapy.

_____ 3. The basic assumption of psychoanalysis is that since maladaptive behaviors are *learned*, they can be unlearned through training.

_____ 4. Transference is the process by which a patient carefully describes his or her problems so the therapist can analyze and solve them.

_____ 5. Although Freud is criticized, psychoanalytic ideas continue to be a force in psychotherapy today.

_____ 6. Plotnik and Kouyoumdjian quote from therapy sessions representing the major approaches; the point is that they all sound pretty much alike.

_____ 7. Carl Rogers' client-centered therapy avoids giving directions, advice, or disapproval.

_____ 8. Aaron Beck's cognitive therapy assumes that we have automatic negative thoughts that we say to ourselves without much notice.

_____ 9. The systematic desensitization technique is essentially an *un*learning experience.

_____ 10. Research suggests that the new technique called Eye Movement Desensitization and Reprocessing (EMDR) will eventually replace all the traditional psychotherapies.

Flashcards 1

_____	1. behavior therapy (behavior modification)	a.	a technique that encourages clients to talk about any thoughts or images that enter their heads
_____	2. client-centered therapy	b.	therapy in which client is gradually exposed to feared object while simultaneously practicing relaxation
_____	3. cognitive therapy	c.	core idea is that repressed threatening thoughts in the unconscious cause conflicts and symptoms
_____	4. dream interpretation	d.	uses principles of conditioning to change disruptive behaviors and improve human functioning
_____	5. free association	e.	client's reluctance to work through feelings and to recognize unconscious conflicts and repressed thoughts
_____	6. intrusive thoughts	f.	the process by which a client expresses strong emotions toward therapist, who is a substitute figure
_____	7. psychoanalysis	g.	a search for underlying hidden meanings, symbols as providing clues to unconscious thoughts and desires
_____	8. resistance	h.	therapist shows compassion and positive regard in helping client reach full potential, self-actualization
_____	9. systematic desensitization	i.	thoughts that we repeatedly experience, are usually unwanted or disruptive, and are very difficult to stop
_____	10. transference	j.	assumes we have automatic negative thoughts that distort our perceptions, influence feelings, and behavior

Flashcards 2

_____	1. clinical psychologists	a.	release of mental patients from hospitals and their return to the community to develop independent lives
_____	2. common factors	b.	go to graduate school in clinical psychology, earn doctorate including one year of work in an applied clinical setting
_____	3. counseling psychologists	c.	basic set of procedures shared by different therapies (supportive relationship, accepting atmosphere, etc.)
_____	4. deinstitutionalization	d.	involves use of various psychoactive drugs to treat mental disorders by changing biological factors
_____	5. eclectic approach	e.	go to medical school, receive M.D., take psychiatric residency and additional training in psychotherapy
_____	6. insight therapy	f.	therapist and client talk about the client's symptoms and problems to identify cause of problem, possible solutions
_____	7. medical therapy	g.	involves combining and using techniques and ideas from many different therapeutic approaches
_____	8. moral therapy	h.	reform movement; belief that mental patients could be helped to function better by providing humane treatment
_____	9. phenothiazines	i.	block or reduce effects of dopamine, thereby reducing schizophrenic symptoms (delusions, hallucinations)
_____	10. psychiatrists	j.	go to graduate school of psychology or education, earn doctorate, including work in a counseling setting

Multiple Choice

____ 1. Plotnik and Kouyoumdjian begin the module with the story of Anna O. to make the point that
- a. Freud had some notable failures as well as famous successes
- b. talking about your problems seems to help
- c. the real credit for inventing psychoanalysis should go to Dr. Breuer
- d. talking won't help unless the client also does something positive

____ 2. John B. Watson's famous experiment with Little Albert was designed to show that
- a. ethical standards of psychological research are much more stringent today
- b. psychological problems affect babies as well as children and adults
- c. fear of rats is almost natural and may be inborn
- d. emotional problems can be understood as learned behavior

____ 3. In the history of the treatment of mental illness, Dorothea Dix is famous for
- a. charging admission to watch the crazy antics of the "lunatics"
- b. inventing early treatment techniques like the strait jacket and bleeding
- c. publicizing the terrible living conditions and poor treatment of the mentally ill
- d. emptying the mental hospitals of almost half of their patients

____ 4. The effect of the phenothiazines on schizophrenics is to
- a. increase the effects of the neurotransmitter dopamine
- b. reduce symptoms like delusions and hallucinations
- c. promote clearer thinking, but at the cost of longer hospital stays
- d. promote clearer thinking, but at the cost of emotional agitation

____ 5. The discovery of antipsychotic drugs led directly to
- a. deinstitutionalization
- b. the reform movement
- c. reinstitutionalization
- d. the community mental health center

____ 6. Deinstitutionalization has led to homelessness, a sad result best explained by a/n
- a. side effect of antipsychotic drugs that makes schizophrenics afraid to be inside
- b. lack of funding and adequate supervision of halfway houses
- c. reluctance of families to allow the "crazies" to come home again
- d. high cost of treatment in community mental health centers

____ 7. A main reason why many people needing professional help do not seek it is the
- a. social stigma attached to having a mental disorder
- b. embarrassment and humiliation when therapists discuss their patients in public
- c. requirement of most therapists that new patients spend a period in the hospital first
- d. refusal of insurance companies to cover mental disorders

____ 8. In order to become a ________, you need a medical degree and a residency with further training in psychopathology and treatment
- a. clinical psychologist
- b. psychiatrist
- c. social worker
- d. counseling psychologist

_____ 9. _________ therapy is a good example of the eclectic approach to therapeutic technique
a. Psychodynamic
b. Behavioral
c. Cognitive-behavioral
d. Medical

_____ 10. How effective is psychotherapy? Studies suggest that it is
a. an effective treatment for many mental disorders
b. no more effective than just waiting
c. no more effective than doing nothing
d. an effective treatment, but only if continued for more than a year

_____ 11. The central idea of Freud's psychoanalysis is that each of us has a(n)
a. unconscious part that contains hidden, threatening desires or thoughts
b. conscious mind containing ideas that can be clarified and made more logical
c. history of learned behavior patterns that reveals why we act in certain ways
d. need to grow and develop our full potential as human beings

_____ 12. All the following are assumptions of psychoanalysis *except*
a. free association
b. dream interpretation
c. schedules of reinforcement
d. unconscious conflicts

_____ 13. Free association seems like a great time waster, but Freud insisted on it because
a. he knew people enjoy talking about themselves, and this would relax them
b. he was billing patients by the hour and could not charge high fees like surgeons
c. patients need encouragement to talk about scary things like rats and wolves
d. patients have little conscious knowledge of what their unconscious problems are

_____ 14. Freud used dream interpretation because he thought dreams represent
a. the purest form of free association
b. sick thinking, which needs to be corrected
c. nonsensical ideas, which the therapist should expose
d. the souls of deceased ancestors attempting to speak to us and help us

_____ 15. Transference and resistance are technical terms for what happens in therapy, but perceptive students may also recognize the workings of these processes in their own
a. thoughts about trying a new school, despite their parents' objections
b. attempts to apply knowledge gained in one course to the next higher course
c. desires to find and win over a new sweetheart
d. feelings about their instructors and troubles with some courses

_____ 16. Psychoanalysis has a famous place in psychology, but what is its current status?
a. it remains as a great story, but few therapists use its odd ideas anymore
b. its key concepts (unconscious forces and defense mechanisms) are not supported by research
c. modified forms of psychoanalysis continue to be important in psychotherapy
d. most psychologists today consider Freud's outlandish ideas a bad joke on psychotherapy

_____ 17. The central assumption of Carl Rogers' client-centered therapy is that
a. each person has the tendency and capacity to develop his or her full potential
b. psychotherapy must be freely available in community mental health centers
c. we must struggle to overcome our basic human selfishness and hostility
d. therapy should focus on real behavior, not vague thoughts and feelings

_____ 18. Aaron Beck discovered that depressed people tend to interpret the world through
a. carefully planned negative statements
b. thoughtless repetitions of what other people believe
c. secretly hostile beliefs
d. automatic negative thoughts

_____ 19. In his cognitive therapy, Beck attempts to make clients aware of
a. the importance of education in the contemporary world
b. adaptive thought patterns like open-mindedness, acceptance, love, and will power
c. maladaptive thought patterns like overgeneralization, polarized thinking, and selective attention
d. how much better they could be if they would just "think about it"

_____ 20. Behavior therapy (behavior modification) differs from the insight therapies in that the therapist
a. encourages the client to free-associate
b. repeats or reflects what the client says
c. discusses the client's tendency to automatically think negative thoughts
d. identifies the specific problem and discusses a program for change

_____ 21. Which one of the following is *not* a step in the systematic desensitization procedure?
a. relaxation
b. stimulus hierarchy
c. stimulus sensitizing
d. exposure

_____ 22. A popular new therapy that combines insight into thinking with principles of learning is called
a. self-help programming
b. cognitive-behavior therapy
c. short-term dynamic psychotherapy
d. behavior modification

_____ 23. The controversial new form of treatment called cybertherapy is therapy that
a. takes place in a space-age office
b. takes place face-to-face
c. is a form of tough-love provided by a psychologist who acts like Judge Judy
d. is delivered over the Internet

_____ 24. Plotnik and Kouyoumdjian's fascinating example of a local healer (the balian) in Bali suggests that the success of Western psychotherapy
a. demonstrates the superiority of modern medicine
b. owes much to what are called common factors in psychotherapy
c. depends on having intelligent and educated patients
d. results from its assumption that the problem lies inside the sufferer

_____ 25. Francine Shapiro's new therapy does seem to work, but the question about EMDR is whether the
   a. same results could be obtained on traumatic memories
   b. successes could be achieved without first hypnotizing the patients
   c. eye movements are really important and why
   d. successes are due to the magnetic personality of Francine Shapiro

Short Essay

1. Who was "Anna O.," and why is she so famous in the history of psychotherapy?

2. How did the discovery of the drug chlorpromazine revolutionize treatment of the mentally ill?

3. How are the Freudian techniques of free association and dream interpretation linked to the treatment of neuroses?

4. Put yourself on the couch for a moment! Can you find any illustrations of the Freudian concepts of transference or resistance in your struggles as a student?

5. Describe the EMDR treatment and explain why it is controversial.

Time to Read

With the end of the term approaching, you will soon have time to read again. One of the paradoxes of education is that just when we should be reading most, we have the least time. (It's also true for teachers!) Plan to read a good book you have heard about. Now that you know more psychology, you will find that novels and biographies are more interesting than ever. What will you read over the interim?

Answers for Module 24

The Big Picture (explanations provided for incorrect choices)

A Despite common factors, there are real differences between the work of a balian and a Western psychotherapist.
B Correct! You see the "big picture" for this Module.
C This is simply not true. Research does not yet support the superior effectiveness of EMDR.
D This assumption belongs to psychoanalysis. Other theories of psychotherapy differ.
E It's just a joke!

True-False (explanations provided for False choices; page numbers given for all choices)

1	F	556	Sadly, the history of psychological treatment is also about inhumane treatment of the mentally ill.
2	T	559	
3	F	560	Psychoanalysis is based on insight into the unconscious, not learned behavior.
4	F	562	Transference is projecting feelings about important people in the patient's life onto the therapist.
5	T	563	
6	F	564	Each therapist quoted shows signs of a particular approach to psychotherapy.
7	T	564	
8	T	565	
9	T	567	
10	F	573	The effectiveness of EMDR remains unproved until scientifically compared to other therapies.

Flashcards 1

1 d 2 h 3 j 4 g 5 a 6 i 7 c 8 e 9 b 10 f

Flashcards 2

1 b 2 c 3 j 4 a 5 g 6 f 7 d 8 h 9 i 10 e

Multiple Choice (explanations provided for incorrect choices)

1
a Anna O. was Dr. Breuer's patient, not Freud's.
b *Correct! See page 555.*
c Dr. Breuer treated Anna O., but it was Freud's genius to see the deeper implications of the case.
d The point was that just talking about problems can help.

2
a True, but Plotnik is making a point about psychotherapy.
b True, but Plotnik is making a point about psychotherapy.
c Little Albert was not afraid of the rat until it was associated with the loud noise.
d *Correct! See page 555.*

3
a Some did this, but not the reformer Dorothea Dix.
b This was not the humane reform work of Dorothea Dix.
c *Correct! See page 556.*
d This did not happen until the invention of antipsychotic drugs in the 1950s.

4
a They work by blocking or reducing the effects of dopamine.
b *Correct! See page 557.*
c They do promote clearer thinking, but also lead to shorter hospital stays.
d They do promote clearer thinking, and also calm patients down.

5
a *Correct! See page 557.*
b The reform movement came much earlier, in the previous century.
c This is not a term used in psychiatry.
d Community mental health centers provide care to people who might not have access to private treatment.

6
a There is no such side effect with antipsychotic drugs.
b *Correct! See page 557.*
c Before they can return to their homes, the ex-patients need care and support in good halfway houses.
d Community mental health centers offer low-cost assistance, but there are not enough of them.

7 ***a*** *Correct! See page 558.*
b Psychotherapists are required to protect the confidentiality of their clients, and would not talk about them.
c There is no such common requirement.
d Insurance is a problem, but many employers offer some coverage for mental disorders.

8 a A clinical psychologist has a Ph.D. and clinical experience.
b *Correct! See page 558.*
c A social worker has a master's degree and may have special training in psychotherapy.
d A counseling psychologist has a Ph.D. and counseling experience.

9 a The psychodynamic approach to therapy is based on a unified theory.
b The behavioral approach to therapy is based on a unified theory.
c *Correct! See page 559.*
d The medical approach to therapy is based on a unified theory.

10 ***a*** *Correct! See page 559.*
b About two-thirds of all psychotherapy clients experience some improvement.
c About two-thirds of all psychotherapy clients experience some improvement.
d Many short-term therapies are quite effective.

11 ***a*** *Correct! See page 560.*
b This would be true of Beck's cognitive therapy.
c This would be true of behavior therapy.
d This would be true of Rogers' client-centered therapy.

12 a Free association is the key to how psychoanalysis works.
b Interpretation is very important in psychoanalysis.
c *Correct! See page 561.*
d Unconscious conflicts are very important in psychoanalysis.

13 a Free association is not always relaxing (try it and you will see that it also can be anxiety provoking).
b OK, so now we know you are an anti-Freudian!
c In therapy, it is the *unconscious* meaning of rats and wolves that is frightening and needs to be explored.
d *Correct! See page 561.*

14 ***a*** *Correct! See page 561.*
b Freud would not accept the idea of "sick" thinking nor believe mental processes need to be "corrected."
c Dreams may appear to be nonsense, but Freud believed they disguised important problems.
d This is believed in some cultures, but certainly was not accepted by Freud.

15 a In psychoanalysis, it is thoughts and feelings, not course credits, which are being transferred.
b In psychoanalysis, it is thoughts and feelings, not learnings, which are being transferred.
c In psychoanalysis, it is thoughts and feelings, not charm bracelets, which are being transferred.
d *Correct! See page 562.*

16 a Many of Freud's insights, if not his whole theory, continue to influence psychology and treatment.
b These two concepts have received research support; others have not.
c *Correct! See page 563.*
d Some psychologists are very critical, but Freud continues to hold a respected place in psychology.

17 ***a*** *Correct! See page 564.*
b This statement sounds more like the beliefs of community mental health workers.
c This might be truer of psychoanalytic therapy.
d This is truer of behavior therapy.

18 a The negative thought patterns of depressed people are not deliberate or planned.
b This is not a characteristic Beck identified in depressed people.
c This is not a characteristic Beck identified in depressed people.
d *Correct! See page 565.*

19 a A noble idea, but it has nothing to do with Beck's cognitive therapy.
b These are not goals of Beck's cognitive therapy.
c *Correct! See page 565.*
d This (wrong) answer comes from an old *Saturday Night Live* skit.

20 a This is what the therapist does in psychoanalysis.
b This is what the therapist does in client-centered therapy.
c This is what the therapist does in cognitive therapy.
d *Correct! See page 566.*

21 a Relaxation is an essential ingredient in desensitization.
b A stimulus hierarchy is an essential ingredient in desensitization.
c *Correct! See page 567.*
d Exposure is an essential ingredient in desensitization.

22 a Self-help programs are derived from cognitive-behavior therapy.
b *Correct! See page 568.*
c Short-term dynamic psychotherapy is a modified version of psychoanalysis.
d Behavior modification is a form of behavior therapy, and does not use cognitive principles.

23 a The word cyber sounds modern, but it means pertaining to computers and information systems.
b Just the opposite is true — that's the point.
c Tough-love is not involved in cybertherapy.
d *Correct! See page 571.*

24 a People who consult a balian do experience relief from symptoms.
b *Correct! See page 572.*
c The village people who consult a balian are neither especially intelligent nor highly educated.
d The truth *might* be just the opposite.

25 a Those are precisely the problems it was designed to alleviate.
b Hypnosis is not part of the EMDR treatment.
c *Correct! See page 573.*
d Today EMDR is used by many other therapists as well.

Short Essay (sample answers)

1. Anna O. was an intelligent young woman who began to experience strange physical symptoms while caring for her seriously ill father. Dr. Joseph Breuer was consulted, but could find no physical causes for her symptoms, so he listened as she talked. Each time she recalled a past traumatic experience, a physical symptom associated with that trauma would vanish. Breuer discussed the confusing case with his colleague Sigmund Freud, who quickly understood Anna O., and went on to originate psychoanalysis.

2. The accidental discovery in the 1950s that chlorpromazine, one of the phenothiazines, could block or reduce the effects of the neurotransmitter dopamine and reduce schizophrenic symptoms, led to a revolution in psychiatric treatment. Freed of disabling delusions and hallucinations, patients who had been "warehoused" in mental hospitals for years could be discharged. But the triumph of deinstitutionalization was followed by the tragedy of homelessness, as society failed to provide adequate support and treatment on the outside.

3. The psychological problems that Freud called neuroses are maladaptive thoughts and actions that arise from some unconscious thought or conflict and indicate feelings of anxiety. But if the problem is unconscious, how can it be discovered? Freud proposed free association — that the patient says anything that came to mind — as the basic rule of psychoanalytic treatment. Dreams, less consciously controlled and thus the purest form of free association, also can be interpreted. Eventually, the truth will come out.

4. Have you wondered why you like a certain professor so much, or why you seem to be constantly struggling with another professor? Does it seem odd that a subject you could easily master is giving you so much trouble? Could it be that earlier attachments to and interactions with your parents are reflected in your current student life? See if you can discover examples of Freud's provocative concepts of transference and resistance in your academic work. Just lie back, relax, and think about anything that comes to mind!

5. Francine Shapiro's EMDR (Eye Movement Desensitization and Reprocessing) involves having the client talk about or imagine a troubling traumatic memory while visually focusing on and following the back-and-forth movement of a therapist's hand. EMDR is controversial because it seems too unusual, too simple, and too quick. Some therapists find it surprisingly effective and others see it as a kind of placebo effect. Research has given some support to the effectiveness of EMDR, but has not solved the mystery of why it works.

Module 25

Social Psychology

Sophisticated Ideas about Everyday Activity

Once you become familiar with the way sociologists look at people, you will never again take human behavior for granted. You will see it as a familiar drama, a performance you now understand. But first you must gain appreciation for what has been called "the sociological imagination," a special way of seeing people as playing social roles according to social rules. Grasping this new viewpoint appears difficult at first, but here's an idea that may make it easier.

Because you are a human being, you have been a social psychologist all your life. If there is one essential human skill, it is how to live with each other. I don't mean this in a preachy way, but in the sense that our instincts, what few we have, tell us very little about interacting with others. Therefore, literally from the first moments of life, we learn to observe, understand, and predict what other people will do (and what we will do) in any given situation. We soon become experts in human interaction. See? You've been studying this stuff all your life!

The beauty of social psychology is that it can take us outside ourselves and help us see our behavior more objectively, and hence more clearly. Such awareness, which social psychology owes to anthropology and sociology, helps correct the tendency of psychology to focus too much on individual, internal factors. There's a price you pay for this insight, however: theories in social psychology typically involve fancy names and complicated explanations. Don't be afraid. The social psychologists you'll study are talking about what you do every day. Try to understand it that way. Give yourself credit for understanding what seems obvious. Translate what does not seem clear into the language of your own experience.

The Cross-Cultural Approach to Psychology

If you counted them, you would discover this module has more key terms in this module than almost any other. Another module with almost the same number of key terms is Plotnik and Kouyoumdjian's presentation of "The Incredible Nervous System." That's no accident. Just as Module 4 helped define the psychobiological approach to psychology, Module 25 defines the other end of the spectrum — the cross-cultural approach (some might call it the sociocultural approach). In the earlier module, we were almost off the chart into biology, hence the need for many new terms. Here, we are deep into sociology, and once again need a whole new vocabulary.

One problem sociologists have is that they talk about things that are utterly familiar, like attitudes, helping, groups, and aggression. Sometimes it almost seems like they invent fancy names for such concepts because what they are describing is so familiar. But they wouldn't do that, would they?

Effective Student Tip 25

Honor Your Need to be Effective

Most of my tips have been quite specific, because I wanted them to be actions you could take immediately. If they worked, you won a victory here and there and perhaps did better in the course. I hope they also contribute to a body of strategies that will make you a stronger student in the courses still to come.

In truth, however, I have an even larger goal in mind. That goal is for you to begin to understand that the need to be effective is the essence of your human motivation. If I am right, you feel a need to be effective not only in your schoolwork but, more importantly, in *everything* you do.

My argument is simply this: we humans have almost no instincts to guide us. The only way we can tell whether what we are doing is right is the extent to which it gets the job done. We know our actions are working when they cause the world to give back what we want and need. In other words, the extent to which the actions we take are effective becomes the measure of our happiness and satisfaction in life.

Whatever situation you may be in, a class or a job or a relationship, honor your need to be effective by paying attention to how well your actions are working for you and how good you feel about what you are doing.

Your response…

I am convinced that we all have a constant need to be effective. Do you feel that need in yourself?

Learning Objectives

1. Understand social psychology as a broad field whose goals are to understand and explain how our thoughts, feelings, perceptions, and behaviors are influenced by interacting with others.

2. Learn the basic mechanisms of perceiving others through the social lenses of physical appearance, stereotypes, and schemas.

3. Learn how our thoughts and behaviors are influenced by attributions, attitudes, and group influences.

4. Understand the classic experiments and findings of social psychology in conformity, compliance, obedience, helping and prosocial behavior, group dynamics, behavior in crowds, and group decisions.

5. Explore the critical human problem of aggression — its origins in nature and nurture, social and personality factors, situational cues, and sexual harassment and aggression.

6. Appreciate how national attitudes and social behaviors are influenced by cultural differences.

7. Apply the insights and research findings of social psychology to the problems of controlling aggression in children, anger in adults, and sexual coercion.

Key Terms

These terms help define the cross-cultural approach to psychology and sum up the field of social psychology.

actor-observer effect
aggression
altruism
arousal-cost-reward model of helping
attitude
attributions
bystander effect
catharsis
central route for persuasion
cognitive dissonance
cognitive miser model
cognitive social psychology
compliance
conformity
consensus
consistency
counterattitudinal behavior
covariation model
crowd
debriefing
decision-stage model of helping
deindividuation
diffusion of responsibility theory
discrimination
distinctiveness
Electroencephalography (EEG)
event schemas (scripts)
external attributions
Functional magnetic resonance imaging (fMRI)
foot-in-the-door technique
frustration-aggression hypothesis
fundamental attribution error
group cohesion
group norms
group polarization
groups
groupthink
hazing
informational influence theory
internal attributions
modified frustration-aggression hypothesis
obedience
peripheral route for persuasion
person perception
person schemas
prejudice
Positron emission tomography (PET scan)
prosocial behavior (helping)
rape myths
role schemas
schemas
self schemas
self-perception theory
self-serving bias
social cognitive theory
social comparison theory
social facilitation
social inhibition
social neuroscience
social psychology
socially oriented group
stereotypes
task-oriented group
Transcranial magnetic stimulation (TMS)

Outline

- *Introduction*
  1. Stereotypes (Lawrence Graham)

☐ What does "cognitive" social psychology add to traditional social psychology?

  a. **Social psychology**

  b. **Cognitive social psychology**

  2. Behavior in groups (violent hazing)

A. Perceiving Others

1. **Person perception**
   a. Physical appearance
   b. Need to explain
   c. Influence on behavior
   d. Effects of race
2. Physical appearance
   a. Attractiveness
   b. Evolution
3. **Social neuroscience**
   a. Human empathy (mirror neurons)
   b. Rejection and pain
4. **Stereotypes**
   a. Development of stereotypes
      (1) **Prejudice**
      (2) **Discrimination**
   b. Functions of stereotypes
      (1) Thought-saving device
      (2) Alertness and survival
5. **Schemas**
   a. Kinds of schemas
      (1) **Person schemas**
      (2) **Role schemas**
      (3) **Event schemas (scripts)**
      (4) **Self schemas**
   b. Advantages and disadvantages

B. Attributions

1. Definition: **attributions**
2. Internal versus external (Fritz Heider)
   a. **Internal attributions**
   b. **External attributions**
3. Kelley's model of covariation
   a. **Covariation model** (Harold Kelley)
      (1) **Consensus**
      (2) **Consistency**
      (3) **Distinctiveness**
   b. Applying Kelley's covariation model
4. Biases and errors
   a. **Cognitive miser model**
   b. Common biases in making attributions
      (1) **Fundamental attribution error**
      (2) **Actor-observer effect**
      (3) **Self-serving bias**

C. Research Focus: Attributions & Grades

1. Can changing attributions change grades?
2. A study of attributions and grades
   a. Kinds of attributions
   b. Method: changing attributions
   c. Results and conclusions

D. Attitudes

1. Definition: **attitude**
2. Components of attitudes
   a. Cognitive component
   b. Affective component
   c. Behavioral component
3. Attitude change

☐ Read the famous "boring task" experiment several times, until you really understand it.

   a. **Cognitive dissonance** (Leon Festinger)
      (1) Adding or changing beliefs
      (2) **Counterattitudinal behavior**
   b. **Self-perception theory** (Daryl Bem)
4. Persuasion

☐ Can you think of examples from current politics for the two routes to persuasion?

a. Two routes to persuasion

(1) **Central route for persuasion**

(2) **Peripheral route for persuasion**

b. Elements of persuasion

(1) Source

(2) Message (one- versus two-sided messages)

(3) Audience

E. Cultural Diversity: National Attitudes and Behaviors

1. Nigeria: beauty ideal
2. Japan: organ transplants
3. Egypt: women's rights

F. Social & Group Influences

1. Conformity (Solomon Asch)

a. **Hazing**

b. **Conformity**

c. Asch's experiment

(1) Procedure

(2) Results

2. Compliance

a. **Compliance**

b. **Foot-in-the-door technique**

3. Obedience (Stanley Milgram)

a. **Obedience**

b. Milgram's experiment

(1) The setup

(2) The conflict

c. Milgram's results

d. Why do people obey?

e. Were Milgram's experiments ethical?

(1) **Debriefing**

(2) Experiments today

4. Helping: prosocial behavior

a. **Prosocial behavior (helping)**

b. **Altruism**

5. Why people help

a. Empathy, personal distress, norms and values

b. **Decision-stage model of helping** (five stages)

c. **Arousal-cost-reward model of helping**

6. Group dynamics: **groups**
    a. Group cohesion and norms
        (1) **Group cohesion**
        (2) **Group norms**
    b. Group membership
        (1) **Social comparison theory**
        (2) **Task-oriented group**
        (3) **Socially oriented group**
7. Behavior in crowds: **crowd**
    a. Facilitation and inhibition
        (1) **Social facilitation**
        (2) **Social inhibition**
    b. Deindividuation in crowds
        (1) **Deindividuation**
        (2) Internal standards
    c. The bystander effect
        (1) **Bystander effect**
        (2) **Informational influence theory**
        (3) **Diffusion of responsibility theory**
8. Group decisions
    a. **Group polarization**
        (1) Risky shift
        (2) Polarization
    b. **Groupthink** (Irving Janis)
        (1) Mindguard, ingroup, outgroup
        (2) Avoiding groupthink (vigilant decision-making)

G. *Social Neuroscience*

1. Definition
    a. **Social neuroscience**
    b. Research
2. Methods
    a. Positron emission tomography (PET scan)
    b. Functional magnetic resonance Imaging (fMRI)
    c. Electroencephalography (EEG)
    d. Transcranial magnetic stimulation (TMS)
3. Findings
    a. Mirror neurons
    b. Racial bias

H. Aggression

1. Genes and environment: **aggression**

☐ Do you believe that human beings are naturally aggressive?

   a. Genetic influences in animals

   b. Genetic influences in humans

   c. Genes interact with good/bad environments

   d. Genes interact with child abuse

2. Social cognitive and personality factors

   a. **Social cognitive theory** (Albert Bandura)

   b. Televisision/video games

   c. Model of aggression

3. Situational cues

   a. **Frustration-aggression hypothesis** (road rage)

   b. **Modified frustration-aggression hypothesis** (Leonard Berkowitz)

4. Sexual harassment and aggression

   a. Characteristics and kinds of rapists

      (1) Power rapist

      (2) Sadistic rapist

      (3) Anger rapist

      (4) Acquaintance (date) rapist

   b. **Rape myths**

I. Application: Controlling Aggression

1. Case study (Monster Kody)

2. Controlling aggression in children

   a. Cognitive-behavioral deficits

   b. Programs to control aggression

      (1) Cognitive problem-solving skills training

      (2) Parent management training (PMT)

3. Controlling anger in adults

   a. **Catharsis**

   b. Cognitive-relaxation program

4. Controlling sexual coercion

   a. Socialization of males

   b. Knowing the risk factors

How English Works

Words in the Textbook

p. 581 A **posh country club** = a fancy private recreation center

the **exclusive** Greenwich Country Club = limited to rich upper class people

hired to be a **busboy** = waiter's assistant who removes dirty dishes

diction like an educated white person = clear pronunciation

an **associate** in a New York law firm = partner

move up the social ladder = rise to a higher social position

The **touch football game** = a more casual version of football with limited contact

rite of passage = an activity that is connected with moving up a level in rank or age

some minor **hazing** = unpleasant rituals used to join a group

well-to-do Chicago suburb = wealthy

fish guts = the inner organs of a fish

p. 583 **rave parties** = large dance music parties, especially with drug use

p. 584 females were not considered **retainable** for a career = could not be kept in the job

p. 585 this **umpire** = judge in baseball games

passed over for promotion = not considered

p. 586 highest ranking female **CEO** = chief executive officer, top officer in a company

keep the **status quo** = the condition or state of affairs that currently exists

people **of color** = non-white

p. 588 **conventional** medical treatment = commonly practiced

p. 589 having to take **scalding** showers = burning hot

p. 590 an **out-and-out hatemonger** = open, unhidden person who encourages hate

white supremacist = general belief that whites are superior to non-whites

p. 593 used by **telemarketers** = telephone salespersons

drivers who **run** red lights = drive through

an **accomplice** of the experimenter = partner, helper

ask the learner **over an intercom** = using an electrical speaker system

p. 595 only inches to **spare** = barely more than what is needed

the only **onlooker** = a person watching, a bystander

do things that **touch our hearts** = give us a good feeling

help **perfect** strangers = total, complete

p. 597 a runner has a **spotty** history = uneven, inconsistent

arrested for **looting** = stealing during riots

p. 598 the **brink** of nuclear war = edge, border

Watergate cover-up = 1973 scandal concerning illegal actions by President Nixon

Challenger disaster = explosion of U.S. space ship (1986), killing all astronauts on board

p. 600 put ourselves in **other people's shoes** = see things the way other people see them

why yawning is **contagious** = transmitted from one person to another

on a more **upbeat** note = like a musical note that is full of optimism or cheerfulness

adamantly report being **race-blind** = claiming to not notice another person's race

p. 603 **penal** institutions = punishment (especially prison)

petting = beginning love-making

things **get out of hand** = go out of control

p. 605 **rant and rave** = complain loudly

Vocabulary: More Opposites

Here are some more **opposites** from this module and earlier ones. Draw a line connecting each word on the left with its opposite on the right.

hardy	conservative
liberal	debilitating
pro	unknown
prominent	con
proponent	weaken
reinforce	opponent

Do you want to try some more? Here are some from earlier modules:

attraction	extrinsic
inductive	terminate
initiate	veteran
intrinsic	aversion
novel	deductive
novice	age-old

Answers

hardy	=	debilitating
liberal	=	conservative
pro	=	con
prominent	=	unknown
proponent	=	opponent
reinforce	=	weaken

attraction	=	aversion
inductive	=	deductive
initiate	=	terminate
intrinsic	=	extrinsic
novel	=	age-old
novice	=	veteran

The Big Picture

Which statement below offers the best summary of the larger significance of this module?

A Understanding the behavior of people in group situations involves a complicated mathematics of combining all the individual tendencies to arrive at an average that will determine how the individuals will behave.

B Plotnik and Kouyoumdjian have discussed the famous nature-nurture question in several modules of this textbook. With their description of the many elegant experiments in social psychology, the answer finally becomes clear: our behavior is mainly determined by the forces of nature.

C No matter how many experiments social psychologists conduct on group influence, the fact remains that we are unique individuals. If we exercise our freedom of choice, no one can make us do anything against our will.

D We like to think of ourselves as rugged individuals, but social psychology has demonstrated that our behavior, our thinking, and even our feelings are highly sensitive to group pressures and the social situations we are in.

E How many social psychologists does it take to change a light bulb? Three: one to give the order, one to change the bulb, and one to record whether the order was obeyed! (And so we end as we began.)

True-False

_____ 1. Prejudice refers to an attitude or belief; discrimination is an act.

_____ 2. A schema is an unfair stereotype we apply to a person who is different.

_____ 3. Attributions are our attempts to understand and explain people's behavior.

_____ 4. An attitude is a tendency to respond to others in a quirky, overly sensitive manner.

_____ 5. Cognitive dissonance occurs when an audience hears so many contradictory arguments that they lose sight of the main issue.

_____ 6. Advice for all you budding politicians: if the facts are on your side, take the central route to persuasion; if they aren't, take the peripheral route.

_____ 7. The famous "electric shock" experiment showed that if you pay people enough they will follow just about any orders.

_____ 8. It is the social-psychological phenomenon of deindividuation that can make a crowd dangerous.

_____ 9. Because of the pooling of many talents and ideas, group decisions are usually superior to individual decisions.

_____ 10. Rape myths are misinformed, false beliefs about women, and these myths are frequently held by rapists.

Flashcards 1

_____	1. actor-observer effect	a.	a state of tension that motivates us to reduce our cognitive inconsistencies by making our beliefs consistent
_____	2. cognitive dissonance	b.	tendency to attribute our own behavior to the situation, but others' behavior to their personality traits or dispositions
_____	3. event schemas (scripts)	c.	noninvasive technique that sends pulses of magnetic energy into the brain; to activate or suppress brain activity
_____	4. external attributions	d.	mental categories that are based on the jobs people perform or the social positions they hold
_____	5. fundamental attribution error	e.	our tendency to explain a person's behavior by focusing on his or her personality traits and overlooking the situation
_____	6. internal attributions	f.	explaining our successes by attributing them to our personality traits, but our failures to the situation
_____	7. person schemas	g.	explanations of behavior based on a person's internal characteristics or dispositions
_____	8. role schemas	h.	mental categories that include our judgments about the traits that we and others possess
_____	9. self-serving bias	i.	explanations of behavior based on the external circumstances or situations; situational attributions
_____	10. Transcranial magnetic stimulation (TMS)	j.	mental categories that contain behaviors that we associate with familiar activities, events, or procedures

Flashcards 2

_____	1. altruism	a.	any behavior you perform because of group pressure, even though it might not involve direct requests
_____	2. bystander effect	b.	behavior performed in response to an order given by someone in a position of power or authority
_____	3. central route for persuasion	c.	emphasizing emotional appeal, focuses on personal traits, and generates positive feelings
_____	4. conformity	d.	increased tendency for irrational or antisocial behavior when there is less chance of being identified
_____	5. deindividuation	e.	helping, often at a cost or risk, for reasons other than the expectation of a material or social reward
_____	6. foot-in-the-door technique	f.	says that an individual may feel inhibited from taking some action because of the presence of others
_____	7. group cohesion	g.	presenting information with strong arguments, analyses, facts, and logic
_____	8. groupthink	h.	occurs when group discussions emphasize sticking together and agreement over use of critical thinking
_____	9. obedience	i.	increased probability of compliance to a second request if person complies with a small, first request
_____	10. peripheral route for persuasion	j.	group togetherness, determined by how much group members perceive they share common attributes

Multiple Choice

____ 1. Plotnik and Kouyoumdjian introduce us to Harvard Law School student Lawrence Graham to make the point that
   a. anyone who has the guts to start at the bottom can work his way up
   b. African American men are overly sensitive to good-natured kidding
   c. how people behave is more significant than what they believe
   d. how we perceive and evaluate others has powerful consequences

____ 2. Plotnik and Kouyoumdjian also give us an example of violent hazing, to illustrate the idea that
   a. group pressures can cause people to do things they would not normally do
   b. young men in gangs are dangerous when challenged by rival gangs
   c. a strong leader can cause normally peaceful people to take violent actions
   d. prejudices that are normally suppressed can emerge under the influence of alcohol

____ 3. According to the new evolutionary psychology approach, men are attracted to
   a. thin women who are a little underweight, which suggests they won't ever get fat
   b. youthful women who have an hourglass figure, which signals a childbirth advantage
   c. older women who are not especially attractive, because they won't leave a man
   d. overweight women, whose rolls of fat are considered attractive signs of family wealth

____ 4. We don't hire any of those people [this is an example of…] because they are too lazy to work hard [this is an example of…]. The correct terms in order are
   a. stereotypes / discrimination
   b. prejudice / discrimination
   c. person perception / person schemas
   d. discrimination / prejudice

____ 5. When we ask someone, "What do you do?" we are trying to get more information about the person by drawing on our
   a. person schemas
   b. role schemas
   c. event schemas
   d. scripts

____ 6. In the language of social psychology, __________ means things we point to as the causes of events, other people's behaviors, and our own behaviors
   a. schemas
   b. covariations
   c. attributions
   d. distinctiveness

____ 7. If I look for the causes of your behavior in your disposition and personality traits, and overlook how the situation influenced that behavior, I am guilty of the
   a. fundamental attribution error
   b. covariation model
   c. actor-observer effect
   d. self-serving bias

_____ 8. "I aced the chem exam because I studied my butt off! The psych exam I flunked? Well, you know he always asks tricky questions." Sounds like the __________ in action, doesn't it?
   a. fundamental attribution error
   b. actor-observer effect
   c. self-serving bias
   d. whiner effect

_____ 9. "Attitude" has been called the single most indispensable term in social psychology, because this concept
   a. reveals how feelings are all we need to know in order to understand other people
   b. explains how we think about other people, and beliefs are what count
   c. is just vague enough to be applied to any situation without being challenged
   d. ties together beliefs, feelings, and behavior to explain human social activity

_____ 10. Which one of the following is *not* a component of an attitude?
   a. cognitive
   b. genetic
   c. affective
   d. behavioral

_____ 11. In Leon Festinger's "boring task" experiment, the subjects who were paid only $1 to tell other students it was interesting (a lie) dealt with their cognitive dissonance by
   a. convincing themselves that it was somewhat interesting after all
   b. hoping the students they lied to realized it was just part of the experiment
   c. insisting that they should also be paid $20 for telling the lie
   d. begging Festinger and his assistants not to reveal their names

_____ 12. Candidate Roberta Reformer, who has an excellent plan for better government, will take the __________ route to persuasion; her opponent Boss Bluster, who plans to label Roberta a hysterical feminist, will take the __________ route
   a. direct / indirect
   b. honest / dishonest
   c. central / peripheral
   d. logical / emotional

_____ 13. A clear example of the extent to which national attitudes shape behavior is the
   a. almost zero possibility that a women will ever be elected President of the United States
   b. rapid improvement in sexual, political, and legal rights for Egyptian women
   c. the unchanging Japanese opposition to organ transplants
   d. recent change (from full to slender) in Nigerian ideas about female beauty

_____ 14. In recent years it has become popular to carry your own bottle of water, a practice we can attribute to
   a. compliance
   b. conformity
   c. obedience
   d. hazing

_____ 15. When Solomon Asch had his confederates deliberately choose an obviously incorrect matching line, the lone naive subject __________ went along with the group
   a. always
   b. never
   c. often
   d. rarely

_____ 16. Tell you what… before you quit just do one more of these questions, okay? [I'm using the __________ technique on you in my efforts to get you to do all the questions.]

a. foot-in-the-door
b. compliance
c. conformity
d. soft-soaping

_____ 17. In Stanley Milgram's electric shock experiment, most subjects continued to give shocks

a. only up to the point they considered dangerous
b. even beyond the point they believed was dangerous
c. only if they had been paid a considerable amount to participate in the experiment
d. only as long as the shocks seemed to be helping the "learner" do better

_____ 18. Milgram's famous experiment could not be conducted today because

a. people today are too rational and scientific to obey orders they don't agree with
b. the experiment has been so widely written about that everyone is in on the secret
c. few would be fooled by the fake lab, since psychologists are known for deception
d. a new code of ethics screens experiments for potential harm to the subjects

_____ 19. Sometimes an individual may feel inhibited from taking some action because of the presence of others; this is called

a. the bystander effect
b. social facilitation
c. group polarization
d. deindividuation

_____ 20. Which one of the following political decisions was a classic example of groupthink?

a. atomic bombing of Japan in World War II
b. assassination of President Kennedy
c. Bay of Pigs invasion of Cuba
d. introduction of New Coke, which the public rejected

_____ 21. The explanation of human empathy by the discovery of mirror neurons in the brain is a contribution of the new field of

a. social comparison theory
b. cognitive dissonance
c. social neuroscience
d. self-perception theory

_____ 22. Many people who adamantly report being race-blind may unknowingly hold unconscious racial biases — a finding that has been demonstrated by

a. electric shocks delivered when "learners" gave wrong answers
b. brain scans of reactions by subjects to subliminal stimuli
c. deliberately wrong answers given by confederates of the researcher
d. secretly recording quarrels between husbands and wives

_____ 23. Why is rape so common? Researchers point to the fact that
- a. there are other motivations for rape, like aggression, power, and control, that may be more important than sex
- b. women are much bolder today, yet still like to be actively pursued, a situation that leaves men confused about what women really want
- c. Hollywood movies keep our sexual urges in a state of almost constant arousal
- d. unfortunately, rape is as natural as male hormones and female flirtatiousness — but it gets reported more often today

_____ 24. Catharsis is a popular idea for reducing and controlling aggression through
- a. enrolling parents in parent management training (PMT)
- b. learning to "keep the lid on" aggressive impulses instead of expressing them
- c. releasing anger or aggressive energy by expressing or letting out powerful negative emotions
- d. engaging in one of the new cognitive-relaxation programs

_____ 25. An important reason why sexual coercion is so prevalent is that, thanks to the media,
- a. males believe that they need a sexual catharsis more often than women do
- b. abstinence seems like a wimpy or "loser" belief
- c. modern women are afraid to say "no"
- d. sexually coercive males misperceive women as showing interest when in fact they are not interested

Short Essay

1. How does the story of Lawrence Graham, the busboy with a Harvard degree, illustrate the concepts of stereotypes, prejudice, and discrimination?

2. Summarize Leon Festinger's boring task experiment. What did Festinger demonstrate?

3. Summarize Solomon Asch's line judging experiment. What did Asch demonstrate?

4. Summarize Stanley Milgram's electric shock experiment. What did Milgram demonstrate?

5. Plotnik and Kouyoumdjian discussed ideals of beauty in Nigeria, organ transplants in Japan, and women's rights in Egypt. What is their point and how does each example support it?

Classic Experiments

The famous experiments in social psychology are among the most elegant in psychology, if not in all of science, but they may seem complicated on first reading. Go through the explanations in the textbook more than once, and make sure you understand the logic of each experiment. The research Plotnik and Kouyoumdjian write about is well worth understanding and remembering. These experiments are important building blocks of modern psychology, and you will come across them repeatedly in your further studies. In fact, many of these classic experiments have become part of the general knowledge of educated people.

There is a great irony surrounding these memorable experiments: most of them could not be conducted today. Plotnik and Kouyoumdjian explain why in their discussion of the ethics of psychological research.

Answers for Module 25

The Big Picture (explanations provided for incorrect choices)

A There is no such mathematics of social behavior.
B Even if you believe that social psychology settles the debate, the answer would be nurture, not nature.
C Social influence is powerful. We may be unique individuals, but only in a common shell of cultural and social forces.
D Correct! You see the "big picture" for this Module.
E It's just a joke!

True-False (explanations provided for False choices; page numbers given for all choices)

1	T	583	
2	F	584	Schema refers to a mental explanation of a person, group, or behavior.
3	T	585	
4	F	588	An attitude is an opinion or belief that predisposes one to act in a certain way.
5	F	590	Cognitive dissonance can result from an imbalance between belief and action.
6	T	591	
7	F	593	Subjects were motivated by a tendency to obey authority, not by money (the pay was small).
8	T	597	
9	F	598	Group decisions (groupthink) do not necessarily represent the best thinking of the group members.
10	T	602	

Flashcards 1

1 b 2 a 3 j 4 i 5 e 6 g 7 h 8 d 9 f 10 c

Flashcards 2

1 e 2 f 3 g 4 a 5 d 6 i 7 j 8 h 9 b 10 c

Multiple Choice (explanations provided for incorrect choices)

1 a Plotnik and Kouyoumdjian's point is about the power of prejudicial attitudes and discriminatory behavior.
b The prejudices expressed in this case were neither good natured nor kidding.
c Good point, but here Plotnik and Kouyoumdjian are showing the connection between attitudes and behavior.
d Correct! See page 581.

2 *a Correct! See page 581.*
b The high school girls doing the violent hazing were not members of gangs.
c The violent hazing was more spontaneous than urged on by a leader.
d The senior girls were hazing junior girls just like themselves.

3 a This may reflect a common prejudice of many men, but it does not come from evolutionary psychology.
b Correct! See page 582.
c A nice example of male chauvinistic thinking.
d Once true of many traditional societies, but not from evolutionary psychology.

4 a This might work if the terms were reversed, but prejudice is a stronger term in this example.
b These are the correct terms, but they are reversed (not attached to the right parts of the statement).
c These terms are more general, and do not get at the discrimination and prejudice involved.
d Correct! See page 583.

5 a Person schemas include judgments about personal traits.
b Correct! See page 584.
c Event schemas contain behaviors we associate with familiar activities, events, or procedures.
d Event schemas are sometimes called scripts.

6 a Schemas are mental categories containing knowledge about people, events, and concepts.
b Covariation refers to things that vary together in a regular way (if A is present, so is B, etc.).
c Correct! See page 585.
d Distinctiveness refers to how differently a person behaves in one situation compared to other situations.

7 ***a*** *Correct! See page 586.*
b The covariation model refers to factors present when the behavior occurs and absent when it does not occur.
c The actor-observer effect refers to explaining our own behavior differently from that of others.
d The self-serving bias refers to explaining our own successes and failures.

8 a The fundamental attribution error would only explain half of this situation.
b The actor-observer effect refers to explaining our own behavior differently from others.
c *Correct! See page 586.*
d There is no whiner effect (although *Saturday Night Live* had a skit called "The Whiners" a few years back).

9 a Feelings are very important, but beliefs and behaviors are also crucial to understanding people.
b Beliefs are very important, but feelings and behaviors are also crucial to understanding people.
c This answer doesn't show much faith in social psychology to help explain the world!
d *Correct! See page 588.*

10 a Cognition is one of the three components of an attitude.
b *Correct! See page 588.*
c Affect (emotion) is one of the three components of an attitude.
d Behavior is one of the three components of an attitude.

11 ***a*** *Correct! See page 589.*
b This did not happen in the experiment.
c This did not happen in the experiment.
d This did not happen in the experiment.

12 a Makes sense, but these are not the social-psychological terms used.
b Perhaps true, but this is only an opinion.
c *Correct! See page 590.*
d Makes sense, but these are not the social-psychological terms used.

13 a Do the initials H.R.C. mean anything to you?
b Sadly, very little of this is happening in Egypt.
c The Japanese opposition to organ transplants is changing due to a new definition of death.
d *Correct! See page 591.*

14 a Compliance would mean that we felt social pressure to carry bottles of water, even though we didn't want to.
b *Correct! See page 592.*
c Obedience would mean that we were ordered by a person in authority to carry a bottle of water.
d Hazing refers to parts of a group's initiation ritual that are humiliating and unpleasant or even dangerous.

15 a This did not happen.
b This did not happen.
c *Correct! See page 592.*
d If this were the correct answer, what would make the experiment significant?

16 ***a*** *Correct! See page 593.*
b Compliance is giving in to social pressure but not changing our beliefs.
c Conformity is performing some behavior because of group pressure.
d This common expression is not a correct technical term in social psychology.

17 a This statement about Milgram's experiment is untrue.
b *Correct! See page 593.*
c This statement about Milgram's experiment is untrue.
d This statement about Milgram's experiment is untrue.

18 a Perhaps we are less conformist today, but people still obey orders.
b Only a few well-educated people (like you) know about this experiment.
c Deception is still successfully used in many experiments.
d *Correct! See page 594.*

19 ***a*** *Correct! See page 597.*
b Social facilitation refers to an increase in performance in the presence of a crowd.
c Group polarization refers to the effects of group discussion on decisions taken.
d Deindividuation refers to the tendency to behave irrationally when there is less chance of being identified.

20 a The decision to use the atomic bomb was made by President Truman.
b The decision to assassinate President Kennedy was made by Lee Harvey Oswald.
c *Correct! See page 598.*
d New Coke was not a political decision, nor do we know if groupthink was involved in the company decision.

21 a Social comparison theory says we compare ourselves to others to measure the correctness of our beliefs.
b Cognitive dissonance is a state of psychological tension motivating us to make our beliefs more consistent.
c *Correct! See page 600.*
d Self-perception theory says we first perceive our own behavior, then, as a result, we change our attitudes.

22 a This was the setup in Milgram's famous study of obedience.
b *Correct! See page 600.*
c This was the setup in Asch's famous study of conformity.
d This was not a research study but an anecdotal report of unconscious bias.

23 ***a*** *Correct! See page 603.*
b If you chose this answer, you've been watching too many talk shows.
c Rape is not primarily about sex.
d *Down, boy, down!*

24 a PMT is a program designed to help parents decrease aggressive behavior in the home and at school.
b Catharsis is just the opposite — releasing aggressive energy by expressing negative emotions.
c *Correct! See page 605.*
d The cognitive-relaxation program works by self-monitoring angry thoughts and learning relaxation methods.

25 a This outdated stereotype wouldn't explain why many men believe sexual coercion is acceptable.
b Not all young people believe this, and even if they did it wouldn't justify sexual coercion.
c No, they are not, but too many men don't recognize that "no" really means "no."
d *Correct! See page 605.*

Short Essay (sample answers)

1. Lawrence Graham, a Harvard Law School graduate who earned $105,000 a year at a New York law firm, could not join a country club. He decided to work for a country club to learn more about it. The best job he could get was busboy. Members were surprised by his diction, but spoke about him as though he were invisible. Lawrence Graham learned firsthand about *stereotypes* based on his appearance, the *prejudice* that members felt toward African Americans, and the *discrimination* that denied him membership.

2. Leon Festinger devised an extremely boring task, then asked participants to lie to new subjects by saying the task was interesting. Some were paid $1 to lie and others $20. The latter, having been well paid, had no problem with lying. But those paid $1 had to justify telling a lie for a small amount. They resolved their cognitive dissonance (what they said versus what they believed) by changing their beliefs, agreeing that the task was interesting after all! Festinger showed that engaging in opposite behaviors could change attitudes.

3. Solomon Asch set up a simple experiment in which participants were asked to judge line lengths. But there was only one real subject; the others were confederates. At some point, all the other participants began agreeing on an obviously wrong answer. What would the real subject do — say what his eyes saw or agree with the others? An astounding 75 percent of subjects conformed on some trials (although 25 percent never conformed). Asch's experiment was the first to clearly show that group pressures can influence conformity.

4. Stanley Milgram's famous experiment on obedience was based on an elaborate but fake "laboratory" in which subjects playing the role of "teachers" were told to administer electric shocks to "learners." In fact, no shocks were given. According to the labels on the shock machine, the shocks soon became painful, and learners pounded on the wall and protested. But 65 percent of the subjects kept going until the shocks, if real, would have been lethal. Milgram had demonstrated a frightening level of obedience to authority.

5. Throughout the textbook, Plotnik and Kouyoumdjian emphasize the cross-cultural dimensions of psychology. They offer three examples of how culture shapes our attitudes. In Nigeria, traditional concepts of female beauty put a premium on fullness. But in a recent attitude shift Nigerian young women today aspire to thinness. In Japan, people did not get organ transplants, because dead was defined as having no heartbeat. In Egypt, a long struggle for equal rights for women continues to be frustrated by powerful traditional forces.

TO THE OWNER OF THIS BOOK

May I ask a favor? It would be very helpful to the publisher (Wadsworth) to know how well the Study Guide worked for you. We would like to have your reactions to the different features of the guide and your suggestions for making improvements. Please fill out this form, fold and seal it, and drop it in the mail. Thanks!

Matthew Enos

School ______________________________

Instructor's name ______________________________

Used this Study Guide because: Required _____ Optional _____ Comment ______________________________

Did this Study Guide help you with the course? ______________________________

____

Was this Study Guide interesting and informative? ______________________________

____

What did you like most about this Study Guide? ______________________________

____

Please check ☑ the parts of the Study Guide you used and tell us how useful they were:

- ☐ Module introductions ______________________________
- ☐ Effective Student Tips ______________________________
- ☐ Learning Objectives lists ______________________________
- ☐ Key Terms lists ______________________________
- ☐ Outlines ______________________________
- ☐ "How English Works" sections (by John Thissen) ______________________________
- ☐ The Big Picture quizzes ______________________________
- ☐ True-False questions ______________________________
- ☐ Flashcards matching questions ______________________________
- ☐ Multiple-Choice questions ______________________________
- ☐ Short Essay questions ______________________________
- ☐ Special boxes and quizzes ______________________________

Additional comments about this Study Guide ______________________________

____

OPTIONAL

Your name ______________________________ Date ______________________________

May Wadsworth, the publisher, quote you in promotions for the Study Guide or in future publishing ventures?

Yes _____ No _____

Note: You can also send me comments by e-mail! **<profenos@mac.com>**

Psychology Editor
20 Davis Dr.
Belmont, CA 94002

EVIL IN THE MAHĀBHĀRATA

EVIL IN THE MAHĀBHĀRATA

MEENA ARORA NAYAK

OXFORD
UNIVERSITY PRESS

OXFORD
UNIVERSITY PRESS

Oxford University Press is a department of the University of Oxford. It furthers the University's objective of excellence in research, scholarship, and education by publishing worldwide. Oxford is a registered trademark of Oxford University Press in the UK and in certain other countries.

Published in India by
Oxford University Press
2/11 Ground Floor, Ansari Road, Daryaganj, New Delhi 110 002, India

First Edition published in 2018

ISBN-13 (print edition): 978-0-19-947774-6
ISBN-10 (print edition): 0-19-947774-4

ISBN-13 (eBook): 978-0-19-909183-6
ISBN-10 (eBook): 0-19-909183-8

Typeset in ScalaPro 10/14
by The Graphics Solution, New Delhi 110 092
Printed in India by Replika Press Pvt. Ltd

For Daddyji

Contents

Acknowledgements

My deepest gratitude to Dr Indrani Sanyal for mentoring me and for spending hours with me on the phone—long distance—discussing the ethical arguments. This book would not have been possible without her help. My warmest thanks to Dr Beverly Blois for his unshakeable faith in me. I also want to thank him for inviting me to help organize three India Institutes funded by the National Endowment for the Humanities. Not only was this a very special privilege and honour, but these India Institute studies helped me gain a deeper understanding of the historical basis of Hindu mythology. And finally, I must thank my dear friend and colleague Bridget Pool. When I worried that I would not have enough time to work on the book, she made it simple for me by aligning my teaching life with my writing life.

Note on the Text

TEXTS CITED

The Devanāgrī Edition of the Mahābhārata (Calcutta), translated by M.N. Dutt and edited by Dr Ishwar Chandra Sharma and Dr O.N. Bimali (Parimal Publications, Delhi, 2006), has been employed for most of the book, with occasional cross-references from J.A.B. van Buitenen's English translation (Books 1–5) of the *Critical Edition* (University of Chicago Press, 1973–8). Additionally, all Gītā references are from *Bhagavad Gītā As It Is,* translated by Bhaktivedanta Swami Prabhupāda (The Bhaktivedanta Book Trust, Los Angeles, 1983), unless otherwise noted.

ABBREVIATIONS USED

AV	*Atharva Veda*
BG	*Bhagavad Gītā*
BP	*Bhāgavata Purāṇa*
Mbh	*Mahābhārata*
RV	*Ṛg Veda*
TB	*Taittirīya Brāhmaṇa*
VaP	*Vāmana Purāṇa*
VP	*Viṣṇu Purāṇa*

TRANSLITERATION AND TRANSLATION

Names of characters and technical terms are in the standard transliteration employed by J.A.B. van Buitenen in the *Critical Edition*, except in quotations from other authors; in which case, the spelling is as used by these authors. The exceptions are the *ślokas* from the M.N. Dutt text; while Dutt uses simplified transliteration, the present work employs the standard for the sake of consistency. Also, the English translation of ślokas quoted in the book are an adaptation of M.N. Dutt's translation.

Glossary[1]

ācār	conduct; behaviour; manner of life
ādarśa	ideal, exemplar
adharma	unrighteousness; immoral; opposite of *dharma*
Adhvaryu	Vedic priest responsible for the physical details of the sacrificial site (for example, measuring the altar space, building the altar, etc.)
agni	fire—sacrificial, digestive; also, god of fire
agyātavāsa	living incognito
ahiṁsā	nonviolence
akrodha	lack of anger
akṣauhiṇī	an army unit consisting of 21,870 elephants, 21,870 chariots, 65,610 horses, and 109,350 foot soldiers
amāvasya	new moon; start of the lunar month
aṃśa	portion; part
an-ārya	not Aryan; considered outside the Aryan fold
anuśāsana	administration; discipline
āpad	emergency situation
apsarās	celestial nymphs of great beauty, often associated with *Gandharvas*
ardharatha	half a warrior; Bhīṣma's insult to Karṇa

[1] Words in italics are independent entries in the glossary.

arghya	offering to an honoured guest, normally of water in which rice, curd, milk, honey, etc., is mixed
artha	material wealth and prosperity
āśrama	one of the age-based four stages of life for a Hindu—studentship, householder, retirement, and renunciation; also mode of life related to *varṇa*
asura	celestial being; opponent of the gods
Aśvamedha	a Vedic horse sacrifice
avatār	descent of a deity on earth; reincarnation of a celestial being; for example, Viṣṇu
bhakta	devotee; worshipper
bhakti	devotion; worship
bhrātadharma	dharma and duty of a brother towards his siblings
brahmacarya	first stage in the four āśramas of life—that of celibate studentship
brahmarṣi	a sage who has divine powers and has studied the Vedas
Brahmāvarta	the holy land; the heartland situated between Sarasvatī and Dṛṣadvatī rivers
brāhmin	member of the *varṇa* that is considered highest in the order of the caste system; priest
chakra	disc; Kṛṣṇa/Viṣṇu's weapon (Sudarśana Chakra)
daivya	fate; divine power
dakṣiṇā	fee paid to a brāhmin for services
dāna	charity
dānava	same as *asura*; a class of beings constantly in battle with the gods
daṇḍa	punishment
dānavīra	generous; munificent; a title of Karṇa
dāsa/dasyu	someone in servitude, *an-ārya*, later seen as quality of *śūdra*
dayā	mercy

deśa	place; region; country
devabhūmī	the land of the gods
dharma	morality, righteousness, duty
dharmaśāstra	doctrine; a body of precepts codified by dharma laws; book of ethical laws
Dvāpara	second of the four great ages or *yugas*, with an environment of half *dharma* and half *adharma*; the second best throw in dice
dvija	twice-born; the three upper castes in the caste system
dyūta	gambling, especially with dice
Gandharva	celestial musicians
guṇa	strain; quality; attribute; in Sāṃkhya philosophy, the character or nature of a being or thing is determined by the proportion of three guṇas—*sattva* (goodness, harmonious) *rajas* (passion, activeness), and *tamas* (darkness, chaos)
hiṁsā	injury; harm; violence
Hiraṇyagarbha	golden foetus; Brahmā, who is born from a golden egg
Hotṛ	Vedic priest, reciter of invocations in a sacrifice
itihāsa	literally, 'thus it happened'; tradition; history
kāla	time; suitable situation
Kāla	Great Time; celestial manifestation of time
Kali	asura; personification of Kali Yuga
Kālī	goddess; dark form of Pārvatī; consort of Śiva
kalpa	aeon; a day of Brahmā consisting of 1,000 *yugas*
kāma	desire; sexual desire
karmayogi	practitioner of karma yoga; one who performs austere action
kāvya	poetic composition
Kṛta Yuga	the first and most evolved of the four great ages; constitutes an environment of total *dharma* and no *adharma*; also the best throw in dice

kṣatriya	member of the *varṇa* that is considered second in the order of the caste system; warrior
kṣetra	field; sphere
kṣetrajñāna	knowledge of the field
laukika	worldly; temporal; customary
māyā	supernatural power; illusory; magic
māyāvi	one who has magical powers; magical
moha	attachment; delusion
niṣkāma karma	desireless action
nīti	polity; ethics; statesmanship
nivṛtti	a life of contemplation, ceasing from worldly acts (as opposed to *pravṛtti*)
niyati	destiny; fate
Plakṣavatarana	manifestation of the cosmographic continent of Plakṣa (peepul tree). Various Purāṇas describe the world as divided into seven *dvīpas* (islands or continents) Jambūdvīpa, Plakṣadvīpa, Śālmalidvīpa, Kuśadvipa, Krauñcadvīpa, Śākadvīpa, and Puṣkaradvīpa. These are concentrically separated by seven oceans of saltwater, sugarcane juice, wine, ghee, curd, milk, and water respectively. In ancient times, India was referred to as Jambūdvīpa, which is in the centre.
pāśa	noose; Varuṇa's weapon to catch and punish miscreants
patidharma	*dharma* and duty of a husband towards his wife
patnīdharma	*dharma* and duty of a wife towards her husband
piśācas	class of demons who were flesh eaters
prakṛti	in Sāṃkhya philosophy, the creative power of the material world consisting of the three *guṇas* (as opposed to *puruṣa*); energy as personified by Śaktī
pralaya	apocalypse; total annihilation
pravṛtti	active life (as opposed to a life of *nivṛtti*)
prema	love

priyavācana	kind words
purāṇa	a work dealing with ancient Indian history, legend, mythology, and theology
Puruṣa	primeval man; soul of the universe (as described in the *Puruṣa-Sūkta* hymn of *Ṛg Veda*); in Sāṃkhya philosophy the animating principle; the world spirit as passive in relation to the creative force of *prakṛti*
puruṣārtha	the four goals of life—*dharma, artha, kāma,* and *mokṣa*
puruṣkāra	human effort (as opposed to *daivya*)
putradharma	*dharma* and duty of a son towards his parents
rājadharma	the *dharma* of a king; a king's duties towards his kingdom and subjects
rājarṣi	a rāja or a king who has attained high spiritual knowledge
Rājasūya	ceremonious ritual of consecrating a king
rākṣasa	malignant and demonic being; demon
ratha	warrior
ṛṣi	sage; one who has attained spiritual wisdom through rigorous training
ṛta	cosmic, divine, human order in Vedic times; also, law that governed these
sadācāra	rightful behaviour
sadasya	member of sacrificial assembly
sahasracakṣu	a being with thousand eyes
śaktī	power; energy; personified as goddess
samprajñāna	mindfulness; clear comprehension
samudra manthana	churning of the ocean (a creation myth)
Saptasarasvat	confluence of seven Sarasvatīs
sarovar	lake; tank
sarpasattra	snake sacrifice
śāstra	scripture; a book of knowledge regarded as divine authority
Śāśvatadharma	*dharma* of eternal liberation

śatru	an enemy
satya	truthfulness
śiṣṭācāra	cultivated behaviour; good and proper conduct
śiṣtas	those who cultivate and practise good and proper behaviour; refined
śloka	song; stanza; verse line in the Anuṣṭubh metre most commonly used in Vedic and classical Sanskrit poetry
Smṛiti	a body of sacred brāhmanical tradition as 'remembered', rather than revealed (as opposed to *Śruti*)
soma	elixir of immortality; ambrosia
śreyas	excellent; auspicious; facilitates in securing happiness
Śruti	the instituted tradition of the Vedas; literally, something that is heard; hence the Vedas are accepted as 'heard' revelations
strīdharma	dharma of a woman or wife
śūdra	member of the *varṇa* that is considered lowest in the order of the caste system; menial worker
sūta	member of charioteer class; bard; of mixed race
svārthatyāga	selflessness
svayaṃvara	a custom by which girls of royal families could choose their own husbands from an assembly of suitable men
tamas/tamasic	the quality of darkness (a *guṇa* in philosophy); ignorance; one who displays these qualities
tapas	asceticism
tējas	fiery energy; irradiating
tīrtha	place of pilgrimage
Tretā Yuga	second of the four great *yugas*; constitutes three-quarters of *dharma* and one quarter of *adharma*
trivarga	three (of four) goals of *puruṣārtha—dharma, artha*, and *kāma*

Udgātṛ	One of the four chief Vedic priests in a ritual sacrifice (the other three are *Hotṛ, Adhvaryu, and Brāhman)*; the priest who chants the hymns from the *Sāma Veda*
Uttaravedī	upper altar area of a sacrificial site
vāhana	vehicle
vaiśya	member of the *varṇa* that is considered third in the order of the caste system; merchant, tradesman, agriculturist
vajra	lightning; diamond; having the indestructible and irresistible properties of both; Indra's weapon
varṇāśrama	mode of life related to class/caste; one of the key *dharmas*. See also *varṇa and āśrama*
varṇa	caste; colour; classification on the basis of these
vidhi	ordinance or rite
vidhi aparādha	fault or error in the performance of a rite
yajamāna	one who performs sacrifices
yajña	ritualistic sacrificial ceremony
Yakśa	spirit deities of nature associated with fertility and wealth
yoga	yoke; connect; a meditational practice through which the individual soul can be united with supreme spirit
yuga	an age of the world; period of time

Introduction

MYTH AND ETHICS

In most Hindu cultures, ethical ideas are generally not derived from theistic commands of an omnipotent God (unlike in Abrahamic cultures). In these theistic models, the original good is God and the original evil is his antithesis, which means that God is the authority who formulates normative ethics and who guides moral behaviours. Hindu ethics, on the other hand, are based on the *Śrutis*, and they are interpreted and understood through the *Smṛitis*, which establish ethical values as traditions; traditions, in turn, guide customary law and moral behaviours. Moreover, traditions inferred from myths in the Smṛitis are inculcated by *śiṣṭācāra* and *sadācāra*—moral conduct that exemplifies the actions and behaviours of characters who symbolize goodness in mythological texts such as the Mahābhārata.

However, this delineating of ethical traditions through myth creates some of the problems of evil in Hindu cultures, because these traditions misrepresent myth. The myths of the Mahābhārata are layered narratives in which truths of the human experience are embedded—truths that tell of life's perfections as well as its imperfections. Therefore, these myths include experiential values of both morality and immorality, which are explored in the actions, behaviours, and relationships of the mythical characters, and in the moral and immoral choices these characters make. Consequently, in the Mahābhārata, no character is just an archetype of good or evil, and his or her behaviour cannot be held up as an exemplar of these polarities. The Mahābhārata calls itself the 'book of rules for the conduct of mankind', and it is a true reflection of the human experience (*Mbh* 1.1.41). However, the tradition of good versus evil that has been educed from the Mahābhārata portrays divine apotheoses and mortal heroes as being representative of a priori good—even though they commit morally questionable acts. But when these 'good' characters are examined in the context of praxes and real-world behavioural paradigms, they are revealed as morally flawed, and their actions, too, are often a consequence of those flaws. By deifying these characters, tradition has created a potential for people to emulate their moral deficiencies.

Furthermore, not only have Hindu ethical traditions limited empirical proof of morality and immorality that can be found in texts like the Mahābhārata, but also, these traditions have resulted from an exploitation of myth's protean nature. By virtue of its ability to evolve and incorporate new and changing meanings, myth is open to interpretations of *deśa* and *kāla,* and also to interpolations by *śiṣtas.* But this fluid nature of myth has been exploited by śiṣtas, who have used the moral imperatives of the mythical characters 'to mobilize support for [their own] ideological position' (Thapar 1989: 4). For example, in the Mahābhārata, tradition mobilizers of *varṇa* ideologies have evoked the characters' *varṇāśrama dharma* obligations to establish the predominance of one varṇa over the other. They have also interpreted myth from a perspective that has aggrandized their own position in society. This is especially so in the case of brāhmins, who have portrayed themselves in the myths as elevated beings worthy of the reverence given to the gods. This exploitative use of the Mahābhārata's myths has resulted in customary laws that continue to cause pain and suffering for many people in Hindu society. Moreover, these misrepresentations of myth have the potential to cause immoral behaviours in ordinary people, who generally follow customs and traditions without questioning their moral worth. Unfortunately, the myths of the Mahābhārata are rarely ever examined free from the influence of these biased perspectives.

Added to this pitfall of śiṣtas misusing the shifting and emulative nature of myth is the fact that the Mahābhārata houses the Bhagavad

Gītā. This justifies the Mahābhārata's view of itself as a spiritual guide that 'dispels the ignorance of man' (*Mbh* 1.1.86). However, there is a disconnect between the narrative of the Mahābhārata and the metaphysics of the soul that the Gītā teaches. In actuality, the conduct of the people in the narrative is rarely guided by the liberating doctrine of the Gītā. Instead, the characters, including Kṛṣṇa himself, and those that are influenced by him and his Bhagavad teachings, actually pursue *pravṛtti* goals of *trivarga* (*dharma, artha,* and *kāma*) rather than *puruṣārtha,* which includes the *nivṛtti* ideals of *mokṣa.* In fact, aside from the peripheral story of Vyāsa's son Śuka, who achieves mokṣa, and Yudhiṣṭhira's occasional courting of the idea of mokṣa, there is little evidence in the Mahābhārata of *mokṣa dharma.* Moreover, even the spiritual message of the Gītā, which is given to Arjuna as a legacy for everyman, is lost in the narrative, so much so that this very character declares to Kṛṣṇa in the *Anu Gītā,* after his 'ignorance is [supposedly] dispelled', that he has forgotten the lessons he learnt (*Mbh* 14.16.6). Therefore, while the Gītā constitutes a doctrine which can be seen as a guide to transcendence, its inclusion in the Mahābhārata seems to serve little purpose; neither does it influence the actions and behaviours of the characters, nor does it guide them on the path of mokṣa. Yet the Mahābhārata has been established in the Hindu mind as a *dharmaśāstra*—a text whose good characters are necessarily guided by both the ethics of dharma and the liberating truths of mokṣa.

The ordinary Hindu, who probably never reads the voluminous text of the Mahābhārata, never learns that its Gītā tradition and its narrative tradition don't cohere. Instead, this Hindu tries to see a continuum between the desire-based karma of trivarga and *niṣkāma karma* of the Gītā, between the mores of individual dharma and Kṛṣṇa's ultimate dharma, between the theodicy of Kṛṣṇa as a theistic divine and his moral evil in the non-theistic context of the narrative. This Hindu then, aspiring to the truths of the Gītā and yet emulating the pravṛtti behaviour of the mythical characters, is not able to reconcile these contradictions. If this Hindu were able to address the ambiguities of this Smṛiti's traditions, he or she may be better equipped to comprehend its ethics. Also, acknowledging the discrepancies of the tradition may facilitate a questioning of the ethical and moral problems in the text itself that have created a potential for evil. Consequently, this may lead Hindus to re-examine their own dharmas according to their own human impulses and natural inclinations.

VALUE PLURALISM

When, around the 5th–3rd century BCE, the era of Śruti literatures—the original mythos—passed, and the fixity of the cosmological order contained in them became transformed into protean logos of the Smṛti, *itihāsa* texts that explained and interpreted the truths of the Śruti through myth gained authority. The Mahābhārata emerged at this time, still touting the normative codes from Śruti literature, but in a new construct that included the ritualistic injunctions of the Vedas, the metaphysics of eschatology and liberation of the Upaniṣads, and pravṛtti myths and narratives of everyday life to which ordinary people could relate.

In addition to being an amalgamation of a variety of value systems, this new literature gained credence as a scriptural and popular text, because its authorship was attributed to an elevated being who was connected to the human world. Case in point: the Mahābhārata's authorship is attributed to Vyāsa,[1] who is not only an *aṃśa* of Nārāyaṇa, but he also corresponds to Brahmā in his triple role of representing brāhmanical orthodoxy, creating and disseminating the Vedas. Additionally, he acts as grandfather to both the Pāṇḍavas and Kauravas, just as Brahmā is the progenitor of both the *devas* and *asuras* (Sullivan 1999: 81). Hence, it is no wonder that this text was seen as a new kind of creation—the fifth Veda—created by Vyāsa, just as Brahmā created the world. This divine and human connection continued in the text's recensions, and, in later interpolations, its scribe became Gaṇeśa—a

[1] The most common scholarly perspective of Vyāsa is that he is mythical, because his existence is difficult to prove. Scholars also believe that the Mahābhārata is a product of multiple authors and editors; hence its author, Vyāsa, is symbolic because that name means 'division' or 'divider' (Sullivan 1999: 1).

god whose main attributes and functions are directly connected to the wellbeing of mortals.[2]

There are also secular aspects to the Mahābhārata. Firstly, many of its myths and stories were adoptions from the folklore of non-Aryan tribes with whom Aryans were forming exogamous relationships. And secondly, this narrative was recited not by the elite brāhmins (as was the case with the Śrutis), but by bardic *sūtas*, who were so much of the hoi polloi that often they were even outside the caste system, because they had hybrid bloodlines. However, while the Mahābhārata demonstrates temporality and fluidity and makes people active collaborators of custom, factors that make the tradition dynamic and alive, it fails as a moral guide. Instead of bridging the gap between the text's different value systems—of the Vedas, Kṛṣṇa theism, puruṣārtha, and tribal and secular beliefs—with a cohesive moral code, it leaves moral lacunae that are open to interpretations.

Its inclusion of Vedic precepts creates the impression that Vedic ideals are in alignment with theistic morality and dharma ethics; this is not so. While the Vedas do constitute an ethical system, they are non-theistic, amoral, ritualistic texts that, through the injunctive practice of sacrifice, unite the cosmological and temporal worlds. This Vedic aesthetic natural order—*ṛta*—appears ethical; hence it is seen in accord with Mahābhārata's ethics. However, in the Mahābhārata, while the aesthetic order of the Vedas still exists to a certain extent, the idea of ṛta is no longer relevant, and the Vedic *vidhi* of sacrifice is transformed into the trivarga of puruṣārtha.

This desire-oriented concept of puruṣārtha is a new form of ethics and ritual activity that, while ensuring material order, is not binding

[2] The earliest iconography of Gaṇeśa dates to the Gupta period (4th–5th century CE). His *yakśa* and *nāga* characteristics suggest that he may have been of pre-Aryan origin, but it was his transformation as Gaṇapati that awarded him a place in the Purāṇic pantheon (Bhattacharji 2000: 183). One of Gaṇeśa's main appellatives is *Vighneśvara,* meaning remover of obstacles; hence he is also invoked as the god of good beginnings. The Critical Edition does not recognize the scribe Gaṇeśa as part of the original Mahābhārata; the story of how he became a scribe is only mentioned as a footnote.

(as ṛta was), because its pursuit is an individual obligation. Additionally, while dharma, the overarching guiding principle of puruṣārtha, appears to be like ṛta (because it suggests symmetry between individual effort and divine operations), in actuality, it subverts the order of the divine and cosmic worlds to a wholly earthly scheme. This secularity gives the system a moralistic character, but it also makes it more susceptible to evil than the Vedic system. Vedic ṛta, although amoralistic, was absolute, all encompassing, and all inclusive; and it was kept incorruptible by Varuṇa of the *sahasracakṣu*, who threatened punishment with his *pāśa* to anyone who broke the order. Dharma, on the other hand, while being normative and pertaining to the whole society, also invests the values of right and wrong in each individual's action, thought, and behaviour, and it determines right and wrong from the consequence of these behaviours. Therefore, dharma is individualistic, in both consequentiality and accountability; this is where the problem occurs, because individuation not only creates malleable values, but also a scope for opportunism. When a code of conduct is an individual obligation, and an individual is accountable only to himself, the powerful can manipulate the values of right and wrong to suit their purpose. The Mahābhārata is a perfect example of this vulnerability, because all its characters commit adharmic actions but justify them with their own interpretation of dharma.

Moreover, the multifariousness of this text necessarily perpetuates a multitude of experiences and moral behaviours, each of which is not only a different interpretation of dharma, while it also does not correspond with the ethics that normative dharma delineates. Therefore, one of the basic problems in the text is that there is a dichotomy between ethics and morality, because what ought to be done is not what is actually done by its characters. While a foundation of ethics is provided through the ideals of puruṣārtha; morality is made an individual obligation,[3] and it is practised differently by its moral agents, based on their own interpretation of good and evil.

[3] Ethics and morality are distinguished based on three factors: (1) the roots of the two words: 'ethics' whose Greek root translates into 'ethos' and means the accepted general customs, beliefs, and practices of a whole culture

The Mahābhārata also includes normative codes of varṇa, dharma, karma, and mokṣa, which allow for even more flexibility of ideas. While different varṇas have their own prescribed actions and behaviours, following an ethical hierarchy in which each varṇa adheres to a different set of morals and rules, the concept of mokṣa caters to various levels of spiritual development, evoking even more individualism. Additionally, this multitude of behaviours is made more complex by the fact that there is no regulative standard that establishes rightful and wrongful conduct; each moral and immoral action of the characters is its own measure of good and evil, based on the situation. Moreover, the theory of karma, which could be regulatory, is not only minimally utilized in the text, but also, when it does come into play, it is impaired by other factors, such as divine intervention and fate.

Adding to the problems of ambiguity in the Mahābhārata is the ideal of dharma itself. This ideal overarches all beliefs and systems that the text tries to integrate into the governing order of puruṣārtha, or, more accurately, the trivarga of dharma, artha, and kāma. However, dharma is tractable and constantly in danger of allowing moral slippage.

Hence, the Mahābhārata accommodates many values that do not cohere, with the result that the text is an assortment rather than a unified guiding system.

---

or society; and 'morals', whose Latin root translates into 'mores' and means behaviours that embody an unquestioned system of practices (*Oxford English Dictionary*). (2) the general understanding that arises from the etymology of the words, and which suggests a subtle difference between them is that ethics is the philosophy and ideology behind a code of conduct for a whole society, and morality is how individuals in the society adopt this code of conduct in their actions and behaviours. Hence, while ethics is what ought to be done; morality is what is done. And since Hindu values are attribute-based and experiential, the praxes of 'what is done' is distinct from the theoria of 'what ought to be done'. (3) The Mahābhārata, while suggesting in its didactic chapters that a unification of ethics and morality would be ideal, portrays through its characters that moral practices can be different from ethical obligations.

KURUKṢETRA AS *DHARMAKṢETRA*

Kurukṣetra, the field of war in the Mahābhārata, is established in the Hindu mind as a *dharmakṣetra* that dates back to the Vedas. It is a *devabhūmī* which has been attributed with a number of reverential aspects from the time of the *Ṛg Veda*. Explaining this piety, O.P. Bharadwaj (1991: 60) says, 'The fabric of Indian mythology is woven around gods most of whom are associated with Kurukṣetra in one way or the other. Manu gives the name of Brahmāvarta to the heartland of Kurukṣetra ... and the oldest Vedic works place the earliest religious and political activities in this region. It is generally agreed that the bulk of the Vedic literature was composed here.' In addition, the holiest of rivers, the Vedic Sarasvatī, in her seven forms, appears as the Saptasarasvat in Kurukṣetra (*Mbh* 9.38.1–26). And there is evidence that even the Vedic Dṛṣadvatī flowed close to the city of Hāstinapura (Bharadwaj 1991: 47). Also, according to *Vāmana Purāṇa*, it was in the Sannihati Sarovar in Kurukṣetra that Hiraṇyagarbha was born, from which creation resulted. This is the *Uttaravedī* of Brahmā (Bharadwaj 1991: 60), and a dip in this sarovar on *amāvasya* is believed to bestow the merit of a thousand *Aśvamedhas*. Moreover, the *Taittirīya Āraṇyaka*, describing the geographical parameters of the land, calls it the sacrificial altar of the gods (quoted in Bharadwaj 1991: 60), and, according to the *Vāmana Purāṇa*, this is where King Kuru tilled the field to create the boundaries of Kurukṣetra. The myth that accompanies this act of King Kuru further establishes the reverence of the land: when King Kuru decided to till, Indra came to ask him what he intended. Kuru's response was that he would sow the seeds of meditation, truth, forgiveness, charity, yoga, and righteousness in this field to make it a true dharmakṣetra. When Viṣṇu asked him what he would use as seed, King Kuru replied that the seeds were in his body. Then he extended his right arm and Viṣṇu cut it up into a thousand pieces. Subsequently, the king offered up his left arm and then his head so that the 'seeds' could be extracted, and Viṣṇu, satisfied that the king's vision was true, granted him the boon that the land of Kurukṣetra would be exactly as he envisioned it (*VaP* 22.22–37).

Altogether, there is no doubt that Kurukṣetra holds tremendous religious and dhārmic importance for Hindus. In fact, even Buddhist texts validate the significance of the region. For example, referencing the *Vinaya* of the *Mūlasarvāstivādins*,[4] Bharadwaj (1991: 75) explains that Buddha, too, made at least one journey with Ānanda, his first cousin and principle disciple, through Hāstinapura and westward, because he was aware of the city's import. And in the Mahābhārata itself, the sanctity of Kurukṣetra is more than evident. It is called the *tīrtha* of Plakṣavatara, that is, 'the gate of heaven' (*Mbh* 3.129.13–14).

In addition to Kurukṣetra and its surroundings[5] being sanctified land, the battlefield of Kurukṣetra is acknowledged many times as a veritable dharmakṣetra; even the warriors of the *Mahābhārata* proclaim it such: Dhṛtarāṣṭra calls it the 'holy field of Kurukṣetra' (*Mbh* 6.25.1), and Karṇa calls it the 'altar for the sacrifice of weapons' where each attribute of war and the warriors will be an ingredient of the sacrificial ritual (*Mbh* 5.141.29–31); hence, Kurukṣetra is 'the holiest spot in all these worlds' (*Mbh* 5.141.53). Considering these testimonials, it is natural for Hindus to believe that any battle fought in this field would be for dharma's sake, and that victory, too, would undoubtedly be dharma's. Thus, the orthodox Hindu cannot conceive of any transgressions of dharma to have occurred in Kurukṣetra, especially perpetrated by the Pāṇḍavas, who are perceived as virtuous dharma heroes.

However, perhaps a popular legend that is often told to explain why the Kurus chose the battlefield of Kurukṣetra to fight their war is the one that tells the true story of not just the war that occurred there but

[4] Vinaya texts are canonical Buddhist texts that lay out the framework and monastic rules for the *sangha* or community of monks. They are based on the *Vinaya Pitaka* ('basket of disciplines') scripture. Mūlasarvāstivāda was one of the early schools of Buddhism in India, and the *Mūlasarvāstivāda Vinaya* is dated to about 2nd-1st century BCE. It is used in the Tibetan tradition.

[5] In the Vedic age, the Kuru region extended up to the Sutlej in the northwest and beyond the Ganga in the east. In later times, Kurukṣetra gradually shrank and came to 'denote first the Sarasvatī-Dṛṣadvatī doab and more recently only the Thanesar tīrtha complex' (Bharadwaj (1991: 11).

also the environment of Kurukṣetra: When the envoys of the Pāṇḍavas and Kauravas were seeking a suitable battlefield which would accommodate eighteen *akṣauhiṇī* of soldiers, they petitioned numerous kings for their land, but no king agreed, because they foresaw the massacre that would occur. But then, returning to Hāstinapura, the envoys saw a farmer tilling his field in Kurukṣetra. As he irrigated it, a levee broke and, despite all his efforts, he could not fix it. The farmer then grabbed his young son, who was playing close by and, killing the boy, he secured the levee with his dead body. When the envoys witnessed this incident, they knew that they had found the battlefield they sought, because this field of Kurukṣetra was obviously cruel enough to bear the burden of a war where blood would turn against blood and all dharma codes would be breached.[6] And they were not wrong, because the Mahābhārata is a testament that the war which occurred in this dharmakṣetra was indeed one in which blood turned against blood, and dharma was flouted and used for personal agendas.

The story of the farmer in the field of Kurukṣetra is a legend found mostly in oral narratives, but legends have a way of capturing and expressing the truth that official chronicles may not want to acknowledge. Perhaps the story of the farmer is true, and perhaps, the people of Kurukṣetra were aware that a land that sanctions blood-letting, even if it is to right a wrong, can hardly be called a holy land. In fact, perhaps, this was the message that the earliest narrative traditions of the Bhārata War contained—that the war which took place on this land was one in which there was a total breakdown of dharma on both sides, tantamount to a father killing his son for his personal gain. But, instead of decoding this message to teach people the moral dangers of such behaviour, the brāhmins, who formalized the myth to ensure their own hegemony and to aggrandize their own status as keepers of dharma, validated the battlefield as dharmakṣetra and concretized the war as dharmayuddha. Or, perhaps the real culprit that misled people into believing the sanctity of Kurukṣetra was the metaphor of

[6] This legend is found in almost all local publications that are available at any tourist site in Kurukshetra.

Kṛṣṇa as the divine charioteer, guiding everyman's chariot of mortal life through the proverbial life-field of Kurukṣetra. This metaphor of Kṛṣṇa became such a panacea that it not only cured the wounds delivered in the battlefield of Kurukṣetra, but it also continues to absolve people from accountability of their immoral actions.

ARYAN IDENTITY AND 'THE OTHER'

Since the focus of this study deals with Aryan society in epic times, it is important to explain who the Aryans of this era were. Also necessary is an interpretation of Aryanism, because part of the proof to the argument that there are problems of evil in the Mahābhārata that have impacted Hindu traditions rests in the perspective about who or what is Aryan.

For this work, which pertains to the epic Aryans and their societal norms, the debate about whether the Aryans were indigenous to India or migrants is only peripherally relevant. In addition, it is not important to determine what the original home of the migrant Aryans (of the standard view) was; therefore, this study will not go into the details of the debate. However, it is necessary to state which view is supported here, because in order to present arguments about epic Aryan society and its ethics and morals, it is necessary to establish whether the legacy of the Aryans was of a continuous race from the earliest times, or whether their 'race' and its racial biases were a product of later developments in the society they formed. This book accepts the standard view for a number of reasons, main among them being the language theory, which propounds that the Sanskrit of the Vedas belongs to the Indo-Aryan group of languages with which it shares etymological roots.[7] Perhaps the greatest proof of Aryan migration is the closeness of Aryan language and culture to Indo-Iranian.[8]

[7] For example, words related to birds, fowl, plants, cows, and horses are similar.

[8] Second century linguistic Indo-Iranian records show similarities to the Indo-Aryan language, which has been established as the source of Avestan

Also, the Mitanni records from the upper Mesopotamia kingdom of Mitanni show a similarity between the Indo-Iranian branch of language and rituals and Vedic culture.[9]

The standard view language theory discounts that 'Aryan' was a name of a race. Rather, it proposes that the Vedic Aryans were those who could be distinguished linguistically as speaking a specific language—Sanskrit—as opposed to any of the Dravidian languages. These people referred to themselves as Aryans. Consequently, because of their distinguishing linguistic traits, at some point, they also began to see themselves as having a culture distinct from people speaking a different language.

However, as these Aryans migrated eastwards and westwards, they also adopted language and culture traits of the indigenous people, the non-Aryans. Giving one such example, Kosambi (1965: 81) cites the case of the Vedic king, Sudāsa of the ten king confederacy, son of Divodāsa, and points out that *dāsa* or *dasyu* was a reference to non-Aryan (not slave), yet it is curious that 'so early a name of an Aryan king should end in *dāsa*'. Kosambi also suggests that this means 'there was some recombination between Aryan and non-Aryan soon after 1500 BCE'. This assimilation becomes even more significant in light of Kosambi's insight into Sudāsa's background. He was chief of a tribe that bore the name Bhārata, or perhaps a special branch of the Bhāratas called the Tritsus. (It is common knowledge that the modern official name for India is Bhārata.) Kosambi also says that these Vedic Bhāratas 'were definitely Aryans'. It is evident that even at this early stage, there was clear cross-cultural flux, with the Aryans adopting

---

and Vedic Sanskrit. Many of the significant words of ritual and worship are similar. For example, *hoama* (soma); daeva (*deva*—a word used in Avestan for 'evil spirit'); *ahura* (god, which is possibly the asura of the Vedas). Scholars also point out that the word, 'Iran' is directly derived from 'the country of Aryas'—airyanam or āryānām (Mehendale 2005: 46–61).

[9] Most cited is the 1360 BCE treaty of the Hittite king with the Mitanni king, in which there is mention of gods who sound very much like the Vedic gods Indra, Mitra, Varuana, and Nastasya.

loanwords and practices from the autochthonous people and the Dravidians becoming Aryanized.

These non-Aryans, the dāsas or dasyus of the *Ṛg Veda*, were not dark-skinned *(tvacam kṛṣṇām)*, on which the racial theory is based, as Romila Thapar (2005: 125) suggests; but this 'dark skin' may be a reference to a name of an asura. Also discounted is the '*anās*' (noseless) theory, a word which many scholars, including Thapar, now see as *an-ās* (without a mouth)—speechless—meaning, not knowing the speech of the Aryans, the speech of the Vedic hymns. Thapar (2005: 123) also points out that the negative probably, and simply, was a reference to the cultural difference: the non-Aryans did not perform the rites of the Vedic Aryans and did not believe in their deities.

In the standard view, the Aryan incursion into India is grouped linguistically into three categories: Old Indo-Aryan (Vedic), Middle Indo-Aryan (MIA) (5th century BCE to 100 CE), and New Indo-Aryan (NIA) (post 1st century CE.) The Mahābhārata falls into the cusp of Old and Middle Indo-Aryan. Within this time, Sanskrit was incorporating the spoken dialects of the region, as defined by Pāṇini's *Aṣṭādhyāyī* (Mehendale 2005: 48),[10] and it was influenced by Prākṛta and Pālī; this became classical Sanskrit. However, there was a distinction between people who used *saṁskṛta*, the 'refined' speech, and prākṛta, the 'natural' and 'unsophisticated' speech (Mehendale 2005: 49). But, by the time the epics were composed, much of the population was linguistically Aryanized. In fact, there was almost a clear bilingualism, which Thapar (2005: 124) says, was 'a mixing of at least two distinctive language systems, the agglutinative Proto-Dravidian and the inflectional Indo Aryan'.

However, notwithstanding the assimilation of Dravidians with the Aryans, other significant elements were distinguishable in the society

[10] M. A. Mehendale explains how Patañjali refers to Pāṇini's definition of this territory in his *Vyākaraṇa Mahābhāṣya* in answer to the question: *kaḥ punar āryāvarṭaḥ* (What is Āryāvarta?) He names the territory of Ādarśa, which has been identified as Kurukṣetra, in the west. Kālakavana (identified as Allahabad) is in the east, Himavat in the north, and Pāriyātra (Vindhya) in the south.

that was formed by Aryans who migrated to the Doab. These elements in the Aryan definition also came to mean people with certain behaviours and characteristics. Madhav Deshpande (2005: 79) gives the following characteristics of the people who called themselves Aryans at the time of the Ganges civilization, which was probably between 1100–600 BCE:

1. A person who speaks the Aryan language as his first language is—linguistically speaking—an Aryan.
2. A person who considers himself to be a member of an Aryan (cultural) community and is accepted to be so by the other members is—culturally speaking—an Aryan.
3. A person who is a member of a group defined to be an Aryan on the basis of some physiological characteristics is—biologically speaking—an Aryan.

As Aryans began to realize a cultural identity, the idea of Aryan śiṣṭācāra also began to form. In his *Vyākarana Mahābhāṣya,* Patañjali (6.3.109, quoted in Mehendale 2005: 48) talks about the *ācār* of the people who lived in the region, calling them śiṣṭa—people who lacked greed and arrogance, hypocrisy, folly, and anger. This ideal śiṣṭācāra defining the Aryans was, perhaps, the product of long-standing prejudices against those who observed different practices and remained an-Aryan (perhaps by choice), and this mindset is quite evident in the Mahābhārata. For example, speaking with contempt about a non-Aryan character, Karṇa tells Śalya, 'They are ignorant of the *Vedas* and void of knowledge. They do not perform *yajñas* nor can they help others in them. They are fallen and many of them have been begotten by *śūdras* upon other caste girls; the gods never accept gifts from them.' Karṇa also names the races that were considered non-Aryan: Prasthalas, Madras, Gandharvas, Arattas, Khaśas, Vasātis, Sindhūs and Sauvīras, Bāhilkas, Kāraskaras, Mahiśkas, Kurandas, Kerals, Karkoṭakas, and Virakas (*Mbh* 8.44.34–47). Not only were the non-Aryans denigrated but also, at this time, Aryans began to fear a mixing of races. For example, Arjuna tells Kṛṣṇa in the Gītā that he does not want to be involved in the large-scale killing of *kṣatriyas,* because it would cause a mixing of races which would cause society to crumble (*BG* 1.39–46). As is evident from these examples, by this time, Aryanism had changed from being related to a language group to a people whose actions and customs defined their identity. Hence, 'Aryan' was fast becoming a race.

Aside from creating demarcations about what constitutes proper Aryan behaviour and what does not, epic society also became progressively caste-based. While the caste system created biases which resulted in many problems of evil, such as inequity, impunity of the high-class brāhmins, and perpetration of abuse and violence against lower castes and women, it was only one aspect of epic Aryan society. Aryanism, as a whole, became the hallmark for a superior 'race', thus also proscribing all outside the fold as the 'other'. Mahābhārata myths are testimony to these problems of evil, and as the text's formalization was passed down as tradition, so were these problems. Then, in the 8th century, during Mohammad ibn Qasim's 712 CE Arab invasion, when the people of India (or Al-Hind, as it was termed in pre-Islamic Arabia) were identified as per their religion, and the term 'Hindu' was used for people who 'lived by the book' (Sharma 2002: 5), 'Hindu' came to represent all people who believed in Aryan ideologies. This gave shape to a new social system, but this society also inherited the problems that already existed, which became an integral part of Hindu ethics, and they remain so till today.

HISTORICAL CONSTRUCTS

Although no scientific, archaeological, or historical record to date has proven that a war such as the 18-day war described in the Mahābhārata occurred, numerous references and accounts in oral traditions and extant written texts prove that many of the clans mentioned in the epic existed; there is also a distinct possibility that certain events that could have shaped such a conflict may have occurred.

While the Indian perspective of astronomical dating, which is based on the theory of the four *yugas*, places the text in 3102 BCE, the most plausible dates of the epic's composition are 9th century BCE to

1st century CE, because the socio-political environment of this time was similar to that described in the epic. According to historians, such as D.D. Kosambi, Romila Thapar, A.L. Basham, etc., around the 6th century BCE, forests were cleared in the Ganges valley, and an agrarian system came into existence, which led to the creation of monarchies (such as the Kuru kingdom) that derived their revenue from agriculture. Also, at this time, another form of political entity came into being—the republic—which was a 'reaction to Vedic orthodoxy' of the monarchies (Thapar 1996: 48). Among these republics, Thapar (1996: 48) names the tribal republic of the Yādavas (to which Kṛṣṇa belonged).

Other factors that attest to these dates are literary evidence of monarchical sacrificial rituals, such as *Rājasūya* and *Aśvamedha,* which were prevalent at that time (Thapar 1996: 54), and also place names. For example, around the time of the Buddha's death in 486 BCE, the city of Takṣaśilā, which was probably part of Gāndhāra, is mentioned as being a centre of learning and trade (Basham 1995: 48). In the Mahābhārata, Takṣaśilā is the city from which Janamejaya returns victorious when he learns how his father, Parikṣit, was killed by Takṣaka (*Mbh* 1.3.162). This, then, leads to the snake sacrifice.

It is also most likely that the Mahābhārata was composed over a period of many centuries, and that many authors added their insertions in it. The epic itself indicates at least two separate recitations—first by Vaiśaṃpāyana and then by Ugraśravas, and even between these two, the epic swelled from 2,400 verses as *Bhārata* to over 100,000 as *Mahābhārata* (*Mbh* 1.1.101–7). The epic reflects varying, and sometimes contradictory, interpolations, and an exploration of these can provide insights into the historiography for specific events and practices. For example, there is evidence in the *Śāntī Parva* of Arthaśāstra's *Daṇḍanīti,* which is considered a 4th-3rd century BCE composition. Some of the ethical and societal ordinances are also reflections of other texts, such as the *Dharmasūtras.* However, since these texts themselves spread over a period of six centuries (P.V. Kane as quoted in Olivelle 2000: 9), it can be said that the epic was still in the process of evolving during these centuries, because it reflects fluctuating proprieties as mentioned in the dharma texts. For instance, as the attitudes regarding women got stricter from Gautama to Vasiṣṭha, so did this treatment in the Mahābhārata: Gautama counts a sonless man's wife as one of the beneficiaries of his property after his death (Olivelle 2000:187, *Gautamadharmasūtram* 28.21), but Vasiṣṭha lists women as property, putting them in the same category as 'a pledge, a boundary, property of minors, an open deposit, a sealed deposit, and the property of the king or Vedic scholar' which always belongs to the 'owner even if they are used by someone else' (Olivelle 2000: 413, *Vasiṣṭhadharmasūtram* 16.26). Perhaps these gender-debasing standards are what account for Draupadī's treatment as property in the dice game. Therefore, her subsequent questioning of the status of women was really a questioning of these conventions established in the dharma texts. Olivelle (2000: 7) even mentions that *Vasiṣṭhadharmasūtram* contains discussion of 'land of the Āryas' and 'legal assembly.' Therefore, considering the dates of Vasiṣṭha's *Dharmasūtra* (300–100 BCE), it can be said that Draupadī's role in the dice game was an interpolation, and, more than likely, it may have occurred closer to the latter date, because standards must be in vogue for a while before people begin questioning them.

Many elements of the Mahābhārata, from geographical to civic and political to economic, also have a historical grounding. For example, O.P. Bharadwaj in his *Ancient Kurukṣetra* (1991: 61) lays out a geographical context that validates the history of the Kuru *rāṣtra*. Referencing *Taittirīya Āraṇyaka*, he describes the territory: the region between Gangā and Yamunā was Kuru proper, with its capital at Hāstinapura (near Meerut); the area between Sarasvatī and Yamunā was Kuru Jāṅgala, and the north of Srughna was Uttara-Kuru. Hence, he says, the Kuru kingdom's heartland comprised the Sarasvatī-Dṛṣadvatī doab. Therefore, it can be assumed that if the Kuru rāṣtra existed, then the ideologies of the Kurus, as described in the epic, must also have been a way of life for a people who lived in the heartland of India. For example, Bharadwaj (1991: 108) states that Karṇa's denouncement of the Madras territory as 'defiled' may have been based in fact, because after the Yāvanas' influence, Madras was pervaded by many social customs, such as drinking wine and eating beef, considered 'reprehensible' by orthodox Aryans.

Other historical proof about certain political practices reduces the gravity of the Pāṇḍava exile. D.D. Kosambi (1965: 88) points out that in the early tribes in Aryan society, the lowest unit within a tribe was a *grāma,* with its own official or *grāmani.* And if two grāmas were in conflict because of some intrigue, the chieftain would drive out one in forced exile in order to preserve peace. If peace-keeping is seen as a reason for the Pāṇḍava exile, then it reduces the blame and evil intent with which the Kauravas are maligned.

Economic imperatives of the time also provide more proof that events in the epic may have actually occurred. Historians like Kosambi and Thapar give a historical basis to the burning of the Khāṇḍava forest which, they say, was to clear out the area for farming. Kosambi emphasizes a reference to such heavy forest burning in the *Śatapatha Brāhmaṇa* (before 700 BCE), and Thapar (2004: 135 & 143) suggests that before this, only light jungles were burnt for agriculture. The purpose of this vast burning could also have been to extract iron ore, whose uses were just being discovered. These speculations have credence because, in the context of the epic, the palace that was built for the Pāṇḍavas by Māyā, after the burning of the Khāṇḍava, is described to be full of new innovations in both design and material, and it is possible that the newly discovered iron ore was used in parts of the palace that seemed 'magical' or full of *māyāvi* creations—definitely an innovation that went beyond the simplicity of agrarian living.

Another matter of discussion among historians and scholars of the Mahābhārata has been whether there really was a war or not. Kosambi (1965: 8, 91 & 92) suggests that this fight may actually have occurred during the time of the *Ṛg Veda,* and the war in the Mahābhārata is a retelling; albeit an exaggerated one. He points out references to the Bhāratas in the *Ṛg* and suggests that they were an Aryan tribe, who, with their tribe leader, Sudāsa, defeated ten kings, some of whom were also Aryan. However, he thinks that the Mahābhārata was probably a small battle between neighbouring tribes, because production at that time would not have supported large-scale armies. Additionally, identifying main tribes of that era, he avers that the Bhāratas were enemies of the Pūrus (who were also Aryan), and the original settlement in Hāstinapura was of a small, old Vedic Pūru tribe. Other scholarship is conflicted on whether this war is a reference to a war in *Ṛg Vedic* times, and also whether this was a small battle or a full-fledged war. For example, Thapar (2010) not only thinks that this was a war, but she also says that in the *dasharājna* (the battle of the ten rajas) described in the *Ṛg*, 'some of the clans from the Vedic corpus such as the Bhāratas, Pūrus, Yadus and Kuru-Pāñcālas reappear in the Mahabharata as lineage ancestors of the epic protagonists'. Also, in Thapar's view (2010), there is all possibility that not only was there an event such as the Mahābhārata war, there were also warriors such as Yudhiṣṭhira, Arjuna, and Vāsudeva; because, Pāṇini, in the 4th century BCE, refers indirectly to grammatical constructions associated with these words. Sharad Patil (1976: 71) too does not see the Great Bhārata war as a 'small battle' between two tribes, but he also does not see the battle as being the same as that of the ten kings described in the Vedas. He says that in the Ṛg Vedic battle, ten tribes participated, with about 10,000 troops (*RV* 7.18.4–25). But the *Mahābhārata* conflict was substantially bigger; we know that it lasted for 18 days, and at least 18 tribes participated in it; therefore, the number of warriors that participated could have been close to 18,000.

If there was an actual war, whether great or small, who were the warriors? From scholarly accounts, it seems that, quite likely, some of the actors portrayed in the Mahābhārata were actual warriors, because their names are also referenced in other literatures. Bharadwaj (1991: 62–68) mentions at least six references to the Kuru ancestry in Vedic literature, and also points out that some of these refer to Kuru-Pāñcāla enmity, which is quite evident in the Mahābhārata, starting from Drona and Drupada's rivalry, and ending with the death of all the remaining Pāñcālas in Aśvatthāman's night raid. However, while the Pāñcālas may have existed, the Pāṇḍavas were, most likely, fictitious. Ruth Cecily Katz (1990: 50–51 & 261) says that Aśvatthāman's destruction of all the Pāñcālas during his night raid casts doubt on the existence of a clan of Pāṇḍavas, because Draupadī's own sons die in this raid, and they are referred to as Draupadayas, but there is not one reference to their patrilineal names (as the Pāṇḍavas are sons of Pandu). Katz (1990: 38, 51 & 261) also suggests that the Pāṇḍava heroes were probably created by the authors to be superimposed on existing warriors. She argues that throughout the epic there is an attempt to connect the Pāñcālas with the Pāṇḍavas by creating parallels. For example, there is a double leadership of the Pāṇḍava army—the Pāṇḍava, Arjuna, and the Pāñcāla, Dhṛṣṭadyumna. Also, the Pāñcālas, Yudhāmanyu and Uttamaujas protect Arjuna's chariot wheels. To add to the parallelism is also the fact that the Pāñcālas were five tribes, as is the number of Pāṇḍavas. This artificial grafting becomes even more obvious because the Pāñcālas are completely wiped out in the Sauptika *Parva*, and Draupadī is left with no progeny, which makes her marriage to the Pāṇḍavas meaningless.

Other scholars also make similar speculations: J.A.B van Buitenen (1973: xxv) points out that Janamejaya is mentioned in the *Śatapatha Brāhmaṇa*, along with his brothers, Ugrasena, Bhīmasena, and Śrutasena, as having performed an Aśvamedha. Even in a late section of the *Atharva Veda*, Janamejaya's father Parikṣit is glorified, and 'his descendants are known as the "vanished dynasty"'. Similarly, there is evidence of various Kuru names in both Buddhist and Vedic literatures, but there is a noticeable absence of the names of the Pāṇḍavas.

Asko Parpola (2002: 362), on the other hand, does not discount the existence of the Pāṇḍavas; he says that they were foreign raiders who may have arrived in the area of the Doab between 800 and 400 BCE. He suggests that they may have been Iranian, and he supports his view with examples such as their polyandrous marriage, which he cites from Herodotus as a practice belonging to the Massagetae Iranians. He also bases his argument on their fair complexion, especially of Pāṇḍu and Arjuna. (Other scholars see Pāṇḍu's 'paleness' as a skin disease.) Also, citing Weber, Parpola points out that the Pāṇḍavas *are* mentioned in the Buddhist texts, but are called 'marauders' roaming over a wide area in North India.

On the other hand, one of the few scholars who does consider the Pāṇḍavas as part of the Kuru clan is Bankim Chandra Chatterjee

(1991: 18). He offers a logical explanation: the Pāṇḍavas were called Kurus, just as the Kauravas were, because they both belonged to the Kuru clan; that is why they were never referred to as Pāṇḍavas, and just like there is no mention of Dhṛtarāṣṭra, there is no mention of Pāṇḍavas. Chatterjee also says that it is possible that when war broke out, it was between the Kurus and Pāñcālas, and the Pāṇḍavas fought with the Pāñcālas because of their marital connection. This would also explain why Bhīṣma and Drona fought with the Kauravas instead of the Pāṇḍavas, who they favoured, because their allegiance was to the Kuru kingdom.

However, no matter who the Pāṇḍavas were, one element of their presence in Mahābhārata seems to stand out: they were superimposed on a heroic narrative. But why? To give them the credibility of real heroes? To convey superlative standards of warriorship? To serve some other purpose that was over and above a tale of war between tribes? Perhaps the reason for the Pāṇḍava overlay on the epic was to sow the seed of change. Considering the historical socio-religious climate at this time, using the most accepted dates of the epic's earliest compositions (9th–5th century BCE), it is clear that brāhmanical practices were losing popularity, heterodoxies were rife, and various cults were struggling to establish supremacy or to co-exist. In this atmosphere of flux, what was to become of a system that had existed as supreme for centuries? The keepers of that system needed a unifying factor to bring about a social change—something that would bring all these differing ideas under one umbrella, allowing them to counter the threatening heterodoxy, while retaining leadership. The unifying factor had to be familiar yet different—trustworthy, divine warrior heroes, who not only had a seamless connection to past heroes and divinities, but who also incorporated all new changing beliefs—heroes who had faith in orthodoxy, but who were practitioners of the new, changing morality. Obviously, hero gods, such as Indra, who had once awed people with their violence and treachery, would not do, because these gods had now been rejected in a society becoming more morally and socially conscious. Besides, people were too familiar with these gods and their exploits, their attributes, and their specific type of divinity.

What was needed was something and someone new, someone about whom people did not have preconceived ideas—new heroes and new gods. Thus, the Pāṇḍavas and Kṛṣṇa were the new kids on the block. D.D. Kosambi (1965: 95) explains how this brāhmin strategy worked to ensure the survival of society: discordant groups such as 'late-Vedic Aryans, Nāga food-gatherers of the forested divide, and Krishna's neo-Vedic cattle herders could together form a more efficient food producing society [especially since iron ore was still hard to come by] if they stopped fighting each other ... So the myths had to coalesce.' Hence, with 'acculturation' in the original battle lore of the Mahābhārata, society was brought together.

Furthermore, to sustain the social change in this atmosphere of fragmentation, a special adhesive was necessary. That adhesive was the Kṛṣṇa factor. The reason why the idea of Kṛṣṇa worked is simple: it is common knowledge that if a change has to be lasting and sustainable, the very psyche of people has to change—attitudes, beliefs, behaviours, ways of life, and ways in which people relate to the transcendental—and such changes can be concretized by an individual so charismatic that others cannot help but follow him. This individual must be able to touch the very core of people, the core which connects them not only to their own humanity, but also to their divine. People are constantly seeking the divine, whether within themselves or outside of themselves, because this divine is what allows them to make meaningful relationships and to transcend their mundane existence. And if an individual (like Moses, Jesus, Muhammad, Buddha, or Kṛṣṇa) can show them a path to the divine, they can be converted to a new way of thinking and living. However, these conversions are most effective when a system, rather than being completely destroyed and recreated, is allowed to transition from the old into the new, assimilating both idea-sets. If people are made to feel that what they believed and practised was wholly wrong, they are more likely to reject the new idea; therefore, the old must be allowed to continue to exist, but in a better and improved form. Hence, in the Mahābhārata, in the context of a changing society, the orthodox Vedic beliefs and gods were not denounced; rather they were moulded into a new system. In other words, the new system was a reincarnation of the old. Sukumari Bhattacharji (2000: 291) explains how

> [t]he totem-worshipers, the animists, the hero-worshipers, all had to find their respective places in this Neo-Brāhmanical religion. This could only be done by acknowledging them as manifestations of one fundamental theophany. With the idea of metempsychosis accepted on human level, it needed but one-step of sublimation to transfer it on to the divine, and thus unite the different cults and people into one fold harmonizing their faiths.

Thus, the unifying force was the belief in reincarnation on both the divine and the human levels; hence the idea of Kṛṣṇa being an incarnation of an older god, Viṣṇu, caught on, and it resulted in the new cult of Kṛṣṇaism.

Kṛṣṇa's history is complex and paradoxical, and there is much scholarly speculation about his background. But there is no doubt about his evolution into supreme godhead. In other words, regardless of whether scholars believe that there really was a Kṛṣṇa or not, history shows that the *idea* of Kṛṣṇa definitely existed and evolved, making him a supreme god. The Kṛṣṇa phenomenon was the amalgamation of the old and the new, the Aryans and the indigenous, and it was very much a part of people's lives during the composition of the Mahābhārata. In fact, his stardom was so pervasive that even the Vedic philosophical systems capitulated to it.

It is clear that Kṛṣṇa's rise to supremacy was a consequence of and an attempt to amalgamate divergent trends, but it is still not clear how this was connected to the itihāsic story of the Pāṇḍavas that was also prevalent at this time. Was Kṛṣṇa's ascendency a functionary of the eulogized war story? Did the two develop individually and then were merged by the authors? Or was the Vṛṣṇi leader truly a part of the war? And if he was, did his cultish fame add credence to the story, giving the Pāṇḍavas the necessary edge they needed? Or, perhaps the Mahābhārata was simply the perfect field in which to sow the seeds for a new kind of fruition. Whatever the case may be, one significant element that comes across as not just the connective, but also a catalyst of social change is the Nara–Nārāyaṇa connection. This interrelation establishes both Kṛṣṇa and Arjuna as the chosen ones to lead the change, and it is key to understanding why the changes became so pervasive and popular. This partnership soldered mortal and divine—Kṛṣṇa as the divine and Arjuna as a representative mortal. 'Kṛṣṇa does not fight but leads the warriors, supplies the motive, the urge and the impelling force ... This image of Kṛṣṇa and Arjuna was so effective aesthetically, and so satisfying philosophically that the hazy concept of the god–man pair was transmuted into a concrete archetype in Nara–Nārāyaṇa which explains the power of the Kṛṣṇa–Arjuna image' (Bhattacharji 2000: 294).

The impact of all these collaborations—between Aryan and non-Aryan ideologies and between warrior heroes and the Kṛṣṇa concept—was immense, like a force of nature that forever changed the relationship between mortal and divine. However, while it gave people a vision of themselves as divine, it also created a maelstrom that took everything into its tumultuous fold—the foundation of order, societal codes, and normative values.

This book takes into account all the above mentioned factors of the Mahābhārata that contributed to creating problems of evil in Hindu society. It reinterprets and examines mythological tales to show how certain groups, such as the asuras and the nāgas were persecuted as 'the other'. It provides an ethical framework of the epic and investigates how the ambiguous traditions of dharma were manipulated to sanction with impunity actions and behaviours of inequity, prejudice, and violence. It analyses the concepts of dharmakṣetra and adharmakṣetra through the myths of the main characters who define the kṣetra and fudge the lines between good and evil. And, finally, it examines the practicability of dharmayuddha to show how it became a credo of dangerous paradigms.

1 Nāgas and Asuras

The Origin of Evil

The two key agents that can be considered pivotal to the concept of evil in the Mahābhārata are the nāgas and the asuras—the former, mostly recipients of evil meted out by the Aryans, and the latter, ostensible perpetrators of evil against the Aryans. Both of these are the subjects of various myths and myth cycles in the epic, which have been misinterpreted to create faulty traditions of good and evil.

The evil meted out to the nāgas is often underplayed, not just in the epic itself but also in scholarly studies on the epic. Perhaps this is because the majority of the nāga myths are only in the *Ādi Parva* and comprise the 'false' beginning of the epic, which is seemingly unrelated or, at best, peripheral to the main frame story of the war.

These myths appear to simply be a collection of folkloric side stories about serpents that loosely link to create a minor climactic event that results in King Janamejaya organizing a *yajña* to sacrifice all serpents. Most of these myths, that is, stories of Upamanyu, Utanka, Ruru, Dundhuba, Kadrū, and Vinatā, are tales in which nāgas are either condemned or cursed for alleged infractions. Finally, a critical curse kills Rājā Parikṣit. This curse is uttered by the brāhmin boy, Śṛngin, who curses the king to be bitten by the serpent king, Takṣaka.

Consequently, Parikṣit's son, Janamejaya, vows to avenge his father's death by exterminating all serpents in a *sarpasattra*.

Innumerable serpents are sacrificed in the fire, but the yajña is eventually halted by Āstīka—the son of a brāhmin father and a serpent mother—to save the serpent race. Takṣaka, the chief alleged culprit, escapes, along with all the remaining serpents, and so ends this 'false' beginning of the epic with a simple declaration by Sauti that he has narrated this story to dispel the fear of serpents (*Mbh* 1.58.28). And that is that.

Immediately after this, Śaunaka requests Sauti to narrate the actual *Bhārata*, the story of the war, which has already been introduced as synopsis in the *Anukramaṇikā Parva*, prior to the serpent stories.

This structure of the epic—the inclusion of a second beginning that seems unrelated to the main story—is a curiosity. But the question is: are these nāga stories narrated only to alleviate the fear of serpents of the great sages attending Kulapati Śaunaka's twelve-year sacrifice in Naimiṣāraṇya? Or does this introduction mean something more?

Some Greek writers, such as Onesikratos, describe the Gangetic Plain as a land of serpents; hence, it is possible that these reptiles were a real danger to the Aryans (Vogel 1995: 1)[1]. Therefore, Sauti's effort to create a conducive atmosphere before settling down to relate the long account of the war is quite plausible. Or perhaps Sauti simply narrates the snake lore to fill in the breaks between ritual activities, as was the norm for lengthy *sattras*. However, the occasion of the sarpasattra and the manner of its execution negate these simple assumptions. This sarpasattra was conducted when Vaiśaṃpāyana told the story of the Great War. Also, this sattra did not follow the normal practices of yajñas of similar nature. *Śrauta sarpasattra,* as explained by Baudhāyana in *Sāṃkhyāna Śrautasūtra,* 'wins worlds, sons, and cattle, and whoever performs it is not harmed by serpents' (quoted in Minkowski 1989: 414); but Janamejaya does not perform his sattra for any of these reasons. His desire is to exterminate the serpents and bring about an apocalypse.

[1] Christopher Minkowski (2007: 391, footnote 28) states that Onesikratos, who travelled with Alexander, mentions two snakes, one 80 cubits and the other 140 cubits. But he is the least reliable of the sources.

Considering these antecedents to the sarpasattra, its inclusion in the Mahābhārata's introduction seems to have significance beyond a mere 'filler' story. Moreover, the mythical elements, metaphors, and analogies of the snake sacrifice, and the individual serpent myths that lead up to the sacrifice, are too vivid to have been mere preventative practices to dispel the fear of serpents. In fact, these metaphors are so deeply reflected in the myths of the rest of the epic that this event can be seen as a prototype of the whole Mahābhārata. What occurs in the rest of the epic mimics the elements of the sarpasattra, not only in terms of how the characters behave, but also in the way that the two frame stories are structured and organized. Minkowski (1989: 417) suggests that there is an interrelationship between the Mahābhārata's frame story and the sattra, which has a 'Vedic heritage'. He says, 'It has been shown that the Mahābhārata's frame story makes use of a technique of sustained embedding. Vedic rituals, and especially *sattras*, are composed following an analogous technique. That is, the recursive system of organization is to the yajña what embedding is to the Mahābhārata' (Minkowski 1989: 417).

Additionally, the framework of a yajña gives the snake sacrifice a ritualistic and pervasive significance; so much so that the epic's own 'dominating theme [of] vengeful, apocalyptic practices' (Minkowski 2007: 391) is based on the genocidal strategies described in Janamejaya's yajña. Furthermore, the snake narrative, as a whole, is like a metanarrative for the epic, because it capsules the story of the Mahābhārata. This 'fake' beginning is so significant, in fact, that D. D. Kosambi (1965: 93) says, 'It is much more important than has been realized...The Mahābhārata as it now stands is not primarily the account of the great war but of the great yajña [the snake sacrifice]'.

The sarpasattra yajña and the treatment of the nāgas by the Aryans is indicative of evil practices in Aryan society. This is apparent in the framework of the nāga sacrifice and also in the individual myths within this framework. The basis and consequence of nāga persecution can be traced to the *Ṛg Veda*, in which there are many references to Aryan usurpation of the wealth of the nāgas. Then, the transformation of the nāgas in the Smṛti literatures, especially as it is delineated in the Mahābhārata, makes them more of a metaphor for the concept of 'the other'. Hence, the persecution against them is more symbolic; but, together, these factors have contributed to myth-based traditions of discrimination and subjugation.

Unlike the nāgas, who are victims, the asuras in the Mahābhārata are portrayed as perpetrators of evil because they are assumed to embody the quality of evil. However, it is important to note that the appellative 'asura' is not used in the Mahābhārata for everyone who displays this quality. The main perpetrators of evil in the Mahābhārata are postulated to be the Kauravas, specifically Duryodhana, and the main cause for his culpability is attributed not so much to his qualities of asura-ness but to his essential nature of being an asura; hence, his equivalency to evil is established as a priori. Duryodhana's actions are considered those of an asura because he is born an asura (although in a non-asura family), and everything he does to oppose the Pāṇḍavas is deemed as evil, hence establishing the Pāṇḍavas as the diametrically opposing, a priori good. Asura, then, is the negative pole of the polarity of good and evil, and, for this reason, for Hindus, 'demons are dangerous by definition regardless of intention' (O'Flaherty 1988: 98).

However, these absolute claims of good and evil (asura = evil and deva = good) cannot be presumptive, because, in Hindu mythology, evil itself is indeterminate; it is neither an absolute value nor is it an unethical one. Therefore, the term, as an epithet or as an adjectival, is a misnomer, because, in actuality, the asura is not even part of the ethical framework of the Mahābhārata, let alone a perpetrator of evil. If, on the other hand, 'asura' is to be seen as a stand-alone term, denoting debased or unethical behaviour, then every character in the Mahābhārata (including the divine Kṛṣṇa) is an asura at some point or another.

In actuality, the word 'asura' cannot be considered as a part of the good and evil paradigm; the misconception creates many ambiguities in moral and ethical codes. Hence, applying this term to people (such as Duryodhana) to describe their 'evil' actions warps the moral–immoral equation of not just those characters but also, by comparison, of the good characters. The very etymology and definitions of the word explain how it suffered degradation from the earliest Ṛg Vedic times to the Mahābhārata. Although the word is as old as (if not older than) the *Ṛg Veda*, its meaning underwent many changes. Each change, while adding a new perspective, retained an association—through myth and allusion—to the preceding meanings, many of which were non-ethical. Hence, it cannot be considered simply in its stand-alone definition, as indicated in the Mahābhārata.

Furthermore, the concept of asura in various asura myths in the Mahābhārata can be interpreted to show that the asuras were a part of Aryan society and not representative of an a priori. However, because of the debasement of the word 'asura', they 'fell' from grace. This fall created a mythos of evil for which they were held responsible, and, consequently, victimized.

To understand this metaphor of persecution that both the nāgas and the *asuras* create, it must be determined who or what were the nāgas and the asuras—were they real people or simply an Aryan concept of symbolic evil? However, even if they were a mythical construct, the very idea that their victimization becomes archetypal speaks of a culture in which evil became systemic.

THE NĀGAS

Who are the Nāgas?

The question of whether the nāgas were a real people or only a symbolic idea of the Aryan concept of evil must be dealt with before any causative problems of evil or flaws in the epic tradition can be defined. Records from early Kashmir indicate that there were tribal people—Nāgas—who were aboriginal inhabitants in that region; it is quite possible that some of the first encounters of the second wave of Aryans (who were moving westward from the Indus Valley) with the indigenous people may have occurred in Kashmir. Citing the *Nīlmata Purāṇa*, R.L. Raina (1993: 24) suggests that the 'Aryans penetrated into Kashmir from the southern routes, while the valley was already inhabited by the Nagas and the Pishachas, who did not see eye to eye with each other'. Raina gives evidence, dating back to 2400 BCE, of indigenous settlements in Kashmir in Burzahom, 16 kilometres east of Srinagar. He explains that Aryan advance into the valley did not go unprotested in the beginning, but, as time passed, the Aryans assimilated the local traditions. He also gives an example of 'Chandradeva, the first enterprising Aryan settler, who had to accept all the conditions laid down by the Naga chief Nila' (Raina 1993: 24). D.R. Bali also cites from *Nīlmata Purāṇa* to explain that the people in Jammu and Kashmir had a Nāga connection. He gives the example of a Nāga chief exiled from Kashmir to Jammu, who was allotted rulership of Mount Usiraka in Jammu by Kashmir's Nāga king, Vibhunga. As evidence, Bali (1993: 29) mentions that, in the Śiva temple of Sudh Mahadeva in Jammu, a broken *triśūl* has been found with the name 'Vibhunga' inscribed on it in Sanskrit. It is believed that this triśūl is from 1000 BCE (Sudh Mahādeva),[2] which was around the time when the Aryans were settling in the area.

J. Vogel (1995: 215) also connects the Nāgas to kingship in Kashmir and suggests an association between their historiography and mythology. He cites an example of the illustrious Rājā Lalitaditya of Kashmir, who boasted of belonging to the line of Nāgarāja Karkoṭaka, a serpent king mentioned in the Mahābhārata as a devotee of Baladeva, who himself is considered a reincarnation of Śeṣa Nāga. This perception, that nāgas were actually the Nāga tribe and that they were not only indigenous to Kashmir but were also related to demi-gods, is furthered by R.L. Raina, who points out that 'nāga' in Kashmiri means 'a water-spring', and each spring has a tutelary deity in the form of a nāga. 'This is a distinct feature of the Kashmiri Nagas and it may lead us to suppose that the Nagas [were] settled around water springs in mountainous valleys' (1993: 23).

In fact, the popular folk legend from the *Rājataraṃgiṇī* about Kashmir's formation not only situates Nāgas in Kashmir but also credits Kashmir's very creation to the relationship between nāgas, *ṛṣis*, and

[2] Sudh Mahādeva is one of the most ancient Śiva temples in Jammu. It houses a black Śiva *linga*, a triśūl, and a mace believed to be Bhima's.

gods. According to this legend, the Nāgas lived in Lake Satisar. When a demon called Jaladeo (perhaps an Aryan enemy), began to harass them, their father, Ṛṣi Kaśyapa, did penance and acquired Viṣṇu's help to dewater the lake and destroy the demon. The Nāgas called this land Kaśyapa-mir (which corrupted into Kashmir). Thus, all this evidence, whether it is folkloric or archaeological, suggests that Nāgas were not only real people, but also indigenous inhabitants, and may have been natives of Kashmir.

Aside from determining the humanness of the nāgas, this evidence also strongly suggests the reason why the Vedic Aryans could have borne animosity towards the Nāga people, and it indicates the crimes they could have committed against them. It can be surmised that the Aryans, migrating to areas that were already inhabited, desired to acquire the resources of the land but the indigenous people opposed the incursion. Therefore, the Aryans seized what they desired by whatever means possible.

Scholarly evidence not only suggests that the Aryans were emigrants, but also validates the culpability of the Aryans as that of a foreign community usurping the wealth of the original inhabitants. No matter the perspective—migrationist or indigenous Aryanist—the inflictions that the Nāga people suffered at the hands of the Vedic Aryans is quite evident; thus, it can be said that the basis of injuring nāgas was established long before the Mahābhārata's snake sacrifice, in which King Janamejaya tried to exterminate them. In fact, as Christopher Minkowski (2007: 386) says, the story of the snake sacrifice has 'more Vedic precedent than the Bhārata story itself'.

This early Aryan–Nāga enmity over the earth's resources of land and water is not difficult to believe, especially in the context of the migrationist view, because the Aryans, as new arrivals to the land, needed these resources for their survival. The enmity turned to violence that the Aryans perpetrated against the Nāgas, because the Nāgas proved to be a daunting enemy, and this practice of persecution became the bedrock for later interpolations and myth-making. Sukumari Bhattacharji (2000: 256) explains:

> Enemy chiefs ... can withhold the water supply to an invading enemy and thus virtually create the conditions of a siege (for the invader) .... In later mythology cosmic interpretations were given to what was perhaps originally a military situation. This became [Indra's] cosmic function, when his military prowess had ceased to retain the former glory because the invaders were already settled in the land. Once they had become a peacefully settled agricultural people, the memory of early warfare became transmuted to suit the needs of the day'.

Bhattacharji (2000: 253) equates asuras and nāgas in the context of Vedic Indra's battles. However, this synonymy discounts the evidence which indicates that, unlike the Nāgas, the asuras were either one of the five Aryan tribes or, at least, within the Aryan fold. It is also important to note that, in epic times, the terms nāga and asura were not at all equivalent. In fact, in epic literatures, nāgas gain ascendency, while the asuras suffer degradation.

Perhaps the reason Bhattacharji and other scholars see an equivalency of nāga and asura is because of the Vedic asura chief, Varuṇa, and his association with water, rivers, and *māyā*—aspects that were also related to the serpents. After Varuṇa's degradation from being the divine asura and keeper of *ṛta* in the *Ṛg Veda* to simply lord of waters, he lives with his consort, Varuṇī, beneath the waters, where he is surrounded by serpents of all variety—the most notorious and the most pious, such as Takṣaka, Airāvata, Padma, and Vāsuki—who pay homage to Varuṇa in his underwater palace (*Mbh* 2.9.1–14).

It is also possible that the animosities the Aryans bore the asuras and Nāgas came to be seen as equivalent, because both were a threat to the Aryans. Hence, in Vedic literatures, they were both seen as practitioners of *an-ṛta* which, in Vedic Aryan vocabulary, was an evil against them. As Briffault (quoted in Patil 1974: 33) explains, 'power in egalitarian primitive society is intrinsically an evil thing; it is synonymous with power to harm'.

Using Briffault's perspective, it can be said that the Vedic Aryans saw the Nāgas as 'evil', because they seemed to have power equal to Aryan divines. Case in point is Vṛtra, possibly a Nāga, who matched

Indra in strength and surpassed him in wealth. Jaan Puhvel (1989: 50) calls Vṛtra a 'monstrous adversary', and his explanation of the word 'Vṛtra' lends meaning to the adversarial relationship between Aryans and Nāgas.

Puhvel (1989: 50) states that 'Vṛtra's name is an original abstract noun...from the same root ["vr" meaning "to confine" or "to restrict"] that yields Varuṇa, thus literally "Confinement", and then actively "Confiner, Obstructer". Monier-Williams (2005: 922) also defines 'vṛtrī' as one who 'keeps back or wards off' or an 'expeller'. Puhvel (1989: 50–1) goes on to explain that 'confinement' can be for good or evil, just as māyā, which both Varuṇa and Vṛtra use. Since Varuṇa uses it to maintain ṛta, his māyā and 'confinement' can be considered for good, whereas Vṛtra's māyā and confinement is to bring evil. Puhvel's explanation of the etymology of Vṛtra and Varuṇa can be used to arrive at a new understanding of Vṛtra. It is possible that Vṛtra was not the name of a single Aryan enemy but a generic name to refer to the quality of someone who 'confines' a desired object, is powerful, and hence a threat. For example, in the famous Indra vs. Vṛtra Ṛg Vedic myth, although Vṛtra is not specifically defined as a nāga, his 'shoulder-less' (*RV* 1.32.5, O'Flaherty 1981: 150) and 'encircling' (*RV* 4.18.6, O'Flaherty 1982: 142) characteristics could simply have been a metaphor to describe him as similar to a serpent who coils around something he wishes to protect or confine.

The idea that Vṛtra was a name used for someone powerful, perhaps a chief of a Nāga tribe, is further evidenced in other Vedic hymns, in which nāgas oppose the Aryans in the way Vṛtra does. For instance, in the *Ṛg Veda*, many of Indra's battles to release the waters are against Ahi—a term that has cognate Greek forms 'Ophis' and 'Echis', meaning serpent (Bhattacharji 2000: 255). As an example, in the following hymn, Indra slays Ahi to cleave the waters from the mountain.[3]

[3] Ralph Griffith, in his translation of the *Ṛg*, translates Ahi as the serpent dragon.

> I will declare the manly deeds of Indra, the first that he achieved, the Thunder-wielder. He slew the Dragon [Ahi], then disclosed the waters, and cleft the channels of the mountain torrents.[4] (*RV* 1.32.1)

And in this hymn, Indra once again slays Ahi to free the seven rivers.

> Who slew the Dragon [Ahi], freed the Seven Rivers, and drove the kine forth from the cave of Vala, Begat the fire between two stones, the spoiler in warrior's battle, he, O men, is Indra. (*RV* 2.12.3)

In these hymns, Ahi could have been a term used to refer to the nāgas, whose chief was the 'confiner' or Vṛtra, who opposed the Aryans' acquisition of water and was a 'roadblock on the path of Aryan progress' (Puhvel 1989: 50). His elimination was necessary for Aryan prosperity. In addition, Puhvel (1989: 50) states that the good and evil of 'confinement', too, depends on who is jailed and who is the jailor; hence suggesting that while Indra may have been fighting Vṛtra for Aryan interest, Vṛtra, who became the Aryan victim, may have been represented as the evil criminal because he opposed Aryan interest by holding back the water, and his power threatened to bring harm to them.

The case that the Nāgas were seen as evil by the Aryans, because they were powerful and not easy to subjugate, can be strengthened by examining the metaphor that snakes may have created in the Aryan mind. The Aryans may have known snakes in their own land of origin. J. Vogel (1995: 6) points out that the word 'nāga' is Indo-Germanic in origin, which, from a migrationist perspective, suggests that the Aryans already had a vocabulary for snakes. In addition, the Aryans may have also encountered venomous snakes in India; therefore, when they met powerful human adversaries who they felt reflected the attributes of the reptiles that were baneful to their existence, they saw an equation. This then may have contributed to the Aryans creating

[4] Quotations from the *Ṛg Veda* are from 1896 translation by Ralph T.H Griffith, *The Hymns of the RG Veda*, unless otherwise noted.

myths, not only about enemy Nāgas but also about their own gods, who they invested with powerful qualities similar to or superior to the nāgas so that they could combat the foe. For example, in some Ṛg Vedic hymns, Vedic Agni is given snake-like qualities. 'He [Agni] in mid-air's expanse hath golden tresses; a raging serpent, like the rushing tempest' (*RV* 1.79.1).

Coomaraswamy (1935: 278) points out that this fire is 'more correctly, Agni ab intra as Ahi Budhnya, Śuṣṇa, the "flesh-eating, man-hurting" (*kravyāt ...puruṣa-reṣaṇah*) Agni of Atharva Veda 3.21.8–9, against whom we have the prayer *mo aham ṛṣam* "may I not be hurt" in *RV* 10.18.13.' Perhaps the bite that the venomous serpents delivered, which, in some instances, was capable of delivering instantaneous death, was seen by the Aryans as lethal as Agni's flesh-eating. For the Aryans, Agni's heat was a result of his *tējas*, and they may have felt that the serpents possessed the same tējas (Vogel 1995: 15).

The Nāgas also may have been seen to possess qualities that were beyond Aryan comprehension—qualities that bordered on divine mysteries. For example, Sukumari Bhattacharji (2000: 149) suggests that the Nāgas probably lived 'on the other side of the forest,' or it can be surmised, from Ṛg Vedic hymns, that they lived beyond water bodies. In other words, the Nāgas lived in places that were hard for the Aryans to traverse. These were probably dense forests and deep water bodies that the Aryans were afraid to cross, but the Nāgas, who were more familiar with the lay of the land, were able to not only cross but also disappear into these areas after executing surprise attacks. This ability to disappear is what the Aryans equated with the serpents that vanished into the earth after delivering a death bite and becoming 'invisible', and this was, perhaps, the most mystifying, because it suggested a quality of māyā or illusion. In the Aryan mind, this was a divine attribute, albeit of a dark nature; therefore, in their myths, both Varuṇa and Indra were made to possess māyā—an attribute, which, significantly in earlier hymns, meant wisdom, extraordinary or supernatural power, and later came to mean illusion, unreality, deception, fraud, trickery, sorcery, witchcraft, and magic (Bhattacharji 2000: 35).

Another cause of envy bordering on awe may have been the Aryan belief that the Nāgas had the secret to immortality, because the serpents, who the Nāgas resembled, were able to cast off their skin and live in a new body, thus giving the impression of immortality. And the Aryans wanted to possess this secret. In fact, a hymn in the *Ṛg Veda* compares a serpent gliding out of his skin to a stream of soma, the elixir which was seen as a means to attain immortality:

> Sing forth to Pavamana skilled in holy song: the juice is flowing onward like a mighty stream. He glideth like a serpent from his ancient skin... (*RV* 9.86.44)

Vogel (1995: 14) gives another example from the *Tāṇḍya-mahābrāhmaṇa* of how the serpents' ability to discard their skin made them equal to the deathless Ādityas:

> By this sacrifice, verily, the serpents have conquered death; death is conquered by those who will perform this sacrifice. Therefore, they cast off their old skin; and having cast the same, they creep out of it. The serpents are Ādityas; like unto the splendor of the Ādityas is the splendor of those who perform this sacrifice.

These qualities that rendered the snakes immortal, full of tējas, and *māyāvi* are what made the Nāgas not only more powerful than the Vedic Aryans but also more wealthy, because they possessed treasures that were beyond material assets. All this power and wealth is what the Aryans desired to 'steal' from the Nāgas so that they could empower themselves and their divines.

Conversely, these were also qualities that, perhaps, came to be seen as evil, because they made the Aryans feel threatened, and, consequently, inferior. Therefore, to overcome this sense of inferiority, they not only attacked the Nāgas and stole from them, but they also hailed their own actions as victories. And to expiate the wrongfulness of their actions, they attributed them to divine help. For example, in the following hymn from the *Rg Veda*, Indra is praised for helping his worshippers kill their enemies and win riches:

> For success in this battle where there are prizes to be won, we will invoke the generous Indra, most manly and brawny, who listens and gives help in combat, who kills enemies and wins riches. (*RV* 3.31.22, O'Flaherty 1981:154)

And, in this following myth, Indra helps the worshippers overcome weakness so that they can subdue the enemy:

> We call on thee, King. Mighty amid the Gods, Ruler of men, to succor us All that is weak in us, Excellent God, make firm, make our foes easy to subdue. (*RV* 6.46.6)

Aryan envy of the Nāgas may actually have destroyed the Nāgas and their way of life and, in a broader sense, may also have brought about the end of the Indus Valley Civilization. D.D. Kosambi (quoted in Thapar 1995: 101) states, 'The decline of the Indus civilization is attributed to the Aryans who destroyed the agricultural system by breaking the embankments' (which were perhaps, created by the Nāgas), which action, he maintains, 'is symbolically referred to in the Ṛgvedic descriptions of Indra destroying Vṛtra, and releasing the waters'.

Scholars like Promatha Nath Mullick and M.N Dutt (1934: 35) suggest that the Nāgas may have been deities of the indigenous people, and the *Ṛg* Vedic killing of Vṛtra by Indra could have been a symbolic killing between divines. This usurping is even more destructive than the material theft of land, water, and wealth, because it strikes at the very edifice of cosmic order—a society's connection with the mythic divine. Thus, Aryan actions destroyed not just the land and its resources, but also, perhaps, a belief system about which we may never learn.

There is much speculation about the pre-Aryan, indigenous theology of the Indus Valley people and whether the solarity of the Aryan male divines may have supplanted the lunar Earth/Mother goddess and possibly also a male nature god.[5] The extant literature from those

[5] Some early scholars suggest that this was Śiva's Paśupata form, but many more scholars have expressed doubt that this figure in the Indus Valley seals is a Śiva prototype.

early times is only Aryan, since the Indus Valley seals are yet to be deciphered, and it eulogizes mostly solar male gods. This indicates not only a one-dimensional gender-biased pantheon, but also that the Aryans negated the gods of the indigenous people (so as to install their own cosmology and the supremacy of their own divines).

In the Mahābhārata, too, there is no real evidence of Nāga deities or the Nāga cosmos, or even the Aryans' persecution of the Nāgas, except in the snake sacrifice. It is also not clear whether there were actually humans belonging to the Nāga race in epic times, because in the myths of the Mahābhārata, the nāgas appear both as humans and as serpents, and since myth-making is most often symbolic and metaphoric, it is hard to determine whether the stories in the myths are about Nāgas who were human, about humans who were serpent-like in appearance and/or attributes, or about serpents who were human-like. A good example of this ambiguity is the story of Śeṣa Nāga in *Ādi Parva* (*Mbh* 1.36.1–24): Śeṣa Nāga, unlike the other sons of Kadrū, who are of 'wicked hearts', is a virtuous and pious ascetic, practising great penances. When Brahmā sees him 'with knotted hair, clad in rags, his flesh, his skin and sinews dried up [looking like a snake]', he asks him what he is doing and why. Śeṣa tells him that he wants to discard his body so that he is not associated with his younger brothers. Brahmā then gives him a boon that he will hold the earth steady 'for the good of all creatures', and he directs Śeṣa to go underneath the earth through a passage that Earth herself will forge for him. Śeṣa enters a hole in the earth and, going to the other side, takes on the duty of keeping the earth steady. Clearly, in this myth, Śeṣa's appearance, after he spends years in penance, becomes like a serpent's, and the fact that he is able to burrow into the earth is a serpent's characteristic. This myth suggests that Śeṣa is a human being with serpent-like qualities, which in turn suggests that there may have been a Nāga race—or, at least, a brethren community of Nāgas—a people that may have had physical attributes that resembled serpents. But, on the other hand, the fact that Śeṣa is born to Kadrū, the mother of serpents, creates ambiguity about his humanness.

Another example of this cryptic nature of nāga reference in the Mahābhārata is provided by Śiva and his association with nāgas, but this becomes integral to the portrayal of his divinity. For example, Śiva's Paśupata weapon is a serpent. When Arjuna, in his dream, visits Śiva to ask him for this weapon so that he can destroy Abhimanyu's killer, he and Kṛṣṇa see a 'terrible serpent' and another 'foremost of serpents possessing a thousand hoods...vomiting terrible flames' (*Mbh* 7.81.13).

When Arjuna and Kṛṣṇa praise Śiva, the two serpents assume the form of a bow and arrow (*Mbh* 7.81. 82). In addition to using serpents as weapons, Śiva is Nīlakaṇṭha because he swallows the deadly poison Halāhala during the churning of the ocean (*Mbh* 1.18. 41–2), and since poison is the tējas of serpents, by swallowing it, Śiva takes this tējas within him and becomes one with them. Thus, in these myths, although the human element of nāgas is missing, it can be inferred that the serpents were either themselves deities of a community whose divinity Śiva assumes or that Śiva himself was a divine for a people who were nāga-like; that is why Śiva embodies their most powerful and transcendent qualities.

This equation that Śiva has with the nāgas could be one reason why he was considered 'other' and, thus, outside the fold of the epic pantheon until much later, as suggested in the Śiva-Sati myth of Dakṣa's sacrifice.

This concept of 'the other' is also the nature of nāgas in Vedic myths, and this otherness became the metaphor of evil in the Aryan mind, which ultimately became nāga legacy in the epic and is portrayed in the serpent myth cycle and the snake sacrifice. This legacy, along with their assets, were the reasons for their near annihilation in a sacrificial ritual, through which the sacrificers hoped to acquire the wealth and destroy 'the other'. How possession through extermination can be accomplished with a ritual sacrifice is explained by Mircea Eliade. He says that a sacrifice is a 'taking over' or an establishing of a new 'fixed point' or a sacred space: 'possession of a territory...becomes legally valid through the erection of a fire altar consecrated to Agni...; the space of the altar becomes a sacred space' (Eliade 1959: 32). He further explains that 'the erection of an altar to Agni is nothing but the reproduction—on the microcosmic scale—of the Creation (*Śatapatha Brāhmaṇa* 1.9,2,29, etc.). Hence the erection of the fire altar—which alone validates taking possession of a new territory—is equivalent to a cosmogony' (Eliade 1959: 33). This 'taking possession' of the nāga world is not only the key motif in the entire nāga myth cycle in the Mahābhārata, it also signifies a real-world societal paradigm.

INTERPRETING EVIL IN NĀGA MYTHS

Utanka and the Usurping of the Nāga World

There are a number of myths within the framework of the snake sacrifice in the Mahābhārata that depict Aryan persecution of the nāgas, but the myth which makes this Aryan usurpation of the nāga sacred space and cosmos most evident is the myth of Utanka (*Mbh* 1.3.1-187). This is an elaborate myth with many layers, each one yielding immense meaning and lending credence to the argument that the nāgas' world was wrested by the Aryans. This myth is also rich with symbolism that suggests many problems of evil, but its main focus is how the nāgas are the 'other' and their world was one that the Aryans hoped to control and subjugate, or, as Mircea Eliade (1959: 32) says, to 'cosmocize' in their own traditions. Eliade also states that this 'taking possession' is given a divine quality to justify it, because 'the cosmocization of unknown territory is always a consecration; to organize a space is to repeat the paradigmatic work of the gods'.

In the Utanka myth, a key symbol of this cosmocization is the stick that Utanka uses to dig a hole in the ground where Takṣaka has disappeared with the gold earrings Utanka had obtained from King Pauṣya's queen to give to his guru's wife as his *guru dakṣiṇā*. This stick represents a sacred pole. Explaining the meaning of this stick/pole, Eliade (1959: 33) says that one way to cosmocize the territory is to plant a sacred pole to establish the fixed point, and it is around this point that the territory can be anointed. The prevalence of cosmocizing a territory with a pole is so significant in creating a new sovereign order that even the Kuru dynasty in the Mahābhārata is established through it: Indra gives Vasu, king of Cedi, a bamboo pole to erect, so as to 'protect the honest and peaceful', and Vasu plants it and worships Indra (*Mbh* 1.63.15). This is the fixing of a new cosmic order, and this order is the orientation for the Kurus: Vasu's semen, spilled from his desire for his wife, Girikā, is swallowed by an *apsarā* in the form of a fish who then gives birth to twins—a boy, Matsya, and a girl, Matsyagandhā, who later becomes Satyavatī—and Satyavatī becomes the matriarch of the Kuru family (*Mbh* 1.63.37–78). Thus, the Kuru cosmic universe is created by connection with Indra, and then the order is sustained by the passage that is created from the planting of Indra's pole, which creates a bridge between the worlds.

Therefore, this pole not only sustains the cosmic order, but it is also instrumental in building a bridge to the 'other side', which can be either the much-desired world of one's own divine above or the underworld of the abhorred 'other' below. Eliade (1959: 33) also explains that the sacred pole must be kept intact in order to channelize the communication between the worlds; the pole's destruction would lead to catastrophe and chaos.

In the Utanka myth in the Mahābhārata, the stick that Utanka is using breaks; this heralds a loss of Aryan sacred space and order, but Indra immediately replaces Utanka's broken stick with his thunderbolt—a sacred pole of energy. Hence, Indra not only prevents the 'chaos' (in the Aryan construct) which could have resulted from Utanka's broken stick, but he also creates a divine bridge to the other side. Descending through this bridge, Utanka becomes instrumental in Aryanizing the other side. Thus, this myth is about the invasion of the 'other's' sacred space by the Aryans and the establishment of their own symbolic cosmogony. The point where Takṣaka has disappeared into the ground after stealing the earrings is the 'fixed point' or ṛta of the Nāgas, and Utanka digging the stick at this very sacred fixed point is the usurpation of the others' cosmic order by creating an Aryan world.

When Utanka's stick breaks and Indra intervenes with his thunderbolt, it becomes the perfect symbol of Aryan hierophany, and through its piercing, the other side is consecrated. Hence, what Utanka finds on the other side are parallels in time and space to the Aryan world above: Dhāta and Vidhāta, who are weaving a cloth with threads of black and white to represent the universe and the beings that inhabit it; six boys, representing seasons, turning a wheel that has twelve spokes marked by twenty-four divisions to mark the lunar changes; even a parallel Indra wearing a black cloth to display the truth and untruth of the world. Indra is able to invade this world, and his purpose is also clear: when he grants Utanka control of this world, he consecrates it with the agni he creates from his horse's nostrils. In fact, the horse Indra is riding is Uccaiḥśravas, a form of Agni himself, and the fire that Agni emits is the sacrificial fire to destroy the nāga world and replace it with Indra's Aryanization.

Hence, by sacrificing the nāga world in the consecrating flames of Agni, Indra and Utanka threaten to not only replace the nāga cosmos with an Aryan one, but also to exterminate the nāgas, unless the creatures of the other world comply with Utanka's demand of returning the gold earrings that Takṣaka has stolen. Sure enough, Takṣaka returns the earrings to save his race, if not their way of life.

What is even more significant about the Utanka myth is that it echoes every other genocidal sacrifice in the epic: the burning of the Khāṇḍava in which Arjuna and Kṛṣṇa slaughter every creature living in it; the demolition of earth caused in the churning of the ocean; and, most importantly, the carnage of the Bhārata War. Although the latter two annihilations are not consecrated by a fire altar; both of them can be seen as sacrificial: the churning of the ocean is made a sacrifice by the planting of Mount Mandara as a sacred pole, and the Bhārata War is a 'sacrifice of weapons', complete with the symbolism of officials like *adhvaryu, udgātṛ, hotṛ,* and *sadasyas,* and items like the sacred ladle, ghee, mantras, and *kuśa* grass (*Mbh* 5.141.30–46).

What the Utanka myth reveals about the epic Aryans is that even as they emerged from the atheistic, amoral Vedic system into a dharma-based, theistic society, they carried with them tendencies that the new dharma construct would classify as evil, such as extreme violence, as perpetrated in the cited incident. While such actions in Vedic times were absolved by the ṛta of ritual sacrifice; in the epic period, when sacrifice was replaced by *vidhi* and individual actions became a matter of personal accountability, this violence became an immoral act of *adharma*. It also thoroughly violated the new, evolving general ethics of *ahiṁsā* that the epic continually touts. Moreover, considering that in the narrative's sequence, the snake sacrifice occurred after the Great War, the evil of hiṁsā against the nāgas becomes even more inexcusable because, by this time, the ideals of non-violence had already been incorporated into Aryan societal codes. Therefore, not only did the paradigm of the Utanka myth promote violence against the 'other', it also resurrected evil practices that the system had already expunged.

Vinatā and Kadrū: Subjugation of the Feminine

Another myth that is not only archetypal but is also replete with mythical, symbolic, and sociological evil is the frame myth in the snake sacrifice cycle of Kadrū and Vinatā and their wager (*Mbh* 1.14.17, 21–35, and 37–58). One of the key symbolic interpretations of this long myth is that of wresting power from a feminine divine and/or an Earth Goddess to give to a 'new' male god, thus creating prototypes of cosmogonic annexation and female suppression.

According to the Great Goddess theorists, (Marija Gimbutas, Johann Jakob Bachofen, Sir James Frazer, et al.), the serpent was one of the significant symbols of the Earth Goddess, because its natural inclinations represented many of her attributes, such as her unending natural cycle (of menstruation). This was considered equivalent to immortality, and was mirrored in the snake's shedding of skin, which in turn embodied the cyclical and triple nature of creation—birth, death, and re-birth—as opposed to the linearity of the life and death of male gods. Another such element was the snake's ability to live in three realms: burrow in the ground, swim in the water, and live on land, which symbolized the triple role of archetypal divine triad. Also, and most importantly, since the Earth Goddess was constantly present with man—in the animals he hunted and the earth he tilled—and he communicated with her at his own level of existence—literally and figuratively—similarly, the serpents' earth-/water-bound existence exemplified this close relationship.

In the male-god era, on the other hand, the intimate relationship between humans and divine severed, because the divine was no longer in close proximity to them; he became distant, represented as a fearsome being living somewhere above and, of course, only the males claimed to know the secrets of reaching him. One of these secrets was flight (since the gods were up and above, flight represents man's transcendence to reach divinity). In the snake sacrifice myths, the king of birds, Garuḍa, is a symbol of this transcendence.

As male power became dominant, the Great Goddess and her symbol, the serpent, were declared threatening demons and they were ousted from power and relegated to the underworld. There are many examples of degradation of the serpent Earth Goddess in world mythologies: for example, the Norse Jörmungandr; the Greek Ophion; and the Judaic and Christian Serpent in the Garden of Eden.

Another degradation of the mother goddess and condemnation of her symbols can be deduced from the archetypal symbol of the moon. The moon was associated with soma, which, by virtue of being an elixir of immortality, was connected to the goddess, and consequently, to the serpents. Heinrich Zimmer (1972: 60) reasons how this inter-symbolism came about: the heat in India was often life threatening, and the moon was a refreshing element. Also, since the moon controlled the waters and water sustained life, it was naturally *Amṛta* (a-mṛta—not dead). Thus, dew or water was soma, and the moon was its cup. Earth goddess theorists also suggest that the moon may have been one of the earliest symbols of the goddess, its waxing and waning representing women's monthly cycles.

However, after the linear traditions of the male god became the norm, the lunar divinities were associated with darkness and relegated as 'demonic', while their godly attributes were usurped by the solar gods. A good example of this is the Vedic dark goddess Nirṛti who, scholars believe, was a pre-Aryan earth goddess associated with the moon. Shard Patil (1974: 32) suggests that not only was Nirṛti a pre-Aryan goddess, but she was also highly auspicious in pre-Aryan society. He gives an example of the non-brāhmanical records in the *Kalpa-sūtra* of Mahāvira's passing on the most auspicious night of the new moon called 'Devānandā surnamed Nirṛti'. However, when the Aryans adopted Nirṛti, they made her, her symbols, and her rituals a dark juxtaposition to offset their own goddesses of light (who only played a minor role in Vedic cosmogony) so that they could ensure their own male ascendency. Hence, while Aditi was made the mother of the Ādityas, Nirṛti was relegated to dark designs of death and calamity. One of the main reasons for slandering the lunar earth goddess was that she possessed soma or immortality, and she was also the goddess of fertility. (In the *Ṛg Veda* she is married to Soma, who is called the king of plants [*RV* 10.97.18].) According to the *Śatapatha Brāhmaṇa*, the new moon is the occasion of the marriage between Earth and the king of soma, who is the moon, and since the old moon dies and a new one is born, it is said that within death is immortality (Patil 1974: 37). Thus, the Aryans degraded the earth goddess and wrested the soma from her to give to their own solar god.

The Great Goddess theories may be conjectural, but in the Vinatā and Kadrū myth, all of these elements of earth mother and her persecution are vividly apparent. Kadrū, by virtue of being the mother of serpents, can be seen as an earth goddess, who the *Taittirīya Saṃhitā* refers to as '*Sarpa-rajnī*' (cited in Patil 1974: 52).

Monier-Williams (2005: 248) defines Kadrū as tawny brown (the colour of the earth), and points out that according to the *Brāhmaṇas*, she is 'the earth personified'. In addition, Monier-Williams describes '*kadrū*' as a brown soma vessel, and says the word is related to legends about bringing down soma from the heavens. Kadrū is even referred to as 'Surasā' in the *Rāmāyaṇa* (*Śrīmad Vālmīki-Rāmāyaṇa* 1.144–51), a word that is defined by Monier-Williams (2005: 1234) as 'juicy,' 'well-flavored,' 'full of moisture'. All these meanings unquestionably make Kadrū the earth goddess and possessor of soma.

On the other hand, Vinatā is called Suparnī, mother of Suparna, another name for Garuḍa (*Mbh* 1.33:7, 24), a word for which Monier-Williams (2005: 1227) gives many meanings, all related to 'beautiful wings' or 'large birds of prey'. Vinatā is the mother of Garuḍa and Aruṇa, both of whom not only have the ability to fly, but are associated with solarity; hence, they represent the male god. Aruṇa is half-formed, because Vinatā breaks his gestation egg prematurely, but he flies to the sky to be the sun's heralder (*Mbh* 1.16.18–23); Vinatā's second son is Garuḍa, who, immediately after birth, not only has the ability to fly (*Mbh* 1.16.24)— and hence knows the secret of transcendence—but also becomes Vishnu's *vāhana*. Additionally, he is given the boon to be 'the eater of snakes' (*Mbh* 1.34.15). Aside from representing male power, Garuḍa is so empowered that he has to reduce his tējas so as not to burn the world in his divine agni (*Mbh* 1.24:2), thus displaying the condescending arrogance of the male divine who is benevolent to the world. Hence, Garuḍa is equated to Viṣṇu himself, who is a solar god and the embodiment of supreme maleness, divinity, and benevolence.

However, contrary to the male divine's seizure of the feminine divine's eminence in the serpent myth in the Mahābhārata, it is Kadrū who enslaves Vinatā through treachery for five hundred years. She coerces her serpent sons to braid themselves in the white tail of the divine horse, Uccaiḥśravas, so that she can win a wager against her sister. Most likely, the years of Vinatā's slavery signify the time it took the Aryans to replace the feminine divines of the indigenous people with their own solar male gods (the number of years can be considered mythical time). Moreover, the fact that Kadrū accomplishes Vinatā's bondage through devious means shows that the Aryans, who, aside from having a male-dominated pantheon, communicated with their gods through male brāhmins, considered the dominance of the feminine divine perverse and threatening. Thus, it is not surprising that when Garuḍa seeks to release his mother from enslavement, the result is the elevation of male gods and catastrophe for female power: In this myth, soma is guarded by two ferocious serpents in Indra's heaven, which clearly indicates that in the Aryan mind, the earth goddess knew the secret of immortality, or the knowledge of life, death, and renewal, and she guarded this secret fiercely. Therefore, to gain access to this soma, Garuḍa fights the serpents, and, shredding them to pieces, steals the soma (*Mbh* 1.33.1–10)—clearly a violent act of destroying the pre-eminence of the goddess to claim possession of her attributes.

To compound this violent theft, the goddess is alienated and made to suffer grave indignities. This is described in the myth when, on his way to earth, Garuḍa carves friendships with the male divines, Indra and Viṣṇu, and exchanges boons with them, thus not only strengthening the power of the male, but also creating a sort of exclusive 'males only' private club. And when Garuḍa does bring the soma to the serpents (which was the deal he had made with them to get his mother released from slavery), he places the bowl before them and sends them off for a ritual bath to purify themselves, but by the time they return, Indra, with whom Garuḍa has already planned this strategic deceit, swoops down and takes away the bowl. Hence, the serpents are reduced to merely licking the *kuśa* grass on which the bowl of soma had been placed, which further diminishes them, because their tongues become forked—a distortion for which they are forever reviled (*Mbh* 1.34:24). This alienation and powerlessness of the progeny of the feminine divine in a male-dominated system was a deliberate subjugation, and the subsequent shredding of their dignity was the final death-blow—a total degradation of the feminine, from which women have been suffering ever since.

This myth also has many reflections in the main story of the Mahābhārata, which further belittles women. It is obvious that Gāndhārī, the mother of a hundred sons, is a representation of the earth goddess, Kadrū, and her offspring, the Kauravas, typify the nāgas. She is the incarnation of goddess Matī (*Mbh* 1.67: 136), who Monier-Williams (2005: 783) defines as 'resolve', 'understanding', 'intelligence', and a daughter of Dakṣa and wife of Soma. Hence, not only is she associated with the earth goddess, but she also has the steadfast and sagacious qualities of the earth. And the fact that Gāndhārī blindfolds herself when she marries Dhṛtarāṣṭra, so as not to be superior to him in any way, indicates the feminine's surrender of her powers to the male. On the other hand, Kuntī is an image of Vinatā, because her sons are not only progeny of divine beings, but, like Garuḍa, they also have divine connections. Very similar to Garuḍa's friendship and male bonding with Viṣṇu and Indra, Arjuna has close relationships with Indra and Kṛṣṇa. And, just as this divinity facilitates Garuḍa's claim to dominance and sabotage of the serpents, so does the Pāṇḍavas' celestial relationship makes them sanctimonious and always contemptuous of the Kauravas. Considering these correlations, it can then be surmised that just as Garuḍa, with the help of divine treachery, is able to not only re-empower his mother but also keep the serpents bereft of the soma that was their birthright, so are the Pāṇḍavas, with the help of divine manipulations, able to gain the kingdom and keep the Kauravas bereft of the wealth that was theirs to begin with. In fact, in this correlation, some specific parallels can also be drawn. For example, when Gāndhārī attempts to make Duryodhana's body invincible by removing her blindfold and looking upon her son's naked body with the tējas of her vow, Kṛṣṇa, like Indra stealing the bowl of soma from the duped serpents, sabotages Duryodhana by misleading him into wearing a loincloth, thus rendering his groin area vulnerable to Bhīma's death blow.[6]

There are other examples in the main frame story of the Mahābhārata that mirror the Vinatā and Kadrū myth, and these also raise ethical questions about the standards that were established for the sanctity of women's social relationships and behaviours. For example, mother and child relationships are subverted by both mothers—Vinatā and Kadrū. Vinatā damages the wellbeing of her first born, Aruṇa, by forcing open the egg before its gestation period is completed; hence, Aruṇa is half formed when he is born. And Kadrū coerces her children to commit an act of treachery to cheat her sister by having her sons braid themselves into the tail of the white divine horse, Uccaiḥśravas, so that the horse appears black and she can win the wager against her sister. In the main narrative, too, although the culpability is reversed, the actions of the mothers are just as damning: Gāndhārī forces the birth of her sons by striking her belly with an iron rod, just to remain at par with Kuntī, who has already birthed

[6] This incident is not included in the Critical Edition or Devanāgri editions of the Mahābhārata. However, it is included in other popular folklore and the North Indian editions of the epic, where this incident ends *Bhāgavatyana* of the *Udyoga Parva*.

Yudhiṣṭhira (*Mbh* 1.115.10–14). In fact, the implication of the iron rod that Gāndhārī uses on her womb reaches beyond the subverted birth of the Kauravas. By using this iron rod to wittingly bring harm to her unborn children, Gāndhārī implements the destruction of her own race, which is, perhaps, a mythical exoneration of the Aryans from this heinous crime, because, in a reversal of Eliade's sacred pole symbolism of consecrating and sustaining a society, Gāndhārī's misuse of this iron rod violates its sacredness and use. Ironically, the evil use of this iron rod can also be intertextualized with 'the rod of punishment held by the celestials' (Mbh 16.1.18) that is 'born' as an iron bolt in the Vṛṣṇi clan and becomes the cause of Kṛṣṇa's destruction of his own race (*Mbh* 16.3.31–41).

To further degrade the feminine, even Kuntī, who is portrayed in the epic as the ideal mother of the sovereign male, violates her dharma as a mother. To keep her own good name, like Kadrū, she commits the evil of a grave untruth. By keeping the secret of Karṇa's birth to herself, she impels her five sons to commit the grievous sins of first denouncing their brother, then maligning him, and, finally, killing him. In fact, Kuntī's abandonment of Karṇa completely undermines the role of woman as nurturer.

The environment created by the degradation of women through the Kadrū and Vinatā myth brings to light certain other problems of evil in the tradition of the Mahābhārata, such as loss of dignity, and even identity, that the 'other' had to suffer just to survive. This is apparent from the ambiguity of why some nāgas, such as Vāsuki and Śeṣa, are not only considered saintly, but are also co-creators of the Aryan universe. Also, the snake sacrifice is halted and the surviving serpents are ultimately saved by these very brethren, Vāsuki, Ananta or Śeṣa, and, especially, Āstīka, a child of the brāhmin, Jaratkāru, and his serpent wife and sister of Vāsuki, also named Jaratkāru (*Mbh* 1.13.28–31, 1.14.1–7, 54, 55, 56). Āstīka is able to stop the massacre of his race because he introduces himself to Janamejaya and his priests at the sarpasattra, not as a nāga, nor as a nāga-brāhmin hybrid, but as a brāhmin, and he humbles himself to propitiate the king, in adherence to Aryan dharma. Āstīka's denial of his nāga identity is his desperation to secure the survival of his race, and it is obvious that this rescue is a last resort, because extinction is suggested by his mother's name: 'Jara' means 'wasted' and 'kāru' means 'huge,' which implies the impending extermination of the whole snake clan. Admittedly, his father's name is also Jaratkāru, but that is because he has reduced his body, which used to be huge, by 'wasting' it in penances of celibacy for his own merit (*Mbh* 1.40.4). This too implies the reduction of a clan, but unlike the snakes' dire threat of a genocide, the brāhmin Jaratkāru's race of Yāyāvara is dying because of his own adharmic choice.

Āstīka's propitiation shows that even though the serpents who are able to plead the snake case are followers of the Aryan dharma (as opposed to their own), they have to prove their good, or more appropriately, *ārya* behaviour to be allowed rights—even the right to life. Whereas, the brāhmin race is protected under Aryan law, even if members of this caste indulge in selfish and evil behaviour. Another example of this inequity is when ravenous Garuḍa is directed by his mother, Vinatā, to satisfy his hunger by consuming all the people in the low caste Niṣāda tribe but never to slay any brāhmin, 'although he maybe always engaged in sinful practices' (*Mbh* 1.29.71). Thus, clearly evident in these myths are Aryan discriminatory practices that became the norm: the powerful, although immoral, continue to thrive, whereas the powerless can only be allowed to survive if they play by the rules, even if they have to go against their *svadharma* and deny their identity.

The Snake Sacrifice Myth and Its Evil Implications

It can be argued that Āstīka's very existence and the fact that he is able to stop the snake sacrifice and save the snakes prove that Aryan society, during epic times, was becoming assimilative, and hybrid bloodlines (such as that of Āstīka) were being accepted. However, blood feuds, especially against those perceived as the 'other', were also very much a part of this society. In fact, genocide was gaining the new sanction of *dharmayuddha*—that is, a war against anyone who was perceived as a threat to one's *dharma, artha,* or *kāma*. A clear example is Arjuna's burning of the Khāṇḍava forest and forest creatures, which he undertakes as a pretext to fulfil his vow to Agni—his *kṣatriya* dharma—but the real reason, which is never revealed in the story, is that Khāṇḍava is the home of Takṣaka, king of serpents, and Arjuna's massacre is to usurp his wealth. This land, as Minkowski (1989: 414), quoting Baudhāyana, states, was not only another name for Indraprastha, the city that the Pāṇḍavas create after burning the Khāṇḍava forest, but also where the original Vedic sarpasattra took place.

Other examples of mass killings through a dharmayuddha in the Mahābhārata include Rāma Jamadagni's annihilation of the kṣatriyas, Aśvatthāman's night slaughter of the Pāṇḍavas, including his attempted foeticide of Uttarā and Abhimanyu's son, and, of course, the Bhārata War, which itself results in the complete massacre of the Kurus and Pāñcālas, and relationally, the Yādavas.

This theme of a genocidal dharmayuddha is not only a leitmotif in the epic, but it also leads to a whole cycle of vengeance and vindication. One peripheral tit-for-tat cycle of vengeance begins with the sisters Vinatā and Kadrū and is carried through by their progeny, the serpents and Garuḍa; this hostility between birds of prey and snakes has even become proverbial. The other, more significant, cycle of killings begins with Arjuna's evil action of burning the Khāṇḍava and killing Takṣaka's family; Takṣaka's son, Aśvasena, in turn, seeks vengeance from Arjuna in the war. Then, the cycle is furthered by the brāhmin boy Śṛngin, who curses Arjuna's grandson, Parikṣit, to be bitten by Takṣaka. On the micro-scale of this myth, Śṛngin evokes the on-again-off-again friend–foe hostility between brāhmins and kṣatriyas by cursing Raja Parikṣit, but, in actuality, in a master stroke, he brings the animosity between the Aryans and the nāgas to a head by naming Takṣaka as the assassin of Raja Parikṣit. Finally, in a full circle, Takṣaka kills Parikṣit, and Parikṣit's son Janamejaya burns all but a few snakes in the sarpasattra.

Another significant problem of evil in this genocidal sattra is that it occurs at that liminal time between two *yugas*, when a new order is just about to be established. Hence, the blood feud that fuels this sacrifice spans both yugas, and the massacre of the 'other' at the very outset of the new yuga is like a commandment that will guide this epoch. Also noteworthy is the manner in which this sacrifice is performed and for what purpose. Unlike sarpasattras of earlier times, such as those cited in the *Pañcavimśa-brāhmaṇa* and *Śrautasūtras*, where the rite was performed not to harm anyone, but to provide the sacrificers with benefits of wealth, sons, cattle, and victory over death (Minkowski 2007: 388–9); this snake sacrifice does not seem to be for any material or abstract gain; it is to kill all snakes. They are burnt, not because of any crimes they have committed, but only because they exist and are the 'others'. Hence, their elimination by the Aryans can be seen as a call to ethnic cleansing.

The purpose of the sattra in the Mahābhārata becomes more suspicious in light of the fact that it has the same structure as the 'ætiological myth' of sarpasattra, which Minkowski (1989: 414), referencing Baudhāyana, states was originally 'performed by the serpents themselves, who gained their poison and became biters (*daṃśuka*) as a result of it'. Considering that many of the names of nāgas who performed the first sattra are names of brāhmins and kṣatriya kings in the Mahābhārata, the objective of Janamejaya's snake sacrifice becomes even more suspect. For example, the brāhmin of the original sarpasattra was Dhṛtarāṣṭra Airāvata, and one of the adhvaryus was Janamejaya. Minkowski (1989: 415) also points out that sadasyas of the Mahābhārata sarpasattra—Vyāsa, Śamanṭhaka, Uddālaka, Śvetaketu, Asita Devala, Nārada, Pārvata, Ātreya, Kutighata, Vātsya Śrutaśravas, Kahoda, Devaśarma, Maudgala, and Śamasaubhara are 'the most Vedic of *brāhmins*'. These equivalents suggest that in the snake sacrifice, Janamejaya and his brāhmins hope to wipe out the serpents and assume their venomous power—a diabolic supplanting through the means of a consecrating fire altar.

It is clear that the sarpasattra in the Mahābhārata has a diabolic purpose, because it is necrophilic in execution—a practice, which, ironically, may even have been non-Aryan. This is suggested in the manner and appearance of the priests who perform the sacrifice at Janamejaya's behest: they are dressed in black, 'their eyes red from smoke, [they pour] ghee in the sacrificial fire, according to Vedic mantra' (*Mbh* 1.52.1). Minkowski (2007: 391) thinks that the black dress here could be associated to the Vrātyas of *Atharva Veda*, who were outside the Aryan fold and had their own ceremonies and sacrifices. Minkowski also suggests that this non-śrauta, *abhicāra* influence of sorcery in the snake sacrifice suggests an uncalled-for maliciousness.

This malevolent intent becomes more egregious when it is seen in the context of the elevation that the nāgas had gained in post-Vedic literature. While, in the earliest Vedic hymns, the serpents and their metaphors were mostly negative and, possibly, resulted from the threat that the serpents posed for the Aryans, in the later literatures, the characteristics of the serpents came to be seen as not just positive but also as representing superior warriorship. In these literatures, the Aryans acknowledged nāga power and elevated the nāgas to almost divine status. For example, Vogel (1995: 8) quotes a verse from the *Atharva Veda*: 'Homage to Asita, homage to Tiraśchirāji, homage to Svaja [and] Babhru, homage to god-people.' And he explains that 'The four terms, *asita* ('black'), *tiraśchirāji* ('cross-lines'), *svaja* ('adder'?), and *babhru* ('brown') ... are commonly explained as denoting certain extant species of serpents ... [and could be] personal names of snake-demons which apparently are associated with four quarters of the sky'. Vogel (1995: 10) further mentions that in the *Atharva Veda* the serpents are referred to as '*devajana*' and associated with *Gandharvas, Apsarās,* and *Yakśas.*

In the Upaniṣads the metaphor of a serpent even came to represent the highest metaphysical truth. For example:

> As an anthill lies a slough of a snake, dead and cast off, so does lie this body dead and cast off. Brāhmaṇa, the Alone, is this immortal breath non corporeal, the Light indeed is it. (quoted from *Bṛhadāraṇyaka Upaniṣad* 4.4.7 in Gupta 1991–2008: 1029)

In his commentary to this verse, Som Nath Gupta (1991–2008: 1030) explains that the person who is liberated emerges from his dead body just as a snake emerges from its skin. Hence, 'Living though in that body, the liberated one, that self of all, that "snake" of the symbolism, lives in every truth, without the body, no more connected to it'. The

Mahābhārata further uses the serpent as a metaphysical symbol of discarding evil:

> As the Ruru deer casting off its old horns or the snake casting off slough passes on without arresting notice, similarly a person who is unattached renounces all his sorrow. (*Mbh* 12.219.48)

There may have been many reasons why the serpents gained ascendency in the Mahābhārata. Since this is a liminal text reflecting a syncretism of the old and the new, the new social norms included mythical elements and divines that were not a part of Vedic Aryan traditions. These could have been in existence in the Indus Valley before the Aryans established themselves, but with their inclusion, Aryan society grew more secular and tolerant. For example, in this new order, there was a resurfacing of a powerful goddess, Devī (the Vedic goddesses, such as Uṣas, Aditi, Virāja, Vāc, Śacī, etc., were almost colourless), and Vedic divines, such as Indra and Varuṇa, were degraded to allow the accession of more secular gods like Viṣṇu. Another factor could have been exogamy, through which the non-Aryan partners could have brought their own beliefs into the ethos, and these, along with the principles of nonviolence advocated by the Aryans' own post-Vedic texts, such as the *Upaniṣads*, created an atmosphere of tolerance and coexistence. Then there was the heterodox influence of Buddhism and Jainism, which spread a different set of ideas. It can thus be assumed that the non-Aryan tribes that had opposed the Aryans in the early days had either assimilated with the Aryans, or at least become friendly over time. In fact, the ambiguity of the dhārmic nature of saintly nāgas like Vāsuki, Airāvata, and Śeṣa indicates that many of the Nāga tribal leaders had joined forces with the Aryans, adapted to their ways, and accepted their divines. It is true that there were other nāgas that continued to be antagonist; for example, the reference to the land of Takṣaśilā, where Utanka goes to garner king Janamejaya's help to kill Takṣaka, is very evocative (*Mbh* 1.3.161), and it is possible that the Aryan king Janamejaya's attack on Takṣaśilā was on the city of his enemy ruler, Takṣaka, who may have belonged to the Nāga race. However, perhaps there was also a time when Takṣaka was not an Aryan enemy, because when the Pāṇḍavas are born, among those who come to celebrate the birth are the nāgas, such as Karkoṭaka, Vāsuki, Kaśyapa, Kuṅda, and even Takṣaka (1.123.45). Perhaps it was Arjuna's reprehensive actions in Khāṇḍava that angered Takṣaka and turned him against the Kurus. But, aside from Takṣaka, there are no major epic nāga enemies at this time. Hence, in the Mahābhārata, other than the snake sacrifice, there are very few nāga victims or myths in which the nāgas are persecuted. Instead, in the epic, not only are the nāgas respected for their good qualities, but they are also in amicable relationships with the kṣatriya warriors. For example, Arjuna has a marital relationship with the nāga princess, Ulūpī, and has a son by her. Moreover, Ulūpī is portrayed as an intelligent and strong woman with characteristics that are superior to most women's; consequently, Ulūpī not only saves Arjuna's life but also redeems him from his sin of killing Bhīṣma by treachery (*Mbh* 14.80.18–56, 14.81.9-14). Bhīma, too, after being poisoned by Duryodhana, ends up in Nāgaloka and is not only saved by his nāga grandfather but is also gifted by him the strength of ten elephants and the antidote to snake venom (*Mbh* 1.128. 48–72). Even Garuḍa, the eternal enemy of the serpents, is forced by Viṣṇu to forge a friendship with serpents when Indra's charioteer Mātali chooses a nāga bridegroom for his daughter (*Mbh* 5.105.61).

In addition to this reconciliation between the Aryans and the nāgas, the admirable attributes of the serpents, which, in Vedic times, seemed to be such a cause of acrimony, become exemplary of the highest levels of strength and acumen in epic times; so much so that throughout the war, serpent similes are used to extol Kuru warriors' valour and warriorship. For example, in *Udyoga Parva*, proclaiming his fear and awe of the Pāṇḍavas, Dhṛtarāṣṭra tells Saṃjaya, 'With the children hard to vanquish, the sons of Draupadī of noble souls, who are like serpents, will the Pāṇḍavas fight' (*Mbh* 5.50.38). Or 'Like a venomous snake having accumulated its poison for a long time, he (Bhīma) will fling his strength on my sons in the field of battle' (*Mbh* 5.51.41). Moreover, the verses pertaining to combat often use snake similes to describe the precision and deadliness of arrows and darts shot by the warriors from both sides. For example, Bhīṣma's lance is 'decked with gold, charged with great velocity and looking beautiful like a daughter of a nāga' (*Mbh* 6.105.31). Even Kṛṣṇa is compared to a snake, when in rage he jumps off the chariot in the midst of war and charges Bhīṣma, who has debilitated Arjuna in war: 'Keśava, who was then breathing like a snake and whose eyes were rolling in wrath ...' (*Mbh* 6.107:72). It is obvious from these examples that, by the time of the epic, the Aryans had begun to respect the nāgas for their superior skills.

It also appears from other, surprising similes used in the war that even those nāgas who were seen in negative light in earlier times, are not recalled for their assumed transgressions but for their strength, and, on the other hand, the negative behaviour of certain Vedic divines is acknowledged as such. This reversal suggests unexpected connotations, fudging the lines of distinction between the Vedic divines and nāgas and, by association, Pāṇḍavas and Kauravas. For example, in the war, Duḥśāsana is compared to Indra, while Arjuna is compared to Vṛtra: '[Duḥśāsana] endued with bravery, and prowess, again began to check Pārtha [Arjuna] with well-sharpened shafts like Indra resisting Vṛtra' (*Mbh* 6.111.48). Other similes compare Bhīṣma to both Takṣaka and Vṛtra: 'The mighty puissant Bhīṣma possessed of sharp weapons and inflamed with rage in battle, appears like the mighty snake Takṣaka of great ferocity and virulent venom' (*Mbh* 6.108.15). And '... seeing him [Bhīṣma] who resembled the unconquerable Vṛtra when he had been vanquished in days of yore by Vasva ...' (*Mbh* 7.3.1). These examples are only a sampling of the nāga-centric epithets and analogies used to describe the warriors in the epic, and they show that the nāgas not only became analogous to superior kṣatriya skills, but they were also given the same transcendent qualities as the Vedic divines.

The final and ultimate elevation of the nāgas in the Mahābhārata comes at the end of *Śāntī Parva* in the story of the nāga king Padmanabha of Nāgapur, who, in a reverse cyclicity, has the resonance of Viṣṇu (*Mbh* 12.357-363). He is so evolved that he is reputed to be the knower of a householder's dharma and also of the ultimate dharma of mokṣa, so much so that a brāhmin goes to this nāga for instruction on mokṣa and tells him, 'O you of great wisdom, O Nāga, who have acquired a knowledge of the Soul. It is very true that the gods are not superior to you in any respect' (*Mbh* 12.364.7). By virtue of his sharing Viṣṇu's name of Padmanabha (lotus navel), he is connected to cosmic creation, and by virtue of his snake-ness he is Śeṣa Nāga. In addition, he also shares Viṣṇu's solar divine function, because when the brāhmin comes to learn from him, he is away on a fortnight-long task of drawing the sun's chariot, thus displaying his beneficence towards all mankind. Hence, in this tale, the serpent, who in the Vedic time was victimized, is now eulogized and made equivalent to the supreme divine. This transformation seems surprising but also fitting, particularly at this time in the epic, because this is the concluding tale of the *Śāntī Parva*. Hence, the words that the brāhmin speaks not only emphasize the prevailing ideas of mokṣa, but they also show that all differences between the Aryans and the Nāga race have been reconciled: 'He that is yourself is verily myself, as that is myself is truly yourself. Myself, yourself, and all other creatures, shall all have to enter into the Supreme Soul' (*Mbh* 12.364.8).

However, this ascendency of the serpents in the Mahābhārata is glaringly negated by the fact that at the end of war the nāgas are subjected to the evil of genocide. Thus, the question that needs to be asked is, if the nāgas had become so much a part of what was 'good' in Aryan society, why did Janamejaya and the brāhmins want to wipe them out? The answer to this question seems to be much bigger than the mere cause of Janamejaya's personal vendetta or even the cycle of revenge that Arjuna and Takṣaka begin; in fact, it seems to point to a systemic problem of evil, most likely created by the brāhmins who needed to eliminate any and all threats to their power, which the Nāgas were posing. Buddhist records indicate that some of the Nāga rajas listed in *Mahāvyutpati* (the Buddhist Sanskrit Glossary) are the same as the Aryan kings in the Mahābhārata. Also, in Buddhism, the nāgas, even when presented as serpents or as metaphors of serpent traits, have the best of human characteristics. Additionally, and most importantly, they are devotees of the Buddha, such as Muccalinda, the

Nāgarāja who sheltered the Buddha from torrential rain for several days by spreading his hood like an umbrella over the Buddha's head. What this Buddhist connection suggests is that the brāhmins saw the Nāgas as a people who could become non-cooperative with the Aryans, choosing instead to side with the heretical propounding of Buddhism; hence it was necessary for the brāhmins to eliminate them. It is also possible that since a nāga—Śeṣa—figured prominently in the very creation of the Aryan cosmos, it was necessary for the brāhmins to demonstrate that they were tolerant only to those Nāgas that were loyal to Aryans; the others, who did not show a devotion to Vaiṣṇavism, would be eliminated.

Another possible cause of the snake sacrifice may have been the brāhmins' megalomaniacal lust for power. Perhaps they really did believe that they could possess the proverbial nāga attributes of immortality and death-delivering skills through the transformative ritual of a Vedic fire sacrifice, and they used Janamejaya's revenge as an excuse to execute this transformation. This argument is not as farfetched as it may sound. Brian Smith and Wendy Doniger describe how this transfer of power is actually possible through a sacrifice. They explain that in a sacrifice, the sacrificed is, in fact, the sacrificer himself, but, instead of the sacrificer actually sacrificing himself, he uses a substitute. Quoting Henri Hubert and Marcel Mauss from *Sacrifice: Its Nature and Function* Smith and Doniger (1989: 190) state that this substitute in 'the sacrificial ritual (including the priest who acts as a buffer and guide between the sacred and profane realms) is the ritual victim'. The victim represents or 'becomes' (and thus substitutes for) both the invisible divine recipient of the offering and the human being who makes the offering. 'Through this proximity the victim, who already represents the gods, comes to represent the sacrifier [= sacrificer] also. Indeed, it is not enough to say that it represents him: it is merged in him. The two personalities are fused together.' What Hubert and Mauss mean and what Smith and Doniger explain through this statement is actually a double substitute, and when interpreted in the context of the snake sacrifice, it reveals interesting insights: in the first and most obvious substitution, the brāhmins at Janamejaya's fire sacrifice offer themselves as a sacrifice to gain benefits. The usual animal substitutes in Vedic fire sacrifices used to be horses and/or goats. However, in Janamejaya's sacrifice, the sacrificers not only perform a sarpasattra, but they also sacrifice as substitutes not one or two, but all the serpents. Hence, the second substitution in this sacrifice is a sarpasattra itself, which, as mentioned above, was originally performed by the Nāgas to acquire venom. Therefore, in Janamejaya's snake sacrifice, the brāhmins figuratively assume the identity of the Nāgas and perform a real sacrifice, using all the serpents as substitutes in order to fuse with them: brāhmin = Nāga = serpent. The reason for this double fusion is the gains that the sacrifice promises. Normally, the gain from a ritual sacrifice included longevity and prosperity; however, this time the brāhmins wanted more than longevity and prosperity; they wanted what the Nāga race had: the most powerful venom to destroy the enemy, wealth hidden away beneath the earth, and the secret of immortality that the serpents possessed by virtue of being the progeny of the earth goddess.

It is possible that this alteration of the equation of the sacrificer and sacrificed was the brāhmin way of dealing with the devastation of the war, in which everything was destroyed—life, property, power. In addition, the belief systems and ideologies were changing; hence, a ritual sacrifice in Vedic style promised not only a salvaging of what little remained of the Aryans but also an appropriation of the ancient and famed glory of the mystical Nāgas. It is also possible that in the re-telling of the Mahābhārata, when Sauti begins the tale of war and devastation with the story of Janamejaya's snake sacrifice, he wants to issue a warning that war can be ravaging, and it can unleash so much violence that after it ends, even the attempts at renewal are violent. However, Sauti also absolves the sacrificers of their crimes by affirming their clemency. He ends his narration of the Mahābhārata by bringing Āstīka, the survivor and saviour of the Nāga race, back into the story: 'Āstīka having rescued the snakes (from a fiery death) became filled with joy' (*Mbh* 18.5.32).

However, despite the final outcome, the fact is that this sacrifice is actually a perpetration of 'three crimes from which it is otherwise indistinguishable—suicide, murder, and deicide' (Smith and Doniger 1989: 189). Therefore, its inclusion in the Mahābhārata tradition and the replication of its metaphors in the various events of the epic create a paradigm of behaviour that makes victims of anyone who does not conform, or who owns wealth that others want to appropriate. Sadly, since the proponents and practitioners of this evil behaviour are supposed dharma heroes, the paradigm has become a problematic exemplar in Hindu society.

THE ASURAS

Who are the Asuras?

In the sixteenth chapter of the Bhagavad Gītā, Kṛṣṇa describes to Arjuna the dark side of man—his asura side:

> dambho darpobhimānaś ca
> krodhaḥ pāruṣyam eva ca
> ajñānaṁ cābhijātasya
> pārtha saṃpadam āsurīm
> [Hypocrisy, pride, conceit, wrath, rudeness, and ignorance, O Pārtha, belong to him who is demoniac.] (*BG* 16.4)

And the converse:

> Ahiṁsā satyam akrodhas
> tyāgaḥ śāntir apaiśunam
> dayā bhūteṣv aloluptvaṁ
> mārdavaṁ hrīr acāpalam
> [Observing non-violence, truth, freedom from anger, renunciation, tranquillity, freedom from fault-finding, compassion for all, absence from covetousness, gentleness, modesty, absence of restlessness.] (*BG* 16.2)

> Tejaḥ kṣamā dhṛtiḥ śaucam
> adroho nātimānitā
> bhavanti saṃpadaṁ daivīm
> abhijātasya bhārata

[Vigor, forgiveness, firmness, cleanliness, absence of quarrel, freedom from vanity, O Bhārata, belong to one who is god like.] (*BG* 16.3)

These and most of the ślokas in this chapter are about the unethical quality of asura-ness and its ethical antithesis. However, in pre-epic texts, the word 'asura' was not related to ethics at all, and it did not define anyone's morality or immorality, let alone absolute values of the same. Evil, as we know it, suggests everything bad: pain, death, disease, violence, etc. In many religions there is a demon, the absolute embodiment of evil, who engenders all evil, and he is as coeternal as god, who is an absolute good. However, in Hindu mythology, there is no such one absolute evil being responsible for all evil. So the question of asura being a representation of this absolute evil does not arise. In addition, in the earliest uses of the term and in subsequent myths, asura is not even equivalent to the psychological inclinations that create evil, such as *tamas* and *avidyā*—qualities that create mythical beings like Mara of early Buddhism. In fact, in Hindu myths, asuras are often more evolved, more ascetic, more adhering to the principle of dharma than devas, brāhmins, or honoured kṣatriyas. Wendy Doniger O'Flaherty (1988: 62) says demons and gods are consubstantial—enemies and brothers from the earliest times. Asuras and devas are not opposite sides of the ethical paradigm—good and evil. The only distinguishing feature of their relationship is the battle in which they are constantly and cyclically engaged, and only in that they are on opposite sides. And this battle is not about good against evil. In fact, this battle has no moral content or context; it is not fought because one side is moral and the other side is immoral; it is simply a cyclical archetype of a conflict. So, 'when the later myths begin to apply new moral codes to the characters of individual gods and demons in myths, a number of inconsistencies arise, for the two groups, as groups, are not fundamentally *morally* opposed' (O'Flaherty 1988: 58). Therefore, when the asuras in the Mahābhārata—especially Duryodhana—are relegated to an a priori asura-ness even before their actions can be gauged against any empirical and relational truths, both the ethical correctness of the word's usage and the scriptural value of the epic, especially the Gītā, become questionable.

Many scholars believe that the Gītā was a later interpolation in the Mahābhārata. Perhaps that is why the meaning of the word 'asura', and its antonymic 'deva' and *daivic* qualities, as described in the Gītā, are not quite in accordance with the rest of the epic. In fact, through the lens of the Gītā and its declaration of asura qualities, not just Duryodhana and his cohorts are suspect, but also most of the daivic heroes and many of the high brāhmins, because they all, at some point or another, display anger, arrogance, or lack of forgiveness. Even Yudhiṣṭhira, who can be considered the epitome of daivic qualities, suffers from lack of tranquillity in his addiction to gambling, and he deviates from the truth when he declares to Drona the death of Aśvatthāman. In addition, the brāhmins, including those that are highly respected and cited as exemplary, such as Jamadagni Rāma, Agastya, Vasiṣṭha, and Mārkaṇḍeya, are actually unforgiving and wrathful, and some, like Drona, also covet another's wealth.

Other scholars consider the Gītā as integral to the Mahābhārata. But whether the Gītā was part of the text from the beginning or a later interpolation is not of importance here, except to present a perspective: if the Gītā is considered an interpolation, then this new meaning of asura has no relationship to the asuras in the Mahābhārata, because their character cannot retrospectively be measured against an ethical quality that did not exist in the context that shaped their characters. And if the Gītā is not seen as an interpolation, then the predilection it attributes to the asuras is discordant with the other aspects of asuras in the epic, which are a composite of the asura concept dating back at least to the *Ṛg Veda*, if not prior.

Thus, to understand how asura-ness was distorted into evil, the concept must be traced through its origin, transformation, and concretization. Monier-Williams says that asura is a derivative from '*asu*' which, in the *Ṛg Veda*, means life breath. In the *Atharva Veda* it also means life of the spiritual world; but in the *Bhāgavata Purāṇa*, the meaning shifts to life of a different kind—that of worldly pleasure (which is neither evil nor against the principles of *puruṣārtha*). Additional definitions by Monier-Williams (2005: 121) also add to the word's ambiguity: 'spiritual, incorporeal, supreme spirit but also evil spirit, and one who is an opponent of the gods'. These diametrically opposing meanings are a result of the changes this term went through, even early on in the *Ṛg Veda* itself; in fact, the chronology of the use of 'asura' in the *Ṛg Veda* indicates this change. In the earliest books, 2–7, asura is used in a favourable sense, especially when it refers to Varuṇa, and it is replaced by the pejorative meaning in the later books, 8–10. Sukumari Bhattacharji (2000: 35) believes that the very root, '*asu*', could also be a reason for this transformation, because according to Monier-Williams' definition—'life of the spiritual world or of the departed souls' is connected with '*pitarah*', dead ancestors. Eventually, as Indra supplanted Varuṇa, the latter came to mean only chief, or the chief of the evil spirits, because he was associated with the spirit world.

Suggesting a positive denotation of 'asura' in its earliest meaning is its most commonly accepted etymological association with the Avestan Ahura Mazda. It also applies to the six Amesha Spentas, the associates or divine sparks of Ahura Mazda. Bhattacharji (23) notes that in the *Avesta*, Ahura Mazda is the lord of high knowledge and his concrete name, Varana, is the same as Varuṇa in India. Some historians now contend that 'asura' can also be equated to the Assyrian god, Ashur, who was the head of the Assyrian pantheon.

From its Avestan and Assyrian associations, and from its early usage in the *Ṛg Veda*, it appears that the appellative, asura, mostly signified lordship, perhaps, for someone who was also exemplary of a 'spiritual life' and who provided spiritual guidance. In the earliest hymns of the *Ṛg Veda*, Varuṇa is the chief asura or lord. Wash Edward Hale (1999: 6) also claims that in many of the earlier hymns in the *Ṛg Veda*, the meaning of the word, asura, signifies not only lordship but also leadership, or even someone who has a fighting force behind him. In addition, he suggests that this honour of lordship was not just reserved for the gods but was also used for humans, and sometimes, even for enemies. So anyone who had power was an asura. For example:

> The leader of the raid, the asura who is more excellent than any other patron, has given me two cows together with a wagon. Tryaruṇa, son of Trivṛṣṇa, has distinguished himself with ten thousand, or Agni Vaiśvānara. (*RV* 5.27.1, quoted in Hale 1999: 48)

Hale believes that in this hymn the asura Tryaruṇa is human, and he has a fighting force with whose help he has conducted a raid against his rivals.

Hale's interpretation also answers another very important question: were the asuras simply mythical beings fabricated by the Aryans to describe the enemy of mythical battles or were they real people? It is essential to address this question, especially in an exploration of ethics, because while a people's gods may be invested with qualities that define the ethical paradigms of a society, it is the people themselves who are the real agents of behaviour that can be classified as ethical or unethical. Hale's interpretation of Tryaruṇa as being human and the other attributes and actions associated with the asuras in various myths demonstrate that the asuras were not just mythical beings; they were human—perhaps a clan of people whose role in Aryan society was capsuled in myth, as is the nature of myth's creation. Besides, the asuras' own behaviour, their treatment by and their interaction with other Aryans are all three-dimensional and human-like aspects that cannot simply be considered mythical allegory. And also, if Aryans are accepted as human, then, by the same standard, so should the asuras be accepted.

The *dāṣa* and asura connection is another argument that proves the humanness of asuras. Hale (1999: 130) points out that the use of '*dasyu*' becomes rare after the *Atharva Veda,* and it drops out of usage about the same time that 'asura' begins to be used in the pejorative sense, so the appellative 'asura' replaces 'dasyu' and assumes the meaning of the latter. Even Monier-Williams (2005: 477) defines 'dāsa' as 'fiend, demon; a certain evil being conquered by Indra (for example, Namuci, Pipru, Śambara, Varcin)', and its Ṛg Vedic meaning is given as 'savage barbarian infidel ... opp. to *ārya*'. Moreover, in the *Ṛg Veda,* 'asura' is sometimes connected to the quality of darkness, and this could have been the reason for the derivative, 'dāsa':

> O Surya, when the Asura's descendant, Svarbhānu pierced thee through and through with darkness
>
> All creatures looked like one who is bewildered, who knoweth not the place where he is standing, (*RV* 5.40.5)

The equivalency of 'asura' with 'dāsa' continues in the *Brāhmaṇas.* Eventually, as 'asura' came to denote the opposite of 'deva', 'dāsa' became closer to meaning of '*śūdra*'. The passage below from the *Taittirīya Brāhmaṇa,* describing the battle between brāhmin and śūdra, clearly replaces the ritual, archetypal battle of the gods and asuras:

> The gods and asuras fought. They contended for the sun. The gods won it. Both a brāhmaṇa and a śūdra fight for a piece of leather. Indeed the brāhmaṇa is the daivic varṇa, the śūdra asuric. Then one should say, 'These prospered; these made good prosperity.' The other (should say), 'These making it inhabited, these made bad prosperity.' Thus what is done well of these, what is success, the one causes that. What is badly done, what is failure, the other strikes that. The brāhmaṇa wins. Thus they find the sun of the rival. (*TB* 1.2.6.6-7 quoted in Hale 1999: 173-4)

Hale's commentary (1999: 174) to this passage explains that the brāhmin and śūdra perform a ritual in which they act out the battle of the gods and asuras over the sun, which is represented in the ritual by a round piece of leather. The brāhmin plays the part of the gods and the śūdra the part of the asuras. Hence this passage says that the śūdra is the asuric varṇa.

This equivalency of dāsa/śūdra and asura could possibly mean that dāsas were *an-ārya,* because they were rivals of the brāhmins and did not subscribe to their practices; hence they were outside the Aryans' fold. Or, it could refer to those Aryans who were born Aryan but did not believe in the practices ordained by the brāhmins, and hence they were relegated to the status of dāsa and disowned by the brāhmins, who also forbade the other Aryans to acknowledge them as anything but outside the fold. Hale (1999: 174), however, believes that 'this statement could also be a recognition that the śūdra varṇa consists of descendants of the original inhabitants of the land, the dasyus, who in later texts, were called asuras'.

While it is possible that, as Hale suggest, dāsas may have been descendants of the historical human asuras; his suggestion that the asuras could have been the descendants of the original people is questionable. The asuras were, most likely, a distinct faction of the

Aryans who were denigrated and made the lowest of the low and called dāsa as an insult to them. The asuras were probably Aryans at one time, or at least they belonged to the five Aryan tribes; at some point, they separated, and the cause of their separation was given the attribute of asuric. In the Mahābhārata the asuras are clearly included in the Aryan clans. This is also suggested by D.D. Kosambi (1967: 33), who proposes that according to Vedic myth, the Aryan clans of the Mahābhārata could have been the descendants of the Vedic Five Tribes, which are referenced a number of times in the various books of the *Ṛg Veda* as *janāḥ* and *jātāḥ*: the five Humans (*mānuṣāḥ*), The Five Nations (*kṛṣtayaḥ*), The Five Mobile Peoples (*carṣaṇyaḥ*). This reference categorizes Ṛg Vedic Aryans not only as ancestors but also as belonging to the same system of clanship and pastoralism. Kosambi (1967: 33) also points out that the names of these five tribes appear in different hymns separately, but in one hymn to Indra and Agni, all five appear together:

> If with the Yadus, Turvaśas, ye sojourn, with Druhyas, Anus, Purūs, Indra-Agni! Even from thence, ye mighty Lords, come hither, and drink libations of the flowing Soma. (*RV* 1.108.8)

This hymn denotes that all five tribes also propitiated the same gods, had the same belief system, and followed the same practices. For example, in the Mahābhārata, both devas and *dānavas* are equally involved in the churning of the ocean, which could have been an amalgamated raid of all Aryans against the indigenous people to acquire their wealth.

Another example that suggests the Aryan background of the asuras is in the *Ādi Parva,* when Ganga hands over Devavrata to Śaṃtanu and tells him how well versed Devavrata is in the Vedas and other conventions. She says, 'Both the celestials and the *asuras* look on him with favor' (*Mbh* 1.8.100), suggesting not only that the asuras were part of the same equation, but also they had equal status as devas in the Aryan community, as per the Vedas. In fact, Bhīṣma tells Yudhiṣṭhira in the *Śāntī Parva* that the dānavas did not even live on earth till the *Tretā* Yuga (*Mbh* 12.207.41), which suggests that prior to that, in the

Kṛta age, they were as celestial as devas, and, therefore, were as much a part of the Aryan cosmological cycle as the devas.

It is possible that, over time, rivalry grew among the various Aryan factions—the five tribes—and they began to see each other as separate. But they eventually came back into the fold, either through exogamy, or simply because, as is the nature of families, they reconciled their differences.

Aryan marriage practices are further proof of the asuras belonging to the same society. Asura marriage was an integral part of the Aryans' marital system. According to Manu, it is sixth on the list of favoured methods. He explains that the first six kinds of marriage should be considered lawful by brāhmins—the last four (*Gandharva, Asura, Rākṣasa and Piśāca*) for kṣatriyas, and the asura marriage is recommended for vaiśyas and śūdras (*The Laws of Manu* 2006: 111.13). Āpastamba, too, in his *Dharmasūtra* describes asura marriage as an accepted norm—one in which the bridegroom gives a bride price according to his free will and ability (2.12.1, Olivelle 2000: 91). In fact, Subhadra's marriage to Arjuna is even lower than an asura marriage; it is a rākṣasa marriage and is still considered lawful. If the asuras were evil, demonic, or even the 'other' (indigenous people), would their practices of marriage have been part of Aryan societal norms, especially since marriage ensures the continuance of family, kingship, and tradition?

But, long before they were epic cousins and even before the dāsa connection, when asura was still an appellation for lord and/or leader with power, the word had already begun to degrade.

One reason for this degradation in Vedic times could have been that the appellative honour of lordship was given indiscriminately—regardless of whether the recipient was mortal or divine; the word 'asura', was used for anyone who displayed power, and, perhaps, it was the significance of this power that caused the process of deterioration. In the earliest Ṛg Vedic hymns, power was not evil; but when the other Aryans began to encounter threats to their power, the might of the opposition came to be seen as threatening. This element of threat is the key to understanding the negative transformation of the word, because the feeling of being threatened is subjective and, in the threatened, it always evokes fear, anxiety, anticipated pain, and sorrow—all feelings that can be deemed a consequence of evil. Therefore, the cause of that threat is what could have been seen as asura: a powerful human leader could be a cause of threat to the gods; the ever-increasing power of the gods could be a threat to humans; or one Aryan faction's leader could have been a threat to another faction's leader. Most likely, it was this element of threat that finally sealed the fate of the word. It was also this threat that brought Indra into the limelight as an 'asura killer'. From the many Indra hymns, the nature of the threat becomes even clearer; not only does Indra subdue the power of the enemy asuras, but he also steals their wealth to give to his loyalists, which suggests that the power of the opposing factions could have been in physical might or in material wealth, or both. However, a significant point to note in these hymns is that in all the implications of lordship, leadership, power, and even threat, or even in Indra's reasons for enmity, there is no indication that the asura is evil, equivalent to evil action, or even that his actions result in pain to others. The asura's only crime seems to be that he is powerful and/or intoxicated with his power. Ironically, this intoxication is also Indra's quality and a quality of the brāhmins in post Vedic texts. They, too, are constantly intoxicated with their power; furthermore, unlike the asura, who is punished for growing too powerful or becoming too consumed with his power, Indra and the brāhmins destroy with impunity anything or anyone that comes in the way of their power. Therefore, if there is any consequent evil, it results from the actions of those who are not deemed asura, such as the brāhmins and the Aryan gods.

Hence, if the power of the gods and the brāhmins was not a threat; why was the lordship and power of the asuras considered a threat by the Aryans? A reason could have been the necessity of the sacrifice. In the later books of the *Ṛg Veda*, after the degradation of Varuṇa, sacrifice was seen as the only way to preserve ṛta, and anyone who opposed ṛta and, by extension, sacrifice, was condemned and debased. Since ṛta was the Aryan concept of aesthetic order; it was a reflection of the 'paradigmatic work of the gods' (Eliade 1998: 33). The Aryans saw this order in the wonders of nature around them and were in wonderment at how it was constantly in flux, constantly cyclical, but always coming back to a fixed point. It was around this dynamic fixed point that they created their cosmology and myths, and, henceforth, strove to preserve it. Initially, the natural phenomena were the mythological gods: Mitra/Varuṇa, Agni, Savitar, Vāyu—all different aspects of the same ṛta—the same fixity. These were impersonal gods with no anthropomorphic qualities—simply phenomena that sustained creation. In the time of Indra as preserver of ṛta, the key means of this preservation was the ritual of sacrifice. Perhaps there were factions in the Aryan society who did not subscribe to this particular actualization of ṛta and had their own ways of cosmocizing the fixed point. Or, perhaps, they did not see the Indra faction's fixed point as a sacred space and had their own version of it.

In the earliest time, during Varuṇa's lordship, sacrifice was not the supreme means to preserve ṛta; instead, Varuṇa, the chief Asura, was synonymous with the cosmic order and was also the keeper of ṛta. Therefore, asuras were adherents of Varuṇa's ṛta. In fact, in an early hymn, these asuras/divines were

> upholding that which moves and that which moves not, Ādityas, Gods protectors of all being/Provident, guarding well the world of spirits, [protecting *asuryam*] true to eternal law [ṛta], the debt. (*RV* 2.27.4)

As per this hymn to Ādityas, *asuryam* (asuraship) is an adjectival quality of the devas; it is a part of their character and not separate (Hale 1999: 59). This also proves that, initially, the asuras were not only within the fold of ṛta but were also protectors of ṛta.

Furthermore, this ṛta-protecting asuryam did not stop at the fixity of the cosmic order; it was echoed as prescriptive for people. Just like the forces of nature were moved to fixity to sustain creation, so were the people supposed to live a life within the order. Whatever action a person performed had to conform to the cosmic order in harmony with nature, because just as the cosmic order was fixed, recurrent and true, so was the rhythm of 'life breath'—'asu', (as defined by

Monier-Williams). Those who acknowledged the equivalency of these rhythms of physical nature and physiology were asuras, and for them ritual and sacrifice, which was also performed with the same regularity, not only ensured this conformity but also rectified any transgression. This was the immutable law of ṛta. In fact, to emphasize this synonymic relationship, the *Ṛg Veda* also contains hymns that tell us what kind of actions men needed to follow—actions that nature itself followed, such as generosity, as described in this hymn to the waters:

> Waters, you are the ones who bring us the life force. Help us to find nourishment so that we may look upon great joy
>
> Let us share in the most delicious sap that you have, as if you were loving mothers
>
> For our well-being let the goddesses be an aid to us, the waters be for us to drink. Let them cause well-being and health to flow over us. (*RV* 10.9.1–4, O'Flaherty 1981: 231)

And this connection of the moral order in the cosmos was reflected in the moral order humans followed—a symbiosis.

> The father sacrifices for his son, the comrade for his comrade, the favorite friend for his friend
>
> So let praises flow back and forth between the two, between us who are mortals and you, the immortals. (*RV* 1.26.3 and 9, O'Flaherty 1981: 100)

Hence, all actions of men—to make a living, cultivate land, form relationships, etc.—were to follow the principle of ṛta, because man's actions not only impacted society, but they also reaffirmed the fixity of the sacred space.

But did they? Did humans align their actions to the sanctity of the fixed point? While the order in nature was obvious and seemingly controlled by outside forces, how did the order in personal life follow the order of nature? And, could life be fulfilled by following the orderliness of nature? Also, who determined what the order was? From historical accounts and from the verses of the *Ṛg Veda*, we know that the Aryans were a civic-minded people with a developed sense of polity. Therefore, to sustain their own society, they not only needed a form of social order, but they also needed to ensure that this order was not disrupted, and it remained supreme above all other orders. But, as is the normal inclination of man—despite acknowledging social ethics and a need for personal morality, man transgresses. Most scholars accept that for the Aryans, cosmic order and human order were not only connected but also, if there was a breach, it was punished. For example, quoting Kaegi's translation of the *Ṛg Veda*, Surendranath Dasgupta (2004: 1.15) says, 'The hymns strongly prove how deeply the prominent minds in the people were persuaded that the eternal ordinances of the rulers of the world were as inviolable in mental and moral matters as in the realm of nature, and that every wrong act, even the unconscious was punished as the sin expiated.' In the beginning, it was the Lord of ṛta, Varuṇa, who watched men with his *sahasracakṣu*, punished miscreants, and made sure society remained within the periphery of this order. And people within the fold realized this, begging him for forgiveness if they committed any an-ṛta or offense. There are many hymns in the *Ṛg Veda* attesting to this. For example:

> If we have committed an offense against a hospitable friend like Āryaman or a close friend like Mitra, or against one who has always been a comrade, or a brother, or a neighbor—one of our own or a stranger—loosen that offence from us, Varuṇa. (*RV* 5.85.7, O'Flaherty 1981: 211)

However, later, during Indra's supremacy, there might have been others who did not see their actions as transgressions in the changing society, or, if they did see them as such, they did not prescribe to Indra's form of punishment. Or, perhaps, there were some who did not transgress, but were wrongfully accused; hence they resented the order. These non-conformists could have been called asuras.

Also, this system of order and punishment had an essential anomaly, which was related to nature itself. While man's transgressions could be punished with Varuṇa's noose, how could one punish nature, which was also flawed, and also transgressed? This flaw was that part of divine nature that was not benevolent, such as floods, earthquakes, etc., which caused the suffering of innocent people and even of those who were deeply immersed in keeping the order. This aesthetic evil—the evil in the cosmic order itself, which, independently of human action, prevented the flux of nature from converging into the fixed point—how did one explain that? How did the cosmic order remain true with such anomalies? And, above all, how did one punish nature for acting against these truths of ṛta? The Aryans had no answer to these questions, just as these continue to plague the theist today. To avert such cosmic evil, ritual and sacrifice was the only answer—to appease the powers, so to speak. And the less the Aryans understood, the more important sacrifice became. And, if the result that occurred from the ritual was not what was desired, the sacrifice was blamed. But the one to suffer the most grievous blame was the sacrificer, because he was seen to have committed errors in the rituals, which led to the adverse result. So, every time nature became disorderly, people accused those who failed to ensure the order; and perhaps these accused were considered asura.

Furthermore, over time, not only could there have been men who threatened the order and broke ṛta, but the gods themselves may have been blamed for breaking the order. The very same evil that the Aryans saw in the natural order became inherent in the gods that represented that natural order. Thus, evil pervaded a god's goodness, and as the gods perpetuated this evil, the very gods who were Asura—and good and powerful—were blamed for weakening the order, and they themselves became representative of negativity. A good example is Varuṇa, who, despite his thousand eyes, could not prevent the breakdown. Hence, this asura was replaced by a more powerful, proactive god—deva.

What is ironic is that 'deva' may have been used not for his qualities of goodness and orderliness but for his evil. The word 'deva' can be etymologically associated with the Avestan '*daeva*', the false god, wrong god, or more fittingly, '*daebaaman*', the deceiver. Perhaps, with Varuṇa and his host of asura gods having failed them, the Aryans decided to put their faith in the daebaaman, hoping to deceive the vagaries of nature with the deceiver himself, and when this deceiver was able to win the Aryans wealth and waters, despite the caprice of nature, Varuṇa, the asura, and his righteousness were devalued. And, perhaps, because of the evil nature of these devas, who were now given eminence, there were some in the Aryan tribes who rejected this idea and chose to remain loyal to the original divine Asura; and hence they were relegated to being asura themselves.

Thus, eventually, the asura humans were banned from the Aryan sacrifice. They were banned from the divine experience that the Aryans evoked through the hierophany of their daivic sacrifice. Perhaps angry at this rejection, the asuras began to gatecrash the sacrifice and corrupt it so that the Aryans could not have the perfect communication that they hoped to achieve with their new divines. Or perhaps they began to steal the sacrifice to sustain their original fixed point—the sacred space and cosmology that had been initially created. And the enmity continued to grow, until everything imperfect and disruptive was seen as asura. The Mahābhārata suggests this schism between the deva-believers and the asuras in a number of myths and passages, which also shed further light on how the asuras belonged to Aryan society, but their degradation and consequent fall created acrimony between them and the gods and their resulting factions. The mythos this rift created also made good and evil amorphous, because the very idea of what was good and virtuous was in flux.

The decline of virtuousness was attributed to the asuras as a consequence of their 'fall'. For example, in *Vana Parva*, Hanuman tells Bhīma that in an earlier time there was no varṇa, no distinction between dānava and deva (perhaps suggesting that all five tribes of Aryans had a common goal in the new land) but after the deterioration of virtues (perhaps virtue of the sacrifice), societal norms and traditions were established to sustain society. In the new order, the celestials are established and sustained by sacrifice, and men maintain themselves by following the ordinances of Bṛhaspati and Uśanas.[7] In other words, men maintain themselves by following the tradition of either devas or dānavas (*Mbh* 3.9.418).

[7] Uśanas is Śukra, guru of the dānavas, and Bṛhaspati is priest and advisor to the devas.

Another example explaining the fall is of Rāhu's sabotage of soma: In this *Ādi Parva* myth, Rāhu, disguised as a deva, drinks the ambrosia; consequently, Nārāyaṇa cuts off his head with his discus. Rāhu's head rises to the sky and then falls to the earth. This sabotage becomes the genesis of the eternal enmity between Rāhu and Candra and Sūrya (*Mbh* 1.5.19). Hence, given that Candra and Sūrya are emblems of natural order, Rāhu is the breaker of this order of the Aryan ṛta, and his transgression causes his fall. However, it must be noted that Rāhu is not evil, nor is his theft of soma evil, because soma did not belong to devas in the first place. Candra and Sūrya precipitate his fall simply because he opposes the ascendency of devas. Nevertheless, the consequence of Rāhu's fall is that it condemns the dānavas to not only eternal degradation but also habitation on earth. The order that comes into existence on earth is 'new', as Hanuman states, but even in this new order devas and asuras[8] inherit the legacy of the conflict.

Hence, it can be concluded that the asuras were part of Aryan society, but over time, their actions and behaviour came to be seen in opposition to the Aryan norm, and they suffered a symbolic 'fall'. This degradation was seen as equivalent to evil.

INTERPRETING EVIL IN ASURA MYTHS

Devas and asuras are part of the same family tree, as is evident in many myths in the Mahābhārata. The genealogy goes back to Brāhmaṇa and his mind-born sons, one of whom was Dakṣa, a Prajāpati, who was born from Brāhmaṇa's toe. Dakṣa had thirteen daughters, including Dānu, Diti, and Aditi, and all of them were married to Kaśyapa, who was Marīci's son (another of Brāhmaṇa's mind-borns). From Dānu, who was the elder sister, were born the Dānavas, and from Diti were born the Daityas, and the progeny of Aditi were the Ādityas, who were

[8] In the *Smṛti* texts, the terms 'dānava' and 'daitya' are often interchangeable with asura. (They belong to the same race). The term 'asura' is a conjunctive of a+sura, which means without '*sura*' or soma; hence beings deprived of soma = asura.

devas. Hence the Dānavas (of asura race) were the elder cousin brothers of the Ādityas. This fact of asuras being older in the same family is another key to understanding the asura concept; the generation gap between old and new caused perpetual conflict.

Madhu and Kaiṭabha: Asuras and Creation

In one Mahābhārata creation myth, when Brahmā is born from the lotus arising from Viṣṇu's navel, the dānavas, Madhu and Kaiṭabha, prevent him from creating a new universe, because their older cosmic order already exists. Interestingly, this older order is within the parameters of the same cosmology that Brahmā hopes to establish in the new order. Madhu and Kaiṭabha state, 'We are always firm in truth and morality. None is equal to us in strength, appearance, beauty, virtue, asceticism, charity and goodness and self-control' (*Mbh* 3.203.28-29). It is clear from these words that not only is the older order of moral codes Aryan, it is also not evil, because these behaviours described by the dānavas are part of Aryan ethics. Therefore, Brahmā is hesitant (or afraid) to create a new order to replace it. But Viṣṇu, who, in the new order, needs to be established as the new supreme divine, manipulates Madhu and Kaiṭabha to end the old order by tricking the two dānavas into asking for a boon. They respond by saying that they are the ones who should be giving boons, since they are elder. And Viṣṇu does ask them for a boon—that Madhu and Kaiṭabha allow Viṣṇu to kill them so that he can get on with his act of creation. The two dānavas agree but place two conditions: that they should be killed in an open space, and they should be born as Viṣṇu's sons in the new creation. Viṣṇu agrees, and seeing his uncovered thighs as the only open space, kills them there (*Mbh* 3.203.35), thus eliminating the older order to make place for the new order.

Aside from the fact that the dānavas existed before the devas and had already created the cosmology and system of ṛta, many other elements are also revealed in this myth: their request to be killed in an open space suggests that a new sacred space of the new order must be open and not interfere with any of the spaces already occupied.

But since Madhu and Kaiṭabha allow themselves to be killed, it indicates that, for the new order to come into existence, the old must be destroyed. In addition, Viṣṇu gets the dānavas to reconcile to the creation of this new order. Moreover, they ask to be born again as Viṣṇu's sons, which suggests that they are not only willing to remain in the fold, but they also want to be part of the new Aryan continuum of reincarnation—a concept that was gaining prevalence at this time. Hence, if Viṣṇu, in the new order, is the daivic supreme and creation flows from him, then in this order, both devas and dānavas are his sons—reincarnation of earlier Aryans.

Another important attestation to the fact that the dānavas and devas are part of the same system is that Viṣṇu destroys this existing order on his thighs. This specificity of the thighs is very revealing: Thighs are not only a part of the body, they are also considered most vulnerable. Additionally, according to the Ṛg Vedic *Puruṣa Sūkta* hymn, the varṇa that originates from the thighs is the vaiśyas—the varṇa related to business, farming, and financial prosperity. This is an insight into why a new Aryan order needed to be created: at stake was the economic stability of evolving Aryan society. Earlier Aryans had relied on more primitive means of survival, and that system was the most vulnerable in current Aryan society; it needed to be overhauled. In fact, this factor also reveals the reason for Duryodhana's death in the frame story of the Mahābhārata. The fatal blow that kills Duryodhana is the one Bhīma strikes on his thighs. In the context of this myth, Duryodhana's killing can be seen as both—the strike against his wealth and prosperity and the destruction of an old order within the same system.

This myth of Madhu and Kaiṭabha is also repeated in *Śāntī Parva* (*Mbh* 12.347.66–73), and in this later interpolation the two dānavas are born from two drops of water in the divine lotus itself; thus further suggesting that they share the same cosmographic space and originate from the same primordial waters. But what is curious about this second version of the myth is that now the two asuras are not evolved, and they lack dharma (unlike in the earlier myth); now they are, in fact, embodiments of darkness and ignorance and steal the Vedas. That is why Hari has to kill them to retrieve the texts—so that creation can be accomplished, and the new order can be established on the old foundation of the Vedas. However, even this negative characteristic puts the asuras in the Aryan fold, because they are symbolic of the post-Vedic Aryan metaphysics of evil, which was seen as equivalent to ignorance and which always had the potential of evolving into knowledge. Thus, the suggestion here is of Viṣṇu dispelling pre-creation darkness and chaos by facilitating a figurative death of ignorance and establishing an order through the knowledge of the Vedas.

This ignorance is the presumptive evil that came to be seen as the decline of righteousness after the fall of the asuras, which is hinted at in earlier texts. For example, in *Śatapatha Brāhmaṇa,* the asuras' ignorance causes the gods to trick them out of heaven, and in *Chāndogya Upaniṣad,* the asuras put the sacrifice in their own mouth instead of in the fire; therefore, they lose virtue and themselves (quoted in O'Flaherty 1988: 68). Hence, the fall became complete, and from there, it was only a very short step to the concept of asuras as mythological demons.

Yayāti: Asura Origin of the Kurus

The familial relationship between devas and dānavas is not limited to the mythical; it also extends into the genealogy of the families of the Mahābhārata. This is portrayed in the Yayāti myth, which is an extension of the five Vedic tribes that D.D. Kosambi mentions. In this myth, Yayāti has five sons—two from his brāhmin wife, Devayānī, and three from his asura wife, Śarmiṣṭha (*Mbh* 1.78–84). When the brāhmin, Śukra, discovers that Yayāti, despite being married to his daughter, Devayānī, has been keeping a separate household and procreating with the dānava princess, Śarmiṣṭha, he curses the king to lose his youth. Yayāti then begs each of his sons to exchange their youth with his decrepitude. Only Pūru, Śarmiṣṭha's youngest son, fulfils his dharma and gives his youth to his father. Yayāti curses the sons who refuse him to be chiefs of different clans that lack kingship and prosperity, and to reward Pūru, he declares him his successor. It is this asura, Pūru, who starts the dynasty of the Pauravas, of which the Pāṇḍavas and the Kauravas are descendants, as is Janamejaya. Hence, the whole Kuru lineage has an asura bloodline.

This myth of Yayāti not only defines the lineage of the heroes of the Mahābhārata, but it also gives very interesting insights into asura aspects. The first and most obvious point is that if asura-ness is to be considered a fault at birth (as with Duryodhana), then all the heroes (Pāṇḍavas and Kauravas) of the Mahābhārata have that fault. Also, it is evident from this myth that the asuras are not only considered part of the Aryan fold, but are also unrelated to the ethics of evil and good; case in point: when Yayāti marries Devayānī, he carries on an affair with Śarmiṣṭha. If her asura birth were a matter of shame or even evilness, would Yayāti be involved in this alliance? In fact, when Śarmiṣṭha propositions Yayāti, she tells him she is 'high born' and he acknowledges it and even fathers three sons with her. Moreover, the asura quality is not seen as evil even by the brāhmins, because when Śukra discovers Yayāti's indiscretion, he is angry that his son-in-law is having an extra-marital affair and is cheating on his daughter but not at the fact that Yayāti has been carrying on an affair with an asura princess. Śukra curses Yayāti to curb his youthful and uncontrolled sexual desire, not because of his involvement with a girl who could potentially be evil. Also, if asura behaviour were evil and against dharma, Pūru certainly doesn't show it. Instead, it is the other brothers—sons of the brāhmin girl, Devayānī —who disregard *putradharma*. Pūru, on the other hand, is the epitome of dharma, and Yayāti rewards him by naming him his successor. Admittedly, the priests of his court oppose his choice of heir apparent, but that is only because Pūru is the youngest, not because he is the son of an asura mother. This suggestion that the dānavas were accepted simply as another (sometimes rival) faction of the Aryans and not considered evil and abhorrent is also clear from the fact that Śukra, a high and respected brāhmin, serves as the guru of dānavas. In fact, Śukra, himself, as Uśanas was declared by goddess Umā as her son, after he passed out of Śaṃkara's stomach through his urethra (*Mbh* 12.289.34–5).

These myths demonstrate that the asuras were accepted back into Aryan society by the time of the Mahābhārata's composition. They prospered alongside the Aryans, they were also productive members of the community, and there was intermarriage between them and the Aryans. However, the notoriety of the fall that they suffered in earlier texts was their legacy. Despite their inclusion in society, they remained suspect and were condemned if they perpetrated any infractions of dharma; and, if their power and prosperity threatened anyone, they were not only belittled for their asura-ness but were also often destroyed. This new status of the asuras is evident in many epic myths about the battles between devas and asuras, and the repeated defeat of the latter. However, despite their fall and loss of virtue, the battle is still not of good vs. evil. It is simply archetypal and perpetual, because, as O'Flaherty (1988: 87) states, the gods keep demons alive to keep men beholden to them: 'That is why the victory of the gods is never complete—not because they are unable to conquer the demons but because they do not wish to do so. For without the demons there would be no reason for the gods to exist at all; without Untouchables there would be no brāhmins.'

Indra-Vṛtra: The Deva–Asura Battle Paradigm

While the battle between devas and asuras is certainly archetypal, that is not the only classification for it. Just like the initial Indra/Vṛtra battle, which had a real cause and effect, but whose implications became paradigmatic for other battles, the many battles between devas and asuras in various Mahābhārata myths have their real causes and effects, even as they mirror the archetype in that the asuras are always more powerful and the gods are always threatened. Also, the gods always win (by whatever means possible) and the asura is either destroyed or at least shown his inferior place, but never wholly conquered. It is this archetype that scholars cite as the victory of good over evil, or that the battle is perpetual because it is between good and evil. Other scholars, such as Aurobindo (1997: 470), call it a 'struggle between the Gods and their dark opponents, between the Masters of

Light, sons of Infinity, and the children of Division and Night, a battle in which man takes part and which is reflected in all his inner life and action'. Aurobindo (1997: 470) also distinguishes between two kinds of people—those with asuric nature that obstruct god-knowledge, salvation, and perfection, and those of daivic nature. For these scholars, the symbolism of good and evil or an interplay of the three *guṇas* of *sattva, rajas,* and tamas, are all-important perspectives of the archetypal battle. However, there are other factors that must be considered. For example, one causative for the battle may have been economic rivalry, as is evident in the first battle of Indra and Vṛtra (*RV* 1.32.12) and in the subsequent hymn about his feats in which he is called 'Wealth-bestower' (1.33.1, 4, 10). Also, in the former hymn, the rivals of the god—the asuras—the ones who are supposedly an 'obstruction' to goodness, if measured by post-Ṛg Vedic ethics, are actually more virtuous and more evolved in *sātvic* tendencies than Indra. Moreover, the consequence of the battle, as depicted in this hymn, is that Indra's exemption from the criminality of theft and killing of a virtuous being in the ruse of enmity is established as a normative code, which also differs from the original code of ṛta, because it corrupts the aesthetic order by diverting human action away from the sacred fixed point.

The narration of the very same battle between Indra and Vṛtra occurs thrice in the Mahābhārata and, interestingly, in each telling, Vṛtra not only becomes more virtuous, but also more of a victim, and, most importantly, his very asura-ness appears synonymous to godliness. This suggests that the Aryans were aware of the evilness of destroying someone who was good simply because he was the enemy, but having accepted it as a dictate of their new supreme divine, Indra, and the alteration in ṛta, they followed it as customary behaviour.

In the second retelling of this Indra/Vṛtra myth (*Mbh* 5.9.3-7), Tvaṣṭar is a 'great devotee and lord of all beings and chief among gods'. Indra is afraid of Tvaṣṭar's power, more so because the latter creates a virtuous son with three heads who can be considered a deva three times over: with one mouth he reads the Vedas, with the other he drinks soma, and, with the eyes of the third, he sees the cardinal points. Indra kills Tvaṣṭar's son with his *Vajra* (after failing to entice him with apsarās and kāma). However, despite killing him, Indra's fear does not diminish; instead he grows even more afraid and asks a passing woodcutter to cut off the head of the slain 'Viśvarūpa'. The woodcutter denounces Indra's action and calls the dead son of Tvaṣṭar a 'son of a *ṛṣi*' and a brāhmin. Hence, Indra is condemned as a brāhmin killer. Tvaṣṭar, enraged at the death of his son and creates another son, Vṛtra, to avenge the death of the former. Vṛtra is a huge being and supremely powerful, and because no one can oppose him, he is referred to as 'Mahāsura' (Great asura) (*Mbh* 5:10.33–5). He is so invincible that Indra needs Viṣṇu's help to destroy him, and together, through treacherous means, they kill him. But now Indra is so guilty that he loses his godly power and hides in a lake in a diminutive form, 'as restless as a snake' (*Mbh* 5.10.46).

In this myth, Vṛtra is both an asura and a deva. Prior to Indra's killing him, when the celestials come to Vṛtra to request him to accept Indra's friendship, Vṛtra refers to himself as 'deva,' saying, 'How can there be peace between us two—myself and Śakra? How can there be friendship between two gods who are both powerful?' (*Mbh* 5.10.22), thus, suggesting that the battle is a power play between two equals—not good and bad or goodness and evil. Also, when Indra kills Vṛtra, the latter is even referred to as the fearful 'god' Vṛtra *'devabhayankara'*—a word that has connotations of Mahāasura. Furthermore, this myth gives a clear indication of how asura power came to be seen as enemy power: all beings that practised Aryan virtue were a form of devas, but if one was considered a threat by the other, he was termed an 'asura' by the threatened. In fact, it is possible that the Vṛtra faction also referred to Indra as asura, but since this story is told from the perspective of Indra's faction, we see only Vṛtra as asura.

A significant element that comes to light in this version of the myth is that while Indra may be a deva in name, he is in no way of daivic nature, because if he were, he would not be 'afraid' of the asura, and most importantly, he would not 'lose' his sātvic qualities by destroying the asura, and his sātvic-ness would not be reduced to the 'restlessness of a nāga'. By the same standard then, neither are Tvaṣṭar's first son nor Vṛtra of asuric nature, because there is no indication that Tvaṣṭar's first son is a '[man] of power who [is] out for the service of [his] intellectual, vital and physical ego,' as Aurobindo (1997: 470) characterizes asuric nature. In fact, it is Indra who seems to fit this characterization. Hence, by extension, neither is Duryodhana of purely asuric nature, which is made evident in the context in which this myth is placed: In the *Udyoga Parva* (5.18.12–13), Śalya compares Yudhiṣṭhira to the Indra of this myth, seeking to maintain his throne, and he compares Duryodhana first to Vṛtra and then to Nahuṣa, who replaces Indra on the throne as king of gods and is later deposed because of his arrogance and disrespect of the brāhmins. From these comparisons, it can be surmised that the reference does not make Duryodhana an evil asura—just as Vṛtra is not evil—but an enemy of equal power and a threat. It is true that Duryodhana is arrogant, as Nahuṣa was, and it is only in that sense that he displays asuric behaviour. But this same arrogance can also be seen as the *rājasic* confidence of any Aryan kṣatriya who needed to keep himself bolstered in order to face the enemy in war. Therefore, while the quality of arrogance may be seen as an asura quality, it can also be considered a natural inclination of a kṣatriya—a quality that is actually demonstrated by every hero in the Mahābhārata, and most especially by the acknowledged divine hero—Arjuna. In addition, and worthy of note in Śalya's comparisons in this event is the fact that Yudhiṣṭhira, on the other hand, portrayed in the character of Indra, comes across as more asuric in behaviour and intention, because he wishes to destroy a righteous enemy whose power threatens his own.

The first retelling of the Indra/Vṛtra myth is in the *Vana Parva* in the Mahābhārata, and it is from the perspective of the Dadhīci story (*Mbh* 3.101–2). In this retelling, we learn the most about the purpose of the perpetuity of battle and its connotational relationship to the conflict between the different factions of the Aryans. In this myth Vṛtra is a Kālakeya of the Dānava tribe and is a dānava by birth. The reason for the battle is that once again the celestials are afraid of the growing power of the dānavas, especially of Kālakeyas, who are led by Vṛtra; hence they must destroy him. To this purpose, Ṛṣi Dadhīci gives up his life so that the celestials can use his bones to make vajra. In the battle that ensues, Indra, with the help of Viṣṇu, kills Vṛtra with vajra. Having lost their leader, the asuras then confer and decide to destroy the asceticism of the brāhmins, and this conference occurs in the ocean where the dānavas use Varuṇa's palace as their enclave. From this base, the dānavas begin to destroy the brāhmins and ascetics in the hermitages of Ṛṣis Vasiṣṭha, Cyavana, and Bharadwaj.

The key element to understand the factional conflict portrayed in this myth is that not only do the dānavas wage their war solely against the brāhmins, but also their warfare seems almost guerrilla-like. They kill at night and disappear into the sea in the morning, and, like guerrillas raiding a place to oust the organized establishment, destroy sites representative of the establishment, such as the sacrificial altars, leaving the contents of broken jars and ghee ladles strewn all over the place. If this behaviour is seen in the context of modern times, it can be perceived as strikes carried out by activists and militants who don't agree with an establishment they think is corrupt and tyrannical, and they rebel against it, often using violent means. The fact that these dānavas hurt *only* the brāhmins is very indicative. It suggests a sense of resentment that certain factions of Aryan society may have felt against the growing power of brāhmins.

Two other meanings of this battle are most obvious: (a) the passing of an old order and its resistance to yield place to new. Varuṇa and his asuras represent the old order, which is coming to an end, and Varuṇa is relegated to the underworld. The brāhmins, who are the target of the guerrilla-like dānavas, are of the new order—representative of the daivic order. But, there is no indication that this new order is a good order, replacing an old, evil order. It is just that—a new order, one whose evilness or goodness needs to be empirically proven. (b) This is a conflict between new establishment and those who are against the change, which is not necessarily for the betterment of society. In fact, from the Bhargava accretions to the epic, the tyranny of the brāhmins in Aryan society and the oppression they meted out on not just the ordinary people but also on the kṣatriyas is evident. Hence, the guerrilla asuras are like militant liberators. Their violent tactics may be wrong, but their purpose is more dhārmic than that of Indra and Dadhīci, who assist in supporting the tyrants rather than sustaining a general good in society.

Sunda and Upasunda: Victims of Māyā

True to the archetype of the deva-asura conflict, the asuras are always in a no-win situation. Despite being virtuous or oppressed, they are destroyed, and, most often, it is because they are victims of duplicity by the gods, which Indra has established as rightful practice within the bounds of ṛta. So, while the asuras fight with true kṣatriya prowess, devas use treachery, which takes many forms, including the employment of a woman's sexuality to entice the dānavas.

In the myth of Sunda and Upasunda (*Mbh* 1.209.2), these two brothers are sons of the asura Nikumbha in the race of Hiraṇyakaśipu. They are inseparable, and together they desire to subjugate the three worlds, so they go to the Vindhya Mountains and practice the most severe of penances. Once again, the gods are terrified of their ascetic power and try everything to disrupt it by using māyā, but the asura brothers are undeterred. Finally, Brahmā appears to grant them boons, and the brothers ask for knowledge of all weapons, māyā, the ability to shape shift, and immortality. The Grandfather grants them all but the last, and tells them to choose their form of death instead. Having implicit trust in each other, the brothers choose that only they be each other's agent of death. Thus, with their super powers, they begin to live a life of pleasure and, tiring of that, begin to subjugate the three worlds, disrupting sacrifices, chasing brāhmins out of hermitages, and killing them. They also disrupt traditions, such as sacred ceremonies, weddings, honour of *pitṛs*, and recitation of the Vedas. Basically, they disrupt the whole cosmic order preserved by the brāhmins—on earth, in heaven, and in the underworld and then they return to Kurukṣetra to live as lords of the worlds, enjoying the asuric order *they* have created by throwing the daivic/brāhmanical system awry. To destroy these brothers, the gods device a treacherous means—Tilottamā—a woman so brilliant and beautiful that even the gods are bedazzled. Tilottamā appears in a single, transparent, red garment before the brothers, flaunting her womanly charms, and soon the brothers are fighting over her. When they both kill each other, the daivic order is restored.

This myth proves a few points at the outset: that asura power was anti-brāhmin and a threat to them; the gods were a brāhmin buffer. In other words, it was the brāhmins who created the gods, and they used these gods to destroy whoever and whatever threatened them. Also, when the brāhmin gods couldn't defeat the asuras in battle, the brāhmins used whatever dirty tricks they could through the medium of gods—in this instance, it is a woman. There is also a clear disparity in the myth: the asura brothers are likened to celestials and respected Aryan kings in terms of their enjoyment of life, but, while the gods and kings are celebrated for it, the asuras are destroyed. For instance, after subjugating the three worlds, when the brothers return to their worldly pleasures, they are compared to the immortals who roam at will in and around gardens and forests. In fact, when they first receive their boons from Brahmā and return home to celebrate with their friends, words such as, 'Eat', Feed', 'Give', 'Make Merry', 'Sing', 'Drink', 'Do as you like' are heard in every house (*Mbh* 1.209.31). These same behaviours and expressions of celebrating life are echoed in the stories of the sixteen worldly good kings that Nārada extols to convince Yudhiṣṭhira after Abhimanyu's death that even the best of kings, who were true practitioners of puruṣārtha, could not save their loved ones from death. This attests to the fact that pleasure is the practice of kṣatriyas and is sanctioned by puruṣārtha. Yet, in the case of the asuras, the same kāma and worldly pleasure are denounced as evil and are made a cause of their assassination. In other words, if the asura embraces puruṣārtha and pursues artha and kāma, even while observing dharma, he is perceived as becoming too powerful and is destroyed, mostly by the gods who, in adharmic ways, exploit his right to enjoyment. If he gives up the pleasure of life and gains ascetic eminence, he is considered a threat to the brāhmins and made to 'fall' from goodness. And if he acts according to his suspected natural inclination, then he is condemned for not making an effort to embrace goodness and rise above his asura-ness. Therefore, this double standard of values always makes the power of the dānavas threatening to the established order. But, to reiterate, the established order is not necessarily a good order.

There are many other myths in the Mahābhārata that are of similar nature and have a similar cause. For example, in the Kāca Devayānī myth (*Mbh* 1.76. 9–12), the gods feel threatened by the asuras because their guru knows the formula of immortality; so, they exploit Devayānī's natural instinct of kāma to arrange for Kāca to learn the formula of immortality from Śukra. Another similar myth is of Samudra Manthan in the *Ādi Parva*, where the gods are afraid to allow the dānavas a share of the amṛta, and when the dānavas acquire it, the gods get Viṣṇu to stop them. Viṣṇu uses his māyā to disguise himself as Mohinī and entices the asuras to give up the amṛta. In these myths, the key facts are the same—asura power is a threat; the asura is destroyed through treachery; and the effect is also the same—downfall of the asura. These myths also demonstrate that asuras are not evil, yet they are perceived as such because of the threat they pose to the hegemony of the gods, that is, the brāhmins. In addition, the asuras are not outside the Aryan fold; they are simply an older order of heterodoxy that the evolving Aryans—that is, the orthodoxy of the brāhmins—sought to replace.

Arjuna and Duryodhana: A New Generation of Devas and Asuras

The perpetuity of one order replacing another is quite evident in the Mahābhārata. In most of these myths in which the order is changed through trickery, the agent of treachery is Viṣṇu and the executer of treachery is Indra (both are brothers and Ādityas). However, in the main story of the Mahābhārata, both Indra and Viṣṇu combine in the form of Arjuna, who takes over the destruction of the dānavas, thus continuing not only the work of the eternal asura killers, but also their continual enmity with the dānavas. A good example of this transformation is Arjuna's destruction of the Nivātakavacas in *Vana Parva* when he, on a quest to acquire celestial weapons, is told by

Indra to kill the Nivāts. He is given no real reason except that Indra sees them as his enemies and asks Arjuna to repay him for the divine weapons by defeating them. Indra simply says that the Nivāts are his enemies—thirty million of them—and asks Arjuna to destroy them (*Mbh* 3.168.71–4). The myth clearly depicts that the Nivāts live peacefully under the ocean, not bothering anyone, in a city more beautiful than that of the celestials, which they obtained with their asceticism and dharma. However, Indra cannot abide this and gets a boon from Śiva that one day he himself, in a different form, will destroy the Nivāts and seize this city from them. Clearly, Arjuna is Indra in a different form; he is the new Indra, and he enters the city and annihilates the Nivāts, using Indra's vajra. Then, on his way back from destroying the Nivāts, Arjuna sees the revolving city of Hiraṇyapura, which the dānavas Pulomā and Kālakeya have won with their asceticism; they live there happily and peacefully without disturbing anyone, but Arjuna destroys this city as well. Here he uses the *rudra*, the weapon Rudra had once used for the destruction of the dānava triple city, Tripura (*Mbh* 3.173.40–57). These weapons—the vajra and the rudra—are the same celestial weapons that Arjuna brings back and uses against the Kauravas, which clearly suggests another transformation: the Kauravas are the new asuras.

Another revealing factor of the Arjuna–Indra connection is that Arjuna is guided by Indra's charioteer, Mātali. Commenting on these battles of Arjuna against the Nivāts and the Pulomās and Kālakeyas, Mātali even reminisces about Indra's battles of bygone days and sees the same pattern in Arjuna's actions. Then Mātali tells Arjuna that he has more prowess than the gods (*Mbh* 3.172.32–3), which, of course, is a clear indication of the commencement of yet another new order—this time of warrior heroes.

Whether the battle is between devas and asuras or between warrior heroes and asuras, these incidents of asura destruction can be seen as the paradigm of the eternal battle which is set up to appear as the battle of good against evil and the victory of the good, but certain illuminating elements clearly negate this: an important factor is that the battle has become causeless. There is no more real reason to destroy the asuras, but the old enmity exists like a custom—an age-old prejudice that has lost its motive; hence the violence perpetrated against the asuras is more pronounced. However, if virtue or goodness is an onus, then, here, the burden of proof must necessarily rest in Arjuna's virtue or lack thereof, since having 'more prowess than even the gods' he is the representative of the new order. Also, he is the sole agent of cause and effect. And he destroys both dānava cities without provocation; in fact, the latter—Hiraṇyapura—is not even a conquest requested by Indra. And, notably, in both cities, he leaves women and children crying and wailing, a testament that his action is evil in that its consequence is the grief of the innocent.

In addition to demonstrating a posteriori evil, which is revealed through Arjuna's action, this myth reverses the roles of the players in the degradation of yugas. This is evident in the statement that Mātali makes when he witnesses Arjuna's destruction of the asuras. He says, 'It has been ordained by Pitāhmāh that this encounter will destroy creation. I see no other reason for this battle' (*Mbh* 3.171.22). He does not say that Arjuna is justified in his actions because they echo Indra's or that the asuras are evil and always need to be destroyed; instead he says *this* battle (unlike the previous battles of gods and demons) is without reason and will destroy all of creation for no reason at all. Thus, Mātali's words point towards a total breakdown of order and cosmology, because according to the myth of time and the four yugas, the final annihilation will occur when dharma has completely deteriorated. So, either this creation's end brought about by Arjuna contradicts the orderliness of Great Time, or Arjuna's unprovoked and pre-emptive battle to destroy the dānavas *is* the total deterioration of dharma; otherwise why would creation be on the verge of destruction? Clearly, it is the latter.

Furthermore, the parallels between these and earlier battles of devas and asuras and the main war in the Mahābhārata cannot be ignored: the Pāṇḍavas are the new devas, with Arjuna as the embodiment of Indra; and the Kauravas are the new asuras, who will be destroyed with the same weapons that the gods used against the asuras of olden times. Also, just as in all battles, the dānavas were simply enemies—not evil—the Kauravas are also simply enemies—not evil. In fact, just as in earlier battles, both wealth and virtue were on the side of the dānavas, and they were defeated by treachery, so it is a foreshadowing that the Kauravas are in the right, and, in a similar vein, they will be defeated by deception. Since this paradigm of consequentiality has already been drawn, we know that the consequence of the main Mahābhārata battle will also bring grief to the innocent, and this will be perpetrated, not by the Kauravas, the reincarnation of the dānavas, but by the Pāṇḍavas, the new gods of the new order.

There is no question that the Kauravas are the asuras of old, not only because of the archetype they represent, but also because this correlation is established in many Mahābhārata myths. The *Ādi Parva* introduces the myth of the origin of the dānavas on earth: 'The sons of Diti (the asuras), having been continually defeated by the sons of Aditi (the celestials) and deprived of sovereignty and heaven, began to take birth on earth.' They took birth among earth creatures, cows, mules, camels, buffaloes, and horses, and some were even born as rākśasas and men, who became sovereign (*Mbh* 1.64.28–32). On earth, the same battles between them and devas are repeated. This not only perpetuates the cyclical battle, but also completes the cosmographic order by taking into its fold all the three worlds. So the action moves from the heavens to the earth, taking its cue from the fall of asuras from heaven. Once again, the ślokas give no indication that the asuras were evil or that their evil was the cause of them being driven out of heaven by the gods. In śloka 28, the words *'nirjita yudhi'* (conquered in battle) simply suggest an opponent in war who has been vanquished; this foe could be evil or good, just as the victor could be evil or good. It can also be assumed that if the dānavas were sovereigns, they governed through a societal system which was not evil, because they *enjoyed* their sovereignty. Therefore, morality is on the side of the asuras, because the verses suggest that heaven was rightfully theirs, since they were there before the gods. Furthermore, they claimed the earth before devas even arrived there. In the context of this symbolic paradigm of the asuras' legitimate right to both heaven and earth, the legitimacy of the throne of Hāstinapura becomes clear; it belongs to the Kauravas, and the Pāṇḍavas are usurpers, just like the gods were in both heaven and earth, because in both realms they arrived after the dānavas and snatched their wealth away from them, all in the guise of being victims of dānava oppression.

This myth describes that on earth, the dānavas continue to have conflicts with the Aryans; and they especially oppress the ṛṣis, a fact which weighs on Earth like a burden, and she goes to Brahmā with a plea to be alleviated of the weight. Brahmā, in turn, calls the celestials, dwellers of heaven, and tells them to take birth on earth according to their respective parts and battle the dānavas to unburden Earth. Hence, devas are born on earth in the form of *brahmarṣis* and *rājarṣis*. Even Nārāyaṇa follows suit, because to him, 'the most exalted of all persons,' Indra, says, '"Be incarnate" and Hari replies, "Be it so"' (1.64.37–54). The transference of the action from the heavens to the earth can also be seen as the devas' bid to re-emphasize their cosmology in the new, evolving era, because they continue to fear the security of their particular order, and they also see the wealth and power of asuras as threatening. So the threat and fear of old remains, as does the need to eliminate both. What is different is that asura-ness has become a legacy of birth, and the asura is now categorized as a race. In addition, the asuras' oppression of the earth-dwelling Aryans with their power and strength can now also be seen as a quality of their asura-ness; even here it is evident that the power of the asuras has the Vedic connotations of a power that threatens but is not necessarily evil.

A noteworthy point of this *Ādi Parva* myth of origins is that, on earth, the dānavas specifically oppress the people of the four varṇas: brāhmins, kṣatriya, vaiśyas and śūdras (*Mbh* 1:64:34), a clear indication that, by this time, the Aryans had established a civic society with human societal codes, which included the social normative of *Varṇāśrama dharma* and puruṣārtha which had replaced the divine order of ṛta. In other words, to use Eliade's idea of sacred space, the cosmological world that the evolving Aryans establish is not only fully affirmed, but it has also increased its sacred space to include earthliness and classes of people. This idea also has historical attestation: by this time, most tribal culture and beliefs of the Aryans were transforming into early kingdoms with a systematic mode of governance, and this governance extended to all people and races within the Aryan fold who were now classified according to their varṇa (Thapar 2004: 119–21). And within this system was also the race of dānavas. In fact, many of the kṣatriya kings and exalted brāhmins who fight in the Mahābhārata are the very same asuras who reincarnated after their fall (*Mbh* 1.67.1–69). Moreover, often the Aryans turn to the asuras for help and use their wealth and knowledge for their own aggrandizement; for example, the asura Māyā builds the Pāṇḍavas' palace at Khāṇḍavaprastha. But this example also shows that the use of asuric wealth is not without its price, and it remains the trigger for conflict because it is Khāṇḍavaprastha and its display of wealth that provokes the next cycle of the battle—the Mahābhārata. Furthermore, this time, there is a twist in the conflict: the one who covets the wealth is not a deva or a daivic representative; it is Duryodhana, who is an asura himself. But, at this time, Duryodhana is unaware that he is an asura; therefore, his covetousness of his rivals' wealth is not an asuric inclination; it is more in keeping with the archetypical, Indra-like behaviour.

Duryodhana is an asura by birth—by legacy of myth, not by lineage. He is born of the Asura Kali, a fact that is revealed in *Vana Parva* when Duryodhana contemplates suicide and is whisked away by the goddess that the sons of Diti have evoked through sacrifices. The dānavas reveal to Duryodhana that the goddess has made his upper body of vajra and his lower body of flowers, and that he was given as a boon to the dānavas by Mahādeva to fight their cause on earth. To help him in this mission, other dānavas have also been born on earth; for instance, Karṇa is the reincarnation of Naraka, whom Nārāyaṇa had killed in an earlier time, and the Samasaptakas are other powerful dānavas who will destroy Arjuna. They also mention that the quality of asura-ness will possess the hearts of Bhīṣma and Drona and make them heartless towards the Pāṇḍavas, so that they will not interfere in Duryodhana's business (*Mbh* 3.252.5–24).

In all of this information that Duryodhana receives from the dānavas, except for Bhīṣma and Drona being possessed by heartlessness (which ultimately is their own free will), there is no mention that Duryodhana is the embodiment of evil or that he will subdue the Pāṇḍavas through evil means. Also, in this 'dream', Duryodhana sees the dānavas as knowers of Veda and practitioners of sacrifices. They are also able to invoke the goddess who has made Duryodhana's lower body of flowers, which, in itself is very notable, because it hints at the respect dānavas have for the feminine principle, as opposed to the devas who constantly use the feminine for treachery. This fact is also indicative that Duryodhana never perverts kāma; instead, sexuality for him is always a flowering. Clearly, here the dānavas, unlike those of earlier battles, are practitioners of high Aryan values of the new era. Also, Duryodhana's upper body is made of vajra, a divine weapon that Viṣṇu and Indra used to destroy Vṛtra. This factor not only makes Duryodhana invincible to Viṣṇu and Indra, but it also gives him moral superiority over them, because while Viṣṇu and Indra use vajra as an offensive; Duryodhana is armoured with it as a defensive.

The evidence from the above examples proves another important factor about the nature of asuras and their role in the Mahābhārata. In these myths subsequent to the dānavas' fall, the enmity of devas and asuras is no longer about the establishment of different cosmological orders; it has shifted to the possession of power and wealth within the same order, and, more importantly, this new order pertains to temporality rather than just divinity. Hence, when Duryodhana returns to Hāstinapura, he worships the brāhmins, celebrates sacrifices, and gives generous dakṣiṇā, following the artha codes of giving and enjoying wealth, which are cited as being the only 'proper use of wealth' (*Mbh* 3.257. 21–2). Thus, he is not only affirming his participation in the divine cosmological order of the Aryans, but he is also participating in Aryan ideology in which the acquisition of material wealth is both a temporal sacrifice and its consecration. However, despite his adherence to these Aryan values, Duryodhana's pursuit and acquisition of wealth is perceived in the Mahābhārata as asuric, because he is born an asura; he is labelled an asura; and whatever action he performs—even if it is ethical—is considered the action of an asura. But, if Duryodhana's desire for wealth is asuric, then the Pāṇḍavas, who also fight to become lords and leaders of this new material order, must be seen as asuric as well. In addition, in light of this materiality, the archetype of the deva–asura juxtaposition becomes inconsequential. In fact, by reiterating the prototypical deva = good and asura = evil imperative, the human imperative and moral agency of not just the asura-Aryans but also the daivic-Aryans is negated, and their myths lose ethical and moral relevance.

Thus, the asuras in the Mahābhārata are human moral agents with human qualities of both good and evil. They also try to adhere to the ethical codes of a societal system in which they believe, but which was rapidly changing. Perhaps the only error on their part is that they resisted change, and the brāhmins, who were the architects of the new social order, could not abide this. Hence, using the degradation of the asura concept that occurred in earlier literatures as a weapon, they targeted the non-conformists and labelled them evil. However, not only are the asuras Aryans, they are also not an embodiment of evil. They are simply the other Aryans.

One of the key problems of evil revealed through the reinterpretation of the nāga and asura myths in the Mahābhārata is the victimization of the 'other' that became instituted. The concept of the 'other' has deep roots; it originated in the Vedic times when the Aryans needed to establish themselves, and it continued through to the epic times. Admittedly, by the time of the Mahābhārata, the imperative for civic and economic stability had facilitated much assimilation, which occurred through various positive means, such as exogamy and acceptance of the 'other', but it also occurred through subjugation and annexation. While this acculturation did breed some tolerance and secularization, the Vedic idea that the 'other' was an-Ārya, hence, nonconforming and a threat, persisted among people, and when ethical ideologies were traditionalized, these characteristics of the 'other' came to be seen as the embodiment of evil, necessarily subject to condemnation. However, there is no evidence that the 'others'—nāgas and/or the asuras—were evil or that their practices were unethical.

In fact, evidence from Mahābhārata myths shows that these 'others' were more exemplary in their actions and behaviours than characters who are considered good. Most often, as in the case of the asuras, these 'others' were actually adherents of the Aryan order, but because the establishment felt threatened by them, they were castigated. The establishment—the creators and keepers of the order—was the brāhmins, who maintained the order with brutal rigidity to ensure their own hegemony. Consequently, this concept of the 'other' created deep societal prejudices, through which both 'others'—the nāgas and asuras—were constantly victimized, sometimes in genocidal proportions, a practice that became a paradigm for future generations.

2 The Ethical Framework of the Mahābhārata

In Hindu society, the Vedas are considered divine word and absolute truth, but, although these texts institute religious rituals and social systems, they only peripherally formulate behaviours and mores. Hindu ethics are largely based on the model established by the conduct of mythical characters in Smṛti texts. This model, instead of being regulated by one fixed, absolute truth, is experiential, and it is also adjusted to circumstance of time and space. Tradition has tried to bridge the gap between the absolute truth value and ethics of behaviour by creating a concept of god and investing in it the qualities of goodness, which perpetuate the wellbeing of humans, and which people can use as a standard (Nayak 1973: 42). By this standard, the contrasting value of goodness would be evilness, which would perpetuate human pain and suffering.

However, this perspective of measuring good and evil in the Mahābhārata only on the basis of a single contrasting value reduces the text, which is actually comprised of a variety of values—some ethical, some non-ethical, some normative, and some descriptive—and the measures of good-ness and evil-ness in this variety are also various. Most of the values illustrated in this text are myth-based, and myth is empirical truth; therefore, in order to measure the good and evil described in the myth, the perpetuity of a multitude of experiences and moral behaviours (of its many moral agents) must necessarily be taken into account. Hence, in the Mahābhārata, it is difficult to standardize the values of goodness and evilness.

Furthermore, by its own admission, the Mahābhārata is a compilation. It contains the three-fold mysteries, the Vedas, yoga and science, and the various books on dharma, artha, kāma; It also contains the histories and discourses and various Śrutis, and it is explained by the Śāstras. It is a great source of knowledge and a delight for readers (*Mbh* 1.1.18–19 & 37–9). Considering this multifariousness, how is it possible to define one value-parameter that confines it all?

Additionally, because this epic is both a mythical and a valuational text, there is a dichotomy between ethical values and moral action; most often, what ought to be done is different from what is actually done. While there is a foundational system of ethics in the text, the morality of behaviours of the mythical characters is dependent not so much on these normative ethics, but on how the characters individually perceive good and evil. Hence, moral action is made an individual obligation, and, therefore, morals are often malleable. The main reason for this disconnect is ambiguity of dharma, which is the modus operandi of the key governing order of ethics—puruṣārtha of dharma, artha, and kāma, and mokṣa. This statute that dictates individual conduct is so protean that it not only makes distinguishing between good and evil almost impossible, it also makes the ethics of artha and kāma pliant. Moreover, other regulatory factors, such as karma (which could be a guiding force of good and evil behaviour), are either peripheral to the ethical context (hence the moral agents are hardly influenced by these), or they are so befuddled by other variants (such as the emphasis on fate and divine intervention) that their conceptual cause and effect lose equilibrium. This lack of fixity, albeit discordant, makes the Mahābhārata dynamic and alive, but it also creates a scope for opportunism, because it allows tradition makers to manipulate values to suit their purpose.

ETHICS AND MORALITY

It would be wrong to say that the scope of Mahābhārata, because of its mythopoeic nature and multitude of values, does not include a system of ethics that can provide for a moral codification. In fact, what underpins the Mahābhārata text is the belief in the good and the rightful; hence, godliness. These values have also transferred into the epic's tradition, and adherence to them is a Hindu's dharma. And to give tradition its due, this conversion is not automatic; it is a deliberate recognition by individuals through a sustained effort of mind and action. This effort blends 'Intellectual conviction and ethical mentality into one and this union of belief and moral nature is indissoluble. Righteousness is a form of God' (Hopkins 1968: 185).

Hopkins' comment can be the ideal for how ethics should work in a society, because it suggests that ethics and moral action are blended though a knowledge base. However, in the Mahābhārata, while this element of blending is visible in its theistic construct, it is only one small component of the text; it is not so clear in the majority of the text, in which the characters do not demonstrate this knowledge base to translate intellectual conviction of ethics into moral action. Hence, while the ethical values of Aryan society come across quite distinctly, the relationship between these values and moral action is ambiguous. Yet, this text is portrayed in tradition as exemplifying both ethics and morality. There are two key reasons for this equivocacy: mythmaking is often henotheistic, and in order to present a mythical character as divine, all his behaviours, whether moral or immoral, are given a godly veneer. Secondly, each moral agent's practice of godliness is tempered with elements of individual puruṣārtha, which often curbs his intellectual conviction and ethical mentality. These factors blur the line between good and evil and prove an imperfection of morality.

The *Anuśāsana* and *Śāntī Parvas* are the two chapters that abound with ethical codes meant to guide moral behaviour, and the principles that are most often cited in these chapters are: never causing pain, giving charity, and speaking the truth. However, aside from charitable giving, the other two are shifting values throughout the text. Even Bhīṣma, the pillar of society, who declares unequivocally that non-injury is righteousness, admits that 'No one describing righteousness can describe it accurately' (*Mbh* 12.109.10–11). Even truth is quixotic, as Kṛṣṇa says,

bhavet satyam avaktavyaṃ vaktavyaṃ anṛtaṃ bhavet
yatrānṛtaṃ bhavet satyaṃ cāpy anṛtaṃ bhavet
[Truth becomes unutterable and untruth utterable, where untruth would pose as truth and truth as untruth] (*Mbh* 8.69.32)

Therefore, truth is time and situation sensitive, and laxity is allowed in various circumstances. Bhīṣma, too, considers truth malleable. In the *Śāntī Parva*, first he states that 'there is nothing higher than the truth' (*Mbh* 12.109.4), but then he advises Yudhiṣṭhira about what men should 'generally' practice: 'There where falsehood prevails as truth, truth should not be said. There again, where truth passes for falsehood, even falsehood should be said' (*Mbh* 12.109.5). In fact, both Bhīṣma and Kṛṣṇa affirm the moral fibre of a person who can lie as per the situation. Bhīṣma says, 'That person is a master of duties who can distinguish truth from untruth [and when to use which]' (*Mbh* 12.109.6). And Kṛṣṇa goes so far as to say, 'He who is bent upon always practicing truth alone is a fool and takes truth to be as it is' (*Mbh* 8.69.34). Therefore, it is evident in the Mahābhārata that while the wise are aware of the ethics of rightfulness, they also acknowledge that it is difficult to convert this wisdom into practical moral action; instead, they think it prudent to let individual moral agents act upon these values according to their own moral perception and circumstance.

This individualized determinant of moral action in the epic becomes problematic in the tradition because, even though it can be said that most people are intrinsically moral beings, they also naturally operate subjectively. Thus, while a moral agent might feel that his/her actions are moral, they might, in fact, affect someone else's well-being, or even violate ethical codes of non-injury to others. This becomes even more pronounced when a moral agent is under duress or in a state of *āpad*. Also, moral agents often become victims of situational and/or cosmic irony, acting according to what they think is moral but discovering later that it was false. For instance, it appears that Yudhiṣṭhira, possessing the wisdom of ethical values, practices moral behaviour throughout the epic, but in the end, his sojourn to *Naraka* falsifies him. And the fact that the first person he sees in *svarga* is Duryodhana—whose behaviour is condemned as asuric and evil throughout the epic—further fuzzes the line between morality and immorality. Does this mean Yudhiṣṭhira's morality lacks goodness, or is Duryodhana's immorality really goodness? Aside from the brief and simplistic explanation about the karmic effect of the lie Yudhiṣṭhira tells Drona, there is no real answer to this question in the epic, except for the admission that the ethics of dharma are subtle. Hence, when the epic's tradition classifies this text as a dharmaśāstra, it sets people up for moral confusion, because a true dharmaśāstra would lay out clear codes of action and behaviour that people can adhere to, and the adherence of which would culminate in expected consequences and soteriological results. Here, the followers of the tradition are left to guess their own moral path, which may or may not be in keeping with the righteousness of ethics.

One key reason for this dichotomy between ethical values and moral action is the inconsistency of ideals. The Mahābhārata includes societal practices going all the way back to the Vedas. It also incorporates the principles of Upaniṣads, *Sāṃkhya*, non-injury of Buddhism, law codes of Manu, and the evolving and new tradition of bhakti. But there is no cohesion between these. For example, while in one śloka the ideal of non-injury is introduced, in the very next verse the significance of a warrior carrying out immense bloodshed is extolled. In addition, these multiple influences create divergent traditions, two of which are especially significant: one, world and life affirming, and the other, life negating; and these two spawn entirely different paths of morality. They are so different, in fact, that it is difficult to say how they originated. Surama Dasgupta believes that both of these emanated from the Vedas, but G.C. Pande believes that the two are such different approaches, that they emanated from two different people—the Aryans and non-Aryans (quoted in Jhingran 1999: 8). On the other hand, scholars like Peter Della Santina suggest that the transcendentalism and liberation through ascetic practices was a Śramaṇical goal; whereas the secular goals of longevity, prosperity, and progeny were brāhmanical; however, these were synthesized in Advaita and legitimized by texts such as the *Muṇḍaka Upaniṣad* and, later, the Bhagavad Gītā (1989: 100). Regardless of who or what is responsible for these divergent trends, what is important is that they are both clearly included in the Mahābhārata and equally available to people.

Adding to this ambiguity is the Bhagavad Gītā, which propounds principles of life affirmation but emphasizes life negation. From the metaphysical perspective of life negation, ideals of non-attachment appear intrinsically moral, because they lead a person to the ultimate goal of liberation, but perceived from the empiricism of the real world values that the Mahābhārata actually portrays, these ideals of *niṣkāma karma* are not only impossible in praxis, but they also justify evil. Yuvraj Krishan (1997: 121), explaining Śaṁkarācārya's commentary on the *Taittirīya Upanishad* (1.1), says, '*kāma*, desire, is the cause of *karma* (*karmahetu*) and is the originator of *karma*'. Hence, whenever action is performed, it is because of desire. Also, all action is causative; therefore, purpose anticipates results, which creates attachment from the get go. Thus, if there is a purpose to kill—such as Arjuna's killing of the Kaurava generals in the war to gain victory—it is motive-oriented action; ergo, attachment. It can be argued that as long as action is dhārmic, it has the potential of good, but dharma-driven karma creates more of a conundrum, because dharma itself is causative; any action performed to fulfil dharma is with the goal to do good. In this case, then, the very idea of goodness becomes a means to attachment; ergo ignorance, and, therefore, evil. Moreover, the ultimate of niṣkāma karma has a goal—the goal of liberation, and, in the process of pursuing this goal, others with whom the aspirant is in relationships, may suffer injury; in which case, the very act of detachment becomes adharma. This perplexity is depicted in the *Śāntī Parva* when Yudhiṣṭhira touts the virtues of renouncing a life of desires to enhance his own virtue and Vyāsa condemns him for it: He chides Yudhiṣṭhira for depriving the Pāṇḍavas of their dharma, artha, and kāma, and then states: 'O king, the virtue that produces affliction on one's own self and on one's own friends is no virtue, at all. It is vice that produces calamities' (*Mbh* 12.33.17). Obviously, Vyāsa sees Yudhiṣṭhira's desire for his own virtue of non-attachment as an impingement on his family's puruṣārtha and happiness. How can this selfishness be considered virtuous? It benefits no one but himself; there is no social consciousness in his virtue. According to Vyāsa, such virtue alone is damaging, because a fulfilled and happy life requires a balance and interdependency of dharma, artha, and kāma (*Mbh* 12.33.17).

Moreover, non-attachment in itself (not just in consequence) is vulnerable to moral slippage—a fact that is amply proved in the Mahābhārata. As long as one was not attached to the action or its result, one could kill, practise treachery, manipulate, etc. For example, a warrior fighting, not for personal gain, but simply to fulfil his dharma of destroying the enemy, would employ means such as deceit and treachery, which are necessary strategies in war. Thus, though his intention appeared to be niṣkāma karma, his actions were not, because the very thought of deceit requires a moral agent to acknowledge that he is breaking a code of *sādhārana dharma* for a particular desire, and he anticipates the resulting fulfilment of that desire through the deceit. This is hardly niṣkāma, because the agent has to acknowledge his egoity in the act of breaking a dhārmic code, and he will only perform this act when he is assured that this particular adharma will be minimized in his own personal karmic account by the greater good it may bring; this, in turn, will maximize his own personal karmic gain. The Pāṇḍavas' actions in the war are proof of how, in the pursuit of niṣkāma karma, morality can be jeopardized to bring about a certain result, even if the moral agent is not attached to the result. In actuality, it is not possible to escape egoity and anticipation of results in any act of immorality. Yudhiṣṭhira's lie to Drona serves as a good example again. He lies to Drona about Aśvatthāman's death because his dharma as a warrior and as a leader of the Pāṇḍavas is to destroy the threat that Drona poses, and it can be believed that he does not anticipate any personal gain from this action. However, it is not possible for him to destroy this threat without employing deceit, even though his act appears selfless, because he sacrifices his clean image of *dharmavīra*; so much so that his airborne chariot falls to the ground. But, as a result of this act, Yudhiṣṭhira is sent to Naraka.

Obviously, this is not a selfless act at all. Not only is it egoity that makes Yudhiṣṭhira consider a choice, but his apparent selflessness and non-attachment are really his unconscious anticipation of results. Such uncertainties of cause and effect are persistent problems in the epic, and they are compounded by the inclusion of the Gītā and its philosophies.

Some scholars go so far as to suggest that the Gītā itself is not an honest portrayal of non-attachment. For example, Hindery (2004: 144) believes that the Gītā only pretends non-attachment to outflank the immensely popular and selfless charisma of Buddhism; therefore, the Gītā's idea of non-attachment is only a gloss without any real depth. This statement has credence in the desire-oriented words and actions of the very characters who advocate desirelessness. For example, despite the lessons Arjuna learns in non-attachment, his actions in war hardly follow that of a non-attached man. While he joins the war and proceeds to kill his enemies/relatives in the guise of non-attachment, his actions are not niṣkāma because he has a clear goal in mind—to achieve victory, not only for the general good, but to prove to the world that his warriorship is superlative. Also, if he truly believed that to war is simply the dharma of a kṣatriya, he would also believe that this is regardless of whether the warrior survives the war or dies in it. Therefore, when Arjuna laments the death of his son Abhimanyu, who actually dies the death of a true kṣatriya, it becomes obvious that neither he nor Kṛṣṇa are able to perceive Abhimanyu's death with non-attachment. Not only is Arjuna immersed in grief at Abhimanyu's death, but he is also resolute in his desire for revenge against his son's killer, Jayadratha. In fact, he vows upon his warriorship to kill Jayadratha before the day is over; thus violating another principle of the Gītā: egolessness. Rather than renounce the conceit of 'I' as the Gītā propounds, and as Kṛṣṇa has supposedly taught him to do, Arjuna allows his I-ness to propel him to single-mindedly kill his son's killer. It is the desire of his own ego that makes him take this vow, and desire makes the action not only causative but also consequential.

Other scholars, however, do see the Gītā as a moral text; for example, according to Nicholas Sutton, the Gītā's qualities of action are full of wisdom—qualities such as freedom from anger and arrogance are all good and moralistic. Sutton (2000: 332) points out that all of chapter sixteen of the Gītā is about morality and immorality. This view, that the Gītā is a moral guide, is most common; however, it is this very quality that separates it from the rest of the text, which is hardly modelled on the principles it advocates. Even the characters that experience its guidance firsthand, such as Arjuna and Kṛṣṇa, are hardly exemplars of its ideals, and their lives, as delineated in the Mahābhārata, do not reflect knowledge of this. The case of Kṛṣṇa is even more problematic, because he propounds this message as his divine word, and he is also playing the role of a mortal; therefore, the onus is on him to live his own ideals to perfection, which he seldom does.

Ultimately, it is clear that what is considered ethical in the scriptural tradition of the Mahābhārata is not what is practised by the epic's characters, including Kṛṣṇa, mostly because these ethics allow the morality of an action to be determined by time and situation. Hence, not only is the former misleading for the practitioner of the tradition, but also the latter is inconsistent with the fixity of norms in the śāstra tradition. Perhaps the authors of the epic were aware of the ambiguity in the system, and perhaps that is why the didactic *Śāntī* and *Anuśāsana Parvas* and the Bhagavad Gītā were added (as per those scholars who believe that these were later interpolations). Or, perhaps, the epic suggests that, in the prevailing system, no one could really align moral action with theorized ethical codes, and the system itself was flawed and needed to be fixed. In that case, perhaps the epic was a plea to bring clarity in ethical and moral values for the betterment of society. However, these remonstrations were lost in the tradition.

KARMA

Another ideology in the Mahābhārata that creates discrepant standards in tradition is karma. In principle, this ideology is not only a law of cause and effect but also a system of checks and balances against which an individual can measure his or her good and evil, make the right choices, and be accountable for their actions. However, in the epic, karma bears many more meanings, and each one deepens the confusion of how this principle comes into play. At times it is *daivya* which seems to impact man without any human effort or causative. At other times, it is *kāla*, which makes all other factors impotent. Sometimes, the causative appears to be a curse rather than a past action, and, only sometimes, it is described as the complex causal chain of action and consequence. Therefore, in the Mahābhārata, the ambiguity with which karma is presented makes its ethics ineffectual, and when these ethics are brought into practice (which is rare), the principle is presented as impractical and inequitable, and, most importantly, it does not serve as a system of accountability.

This release from the liability of consequence is set by Kṛṣṇa himself. In the Gītā, Kṛṣṇa declares himself as not just the knowledge of the supreme self, but also the foremost among causes and effects in a life of *pravṛtti*. He says: 'I am argument of all debtors ...I am the dice-game among cheats, I am the glory among glories. I am victory, I am industry, I am the goodness of the good...I am the rod of the chastiser, and the policy of those that seek victory...Whatever thing there is...know them to be produced from portions of my energy' (*BG* 10: 36). From this perspective of pravṛtti, the Gītā is in alignment with the frame story of the Mahābhārata, which celebrates active life with its full gamut of good and evil of cause, action, and consequence. By definition, this is the theory of karma in play. However, Kṛṣṇa's words indicate that karma is not the cause and effect for which each individual is accountable; instead, its cause and effect are contained in the divine, eliminating individual responsibility of the consequence of action.

This exemption of the moral agents is a key problem in the epic, and it is most evident in the behaviour of the Pāṇḍavas who commit sins with impunity, because they attribute the resulting suffering of others, not to what they have perpetrated, but to the victims' own formulaic karma and past actions. Bhīṣma tells Yudhiṣṭhira a story about Gautamī (in the *Anuśāsana Parva*) that explains this (*Mbh* 13.1). In the story, Gautamī's son is bitten by a snake and he dies. A fowler, Arjunaka, catches the snake, binds him with a cord, and brings him to Gautamī with the intent of punishing him for the evil he has committed by biting an innocent child. The rest of the narrative explores the ethics of who is really to blame for the death of the child and the suffering of the mother. The narrative then goes on to find the original cause of evil and to determine if the agents that carry out the evil are just as responsible. The cause is linked from the snake to Mṛtyu to Kāla, and then the child and the old woman's karma. Ultimately, everyone is exonerated because the original cause is discovered to be none other than the child and the mother themselves. They both suffer because of their own karmas. Hence, the snake that bites the child is not guilty, because he is simply an agent of Mṛtyu, and Mṛtyu is innocent, because he is sent by Kāla, and Kāla is innocent because he is simply acting on the dictates of the karma of the child and mother. So, the old woman accepts that her own karma is the main cause of her suffering, and the others are freed of blame.

This story establishes that there is no external cause of evil; the individual himself is responsible for his own evil and his own suffering. But suffering, although self-inflicted as a remote cause, needs an agent to act as an immediate cause, and the perpetration is not evil, because the perpetrator is simply an agent. However, the praxes of this formulaic karma not only allow evildoers to escape the consequences of the evil they have committed, but to also justify causeless suffering. Perhaps, the question to ask here is: is there any circumstance under which agents can be considered guilty?

In theory, the answer to that is, 'yes'; by the *principle* of the doctrine, at least under two types of circumstances: (1) If the agent, instead of being an unattached doer carries out the evil act with intent and (2) all evil acts, even if carried out simply as a dictate of kāla and mṛtyu, consequent to the sufferer's karma, incur evil karma and become subject to the principle of causation. Hence, the agent, although unattached to his or her 'unintentional' evil action, gets caught in the cycle of this evil as well. But how does an individual avoid becoming an agent of evil in order to remain free of the effects of evil action? This is not possible, because, unlike the lack of culpability of the agent in Gautamī's story, the fact that an individual is chosen as an agent of evil is already a result of that individual's past action or karma. For example, the snake in this story is actually an agent of Mṛtyu because he incurred some bad karma in his past birth for which he has to pay by becoming a snake and biting the innocent child. And now, in his next birth, he will have to pay for biting the child. So, one evil action leads to another in a complex causal chain of events that extends over innumerable lifetimes. In this story, the agents are not only non-human, but also acting as per their natural inclination (the snake bites, kāla destroys, etc.); however, when this story is applied to human agents, it gains moral relevance. For instance, if the snake is replaced by a human agent, then the killing of the child, despite the karma of its past life would be considered an evil act because killing innocent children is not a natural inclination of human moral agents; it has to be intentional. Similarly, if Mṛtyu and Kāla are replaced with human agents, their commissioning the death of an innocent child would implicate them of diabolic intentions.

This causal chain linking intention, action, and consequence is almost completely lacking in the Mahābhārata, especially in the case of the supposed dharma heroes, the Pāṇḍavas, who do not suffer any of these intentions or consequences. They commit many offences, which are often justified as simply the fruition of the victim's own past actions. In addition, to give the Pāṇḍavas even greater impunity and credulity, these past actions are attached to the victims themselves as a curse, which the Pāṇḍavas righteously fulfil as agents, or they are obligated to do so by a vow they have taken. The Mahābhārata abounds with such examples: the treacherous killing of Karṇa is attributed to his curses and past life; the deceitful killing of Drona is attributed to the fulfilment of Dhṛṣṭadyumna's purpose on earth. Bhīṣma's killing by duplicity is because of Ambā's curse and her endeavour to destroy him; Duryodhana is killed by foul play because of the vow Bhīma had taken; etc.

Another deeply confusing factor in the idea of karma in the Mahābhārata is its interchangeability with fate or daivya. The element of fate has no Vedic precedent, and the Upaniṣadic philosophers did not admit the influence of fate, except to say that everyone makes his or her own fate. But the Purāṇas and epics clearly suggest the prominence of daivya and *niyati*, often, even over human effort, and it is defined severally—an effect of preceding lives, payback for wrongdoings in present life, divine ordinance, kāla, good luck, etc. These various interpretations of fate are very much evident in the Mahābhārata, and most often in situations where the sinful actions of the Pāṇḍavas cause pain and suffering for themselves, for the Kauravas, and for other people. Additionally, fate is held responsible in situations of extreme devastation that do not seem to have a visible cause, and fate is also invoked when the cause is evident but cannot be visibly acknowledged, because other factors have greater sociological significance, such as if a brāhmin commits a sin and causes a distressing event. Also, if someone does not receive an anticipated reward for his actions, he or she accepts the disappointment as fate's doing.

There are numerous examples of all such relegations of karma to fate, but nothing can be more glaring than Yudhiṣṭhira blaming fate for his role in the dice game. Yudhiṣṭhira also refuses to see his brothers' fault in creating situations that cause pain and suffering. Even when Bhīma delivers a death-blow to Duryodhana with blatant deceit, Yudhiṣṭhira does not hold Bhīma responsible; instead he upbraids Duryodhana and tells him that his brothers' deaths is a result of fate: 'For your folly, your brothers, mighty warriors all, and your kinsmen, have been killed by us! I think all this is the work of Destiny' (*Mbh* 9.59. 26). Even Kṛṣṇa uses fate as a scapegoat to exonerate the Pāṇḍavas of their immoral actions. After the war, when he visits Dhṛtarāṣṭra to console him, he too calls the death of the Kauravas 'destiny': 'What else can it be but the effect of Time? Indeed, Destiny always reigns supreme! Do not attribute any fault to the Pāṇḍavas' (*Mbh* 9.63.48). Curiously, even Dhṛtarāṣṭra, who suffers the death of all his sons and the whole Kaurava army at the hands of the Pāṇḍavas, blames destiny and not the Pāṇḍavas, saying:

> When the valiant Bhīṣma having encountered Śikhaṇḍin, died like a lion, killed by a jackal, what can it be but Destiny? When the Brahmin

> Drona, the master of all offensive and defensive weapons has been killed by the Pāṇḍavas in battle, what can it be but Destiny? When Bhūriśravas has been slain in battle, as also Somdatta and king Valhika were killed, what can it be else Destiny? When Bhagadatta, an expert in fighting from the back of elephants, has been killed and when Jayadratha has been slain, what can it be but Fate? When Sudakṣiṇa has been slain and Jalasaṃdha of Puru's race, as also Śrutāyus and Āyutāyus, what can it be but destiny?' (*Mbh* 9.2.30–5)

Even Duryodhana, who, throughout the epic, never forgets that the Pāṇḍavas are his enemy blames everything on fate at the end of the war. 'I was the master of eleven *camus* of troops and yet I have come by this plight...no one can control Destiny' (*Mbh* 9.64.9). There is an abundance of such examples of moral agents attributing the consequences of action to destiny.

In one instance the epic does question the acceptance of fate over responsibility, but this questioning is done by Draupadī—a woman—and not by a warrior hero or a brāhmin; hence, the words do not much impact the prevalent norms. Draupadī condemns fate for its power over men and condemns men for allowing fate to have power over them. Although she accepts that her sorrows in exile are due to fate—Vidhāta—and Creator—Dhāta (*Mbh* 3.30.1)—she condemns both by saying, 'If the act done follows the performer then forsooth, the God himself is contaminated with the sin of every action' (*Mbh* 3.30.42). In addition, she states that if this sin does not touch upon a person, then it is only because of their own power, but the ordinary man who is weak is doomed. Hence, Draupadī questions the very nature of karma and fate and gives precedence to karma, thus redefining ethics of fatalism as ethics of karma. In fact, it is Draupadī alone who also sees fate as escapism from accountability of action that negates the laws of karmic cause and effect: 'The man who believes in chance and who, though capable of work, does not work, does not live long, for his life is one of weakness and helplessness' (*Mbh* 3.32.15). She adds that even fate rewards those who perform pristine action; action itself could be pure or impure—but action is the key. 'If a person were not himself the instrument of his acts, the sacrifices would not bear any fruit in his case' (*Mbh* 3.32.30). It is only because humans are the instrument that they are considered good when they perform good actions, and bad when they perform bad actions. If it were all fate, how could a man performing bad action be considered sinful? Thus, Draupadī removes the consequence from fate's hands and places it in the hands of moral agents and clearly defines the ethics of good and evil. Draupadī's probing questions about ethics of action are, in fact, the only dynamic that can justify the epic tradition's personification of evil in Duryodhana's character. Otherwise, if his hurtful actions against the Pāṇḍavas are passed off as their fate, then Duryodhana himself stands exonerated in the same way that the Pāṇḍavas are.

In actuality, it is in Duryodhana in particular and the Kauravas in general that the concept of karma is realized. The Pāṇḍavas, who are blind to the cause and effect of their own actions, not only see Duryodhana and the Kauravas' actions in a karmic light, they also insistently force the Kauravas to see the cause and effect of these actions and not pass them off as fate. For example, in *Karṇa Parva*, as Kṛṣṇa directs Arjuna to shoot the fatal arrow that will kill Karṇa, and Karṇa, whose chariot wheel is stuck in the mud, points out the violation of a code of war, Kṛṣṇa reminds Karṇa of his past evil actions, saying sarcastically, 'Fortunate, it is, O son of Rādhā that you remember virtue. It is always seen that men, when they are in distress, speak ill of the providence and not of their own evil deeds' (*Mbh* 8.91.1). Also, the retributive aspect of karma spanning many lives is mentioned only in reference to the Kauravas. For example, when Aśvatthāman makes plans for the night raid against the Pāñcālas because he wants to kill 'Those destroyers of [his] father in the night when they are buried in sleep,' he says, 'I care not if I am born as a worm or an insect in my next birth' (*Mbh* 10.5.27), thus implying the accumulation of karmic effect in subsequent lives. Additionally, the distinction between fate and karma is also associated mostly with the Kauravas. For example, advising Aśvatthāman before the night raid, Kṛpa tells Aśvatthāman: 'Generally no act ever becomes fruitless in the world ... There is hardly seen a person who obtains something of itself without having made any exertion, as also one who does not obtain anything even after exertion' (*Mbh* 10.2.13–14).

The idea of karma's retribution is also most clear in Duryodhana's case, when the Pāṇḍavas and Kṛṣṇa constantly remind him of his immoral acts. Even as Duryodhana is dying from the fatal strike that Bhīma has delivered treacherously, Yudhiṣṭhira tells Duryodhana, 'forsooth you suffer dreadful consequences of your own former acts' (*Mbh* 9.59.22). In fact, karma's equitable retribution is made completely clear in a strange twist of words that are evoked by Duryodhana: as he is dying Yudhiṣṭhira tells him that the Pāṇḍavas will suffer more, because while Duryodhana will depart to the other world and go to heaven, they, the 'creatures of hell shall continue to suffer the bitterest grief' (*Mbh* 9.59.28). In the final reckoning then, karma holds the Pāṇḍavas accountable for their actions, and condemns them to suffer the consequence—their own guilt and suffering.

However, there is a glaring inequity in how much the Pāṇḍavas are held accountable as compared to the Kauravas. This is clearest in the *Strī Parva*, when the narrative describes how the war that the Pāṇḍavas helped start causes the suffering of innumerable wives, mothers, and sisters who walk the fields and bewail the dead, questioning the justification of the war. But, sadly, the epic glosses over this dire consequence and treats it not only briefly (there are only 19 verses devoted to the lamentation of the women in *Strī Parva*) but also mildly—a small offence that is easily rectified with a yajña and charity to brāhmins.

One of the reasons karma is ambiguous in the Mahābhārata is that, in epic times, the theory was still evolving. Various forms of karma were derived from all belief systems prevalent at that time, and there was no reconciliation or unification of them. Karma in pre-epic form may have been a system of soteriology; the germ of it is present in the Vedas as *iṣṭāpūrta* (stored up merit of sacred rites), which, in the Brāhmaṇas, came to be known as yajña karma. This karma, as Yuvraj Krishan (1997: 29) succinctly concludes, entailed

> (i) construction of works of public welfare; (ii) the productions of merit or beneficial potency, which is invisible—*adṛṣṭam*; (iii) the storing up (*āpūrta*) of merit in heaven, *svarga*; (iv) the transmigration of the soul (*ātmā*), of the *yajamāna* (performer of the *iṣṭi*) after death, from earth

(*bhūloka*) to heaven (*svarga*); and (v) the enjoyment of the stored up merit by the soul of the *yajamāna*, in heaven.

But, it is important to note that this Vedic form of karma was ritualistic, not moral, and if a *vidhi aparādha* occurred in the ritual which rendered it ineffective, there were ways to expatiate that 'sin' through further ritual.

Wendy Doniger O'Flaherty (2007: 3) suggests that it may have been the theory of 're-death' that predetermined the theory of rebirth. Citing David M. Knipe's *Sapiṇḍīkaraṇa: The Hindu Rite of Entry into Heaven*, O'Flaherty (2007: 3) explains that the funeral rites of *śrāddha* and *piṇḍa* in Vedic rituals were to 'prevent the dissolutions of an afterlife for the deceased. However, she also points out that these rituals indicate a number of inconsistencies and ambiguities and raise questions that plague the theory of karma in later texts (O'Flaherty 2007: 3–4). The Mahābhārata includes this earlier form of the Vedic concept of karma in many of its myths, especially in the way it is portrayed, not as an ethical principle to show that good karma begets good, and bad karma begets bad, but simply as an eschatological practice. In addition, the Bhagavad Gītā also expounds the Upaniṣadic perspective of the nivṛtti-based karma, which binds a soul in an action-consequence chain or *saṃsāra*, and the only release from this bondage is mokṣa, which requires abandonment of desire-based karma.

The Mahābhārata, thus, reflects various ideas about karma that did not quite cohere, because they were derived from various sources. However, the tradition of the epic conjoined the nivṛtti form of karma with pravṛtti-based puruṣārtha, and this created an ethical trap in which a person, on the one hand, is encouraged to enjoy a life of materiality, but on the other hand, condemned by karmic law for his/her attachment to material enjoyment. Moreover, in tradition, the examples of epic heroes—even those as evolved as Yudhiṣṭhira—caught in saṃsāra give people a pessimistic outlook on life, because a person's actions are unceasing, and, according to the karma doctrine, so are their results; when Dharmavīra himself, or Arjuna, who is taught the knowledge of extrication from saṃsāra, cannot break the cycle, how can an ordinary person hope to achieve this? The only solutions tradition seems to offer are that one can either cease all action, or that one can follow the Bhagavad Gītā-devised niṣkāma karma. However, the former is not possible and the latter is not only ambiguous, but also next to impossible.

Another grave danger in the theory of karma that the epic tradition presents, especially through the philosophies of the Gītā, is that it creates inequity in society by drawing rigid lines of varṇa. The Gītā enjoins that one must act only according to one's dharma, and that it is evil to act against it (*BG* 3.35). This injunction must be seen in combination with varṇāśrama, which was an ethical principle of Aryan society and was made binding for moral agents through the Dharmaśāstras. For example, according to Manu, a śūdra must only serve the upper castes, and if he performs any other duty that is the dharma of other castes, these actions will bear undesirable fruit. Also, a śūdra must not listen to the Vedas, and he must refrain from performing Vedic rituals or any ritualistic action to expatiate his sins, or even to improve himself through *jñāna* (*Laws of Manu* 10.122–7, Müller: 428–30). Therefore, in order to perform moral action, the only path a śūdra can follow is the path of *karmayoga*; however, following this path, a śūdra is forever caught up in servitude. The śūdra's only way out is that he perform his servitude to the best of his ability, which means that he can never improve his lot through *puruṣkāra*. In theory, niṣkāma karma for the śūdra seems possible, but in praxis, it is almost impossible. For instance, how can it be expected of a person who cleans out latrines to be happy with his lot in life, and to continue for the rest of his life to clean latrines to the best of his ability without making any effort to get out of that profession, even if he accepts that his life is a consequence of some past karma? And if he does desire to improve himself, he breaks the principle of varṇa dharma, and hence accrues bad karma, which could bring him right back to this sort of life upon rebirth too. In short, he is damned if he does, and damned if he doesn't.

The Mahābhārata does not elaborate on the societal inequities of the śūdras in its myths, because it is mainly a text about warrior heroes and kṣatriya dharma. However, it advocates adherence to one's varṇa dharma in various places, and especially in the Gītā. These references may have been a reflection of the conversations that were occurring in society at that time, but when these were codified by tradition and supported by the decrees of the Dharmaśāstras, they resulted in discriminatory standards in society that persist till today.

Thus, in the majority of the Mahābhārata narrative and myths, karma is actually presented only as a cursory measure that is quite ineffectual in setting clear standards of good and evil, or clear ethical connections between cause, action, and consequence. Hence, the doctrine of karma is neither explored in its retributive fulsomeness, nor in its liberating potentiality. In fact, in the former case, it is almost non-existent, because the epic never describes the consequences of actions in rebirth. No character's preceding births are presented in connection to their karma; therefore, there is no evidence of how a person's present life is a consequence of his/her past life. The only reference to this chain is in some incidental myths, such as Draupadī, in a previous life, asking Śiva for a husband five times, hence obtaining five husbands in her subsequent life; but, even in this, no insight is provided into the good and evil attributes of her actions or behaviours which caused her to be married to five husbands in her next life. Nor is there any mention of the next birth of any individual. The farthest extent of the epic's reach is *svarga* or *naraka lokas*, which are places of simple joy and suffering, respectively, far removed from the reality of life.

Hence, the concept of karma in the Mahābhārata is more of a confusing factor than a guiding principle of ethics and morality. Also, in the epic's depiction, karma's equation with fate and destiny not only make it ineffectual as a measure of accountability, but it also creates a pessimistic and fatalist theme in a Hindu's life, especially because its inexplicable dichotomies make human suffering appear causeless and futile. These problems were further compounded by tradition, adding remedies such as sacrifice, charity to brāhmins, and bhakti to help people circumvent the effects of karma.

PURUṢĀRTHA

The guiding force in the Mahābhārata is a system that is meant to sustain society in all respects. This is the system of puruṣārtha. With dharma as the leading principle in this value system of ethics, the epic is framed within the *caturvarga* of dharma, artha, kāma, and mokṣa. However, at the very outset, the last principle, mokṣa, must be eliminated from the equation, because this is only peripheral at best. Mokṣa is the concept of liberation, but it is at odds with the lives of moral agents in the epic. 'The proper eschatological goal of life dedicated to the realization of the first three goals should have been heaven which has been ... recognized by various religion texts' (Jhingran 1999: 17). But, instead of heaven, which is the natural outcome of living a life of dharma and pravṛtti, liberation is included in the fourth and final goal of human life. G.C. Nayak (1973: 31) says that mokṣa 'is more or less an exhortation to transcend the dichotomy of good and evil and attain a stage of awareness in which all worldly differences ... no longer appear to have any significance or importance'. Hence, in the context of the Mahābhārata, the idea of mokṣa is incongruous, because myths are significantly about the human experience in the realm of good and evil.

Many scholars see mokṣa as amoral, because to achieve mokṣa, all action—good or bad—including moral action, is renounced. Referencing O'Flaherty and P. Hacker, Sutton (2000: 314) says that to attain mokṣa 'modes of behaviour are dictated not on the basis of consideration of right and wrong, but, as with Aristotelian ethics, they bring success to the practitioner, in this case release from the world experience. Hence ethical codes presented in it are not an appreciation of moral rectitude but simply a part of a soteriological technique'. However, Sutton (2000: 316) also adds that, 'it is notable that the term dharma is used for both [moral action and mokṣa]'. In fact, in the Mahābhārata, the concept of mokṣa is made moralistic, because, although mokṣa dharma appears to negate moral content in action, its pursuit requires a discipline which is more vigorous than just an adherence to dhārmic morals of right and wrong; this makes it an ethical guiding principle. But, regardless of the ethics this principle delineates (or not), the fact remains that mokṣa dharma is not practised by any major character in the epic, and it is not at all a part of the narrative of the Mahābhārata (aside from the treatise on it by Kṛṣṇa and Bhīṣma). So, it really cannot be considered in the ethical framework of the epic. And this very fact, that the principle of mokṣa can be eliminated from the discussion about the epic's ethics, is a problem because, while it is easy to discount it in theory, it is not so in a Hindu's life, who has been taught by tradition to recognize it as part of puruṣārtha. It is integral to his ethical goals, and he keeps striving to achieve that which his own life renders unachievable.

The foundational principles of the Mahābhārata are the trivarga of dharma, artha, and kāma, with the observance of all three interwoven, as suggested by Nārada when he enquires of Yudhiṣṭhira after his coronation as king: 'Do you, dividing your time judiciously, follow religion, profit and pleasure?' (*Mbh* 2.5.19). Out of these three principles, dharma is key, because it overarches the other principles and is central to the ethical framework of the epic. In fact, kāma and artha, if pursued without dharma, have the potential of becoming immoral; therefore, dharma is the only right means to achieve the goals of trivarga. 'Just like one may ask "what is ethical?" In the same way one can ask "What is *dharma*?"' (Sutton 2000: 293).

Dharma

In its very basic meaning, dharma is duty, morality, justice, virtue, religion, and all other such principles that guide rightful action. According to its Sanskrit root '*dhr*', it means to hold or uphold, which means that it holds together or upholds society, community, family, and the individual. Hence, an individual, by acting in the way of dharma, holds together in a consequentiality of a domino effect, his family, community, society, the universe, etc. While in the Vedas the determinate of right and wrong and good and evil was ṛta or an-ṛta, and, to some extent, being Aryan or an-Aryan, in the Mahābhārata, the guiding principle is dharma with its antithesis, adharma. In Vedic times, ṛta was order—cosmic order, the order of rituals and sacrifices, and the order of human behaviour. Vedic Aryans believed that their personal lives and gods were subject to cosmic order being upheld; therefore, ṛta was the fixed point from which all other orders emanated and into which all orders converged. In the Mahābhārata, the order is not cosmic; it is a 'moral order which is oriented towards the conservation and realization of moral and spiritual values. It is the belief that the moral law, and not the mechanical forces of nature, governs and controls the world order and all natural processes. It is also the belief in the final victory of justice, better known as truth (*satya*) or right (*dharma*)' (Jhingran 1999: 33). This is to say that the moral quality of one's deeds, thoughts, and desires not only condition one's character but also manipulate the natural order so that one is thrown in external circumstances that are most suited to effectuate the rewards that one's moral character deserves. This is the order of dharma.

Unlike ṛta, which is fixed, dharma is mutable; it is time-, character-, and situation-specific. As Surama Dasgupta (2008: 342) says, 'There cannot be any fixed or rigid standard of duties for all times, because life is complex and ever changing. What appears to be good or right in one context may not be so at another; at most, some general maxims and principles can be laid down'. Moreover, dharma is also consequential, and what people experience or suffer or gain from this order is the very element that determines its mutability. Hence, how people act in these experiences is dharma. This makes dharma normative to a certain extent, but it also makes it descriptive. Because dharma creates models of action and behaviour, and it brings together individuals who interact and relate to one another as per these models of behaviour, it can be seen as the cohesive for social harmony. But this same individual whose dharma is the cohesive can also give up family, community, and society in the pursuit of mokṣa, and that too is dharma—*mokṣadharma*.

Dharma also implies in itself a whole code of conduct about behaviours to be avoided, such as crimes—murder, adultery, theft, spiritual sins—arrogance, envy, jealousy, and all injury of beings, etc. It also includes in its fold following the stages of life and adhering to caste, customs, daily rituals, societal norms, etc. Dharma is all this, and much more. In fact, the meanings of dharma are so various and all-encompassing that dharma is untranslatable, especially into simplistic terms of duty, morality, or virtue. The concept of dharma is present in all its shades in the Mahābhārata, and all the myths, side stories, characters, situations, treatises, are delineated and defined by it in its variousness—from basic rules to complexities of characters and moral dilemmas.

The two primary dharmas that underpin the epic's framework of ethics are *varṇadharma* and *āśramadharma*, but there are also a few others, such as *naimittakadharma*, *rājadharma*, *strīdharma*, and *kuladharma*, that come into play depending on the situation or event. Āśramadharma is behaviour according to one's stage in life (*brahmacarya*, *gṛhastha*, *vanaprastha*, and *saṃnyāsa*). Hence, what is allowed for a person in one *āśrama* may not be allowed in the dharma for another in another stage of life; for example, it is the privilege and right of a person in gṛhastha to experience and pursue sexual desire, but for a person in brahmacarya, this is forbidden. Varṇadharma entails occupation, duties, and actions to be performed according to one's caste. Hence, what may be dharma for one caste may be adharma for the other. For example, non-violence is prescribed for the brāhmin, but a kṣatriya has to necessarily kill his enemy, and a butcher has to necessarily carve the meat of an animal. These āśramas are like controls that society imposed on the people. Hindery (2004: 90) equates this control of power to morality, because it created order and some justice. However, this control became a real problem of evil in the tradition, because unlike the Vedas, where individuals recognized and practised order, not because it was right or wrong, but because it was a continuum of the cosmic order (a natural state of being), the epic's moral order was necessarily to establish standards of right and wrong (an imposed state of being). Also, no matter how orderly varṇāśramadharma may have been for society, it did not promote justice or equality, because it was biased, not only against women, śūdras, and *Mlecchas*, but also in the hierarchy of the castes.

In the epic's brāhmin-controlled framework of varṇāśrama, there was one set of ethics or ethical bindings for brāhmins and another set for the rest of the people, especially for the śūdras, women, and those outside the Aryan fold. The brāhmins were allowed anything they chose to justify—even those actions that were forbidden in the normative ethics of puruṣārtha and the restrictive order of varṇāśrama. For example, they could change their profession and become kṣatriyas, like Drona. They could indulge in kāma and covetousness, like Parāśara. They could lie, cheat, and even indulge in violence and anger—all with not just impunity but also self-righteousness; for example, Jamadagni Paraśurāma, who metes out extreme violence against the kṣatriyas and is actually deified for it, so much so that tradition considers him an incarnation of Viṣṇu. This dubious environment of contradictions, double standards, and constant self-aggrandizement that the brāhmins created was a hindrance to evolvement in morality. 'The caste-feeling ... not only deprived the slave of "god and sacrifice" and made the mere "people" (that is, the agricultural and mercantile classes) the "food of kings" but exalted the priest to the position of gods on earth' (Hopkins 1968: 59).

In the Mahābhārata, the brāhmins are portrayed as not only powerful but also intolerant of any mutinous element that threatens their supremacy, so much so that they can even manipulate the very scope of creation to ensure that they remain supreme. For instance, in *Vana Parva*, Mārkaṇḍeya tells Yudhiṣṭhira that 'when the world is annihilated by Kalki, I will create a new *Yuga* surrounded by *brāhmins* and will exterminate all the low and despicable *Mlecchas* ... Then exterminating all robbers, I will duly give away this earth at a great horse sacrifice to the *brāhmins* ... In the *Kṛta* age...the *śūdra* will be devoted to the service of the other three orders. Such will be the *Dharma*...' (*Mbh* 3.190.17 & 3.191.1,14). And then he warns Yudhiṣṭhira: 'You should never humiliate a *brāhmin*, for a *brāhmin* if angry can destroy the three worlds by his vows' (*Mbh* 3.191.20). These statements are especially ironic because, in this same parva, Mārkaṇḍeya classifies the four castes as merely different parts of Nārāyaṇa, the supreme deity, and he also states the qualities of a brāhmin as 'devoted to asceticism', 'souls under complete control', 'desirous of knowledge', 'freed from lust and wrath and envy', 'unwedded to earthly things', 'their sins completely destroyed', 'possessing gentleness and virtue', 'free from pride', etc. (*Mbh* 3.189.14). Obviously, these qualities were only a theoretical ideology, because the brāhmins in the epic, including Mārkaṇḍeya, are hardly these paragons of virtue.

The control that the brāhmins wielded can also be seen in how people of other varṇas in the epic perceive this caste. To cite just a few examples: in *Ādi Parva*, Arjuna is told by the Gandharva, Angāraparṇa: 'A king who is without a brāhmin, can never acquire any land by his bravery or nobility of birth only, O spreader of Kuru race, therefore, know that the kingdoms with brāhmins at their heads can be retained for long' (*Mbh* 1.170.79). Another telling example is when, at her *svayaṃvara*, Draupadī chooses Arjuna, who is disguised as a brāhmin, all the attending kṣatriya kings object to her choice; but though they feel insulted, they do not want to call out or hurt the brāhmin, because they believe that '[their] kingdoms, lives, wealth, sons and grandsons and whatever other wealth [they] have in this world all exists for the *brāhmins*' (*Mbh* 1.189.10–11). In these examples, three aspects of brāhmin power come to light: (1) brāhmins were indispensable to kingship, (2) even if the kṣatriyas resented the privileges that the brāhmins had, they could not do anything about it out of fear, and (3) they could violate even marital law by marrying women outside of their caste.

There are many reasons why kṣatriyas accepted the control of the brāhmins: brāhmins oversaw yajñas for special occasions, everyday life, and personal purification—rituals that were integral to Aryan life. They were also well versed in the Vedas and monopolized the imparting of that highest of knowledge to whomever they deemed worthy. They were teachers and gurus of weaponry and claimed to know formulae for divine weapons. Although they were not mediators between a person and the divine, their asceticism gave them the power to fulfil boons and desires, just like the gods. Hence, as Hopkins (1968: 61) says, they were substitutes for the divines, but he also points out that the divinity of brāhmins was only one-sided. They used their power and spiritual inheritance for self-aggrandizement while 'prostituting' much that was pure. Sutton (2000: 55) also speculates about the actual status of brāhmins in epic Aryan society. He says, 'It is tempting to guess at the actual social order that underlay the Brāhmanical view of an ideally structured society presented in the Mahābhārata. The continual emphasis on the respect that must be offered by kings to brāhmins suggests that the position of the latter was somewhat less secure than the authors of the epic would have liked'. Hence, it can be surmised that the brāhmins emphasized caste biases and their high position, because they needed to secure their own dwindling control.

However, it is important to note that at the time of the epic's formulation, the premise of the caste system had not yet become wholly inflexible. Although intermingling of caste duties was frowned upon, an individual's caste was ideologically determined by his actions. A good example of this practice is evidenced in the forest of Viśākhayupa when Bhīma is seized by Nahuṣa, who has been turned into a serpent. He agrees to release Bhīma only if Yudhiṣṭhira answers his questions, most of which relate to caste. Obviously, caste was a crucial issue at that time, and it appears that the Aryans were trying to resolve it. In fact, the answers that Yudhiṣṭhira gives Nahuṣa indicate that people were aware of the rightness behind a more flexible and people-friendly caste system. For instance, when Nahuṣa asks Yudhiṣṭhira who is a brāhmin and who is a śūdra, Yudhiṣṭhira replies that a brāhmin is one who has truthfulness, charity, forgiveness, good conduct, benevolence, asceticism, and mercy. When Nahuṣa argues that even the śūdra can have these qualities, Yudhiṣṭhira states that anyone who does not possess these qualities is not a brāhmin, and if a śūdra possesses them, then the śūdra is a brāhmin. Consequently, when Nahuṣa asks if caste is determined by actions or character, and if so, what purpose does the distinction of caste serve, Yudhiṣṭhira responds by stating that because there is so much exogamy among the caste, it is very difficult to distinguish the various castes (*Mbh* 3.180. 23–6). Yudhiṣṭhira's words not only provide an insight into the amorphousness of the system, but also a sanction for intermingling of caste.

However, in practice, because of brāhmin repression, caste biases and rigidity of caste was very much a reality. And, by the time the epic became tradition, caste had become hereditary and inviolate: thus, a śūdra could never aspire to break from his caste duties. A significant example of how the very preservation of society came to be dependent on an ironclad caste system is Arjuna's rejection of his warrior duty in Kurukshetra at the beginning of the war. Facing the Kaurava forces, he realizes that he would cause the death of numerous warriors, which would deplete the kṣatriya gene pool and, this, in turn would force kṣatriya women to marry into other castes. Not wanting to be responsible for this adharma of mixing of castes, he decides it would be better not to fight at all (*Mbh* 6.26.7) In fact, the lines of separation between castes had become so indelible that Kṛṣṇa's emphatic advise to adhere to one's caste duty is a key element in the tradition-establishing Gītā. Citing verse 48, Sutton (2000: 296) points out that '*vināśāya ca duṣkritām*' is a part of Kṛṣṇa's mission—*vināśa*, not of the wicked or evildoers in a moral sense, but rather of those actions that controvert ritual conduct of life, as per caste. A clear example of Kṛṣṇa's vināśa of such mutinous conduct is the punishment he gives to Aśvatthāman after his night raid (Sutton 2000: 296). Aśvatthāman is of brāhmin varṇa living the life of a kṣatriya, and as a Kaurava warrior, he released an exterminating weapon into the wombs of Pāṇḍava women. For this crime, which is seen as a consequence of his varṇa violation, Kṛṣṇa curses him: 'O wretch, for three thousand years, you shall have to wander the earth without a companion and without being able to talk with anyone...You shall have to live outside the pale of human society in dense forest and dreary moors. The stench of your puss and blood shall come out of your body, and you will wander over the earth suffering from all diseases' (*Mbh* 10.16.11–12).

One reason why caste practices were binding was that they came to be considered as obligatory as rituals that sustained the natural order. Also, these practices were supposed to harmonize behavior with an individual's inherent nature, and this was seen as svadharma. In theory, this dharma is synonymous with free will. It seems to supersede all other dharmas, because it places the individual over social norms, thus empowering him or her. However, in actuality, this aspect of dharma not only added to the ambiguity of ethics, but it also made the system unfair, because while brāhmins and kṣatriyas were free to follow their svadharma, the other two castes were condemned for breaking the codes of varṇāśrama if they tried to rise above their varṇa. The clearest examples of this is Ekalavya, who belongs to the Niṣāda tribe (a śūdra) but feels naturally inclined to be a warrior. He is not only rejected by Drona because of his caste, but he is also made to suffer the extreme consequence of aspiring to be a kṣatriya by cutting off and giving his right thumb to Drona, which deprives him of the ability to use a bow and arrow (*Mbh* 1.132.31–56). Moreover, while the low-caste Ekalavya suffers this grievous injury, the kṣatriya prince, Arjuna, who is the catalyst of this incident, is able to salve his jealousy with impunity. The epic is silent about the wrongness of Drona's and Arjuna's behaviour in this incident of gross injustice. Another example displaying the discrimination that the lower castes had to face if they so much as attempted to fulfil svadharma is Karṇa's first challenge to Arjuna in the *Udyoga Parva*. Karṇa is not only rejected as a warrior, but he is also mocked by the Pāṇḍavas for being the son of a charioteer and aspiring to compete with kṣatriyas in a competition of arms. Ironically, it is Duryodhana who presents the most equitable and just argument here: 'Strength is the cardinal virtue of the kṣatriyas; even a man of inferior birth deserves to be fought with. The sources of heroes and rivers are the same, both are always unknown' (*Mbh* 2.137.12–16). And, although Duryodhana confers the kingship of Anga on Karṇa and raises him to the level of kṣatriyas, the Pāṇḍavas never accept Karṇa as an equal, and Bhīṣma relegates him to only 'half a Ratha', thus negating his superior warrior skills (*Mbh* 5.168.9); they never acknowledge his natural inclination towards warriorship, because he is a just a *sūta*.

Duryodhana's sentiments about the injustice of caste prejudice are repeated in the whole Bhṛgu Bhārgava *samvād* in the *Śāntī Parva* (*Mbh* 12.188–9). This dialogue relates to the ritual of svadharma and its just place in the varṇāśrama, suggesting that the varṇas were actually svadharma-oriented. Hence the two—varṇadharma and svadharma—were supposed to have a natural connection. However, this acknowledgement was only didactical, because, as the examples cited (and many more in the text) indicate, it was not so in practice. In actuality, if an individual tried to act according to his svadharma, most often, he was not only condemned, but also held responsible for the conflicts that his nonconformity caused in the societal order. This was sometimes true for even glorified brāhmins, such as Drona, who, at his death, is derided by Bhīma for taking up the profession of a warrior and is called a *caṇḍāla* (*Mbh* 7.193.39–40). But, it is important to note that despite acting against his varṇa, Drona ascends to heaven (*Mbh* 7.193: 53–7), perhaps because his caste absolves him of his infraction of varṇa dharma. Not surprisingly, there is no evidence of any one of the lower castes enjoying this privilege.

Even more disparate standards occur in the epic when immoral behaviours of the kṣatriya varṇa are accepted because they are the kṣatriya's natural inclination. For example, within rājadharma, drinking and womanizing were considered kingly pursuits, as were cheating, treachery, and lying to achieve a purpose. In fact, in *Vana Parva*, Bhīma even proclaims this as the nature of kṣatriyas and derides Yudhiṣṭhira for being soft: 'You are kind as a *brāhmin*; how have you been born in the *kṣatriya* order? Those born in it (*kṣatriya* order) are generally crooked-minded ... You have heard the duties of kings told by Manu; they are fraught with crookedness and unfairness; they are perfectly opposed to peace and virtue' (*Mbh* 3.35.20–21). And, sometimes, the kṣatriyas even exercised their natural inclination to violence without a purpose. Arjuna is a good example: on his journey from *Indraloka*, he is told by Mātali about the beautiful Asura city of Hiraṇyapura (*Mbh* 3.173.1–62) that the Nivātakavaca asuras have created through much penance. They live there happily and in peace, not bothering anyone, not causing anyone distress or sorrow, but Arjuna enters it and, without provocation, begins killing the asuras, simply on the pretext that dānavas, by nature, are the enemies of the gods. After a long-drawn battle, he is able to destroy the asuras and reduce the city to total distress. 'All their sorrowing wives smitten with grief and with hair disheveled issue out of the home lamenting ...

Mourning for their sons, fathers and brothers, uttering piteous cries of distress for the loss of their lords and beating their breasts they fall down upon the ground, their ornaments falling off from their bodies. The city of the *dānavas*, resembling the city of the Gandharvas, filled with lamentation, afflicted with sorrow and distress, devoid of beauty and deprived of its lords, looks like a lake devoid of elephants or like a forest with all its trees dead, and then vanishes from sight' (*Mbh* 3.173.62–6). This violence, perpetrated by Arjuna, has no apparent cause, except one inconsequential justification of Brahmā's foretelling that a mortal will destroy the Nivātakavacas (*Mbh* 3.173.15). Moreover, the consequence of this violence goes against everything good or right, because it causes unnecessary and uncalled-for suffering on innumerable wives and children of the dānavas. Another example of Arjuna's unprovoked kṣatriya violence is in *Jayadrathavadha Parva*. When Sātyaki and Bhūriśravas are engaged in single combat, Arjuna, hidden from Bhūriśravas' view, cuts off his arm, simply because he boasts of being able to carry out a 'very difficult feat' (*Mbh* 7.142.70–2). In fact, in the epic, Arjuna's natural inclination to violence is more pronounced than any other warrior's, and each of his acts of unnecessary violence is accepted as the demonstration of his exceptional warrior skills. This fact, when considered in light of Arjuna's place in tradition as being everyman warrior, certainly does not bode well for customary behaviour.

Other such incidents of purposeless violence and treachery by kṣatriyas abound in the epic, and they are compounded by the fact that the kṣatriyas who perpetrate these are praised for following their natural inclination as warriors, while those like Yudhiṣṭhira (who is more inclined towards not causing injury to others) are ridiculed, as Bhīma does his elder brother: 'O king of kings, awake and understand the eternal virtues (of one's own order). You belong by birth to an order the acts of which are cruel and are the sources of pain to others' (*Mbh* 3.33.54). Hence, natural inclination, when given free rein (as was the case with brāhmins and kṣatriyas) negated the core purpose of dharma, which was designed for *bhūyo hitam*—the general good.

Another element of dharma that was meant to benefit the majority and sustain order, but really became a sanction for immoral action was that all people were enjoined to perform *tapas*, *yajña*, and *dāna*. However, aside from the obvious purificatory aspect of these practices, they were used by the powerful and wealthy of the upper two castes for expatiation of adharma. Tapas, yajña, and dāna were ways that allowed an individual to extract himself from the effect of bad karma, and because the atonement was so readily available and easy through these three prescriptions, the individual felt no compunction about indulging in adharma. In addition, the practice of these methods negated the suffering of others, because the offender was not required to make reparation to the injured; instead he could simply be cleansed of the adharmic act by a few ritualized practices. The best example of this in the Mahābhārata is when, at the end of the war, Yudhiṣṭhira, filled with remorse at having caused such destruction, is advised by Vyāsa to perform the Aśvamedha yajña. Vyāsa tells Yudhiṣṭhira:

> tapobhiḥ kratubhiś caiva dānena ca
> taranti nityaṃ puruṣā ye sma pāpāni kurvate
> [Those who commit sins can always free themselves from them through penance, sacrifice, and gifts.] (*Mbh* 14.3.4)

There is no mention here of rebuilding, help to orphans and women, succour to bereaved family members—none of that. Instead, Yudhiṣṭhira is told that all he needs to do to absolve himself of the evil of the war he perpetrated is perform a yajña in which he will give away wealth to brāhmins (*Mbh* 14.3.10).

The above example gives further insight into another evil practice which may have been a norm for Aryan kings during epic times: to levy taxes on their subjects after war or any such *āpad* situation, just so they could perform an expiational yajña for their own benefit. This can be surmised from the hesitation Yudhiṣṭhira feels to get involved in a massive and expensive yajña, for which he would have to collect wealth via taxes from his already overburdened and suffering people. Admittedly, in this particular incident, the people are not taxed, because Yudhiṣṭhira's brāhmins furnish an alternative source of wealth—the hidden treasure of an ancestral king, Marutta, in Himavat (14.3.12–21). However, just the fact that Yudhiṣṭhira is concerned about the expense and the methods he would have to use to collect the money suggests that taxing people for this purpose was a common practice among Aryan kings. Additionally, this act, although for the personal benefit of the king, was most likely disguised as being for the general good, because the king's purification represented the purification of his subjects.

The dharma that benefits the majority—*sādhāranadharma*—is a parallel strain that prescribes general principles which pertain to all: people of upper and lower caste, and also people in the different āśramas of life. For the most part, the practices of this dharma are ethical in nature, unlike the inequity of varṇadharma and āśramadharma. They include ideals like *ahiṁsā, satya, akrodha, priyavācana, dayā, prema,* svā*rthatyāga*, etc. These commandments that are for the general good are found in all societies in all ethical and moral systems, and are the ones that are upheld above all else. However, in the dharma demonstrated by the Mahābhārata, when there is a conflict between an individual moral perception of varṇa and āśrama and the ethics of sādhāranadharma, the former takes precedence. For example, the ethics of nonviolence can be violated by a kṣatriya at all times, and especially at the time of war, or the ethics of truthfulness can be violated by anyone, provided there is a justification, such as the twisting of truth that Kṛṣṇa calls permissible (*Mbh* 8.69.29–30). Similarly, the ethics of akrodha can be violated by brāhmins at any time if they are not given the respect they demand. In fact, time and again, brāhmins give in to anger so extreme that the curses they issue and the actions in which they indulge destroy not just individual life, but entire communities, generation after generation.

A more cohesive and just establishment of society's ethics would have been a seamless alignment of sādhāranadharma and svadharma, or even the precedence of sādhāranadharma over svadharma. However, these two dharmas are almost contrary to each other in the epic, and when someone does attempt to bring them into alignment, such as Yudhiṣṭhira, who often considers morality over his rājadharma or kṣatriya dharma, he is considered a weak kṣatriya. Not only is there no reconciliation between the two dharmas, but their applicability is also fuzzy. For example, when Duryodhana who, unlike Yudhiṣṭhira, is a strong kṣatriya, adheres to all the prescriptions of kṣatriyahood—moral or immoral—he is not considered a better man but an asura. Hence, the practice of dharma is like a no-win situation for certain people, and win-win for others. Therefore, when Bhīṣma's only response to Draupadī's question during her ordeal in the dice game is that dharma is subtle, it is tantamount to saying there are no clear standards of behaviour in the realm of dharma.

The Mahābhārata grapples with the nebulousness of dharma and the flexibility of morals within its varṇa and āśrama dharmas, and as traditions, these dharmas still condone grave injustices that violate basic human values and legitimize violence and injustice. Especially vulnerable to these evils are the lower caste and women; in fact, the former are often oppressed, and the latter do not even have an individualized dharma; they are seen only in relation to their male relatives—mother, sister, wife, daughter, etc.—and are often dehumanized.

Artha

The gathering of wealth for personal use and its distribution among brāhmins is what drives the second principle of trivarga—artha. In the Mahābhārata, this puruṣārtha not only plays a key role in everyone's life, but it is also considered part of the rightful order of creation, because Artha is the son of Dharma: 'The Goddess Śrī was born of the lotus. She became the consort of the highly intelligent Dharma. Upon Śrī ... Dharma begot Artha' (*Mbh* 12.59.132). In principle, this puruṣārthic goal, when maintained through dharma, is the means to a happy life of materiality, which, in turn, promotes moral behaviour and goodness. However, in the Mahābhārata, the very fact of owning artha is ethical, and not owning it is unethical. Hence, its purpose and mode of acquisition are either irrelevant or not factors in the moral/immoral equation.

The reason why artha in itself was considered ethical is because it defined kingship. 'All three, viz., Dharma and Artha and Śrī are established in a king...' (*Mbh* 12.59.134). This belief is very significant because the war of Kurukṣetra is to decide who is king, and hence, who owns wealth. Besides the fact that the goal to pursue wealth was one of the four goals of an Aryan, the very raison d'être for the war is wealth and to ascertain its rightful owner. The situation is reminiscent of Indra's battles for wealth in the *Ṛg Veda*; at various junctures, various characters in the Mahābhārata are even compared to Indra—from Yudhiṣṭhira to Duryodhana—in their pursuit of wealth. Also, true to the analogy of Indra's destruction of enemies to secure wealth for self-empowerment and the empowerment of his loyalists, the Aryans in the Mahābhārata, too, pursue wealth to secure power. And the equation becomes even more apt, because both carry out robbery with a holier-than-thou attitude, as though the acquisition of enemy wealth is their sacrosanct right—the ultimate ṛta or dharma. It is as though to gain ownership of enemy wealth is their moral duty, and the enemy's claims to the same wealth is adharmic and immoral. The difference, however, is that while in Vedic times the demarcation between the Aryans and the an-Aryans was somewhat clear, and Indra's robbing of the an-Aryan was a clear case of establishing 'the other', in the Mahābhārata, there is no such clarity. Both the Pāṇḍavas and Kauravas are not only Aryans, but also cousins with an equal claim to the wealth. Hence there is no 'other'. Of course, this demarcating of 'the other' does not exonerate Indra and the Vedic Aryans, and it does not relieve them of moral obligations, but it does, by contrast, emphasize the moral depravity of the Pāṇḍavas who fight and kill their cousins for wealth on sanctimonious grounds—the grounds of dharma, which makes the immorality of the acquisition more pronounced.

But why was the acquisition of wealth, by whatever means possible, of such significance? To answer that, the purpose of wealth must be understood. The most obvious purpose was, of course, to live well and to enjoy comforts and luxuries, which were deemed necessary for happiness. For instance, when, after losing the dice games, the Pāṇḍavas have to live in the wilderness without creature comforts, everyone—the Pāṇḍavas, Kuntī, Dhṛtarāṣṭra, the citizens of Hāstinapura—see it as a great misfortune and suffering. There are many other examples, as well; for instance, Nala, after losing his wealth, becomes so disheartened at not being able to provide for his wife, Damayantī, that he considers himself an unworthy husband and leaves her alone and hapless in the forest. Thus, lack of wealth meant lack of self-worth and lack of happiness.

Another important purpose of wealth is revealed in Yudhiṣṭhira's words right after his arrival in the Kāmyaka forest. Responding to Śaunaka's advice about detachment from the desire of wealth, he says: 'My desire for wealth is not for the purpose of enjoying it when obtained. I do not desire it through avarice. I desire it only for the support of the *brāhmins*' (*Mbh* 2.2.51). He then goes on to talk about the necessity of having wealth for charitable purposes and also for performing his duty towards the brāhmin guests who remain with him in the forest. These two purposes support wellbeing and they were life-affirming; in addition, they denote that the desire for wealth was not necessarily immoral. However, the epic emphasizes another purpose of wealth which, even in epic society, was being condemned in heterodox ideologies. This was the practice of large-scale sacrifices in which a *yajamāna* gave away hordes of wealth to brāhmins, often to the point of his own penury. These lavish sacrifices, which were considered an integral obligation of a householder's life, were performed by kṣatriyas and the wealthy for a variety of reasons—to proclaim power, to display prosperity, to be charitable, to expiate sin, to beget sons, and to follow tradition. However, they created an uneven society, where only the wealthy felt empowered and the brāhmins reaped all the benefits. Most common people could not perform the costly, elaborate, and complex sacrifices, and thus felt left out. Moreover, there was the mandatory dakṣiṇā or priest fee, which was often quite hefty, even for kings; therefore, even if ordinary people wanted to engage in these sacrifices, they could not afford to pay the priests.

Aside from its use or misuse, wealth was actually considered a means to living a moral life of puruṣārtha. A wealthy man was a dhārmic man and a man who was poor or lacked wealth was condemned to live an adharmic life. Arjuna clearly states this in the *Śāntī*

Parva when Yudhiṣṭhira is lamenting the violence of the war and wishes to renounce his wealth and his kingdom. Arjuna equates a poor man to a degraded man or a man without virtue. He compares the disposition of wealth to rivers flowing from mountains and says this wealth begets meritorious acts—all religious acts, all pleasures, and heaven itself. He also says that the man who has wealth is 'sincere' and 'learned'. And that all acts, religious, pleasurable, courageous, or dignified, arise from wealth (*Mbh* 12.8.19–22). Thus, wealth in Aryan society was in itself considered an aspect of ethics because it facilitated pravṛtti.

People were expected to pursue wealth through dharma, but the Pāṇḍavas' perception of artha shows how the pursuit of this puruṣārthic goal also distorted morality. The dialogue about artha between Arjuna and Yudhiṣṭhira at the end of the war represents this potential of evil that the goal of artha included. Arjuna, telling Yudhiṣṭhira about the methods that can be used to acquire wealth, says, just as the gods appropriated the wealth of the dānavas, kings appropriate the wealth of others, and they are regarded as rightful. He reminds Yudhiṣṭhira that this injunction has been laid down in the Vedas, and the gods themselves gained footing in the celestial regions by inciting civil war over the ownership of wealth; hence this war (at Kurukṣetra) cannot be wrong. Arjuna goes on to say that 'wealth is never acquired without doing some injury to others'. The duty of kings is to defeat their enemies and regard enemy wealth as their own. And to expiate the sin of injury to others, the king, through the means of his wealth, can perform the horse sacrifice (*Mbh* 12.8.1–34). Arjuna's statements about wealth, its purpose, and its methods of acquisition unmask the immorality that was disguised in this puruṣārthic goal of artha in Aryan society. Furthermore, with these statements, not only does Arjuna shift the purpose of the war from a dharmayuddha to one over wealth, he also admits to the fact that the Pāṇḍavas incited a civil war to usurp Kaurava wealth. Therefore, Arjuna's words shatter the moral legitimacy of the Pāṇḍavas, and they cast grave doubt on the dhārmic value of artha.

Arjuna's statements are followed by a response from Yudhiṣṭhira, which, while upholding the ethics of wealth, in principle, reduces the moral high ground of some of the epic's exemplary moral agents, such as Bhīṣma. Yudhiṣṭhira says to Arjuna that those who desire and acquire wealth do so with the necessity to continue in goodness. But, often, this is not the case; people acquire wealth by injuring others and then when they do acquire it, they themselves are troubled. And this, he says, is especially true for anyone who is weak-minded and easily swayed by even a little wealth. In fact, he says that such a person oppresses others and incurs a sin as great as brahminicide (*Mbh* 12.26. 20–1). With these words, Yudhiṣṭhira reduces revered elders such as Bhīṣma as not only 'weak-minded' but also sinful, because by his own admission, Bhīṣma has told Yudhiṣṭhira that his reason for siding with the Kauravas rather than with the Pāṇḍavas (even though he believes that they are good) is wealth: 'A man is the slave of wealth, but wealth is no one's slave...I am bound to the Kurus by wealth...It is for this I am like a eunuch...' (*Mbh* 6.43. 41–2). In fact, Bhīṣma repeats this statement—that he is bound by wealth—three times in subsequent ślokas, thus emphasizing the importance he gives to wealth in a man's life, even if it means supporting what he intrinsically believes is the wrongful cause and feeling emasculated. Or, perhaps, Bhīṣma is subtly suggesting that he believes the Kauravas to be the rightful owners of the wealth and kingship of Hāstinapura, and thus he thinks they will be victors; hence, by siding with them rather than with the Pāṇḍavas, he is ensuring his own wealth.

Another aspect of wealth that is demonstrated in the Mahābhārata is how it was considered the true measure of a king's fame, which, as Arjuna states, was the true virtue of a king. Even Vyāsa advocates this purpose of wealth when, after Abhimanyu's death, he tells Yudhiṣṭhira the stories of the sixteen kings who were like Yudhiṣṭhira, but superior to him in wealth and virtue, and had to suffer their own death or the death of a loved one, despite their wealth (*Mbh* 7.56–71). The manner in which Vyāsa narrates the stories is such that it makes the kings' moral behaviour secondary to their prosperity and their success in accumulating gold. This narration also indicates that the significant message for society was not so much that death is inevitable for all—rich and poor—or that virtue is the highest quality, but that a king's rightness is in his pursuit, acquisition, and enjoyment of gold. For instance, one of the stories that Vyāsa tells Yudhiṣṭhira is of King Suhotra who was a skilled and glorious warrior. He was generous to brāhmins and did many great deeds, such as freeing the earth from Mlecchas. However, he performed all this to get gold so that even the river in his kingdom flowed liquid gold, and the alligators and fish in the waters were also gold. He performed a thousand horse sacrifices and a hundred *Rājasūya* yajñas, and gave away gold to brāhmins (*Mbh* 7.56.1–12).

Another example Vyāsa cites is of Sini, son of Uśinara, who, during sacrifices, gave away as much wealth as there are grains of sand on Ganga's bank or stars in the sky, and his palace constantly echoed with words like 'drink', 'eat', and 'do as you like'. It was his wealth that facilitated these kingly rights. Vyāsa even transmutes the philanthropy of Bhagīratha, who brought the Ganga down on earth for all humanity. According to Vyāsa, Bhagīratha is not considered glorious simply because of this act of benevolence, but because, at sacrifices, he used to give brāhmins as much wealth as they desired. Similarly, King Gaya, who lived only on remnants from sacrificial libations for a hundred years, is remembered not so much for his asceticism but for his inexhaustible wealth, the boon he received for his lifelong asceticism.

The conclusion that can be drawn from the stories of these sixteen kings is that these kings were not exemplars of morality when they died; in fact, their morality or immorality was inconsequential. They were considered superior to Yudhiṣṭhira in virtue because of their money power. Owning artha, then, was equivalent to having morality, and the three—morality, profit, and pleasure—were to be seen as harmonious (*Mbh* 9.60.22). However, the cause-and-effect relationship among these three elements is never made clear in the epic, and this ambiguity is intentional: 'Whoever without making distinction between Morality and Profit, or Morality and Pleasure, or Pleasure and Profit, follows all three, viz., Morality, Profit and Pleasure, always succeeds in obtaining great happiness' (*Mbh* 9.60.22). Therefore, morality could equal profit, or morality could equal pleasure, or pleasure and profit (even if obtained immorally) could equal morality. This lack of relational clarity between the acquisition of wealth and morality further implicates an already flawed system.

Kāma

The third ideal of puruṣārtha, kāma, denotes 'desire', in general, and it also means sexual desire. In the Mahābhārata, this ideal is mostly portrayed as either men's desires in association with women or as their outright desire for fulfilment of sexual needs. Hence, by extension, the principle of kāma also establishes traditions about the status of women.

The ideal of kāma is not immoral in itself; in fact, its inclusion in puruṣārtha shows how well the Aryans understood human psyche and behaviour, and how progressive they were in their thinking. Kāma, like artha, is life affirming, and when practised within the bounds of ideal dharma, it procures happiness and enhances the quality of life. However, quite often, this is not the case in the Mahābhārata. In myth after myth, there is evidence that men distorted sexuality by using it to their advantage without any regard to the women they targeted to fulfil their sexual needs. And the women, bound by strīdharma, unable to object, became victims. It is this suffering of the women that makes kāma the most exploitative of the puruṣārthas.

Women in epic society were considered a corrupting and intoxicating force. According to a myth in *Vana Parva*, Ṛṣi Cyavana, in a battle against Indra, created the asura Mada (intoxication), and when the ṛṣi had no more use for him, he distributed mada among women, alcohol, and gambling (*Mbh* 3.125.1–7). In greater measure, women were also seen as the force of darkness and ignorance, as Bhīṣma warns. He says that wise men should not approach women, because 'they are like dreadful *mantra* powers. They stupefy persons shorn of wisdom. They are sunk in the quality of darkness. They are the eternal embodiment of sensuality' (*Mbh* 3.125.1–7). Bhīṣma even describes the feminine as the very first primeval element of ignorance—tamas (*Mbh* 12.342.8). A point to be noted is that this same quality of tamas is also born with the lotus that grows out of Nārāyaṇa's navel at creation, and takes the form of the asuras Madhu and Kaiṭabha (*Mbh* 12.347.61). Therefore, Bhīṣma suggests that this ignorance (represented by asuras and women) is as primeval as the lotus of creation; in fact, it is the polar opposite of the highest form of intelligence (which is symbolized by the lotus[1]), and has the ability to befuddle even the most evolved males, just as the asuras Madhu and Kaiṭabha befuddled Brahmā when he tried to begin the act of creation. Hence, through Bhīṣma, whose words 'pass on earth like the authoritative declarations of the *Vedas*' (*Mbh* 12.54.29) and establish traditions, women are the embodiment of tamas and kāma, both of which are qualities of asuric evil.

However, despite Bhīṣma's directives, exalted men of dharma in the Mahābhārata do not avoid women. They use them, and not just to fulfil their sexual desire, but many other desires. Men in the epic seem to believe that even though women are embodiments of tamas and are filled with mada, their own elevated maleness will counter the negative effects. Or perhaps, since women were considered *kṣetra*, their use by men, who had *kṣetrajñāna*, was to help them evolve from their quality of darkness (*Mbh* 12.213.8–9). Whatever the case, by virtue of their puruṣārtha, men in the Mahābhārata take full advantage of their right to sexual desire. This text abounds with examples of how men not only use women for their kāma, but, often, they also abuse them without compunction.

There are so many such myths in the Mahābhārata that, aside from validating Bhīṣma's words, prove that the degraded status of women was, in fact, the norm, and that men equated women with their right to kāma. They saw them only as objects placed on earth to use for their benefit. An apt example of this exploitation of women is the myth of Mādhavī and Ṛṣi Gālava (*Mbh* 5.106. 21–27 & 5.115–20). Gālava's guru, Viśvāmitra, asks him for a dakṣiṇā of eight hundred white horses with one black ear. With Garuḍa's help, Gālava wanders from

[1] Ironically, the lotus is the key symbol of the feminine divine; it is associated with Sri/Lakṣmī

kingdom to kingdom, looking for these horses till he finally arrives in King Yayāti's kingdom; but the king is not able to give Gālava the horses; instead he gives him his daughter, Mādhavī, claiming that she can beget four sons. Gālava trades Mādhavī's sexuality and womb with three different kings—Haryaśva of Ayodhyā, Divodāsa, king of Kāśi, and Uśinara, king of Bhojas—for two hundred horses each and, to make up for the remainder two hundred, he gives her to Viśvāmitra, who, like the kings, has a son from her and returns her to Gālava. Gālava, having accomplished his purpose and paid his debt, returns her to her father. Mādhavī, now unable to bear any more children, becomes a *brahmacārin*. Ironically, the myth exalts the morality of Ṛṣi Gālava for having fulfilled his duty to his guru and even praises Mādhavī for fulfilling her duty as a daughter and for choosing a life of asceticism. However, not once in the myth is there mention of how the men, seeking to fulfil their obligations, injure a woman. It is a tragic myth in terms of human dignity. After being prostituted by her father and other men, and being treated as no better than a son-making machine, Mādhavī probably feels so violated and repulsed by the consequences of kāma that she renounces all desire.

This subversion of kāma in the Mahābhārata is abundantly evident in one of the gravest episodes of men's exploitation of women, even within the sanctity of marriage. This is the myth of King Sudarśana and his wife, Oghavatī (*Mbh* 13.2). Sudarśana, the grandson of Agni, desires to conquer death and takes a vow that he will do so by following his householder dharma to perfection, and to ensure that his wife will help him fulfil his vow, he tells her: 'You should extend yourself in welcoming guests, even if you have to offer your own body to please the guest' (*Mbh* 13.2.39). Sure enough, one day a brāhmin comes to Sudarśana's home while he is away, and Oghavatī offers him hospitality, but the brāhmin, refusing all else, demands only that she fulfil his sexual desire. Oghavatī is consumed with shame and guilt for having to give herself to the guest, and she is repulsed by the act, but she obeys her husband's command and lets the brāhmin fulfil his kāma. When Sudarśana returns and calls out to his wife, she cannot respond, because she is in bed with the brāhmin, but the brāhmin shamelessly responds to Sudarśana, telling him what they are about. Sudarśana applauds his wife and basically tells the brāhmin to carry on and enjoy himself. Thus, through his wife's sacrifice, Sudarśana's boon of conquering death is granted. What is most disturbing about this myth is that the brāhmin who uses Oghavatī is Dharma himself. He blesses Sudarśana, calling him virtuous and chaste and he applauds him for mastering his kāma. He also absolves Oghavatī of her shame and declares that only half of her will now follow Sudarśana, because the other half will become the river Oghavatī (*Mbh* 13.2.86)—to be an example of how women should sacrifice themselves. In this myth, violation of a spousal relationship and a woman's sexual submission are made equivalent to dharma, just so a male can fulfil an impossible desire. It is not only an endorsement for men to prostitute their wives for personal benefit, but it also declares this immorality as ethical—a societal norm. In addition, on a side note, it reduces the purity of rivers to the analogy of an indiscriminate woman, creating the well-known derogatory adage that women are like rivers who service all men indiscriminately.

It is possible that the ideal of kāma under the umbrella of puruṣārtha was at one time related to marital bliss, and it allowed women more respect. There are instances in the frame story of the epic that uphold the sanctity of marriage over raging kāma, such as Draupadī's relationship with her five husbands, and Gāndhārī's relationship with Dhṛtarāṣṭra. In the best-case scenarios, marital kāma even led to profitable alliances, such as Arjuna's to Ulupi, Chitrangada, and Subhadra, and Bhīma's to Hiḍimbā. However, more often, even in marriage, kāma was vulnerable to the danger of misuse; uncurbed kāma in men led to disaster. For example, when Pāṇḍu desires Mādrī, he dies, and Mādrī considers herself guilty. Also Śaṃtanu's kāma for Satyavatī ultimately becomes the foundation for the war. Even Kuntī's kāma-invoking mantra to call any god without the sanction of marriage results in Karṇa—a child she abandons with disastrous results. In fact, Kuntī is degraded even in marriage. Although it appears that she is empowered by having the power to call upon any man or god and indulge in intercourse, she really isn't. Her 'power' reduces her to being nothing more than a receptacle for her husband's desire to have sons.

Many myths in the epic also demonstrate that if men's kāma went awry, it was not they who were curbed, but the women who were the targets of their kāma, and consequently, proclamations were made to restrict women's sexuality and freedom. A good example of this is the story of Mamata and Bṛhaspati in the *Ādi Parva* (*Mbh* 1.104.10–37). In this myth, Bṛhaspati propositions his pregnant sister-in-law, Mamata, and when she refuses him, he curses her to give birth to a blind son. The blind Dīrghatamas is an indulgent man engaged in many vices, but his wife, Pradveśi, following her strīdharma, takes care of him. When Dīrghatamas is thrown out of the hermitage because of his continuous adharmic behaviour, he begins to oppress his wife even more, till she has no choice but to leave him. Dīrghatamas, who himself is hardly a paragon of virtue, then makes a new edict for women:

> I make this rule among men that every woman shall stick to one husband only all through her life. Whether the husband is dead, or whether he is alive, she must not have connection with another man, She who will have it, will be considered fallen. A woman without a husband will always be liable to be sinful. Even, if she has wealth, she will not be able to enjoy it truly. Calumny and evil report will always follow her. (*Mbh* 1.104.34–7)

A similar story of men's kāma and women's victimization through restrictive laws is of Śvetaketu and his mother (*Mbh* 1.122.11–20). In this myth, Ṛṣi Uddālaka's wife is propositioned by another brāhmin in the presence of her husband and her son, Śvetaketu. Śvetaketu is so angered that he curses not just his mother but also all women and 'establishes the practice' that any woman who is promiscuous will commit a sin as grave as destroying the embryo (*Mbh* 1.122.17). It is true that Śvetaketu also lays a similar law for men who will neglect their own loving wives and go to other women who have taken the vow of purity (*Mbh* 1.122. 17–18). However, the point to note here is that Śvetaketu's mother is not the one propositioning the brāhmin, yet Śvetaketu curses women, as though their very being is responsible for inciting men's illicit kāma. This is what Bhīṣma is referring to when he says women are tamas or when Ṛṣi Cyavana imbues women with a portion of mada. Hence, the fact cannot be ignored that women were blamed for men's lack of mental and physical restraint. This blame transformed into restrictive societal practices for women, which ultimately became binding as tradition.

Uma Chakravarti (2009: 26) thinks that

> The new law laid down by Śvetaketu ... clearly marks an important 'moment' when women's reproductive potential is being bounded within a particular circle of men, closing off access to other men; on the face of it, this is a law to regulate men's access to women by privileging one set of men over others. But, at the same time, it is also denying women the possibility of sexual agency in a consensual relationship; it is also the first stage in institutionally creating a double standard of sexual morality in which women, as wives, bore the burden of the new sexual mores.

According to these new mores, women's desire to fulfil their sexuality was violently condemned. They were considered 'polluted' and their desire was 'unlawful'. The story of Rāma Jamadagni's mother, Reṇukā, is a good example of this restraint over women and their kāma: One day, Reṇukā sees the handsome Gandharva, Citrarartha, and 'becomes polluted with this unlawful desire' (*Mbh* 3.116.6–7). As a consequence, her husband, Jamadagni, asks his four sons, one by one, to kill her. But the sons refuse, and the father turns them into birds and beasts. The fifth son, Rāma, obeys his father and cuts off his mother's head with an axe and is praised for the act. Although, later, Jamadagni grants Rāma a boon and restores Reṇukā's life, the fact remains that just for feeling the pangs of kāma for another man, Reṇukā is punished by the men in her life. Quoting Wendy Doniger in reference to this myth, Chakravarti (2009: 29) says,

> [While] there is a male gaze in this myth, there is also a powerful female gaze: it is by gazing, not being gazed at that Reṇukā discovers, and revels in her eroticism ...she is a subject, not a mere object or victim of a male subject ... [but] precisely because the male author of the

text deems the female gaze unacceptable, Reṇukā must be beheaded, her gaze silenced as it were.

From these and other similar myths, it appears that the creators of the Mahābhārata's tradition could hardly conceive of lustful women in the fold of Aryan society. Most often, those females who were openly lustful and felt empowered to pursue their kāma were not seen as Aryan women, but as rākṣasīs, like Hiḍimbā, nāgas, like Ulūpī, or apsarās, like Urvaśī. Sometimes, even the lustful apsarās were punished for their desire, as is the case with Sarabhī, Samīcī, Budabudā, Latā, and Vargā who desire a brāhmin and are cursed to become crocodiles, and who are later released from it by Arjuna (*Mbh* 1.216–17). Clearly, men had supreme power over women. They could victimize them or save them, as they desired.

In comparison to women, the standard for brāhmin males was beyond the scope of societal laws. When they lusted for women, neither was their desire unholy nor was it unlawful. Instead, it was glorified, and its consequence was praiseworthy. For example, when Ṛṣi Parāśara desires Satyavatī and indulges in kāma, the result is not only that her body becomes fragrant but she also gives birth to Vyāsa, the most exalted of men. Both Drona and Kṛpa are also born of their fathers' uncontrolled sexual desire and both ṛṣis are ennobled in the epic. Vyāsa's own lust for the apsarā Ghṛtācī produces a son Śuka, who is so elevated that he is one of the few in the epic to realize mokṣa (*Mbh* 1.216–17).

A significant point to note in all these brāhmin kāma incidents (aside from Satyavatī, who is probably raped), is that the brāhmins' sperm do not gestate in a woman's womb; the sons that are produced are born in symbolic elements: Drona is born in a vessel, Kṛpa in the weeds, and Śuka through the rubbing together of two sticks. The suggestion here seems to be that because these were 'pure' and 'exalted' brāhmins, they had to remain untouched by the contaminating power of women, and even a woman's womb would have defiled their purity.

Some scholars, like A.N. Bhattacharya (1992: 104), suggest that even though women were mistreated by men, the end result of their sacrifice was 'for the benefit of many'—this is the 'philosophy of utilitarianism'. This is a doctrine based on utility or use of goods and services by and for the satisfaction of the consumer, and the more consumers that are satisfied the more the object's utility. By this definition, Bhattacharya's views are on the mark, because women are certainly 'objects of utility', and the use of their 'goods and services' are made to fulfil the desires of various 'consumers' to their satisfaction. However, even in that, there is no rationale in any of the myths that proves that women's sacrifice benefit many. For example, how does Oghavatī's husband's personal goal to conquer death benefit anyone but himself? How does Mādhavī's prostitution benefit anyone other than her father and the men for whom she bears sons? Most importantly, the so-called sacrifice of women actually creates a tradition which hurts, rather than benefits, the females in society. How, then, is this 'for the benefit of many', unless, of course, only the male members of society are the ones factored into the 'many'? Additionally, it is exactly this condescending attitude towards women that is cemented in tradition and has prevailed in Hindu society. It is also responsible for creating traditions that force women to accept all degradation. They are cajoled into believing that their sacrifice is their strength, because it is for the good of mankind; therefore, women continually subject themselves to abuse and suffering. How is it that men are never held up to any sacrifice? In fact, even the sacrifices they do make are for personal aggrandizement, such as the elevation in status Arjuna and Bhīṣma enjoy as a consequence of the kāma they 'sacrifice': when Arjuna sacrifices his desire for Urvaśī and she curses him to become a eunuch, the curse helps him to live undetected during his year of concealment. And when Bhīṣma sacrifices his kāma to fulfil Satyavatī's wishes, he is elevated from Devavrata to Bhīṣma.

On the other hand, the women of Mahābhārata embody the rigid principles of strīdharma, which does not include kāma, because that would have been empowerment. They are, instead, expected to be servile and mindless. That is the advice even Draupadī gives to Kṛṣṇa's wife, Satyabhāmā: 'a woman is in service of her husband and her goal is to acquire trivialities like jewels, perfumes, clothes, which her husband will bestow on her' (*Mbh* 3.2.4–7). Of course, Draupadī herself does not fall into this category. While she does serve her husbands to the utmost, she feels empowered enough to pursue her kāma and to state her opinions. But, because of her non-traditional behaviour, Draupadī is not held up as a role model even today, (as opposed to Sītā, whose whole life is spent in sacrifice). It is only recently that feminists have made Draupadī a poster child. However, although women like Draupadī and Gāndhārī and, to some extent, Kuntī, can be considered more empowered and independent, we cannot 'push the point too far. Because even these women lack the true evidence of equality and independence' (Sutton 2000: 104).

Most people believe that the idea of equality of genders is a relatively new phenomenon in the world, and it is mostly a western endeavour. Therefore, it is easy to pass off this inequality of women in ancient Hindu texts, such as the Mahābhārata, as true to their time. But this is a misconception. In truth, feminism may very well have been a Hindu tradition, and it involved not just equality between male and female but also, often, supremacy of feminine power. The Hindu goddess myths are a testimony to this. For example, the mother goddesses, Kali and Durgā, individually fulfil the triple function of a supreme divine—creation, preservation, and destruction. Even those goddesses who are consorts, such as Lakṣmī and Pārvatī, have an undeniably high status. They are equal partners to their husbands and, often, the husbands are incomplete without them, because the feminine is the embodiment of *śaktī*, as is portrayed in the Shiva Śaktī myths. In fact, in these consort myths, the very foundation of creation is dependent on a balance of the male and female.

Additionally, contrary to Bhīṣma's condemnation of the female energy as tamas or ignorance, the goddess in the epic is the embodiment of wisdom. In the *Śāntī Parva*, the goddess Sarasvatī is called Truth and is named Ṛta (*Mbh* 12.342.37). In fact, without the feminine principle of the goddess, creation would not have been possible, because when Brahmā does not have the intelligence to create, and he stands before Nārāyaṇa befuddled, Nārāyaṇa, with the help of yoga, 'applies to the Goddess of Intelligence' and requests her to help

Brahmā accomplish the task by entering Brahmā. Thus, only when the goddess has infused herself into his befuddled being, can he fulfil his desire to create (*Mbh* 12.349.15–20). The goddess is actually so revered in the epic that she is called to give her blessing even before the gods, such as in *Vana Parva*, when Arjuna decides to acquire divine weapons, Draupadī prays for him and calls upon the goddesses Hrī, Śrī, Kīrtī, Dhṛtī, Puṣtī, Umā, Lakṣmī, and Sarasvatī to protect him on his journey (*Mbh* 3.37.32-33).

These myths are proof that the goddess was respected at the time of the Mahābhārata, and that the feminine helped fulfil desires other than sexual. What is surprisingly contradictory is that while the goddess remained transcendent in tradition, becoming not just a part of the Hindu trinity but also a totality, such as the Devī in *Devī Mahātamaya*, women rapidly lost their status in a male-dominated society pursuing kāma. Somehow, the connective natural progression from the goddess concept to women got severed, and, as the two strains of Hinduism—mythical and ethical—progressed separately, most Hindus, while continuing to believe in the mythical and the goddess supreme, practised the ethical codes of the Dharmaśāstras that derogated women, not questioning the disconnect. These dharmaśāstric laws, compounded with the teachings in the epics, especially in the *Śāntī* and *Anuśāsana Parvas* of the Mahābhārata, became deified, and thus they overshadowed the goddess tradition and created a whole new tradition of degradation of women.

This denigration of the divine feminine in the *Śāntī* and *Anuśāsana Parvas* 'does of course raise the question about the status of the epic as scripture ... [in which] values are projected back into a reinterpreted tradition rather than tradition speaking as an authoritative voice to the present' (Sutton 2000: 422–423), and this backward evolution is one of the main problems in the epic tradition. In the formulation of tradition, rather than a reconnection to the positive and ascendant goddess, the goddess myths were reinterpreted to align with the devolving status of women.

While the ethical framework of the Mahābhārata includes ideologies and doctrines that encompass many dynamic traditions, such as karma and puruṣārtha, nivṛtti and pravṛtti, their potentiality is lost in inconsistencies and ambiguities. Rather than reconciling the differences of the multifariousness, the epic tradition deepens the schisms, which has, over time, resulted in misdirection and societal inequities. The Bhagavad Gītā attempts to resolve some of the epic's ethical problems, but sadly, it fails, because there is little affinity between what it expounds and what the moral agents practise and project. Compounding this gap between societal ethics and individual morality is the exemplification of immoral practices and behaviours of characters, which, in turn, created morally corrupt customary laws that are accepted as tradition.

While tradition may be validated by being passed down from one generation to another, its continuance does not prove it to be moral or right or good. Most often, the keepers of tradition were self-serving brāhmins and/or misogynistic elders like Bhīṣma; hence, the traditions of dharma, artha, and kāma that were validated, and are still prevalent in Hindu cultures today, are biased, and they continue to violate the human dignity of many people in various sections of society.

3 *Dharmakṣetra* and *Adharmakṣetra*

Framing the Kṣetra

The Mahābhārata does not define concepts of good and evil, but it shows what they are through their *lakṣaṇa*[1] (Badrinath 2006: 13–14). In other words, the text does not state what a dharmakṣetra or an adharmakṣetra is, but it demonstrates the lakṣaṇa of both. These lakṣaṇa can be gauged through an enquiry into how the events of the epic create kṣetras of dharma and adharma, and what kind of kṣetra the characters evoke with their individual actions and behaviours. This, then, is also how good and evil and dharma and adharma are revealed, and the context in which these are revealed is the kṣetra.

However, it is important to note that the dharmakṣetra of the Mahābhārata is not just the battlefield of Kurukṣetra; in a larger context, not only this battlefield, but also the whole *itihāsa* of the Mahābhārata is symbolized by Kurukṣetra; hence, in actuality, the entire Mahābhārata is a dharmakṣetra in itself. Therefore, this boundless Kurukṣetra cannot be seen from a single dimension of the war

[1] Here, the word *lakṣaṇa* is used not in its philosophical meaning of 'definition', but as 'something symptomatic'—a characteristic or distinguishing feature. In the rest of this book, *lakṣaṇa* will be used in this meaning of the word.

and the actions of the warriors in the war. It must be seen from many levels of behaviour, even those that moral agents demonstrate during peacetime. Moreover, all layers of the Mahābhārata—those that were part of the Ur Mahābhārata, and also all those that may have been interpolations—must be taken into consideration for this enquiry, because even when this text may have been just a *Sauta* literature (a narrative about battle and warriors) it was an enquiry into good and evil. Dr V.S. Sukthankar (quoted in Karve 2008: 6) suggests that the Mahābhārata worked on many levels of dharma even as it was created and told for the first time, and all later levels just added to its meaning. Therefore, any study of the kṣetras of the Mahābhārata must take into account all these layers, because they are part of the same complexity.

In certain strata of the Mahābhārata, such as the archetypal and cyclical battle of devas and asuras, it is difficult to polarize good and evil, because in these levels, dharma is static, similar to the cosmic and fixed order of ṛta of the Vedas. There is no active and empirical morality in these strata, as compared to other layers, in which moral agents experience dilemmas of dynamic and perplexing moral actions in a kṣetra where, as Kṛṣṇa says, '*dharmāṇāṃ gatiṃ sūkṣmāṃ duranvayām*, 'the ways of dharma are subtle' (*Mbh* 8.69.28).

The two most significant active kṣetra-defining layers in the Mahābhārata are Vaiṣṇava and Śaivic sectarianism and the Pāṇḍava–Kaurava conflict regarding the legitimacy of the throne of Hāstinapura. The former, although mythopoeic, is empirical in the kṣetra it creates, because in it, the moral agents act as per their perception of dharma and contend with one another to prove the dhārmic supremacy of the divine to whom they are allegiant—Śiva or Viṣṇu/Kṛṣṇa. Thus, while the kṣetra itself is a juxtaposition of two dharmakṣetras, the cult conflict it generates impels the moral agents into acts of adharma that corrupt both dharmakṣetras. The latter—the framing layer of the Pāṇḍava–Kaurava conflict over the legitimacy of the throne—is in itself a dharmakṣetra that precedes the actual battlefield. However, this kṣetra is contaminated long before the Pāṇḍavas and the Kauravas enter it, because the very foundation—the question of kingship, which is the fulcrum of the war—is polluted by numerous factors that include traditions and normative codes and prior actions of other moral agents, who are father figures, such as Bhīṣma, Vidura, Dhṛtarāṣṭra, and Pandu. Furthermore, even before the battle begins, the Pāṇḍavas are pre-established as dharma warriors and the Kauravas as adharmic. This demonstrates a clear antecedent bias in the kṣetra before dharma is even tested on the battleground.

THE KṢETRA OF SECTARIAN CULTS

By the time Smṛti literatures were created, numerous belief systems had been incorporated into three overarching ideologies—Neo-Vedic Vaiṣṇavism/Kṛṣṇaism, Śaivism, and Śramaṇism. However, in this context of kṣetra-oriented dharma and adharma, the Śramaṇic cult is irrelevant because it dealt with liberation—an ideology in which the practitioners renounced the kṣetra. The Mahābhārata and the Gītā make occasional references to this cult, but it is not a kṣetra on which empirical good and evil can be examined. On the other hand, Śaivism was not only contemporaneous to Kṛṣṇaism, but it was also an aggregate alternative belief system, and, although it was a fringe cult, its practitioners were active moral agents. Therefore, the two key sects that characterized the dharmakṣetra during the time of the Mahābhārata were Śaivism and Vaiṣṇavism. Although both these sects coalesced into one theistic core, their practices differed, mostly because Śaivism's ideology was based on life negation and an annihilative ultimate objective, and Vaiṣṇavism's key principles were of life-affirming puruṣārtha. Therefore, the behavioural kṣetras these two sects characterized also differed. Consequently, the practitioners of these sects were often intolerant of each other's differences; they saw the other cult as adharmic and opposed it, and, in the process, these kṣetras of sectarianism became wrought with violence and injury. Notwithstanding the immorality of these behaviours, they were given the guise of dharma, because they preserved the ascendency of the sect.

A key reason why Śiva was seen as a rival candidate to Viṣṇu is that he was the Destroyer, capable of bringing about the dissolution of all life, which K. Sivaraman (2001: 43) considers 'cosmic operation *par excellence*'. '[Śiva] alone is the causal ground of phenomena who can retract the phenomena wholly without residue unto himself', because in order to recreate, the created world needs to be retracted entirely. Thus, 'Dissolution "precedes" Creation' (Sivaraman 2001: 43–4). From the perspective of this Śaivic *siddhānta*, in the Mahābhārata, both Vaiṣṇavism and Śaivism are juxtaposed to fight for this ultimate cosmic victory; divines of both sects not only reveal creational theophanies but also seek to bring about annihilation—Kṛṣṇa through the eighteen-day war and Śiva through Aśvatthāman's night raid in the *Sauptika Parva*. Kṛṣṇa does destroy the world via the eighteen-day war, and only the five Pāṇḍavas, Kṛṣṇa, Sātyaki, Kṛtavarman, Aśvatthāman, Yuyutsu, Kṛpa, and Karna's son, Vṛṣaketu, survive. In Aśvatthāman's night raid, too, the entire Pāñcāla camp is wiped out, down to the very foetus in Uttarā's womb, but the Pāṇḍavas and Kṛṣṇa escape.

Comparisons between Śiva-centric and Kṛṣṇa-centric incidents are easy to draw in the Mahābhārata. For example, Śiva's two theophanies in Aśvatthāman's night raid are similar to Kṛṣṇa's two theophanies, the first of which occurs after his embassy to the Kaurava court and the second occurs at Arjuna's request, during his recital of the Gītā. However, there is a slight difference in the nature of these theophanies: in his first theophany, Kṛṣṇa is clearly the creator from whom beings emerge; in the second, they retreat into him. In Śiva's first theophany, he is in the form of a sacrificial fire altar from which beings also emanate, but unlike in Kṛṣṇa's emanation, these beings have distorted faces and bodies. In the second theophany, Śiva, converging in the body of Aśvatthāman, is the Destroyer. But the implication of the theophanies is quite similar—both are cosmic forms that are the cause of creation and can also bring about annihilation. In fact, even the words they use to define the purpose of the theophany of destruction are the same: Kṛṣṇa tells Arjuna during the second theophany:

> kālosmi lokakṣayakṛt pravṛddho
> lokān samāhartum iha pravṛttaḥ

> ṛtepi tvāṃ na bhaviṣyanti sarve
> yevasthitāḥ pratyanīkeṣu yodhāḥ
> [I am now the full manifestation of Death and destroyer of the worlds. All these warriors standing in different division will cease to be, even if you do not kill them.] (*BG* 11.32)

And Śiva tells Aśvatthāman that the kāla had come for the Pāñcālas:

> kṛtas tasyaiṣa saṃmānaḥ pāñcālān rakṣat ā mayā
> abhibhūtās tu kālena naiṣām adyāsti jīvitam
> [By protecting the Pāñcālas I have honoured him [Kṛṣṇa]. They have however been assailed by Time. The lease of their lives is over.] (*Mbh* 10.7.65)

Hence, both divines portray themselves as the executors of Great Time.

Both cults also claim to offer liberation. Śiva facilitates Ganga's liberating presence on earth, and as Mahākāla and a close associate of Yama, he has eschatological power. Viṣṇu/Kṛṣṇa, too, takes on this function through the fourth puruṣārtha of mokṣa, which was perhaps added to the trivarga so that Vaiṣṇavism would be on par with Śaivism. In fact, this element of mokṣa even reduced the might of Śiva's significance as the finality, because it gave man the power to his own liberation. This is evidenced significantly in the Mahābhārata, when even the character of Vṛtra, the Vedic arch-enemy of the gods, alters, in order to reflect this Vaiṣṇava aspiration. In the myth that Bhīṣma tells Yudhiṣṭhira, Vṛtra is an aspirant of mokṣa. He is a devotee of Viṣṇu (instead of Śiva, who is most commonly favourable to the nāgas and asuras) and after he dies, he ascends to the 'highest abode'—'the region of Viṣṇu' (*Mbh* 12: 283.60–1). Additionally, Vṛtra's priest Uśanas, who is the guru of the asuras, calls Viṣṇu 'pre-eminent' and 'that Infinite place' (*Mbh* 12.280.2). Thus, the shift of mokṣa's association from Śiva to Viṣṇu is evident from Uśanas' change of kathenotheistic allegiance. Uśanas also invites Sanatkumāra, the mind-born son of Brahmā, to teach Vṛtra about how mokṣa is possible through Yoga (*Mbh* 12.280.1–57). This discipline of Yoga is normally associated with

Śiva, who is Yogiśvara himself, but here Uśanas and Sanatkumāra clearly make Yoga a Vaiṣṇava discipline. Hence, Vaiṣṇavism unmistakably carved out an equal share in all methods of achieving mokṣa, or final liberation, which used to be a Śaivic monopoly. This bid for an equal status is also clear in Bhīṣma's words, who concludes Vṛtra's story by first telling Yudhiṣṭhira that Kṛṣṇa is the final liberation—the Creator and Liberator (*Mbh* 12: 280.58–78)—and then by connecting Śiva and Viṣṇu. He first deifies Nārāyaṇa for retrieving the Vedas from the dānavas Madhu and Kaiṭabha (*Mbh* 12: 347.20–70), as Hayaśiras (the horse-headed), and for being the 'Supreme God, the receptacle of *Vedas*, of Sāṃkhya, of the yoga of renunciation and of the yoga of *Karma*,' and for being 'The deity who is *Puruṣa*' (*Mbh* 12.347.78–96). Then Bhīṣma deifies Śiva as above both Prakṛti and Puruṣa and says it is he [Śiva] who created 'Brāhmaṇa' (*Mbh* 13.14.5–6).

However, most often, the Śaivic element diverges to the point that it becomes a catalyst for many of the key conflicts in the story. Most likely, the reason why Śaivic elements appear more irascible than the Vaiṣṇava elements is because the Mahābhārata is composed by Vaiṣṇava brāhmins, who shifted the blame of the conflicts to their rivals. Perhaps, this is also the reason why Śiva/Rudra's inclusion in the divine triad of Vaiṣṇavism is in the form of Anirudha/Nārāyaṇa's anger that springs from his forehead (*Mbh* 12.341. 11–18).[2] These early forms of Śaivism and Vaiṣṇavism[3] and the conflict between them form a significant kṣetra in the Mahābhārata, because the sectarian battles they trigger evoke good and evil behaviour from the practitioners of these sects.

[2] In the Vaiṣṇava creation myth of the divine triad, Brahmā originates from the Nārāyaṇa's navel-lotus and is Nārāyaṇa's joy, and Rudra originates from Nārāyaṇa's forehead and is his anger.

[3] Considering that the orality of the Mahābhārata is about a thousand years prior to its first Sanskrit composition, it is possible that the Śaivic elements were all later interpolations; however, these were early enough to become integral to the frame story—and even the Critical Edition includes most ślokas related to it.

There are a number of myths in the Mahābhārata which can be seen as inspired by Śaivism, and these become the backdrop for incidents that raise questions about the morality/immorality of behaviours. One of the myths is of Dakṣa's sacrifice and Śiva's destruction of it. Klaus Klostermaier (2007: 111–12) gives a historical basis to this myth and considers the Śiva-Dakṣa myth a Śaiva conquest of Kanakhala, a *tīrtha* close to Haridwar mentioned in the Mahābhārata. Klostermaier believes that this tīrtha was an important one at the time of the Mahābhārata; its holiness was comparable to that of Prayāga, and its occupation was legitimized by Śaivism. Klostermaier (2007: 113) further suggests that this was a real event and it occurred after Vaiṣṇavism had already replaced Vedic orthodoxy. The myth of Dakṣa's sacrifice describes Viṣṇu battling with Śiva, and this violence became a part of each sect's traditions; so much so that each divine receives his identifying marks as a result of the conflict: Śiva throws a burning dart that strikes Viṣṇu on the chest, and his hair turns green, which is why Viṣṇu is also called Munjakeśa. In retaliation, Viṣṇu grabs Śiva by the throat, till his throat turns dark, and from then on he is known as Śitikaṇtha (*Mbh* 12.342.112-115). Notably, in this myth, Śiva is the victor. His Vīrabhadra form battles with the gods and defeats them, and even Dakṣa, the progenitor, loses his head. Thus, to ensure that the sacrifice is preserved, the Vaiṣṇavas not only accept the legitimacy of Śaivism, but they also see Śiva as a god of the pantheon, worthy of the sacrifice. Klostermaier (2007: 115) believes that the historic magnitude of this cannot be ignored because variations of this myth are told in all traditions, Vaiṣṇava, Śaivic, and Śakta. From Bhīṣma's narration of this same myth in the *Śāntī Parva* (*Mbh* 12.284.1-67), it is evident that an attempt had been made to accept Śaivism into Vedic tradition, but it had failed, and the practitioners of the former continued to press their cause, often using violent means to achieve it. In this Bhīṣma version, Dadhīci tells Dakṣa that he should have invited Śiva to the sacrifice, but Dakṣa doesn't agree. Hence, Śiva's anger turns into Vīrabhadra, who is then joined with Mahākālī, hence connecting Śaivism to Śaktism. This connection indicates that the myth may have been a later addition, which means that the sectarianism of the two cults became more compartmentalizing with time.

Perhaps the reason Śiva held on jealously to his monopoly over destruction was because, in many myths, he was not allowed to participate in creation; hence he was denied a key role necessary in the triple functions of creation, preservation, and destruction that is integral to the recognition of a divine as supreme. In *Sauptika Parva*, Kṛṣṇa too cites a similar reason for Śiva's anger. He explains that at the beginning of creation, Brahmā had asked Rudra, the first born, to create the world, and Rudra went away to practise austerities for the purpose, but he was gone for so long that Brahmā asked another being to engender creation. When Rudra reappeared, he was so upset that creation had been completed by someone else, that he broke off his generative organ and threw it into the ocean, because he felt that his ability to create was of no use now (*Mbh* 10.17.11–25).

All these myths about Śiva's anger and the conflicts he had with other gods show that Śiva (who could have been a pre-Aryan god), became a definite contender in the race for being the number one supreme, and his adherents tried to establish this supremacy through means which were often in opposition to the adherents of the Vaiṣṇava cult. While this opposition in itself cannot be seen as adharmic, the way it was executed was clearly indicative of the ethics of good and evil, because it dictated the conduct of the practitioners of the sects. A good example of this causative morality/immorality is in Aśvatthāman's night raid and destruction of the Pāñcāla camp. This incident clearly reveals not only the opposing moral codes of the Śaivas and Vaiṣṇavas, but also the immorality of human behaviour that the sectarian battles evoked. Moreover, the question of the evilness of the act is not left to conjecture or ambiguity but is emphatically measured against the codes of dharma, and is sometimes even opposed by the sectarian god himself. For example, in this incident, Kṛpa, realizing the immorality of Aśvatthāman's plan, pleads with him to refrain from this dastardly act of killing the Pāñcālas in their sleep, because it breaks all kṣatriya codes (*Mbh* 10.5.1-18). He tells Aśvatthāman to wait till the morning and fight a righteous battle, but Aśvatthāman is so full of rage at Dhṛṣṭadyumna's killing of his father that he is willing to forego dharma for revenge. However, in the Pāñcāla camp, he discovers that it is being guarded by a terrible being spewing flames from his mouth and eyes. Aśvatthāman tries to battle with this being, but his weapons prove ineffectual, and when they are exhausted, the sky fills with images of Janārdana (*Mbh* 10.6.4). Obviously, this terrible being is Śiva, but he is syncretized with Kṛṣṇa to protect the Pāñcālas, who are Kṛṣṇa worshippers, and also to remind Aśvatthāman that kṣatriya codes of war are non-sectarian and their violation is wrong in all instances.

This myth has many other elements that convey that the sects shared societal codes; however, sectarian differences were still emphasized to the extent that sectarian gods themselves were personified in the conflict. For example, in the continuing events of this incident, Aśvatthāman, though disheartened, decides to propitiate Giriśa—the same Śiva—and is prepared to give up his own self as sacrifice, another action that was non-sectarian and dhārmic for both sects. However, the interesting point here is that even as Aśvatthāman thinks about this self-sacrifice, a golden, blazing altar appears before him, and a distorted image of Śiva's theophany is presented: the flames of the altar reach across all the cardinal points in the horizon, and in the flames are hundreds of beings in all forms and shapes—animal, human, and bird. There are bodies with no heads but huge stomachs; heads with a thousand eyes and mouths with four tongues; faces that look like conches and bodies garlanded with conch shells. Some of the beings also carry weapons and some hold serpents. Some are blue-bodied, and some are covered with dust. There are beings playing musical instruments, while others run around like wild elephants. Some are flesh eaters and others drinkers of blood. They are worshippers of Mahādeva who have come to see his final act of destruction, and when Aśvatthāman offers his own soul and body as a sacrifice and enters the burning fire of the altar, Śiva finally manifests himself (*Mbh* 10.7.18–63).

Śiva's appearance at this juncture, especially in the form of sacrifice, leaves no doubt that this is an incident of sectarian violence in which Aśvatthāman (who is a Śaiva and a partial incarnation of Śiva) will proclaim Śiva's supremacy, because, like Viṣṇu, Śiva, too, is associated with sacrifice, as described in the *Yajur Veda* (Bhattacharji 2000: 117). However, the fact that this sacrificial altar is fearful, and the creatures emanating from it are deformed, proves that this is a Vaiṣṇava representation of the other cult's 'distorted' beliefs.

The distortion could also indicate that as the purpose of this sacrifice is destruction, its manifestations can only be terrifying; but this view seems unlikely in light of Kṛṣṇa's destruction theophany in the Gītā. In that theophany, Kṛṣṇa is 'adorned with celestial garlands and robes' (*Mbh* 6.35: 11), and he is holding the 'diadem and discus which is glowing on all sides' (*Mbh* 6.35.17). He is also surrounded by all the celestials, and the sun and moon are his eyes. There is a fire, too, that is emanating from his mouth, but, instead of being fearful, this fire is 'heating the universe with [Kṛṣṇa's] energy' (*Mbh* 6.35.19). The only fearful image in this theophany is that tusks thrust out of Kṛṣṇa's mouth, but that is only a magnified representation of Viṣṇu's Varāha (boar) incarnation—one in which he retrieved the Vedas and re-established Vaiṣṇavism. Obviously, this difference in imagery is the Vaiṣṇava attempt to show that while Śiva may be the final god of destruction, his destruction is ugly and deformed as compared to Kṛṣṇa's, who too could bring about destruction, but his annihilation will be gentle and splendid.

The various other exchanges and stories in the *Sauptika Parva* also reveal interesting insights into how rampant sectarianism was. For example, Śiva tells Aśvatthāman that he has protected the Pāñcālas because he has been worshipped by Kṛṣṇa, who is very dear to him, and that by protecting the Pāñcālas, he has honoured Kṛṣṇa. Now, however, he says, the time of the Pāñcālas has come (*Mbh* 10.7.65). It is almost as though, reminded by Aśvatthāman of their separate identity, the Śaivas needed to reclaim their power and prove that they were not subordinate to followers of Kṛṣṇaism. Furthermore, when Dhṛtarāṣṭra asks Saṃjaya why Aśvatthāman had not performed this massacre before, Saṃjaya tells him that Aśvatthāman was afraid of the Pāṇḍavas and Keśava (*Mbh* 10.8.154), which could mean that the practitioners of Śaivism were aware of the power of the Vaiṣṇava cult and may have been threatened by them on occasion. This is made evident in another verse in this parva as well, where there is undisguised enmity between sects. In a dialogue between Kṛṣṇa and Yudhiṣṭhira, Kṛṣṇa reveals that Aśvatthāman had come to him to request him for his disc because he had learnt that he could not use the *Brahmaśiras* weapon, which would bring complete destruction. Kṛṣṇa had given him the disc, but Aśvatthāman could not lift it, and was very disappointed. When Kṛṣṇa asked Aśvatthāman why he wanted the disc, Aśvatthāman replied, 'to fight you' (*Mbh* 10.12.15-36).

This violent power struggle between the two sects—made evident through the active participation of their gods—becomes the key theme of *Sauptika Parva,* and also of the whole Mahābhārata. Once Aśvatthāman propitiates Śiva, the god of destruction gives Aśvatthāman a sword and enters his body, infusing him with his own energy. Hence, Aśvatthāman, filled with Śiva and accompanied by invisible beings and rākṣasas, goes into the Pāñcāla camp and massacres everyone 'like animals in a sacrifice', including Dhṛṣṭadyumna, Śikhaṇḍin, and Draupadī's sons with 'superhuman force', 'thundering like a lion', till he is 'bathed in blood' 'appearing like death himself' (*Mbh* 10.7.66–68 & 10.8.1–87). In fact, in this massacre, Aśvatthāman is called the 'Great Destroyer himself let loose by Time' (*Mbh* 10.8.77) and is also equated to 'Destiny' (*Mbh* 10.8.75–76). The warriors in the Pāṇḍava camp see him as 'Death-night of black visage, having a bloody mouth and bloody eyes, wearing crimson garlands and smeared with crimson unguents, clad in single piece of red cloth, with a noose in hand, and resembling an elderly lady, singing a dreadful song, standing erect before their eyes, about to lead them away' (*Mbh* 10.8.70). When morning comes, Aśvatthāman is covered in blood and is holding the sword so tightly that his hand and sword seem like one, and he 'looks like the blazing fire at the end of the cycle, reducing all creatures to ashes' (*Mbh* 10.8.143–4).

Obviously, here, Aśvatthāman has not just assumed Śiva's kathenotheism in the sectarian battle, but he has also assumed his function of *pralaya.* A function that Śiva fulfils exclusively. Even Kṛṣṇa states that in the night raid 'it was not Drona's son that performed that act. It was done through the power of Mahādeva' (because Mahādeva is the master of pralaya) (*Mbh* 10.18.26).

The paradigmatic cosmic theme of Śiva's destructive powers and Aśvatthāman's divine transformation revealed in this incident raise important questions about the relationship of myth and ethics. The fact is that myth, even in its simplest definition, reveals the truth of the human experience, and the truth here is that in this myth Aśvatthāman is not simply a symbolic manifestation of Śiva and his cosmic pralaya. He is a moral agent accountable for his dharma/adharma, whose lakṣaṇa defines the kṣetra as good or evil. What he does and how he acts needs to be judged on the scale of dharma's ethics, and there can be no doubt that this moral agent commits extreme violence and, consequently, corrupts the dharmakṣetra.

Aśvatthāman's behaviour, when seen as that of a moral agent, also sheds light on the immorality of the other side—the Kṛṣṇa side, which parallels the Śaiva one in similar evil acts of mass killing. A good example of this is Arjuna's and Kṛṣṇa's burning of the Khāṇḍava. The two incidents are so similar, in fact, that even the description of the massacred Pāñcāla bodies is similar to that of the massacred animals and birds in the Khāṇḍava. In addition, just as some beings escape the Khāṇḍava fire, such as Takṣaka's son, Aśvasena, the demon Maya, and the *Śāranga* birds, in the *Sauptika* pralaya, too, the Pāṇḍavas escape. Hence the destruction (from either side) is not complete. But, in moral terms, both Arjuna and Aśvatthāman perpetrate ruthless acts of violence and evil in the name of sectarianism. Additionally, when seen in comparison, Arjuna's actions in the Khāṇḍava appear more heinous because his violence is purposeless, as opposed to Aśvatthāman's, who at least is avenging his father's death and fighting for the cause of victory. Admittedly, Aśvatthāman goes a step further and tries to complete the destruction by releasing the *Brahmaśiras* weapon 'which appears capable of destroying the three worlds like the all-destroying Yama at the end of the cycle' (*Mbh* 10.13.22). But then, at this time, Kṛṣṇa, too, impels Arjuna to discharge his Brahmaśiras. The world is saved by the Vaiṣṇava brāhmins, Nārada and Vyāsa, who intervene and tell the heroes to withdraw these weapons that could bring about total destruction to the world, and true to sectarian biases, while Arjuna, who is considered more ascetic, is able to withdraw his weapon, Aśvatthāman is not; hence he directs it to the wombs of the Pāṇḍava women and kills the foetus in Uttarā's belly (*Mbh* 10.14.12–16, 10.15.1–35 & 10.16.1).

This whole exchange clearly depicts the conflict that existed between the two sects. Though each tried to best the other, once again the Vaiṣṇava cult is shown to be superior, because it is represented by Arjuna who is considered to be full of dharma, practises brahmacarya, and is an observer of vows. Also, Kṛṣṇa revives the foetus in Uttarā's womb, (10-16.2–3), so the destruction that Śiva/Aśvatthāman tries to bring about is countered through Kṛṣṇa's māyā. On the other hand, Aśvatthāman, who does not have brahmacarya qualities and, to make matters worse, is living the life of a kṣatriya while being a brāhmin, is cursed to wander the earth (just like Śiva). From a sectarian point of view, Aśvatthāman's lack of brahmacarya and his adharma is a Vaiṣṇava condemnation of what is really Aśvatthāman's belief in Śaivism. And, of course, Arjuna is full of dharma because he is a Kṛṣṇa worshipper. Perhaps this is also why Arjuna's and Kṛṣṇa's act of destruction in the burning of the Khāṇḍava is never questioned; instead, they are both held up as models of dharma fighting in a dharmakṣetra as opposed to Aśvatthāman's kṣetra, which is seen as adharmic. But, if Aśvatthāman's act is defined as evil and he is penalized for it, what is it about Arjuna and Kṛṣṇa's act that changes the definition? Scholars consider Arjuna's and Kṛṣṇa's actions in the Khāṇḍava as a glimpse into pralaya; hence, devoid of moral/immoral value. But from this perspective, the violence Aśvatthāman perpetrates is also pralaya, and this is more validating of Śiva's *yugadharma*, because it is a divine function normally associated with Śiva. This would actually exonerate Aśvatthāman, but the Mahābhārata tradition is biased; the extreme violence that the Vaiṣṇavas and their divines commit is often passed off as simply necessary. Moreover, justifying these sectarian acts of violence as perpetrated by pralaya-evoking divines makes the Mahābhārata predominantly apocalyptic, whereas it is obvious from its treatment of human behaviours that the text is much more complex than that.

The juxtaposition of the sectarian divines is also worthy of note. Śiva often poses situations which test not only the dharma and adharma practices of the Vaiṣṇavas but also the imperatives of their divines. Śiva's dice playing in the *Ādi Parva* is a good example of this. In this incident, Śiva contravenes the very norms of Vaiṣṇava societal codes and, consequently, creates a catalytic situation that causes the Vaiṣṇava kṣetra to become a yuddha kṣetra—a kṣetra where good and evil is clearly in conflict. First, Śiva decides the fate of five Indras with the throw of dice, then he curses the Indras to reincarnate on earth as the Pāṇḍavas, which is followed by Śrī reincarnating as Draupadī, and a portion of Viṣṇu as Kṛṣṇa and Saṃkarṣaṇa (*Mbh* 1.197.15–35). On the surface, this myth appears quite innocuous—unrelated to sectarianism. It is told as one justification for Draupadī's marriage to five husbands; hence it seems unrelated to anything else that follows. In actuality, Śiva's role in this myth not only delineates the very kṣetra on which good and evil actions occur, but it also creates the catalyst that leads to the war. In addition, it disorients the Kṛṣṇa/Pāṇḍava camp and tests the conduct of all moral agents, including the dharma-knowing, Kṛṣṇized elders, such as Bhīṣma and Drona. Moreover, through the fruition of this myth, Śiva and Kṛṣṇa themselves are cast in the roles of moral agents.

Śiva's dice playing parallels the main dice game in the *Sabhā Parva*, which is the key catalyst of the war. Hiltebeitel (1991: 93–6) states that Śiva actually 'orchestrates this game' that is set at Yudhiṣṭhira's Rājasūya, a yajña which must end with a dice game, and in which the very wood for the yajña altar must be from the house of the *akṣāvāpa* (dice keeper). He also suggests some key points of comparison between Śiva's dice playing and the *dyūta* between the Kauravas and Yudhiṣṭhira: (1) Śiva and Pārvatī's dice symbolize the four yugas, and in the latter, Śakuni is Dvāpara, and Duryodhana is Kali. (2) Śiva's dice brings down the Indras, one after another, and in the Mahābhārata dice game the Pāṇḍavas suffer a synchronous fall. (3) In Śiva's game,

Indra, through his folly, is separated from Śrī; in the dyūta, through Yudhiṣṭhira's folly, Śrī/Draupadī is also separated from the Pāṇḍavas. (4) In Śiva's game, Śrī weeps tears that become golden lotuses; after the dyūta Draupadī's tears and laments are unceasing. (5) At Śiva's command, the Indras must be 'born' on earth, just like the Pāṇḍavas who must be 'born' again after they go through a forest exile and a year in disguise, (6) Viṣṇu approves of Śrī reuniting with the Indras and being born as Draupadī; Kṛṣṇa tells Draupadī that she will once again be the 'queen of kings' (Hiltebeitel 1991: 97).

Notwithstanding the many similarities, it is the differences between the two dice games that test the moral agency of the Pāṇḍavas, and especially of Kṛṣṇa: the two key differences are that Śiva is intoxicated with dicing, but Kṛṣṇa disapproves of dicing. And while Śiva himself is present at the dice game and is playing it, Kṛṣṇa is absent. Hiltebeitel (1991: 97–9) attributes this latter point to the pattern of Śiva always being present when dharma is violated and Kṛṣṇa being absent at these times. Śiva's motives can be seen purely as his deva dharma because he does not play a mortal role. Hence, the dice in which he seems intoxicated is his concentrated role in yugadharma (as is evident from the names of the dice throws). Also, his presence, whenever dharma is being violated, can be considered his yugadharma, because with the change of each yuga, dharma loses more ground. However, on a mortal, sectarian level, the 'orchestration' by Śiva—of Draupadī marrying five husbands, which is a violation of the marital codes—is a deliberate ploy to corrupt Vaiṣṇava societal norms. On the other hand, Kṛṣṇa's absence, even though dharma is being violated, negates his deva dharma because the very purpose of his reincarnation is to restore dharma. In addition, and more importantly, because the Rājasūya yajña cannot be considered complete without the dyūta, Kṛṣṇa's absence from it falsifies him on even the human level, because he obviously doesn't protect the yajña till the end, as he promises to do (Hiltebeitel 1991: 97–9).

Thus, this event of sectarianism tests dharma on both the cosmic and human level. Both divines are responsible for dharma, but from opposite ends: Śiva ensures dharma's decline to usher in another yuga, and Kṛṣṇa is supposed to ensure its restoration. But, while Śiva fulfils his role, Kṛṣṇa doesn't. Therefore, whatever adharma occurs on this kṣetra of cult conflicts must be attributed to Kṛṣṇa. In addition, if Śiva, and by extension the dice game, is to be seen as the catalyst for the war, then, once again, Kṛṣṇa is more at fault, because, while Śiva creates the situation in which to test dharma, it is Kṛṣṇa's duty to preserve dharma. Kṛṣṇa, however, is absent from the dice game. If he had been present, he could have prevented the resulting catastrophe, as he himself admits (*Mbh* 3.13.3).

The dice game, which Śiva cosmically orchestrates, is not just a catalyst—it is also a representation of the war, another situation of extreme conflict and testing of dharma that Śiva creates. There are many indications of this in the *Sabhā Parva*. For example, both Śakuni and Sahadeva claim that Śakuni's dice are like arrows (*Mbh* 2.77. 39). And just as the dice game is part of the sacrifice, so is the war a sacrifice of weapons, as Karṇa tells Kṛṣṇa (*Mbh* 5.141.30). The difference, of course, is that the treacheries and deceits are reversed. Although Kṛṣṇa is absent in this particular dice game and he disapproves of it; he is certainly present in that other game—the war—and even though he does not actively play, he strategizes for the Pāṇḍavas. He is the Śakuni of that game, just as Śiva is the Śakuni of the cosmic dice game. Also, just like the Indras are lost with each throw of Śiva's dice, so is every one of Yudhiṣṭhira's belongings with each throw of Śakuni's dice; and also with each 'throw' of Kṛṣṇa's 'dice', the Kauravas fall: first Bhīma, then Drona, then Karṇa, and then Duryodhana himself. So, the key players in the kṣetra of both games are really Kṛṣṇa and Śiva.

The two dice games—Śiva's in *Ādi Parva* and the dyūta in Sabhā *Parva*—also become the testing ground for the moral behaviour of human agents, especially those who believe in Vaiṣṇavism. This is most evident in Draupadī's situation. Even if it is accepted that Draupadī's unorthodox marriage to the Pāṇḍavas is preordained because of Śiva's orchestration, Śiva only lays the ground for the situation; he does not force the Pāṇḍavas to make Draupadī their joint wife. They, especially Yudhiṣṭhira, have the free will to abide by śāstras and tradition and refuse, or at the least present an argument against it. But the Pāṇḍavas do neither. The text suggests a moral justification of their participation in the violation of dharma—that they are fulfilling their mother, Kuntī's desire. But this raises an important question about Vaiṣṇava customary law: is this the definition of 'good' in Vaiṣṇavism, then, to blindly fulfil the desire of parents and elders, regardless of whether the act or the desire is good or evil? For an answer, the consequence of this action must be considered. While the Pāṇḍavas' polyandrous marriage does unite them in a strange incestuous bond, the physical, mental, and emotional strain on Draupadī to maintain *patnīdharma* towards five husbands must have been tremendous (this is never examined in the epic). Furthermore, this polyandry breeds feelings of jealousy among the brothers, especially in Arjuna. But the one who suffers the gravest repercussion of this act is Yudhiṣṭhira, because when he violates his duty towards Draupadī in the dyūta, he doesn't just victimize his own wife but also the wife of his brothers, and consequently, even the brothers themselves. Hence the kṣetra that Śiva creates is a test of dharma, which all moral agents fail.

Another demonstrative incident of sectarianism and the evil that invades the characters fighting its cause is that of Jarāsaṃdha and his destruction. The incident occurs when Yudhiṣṭhira is to perform his Rājasūya. Kṛṣṇa tells him that his key opposition would be Jarāsaṃdha, and that if he can subjugate him, he can be *samrāṭ*. Jarāsaṃdha's very birth is indicative of his affiliation with Śiva. When he is born split from the wombs of two mothers, he is put together by Jarā, a rākṣasī—a being over whom Śiva has dominion. Also, when Candrakauśika, the Gautama ṛṣi who ordains his birth, blesses him, he tells his father that Jarāsaṃdha will be a powerful ruler full of dharma and that 'with his physical eyes, he will see the god of gods, Rudra' (*Mbh* 2.19.15). That Jarāsaṃdha is a Śaiva is further proved by his enmity with Kṛṣṇa and the Yādavas, and it is actually for this sectarian reason that Kṛṣṇa wants to destroy Jarāsaṃdha, using Yudhiṣṭhira's Rājasūya as an excuse.

When Kṛṣṇa, Arjuna, and Bhīma enter Jarāsaṃdha's kingdom through deceit and meet him in his court, Jarāsaṃdha proclaims himself as a king full of dharma (which is not only the Śaiva dharma he subscribes to, but also the non-sectarian general dharma of a kṣatriya) and all his actions and behaviours described are testimony to this. Yet, Kṛṣṇa urges Bhīma to kill the Magadha king by violating a code of single combat and fighting with the old king non-stop for thirteen days, and thus tiring him to the point of death (*Mbh* 2.23.32–3). This is the very evil for which Śiśupala, consequently, condemns Kṛṣṇa at Yudhiṣṭhira's Rājasūya (*Mbh* 2.42.1–5). Once again, with sectarian overtones, Kṛṣṇa destroys Śiśupala, another Śaiva, to establish his own supremacy. Furthermore, the fact that hundreds of kings witness this killing and applaud Kṛṣṇa's actions instead of objecting to them, proclaims the ruthlessness of sectarian alliances.

On the other hand, Śiva, in his role of sectarian contender, rarely ever kills any Vaiṣṇava; his opposition is more subtle, creating situations in which the dharma of characters is put to the test. For example, many boons that are granted to those who are against the Pāṇḍavas are given by Śiva. The most important of Śiva's boons is to the dānavas through which Duryodhana is born (*Mbh* 3.253.8), and to contend with this particular orchestration, the Pāṇḍavas have to resort to war. Another such boon is to Ambā so that she can destroy Bhīṣma, who, very clearly, is a strong believer in Kṛṣṇa. He is also a mighty warrior, proud of his adherence to Kṛṣṇa bhakti, his oath of celibacy, and his kṣatriyahood. That he is reduced by a woman's power of asceticism could have been a Śaiva ploy to belittle him, and from this perspective, the fact that it is, in actuality, Arjuna (and not Śikhaṇḍin) who kills Bhīṣma could be considered a Vaiṣṇava attempt to rescue Bhīṣma's Vaiṣṇava manhood.

In this kṣetra of sectarianism, aside from the numerous instances of conflict, there are also incidents of compromise, especially when the two divines, instead of trying to best one another, accept each other as equals. Śiva's acknowledgment of Viṣṇu's supremacy and his collaboration with Kṛṣṇa and Arjuna in various incidents may be an interpolation by the Vaiṣṇava brāhmins who took over the telling of the Mahābhārata. Or maybe, considering that the composition of the epic spans centuries, these sectarian battles had their ups and downs—times when the two cults were in bitter opposition and times when there were attempts to unify them.

However, even during the occasional alignment and periods of peace, the moral agents could not uphold dharma. One of the most revealing of these incidents is Śiva's boon to Jayadratha, who propitiates the god after his attempt to kidnap Draupadī and his humiliation at the hands of the Pāṇḍavas. Here, Śiva acknowledges Nārāyaṇa as the 'unmanifest, *Pradhān Puruṣa*' (*Mbh* 3.272.31) and calls the created universe '*Vaiṣṇava*' (*Mbh* 3.272.70). He also validates Kṛṣṇa by telling Jayadratha that he is Viṣṇu's incarnation (*Mbh* 3.272.72). Therefore, when the Sindhu king asks Śiva for the ability to destroy all the Pāṇḍavas, the god does not grant that boon; instead he grants Jayadratha the boon to be victorious in one encounter over all the Pāṇḍavas, excepting Arjuna, who is protected by Nārāyaṇa. The consequence of this boon is hardly moral. In the war, as Śiva promises, Jayadratha is able to hold back the Pāṇḍavas in one encounter; but to what end? To allow a mass of Kaurava commanders to kill Abhimanyu—an act that is clearly immoral—in the context of both the war and society. This, then, is followed by more adharma, and this time it is carried out by both Arjuna and Kṛṣṇa under the pretext of a vow that the Pāṇḍava hero takes to kill Jayadratha. Ironically, and even more incriminating for Arjuna, on the eve of Jayadratha's *vadha*, Śiva helps Arjuna in the battlefield. Arjuna sees this in a dream in which he and Kṛṣṇa visit Śiva, and the god of destruction once again gives him the Paśupata weapon (*Mbh* 7.81.22). Later, Vyāsa tells Arjuna that Maheśvara was protecting him all along (*Mbh* 7.203.21–3). However, despite having both divines on his side, Arjuna fails in dharma. He kills Jayadratha by trickery that Kṛṣṇa orchestrates.

The clearest incident of Vaiṣṇavas and Śaivas working together in the same kṣetra is seen in Arjuna's encounter with Śiva as Kirāta in the *Vana Parva*. Once again, favoured by the two divines, Arjuna is filled with a sense of entitlement and, even supported by them, he falters as a moral agent. In this incident, initially, Arjuna seeks Śiva single-mindedly, performing the most arduous of penances, and when Śiva appears in the form of Kirāta, a mountain hunter, they both strike

Mūka, a dānava disguised as a boar, at the same time. A battle breaks out between them over who first struck the boar, but Arjuna is incapacitated by Śiva's strength and māyā, and when he gains consciousness and realizes who he is battling, he bows before Śiva and praises him as being the supreme being, the creator, preserver, and destroyer and equates him with Viṣṇu, saying, 'You are Śiva in the form of Viṣṇu, and Viṣṇu in the form of Śiva' (*Mbh* 3.39.76). Then, Arjuna asks Śiva for the Brahmaśiras weapon (*Mbh* 3.40.9). This weapon has a 'Brahman head', hence the implication is that it is a cosmic weapon that would destroy the world. Śiva refuses Arjuna this weapon, reminding him that he is a mere mortal, and then he gives him his Paśupata instead (this is a more personal weapon since Śiva himself is Paśupata) (*Mbh* 3.40.15). But the fact that Arjuna feels entitled to an absolute cosmic weapon shows that in times when Vaiṣṇavas felt they had managed to fully bring the Śaivic elements into their fold, they grew vainglorious.

Arjuna is a complete warrior, possessing the power of all the gods; hence there is more responsibility on him to uphold dharma. He could have been an ideal vehicle of a concurrence of the sects. However, in the final analysis, Arjuna fails. In his cosmic act of evoking pralaya to match the power of Aśvatthāman's Brahmaśiras weapon, Arjuna reveals himself to be no more than an unthinking, ignorant mortal (ignorance being analogous to adharma). His intent may not have been to destroy the world, but the fact that Arjuna does not even consider the implications of discharging his own pralaya weapon makes him culpable, because ignorance or lack of foresight is as much an evil as the action itself. In addition, it reeks of abuse of power, which may have been how the Vaiṣṇavas behaved whenever they gained advantage. But the way the brāhmins panic when the weapons are released indicates the destruction this cult conflict could have let loose.

To give the Vaiṣṇavas credit, they sometimes did try to curb sectarian violence; but, to do so, they either discredited Śiva's powers or subsumed them into Viṣṇu—the same was true of Śaivites. These methods made the practitioners of both sects susceptible to acts of adharma. Admittedly, in this warrior culture, it may not have been possible to refrain from all acts of violence. The only other way to stop violence or adhere to absolute dharma would have been by totally ceasing all action. In fact, there is one such incident of non-action in the Mahābhārata which, ironically, is initiated by Aśvatthāman, although he does it inadvertently. This event also indicates that peace between the sects was not wholly impossible; they were just not willing to concede. This incident (*Mbh* 7.202.55–96) occurs when Aśvatthāman uses the Nārāyaṇa weapon after Drona's death. The power of this weapon is such that it destroys anyone who is holding weapons (except for Nara and Nārāyaṇa, who are immune to any weapon or being as a result of a boon from Śiva). The effect of the weapon is rendered useless because Kṛṣṇa, knowing its power, tells all the Pāṇḍavas and their troops to lay down their weapons (only Bhīma continues to defy this). Obviously, the Nārāyaṇa weapon is a weapon of peace, and, most importantly, both Śiva and Nārāyaṇa are responsible for its effectiveness. Thus, while the kṣetra on which Śaivism and Vaiṣṇavism dwelt was a sectarian ground, evoking violence, it was also a kṣetra in which individual moral agents could decide to end the violence. But, in the Mahābhārata, they chose war over peace, and this compulsion continued in tradition.

KṢETRA OF THE FRAME STORY: THE PĀṆḌAVA AND KAURAVA CONFLICT

The key kṣetra of the Mahābhārata which must be examined as a dharmakṣetra is that of the frame story. It is in this kṣetra that the moral agents have no archetypal, mythopoeic, or sectarian excuses. Their behaviour is guided by pure human impulses and adherence or lack thereof to puruṣārthic dharma; hence, their dhārmic or adharmic characteristics define the good and evil of the kṣetra. As Sukthankar (1998: 19) says, the Mahābhārata is 'clearly intended by the author or authors of the poem to portray different aspects of human personality, to visualize the different types of subtle psyche of man' therefore, the characters are 'as active and potent today as they were in the time of the *Mahābhārata*'. Hence, this tradition of the text, in which the 'psyche of man' continues to be dynamically visual, is one of the most important.

This kṣetra is set with the birth of Dhṛtarāṣṭra, Pāṇḍu, and Vidura: 'Thus were begotten on the field (wives) of Vicitravīrya by Dvaipāyana three sons, as effulgent as the celestial children, the expanders of the Kuru race' (*Mbh* 1.106.32), and it reaches fruition with the birth of the Kauravas and Pāṇḍavas, which spawns the question of who will be the legitimate king of Hāstinapura—Duryodhana, the eldest Kaurava, or Yudhiṣṭhira, the eldest Pāṇḍava? Trying to prove legitimacy, the moral agents war—with each other, with their relationships and circumstances, and with their inner selves—but, more often than not, they lose their morality in the process of their battles. Therefore, in this field, the epic is more an adharmakṣetra than a dharmakṣetra. In addition, in this field, dharma itself becomes biased—suspect of partiality—even before the battle lines are drawn; rather, even before the moral agents are allowed to demonstrate their (im)morality, dharma takes sides and predetermines that no matter what nature of puruṣkāra the two sides demonstrate, the Pāṇḍavas will be considered moral and the Kauravas immoral. Hence, victory is already preordained, since it is known that where there is dharma, there is victory. Therefore, the question of dharmakṣetra or adharmakṣetra and the definition of good and evil through the lakṣaṇa of the moral agents becomes moot at the outset.

Corruption of the Kṣetra of Kingship and Legitimacy: Bhīṣma, Vidura, Pāṇḍu, and Dhṛtarāṣṭra

The yuddha kṣetra created by the Kauravas and Pāṇḍavas to decide the issue of the legitimacy is not simply a question of who is the rightful king as per the codes of kingship. If it were, it would be easy to resolve, because then it would be a matter of just matching up the qualities of an ideal king (that Bhīṣma, Vidura, and Nārada describe) with the candidates and declaring the winner. For example, Bhīṣma equates the king to Indra and says he has total power and is the one who sustains dharma and ensures its execution. This ideal king is an independent ruler, and he protects his kingdom from being taken over. Also, when the need arises, he 'assails the kingdom of the stronger one by means of weapons of fire and the administering of poison' (*Mbh* 12.69.15–16). Also according to Bhīṣma, a king satisfies his debt when he defeats his foe or kills him at once. And a good king takes care of 'his own self, his ministers, his treasury, his servants, his friends, his provinces, and his capital' *(Mbh* 12.69.64–5). Considering these qualities, the ideal king would be Duryodhana. He fits all the criteria that Bhīṣma describes. In fact, Duryodhana is such a good king that both his people and the gods attest to it. For instance, just before Dhṛtarāṣṭra goes into the forest at the end of the war, his subjects thank him and tell him that under King Duryodhana, '[they] were well protected and well ruled' and 'they lived depending on [him] as trustfully as [their] own father' (*Mbh* 15.10.20–1). And when the dying Duryodhana himself proclaims his kingly virtues, the heavens shower flowers to honour him, and the Gandharvas, siddhas, and apsarās sing his praise (*Mbh* 10.61.18). Yudhiṣṭhira, on the other hand, may be a man of dharma, but he neither fits the kṣatriya qualities that Bhīṣma describes, nor does he care about his people. If he cared for his people, would he have staked them in a dice game? If he was so worried about Duryodhana's adharmic character, would he have wagered his kingdom, subjecting his people to the immorality of his cousin's kingship? This fact alone would immediately cancel Yudhiṣṭhira's candidacy.

But the question of kingship doesn't just address the qualities of a good king; it also pertains to the matter of legitimacy of birth. It is a right passed down from father to eldest son. This is the key problem. Who is the eldest son, the legitimate heir to the throne of Hāstinapura—Yudhiṣṭhira or Duryodhana? Legitimacy cannot be conclusively determined because of the actions of certain progenitors, who, by virtue of their free will, make the 'wrong choices', thereby creating a domino effect of consequentiality in which legitimacy becomes dubious. The first culprit of this problematic situation is Bhīṣma, a character who is considered exemplary in tradition and also by most scholars. For example, Sukthankar (1998: 45) sees Bhīṣma as the 'Perfect Man', the character whose idealism is unequalled in epic poetry. According to Sukthankar, Bhīṣma is that character of the Mahābhārata who achieves self-actualization, because he acts on *asirdhārāvrata* (a vow as fine-edged as an arrow) and proves his mettle (Sukthankar 1998: 45). However, the fact is that Bhīṣma takes this vow to protect Hāstinapura, yet he forfeits the fate of the kingdom for his own glory; not once, but twice. The first time he chooses putradharma over Hāstinapura. In that choice, he endangers the kingdom, because, to make his father happy, he promises Matsyagandhā's father that he will take the oath of celibacy. He does not once consider whether Matsyagandhā's (Satyavatī's) union with Śaṃtanu will be fruitful or not. What if Śaṃtanu and Satyavatī had not been able to have children? In his haste to be a good son and to prove to the world his asceticism, he allows selfish achievement to cloud his love for Hāstinapura. Then, again, he jeopardizes Hāstinapura for his own glory when his half-brothers, Vicitravīrya and Citrāngada, die without children and Satyavatī requests him to follow the accepted practice of *niyoga* and father sons on Ambikā and Ambālikā, his brothers' widows. Bhīṣma refuses. He is willing to play with the fate of Hāstinapura rather than break the oath that has won him such personal glory amongst both mortals and immortals. Further, trusting Satyavatī's word, he allows Vyāsa to impregnate the queens without considering whether the sons born from that union will be suitable for kingship or not, once again jeopardizing the kingdom. In fact, that is exactly what occurs. The queens give birth to sons who are both unsuited to be king: Dhṛtarāṣṭra is blind, and Pāṇḍu is impotent.

It can be argued that Bhīṣma cannot really be blamed for the infirmities that Ambikā's and Ambālikā's children suffer, because that, as the epic keeps repeating, is daivya or fate. However, Bhīṣma's choices are his own, even when it seems that fate is inexorable. If he had forfeited his oath in lieu of fathering children, the ensuing progeny may have been more suitable. He even had an ideal candidate for motherhood in Ambā, who, unlike Ambikā and Ambālikā, did not shy away from sexual union; in fact, she invited it. Having obscured forever the legitimacy of Hāstinapura's heir, Bhīṣma continues to err. In the process of trying to sustain Hāstinapura, he hurts many people, especially women: Ambikā and Ambālikā are forced to bear intercourse with Vyāsa, a man so ugly that they can hardly bear it; Gāndhārī is married to a blind husband and binds her own eyes forever; and Kuntī and Mādrī are married to an impotent man. He also hurts Ambā, who, consequently, commits suicide, and ultimately causes Bhīṣma's destruction and, perhaps, his salvation too. Then there is the case of Draupadī, which is not directly related to the question of legitimacy of kingship that Bhīṣma muddles, but Bhīṣma's non-action does deepen the obscurity of dharma in this question of kingship, as well as the legality of the issue. He has the authority to stop the dice game, but he doesn't. He just sits there, watching Draupadī's humiliation. In fact, at that moment, if he had fulfilled the role of the grandfather that he is, the protector of Hāstinapura that he proclaims himself to be, the keeper of traditions—the title Kṛṣṇa confers upon him—and had supported the dharma of protecting the *kulavadhu*, the war would have been averted. Irawati Karve (2008: 17) says he does not really do any explicit wrong in this; he is just indifferent to the fate of these women. This indifference is, perhaps, Bhīṣma's greatest wrong, because it is indicative of his apathy towards social justice—whether it pertains to women, legitimacy of kingship, or war. His sin is as grievous as that of a person who watches a woman being raped and does nothing to prevent it, even though he is in a position to do so. Therefore, Bhīṣma is as much to blame, if not more, for Draupadī's suffering, just as the men who directly cause it. Hence, by his lack of action at this crucial time, he becomes instrumental in the violent solution that the two sides find to the problem of legitimacy.

Bhīṣma's 'sacrifices', which scholars like Sukthankar see as ideal examples of niṣkāma karma, are also not as selfless as they appear. Sukthankar (1998: 47) believes that he joins the war and fights on the Kaurava side because he is bound by dharma to fight for the monarch—Dhṛtarāṣṭra. Hence he fights without desire, or rather his desire is desireless. In other words, the motive of his sacrifices is the greater good. However, not only do his sacrifices hurt innumerable people and thrust Hāstinapura in the āpad situation of war, but also his actions are not niṣkāma. By his own admission, one of his motives to join the Kauravas in the war is his desire for wealth, and his actions in the war are ruled by his hubris and his desire for power. The consequence of the latter is one of the reasons for the thorough massacre in Kurukṣetra: Arjuna cannot touch him, because he is the grandfather, Duryodhana cannot remove him from the commandership of his armies out of respect for him, and he himself cannot die because of his boon. So, instead of a quick war, the Kauravas and Pāṇḍavas have to massacre many, many enemy warriors over eighteen days to gain victory. Additionally, Bhīṣma's refusal to let Karṇa fight is because his ego will not allow him to acknowledge that Karṇa may be a greater kṣatriya *and* warrior than him. Perhaps, if Karṇa had been actively fighting in the war from day one, the outcome would have been decided without the total bloodbath. Tradition upholds Bhīṣma as the ideal man, whose choices in life are all for the service of others and for the kingdom. The truth is, Bhīṣma, through his bad choices and adharma of hubris, can be seen as a character who lays not only the first seeds of adharma in this kṣetra but also many rotations of bad seeds, including the seed of a disputed kingship.

The other culprits who complicate the question of legitimacy are the fathers, Pāṇḍu, Dhṛtarāṣṭra, and Vidura. The culpability of Pāṇḍu and Dhṛtarāṣṭra can be demonstrated through a dialogue that Kṛṣṇa and Nārada have in the *Śāntī Parva*: when Kṛṣṇa, distressed by the disunity in his own clans of Bhojas and Vṛṣṇis over distribution of wealth, seeks Nārada's advice, the ṛṣi tells him that this is a result of his own actions. Kṛṣṇa gave away the kingdom to Babhru and Ugrasena, who were Vṛṣṇis, thus upsetting the Bhojas, and this, Nārada says, is the root cause of the disunity. He says to Kṛṣṇa, 'You cannot take back that wealth, even as you cannot swallow again the food that you have vomited yourself.' Taking it back would create intestine feuds (*Mbh* 12.81.16–17). Nārada also warns Kṛṣṇa that 'even if the attempt succeeds, it will do so after... a great slaughter and a great loss of wealth ... perhaps even total destruction' (*Mbh* 12.81.18). Nārada's statements echo the very situation in Hāstinapura: Pāṇḍu gave away the kingdom to Dhṛtarāṣṭra; now his sons, the Pāṇḍavas, cannot take it back. Similarly, Dhṛtarāṣṭra does give a portion back to the Pāṇḍavas and creates more 'intestine feuds'. Then, Yudhiṣṭhira gives away his wealth and kingdom to Duryodhana in a dice game, once again creating more disunity and inviting slaughter. Therefore, how can Duryodhana be blamed for fighting over what was his two times over, and how can the Pāṇḍavas claim a right to it? And, to make matters worse, there is Kṛṣṇa's meddling. He created problems in his own clans with his interference, despite Nārada's warning to him that 'disunion will create destruction' and that he, being the 'foremost among them', should act in such a way that the two parties 'may not meet with destruction' (*Mbh* 12.81.25). And now he is causing similar discord between the Pāṇḍavas and Kauravas.

The other question that must be raised here in terms of legitimacy is that of birth and birthright. The throne is contested because the Pāṇḍavas are considered Pāṇḍu's progeny by niyoga, but who are the Pāṇḍavas? Who are their fathers? In this patrilineal society, the identity of the fathers was imperative. The divine parentage of the Pāṇḍavas is only mythic. In reality, Pāṇḍu was probably impotent (or from a myth perspective, rendered impotent by Kiṃdam's curse), and Kuntī and Mādrī had five sons between them. Who really fathered these five sons? Scholars like Irawati Karve (2008: 69) believe that Yudhiṣṭhira, who is the chief candidate for kingship, is really Vidura's son. From this perspective, Vidura is the third father and culprit of this situation.

Right at the outset in this question of legitimacy, it is important to state Vidura's status in the hierarchy of caste. The king could only be a kṣatriya or, in certain situations, a brāhmin, but not a vaiśya, and never a śūdra. Vidura is the son of a śūdra woman (*Mbh* 1.108.9). There is quite a bit of proof in the Mahābhārata that shows that Vidura is Yudhiṣṭhira's father: Vidura is Dharma himself, but cursed to be born as a low caste. This incarnation of Dharma in both Vidura and Yudhiṣṭhira implies the father–son relationship between the two. This fact is also supported by numerous statements in the epic; for example, when Dhṛtarāṣṭra, Gāndhārī, and Kuntī give up their mortal bodies, Nārada tells them that they will go to their desired places and Vidura will 'enter into the high soul of Yudhiṣṭhira' (*Mbh* 14.20.20), and by Yoga power, Vidura enters the body of Yudhiṣṭhira limb by limb;

he unites his vital airs with those of Yudhiṣṭhira, and his senses with Yudhiṣṭhira's senses (*Mbh* 15.26.20). And when Yudhiṣṭhira wants to cremate Vidura's body, a heavenly voice tells him not to, because 'In him is your body' (*Mbh* 15.26.25). These are the very words Ulūpī had used to introduce Arjuna to his son Babhruvāhana, who had struck him dead during the horse wandering of the Aśvamedha. Ulūpī's words were: 'The son is one's own self' (*Mbh* 14.81.18)—words that are also echoed in the *Law Code of Manu* (9: 32–56 and 9: 132; Olivelle 2004: 156, 164).

To further support this argument of Yudhiṣṭhira's parentage is Vidura's unwavering support of him. Just as Dhṛtarāṣṭra dotes on Duryodhana like a favourite child, so Vidura supports and protects Yudhiṣṭhira in subtle and not-so-subtle ways. For example, when Vidura warns Yudhiṣṭhira of the incendiary nature of the house of lac, he sends him a message in the Mleccha tongue that only the eldest Pāṇḍava understands. This is a language that Bhīṣma considers sinful, because Mlecchas are outside the Aryan fold (*Mbh* 12.188.17), but Vidura knows it, perhaps because of his caste. The fact that Yudhiṣṭhira too knows it, suggests that Vidura spoke Mleccha often enough that his 'son' picked it up. Otherwise, why would Yudhiṣṭhira, who is supposedly a dharma- and caste-bound Aryan prince, be allowed to learn a language that was considered sinful and outside the bounds of Aryanism? Another fact that is suggestive of their filial bond is Kuntī's intimate relationship with Vidura. That is why, when the Pāṇḍavas go to the forest, Kuntī decides not to join them in exile but chooses instead to stay with Vidura. All these are subtle references to the father–son relationship between Vidura and Yudhiṣṭhira, but in the *Āśramavāsika Parva*, Vyāsa states this father–son bond quite clearly. He tells Dhṛtarāṣṭra: 'He [Vidura] was a deity of deities ... and from that Deity of Virtue, through Yoga power, the Kuru King, Yudhiṣṭhira also took birth.' And also, 'He who is Dharma is Vidura, and he who is Vidura is the eldest son of Pāṇḍu' (*Mbh* 15.28.16 &118). Thus, it is more than likely that Vidura is Yudhiṣṭhira's father; therefore, by virtue of his low-caste parentage, Yudhiṣṭhira has no claim to the throne.

Yudhiṣṭhira's parentage changes everything, and the question of 'who is king' need not even be asked. In fact, in this respect, there is even precedent for why Yudhiṣṭhira cannot be king: when both Dhṛtarāṣṭra and Pāṇḍu were seen as unsuited for kingship, their half-brother, Vidura, who was the epitome of dharma, and was able-bodied, could not be made king because his mother was a śūdra, even though his father was Vyāsa himself. In Yudhiṣṭhira's case, Aryan paternity law of kingship is even more against him, because it is his father who is a śūdra. On the other hand, Duryodhana is a legitimate, unquestioned son of the kṣatriya princess Gāndhārī and the king of Hāstinapura, Dhṛtarāṣṭra. The answer to the question of who should be king is clear. But it isn't because, obviously, this story is about more than just the legitimacy of a kingship or, even if it is, these determinations are not conclusive. Hence, the onus now falls on dharma; and, therefore, the kṣetra on which the question of kingship rests becomes a true dharmakṣetra. So now the initial question of who is the legitimate king can be qualified as: who, *by virtue of dharma*, is the legitimate king? The answer to this can also be simple, because one of the candidates (even though his birth is cast in doubt) is Dharma manifest; therefore, he can be crowned the winner. But this claim is also equivocal, because dharma itself is ambiguous, and by the same standard adharma too is indistinguishable. There are no litmus tests to prove the red and blue of these opposing factors and whether Yudhiṣṭhira truly is the dharma king.

A Biased *Kṣetra* of War

Since dharma is ambiguous and the legitimacy of the throne cannot be proved otherwise, the only deciding factor is battle, because one seemingly irrefutable fact of this battle of good and evil is that *yato dharmas tato jayaḥ*. This means that victory itself is equivalent to dharma, or that dharma itself is victory. Thus, it can be assumed that the faction which gains victory in the war will be emblematic of dharma. Clearly, in the battlefield of Kurukṣetra, one faction is the victor, and this faction does become emblematic of dharma. But does this faction truly display the lakṣaṇa of dharma? The answer to this question will determine whether this kṣetra is a dharmakṣetra or not, and if it is proved that this faction did not uphold dharma, then the very truth of the dharmakṣetra and of the statement, 'yato dharmas tato jayaḥ' is falsified. In this case, Kurukṣetra becomes an adharmakṣetra.

One of dharma's explicit and unequivocal qualities is goodness; therefore, this quality can be accepted as the barometer of the kṣetra. If the Pāṇḍavas are to be accepted as embodiments of good by virtue of their birth, and their yuddha with the Kauravas is for the victory of that good, their victory must be unequivocally good. There are two determinants to decide this: firstly, if karma (action, which is the means) is undertaken with the intent of good and, secondly, if the consequence (the end) of that karma is also good, then it can be said that the good, that is, the Pāṇḍavas, has been victorious. Since the intent of war is tied up with the ambiguity of legitimacy, it cannot be determined if the Pāṇḍavas are fighting for right and their intent was good. However, what is not at all ambiguous is that the consequence of their actions hardly begets good. In fact, after the war, even Kurukṣetra itself, the field on which this battle of the victory of good is fought, is left as ugly as sin:

> Covered with numberless killed men, horses and elephants ... The bodies that were adorned with golden trappings are now covered with blood ... carcasses of killed horses, mangled with arrows, breathing hard in agony and vomiting blood ... the elephants with shattered tusks, vomiting blood, crying piteously in anguish ... strewn with the heads of bodies of thousands of heroes wounded with arrows ... covered with dead bodies of Kuru and Sṛñjaya warriors ... the entire field is blackened with carcasses, corpses, broken chariots and arrows that Arjuna and Karṇa shot. (*Mbh* 8.94.1–16)

In fact, even the victory itself is equivocal; Yudhiṣṭhira's words at the end of the war testify to this: 'The enemies who were defeated have become victorious. Ourselves, again, while victorious are defeated' (*Mbh* 10.10.11). Furthermore, he says, 'Misery appears like prosperity, and prosperity looks like misery. This, our victory, is turned into defeat ... Having gained victory, I am obliged to grieve as an afflicted wretch ... In sooth, I have been doubly defeated by the enemy' (*Mbh* 10.10.12–15). In addition, it is revealed that after the war, the celestial paraphernalia that Arjuna had received to fight this battle for good disappear—the celestial ape that was on the banner of his chariot vanishes, and the chariot itself, along with its quivers, reins, horses, yoke, and shaft suddenly bursts into flames and is instantly reduced to ashes (*Mbh* 9.62.12–14). The explanation Kṛṣṇa provides is that the chariot, which had earlier been burnt by Drona and Karna with various weapons, was holding together because he (Kṛṣṇa) was sitting in it, and now that the war's objective was achieved and Kṛṣṇa was no longer in it, it became ashes (*Mbh* 9.62.18–19). However, the objective of the war was not just victory; it was victory of dharma. If dharma had been the purpose, dharma the means, and dharma the end of this dharmayuddha, wouldn't Arjuna's accoutrements of battle remain as emblems of his dharma and warriorship, especially since these were given to him by Varuna, the 'protector of the world' and 'foremost of all the Lokapālas' to accomplish great warrior feats to benefit the world (*Mbh* 1.225.3–4)? Isn't that how dharma sustains? Especially of note is that, conversely, Duryodhana's beloved golden mace, with which he fought valiantly in every battle, 'does not abandon the illustrious hero' and remains right beside him 'like a loving wife', even as he dies (*Mbh* 10.9.11–13). Thus, in this equivocation, even the lucidity of the quality of goodness is lost in the falsity of the dharma that the Pāṇḍavas demonstrate.

One key element to consider in this misconstrued dharma victory of the Pāṇḍavas is that it is actually predetermined by many factors. One of the most elemental factors is that the Pāṇḍavas and Kauravas themselves are the archetypal representation of gods and demons. Even Saṃjaya in his description of the troops presents them as such to Dhṛtarāṣṭra. He says, '*daityendra seneva ca kauravāṇāṃ; devendra seneva ca pāṇḍavānām*' [the Kuru troops looked like the army of the *dānava* chief, while the Pāṇḍava troops looked like the army of the celestials] (*Mbh* 6.20.5). But, while the archetypal predetermination of the ultimate victory of the gods can be accepted on an allegorical level (because in this victory dharma is static), on the material plain, dharma must be determined empirically through its lakṣaṇa. However, in the battlefield of Kurukṣetra, dharma is not given a chance to prove itself through its lakṣaṇa. The Pāṇḍavas are made emblematic of dharma even before the battle and even before they prove their dharma.

There are many factors that establish the outcome of the war, and all these become unfair advantages for the Pāṇḍavas. The following are just a few key instances: Draupadī is wedded to the Pāṇḍavas, which is a clear indication that they will be the victors, because she is a reincarnation of Śrī, who is prosperity and also the goddess who determines kingship with her favours (*Mbh* 1.197.29). In the *Śānti Parva*, Bhīṣma tells Yudhiṣṭhira that Śrī was born from the lotus that sprang from Viṣṇu's brow. She then became Dharma's consort and Artha was born from their union. Hence Dharma, Artha, and Śrī are established in a king (*Mbh* 12.59.132-134). Bhīṣma also eulogizes Śrī by citing from the response she herself gave Nārada when he questioned who she was: 'I am called Lakṣmī, Bhūtī, and Śrī ... I am Faith; I am Intelligence; I am Affluence; I am Victory and I am Immutability ... I am patience. I am success and I am prosperity. I am Svāha, I am Svadhā, I am Reverence, and I am Fate, and I am Memory ... I live at the vanguard and on the standards of victorious and virtuous kings, as well as in their homes, cities, and kingdoms' (*Mbh* 12.228.18–23). Thus, 'Śrī is associated with prosperity, well-being, royal power, and illustriousness ... She is the embodiment of these qualities, and it is commonly understood that when these qualities are evident, Śrī herself is present or reveals herself' (Kinsley 1988: 19). Hence, the fact that Śrī wholly favours the Pāṇḍavas determines that they will gain victory. Although Yudhiṣṭhira foolishly loses her in the dice game, Śrī does not only continue to favour the Pāṇḍavas, she also helps them gain her back.

In addition, with Draupadī, the Pāṇḍavas also have the power of Kṛṣṇa, because she is not only his mortal 'sakhī' but also his celestial consort: 'Krishna incarnate[s] Viṣṇu, and Draupadī quite emphatically incarnates Viṣṇu's consort Śrī (Hiltebeitel 1991: 62). Also, because Draupadī bears the name of Kṛṣṇā, Hiltebeitel (1991: 63) connects her and Kṛṣṇa through the colour black. He says that since Kṛṣṇa assumes different colours—*śukla, rakta, pīta, kṛṣṇa* (white, red, yellow and black)—for the various yugas and his colour is black for *Kali Yuga*, so is Śrī/Draupadī 'similarly related to periodic coloric' to show 'mythological consolidarity'. Therefore, having Draupadī on their side is a guarantee that the Pāṇḍavas cannot lose this war, because not only are they married to Śrī incarnate, but also, through her, they have the benefaction of Kṛṣṇa.

Kṛṣṇa then is the other unfair advantage that the Pāṇḍavas have—both in his individual divinity and in the Nara–Nārāyaṇa connection between Arjuna and Kṛṣṇa, but especially the latter, because it gives Arjuna a special status. Kṛṣṇa openly declares this connection many times but never so clearly as in *Drona Parva*, when, for the second time, he intends to break his vow of unarmed alliance. After Abhimanyu's death and Arjuna's vow to either kill Jayadratha the following day or self-immolate, Kṛṣṇa tells Dāruka, his attendant, 'Tomorrow Dāruka, you shall see the army crushed with my discus and overthrown by my enraged self for the sake of Arjuna. Tomorrow the celestials, the Gandharvas, the *piśācas*, the nāgas and the rākṣasas will all know me to be the true friend of Savyasācin. He that injures him injures me, and he that follows him follows me' (*Mbh* 7.79.31–33). With Kṛṣṇa ensuring Arjuna's victory, even at the cost of his own vow, how can Arjuna lose?

Pratismṛti or foreknowledge is another element that acts in Pāṇḍava favour. This advantage is given to the Pāṇḍavas by Vyāsa, when in *Vana Parva*, he gives them the ability to know the future. Vyāsa even calls it 'success personified' (*Mbh* 3.36.24), and he advises Arjuna to go and seek weapons from the gods so that he can bring this knowledge to fruition. Hence, the Pāṇḍavas not only have knowledge of the future, they are also aided by Vyāsa and the celestials. On the other hand, the pratismṛti of victory that Duryodhana receives in a dream from the dānavas after they reveal the truth of his birth, is false, because it is provided by the dānavas, who are always falsified by the devas. Therefore, even before they go to war, the Pāṇḍavas know they will win, because their foreknowledge of victory is true.

The most significant unfair advantage that the Pāṇḍavas have, and it also becomes a lakṣaṇa of adharma, is the fact that Bhīṣma and Drona, two of the Kaurava generals, though fighting for the Kauravas, are not only rooting for the Pāṇḍavas but are also sabotaging the war. This is made clear when Bhīṣma becomes general and openly declares that he will not kill the sons of Pāṇḍu (*Mbh* 5.156.20). And then he sets another condition: that either he will fight or Karṇa will, and Karṇa lays down his weapons, swearing that as long as Bhīṣma is alive, he will not fight (*Mbh* 5.156.23–24). Bhīṣma's enmity and denigration of Karṇa is inexplicable, and his insult to Karṇa, that he is only half a ratha (*Mbh* 5.168: 8) because he has lost his earrings and protective mail, breaks Karṇa's spirit, a fact that cuts at the very certainty on which Duryodhana's victory is dependent. Bhīṣma's double-cross is quite evident when Karṇa says to him in disgust that his partiality to the Pāṇḍavas already puts his allegiance in doubt and he is really an enemy of Duryodhana rather than an ally (*Mbh* 5.168.12–13). Bhīṣma and Drona's sabotage is further proved by Saṃjaya who, describing the behaviour of warriors, tells Dhṛtarāṣṭra that when Drona and Bhīṣma rise in the morning, they pray to the gods with concentration for 'Victory to the Pāṇḍavas' (*Mbh* 6.17.9).

The role of the key charioteers, Kṛṣṇa and Śalya, also works to the Pāṇḍavas' advantage. Kṛṣṇa's role is, of course, key to Pāṇḍava victory, but Śalya's betrayal is a crucial factor in the Kauravas' defeat. While Kṛṣṇa is the epitome of a charioteer in both the literal and symbolic sense, and his guidance helps Arjuna win the war, Śalya, who becomes Karṇa's charioteer, misguides Karṇa and breaks his confidence, as per his promise to Yudhiṣṭhira prior to the war, instead of encouraging and guiding him as a charioteer would do. This promise is in itself a double violation—of the traditions of hospitality that Śalya fails to honour and yuddha dharma that Yudhiṣṭhira corrupts. Śalya pledged to fight for the Kauravas because Duryodhana's hospitality had won him over, but Yudhiṣṭhira emotionally blackmailed him to make a traitorous promise that he would 'kill the energy of the son of *Sūta*

[Karṇa] and do what is calculated to bring his defeat' (*Mbh* 5.8.44), and this Śalya does throughout the time that he drives Karṇa's chariot. So Karṇa is brought down not just by his enemies but also by his own charioteer.

Thus, the framing of the kṣetra reveals that not only do the Pāṇḍavas have many unfair advantages even before they go to war, but also many of these advantages are established through violations of dharma and through elders who, as custodians of dharma, warp norms and traditions to their own advantage. These are clearly indicative of how the war will play out and how the two sides will serve dharma. Yet, the war begins with the illusion that dharma is with the Pāṇḍavas, and that their chief opponent, Duryodhana, is the embodiment of adharma. Hence the Kauravas must necessarily lose because this is a dharmakṣetra in which dharma must be victorious. Adding to the tilt is the precarious sectarian slope of Śaivism and Kṛṣṇaism, which keeps the moral agents on both sides constantly grappling with each other to gain elevation. But, because Kṛṣṇaism was the call of the day, those who did not hearken to the call were labelled evil, regardless of their dharma lakṣaṇa, and conversely, those who embraced Kṛṣṇa were perceived as dharma heroes, irrespective of their morality or immorality. This hypocritical dharmakṣetra is what the Mahābhārata tradition upholds; therefore, this is the paradigm of good and evil that ordinary Hindus know and practise in the kṣetra of their own lives. To discern these false perceptions, both dharma and the characters who demonstrate it must be re-examined.

4 Dharmakṣetra and Adharmakṣetra

Delineating the Kṣetra

The good and evil in Mahābhārata's kṣetra appears to be a reflection of how its characters are perceived. However, this delineation is a static form of dharma, because it does not encompass thought-provoked intent and consequence. It is more a mirror of the deva–asura archetype, in which the Pāṇḍavas are semi-divines, all having gods for fathers, and the Kauravas are born through Gāndhārī's unnatural, asuric act of inducing a near miscarriage by striking her belly. Thus, while the Pāṇḍavas are born full-bodied, beautiful, and effulgent like the gods, the Kauravas are birthed by Gāndhārī as a ball of flesh that has to be sliced into a hundred plus one pieces. In addition, at Duryodhana's birth, bad omens portending the destruction of the Kurus are seen and heard, leaving no doubt that he will be the embodiment of evil. Moreover, throughout the epic, Duryodhana is given no benefit of free will and puruṣkāra to change his pattern of karma. Hence, no matter what the Kauravas do, they are condemned as evil, and no matter what the Pāṇḍavas do, they are seen as good, and their immoral actions are either immediately forgiven or justified by fate.

To examine the Mahābhārata as an active dharmakṣetra, it is imperative to see its characters not only through an unbiased lens but also as dynamic moral agents; only then will their lakṣaṇa truly determine morality and immorality.

The Bhagavad Gītā begins with Dhṛtarāṣṭra's query to Saṃjaya:

> dharmakṣetre kurukṣetre samavetā yuyutsavaḥ
> māmakāḥ pāṇḍavāś caiva kim akurvata saṃjaya
> [What did my sons and the Pāṇḍavas do, O Saṃjaya, when desirous of battle they all assembled on the dharma field of Kurukṣetra?] (*Mbh* 6.25.1)

Thus, Kurukṣetra is laid out as the field on which dharma will be tested, or the field on which a battle will be fought for dharma, or a field in which the battle that will occur will prove the victory of dharma over adharma. But this ultimate field of the Kurus will be revealed as equivalent to a dharmakṣetra *only* through the good and evil actions and behaviours of the sons of Dhṛtarāṣṭra and Pāṇḍu—the moral agents.

In this field, it is revealed that Yudhiṣṭhira, believing himself to be the embodiment of dharma, considers his actions so inviolable that he compels everyone into committing destructive acts of adharma. It also reveals how Arjuna, in his kṣetra of everyman warrior, enjoys privileges that hardly make him representative of everyman and how his dilemmas, instead of resolving the issues of dharma, mislead the everyman into paths of adharma. On the other hand, Duryodhana, despite committing many adharmas, delineates this kṣetra through puruṣārthic dharma. In addition, his lakṣaṇa of good and evil are so representative of a moral agent that he is more an everyman warrior than Arjuna. Further, Karṇa's role in the kṣetra shows how, despite the adharmas heaped on him by others, he tenaciously retains his own dharma and does not allow either circumstances or crises to corrupt this dharmakṣetra. Finally, in this level, Kṛṣṇa is revealed as the true delineator of the dharmakṣetra, because his very name is synonymous with dharma and victory: '*yataḥ kṛṣṇas tato dharmo yato dharmas tato jayaḥ*' [where Kṛṣṇa is, there is dharma, where dharma is, there is victory] (*Mbh* 6.66.35). However, Kṛṣṇa not only makes the victory of dharma imperfect, he also makes the dharmakṣetra an adharmakṣetra.

HOW DURYODHANA DEFINES THE KṢETRA

The general perception of Duryodhana is that he is a treacherous, malicious, power- and money-hungry man of asuric nature, who will do anything to become king of Hāstinapura. This is how the Mahābhārata portrays him, this is how he is perceived in tradition, and this is how many scholars of the epic also view him. For example, in his introduction to the English translation of the Critical Edition of the Mahābhārata, J.A.B. Van Buitenen (1973: 15) describes Duryodhana thus: 'Dhṛtarāṣṭra's [son is] vile. It is Duryodhana's undying ambition to possess himself of the throne of Hāstinapura, by any means, but mostly foul ... Surely his character has been blackened even more in the course of time, but equally surely was he cast in the role of the villain from the beginning, treacherous and lawless ...'. Considering these impressions, it seems obvious that Duryodhana in the Mahābhārata would define a kṣetra in which morality and ethics are violated. However, this image of Duryodhana is misconceived. In actuality, there is very little difference between the evil and goodness of Duryodhana and the goodness and evil of the Pāṇḍavas. In fact, in some instances, Duryodhana even surpasses the Pāṇḍavas in goodness and the Pāṇḍavas surpass Duryodhana in evil. Therefore, neither is the tradition that Duryodhana establishes one of evil nor are his lakṣaṇa as a moral agent representative of flagrant adharma.

Duryodhana is possibly the last of the pre-Kṛṣṇized heroes—the last of the heroes of the orthodox Vedic beliefs. He is a kṣatriya of the Indra brand—a Vedic hero who wholeheartedly believes in the pursuit of the trivarga of dharma, artha, and kāma. He is, in fact, the warrior that the Mahābhārata actually extols over and over again, through the words of many—Bhīṣma, the ṛṣis, and even the Pāṇḍavas, Draupadī, and Kuntī. However, although his character and lakṣaṇa are in alignment with the idolized warrior's, Duryodhana as an individual is condemned. In actuality, the behaviours for which Duryodhana is most condemned are the very behaviours that the Pāṇḍavas themselves commend. For example, Duryodhana is maligned for provoking a civil war to acquire wealth; but the advice Arjuna gives to Yudhiṣṭhira echoes these very same reasons. Trying to alleviate the guilt his elder brother feels after the war, Arjuna tells him, 'When the very gods have won their prosperity through civil war, what fault can there be in such quarrels' (*Mbh* 12.8.28). Moreover, Kuntī's words of advice for Yudhiṣṭhira that she conveys through Kṛṣṇa after his Embassy to goad her sons to war are the very words that exactly describe Duryodhana and his actions. She asks Kṛṣṇa to tell her sons, 'Being the reverse of wrathful, you cannot be reckoned among men ...' (*Mbh* 5.133.6). And, 'those are indeed men who are wrathful and who exercise no forgiveness. Being destitute of wrath and given to the exercise of forgiveness is neither a woman nor a man; satisfaction destroys prosperity as does softness of heart. Making your heart one of steel, hunt for the recovery of your lost wealth; one is called a man (*Puruṣa*) for he vanquishes the enemy ... Compassion is only suitable for a coward' (*Mbh* 5.133.32–35). She also uses the example of Indra, saying that he became the great Indra only after he slayed Vṛtra (*Mbh* 5.134.24), and advises her sons that 'the *kṣatriya,* who is born in this world knowing the duties of a *kṣatriya* does not bow to anyone from fear or from consideration of livelihood ... He should stand erect and never bend down; for energy is manliness. One may break down his knots [weaknesses] but he should not bend down. That great-minded man, the *kṣatriya,* should move about like an infuriated elephant ...' (*Mbh* 5.134.38-40). Every single one of these qualities and characteristics that Kuntī loudly declares are the very ones that Duryodhana not only embodies but also proudly demonstrates. In fact, ironically, just prior to this conversation that Kuntī has with Kṛṣṇa, Duryodhana himself declares that he will not bow down from fear before anyone—not even Indra (*Mbh* 5.127.13). However, while injunctions such as these are cited over and over again to lead the Pāṇḍavas to war and to justify their actions, Duryodhana is castigated for following them. The question, of course, is why this inequity?

Duryodhana was that warrior who had no place in the new Kṛṣṇized society that was just then becoming popular. His brand of Indra-like herodom and Vedic and brāhmanical kṣatriyahood, based solely on the trivarga of puruṣārtha, was outdated in the evolving norms of Kṛṣṇa's deification. As Katz (1990: 141) says, '[Duryodhana] is seen as evil specifically because [he] rejects Kṛṣṇa'. Gotimer (1992: 224) too remarks on this 'flaw' of Duryodhana:

> The wrongdoings of Duryodhana tend to be subsumed under a single flaw ... [It is] not Duryodhana's ruthless usurpation of the kingdom, which includes the humiliation of Draupadī. It is not even his opposition to the Pāṇḍavas per se ... all these become his subsumptive sin: opposition to Kṛṣṇa Vāsudeva. In theology this has been taken to mean blindness to Kṛṣṇa's divinity.

But Duryodhana is not 'blind' to Kṛṣṇa's divinity; it is just that his kṣatriya dharma is more important to him, and he refuses to be awed by the Kṛṣṇa factor. He clearly proclaims this when he is dying:

> manyamānaḥ prabhāvaṃ ca kṛṣṇasyāmita tejasaḥ
> tena na cyāvitaś cāhaṃ kṣatradharmāt svanuṣṭhitāt
> [I am not ignorant of the glory of Kṛṣṇa. He did not make me disregard kṣatriya duties.] (*Mbh* 9.65.29)

Most importantly, Duryodhana actually believes that through his passionate adherence to his dharma, he has 'obtained him [Kṛṣṇa]': '*Sa mayā samanuprāpto*' (*Mbh* 9.65.30); but no one in the epic seems to recognize Duryodhana's achievement. He is only seen as a man opposed to Kṛṣṇaism. Even Kṛṣṇa himself, who urges Arjuna to recognize Kṛṣṇa's true essence, is not able to see that Duryodhana is the one who has acquired this wisdom. It is actually Kṛṣṇa who is 'blind' who cannot see that in his opposition to him, Duryodhana is opposing Kṛṣṇa the celebrity phenomenon, not Kṛṣṇa the essence of all dharma. Perhaps this is the reason for Kṛṣṇa's first theophany during his Embassy to the Kaurava court. It is to scare Duryodhana and to awe him; conversely, Duryodhana's intention to bind Kṛṣṇa at this time is, perhaps, his attempt to constrict the fast-spreading wave of Kṛṣṇaism and to curb the mortal Kṛṣṇa's self-importance.

The fact that this theophany of Kṛṣṇa in the Kaurava court is not one of pralaya but one of creation is important in discerning how Kṛṣṇa views Duryodhana: during the manifestation, from Kṛṣṇa's body emerge thumb-sized gods amidst sun-like rays. Brahmā sits on his brow and Rudra on his breast, and the other celestials arise from his arms. From his two eyes issue Arjuna and Saṃkarṣaṇa, and behind them the other Pāṇḍavas and the Vṛṣṇis, and when he raises his arms, weapons and conch shells and dice issue forth, and all the while his mouth emits fire and his body emits rays (*Mbh* 5.131.5–14). It is possible that the reason why Kṛṣṇa shows this 'creation' to Duryodhana is to tell him that a new era is dawning where the gods of his belief—Indra and the other celestials—are re-born through Kṛṣṇa. However, it is important to note that with this theophany Kṛṣṇa is not wooing Duryodhana, nor is he bestowing a vision to a devotee, as he does for Arjuna in his Universal Form during his telling of the Gītā. This theophany is only to re-establish the fact that Duryodhana is outside this circle, because as K. Sivaraman (2000: 44) says, creational theophanies do not bring change: 'Dissolution is logically, objectively prior to creation as it conditions, and is not conditioned by creation ... the seed has to *change* its form before it can sprout ...' Hence, Kṛṣṇa's theophany is not meant to convert or to *change* Duryodhana. Moreover, Duryodhana's own orthodox Vedic roots are too deep; without destroying them, Kṛṣṇa could not hope to plant 'new seeds'. In fact, rather than convert, this display seems to concretize Duryodhana's rejection of Kṛṣṇa and his followers. And Kṛṣṇa, by deriding Duryodhana for his beliefs and by raising the Pāṇḍavas to the level of celestials in the theophany, further alienates Duryodhana. Others present at this theophany, who also experience it—Bhīṣma, Drona, and even Dhṛtarāṣṭra—are already aware of Kṛṣṇa's identity and the former two are already converts. Therefore, obviously, this theophany is to let Duryodhana know that Kṛṣṇaism is the new establishment.

Duryodhana's kṣatriya orthodoxy makes him a dānava/asura in this new system, because he chooses to remain outside its fold. His dream before the war, in which he discovers that he is Śiva's boon to the dānavas, validates this (*Mbh* 3.252.1—27). He awakens from this dream convinced that he will win the war, but the foreshadowing of Kṛṣṇa's theophany has made it clear that he cannot, because his time (and the time of others like him of orthodox views) has passed.

Duryodhana's brand may be passé, but the question is, does his rejection of the new system make him evil? The answer to this must necessarily relate to the context of the societal codes to which Duryodhana prescribed. The milieu that Kṛṣṇaism invaded was wholly kṣatriya-centric; it shaped warriors whose goal was victory in war and whose way of life was the trivarga of puruṣārtha (dharma, artha, and kāma). Kṛṣṇaism, on the other hand, while still puruṣārthic, demanded exclusive loyalty to Kṛṣṇa. But the beliefs of an earlier time cannot simply be classified as immoral if they do not cohere with the beliefs of the current time. Morality must be seen as relational, and, Duryodhana's strict adherence to his own beliefs makes him virtuous. Therefore, if his behaviour is immoral, it is only because the ideal itself may have been flawed. But can a man be faulted or called evil for living by the established codes of the society in which he lives, flawed though they may be? Moreover, it is only in the context of changing norms that these practices came to be seen as unethical. Duryodhana's only fault then is that, while people around him bought into the system of change, he refuses to change. Perhaps he does not believe that the changes are good. In fact, the ethical system that Duryodhana adheres to appears more humane and more tolerant, especially in terms of the biases of the caste system, which, in the changing times, became more rigid. Duryodhana's secularity was a recognized aspect of his character, although the larger Mahābhārata tradition does not acknowledge it because that tradition favours caste stringency. However, this characteristic of Duryodhana is revealed in the text through various subtle descriptions of the hero. For example, bemoaning his son's defeat in the war, Dhṛtarāṣṭra tells Saṃjaya how, as a consequence, the whole earth will suffer because 'even her Mlecchas [nomad tribes] depend on his [Duryodhana's] grace' (*Mbh* 9.32.4). The remnants of Duryodhana's lack of caste prejudice are still evident in oral folk traditions. For example, in the Kolam district of Kerala there is a temple dedicated to Duryodhana and his rājadharma, which was equal and magnanimous towards people of all castes. According to folk belief, the Poruvazhy Peruviruthy Malanada temple is the site where Duryodhana accepted toddy from a śudra woman of the Kurava caste. He had stopped here, tired and thirsty, on his search for the Pāṇḍavas during their exile. When he realized that the woman who had offered him hospitality was of the low Kurava caste, instead of rejecting her, as any caste-conscious kṣatriya of his time would have done, he sat on a nearby hill and worshipped Śiva for the welfare of the people of that area and then gave away hundreds of acres of agricultural land to the community. Even today, the land tax receipts in Poruvazhy village are issued in the name of Duryodhana, and the temple's administrative committee includes special status members from the Kurava caste.

In the Mahābhārata text too, Duryodhana's rejection of caste bias is amply proved through his attitude towards Karṇa. When Karṇa is mocked by the Pāṇḍavas in the archery contest for being a charioteer's son and his own mother refuses to save him, it is Duryodhana who steps forward and, breaking caste barriers, makes Karṇa king of Anga (*Mbh* 1.136.36). No matter what misdeeds are ascribed to Duryodhana, his act of forming a friendship with Karṇa is commendable; even those who see Duryodhana as purely evil acknowledge this.

There are those who say that Duryodhana only makes Karṇa his friend because he hopes to use his warrior prowess against the Pāṇḍavas. This hardly seems the case, because when Karṇa asks Duryodhana what he can give him in return, Duryodhana's response is genuine: '*atyantaṃ sakhyam icchāmīty āha*', 'I am desirous of your friendship' (*Mbh* 1.136.40). The genuineness of this friendship is further proved at Karṇa's death, when a devastated Duryodhana urges his driver to station his chariot at the edge of the troops so that, single-handed, he can hold the enemy at bay and fight Karṇa's killers, Kṛṣṇa and Arjuna, to pay his debt to Karṇa (*Mbh* 9.3.19). These sentiments hardly seem those of man who only wanted personal gain from the friendship. Duryodhana not only uplifts Karṇa but also exposes the evil of a societal norm that had become demeaning in the new system. Whatever Duryodhana's motive may have been, it is evident that the standards he lived by are not only ethical but also applaudable.

In the context of his epic society, Duryodhana's nobility cannot be denied. Even the authors of the text describe him as nothing less than a noble warrior. This is evident from the description of him as he rises out of the lake he is resting in at the end of the war, fatigued in body and dejected in mind at the utter loss of friends and relatives, having solidified the lake's water with the power of his illusion so that he will be undetected and undisturbed for a while. When the Pāṇḍavas accuse him of fleeing from battle and hiding, he tells them honestly that he is not hiding but exhausted, and since he has lost all his men, he needs a little rest before he can join the battle again and fight them single-handedly. However, when Yudhiṣṭhira continues to taunt him, provoking him to get out of the lake and fight the Pāṇḍavas right then and there, he accepts the challenge of a single combat and, choosing Bhima as his opponent, breaks the crystalized water and rises (9.31.39–43 & 9.32.11–36):

> Agitating the waters with great force, that brave warrior rose like a prince of elephants from within the lake, sighing heavily in rage and armed with his heavy and strong mace of iron decked with gold. Cutting through the solidified waters [Duryodhana] rose ... like the sun himself consuming everything with its rays ... resembling a mountain crest or the trident-wielding Rudra himself casting angry looks on living beings ... Indeed all creatures then regarded that mighty-armed chastiser of foes as he stood with his mace on his shoulders after rising from the waves like Death himself armed with a rod. (*Mbh* 9.32.37–44)

This description is of a warrior supreme—an image of flawless perfection. Arjuna, on the other hand, is never portrayed in this light. In fact, Arjuna has a marked flaw—his high cheek bones—or, as suggested by Nīlakaṇṭha, his big calves, or as Daniel H.H. Ingalls suggests—his big testicles (quoted in Katz 1990: 199, notes: 9, 10 & 11), that reduces his nobility. Hence, even without divine parentage, Duryodhana is clearly no less than Arjuna, and combined with his warrior qualities, he is visibly superior to Arjuna.

Duryodhana remains true to his kṣatriya dharma to the very end. He also dies like a warrior, despite the treachery that the Pāṇḍavas deal him; so much so that even the celestials honour him by showering flowers on him. When he is challenged to single combat by Yudhiṣṭhira, he is not afraid, even though he is without armour, and he is tired and wounded. Most importantly, when he accepts the challenge, not only does he refrain from using harsh words for the Pāṇḍavas, but he also sees this fight as not for the kingdom but a way to pay his debt to those who supported him in the war:

> Today I shall release myself from the debt I owe to the many illustrious kṣatriyas, to Valhika and Drona and Bhīṣma and the great Karṇa, to the heroic Jayadratha and Bhagadatta, to Śalya, the ruler of Madras and Bhūriśravas, to my sons, to Śakuni, the son of Subala, and to all my friends and well-wishers and relatives. (*Mbh* 9.32.21)

But, sadly, he is so misunderstood and maligned that Yudhiṣṭhira is still not willing to acknowledge his deliberate and concerted warriorship and kṣatriyahood. Yudhiṣṭhira calls it merely 'good luck' and says it is his 'good luck' that he knows the duties of a kṣatriya and 'good luck' that he is a hero and 'good luck' that he knows the conventions of battle (*Mbh* 9.32.23-24). However, if it were merely 'good luck', Duryodhana could have easily bested the Pāṇḍavas and won back the kingdom by choosing to fight with one of the weaker brothers when Yudhiṣṭhira gives him the option to choose an opponent (*Mbh* 9.32.25). But Duryodhana, who is a consummate warrior proud of his warriorship, picks Bhīma, who he knows is a warrior of strength equal to his. Even Kṛṣṇa recognizes that if Duryodhana had chosen Nakula or Sahadeva, he would have defeated them with his mace in no time at all (*Mbh* 9.33.10).

Additionally, in this incident, while Duryodhana strictly adheres to the codes of single combat, the Pāṇḍavas resort to treachery. During the mace fight, when Bhīma begins to lose, he is directed by Kṛṣṇa to strike Duryodhana on the thigh—a strike considered illegal in single combat. What accentuates the Pāṇḍava immorality even more is that Duryodhana himself remains a true warrior. For instance, when Bhīma tires in the battle, Duryodhana stops to let his opponent rest (*Mbh* 9.58.41-42). On the other hand, after Bhīma fells Duryodhana through deceit, he kicks the fallen warrior's head with his left foot, not once but twice, and would have crushed it if Yudhiṣṭhira had not stopped him (*Mbh* 9.59.4-5 & 14). But, as Duryodhana falls, the cosmos proclaims the injustice of his slaying: the environment is filled with fierce winds, loud sounds, showers of dust, trembling trees, thunder, and meteors; wild beasts and birds begin to scream and screech, and headless beings arise from the bowels of the earth and begin to dance (*Mbh* 9.58.41–60). These omens are noteworthy because these very same omens at Duryodhana's birth had been interpreted as inauspicious, proclaiming Duryodhana as the cause of his clan's destruction. Perhaps, when he was born, the natural omens were portending not his life, but his treacherous death. Even Baladeva, Kṛṣṇa's elder brother, a master mace warrior who taught both Duryodhana and Bhima mace fighting and bore 'the same affection for Duryodhana as he did for Bhima' (*Mbh* 5.157.33), is pained by the deceitfulness of Duryodhana's killing and condemns both Kṛṣṇa and Bhīma. He says the 'fall of Duryodhana through unjust tactics has humiliated even me' (*Mbh* 9.60.9) and, calling Duryodhana a 'dharmātma', he declares his prowess equal to his own. Despite Kṛṣṇa's feeble justification that such acts are in keeping with the Kali age and that whatever happened to the Kuru heroes happened as a result of Duryodhana's own avarice and sinfulness, Baladeva curses Bhīma that he will be remembered in the world as a '*jihm yoddhā*', 'crooked warrior' (*Mbh* 9.60.26), and bestows on Duryodhana the title of '*ṛju yoddhā*', 'upright warrior' (*Mbh* 9.60: 21–28). In fact, Balarāma declares Duryodhana's sacrifice (in battle by the final ablution of glory) completed and successful (*Mbh* 9.60.29).

Duryodhana's death by treachery shames the Pāṇḍavas and creates a kṣetra of not just adharmic yuddha, but also one in which the consequence proves the Pāṇḍavas' guilt for the rest of their lives. Yudhiṣṭhira admits to the dying Duryodhana, 'You will surely go to heaven! We are, on the other hand, creatures of hell, and shall continue to suffer the bitterest grief!' (*Mbh* 9.59.29). If karma is just desert, then this consequence that the Pāṇḍavas have to suffer proves how gravely immoral their acts have been. Duryodhana himself describes the ideal life of a kṣatriya, which he has lived, thus showing the Pāṇḍavas' act as more grievous, making their victory an ethical defeat. Duryodhana declares:

> I have made various studies according to the ordinance, governed the wide Earth with her seas, and trumpeted over the heads of foes. Who is there more fortunate as myself? That end again which is sought by *kṣatriya* observant of the duties of their own order, viz., death in battle, I have also met with mine. Who, therefore, is so fortunate as myself? I have enjoyed pleasures, such as were worthy of the very gods and such as could with difficulty, be obtained by other kings. I have attained the highest prosperity. Who then is so fortunate as myself?' (*Mbh* 9.61.50–3)

Obviously, his dharma was true because fragrant flowers fall from the heavens to celebrate Duryodhana's life, and seeing these signs and 'this worship offered to Duryodhana, the Pāṇḍavas with Vāsudeva at their head are put to shame' (*Mbh* 9.61.58).

However, the immorality of the Pāṇḍavas is such that even their regret is short-lived. They forget their shame immediately after they realize it, when Kṛṣṇa reminds them that all these warriors (Bhīṣma, Drona, Karṇa, and Bhūriśravas) were invincible in war, and if he, Kṛṣṇa, had not used deceit, the Pāṇḍavas would never have won the war. Then Kṛṣṇa justifies the immorality by using the analogy of the archetypal battle of gods and demons, and the Pāṇḍavas blow their conches and are filled with joy at their victory. However, this victory does not prove the Pāṇḍavas' warriorship or their dharma. It simply proves their blind faith in Kṛṣṇa's divinity, which is clearly indicative of the immorality of the new system that is replacing the old system of a virtuous fight. This kṣetra that is supposed to be a dharmakṣetra by virtue of good action and good behaviour is reduced to a system where the end justifies the means. But, the consequentiality of evil actions that prove the adharma of the action cannot be negated, as is evident in Duryodhana's last words to Yudhiṣṭhira, 'This empty earth, O king is now intended for you. What king would like to rule a kingdom divested of friends and allies? Go, O king and rule the Earth destitute of kings, warriors, wealth and without citadels, as you like' (*Mbh* 9.31.48–53). And Yudhiṣṭhira is 'anguished' with these words, because they hit home. If this is a dharmakṣetra, a kṣetra that ensures the victory of dharma, then dharma here is shown as impoverished.

However, despite Duryodhana's righteousness in the battlefield of Kurukṣetra, the overall impression of this eldest Kaurava is that he is wicked and unrighteous. One reason for this impression is that he is labelled as such from birth and is set up with a predetermined future that could only be replete with wickedness: Even as he is born, omens occur at his birth that are seen as inauspicious, and Vidura tells Dhṛtarāṣṭra to abandon him, or else he will be 'the exterminator of [the Kuru] race' (*Mbh* 1.115.35), and Vidura constantly repeats this every time Dhṛtarāṣṭra comes to him for advice. It must be remembered that Vidura is possibly Yudhiṣṭhira's father; hence, his constant berating of Duryodhana, a legitimate contender to the throne to which his own son is aspiring, is to discredit the prince.

However, it cannot be denied that some of Duryodhana's acts are, in fact, immoral. One of the early incidents of Duryodhana's wickedness is when he poisons Bhīma and throws him into the Ganga. This is certainly a vicious and malicious act—one that is meant to deliberately hurt Bhīma. However, before this act is judged, its causality must be taken into account. Prior to this incident, Bhīma has been bullying and humiliating the Kauravas relentlessly. He pulls their hair and then laughs at them. He breaks their bones and throws them in the water till they almost drown. Basically, Bhīma prides himself by tormenting the sons of Dhṛtarāṣṭra (*Mbh* 1.128.16-24), and Duryodhana, just like any other adolescent, cannot bear it any longer, so he finally decides to get even as any bullied child would do. It must be noted that Duryodhana is introduced in this incident with authorial comments that already label him 'wicked and unrighteous' who 'through ignorance and ambition of possessing wealth is inclined to commit acts of sin' (*Mbh* 1.128.26). But, at this time, Duryodhana is a young boy, hardly considering wealth, hardly considering ambition. He is only reacting to Bhīma's constant bullying. Also, can Duryodhana's actions really be condemned as 'evil' at this time, when he is only a child? Especially in light of the societal law that Ṛṣi Animāṇḍavya has already established, stating no sinful act committed by a child under fourteen would be considered a sin. As a matter of fact, this law was made in consequence of Dharma's own act of punishing a child, and it was considered such a wrongful act that Dharma had been cursed for it to be born in the womb of a śūdra woman—as Vidura (*Mbh* 1.108.13). Therefore, these comments that paint Duryodhana as sinful even in his childhood raise questions about the validity of his characterization.

Another incident that is held against Duryodhana is his evil scheme to kill the Pāṇḍavas in the house of lac. The immorality of this act cannot be denied. It was deliberate and it was designed to destroy the Pāṇḍavas. However, this act too must be seen in context, that is, in light of the guidance Duryodhana receives and also in light of the kṣatriya code against enemies—a code that Duryodhana unashamedly follows. Duryodhana is advised by Kaṇika, the 'best of ministers, learned in politics and expert in counsels' that 'a king should first gain the confidence of men, who are his enemies; and then he should spring upon them like a wolf ... As a hooked staff is used to bend down the bough of a tree to pluck ripe fruit. So this method should be used in destroying one's own enemies', because 'the killing of a harmful foe is always praiseworthy. Destroy him by any means open or secret' (*Mbh* 1.140.11–20). Kaṇika goes on to counsel Duryodhana about the means a king should use, even of the greatest cruelty, to destroy his enemies, including burning down their house (*Mbh* 1.140.35). This rājadharma advice is no different from what Bhīṣma gives Yudhiṣṭhira in the *Śāntī Parva:* '[A king] should assail the kingdom of the stronger by means of weapons of fire and the administering of poison' (*Mbh* 12.69.18). It can be argued that Duryodhana is not king and, moreover, the Pāṇḍavas are not enemy kings; they are his cousins. But this point becomes moot because Duryodhana does see himself as future king, much as the Pāṇḍavas see themselves. It is true that the Pāṇḍavas are Duryodhana's cousins, but according to kṣatriya code, 'He, and none else, is one's enemy who has common pursuits with another,' and 'if this be kinsman, then he should be treated as any other enemy' (*Mbh* 2.55.15).

Regardless of the justifications, there is no doubt that this act of Duryodhana is immoral and it causes suffering to the Pāṇḍavas. However, it must be considered alongside the heinous act that

Yudhiṣṭhira commits by deliberately setting fire to the house of lac when a Niṣāda woman and her five sons are in it so that their bodies can be mistaken for the Pāṇḍavas'. Not only does Yudhiṣṭhira murder six innocent people who have done him no harm, but he also violates *atithidharma*, because this family was a guest in his house. While it is true that Duryodhana tries to destroy his cousins' lives to secure wealth, he does it because he truly believes that the wealth is rightfully his, and, more importantly, he owns up to his immoral actions that are impelled by his desire to be king and his jealousy towards his cousins by honestly confessing to his father that these 'consume him like a fire' and 'pierce his heart like a dart' (*Mbh* 1.142.24). The Pāṇḍavas, on the other hand, secretly take six innocent lives to secure their own escape, and they call it fate (*Mbh* 1.148.3). Therefore, while both incidents delineate adharma because they both cause injury to others, Pāṇḍava adharma is more reprehensible in this incident.

Another incident which not only makes Duryodhana a pariah in Hindu society but also becomes the catalyst for the war is his rigging of the dice game and humiliating Draupadī. However, this act, too, cannot be condemned as downright 'evil', because it involves the ambit of the entire epic, and its complexity makes it impossible to view in simple black-and-white terms of good and evil or dharma and adharma. It is important to see the cause of Duryodhana's actions, and then to see what compulsion he had as a moral agent and a human being to commit the act. To begin with, the most precise and basic cause is that Duryodhana is simply human. After he sees the Pāṇḍavas' assembly hall and the splendour of the Rājasūya, he feels jealous. But what is significant and redeeming is that he feels guilty about his jealousy and also realizes that he shouldn't feel this way. In fact, even Śakuni admonishes Duryodhana for feeling jealous and advises him that whatever prosperity the Pāṇḍavas attained, it is through their own energy and efforts; therefore, Duryodhana should not resent them for it (*Mbh* 2.48.3–6). Jealousy is a normal human emotion; everyone has experienced it, and Duryodhana himself accepts that any man would be jealous to see his enemies thrive (*Mbh* 2.47.24–28). Therefore, Duryodhana is like any ordinary human being; however, unlike most ordinary human beings, he recognizes this trait in himself. What he can be faulted for is that despite acknowledging the wrongfulness of this emotion, he acts upon it. From one perspective, it can even be said that Duryodhana actually rises above the inaction, which is inherent in fate, and challenges his fate with action. However, the action he decides on is not ethical, because he allows the *tamasic* nature of his human trait to override his sense of dharma. But Duryodhana is not alone in letting his jealousy goad him. Even Arjuna experiences this emotion on many occasions; especially noteworthy is his reaction to Ekalavya's archery skills. However, unlike Duryodhana, Arjuna's dharma is never questioned; instead his status of being the greatest archer is aggrandized, despite the fact that the consequence and his jealousy culminates in the extreme suffering of the Niṣāda prince.

Duryodhana sees the dice game as a means to an end and, in this sense, Duryodhana's act can be seen as evil. But a point to note is that according to Duryodhana's varṇadharma and rājadharma motive, neither is this dyūta evil, nor is the goal that Duryodhana desires from this means. In fact, Duryodhana's question to Śakuni prior to the dice game proves that his motive is only to destroy the Pāṇḍavas, whom he perceives as his enemies. At the same time, he wants to ensure that this means of destruction will be 'without any danger to [his] friends and other illustrious men' (*Mbh* 2.48.18). It is true that Śakuni and Duryodhana come up with the plan of a dice game in which Śakuni will employ all his swindling skills to conquer the Pāṇḍavas. This treachery is, undoubtedly, evil, and Duryodhana knows it is treachery. Perhaps he also knows that even in kṣatriya code it will be seen as an act against the virtue of a kṣatriya. However, in actuality, no normative codes of kṣatriya dharma condemn it, because ultimately it falls within Duryodhana's rājadharma of destroying an enemy who is becoming powerful. These same norms are also stated by Bhīṣma, who cites them as the advice Bṛhaspati gave to Indra. To teach Yudhiṣṭhira the conventions of rājadharma, Bhīṣma tells him, 'Knowing the beginning, the middle, and the end of his enemy, a king should secretly entertain feelings of hostility towards them. He should corrupt the forces of his enemy, determine everything by positive evidence, creating disunion, making gifts, and administering poison. A king should never live with his foes' (*Mbh* 12.103.14). Moreover, this same advice is what Bhīma gives Yudhiṣṭhira in the *Vana Parva*: 'a man who does not chastise his enemies is a low-born and that if a man destroys his enemy on the day he goes to hell, that hell will become heaven' (*Mbh* 3.35.7–8). Additionally, the precedent of using deceit to destroy an enemy has already been established by Kṛṣṇa himself in the killing of Jarāsaṃdha.

Furthermore, and in all fairness, Śakuni's cheating in the dice game cannot really be classified as treachery because treachery, by definition, is a deliberate act of perfidy, where one person violates another person's trust. In other words, the one who is committing the treachery uses the trust and good faith of the one against whom the treachery is committed for the purpose of cheating him. Śakuni, on the contrary, makes no bones about either his skill in cheating or the fact that he will use his cheating skills in the game. In fact, he openly admits that dicing is all about knowing the secret of winning and losing, and that the skilled dice player knows how to baffle the opponent with deceit. He calls himself a skilled dice player and a master cheater, and he openly declares this to Yudhiṣṭhira, challenging him to refuse to play (*Mbh* 2.59.8). Moreover, it is not just Yudhiṣṭhira who knows that Śakuni will cheat in the game; everyone present in the assembly knows it too. Vidura even warns Yudhiṣṭhira about this when he goes to invite Yudhiṣṭhira to the dice game at Dhṛtarāṣṭra's behest. The king of Khandava is also aware that Śakuni is one of 'the most desperate and terrible gamblers who always depend on deceit in their play' (*Mbh* 2.58.14). Yet, Yudhiṣṭhira makes the choice of his own free will to disregard what he surely knows will happen. He simply attributes it to fate and to his inability to refuse the challenge. Hence, there really is no treachery in the dice game. Śakuni is not cheating in secret. He is openly cheating and openly challenging Yudhiṣṭhira to counter that. Yudhiṣṭhira not only has a choice to refuse to play a swindling gambler, but also to walk away from dicing, which itself is an activity that everyone, even Śakuni, declares as evil.

Another evil act during the dice game for which Duryodhana is condemned is his humiliation of Draupadī. Duryodhana's treatment of Draupadī is certainly reprehensible; it also violates his dharma on many levels—social dharma of honouring women, family dharma of a brother-in-law, and svadharma of humanness that he owes himself. And the insult to womanhood perpetrated in this act creates a kṣetra of such adharma that it shakes the very foundation of Kuru society. However, what has often been misperceived in this incident is that it is only Duryodhana who violates codes of dharma. Actually, not only do both Duryodhana and the Pāṇḍavas make Draupadī suffer utter humiliation, but also Duryodhana's infractions against dharma are slightly mitigated by the glaring violations that are perpetrated by the Pāṇḍavas themselves. Therefore, the issue that must be considered here is the severity of adharmas: Who wrongs Draupadī the most? Her eldest husband, who stakes her like a piece of property and condemns her to a fate of a slave, and those other husbands who have sworn by dhārmic law to protect and honour her at all times but stay silently watching? Or Duryodhana? In actuality, Duryodhana had no intention of bringing Draupadī into the game, or for that matter, the Pāṇḍava brothers; he just wanted the Pāṇḍavas' wealth. Therefore, he sets the game up only as dyūta, gambling with inanimate wealth; it is Yudhiṣṭhira who changes the nature of this game from dyūta to *samāḥvaya*[1]. Additionally, it is Yudhiṣṭhira who decides to wager Draupadī, even though he knows that if he loses, Draupadī will become a slave, and surely he knows how slaves could be treated; yet, without compunction, he gambles with Draupadī's fate. Shamashastry, in his translation of *Arthaśāstra*, which was a contemporaneous text, points out that the practice of keeping a female slave naked, hurting and abusing her, and violating her chastity existed in that society; although such practices could be punished with forfeiture of the value paid for her (*Kautilya's Arthashastra*, 1915: 261). Therefore, it is not likely that Yudhiṣṭhira, who takes his rājadharma very seriously, is unaware of this eventuality. Also, by ordering Duḥśāsana to disrobe Draupadī, who Yudhiṣṭhira has thrust into slavery, Duryodhana, too, is, most likely, aware that he is violating the slave law, but, like

[1] The betting of animate stakes (*Laws of Manu*, 9. 223)

everyone in the assembly hall, he is so aghast at Yudhiṣṭhira's staking of his wife, that in the heat of the moment, he grabs this opportunity and uses it to humiliate the Pāṇḍavas; at that moment, Draupadī's suffering is simply collateral damage. His awareness of this violation is also perhaps the reason why he does not object when Dhṛtarāṣṭra ultimately returns the value for which Draupadī has been wagered—the freedom of her husbands and the Pāṇḍavas' wealth.

Similarly, Duryodhana's sexual overture of baring his thigh to Draupadī, for which he has been condemned over millennia, is really a means to insult the Pāṇḍavas. It is true that this action of Duryodhana is injurious not just to Draupadī but to all women in general, and it is against social laws. But once again, Duryodhana's insults are not targeted at Draupadī but at the Pāṇḍavas, his enemies. Draupadī is simply incidental—a means to get to them. The Pāṇḍavas, on the other hand, have specifically married Draupadī with Vedic rituals and vowed to take care of her and honour her and protect her. Isn't their staking and abandonment of their wife a greater adharma than Duryodhana's? And, it is important to reiterate here that Duryodhana only issues this insult after Draupadī has been staked as property and won and declared a slave.

Then there is the question of Bhīṣma and Drona's silence at this act, which is grievous adharma on the part of the elders—the knowers of dharma, who are fully aware that 'where women are honored, the very gods are said to be propitiated,' and 'if the women of a family, on account of the treatment they receive, are made to suffer grief and tears, that family soon becomes extinct' (*Mbh* 13.46.5–6). Despite Draupadī's repeated pleas to these elders, they remain silent and do nothing. Perhaps this is because they also know that, according to the laws of samāḥvaya and societal mores about the status of women, Draupadī is bound to Yudhiṣṭhira and must suffer the consequence of his actions. As per *Manusmṛti* 'neither by sale nor by repudiation is a wife released from her husband' (*Laws of Manu*, 9.46). Hence, even as Yudhiṣṭhira becomes a slave, so does Draupadī. Thus, technically, Duryodhana's actions are not an infringement of established dharmas. He can, however, be faulted for using Draupadī's situation to his advantage.

It cannot be denied that Duryodhana is full of jealousy, anger, and possessiveness. But these very qualities make him more human than Arjuna, who is hailed as everyman warrior. Even Arjuna's moral dilemma before the war, that is hailed as representing the psyche of every man, is matched by Duryodhana when, during the war, he realizes the consequences of his anger and jealousy. His genuine regret for his many faults makes him more human and ultimately absolves him of them. He says to Drona:

> O Preceptor, behold this great carnage of those whose heads have undergone the sacred coronation bath ... Those allies of ours, desirous of our victory and welfare have gone to the abode of Yama. How can I repay the debt of obligation that I owe to them? Those lords of the earth, who desired for me the sovereignty of the earth, having abandoned all earthly prosperity, are lying on the earth. Coward that I am I have caused this great slaughter of my friends; and therefore cannot encourage myself to believe that I shall be able to purify myself by celebrating even a hundred horse-sacrifices. Desirous of securing victory for myself who is covetous and sinful and a rebel against virtue, these kings have gone to the abode of the sons of Vivasvata. I have fallen from virtue; evil-minded and an enemy to my friends as I am, why not the earth yields me a hole to bury me in .... (*Mbh* 7.151.31–8)

And when Duryodhana meets his friend Sātyaki as an enemy in battle, the tragedy he feel is unmistakable:

> Fie on wrath, O friend, and fie on vindictiveness, fie on kṣatriya urge and fie on might and prowess. In as much as you aim weapons at me and I am directing mine at you ... In the days of childhood, you were dearer to me than my very own life and I also was to you. Alas! All those deeds of boyhood that I recollect of both yourself and mine, become as nothing on the field of battle. Alas! Impelled by rage and covetousness, we are here today for fighting with each other ... where have those sports of our childhood vanished and alas how has this battle come upon us ... urged though we are by a desire of wealth, what use have we of wealth that meeting each other, we now engage in battle, urged by avarice. (*Mbh* 7.190.23–28)

Clearly, Duryodhana not only recognizes his errors but also regrets the pain and suffering he has brought upon his friends and relatives. He might not have followed the strict codes of dharma, but his words make him a human with a heart. His regret is so heartfelt that he even acknowledges the damage he has done to his relationship with his cousins. This is evident in an incident during the combat between Arjuna and Karṇa, when Aśvatthāman urges Duryodhana to make peace with the Pāṇḍavas and jointly rule Hāstinapura with them. At these words, Duryodhana pauses to think for a while (*Mbh* 8.88.20–2). This is a significant point—that he pauses to think—which implies that he is not all brashness and impulsiveness, and also that he does consider the idea of peace and the implication of his continued war. In this instance, after thinking over Aśvatthāman's words, Duryodhana becomes sorrowful and states with regret that Duḥśāsana's violent death by Bhīma rankles in his heart; how then can he make peace? In addition, he says, that when Karṇa kills Arjuna, how will Arjuna's son be able to abide this and his enmity (*Mbh* 8.88.29–31)? Hence, there is no more choice for him but to continue to war.

Then, after Karṇa's death when Kṛpa advises Duryodhana to make peace, which would most likely result in Kṛṣṇa persuading the Pāṇḍavas to give him the kingdom and make him king, Duryodhana tells Kṛpa, in all honesty, that he would not expect the Pāṇḍavas to accept his peace terms, considering that he defeated them wrongfully at the dice game and also mistreated Kṛṣṇa when he came to him as an emissary. In addition, he knows that Draupadī, who was made to weep piteously in the middle of the assembly hall, will not forget or forgive these grievances. Also, he doubts that Kṛṣṇa and Arjuna, who still mourn Abhimanyu's death, will forgive him (*Mbh* 9.5.3–6).

All these examples prove that Duryodhana holds himself accountable for all the infractions that have occurred; but then, like the true warrior that he is, he stands proud and talks about all that he has enjoyed and done according to dharma and life's affirmation, and he does not see himself begging for his kingdom back when, as a kṣatriya, his greatest honour is to die at war (*Mbh* 9.5.20–1). In addition to his regret, Duryodhana truly appreciates his friends and the sacrifices they have made for him. He recollects with gratitude all the heroes who have given their lives for him and wants to pay his debt to them rather than think of acquiring a kingdom: 'It will be useless for me to enjoy the kingdom destitute of kinsmen and friends and well-wishers and submitting to the son of Pāṇḍu. I, who was the master of the universe will now acquire heaven by fair fight. It will not be otherwise' (*Mbh* 9.5.26–47).

Another significant point that redeems Duryodhana is the fact that he takes the blame for the carnage left in the wake of tha battle at Kurukṣetra, and despite his anger towards the Pāṇḍavas, he does not call them evil or wicked even once. He derides and blames them for their treacheries but not once for the massacre, which, he realizes, is as much his fault as it is theirs. On the other hand, the Pāṇḍavas, even in the midst of their grief at the end of war, do not accept their responsibility for any of the deaths and killings that have occurred in Kurukṣetra; instead, they only continue to blame Duryodhana. For example, on the verge of victory, on the eighteenth day, Arjuna tells Kṛṣṇa that Duryodhana was foolish and wicked-minded for not stopping the 'slaughter' after the death of each of his commanders (*Mbh* 9.24.11–24). But weren't the Pāṇḍavas equally responsible for the slaughter? If the Pāṇḍavas were so aggrieved by it, why didn't they stop it? This statement is only one of many the Pāṇḍavas make that are indicative of the impunity with which they live their lives and the ease with which they shift the blame onto someone else. However, when something is repeated often enough, it begins to sound like the truth, and this 'truth' of Duryodhana's wickedness, repeated by everyone in the Mahābhārata, becomes the accepted truth. Over the years, Duryodhana's character lost more and more morality in people's perception, and today he is seen as the villain of not just the epic, but also of Hindu society; so much so that his 'wickedness' has become part of the Indian idiom.

However, Duryodhana wasn't always perceived as vile or wicked. There was a time, not long after the Mahābhārata had reached its zenith of composition, that Duryodhana was still seen as the noble and humane warrior that he was—not an evil man or a good man, but just a man experiencing the joys and sorrows of life, practising his karma and dharma and recognizing the consequences of his actions. This is the Duryodhana portrayed in the plays of Bhāsa, the Sanskrit dramatologist. And this may actually be the true picture of the Kuru king, because at the time that Bhāsa was writing his plays, the epic was still relatively current in its context. In fact, it had become part of popular culture, and considering Bhāsa's themes, people were quite familiar with the events and characters described in the Mahābhārata.[2] From the manner in which Bhāsa portrays Duryodhana, it is quite apparent that Duryodhana not only engaged people's minds, but he was also seen as a character worthy of being the protagonist. In many of the plays, Duryodhana is portrayed as noble and loyal and also full of compassion. For example, in *Pañcarātram*, a drama about the last few days of the Pāṇḍava *agyātavāsa* in Virāṭa, but before their thirteen-year exile is over, Duryodhana makes an oath to his preceptor, Drona, and promises to give half the kingdom to the Pāṇḍavas if they can be found in five days. While both Bhīṣma and Drona recognize that Duryodhana can be drawn to anger quickly, they also know that he keeps his word and respects his elders. Hence, Bhīṣma and Drona, suspecting that the Pāṇḍavas are in Virāṭa, attack that kingdom in a mock battle to draw out Arjuna and make the Pāṇḍavas reveal themselves (but Duryodhana does not know it is a mock battle). The Pāṇḍavas are discovered, and Bhīma takes Abhimanyu. This appears to be a kidnapping to Duryodhana, who is unaware that the foot soldier who grabbed Abhimanyu was Bhīma. In the last act of the play, Duryodhana is bent upon securing Abhimanyu's release because he says his quarrel is with his father not with his children. 'He is my

[2] According to A. Haksar, 'Bhāsa is considered to have lived sometime in the 1st–3rd centuries BCE (around the same time that the Mahābhārata gained popularity). Although not much is known about Bhāsa himself, his plays were obviously not only well known, but also well respected, because some of the greatest playwrights of India, such as Bāṇabhaṭṭa, mention him as their inspiration.' See 'Introduction' in A. Haksar (ed.), Bhāsa, *The Shattered Thighs and other Plays*, translated by A. Haksar (New Delhi: Penguin Books India, 2008), p. ix.

child first, and only then of the Pāṇḍavas', he says (Bhāsa 2008: 52). What is most interesting is that Abhimanyu is living with the Kauravas in Hāstinapura and supporting them in their fight, indicating that the Mahābhārata was really seen as just a conflict between brothers—not the epic battle of good against evil it eventually came to be considered. D.D. Kosambi says that such constant fighting within the family was common practice, because it increased the power of the king. Also, 'possible rivals, whether princes, former chiefs, or strong oligarchs, had increasingly often to be restrained in some way or driven out (*aparuddha*) to preserve internal peace'. Thus, even the Pāṇḍavas' exile, for which Duryodhana is deprecated as opportunistic and callous, may actually have been his attempt to safeguard Hāstinapura's peace (1965:88).

Throughout this play, there is no indication that Duryodhana is in any way evil or his actions adharmic; on the contrary, he is portrayed as a noble Kuru warrior who cares about his family, friends, and subjects This is especially apparent in the beginning of the drama, where Duryodhana is hailed as a mighty and good king who, through his immense fire sacrifice, has made the world happy and 'all the men and beasts and birds are content'. People also proclaim the 'merits of such a king who makes this earth surpass heaven' (Bhāsa 2008: 27). Obviously at this time, while Vaiṣṇavism and Kṛṣṇa bhakti were the new order, old orthodox Vedic practices were still in vogue and kings were still applauded for following them. Therefore, rejecting Kṛṣṇaism was not considered evil. If the audiences at that time had viewed Duryodhana as immoral or evil, would they have perceived him in such sympathetic light?

Bhāsa's most recognized play is *Urubhaṅgam* (*The Shattered Thighs*), perhaps because this play breaks with the convention of the happy endings of Sanskrit drama and ends in a tragedy—the death of Duryodhana. This is a significant point, that Duryodhana's death is considered a tragedy, *not* vindication or a celebration of the destruction of evil. In fact, in this play, Duryodhana is a tragic hero who has been struck down by treachery. Most of the play focuses on his sorrowful and heart-wrenching last meeting with his parents, his two wives, and especially his son, who wants to sit on his father's lap but is unable to because his father's thighs are shattered. Another significant point about the play is the extreme remorse Duryodhana feels at the devastation of the war and his acceptance of the fact that his pride caused the war. The play also shows that Duryodhana is not a vindictive man through a scene in which Balarāma wants to avenge him and punish Bhīma for his treachery, Duryodhana stops him, and when Aśvatthāman apprises him of his intention of destroying the remaining Pāṇḍavas, Duryodhana tries to stop him too. In this play, Duryodhana is portrayed as a man worthy of attaining heaven. When he dies, he is received with honour by the celestials (Bhāsa 2008: 107–125). It is noteworthy that this last event is retained in the legacy of the Mahābhārata tradition; that is why his presence in svarga appears contradictory, and it has been the cause of much speculation. However, when Duryodhana is seen from Bhāsa's perspective, his heavenly afterlife is hardly surprising.

Bhāsa's plays are proof that Duryodhana was not conceived as an evil man in the early narrations of the *Bhārata*. However, the interpolations that the brāhmins added in the text maligned and debased his character. There could have been many reasons for this. In the atmosphere of ideological differences, Kṛṣṇaism needed to thrive so that it could enfold and unify other beliefs. Also, in order to keep their hegemony, the brāhmins needed to clearly define their perception of good and evil and dharma and adharma, so that they could use the system to their advantage. In addition, and most importantly, since this was a time when ideas of theology and eschatology were rapidly developing, it was necessary to model characters like Arjuna who could represent the everyman facing dilemmas of the evolving human psyche. However, while Arjuna may be seen as the everyman warrior faced with moral dilemmas, experiencing existential crises that would lead to self-analysis and a realization of the self, Duryodhana is the noble warrior, the tragic hero of the everyman warrior's aspect who may not hold up as an ideal, but whose greatness evokes a sense of awe. He lives a noble life, aspiring to the highest goals of puruṣārtha. Admittedly, he is flawed in his hubris, but his genuine regret at the consequences of his errors of judgment make him better than most humans; for, in the fashion of a tragic hero, his own high ideals and hubris devastate him. But, in his devastation, his nobility becomes even more pronounced and awe inspiring. Duryodhana might not be the protagonist of the Mahābhārata, but he is certainly not the evil antagonist that Hindus consider him to be.

If Duryodhana was just a character in an epic tale, this misconception would not be of such great significance. The fact is that the characters of the epic are more than storybook heroes and villains, and their actions are more than mere narrative progressions. These characters are moral agents whose actions establish traditions of dharma and adharma, and they delineate society's kṣetra as a dharmakṣetra or adharmakṣetra. It is true that Duryodhana perpetrates much adharma in his life, but does he define evil to such an extent that his defeat and death by the Pāṇḍavas elevate the kṣetra of the Mahābhārata to a dharmakṣetra where dharma is victorious? The answer, of course, is no. Duryodhana is not evil and his treacherous death by the Pāṇḍavas, who are hardly paragons of dharma, instead of elevating the kṣetra to a dharmakṣetra, is a cause of shame.

HOW KARṆA DEFINES THE KṢETRA

The only Kaurava in the Mahābhārata who is actually a Kaurava by choice and not by birth is Karṇa. The kṣetra that Karṇa inhabits is that of a tragic hero; however, he is not the tragic hero in the classic Western sense of the term. In other words, he is not undone by his own hamartia; rather he is the hero of a tragedy—a tragedy in which, not so much his own actions, but the actions and behaviours of others devastate him. All his life, Karṇa suffers the consequences of other people's choices and actions, especially those of his birth mother, Kuntī. Hence, Karṇa's kṣetra is an adharmakṣetra which is not of his own making; yet, despite this atmosphere of adharma, he attempts to adhere to the codes of dharma throughout the epic.

Karṇa is a mighty warrior, noble and true to a kṣatriyahood that society has denied him. In Karṇa Parva, this is how Kṛṣṇa describes Karṇa to Arjuna:

> I regard that mighty chariot-warrior Karṇa as being equal, if not superior, to you in prowess ... he is valorous like Agni, swift like the speed of the wind, furious like the Destroyer, strong and powerful like the lion ... He is eight *ratnis* in height and of long arms. His chest is expanded and strong and he is almost invincible. He is, moreover, chivalrous and an eminent hero and of graceful figure. He possesses all the necessary attributes of a warrior and is a dispeller of the fears of his friends ... That son of Rādhā cannot be slain by anyone, not even by the gods with Vasva himself at their head ... No one made of flesh and blood, not all the warriors, nor even gods would succeed in defeating that mighty chariot-warrior in fight, even if they combine together to do so. (*Mbh* 8.72.28–31)

Aside from extolling his handsomeness and valour, Kṛṣṇa also tells Arjuna that Karṇa 'has no self-interest in this quarrel with the Pāṇḍavas' (*Mbh* 8.72.34). In fact, what Sukthankar (1998:47) says about Bhīṣma being the ideal man, who acts without desire, is actually true of Karṇa. He is a true warrior who considers the battle to be '*citramtulyarūpam*', 'beautiful like a picture' (*Mbh* 8.79: 61); he sees Kurukṣetra not as a battleground in which one side will gain victory over the other, or as a gauge of good and evil, but as a sacrifice of weapons in which Duryodhana will be the sacrificer, Kṛṣṇa the *adhvaryu* priest, and Arjuna the *hotṛa* priest. In Karṇa's perception, in this sacrifice the Gāṇḍīva will be the ladle, the celestial weapons the mantras, and all the other warriors will play a in one way or another. Karṇa also believes that this sacrifice will only end when Duryodhana himself will be killed and that will make the sacrifice complete (*Mbh* 5.141.21–41). Therefore, for Karṇa, Kurukṣetra, the sacrificial ground, is unquestionably a dharmakṣetra. Karṇa's only desire is to be a part of this sacrifice. He desires to win, but only because it is the dharma of a warrior to fight for victory. He knows he will perish, but for him both death and victory in battle are of equal value. 'Whether I kill them or they kill me, I will stand true to purpose' (*Mbh* 8.79.52), he tells Śalya. But while he considers the battlefield the emblem of a dharmakṣetra, he is not a warmonger. The desire he expresses to Śalya when he faces a celebrated enemy is, 'Perhaps Arjuna will send me this day to my last account, and there will be an end of this [the war] with my fall' (*Mbh* 8.79.55). This is an obvious bid for peace. This is the ideal niṣkāma karma performed for the greater good—the sacrifice that will bring an end to the hostilities.

In addition to recognizing the war as his niṣkāma karma, Karṇa is the true dharma yoddhā who is unwilling to forego his virtue as a warrior just to win. A good example of this is when Karṇa faces Arjuna in the final battle (*Mbh* 8.90.13–31), and Aśvasena, Takṣaka's son, steals into Karṇa's quiver in the shape of an arrow so that he can strike Arjuna and avenge his mother who was killed in the fire of the Khāṇḍava forest. Karṇa is unaware of Aśvasena's stealth and he shoots the arrow, but Kṛṣṇa recognizes Aśvasena and presses down the chariot one cubit into the ground so that the arrow misses its mark and, instead of piercing Arjuna, it strikes his diadem. When Karṇa aims again, he realizes Aśvasena's presence, and the serpent tells him, 'Do what I say. I will help you achieve victory.' To this Karṇa's response is: 'Karṇa does not wish victory today in battle depending on another's strength. I shall not discharge a shaft twice even if I can kill a hundred Arjunas' (*Mbh* 8.90.44–47). It is clear that, compared to Arjuna, who is fighting for the goal of acquiring a kingdom and, that too, with deceit and divine help, Karṇa is fighting a true fight, because for him the fight itself is dharma. And, perhaps, it is for this reason that Karṇa rarely boasts of his warrior prowess, even though he is on par with Arjuna in warrior skills.

Arjuna and Karṇa are equally matched in the war. When the two finally meet in battle, Saṃjaya describes them to Dhṛtarāṣṭra:

> They [are] both skilful in war and possess select weapons and they make the skies ring back with the noise of sounding their arm-pits. Both of them [are] famous for their courage and strength and they are skillful like the asuras and the king of gods in war. Both resemble Kārtavīrya and Daśaratha's son Rāma in battle and look like the god Viṣṇu himself

in prowess, or Bhava himself ... Both of them [have] white horses and select chariots and the best of drivers. Those two warriors look beautiful and brilliant on their chariots. (*Mbh* 8.87.20–8)

In addition to their well-matched appearance, the battle between Arjuna and Karṇa is also balanced. Even Śalya, who is Karṇa's reluctant and traitorous charioteer, cannot help but take pride in him. When Karṇa asks Śalya (just as Arjuna has asked Kṛṣṇa): 'O friend, tell me the truth what would you do if I am killed today by Pārtha?', Śalya replies, 'O Karṇa, if you are today killed by this grey-horsed Arjuna, I alone on a single chariot will put both Mādhava and Phalguna to death' (*Mbh* 8.87.53–59).

Moreover, this battle between the two is so significantly on par that everyone in the cosmic world also takes sides as the two fight. However, all the immortals, even those who the gods normally oppose, and also the beasts associated with the gods, are on Arjuna's side: the asuras, the Yatudhanas, the Guhayakas, the birds, the Vedas, the UpaVedas, the Upaniṣads, Vāsuki, Citrasena, Takṣaka, UpaTakṣaka, the mountains, the descendants of Kadrū, the nāgas, Airāvata, Saurabhī, Vaitakī and Bhojnī and their descendants, the wolves, the deer and wild animals, birds, the Vāsus, the Māruts, the Siddhas, the Rudras, the Viśvadevas, the Aśvins, Agni, Soma, Indra, Pavana... The only ones favouring Karṇa are the vaiśyas, śūdras, and sūtas and, of course, Surya, Karṇa's divine father (*Mbh* 8.87.36–51). The reason for this disparity is that Karṇa sides with Duryodhana, therefore making it seem that he rejects Kṛṣṇa. Hence, when the divines decide the outcome of the battle, they acknowledge that both warriors are superior, but since Karṇa sides with the dānavas, he must be defeated. Basically, the idea is that the entire Aryan cosmos is opposing Karṇa; therefore, this battle too becomes the archetypal battle of devas and dānavas. However, there is a key difference: everyone on the side of devas agrees that Karṇa is a righteous warrior; that is why they decide that even though Karṇa will not win the battle, he will attain heaven (*Mbh* 8.87.71 & 82–3). Hence, although Karṇa himself proves true to the test of kṣatriya dharma, it is the divines who contaminate the dharmakṣetra with the adharma of nepotism.

It isn't that Karṇa rejects Kṛṣṇa; in fact, in *Udyoga Parva*, after his Embassy, when Kṛṣṇa talks to Karṇa to try to persuade him to leave Duryodhana and join the Pāṇḍavas, Karṇa acknowledges Kṛṣṇa's divinity. He also accepts the fact that destruction will occur because of the Kauravas. He realizes that virtue and dharma are seen on the side of the Pāṇḍavas and knows that the Pāṇḍavas will be victorious for the dharma values they represent (*Mbh* 5.143.3–5). However, he has sworn loyalty to Duryodhana and is honour bound, and he is willing to sacrifice his own salvation for his honour. He is not, however, willing to sacrifice his loyalty for the sake of the entire earth, pleasure, gold, or fear (*Mbh* 5.141.12). The ethical question that needs to be asked about Karṇa's undeterred and selfless loyalty towards his friend is whether dharma is served when that loyalty is towards a friend who may possibly be involved in wrongdoing, or is the dharma of loyalty and friendship itself absolving? Simple though this question sounds; it is not easy to answer, especially because none of the texts—the Mahābhārata or the Dharmaśāstras—describe any specific rules of conduct between friends. However, in order to explore this question, an example of another great friendship in the Mahābhārata can be used as a prototype—that of Kṛṣṇa and Arjuna. Aside from the fact that this pair has a history in the concept of Nara–Nārāyaṇa and that Arjuna is representative of Kṛṣṇa-ite theology, their friendship in the Mahābhārata is very human in nature. They enjoy exploits together that bring them closer, such as Arjuna's abduction of Subhadra; Kṛṣṇa is also a constant source of encouragement to Arjuna in his moments of weakness; Arjuna shares his grief and joys with Kṛṣṇa more than with anyone else; and most importantly, Kṛṣṇa is willing to break his vows of dharma to ensure his friend's well-being, such as the two times in the war when Kṛṣṇa picks up his weapon to protect Arjuna, even though he has taken an oath to remain unarmed. If Kṛṣṇa and Arjuna's friendship is hailed as exemplary, then how can Karṇa's friendship with Duryodhana be questioned? And if protecting Arjuna and his vows—despite the wrongness and deceit involved in it—is Kṛṣṇa's highest dharma, then how can it be said that remaining loyal to Duryodhana, even if Duryodhana is wrong, is not Karṇa's highest dharma?

This friendship between Karṇa and Duryodhana can also be seen from another perspective. Perhaps what Karṇa sees in Duryodhana is different from what the Pāṇḍavas see or what the authors of the Mahābhārata reveal. He sees in Duryodhana a mirror of himself: they are both alienated by the Pāṇḍavas, and they are both misunderstood by society. In fact, this equivalency is perhaps what draws Duryodhana to Karṇa in the first place. In addition, Karṇa sees in Duryodhana goodness and virtue similar to his own rather than just shortcomings, and it is to this bond that Karṇa owes the dharma of friendship. Hence, Karṇa and Duryodhana's friendship is their natural inclination, and it is their svadharma to nurture that bond.

Karṇa's motivation in life is only dharma—both in kṣatriyahood and in friendship. However, this is one hero who has to constantly fight the world to remain true to his dharma. His efforts are foiled by his own mother's actions, society's denigration of him as a consequence of his mother's action, and also fate, because situations always turn against him and, despite his adherence to dharma, he seems to have no control over the way his life plays out. He tells Śalya, 'The virtuous always say that virtue protects the virtuous. We, however, always practice virtue to the best of our knowledge and power. But virtue, instead of protecting us, is now destroying us who are its votaries' (*Mbh* 8.90.86). His life is a series of such devastations from the very beginning. His mother, Kuntī, abandons him at birth without even performing the consecratory rituals of a kṣatriya, and he is adopted by Adhiratha and Rādhā of the sūta class. Hence, he grows up as sūta and lives the life of a member of that class, even marrying women of that class. However, in his heart, Karṇa knows he is kṣatriya, and all his life he strives against all odds to be recognized as one—in action, if not by birth. This birthright is what his mother denies him so that she can protect her own name, and it is also his mother's denial that germinates into an adharma that is forced upon his psyche—a deep desire to resolve his identity crisis and be recognized for who he truly is. Sukthankar (1998: 52) points out that 'he [comes] into the world as an indirect and undesired consequence of the almost irresistible curiosity (kautūhala) of his mother, Kuntī'. This brings to mind Pandora from Greek mythology who can't resist opening the box Zeus gifts her out of extreme curiosity (even though she has been warned not to), and brings upon the world all kinds of sorrows and misfortunes. In Kuntī's case, her curiosity releases upon Karṇa all manner of sorrows and misfortunes.

Karṇa's abandonment by Kuntī also dictates how he fulfils his dharma towards his birth mother. But this dharma of Karṇa's is moulded by Kuntī's own behaviour towards him. The common perception of Kuntī is that she is a woman who makes a grave error at a young age but who stands strong for her other sons and forwards their cause of dharma. Perhaps Kuntī's grave error can be forgiven, because she was naïve and foolish. And, if her invocation of Surya can be seen as a rape (as some scholars interpret), then she is even more deserving of forgiveness. Additionally, she can also be forgiven for abandoning her child, because society would have ostracized her and she would have dishonoured her family. However, what cannot be forgiven is her behaviour towards Karṇa later on, when she is no longer in danger of being ostracized or condemned. In fact, when Kuntī meets Karṇa again, she is in such a position that her acceptance of her illegitimate son would have allowed him the status of *kanina* or *sahoda* son[3] (*Mbh* 5.140.8), but she doesn't acknowledge him. When Karṇa comes into the competition of arms to compete with the Pāṇḍavas and is thoroughly insulted by his brothers for his low birth, she does nothing. It is true that she faints when Arjuna and Karṇa face each other in the contest and she is 'seized with fear' (*Mbh* 1.136.29). But once she recovers, she has the choice to step forward and tell the world who Karṇa is, especially when her past actions have caused her son to suffer so grievously. Where are her maternal instincts? Is her desire to remain untainted in the eyes of society so

[3] A son begotten by a woman before her marriage, but given the name and paternity of the man who marries the woman.

paramount that she is able to stand by and see her son suffer? This is a sad comment on her dharma as a mother. The Mahābhārata offers no justification or explanation for Kuntī's behaviour, but tradition in her case is rightfully unforgiving.

Kuntī's behaviour towards Karṇa becomes even more of a damning comment on her because it is only when it suits her purpose that she claims him as her son. However, even in this situation, where his mother plays him false again, Karṇa remains true. Kuntī reveals her identity to Karṇa only when she learns that he will join the war as a Kaurava commander, and since she knows that he is fully capable of killing her other sons, she hopes to emotionally blackmail him to save them. Kuntī is so convinced that her blackmail will work that she does not even pay heed to the fact that Karṇa has already told Kṛṣṇa, 'Not for the sake of this entire earth nor for heaps of gold, not for pleasure, nor owing to fear can I venture to break off the ties [with Duryodhana]' (*Mbh* 5.141.12). In fact, he warns Kṛṣṇa that if Yudhiṣṭhira gave him the kingship, he would just hand it over to Duryodhana (*Mbh* 5.141.22). Therefore, Kuntī is fully aware that Karṇa is resolved to fulfil his dharma towards Duryodhana. But, instead of appreciating Karṇa for acting rightfully, she calls Karṇa 'a wretch' and says she is 'burning up' because he is opposed to the sons of Pāṇḍu (*Mbh* 5.144.17–18). Her selfish motive is clearly evident when she states to Kṛṣṇa that she was seeking her own good when she abandoned Karṇa, and now she is seeking her good again by protecting her sons from Karṇa (*Mbh* 5.144.24).

In contrast to Kuntī's immoral behaviour, Karṇa's words and actions during his meeting with her display a dharma so exemplary that it supersedes his flaw of desiring recognition. At this time, Karṇa knows that he is Kuntī's son, because Kṛṣṇa has already told him, but when Karṇa first sees Kuntī, he deliberately upholds his adoptive parentage, stating that he is '*rādheyo ham ādhirathiḥ karṇas*', 'I am Karṇa, the son of Rādhā and Adhiratha' (*Mbh* 5.145.1). Kuntī immediately responds with '*kaunteyas tvaṃ na rādheyo na tavādhirathaḥ pitā*', 'You are the son of Kuntī and not the son of Rādhā. Nor is Adhiratha your father' (*Mbh* 5.145.2), and then she addresses him as 'my son' in almost every sentence she speaks. But Karṇa is resolute to remain loyal to the parents who adopted him and cared for him. Thus, at this time, Karṇa absolves himself of the adharma he is often accused of—the desire to be recognized. This is his chance to stand tall before the world and be counted in the varṇa that he has aspired to all his life, but he doesn't; instead he establishes a new dharma standard for society—that those who nurture are greater than those who give birth. He also exposes the adharma of parents who abandon their children.

Karṇa holds Kuntī responsible for his miseries and tells her how her abandonment hurt him all his life. Though born a kṣatriya, he was not allowed to be one. 'What enemy can possibly do me a greater injury?' he asks her (*Mbh* 5.146.6). However, despite Kuntī's abandonment of him, her emotional blackmail, and her hypocritical concern for him for her own benefit, Karṇa still fulfils his dharma towards her. He promises Kuntī that he will not kill any of her sons except Arjuna so that no matter who dies, he or Arjuna, she will still have five sons (*Mbh* 5.146.20–23).

Perhaps what absolves Kuntī in some small measure is that she weeps over Karṇa's body after his death. That is when the Pāṇḍava brothers learn that Karṇa was their elder brother. Sukthankar (1998: 54) sees Kuntī's situation as epitomizing the 'silently tragic', because by revealing her secret first to Karṇa and then, after his death, to her sons, she is forced to admit her disgrace to the very people from whom she wanted to keep it. In that sense, Kuntī's situation may be tragic, but it does not negate her adharma of putting her own fear of disgrace above her son's need; so much so that the Pāṇḍavas, who have respected her and exalted her all their lives, blame her, not only because she let them kill their elder brother, but also for the war. Yudhiṣṭhira says to her, 'This terrible carnage, so destructive of the Kurus, would not have taken place [if she had revealed Karṇa's true identity before the war] (*Mbh* 11. 27.24). In fact, Yudhiṣṭhira is so sorrowful at the devastation Kuntī's secret has caused that he curses all women: 'henceforth no woman shall succeed in keeping secrets' (*Mbh* 12.6.10).

This secret of Kuntī's is what causes Karṇa to suffer the mockery of the world for his entire life, especially of the Pāṇḍavas who mock him with words that are sharper than barbs. Bhīma even makes fun of him when Duryodhana confers on the him the kingdom of Anga, saying that he should take up the whip instead of the sword: 'O worst of men, you are not worthy of enjoying the kingdom of Anga, as a dog deserves not the ghee placed before the sacrificial fire' (*Mbh* 1.137.5-7). Bhīṣma also constantly denigrates him, calling him 'low born', 'not even one sixteenth part of the Pāṇḍavas', 'wicked minded', who will single-handedly be responsible for the calamity that will come upon the Kauravas (*Mbh* 5.49.28 & 33–5). It is only when Karṇa visits Bhīṣma's on his bed of arrows and begs his permission to fight in the war that Bhīṣma finally acknowledges the warrior's true birth, but only so he will give up his enmity towards the Pāṇḍavas (*Mbh* 6.124.18–29).

In addition to being mocked about his sūta caste, Karṇa is played false by his charioteer, Śalya, turning what should have been a true dharma friendship of warrior and charioteer into one of misguidance and discouragement. Karṇa requested Śalya to be his charioteer hoping to have a guide as sagacious as Kṛṣṇa; however, he did not know that Śalya had also promised Yudhiṣṭhira that he would break Karṇa's mettle; therefore, instead of guiding Karṇa and boosting his confidence, as Kṛṣṇa does for Arjuna, Śalya constantly provokes Karṇa by deriding him and saying he's no match to Arjuna, reminding him that when Duryodhana had been captured by Gandharvas, it was the 'effulgent like the sun' Arjuna who had liberated Duryodhana, while Karṇa had fled (*Mbh* 8.37.37-38). He also heaps insults on Karṇa, such as, 'You are always a jackal and Dhanaṃjaya always a lion' (*Mbh* 8.39.33). This constant berating hits home and Karṇa's strength shatters. Drawing parallels between Kṛṣṇa and Śalya, Hiltebeitel compares the 'exemplary communication between Arjuna and Kṛṣṇa to the insult ridden communication between Karṇa and Śalya'. He also comments on how this relationship is similar to the 'friendship' that Indra forges with Vṛtra only to trick him, and states, 'Men shall talk of just one death for Karṇa and Vṛtra ... each was undone by the same device: a violation of friendship encouraged and reinforced by his opponents' closest "friend"'. 'Hence, if his mother's actions rob him of his proper place in kṣatriya society, Śalya's treachery robs him of his kṣatriya spirit' (Hiltebeitel 1991:258–64).

Karṇa is perhaps the only character in the Mahābhārata who can be considered a true victim of fate. Unlike the other Pāṇḍavas and Kauravas, who use the excuse of daivya only to shirk the responsibility of actions that they can clearly control, and whose consequences they clearly bring about, Karṇa truly has no control over many consequences, despite his good intentions. A number of curses are heaped upon him for reasons that are either petty or misconstrued. For example, one day, he inadvertently kills a *homa* cow belonging to a brāhmin, and even though he apologizes profusely to the brāhmin and offers him much wealth of cows and gems, the brāhmin curses him that when he is intent on killing his enemy, the wheel of his chariot will be swallowed by the earth, and the enemy will cut off his head (*Mbh* 12.2.19–25). He is also cursed by Rāma Jamadagni, whose student he becomes after Drona refuses to accept him because of his low caste. In order to learn the science of weapons from Rāma, Karṇa lies to him about his varṇa, telling him that he is a brāhmin from the Bhṛgu race. But, once, while Rāma is resting with his head in Karṇa's lap, a worm (that is a cursed asura), pierces Karṇa's thigh. Although in excruciating pain, Karṇa does not cry out or even shift position so as not to disturb his guru, but Karṇa's trickling blood touches Rāma and he awakens with the realization that no brāhmin would have been able to bear the pain. At that time, Karṇa has no choice but to confess that he is a son of a sūta, and Rāma curses him that the Brahmā weapon he has worked so hard to achieve will live in him and he will be a matchless warrior, but the moment he faces another warrior of equal skill in war, he will forget the science (*Mbh* 12.3.1–32). The irony of his desire to serve his guru turning against him is just another misfortune in his life which is so 'beguiled' and 'cursed' that Nārada considers that the very reason for his doom, along with his generous nature, which did not allow him to ever refuse anyone (*Mbh* 12.5.9–15).

Numerous incidents in the Mahābhārata are testimonials to Karṇa's exemplary and boundless generosity, and a number of oral narratives have also developed around Karṇa's spirit of giving. All these add to the Hindus' perception of this hero. One popular story (not included in the text of the Mahābhārata) has Kṛṣṇa showing Arjuna how truly ingrained generosity was in Karṇa: as Karṇa lies dying on the battlefield, Kṛṣṇa disguises himself and Arjuna as brāhmins and, approaching Karṇa, asks him for gifts. The dying Karṇa has nothing to give the brāhmins except his gold tooth, and though he is mortally wounded and bleeding to death, he knocks out his tooth with a rock and holds it out to the brāhmins. When the brāhmins object to receiving something covered in blood, Karṇa washes the blood with his own tears and hands the brāhmins the gold tooth.

In the epic narrative, there are two instances in which Karṇa's generosity reaches its zenith; ironically; these very incidents also become his key adharma, because they go against his loyalty to Duryodhana. One of these incidents is his promise to Kuntī that he will not kill any of her sons in war except Arjuna. Scholars like Irawati Karve (2008: 33) see this boon not as generosity, but as a bolstering of his own ego; and by doing so, he puts Duryodhana's victory in jeopardy, even though the latter only goes to war because he knows Karṇa has the ability to demolish the Pāṇḍavas. Thus, by swearing not to kill the Pāṇḍavas, he makes Kaurava defeat imminent. Karṇa's impulsive oath to Kuntī does undercut his loyalty to Duryodhana; however, his promise to his birth mother does not appear to be a salve for his ego. In fact, it seems that he wanted to show Kuntī that while she may not have fulfilled her dharma of a mother, he will fulfil the dharma of a son and a brother. In addition, and most importantly, he has no desire to kill warriors, especially his younger brothers who are not equally matched to his skills. He tells Kuntī, 'I shall not kill such of your sons as are capable of being withstood and killed by me in battle; in fact, Arjuna alone in the army of Yudhiṣṭhira is worthy to fight me' (*Mbh* 5.146.20–1). He also follows through on this promise, because when he meets Nakula in battle, brings him to the point of helplessness, and then simply lets him go (*Mbh* 8.24.1–51). Then again when he is chasing Yudhiṣṭhira, 'a memory of commitment he had made before Kuntī chains his racing feet' and he says to the eldest Pāṇḍava, 'O king! Karṇa will not slaughter you in battle-field' (*Mbh* 8.49.51–3).

Hence, this vow to Kuntī is Karṇa's sense of kṣatriyahood. It is not ego; it is simply knowledge of his own capability, a mark of a true warrior.

The second key instance of Karṇa's generosity is when he tears off his natural *kavaca* and *kuṇḍala* to give to Indra, who comes to him disguised as a brāhmin to trick him to part with these items of invincibility made of amṛta that have been bestowed upon him by Surya, his father. Even though he has been warned by Surya, he does not hesitate to give them away, simply because he is asked. But Indra, impressed with his generosity, gives him a celestial dart in return, which has the ability to destroy one powerful enemy and then return to Indra (*Mbh* 3.307.12–13 & 3.310.1–25). Sukthankar (1998: 52) too considers Karṇa's adherance to his oath of generosity a bad choice motivated by his ego. Admittedly, to fulfil his oath and remain true to his reputation of *dānavīra*, Karṇa rejects his father's advice and not only makes himself vulnerable, but also does Duryodhana—who is depending on Karṇa's invincibility in the war—a grave injustice. However, while this can be seen as a bad choice, in the kṣetra of oaths, this one is hardly deserving of condemnation, especially when the most damage it does is only to Karṇa himself. While it jeopardizes Duryodhana's position to some extent, Karṇa does make up for it by receiving Indra's dart in exchange. That the dart is used to destroy Ghaṭotkaca rather than Arjuna is not Karṇa's fault. However, the fact that scholars like Sukthankar see Karṇa's oath as an ego-booster and never question the egoity behind the oaths taken by the other dharma characters, such as Yudhiṣṭhira's to never refuse a challenge, and Bhīṣma's to remain celibate, is in itself very telling about the deep-rooted bias that this tradition of the Mahābhārata has established against Kauravas. So much so that even the tragedies borne by the Kauravas are labelled with adharmic qualities of egoity and disloyalty.

The incident in which Karṇa exchanges his invincibility for Indra's dart becomes tragic for him because of Kṛṣṇa's devious machinations. Karṇa saves and worships the dart for a year so that he can strike Arjuna with it in the war, but he has to use it against Ghaṭotkaca, who is destroying the Kauravas with his rākṣasa power (*Mbh* 7.180–54). It is important to note here that it is Karṇa's intention to use the dart only on Arjuna, since the dart has the condition that it will destroy only one enemy and then return to Indra. He considers using it on Arjuna his dharma, and he strives to adhere to this dharma in the kṣetra he has been presented, but this kṣetra is contaminated by Kṛṣṇa who unleashes Ghaṭotkaca on the Kauravas; hence Karṇa is forced to use his dart. Kṛṣṇa's behaviour after the incident clearly demonstrates not only how Karṇa has been cheated by him, but also how he has been used to serve Kṛṣṇa's divine purpose. Kṛṣṇa celebrates and rejoices not just Karṇa's misfortune, but also Ghaṭotkaca's death. The latter is a rākṣasa—a destroyer of brāhmin sacrifices; thus, despite his valour and sacrifice for the Pāṇḍavas, he is seen as a 'wicked-souled' being who needed to be destroyed by Kṛṣṇa (*Mbh* 7.182.27) And, in Karṇa's case, although Kṛṣṇa acknowledges his 'devotion to brāhmins, truthfulness of ascetic practices and vow-observing and mercifulness of his foes' (*Mbh* 7.181.23), he reduces this '*vṛṣa*'[4] warrior to nothing more than a defenceless mortal (*Mbh* 7.181.30) to ensure Pāṇḍava victory. Perhaps this is the divine Kṛṣṇa's motive—to reduce Karṇa to a mere mortal so that his warrior dharma can truly be tested in the kṣetra of mortals, and he can finally prove himself. But, if this is the case, then Kṛṣṇa's deviousness during Karṇa's killing becomes even more questionable: Karṇa's manner of death does not test his kṣatriyahood; instead, it pollutes the kṣetra with conduct that would shame any warrior, but also obscures the ethics of crime and punishment.

Karṇa is killed treacherously by Arjuna who acts on Kṛṣṇa's advice. During the battle, Karṇa's wheel gets stuck in the mud (as per the brāhmin's curse), and as he dismounts to pull it out, he reminds Arjuna about the honourable code of war which forbids a hero from shooting his arrows at an enemy who is dislodged from his chariot (*Mbh* 8.90.101-114). However, instead of honouring this kṣatriya code, Kṛṣṇa mocks Karṇa and reminds him of all the evil actions of the

[4] Monier-Williams defines the word as 'best of men', an epithet used for Indra and Vishnu.

Kauravas, such as Bhīma's poisoning, the house of lac, Draupadī's humiliation, and Abhimanyu's killing. There is no doubt that Karṇa is as responsible as the other Kauravas for Abhimanyu's gang killing and Draupadī's humiliation, and these two acts of adharma definitely mar his character. However, what Kṛṣṇa is justifying here is an eye-for-an-eye form of justice. Moreover, if this quid pro quo is to be considered dharma, then Karṇa should be absolved, because in the dice game he paid Draupadī back for humiliating him during her svayaṃvara by calling him 'sūta's son' and rejecting him, even though he was able to string the bow and bring down the mark to fulfil the terms of competition.[5] (*Mbh* 1.187.23). And he himself was paid back for participating in Abhimanyu's illegal killing by having his own son, Vṛṣasena, killed brutally before his eyes by Arjuna. (*Mbh* 8.85.31–2). However, dharma cannot be minimized by such justifications, especially in a kṣetra where dharma is being tested on a knife's edge. Therefore, none of these arguments can justify Karṇa's adharmas. In fact, in a hero of his stature, who is hailed a 'vṛṣa' in his own time and held up as a standard, these adharmas cannot be excused. But what can also not be excused is Kṛṣṇa's and Arjuna's treachery in his killing. Karṇa's death truly reveals not only how all the odds are against him, but also, and more importantly, how the false dharma of Arjuna and Kṛṣṇa overrides the dharma of the kṣetra.

Despite his wheel being stuck, Karṇa continues to fight, so much so that he is able to shoot an *Anjalika* arrow that pierces Arjuna heart and almost kills him, and in the time it takes for Arjuna to recover, Karṇa jumps down from his chariot to pull out the wheel. In that time, while he is dismounted and unarmed, Kṛṣṇa urges Arjuna to cut off his head, and Arjuna does. Karṇa cannot defend himself or shoot back, because he is unable to call upon the Brahmā weapon he had received from Rāma because of his curse to forget (*Mbh* 8.91.26–8). Karṇa's death is clearly a result of Kṛṣṇa's deceit, but the greatest travesty of this killing is that this is truly a fight of equals on the kṣetra

[5] This incident is not included in the Critical Edition.

of kṣatriyahood, and by interfering with his deceitful advice, Kṛṣṇa forces it to become uneven.

Appropriately, the kṣatriya credit of Karṇa's death belongs to neither Arjuna nor Kṛṣṇa, but to his own misfortune. As Nārada says,

> On account of the brāhmin's curse, as also the curse of the great Rāma, of the boon granted to Kuntī and the illusion practiced on by Indra, of his being belittled by Bhīṣma as only half a chariot warrior, behind Rathas and Atirathas, of the destruction of his energy by Śalya, of Vāsudeva's policy, and lastly, of the celestial weapons acquired by Arjuna from Rudra and Indra, Yama, Varuṇa, Kubera, Drona and the illustrious Kṛpa, Arjuna succeeded in killing Vikrānta's son of solar effulgence. (*Mbh* 12.5.11–14).

However, if not in life, at least in death, Karṇa is recognized for his adherence to dharma and his superlative warriorship. The epic has twenty-two verses describing 'the beauty of Karṇa's countenance' (*Mbh* 8.94.33) even after his death, and also the lamentation of the cosmic elements (*Mbh* 8.94.21–52), because 'He left the world but took away with him his fame which he had won on earth with a fair fight' (*Mbh* 8. 94.41). This hero lived by dharma and understood that to maintain the dharma of a kṣetra is as sacred a duty for the kṣatriya as a ritual sacrifice, and this is how Karṇa is rightfully remembered in the Mahābhārata tradition.

HOW ARJUNA DEFINES THE KṢETRA

Arjuna is commonly acknowledged—both by scholars and by ordinary Hindus—as everyman warrior, because his kṣetra of actions, relationships, moral dilemmas, and psyche are seen as a representative kṣetra of the common man. Especially prototypical is his moral dilemma at the beginning of the war, which epitomizes the dilemmas of the human psyche and raises universal questions of good and evil, violence and non-violence, and duty and conscience. Katz (1990: 134) says that Arjuna's reaction to seeing his relatives on the opposite side on the battlefield are 'human reactions of heroic Arjuna [and they] reduce him to human proportions ... In terms of the Pāṇḍava hierarchy, "central" Arjuna becomes "average" Arjuna, no longer towering above the audience as semi divine but, rather, coming to represent "everyman"'. However, even though the ordinary Hindu recognizes the 'everyman' quality of Arjuna, the fact that he is chosen by Kṛṣṇa to hear the Gītā also suggests that Arjuna is the exemplary hero, the model of quintessential behaviour, the unequivocal dharma hero. And this is where the problem occurs, because this paradox in the perception of his character creates a schism and puts his dharma role in grave danger, as what would ordinarily be forgiven in an everyman cannot be pardoned in someone who is an exemplar of dharma. What creates an even deeper problem is the evidence in the Mahābhārata which proves that neither is Arjuna a true everyman representative, nor is he an exemplary dharma hero.

Arjuna does not quite fit the everyman role, because unlike the ordinary man who is battling with everyday concerns that are every man's lot in life, he is privileged, declared superior from birth, favoured by his gurus and elders, equated to celestials, and protected by Kṛṣṇa. In fact, even in the period of his suffering (his exile), when he is supposed to live a life of deprivation (as would be the ordinary man's situation), he goes off to heaven and rubs shoulders with celestials, sitting in Indra's lap, riding in Indra's chariot, and learning dance and music from Citrasena in the halcyon avenues of *Indraloka*. Moreover, even the cycle of cause and effect, which is the fate of all people, is simply hypothetical in his life because most of his actions are monitored by Kṛṣṇa. Hence the cause of each of his actions is determined by Kṛṣṇa, and the consequence is orchestrated by Kṛṣṇa. It is true that he presents one of the most human moral dilemmas in the epic and becomes representative of humanity, but that too is overtly resolved for him with divine help. Which ordinary man ever has this privilege? Most often, moral dilemmas are never resolved in life. Ordinary men ride the horns of dilemma and make choices. Sometimes those choices lead to good results and sometimes they devastate or create further dilemmas; but whatever the case, ordinary men suffer the consequences of those choices, which Arjuna does not. And yet, despite all these privileges, Arjuna does not even act rightfully; he uses deceit to win victory, unlike ordinary men who, despite being rightful in their actions, have to combat hurdle after hurdle to win, and often victory for them is still elusive. Hence, if the everyman kṣetra is Arjuna's to delineate into a dharmakṣetra or an adharmakṣetra, then Arjuna as an everyman warrior is a poor representative indeed: his privileges makes him better than everyman, and his adharmas make him less than everyman.

Arjuna's superior life is determined at birth. When he is born, a heavenly, invisible voice declares to Kuntī:

> This child will be equal to Kārtavīrya and Śiva in prowess; he will be invincible like Indra himself ... He will maintain the Lakṣmī of the Kuru dynasty ... This greatly powerful hero with his brothers will conquer all the weak kings and perform three great horse-sacrifices ... he will be equal to the son of Jamadagni and Viṣṇu in prowess ... He will gratify in battle the great god Śaṃkara and he will receive from him a weapon named Paśupata, which will be given to him with pleasure ... . He will also acquire all kinds of celestial weapons, and this best of men will retrieve the lost fortunes of his race. (*Mbh* 1.123.39–46)

Hence, from birth, Arjuna is destined for not just greatness, but greatness equal to the greatest gods. The epic does not let the reader forget this, describing his prowess at every opportunity, starting from the time Drona becomes the teacher of the Kuru brothers. For example, even though Drona tries his best to keep Arjuna from gaining superiority over his own son, Aśvatthāman, Arjuna excels. When Drona gives all his pupils narrow mouthed vessels to fill water but his own son a wide mouthed one so that he can accomplish the chore quickly and Drona can use that extra time to teach his son extra skills, Arjuna begins to fill his vessel with the aid of the Varuṇa weapon and returns to Drona at the same time as Aśvatthāman so that he too can have extra time to learn. Then, when Drona instructs the cook never to give him food in the dark, one day the wind blows out the light and Arjuna automatically perfects eating food in the dark; as a result, shooting his arrows in the dark becomes almost a reflex action for him (*Mbh* 1.132.19–25).

Arjuna's accomplishments continue through adolescence and youth. In the first competition of archery, Arjuna, out of all of Drona's students, is able to aim for the target bird's head to the exclusion of everything else (*Mbh* 1.133.1–9), and he is named the greatest archer. And when Drona is seized by an alligator, Arjuna alone has the quickness of mind and skill to shoot the animal to rescue Drona; consequently, his guru presents him the Brahmaśiras weapon and declares to him, 'None will ever be a superior bowman to you. You will be invincible and greatly illustrious' (*Mbh* 1.133.18–22). Then again, in the first competition of arms, competing against other kṣatriya sons and princes, he shows his superior dexterity in the use of all weapons—sword, bow, and club (*Mbh* 1.135.1–26)—and, as a consequence, gains the reputation of the supreme warrior. Additionally, when Drona asks his students for gurudakṣiṇā, which is the defeat of his enemy Drupada, king of Pāñcāla, Arjuna, out of all Drona's students, is the one who strikes the lethal arrows and captures the king (*Mbh*1.138.1–40). As a result, he gains his guru's appreciation and gratitude for the rest of his life.

As a young adult, it is Arjuna's adroitness in archery again that wins him (and his brothers) Draupadī when no other kṣatriya can even string the bow[6] (*Mbh* 1.188.1–18). Furthermore, as an adult, Arjuna challenges even Gandharvas and defeats them to rescue Duryodhana (*Mbh* 3.245.6-30). In fact, in adulthood, his expertise is so great that with skills superior even to Indra, he is able to fight like a celestial, both on earth and in the heavens. For instance, he stops Indra's clouds from raining on the Khāṇḍava so that Agni can burn it, killing every single creature in the forest that tries to escape the flames.[7] Also, as an adult and in his full form of a 'second Indra', he is able to single-handedly destroy the Nivātakavaca and the daityas of Hiraṇyapura. The text devotes five whole chapters in *Vana Parva* (*Mbh* 3.169–73) to

[6] Except Karna, who, at this time, is still a sūta's son, and Draupadī refuses to marry him.

[7] Only the asura Māyā, the nāga Aśvasena, and the Śāranga birds escape the Khāṇḍava fire.

describe these wars and extol Arjuna's prowess. His command of the bow is so remarkable that even when he encounters Śiva as Kirāta, he is able to challenge him by laying claim to shooting Mūka before the god (*Mbh* 3.39.27-28). Obviously, Arjuna is no less than the celestials; so much so that when he, as the eunuch Bṛhannalā, battles the Kauravas in Matsya, the celestials themselves come to watch in awe (*Mbh* 4.56.2–5).

In adulthood, Arjuna becomes more of an immortal warrior than he is at birth because he has acquired celestial weapons. After he burns the Khāṇḍava and Indra descends from the sky with the Māruts to praise him and grant him a boon, Arjuna asks the king of gods for his weapons (*Mbh* 1.234.7–9), and is thus already promised more glory. Through this feat of burning the Khāṇḍava, he also receives his famous Gāṇḍīva and his ape-bannered chariot. To add to his arsenal, Śiva bestows upon him the Paśupata weapon, and declares that '[his] prowess will be incapable of being baffled' (*Mbh* 3.40.6), and this, as has been promised by Indra, is followed by the Lokapālas—Indra, Varuṇa, Kubera, Yama, and Surya—handing over to him their weapons and praising him as Naraor unconquerable (*Mbh* 3.41.31–41). Equipped with these weapons, Arjuna is more than prepared to go to war in the Mahābhārata. His meeting the Kauravas in Matsya is a dry run of how he will use the celestial weapons in the actual war, because these are the very weapons he uses in both kṣetras. Thus, equipped with superior warrior skill, the Gāṇḍīva and the ape-bannered chariot, and celestial weapons, he is now equal to the gods. Ruth Cecily Katz (1990: 55) notes that Arjuna's receiving all the divine weapons and being able to use them makes him similar to Skanda and also to the Devī in *Devī Mahātamaya,* as she is portrayed in the *Mārkaṇḍeya Purāṇa*—both of whom receive powers and gifts from all the gods.

The description of Arjuna's prophecy of birth, his predestined greatness, his skills in weaponry, and his warrior prowess show how different he is, not only from the ordinary mortals that he supposedly represents, but also from the Kaurava heroes who have only ordinary human skills to depend on (except for one or two divine weapons, such as Karṇa's Brahmāstra, which, in any case, he is cursed to forget). Admittedly, Arjuna's acquisition of celestial weapons and his admirable talents can be attributed to what the elders in the epic constantly call his asceticism, his righteousness, and his adherence to dharma. However, despite his prowess, or rather, because of his prowess, Arjuna's behaviour on a human level—a level that would make him relatable to ordinary men—becomes a subject of deeper scrutiny, making his adharmas even more pronounced and his goodness and righteousness questionable.

Indeed, Arjuna's very birth is questionable. He is the son of Indra, and as Dumézil (quoted in Katz 1990: 30) emphasizes, the traits of a father pass down to the son, and the son is seen as identical to father. The epithets used for Arjuna also verify this connection to Indra. In the epic, he is called Aindri, Indrasuta, Vasvaja, Mahendratanaya, Shakrasuta, etc. (quoted in Katz 1990: 30); even his Gāṇḍīva is likened to Indra's vajra. But if Arjuna is to be given the same warrior qualities as his father, Indra, then his actions must also be seen through the lens of the archetypal Aindria pursuits and treacheries—Indra's stealing of water and wealth from the early Aryan enemies and his treachery in killing Vṛtra and the other asuras. It is these very patterns of immoral behaviour that guide Arjuna in his own pursuit of wealth and in his battles against his own dānavas—the Kauravas. The difference is that, while in Vedic times this was not seen as 'immoral', in epic times, through the ethical lens of dharma, these behaviours become adharmic.

Another adharmic trait of Arjuna's that echoes Indra is his jealousy of anyone who may surpass him in warrior skills. Once again, in bygone days, this trait may not have been considered unethical. In Arjuna's time, when dharma became the supreme virtue, jealousy came to be seen as a grievous adharma, because its consequences consumed the moral agent in darkness and destroyed those who suffered its repercussions. An apt example of Arjuna's jealousy is Ekalavya, the Niṣāda prince who, despite his low birth and Drona's rejection, proves his genius by shooting seven arrows in the barking mouth of a dog without killing it. Arjuna is so jealous of the lowborn Niṣāda's exceptional talent that he says to Drona, like a spoiled child, 'You have joyfully told me, embracing me to your bosom, no pupil of yours would be equal to me. Why then there is a pupil of yours in the world [equal to me], the mighty son of the Niṣāda king?' (*Mbh* 1.132.48–49). The grave consequence of Arjuna's jealousy towards Ekalavya is that Drona, despite having rejected him as a student, makes Ekalavya sever his right thumb and give it to him as gurudakṣiṇā, thus incapacitating the Niṣāda prince forever.

A more grievous form of Arjuna's jealousy transforms into his fierce possessiveness of his weapons, especially the Gāṇḍīva—the very weapon that makes him great. His acute attachment to Gāṇḍīva evokes an incident in the war that suddenly reveals deep holes in the roles of not only Arjuna as dharma hero, but also of Yudhiṣṭhira's as dharmarāja and of Kṛṣṇa as dharma guide and mentor. This incident also shows that the loving bond between the Pāṇḍava brothers is a sham, and it reveals the hypocrisy of not just the characters but also of the dharmayuddha they are supposed to be fighting. This occurs when, in the war, Karṇa spares Yudhiṣṭhira's life as per his oath to Kuntī, and Yudhiṣṭhira is so insulted that he cannot bear it. But, unlike Duryodhana who, unable to bear the insult of being rescued from the Gandharvas by the Pāṇḍavas, blamed only himself and sought to kill himself, Yudhiṣṭhira, burning in rage and humiliation, seeks to blame and hurt Arjuna. This incident exposes Yudhiṣṭhira and shows that he is not really the equanimous ascetic that he appears to be; he is actually consumed by fear and insecurities, and he blames Arjuna for not doing anything to help alleviate his anxieties. He tells Arjuna,

> O Dhanaṃjaya, through fear of him [Karṇa], I have not slept in the night nor have I enjoyed comfort in the day for these thirteen years. I am burning with hatred against him. ... Awake or asleep I spent days only in thinking how I would accomplish Karṇa's death. Wherever I go, O Dhanaṃjaya, in fear of Karṇa, everywhere I see his image before me. (*Mbh* 8.66.13–17)

Then Yudhiṣṭhira begins to revile and belittle Arjuna's warriorship because he hasn't killed Karṇa as he had promised. Furthermore, Yudhiṣṭhira denigrates Arjuna and declares that all the prophecies about him are false and that he is a stain on the Pāṇḍava race, and he should have been aborted even before he was born. He proclaims, 'Fie to your Gāṇḍīva! Fie to the strength of your arms, fie to your numberless arrows, fie to your standard bearing the ensign of an ape on it and fie to your car presented to you by the god of fire!' (*Mbh* 8.68.30), and then he tells Arjuna to give up his bow. The consequence of Yudhiṣṭhira's insulting words is quite shocking, because it completely belies the impression that the epic has created about Arjuna's respect for his elder brother. Arjuna looks towards Yudhiṣṭhira, 'whizzing like an angry snake', and pulls out his sword to kill his brother, announcing that he has made a secret vow that he will cut off the head of anyone who tells him to give up his Gāṇḍīva (*Mbh* 8.69.8-11). Of course, the Gāṇḍīva is not just a symbol of Arjuna's kṣatriyahood but also of his manhood, and the fact that Arjuna is ready to kill his elder brother because he disparaged it not only shows how insecure Arjuna is about his warrior prowess but also the hypocrisy of his dharma to an elder brother.

This incident is rife with significance, the least of it being the unmistakable irony of the situation. This very same Arjuna had reminded Bhīma of his dharma to an elder brother and chided him when that Pāṇḍava had threatened to burn Yudhiṣṭhira's hands for staking Draupadī in the dice game. When, in fact, at that time the vows that the Pāṇḍavas broke were so tremendous that they threatened the very establishment of marriage—the entire social system. And yet, now, at this comparatively minor insult to a petty and secret personal vow, Arjuna is ready to kill his brother. This is especially glaring in view of the fact that this same Arjuna has already demonstrated that vows can be easily broken. For example, he breaks the vow of the twelve' years celibacy that he had to observe because he intruded on Yudhiṣṭhira and Draupadī. It is true that in this incident his intrusion was to help a brāhmin, and even Yudhiṣṭhira was willing to absolve him of his vow, but in kṣatriya fashion, Arjuna bound himself in the vow and took exile to observe it. However, in exile, far from remaining a celibate, he married four women (*Mbh* 1.212.28–30). Hence, his extreme reaction to Yudhiṣṭhira's words and his obstinacy to adhere to this injurious secret vow ruins Arjuna's credibility. Besides, who is to say this isn't a vow he has furnished on the spot to appease his resentment against Yudhiṣṭhira. After all, Arjuna's vow is 'secret' and no one has ever heard it before, not even Kṛṣṇa with whom Arjuna shares all his hopes, desires, insecurities, and fears. In fact, Kṛṣṇa, his constant supporter, offers no praise for the vow or endorsement for it. Instead he calls this vow 'childish' and repudiates Arjuna for his anger and, most importantly, questions Arjuna's comprehension of the Gītā and tradition. Kṛṣṇa says to Arjuna, 'You have never attended upon the old, since you, O mightiest of men, have been overcome with anger at a time quite out of season' (*Mbh* 8.69.16). Kṛṣṇa tells Arjuna that he has become benumbed and befooled in discriminating between what ought to be done and what ought not. 'Everything can be learnt with the help of the scriptures. You are, however, a stranger to them' (*Mbh* 8.69.21–2). It is important to note that Arjuna not 'attending upon on the old' does not mean that he did not hear the lessons of the Gītā. Rather, this is proof that the Gītā never impacted Arjuna's thinking. Thus, it can be said that if Arjuna was chosen to receive the Gītā for the benefit of every man, then he has failed every man because, holding on to insecurities, egoity, and selfish resolves, he has squandered the knowledge.

This incident does not just implicate Arjuna, it also implicates Kṛṣṇa and his role as guide, because it shows Kṛṣṇa trapped in his own contrariness, trying to make dharma arguments that don't hold up. For example, in direct contradiction to his own words in the Gītā about a kṣatriya's dharma of honour killing, Kṛṣṇa now tells Arjuna, 'You believe yourself to be virtuous but you know not, O Pārtha, that it is a sin to slay living beings' (*Mbh* 8.69.22). Then Kṛṣṇa gives Arjuna lessons about rules of war which contravene his and the Pāṇḍavas' role in the killing of Bhīṣma, Drona, and Karṇa. He says to Arjuna, 'O Bhārata, the slaying of a man who is not engaged in a fight, or is unwilling to fight, or takes to flight, or seeks your shelter ... be he even a foe, is never upheld by the righteous' (*Mbh* 8.69.25-26). These words make all the Pāṇḍava treacheries in the war adharmic. In addition to this, Kṛṣṇa extols the virtue of truth, saying nothing is higher than the truth, and then he contradicts his statement by relating confusing stories in which both nonviolence and truth are shown as relative values, violable at any time.

One of the stories that Kṛṣṇa tells is of the hunter, Balāka, who kills a blind beast of prey to feed his family and is rewarded for his hiṁsā against this seemingly helpless animal because the beast treacherously used his blindness to lure animals and then killed them. The next story is of a brāhmin named Kauśika who had vowed to tell the truth; this brāhmin is sent to hell because in telling the truth, he reveales the whereabouts of innocent people who were hiding from robbers (*Mbh* 8.69.32–45). Using these stories as analogies, Kṛṣṇa first labels the Kauravas as the blind beast, and then he compares Arjuna's vow to that of the brāhmin Kauśika's—immoral because it would hurt the innocent Yudhiṣṭhira. However, these analogies are not only weak, they are also inaccurate: the beast that Balāka kills cannot be called treacherous because although he was blind, being an animal of prey, he mostly likely had an excellent sense of smell with which to track his prey. And Balāka, being a hunter, would have known this; therefore, his comparison to the Kauravas actually makes them honest warriors. Similarly, Yudhiṣṭhira is not innocent: he has just insulted his younger brother for his own fear and humiliation. Perhaps what Kṛṣṇa's words mean is that the actions of an individual need not meet the strict standards of morality, provided the consequence of action is to benefit others; hence, what matters is the end, not the means.

Obviously, Arjuna accepts Kṛṣṇa's guidance about ends and means, because he agrees not to kill Yudhiṣṭhira if he can find a way to also keep his vow. With these statements, Arjuna and Kṛṣṇa have left the kṣetra open for further equivocacy: about means and ends, about rightfulness in observing oaths that injure others, and about the truth of vows and oaths. Additionally, it brings to light the possibility that any and all vows in the epic that cause such havoc could have been circumvented, because Arjuna's words indicate that there is always a way out. In this instance, too, Kṛṣṇa shows Arjuna the way out. He advises Arjuna to kill Yudhiṣṭhira figuratively by verbally dishonouring him, because a dishonoured man 'dies at heart' (*Mbh* 8.70.2).

By acting on Kṛṣṇa's solution of ends and means, Arjuna digs a deeper hole for himself in his kṣetra of dharma, not only revealing his own hypocrisy but also completely falsifying his dharma to his elder brother. Given this sanction by Kṛṣṇa, Arjuna spews out all the resentment he feels towards Yudhiṣṭhira. He begins by calling Yudhiṣṭhira a coward, telling him that he remained at a distance from the fray of battle. Then he calls him a wanton and says he is tired of Yudhiṣṭhira toying with the lives and souls of his brothers, their wives and their sons. Then the jealousy Arjuna feels for sharing Draupadī with Yudhiṣṭhira spills out with venom. And finally, Arjuna blames Yudhiṣṭhira for jeopardizing his and his brothers' happiness with his addiction to gambling and worse, he says, having committed this sin of gambling, Yudhiṣṭhira is trying to get back to his enemies by using his brothers. He believes that all the evil that befell the Pāṇḍavas was a result of Yudhiṣṭhira's own actions. In fact, he even blames Yudhiṣṭhira for the death of Kaurava heroes and states that he does not approve of Yudhiṣṭhira being restored to sovereignty (*Mbh* 8.70.2–20). Ultimately, the truths that are disclosed in this incident invalidate almost all dharma claims that the epic makes about the Pāṇḍavas: the unity of the Pāṇḍava brothers, the decisiveness of their kṣatriya traits, the legitimacy of their kingship, and the correctness of Kṛṣṇa's guidance.

Even more astonishing than this revelatory exchange between Arjuna and Yudhiṣṭhira is how this incident is perceived by the authors of the epic. Describing the incident to Dhṛtarāṣṭra, Saṃjaya says that the 'calm, virtuous and conscientious Savyasācin having addressed to Yudhiṣṭhira such harsh and exceedingly cruel words and having thus slightly sinned became cheerless' (*Mbh* 8.70.22). This śloka appears only in the Devanāgri edition of the epic, but it is worth mentioning, because it sheds more light on how the authors of the epic glossed over Arjuna's infractions. The words *pātakam kiṃcivedaṃ* (slight sin) are not only ironic, but also misleading. Firstly, the fact that Arjuna has completely denounced his elder brother and the Pāṇḍava rectitude is hardly 'kiṃcivedaṃ' (slight). Secondly, how does one 'sin slightly'? A sin is a sin. It is true that in its immediate execution, one sin can be graver than another, depending on the offense against established dharmas, but actions are perceptible, all karma is retributive, and all sins are against dharma. In addition, in this instance, if keeping a vow is considered more important than respecting an elder brother, then doesn't it catapult Arjuna into the grave adharma of extreme egoity? To add to the confusion of this incident, when Kṛṣṇa sees Arjuna ready to drive the sword through his own body to sacrifice himself for insulting his elder brother, Kṛṣṇa stops him by saying that he will help him 'gain [his] desired gain'. Hence, not only are the lessons of desireless action, which Kṛṣṇa himself has propounded, perverted, but Kṛṣṇa's next piece of advice proves another adharma—that one's guilt can be appeased by transferring the violence onto someone else. Kṛṣṇa tells Arjuna that instead of killing himself, he should find Karṇa and kill him, because this will bring him his 'desired gains' (*Mbh* 8.71.8–9). In other words, killing Karṇa will help Arjuna appease his own guilt. Therefore, in these few words, Kṛṣṇa opens a Pandora's box full of immoralities. To name just a few: violence, negation of accountability, questionable means to reach a desired end, pursuit of desires, and transference of guilt. In fact, this incident is so wrought with ethical contradictions and fallibility that the very idea of these characters creating a dharmakṣetra with their lakṣaṇa and fighting a dharmayuddha becomes unbelievable.

Another such incident of dubious morality is Arjuna's burning of the Khāṇḍava forest. This incident prompts an important question about the role of a kṣatriya and the misuse of warrior prowess. And if that expertise is attained by asceticism, as Arjuna's is supposed to be, then the question becomes even more grievous. Ruth Cecily Katz, who justifies many of Arjuna's faults, also finds it hard to justify Arjuna's actions in this incident. She states (1990: 72–3),

> The episode of the Khandava Forest burning is one of the most difficult sections of the epic to understand. For not only does it offend modern sensibilities (both Hindu and Western); it also goes against the morality propounded by the extant epic. This it does not only by

> deliberately flouting the doctrine of non-violence, which is important in classical Hinduism and is advocated in many of the *Mahabharata* didactic passages. The behavior extolled as heroic in the episode also violates the rules of warfare, the Kshatriya codes set forth throughout the *Mahabharata*, which state clearly that innocent bystanders are never to be slain in battle. The Khandava episode, on the contrary, depicts a berserker ideal of martial ecstasy, as Arjuna and Krishna, laughing, slay all creatures who cross their path.

A possible justification for this incident can be that this is permissible violence, as in a Vedic sacrifice that sustains cosmic order, or it can be considered mythical, as in the parallel myth of the churning of the ocean. However, these justifications are not strong enough to excuse the Khāṇḍava incident's flagrant and causeless violence. Besides, if the burning of Khāṇḍava is to be seen as a Vedic sacrifice, then Arjuna is given Vedic sanctification, which not only equates him with Duryodhana, who is maligned for his adherence to Vedic practices, it also negates his flag-bearing role in the Kṛṣṇa theocracy. Furthermore, in the co-relation of the burning of the Khāṇḍava and the churning of the ocean, it must be noted that the latter myth, while causing cosmic destruction, is creational. It facilitates the procurement of Śrī, the acquisition of soma by the gods, the creation of divine beings that arise from it, and the establishment of Śiva's role as protector of the creation when he drinks the poison. To some extent, the Khāṇḍava incident does imitate a pralaya in its annihilation, and it does contain elements of creation in Arjuna receiving the Gāṇḍīva and his ape banner chariot, Kṛṣṇa receiving his discus, and asura Māya's building of Khāṇḍavaprastha. However, Arjuna's and Kṛṣṇa's munitions disappear at the end of the war and the creation of Khāṇḍavaprastha actually leads to the potential of an even bigger destruction—the war.

Arjuna's behaviour in the Khāṇḍava forest can, perhaps, be excused on a mythic level, because this incident is a credible way to elevate Arjuna's status from human to cosmic. He is thrown in the role of destroyer or Śiva, alongside Kṛṣṇa. He is already equated to Viṣṇu, and later, when Śiva himself becomes destroyer again through Aśvatthāman, Arjuna will become preserver by saving the world from total annihilation from Aśvatthāman's Brahmāstra. However, on the level of the dharmakṣetra, where moral agents chart out good and evil through their actions and behaviours, it is irrelevant whether Arjuna reflects the divine. On this level, it is relevant only to see him and his actions on the human plain, a kṣetra in which moral agents act, and on this kṣetra, Arjuna's actions are deplorable and against any codes of dharma. Therefore, no matter how this episode is perceived, from a human level, it is hard to justify.

In addition, and even more shameful, is the fact that this incident is an example of the extreme destruction of an entire ecosystem—and not just from a modern perspective. Preservation of ecosystems was something about which the Pāṇḍavas themselves were conscious, and practised. For example, during their exile, when they are living in Dvaitavana for a while, Vyāsa advices Yudhiṣṭhira, 'Because you support numerous brāhmins ... your continued residence here may exhaust the deer of the forest and may be destructive of the creepers and plants.' So the Pāṇḍavas leave Dvaitavana and move to Kāmyaka (*Mbh* 3.36.35–41). Also, while in exile, as they hunt, they only use non-poisonous arrows (*Mbh* 3.36.45) so as not to cause the animals suffering. Therefore, it is obvious that ecological and environmental concerns were very much a part of epic Aryan society and dharma. Hence, it is difficult to reconcile Arjuna's indiscriminate and painful destruction of plant and animal life in the Khāṇḍava.

Historians like D.D. Kosambi (1965: 117) say that the burning of forests was necessary to clear the land for agriculture and living—to build societies. But, even if the historical evidence can be accepted that the Khāṇḍava had to be burned to clear space for building Khāṇḍavaprastha, it is still incomprehensible why Arjuna and Kṛṣṇa deliberately trap the animals and torture them to death, while gleefully enjoying the experience. These actions reek of unconscionable violence. Therefore, the suffering that the Pāṇḍavas experience after this incident seems like a direct consequence and fitting: Asura Māyā escapes the fire and the Pāṇḍavas befriend him, because he promises to build their palace with 'gold' he himself has stashed away (perhaps the iron-ore that had just come into use). He creates a palace that is so māyāvi that even Duryodhana is baffled. But, by befriending Māyā, the Pāṇḍavas themselves are trapped in māyā, the asuric illusion that can befuddle a person's mind. Noteworthy is that before the burning of Khāṇḍava, the Pāṇḍavas adhere to every dharma. They are the good guys. But after they move into Indraprastha, there is a marked reversal in their behaviour and psyche, starting from Yudhiṣṭhira's extreme addiction to dyūta, followed by the war in which the Pāṇḍavas, who had remained righteous despite Duryodhana's ploys to kill them, employ all kinds of treacheries to destroy their enemies. Even Draupadī's humiliation is connected to this palace, because it is here that she insults Duryodhana as being the blind son of a blind father, and he takes the insult to heart. Thus, the evil occurrences connected to the palace at Khāṇḍavaprastha can be seen as proof that unrighteous means cannot produce a righteous end. Also worthy of note is that after the war, the Pāṇḍavas do not move back into Khāṇḍavaprastha but into Hāstinapura. In fact, after the war, nothing is heard or said about Khāṇḍavaprastha. It can thus be concluded that it is only when the Pāṇḍavas abandon the place whose foundation is evil that they are able to rule righteously and sustain society.

Other incidents that cast doubt on Arjuna's roles of everyman warrior and dharma hero involve his actions in the actual war and his participation in the treacherous killings of the Kaurava commanders. The first of these is of Bhīṣma, who, committing his own traitorous adharma, tells the Pāṇḍavas the means to his death (*Mbh* 6.108.77–88), thus jeopardizing Duryodhana's whole game plan. Using Bhīṣma's secret, Arjuna stands behind Śikhaṇḍin and shoots lethal arrows, but everyone believes that Śikhaṇḍin has killed him, and no one knows that Arjuna broke a cardinal rule of law by killing a warrior with whom he was not engaged in battle, and especially in this treacherous manner. This lie itself further convolutes the dharma of truth-telling. For instance, when Bhīṣma finally dies and his mother, Bhagirathī (Gangā), arising from the water, bemoans that her, 'powerful son who defeated even Rāma was killed by Śikhaṇḍin [a transgender]', Kṛṣṇa tells her that her son was actually killed by Dhanaṃjaya (Arjuna) (*Mbh* 13.168.31–32) so as to console her. But then, in the

Aśvamedha Parva, when Kṛṣṇa is recounting the story of the war to his father, he wants to take the blame away from Arjuna and says that Śikhaṇḍin killed Bhīṣma (*Mbh* 14.60.11). This shifting of truth is not new for Kṛṣṇa—and it keeps dharma constantly tottering on the verge of adharma—but, most importantly, it disguises Arjuna's sin of unfairly killing Bhīṣma. However, as mentioned above, each action is perceptible, and no action remains disguised in the scope of karma. This is proved true when, during the Aśvamedha, the horse Arjuna is following is seized by his son Babhruvāhana, Citrāngada's son, who strikes a death blow to Arjuna. But Arjuna's second wife Ulūpī arrives and, reviving him, informs him that he had been cursed by the Vāsus and Ganga for Bhīṣma's unfair killing. The expiation of that sin is that Arjuna's own son would cause him to fall on the ground in a field of war (*Mbh* 14.81.7-8). Admittedly, this cycle of karma is moralistic, and because it is exemplified in Arjuna's life, it makes Arjuna a paradigm for everyman; but the fact that Arjuna himself is unmindful of the implications of his evil actions makes him more a one-dimensional prototype than a three-dimensional moral agent.

There are many other treacheries that Arjuna commits in the war: not condemning the lie that kills Drona; urging Bhīma to strike Duryodhana on the thigh; randomly lopping off of Bhūriśravas' arm; and dropping Jayadratha's head in his father Vṛdhakṣatra's lap, so that when the old king stands up after his *sandhyā* prayers, his son's head falls to the ground, thus shattering his own head, as per the boon he had received (*Mbh* 7.146.104-130). Arjuna's gravest deception is his killing of Karṇa, which has evoked much polemic among the scholars of the Mahābhārata. In light of these killings, the Kauravas are vindicated, because they are no longer the only unrighteous ones. Instead of being perpetrators of evil, they are revealed as victims. Additionally, if these incidents are rationalized as using deceit to counter deceit as per Kṛṣṇa's constant advice, then what is established is the standard of an eye-for-an-eye justice and ends justifying means. This completely falsifies the dharma of the kṣetra, because dharma is not just what results from action but also the action itself.

An important point to note is that in many of the cited incidents, Arjuna wants to abide by the codes of war and is deeply conflicted about breaking the codes. Firstly, this itself proves that the acts Arjuna commits are adharmic because his conscience is aware of the wrongness of these acts. In the killing of Karṇa, too, Arjuna wants to wait for Karṇa to free his chariot wheel, but he is advised by Kṛṣṇa to strike him while he is down. It can be said that, technically, Arjuna is not responsible for the *karma phala* of this act. After all, Kṛṣṇa is god and Arjuna has already received the Gītā and knows Kṛṣṇa's true identity; hence he believes that Kṛṣṇa's advice is infallible. Besides, it is Karṇa's own bad karma (his role in killing Abhimanyu and in humiliating Draupadī), as Kṛṣṇa points out, that is responsible for his death. Arjuna is simply the agent—a means. Secondly, this evokes a number of important questions about the morality of the action performed by agents: Is the moral agent committing the action accountable for the action he performs, or is the one on whom the action is committed responsible for his own suffering? In addition, in this complex causal chain of cause and effect in the eye-for-an-eye form of justice, who is really accountable? This is an issue of karma's ambiguity, and is one of the gravest problems of evil in not just this kṣetra that Arjuna delineates but also in the entire Mahābhārata tradition. This aspect has also been discussed in Chapter 2, especially in the example of Gautami's story of moral agency and the exoneration of moral agents from their acts. In fact, Gautami's story and Bhīṣma's explanation for it are key to understanding not only Arjuna's blamelessness but also the Hindu psyche. On one level, it is a dangerous prototype that caters to the escapist attitude that negates accountability, because evildoers can justify all evil acts by simply labelling them the karma of the one who is injured through his or her own evil actions. On a more significant level, the practicality of this logic is dubious: unlike the snake and Kāla in Gautami's story, who are not human moral agents but are simply acting from natural instincts, moral agents are human and they act not only from natural instinct, but from a combination of factors—their *pravṛtti* and *saṃskāras*, their effort to improve the demerits of their previous karma, and their motive to do good or evil to another, and most importantly, as a consequence of their ego, their I-ness, and their personal desires. Hence, their actions are always ruled by intent, they always have a consequence, and there is always the choice of free will. For human moral agents, one action (good or evil) sets off another action in a complex causal chain of events that extends over many lifetimes. Moreover, if the individual's intent to act is evil or to fulfil a personal desire, and also the consequence of the action causes the breakdown of dharma and the suffering of another, then under no circumstance can this agent be considered free of adharma or unaccountable.

In Arjuna's case there is no doubt about his intent and his hope for a desired consequence. In fact, in the incident of Karṇa's death, not only is Arjuna intent on killing Karṇa because he is an enemy, but also because Karna threatens his status of supreme warrior. Additionally, Arjuna means to make Karṇa suffer for his role in Abhimanyu's death and Draupadī's humiliation. Thus, even if it is Karṇa's own karma that is causing him to suffer, Arjuna is responsible for the action he himself is committing and he and he alone is responsible for his action. Moreover, even if Arjuna is acting on Kṛṣṇa's dictates (as the snake was acting on Kāla's dictates in the Gautamī's story), his free will (unlike the snake's, who was acting from natural instinct) affords him a choice. He has every choice to say no to Kṛṣṇa and not commit this sin, but he chooses to bind himself in the bad karma of a deceitful killing. Hence, Arjuna's adharma is not so much that he causes Karṇa's death, which is simply a karma that will bind Arjuna in a chain of causality, but his bigger adharma is this intentional treachery which he agrees to commit.

Perhaps Arjuna too is caught up in the complacency of the prototype that Gautamī's story creates, believing that he is simply an agent acting on the dictates of Karṇa's karma, and that he is not responsible for what happens to Karṇa. Or perhaps he would have been able to see the injustice of his action if his mind hadn't been befuddled by Kṛṣṇa's words. In either case, is he worthy of the role of everyman that he has been given? Unlike Arjuna, everyman cannot escape the justice of karma by pleading prototypical complacency or befuddlement.

Everyman is actually held accountable for the choices he makes through the agency of his free will.

On a separate note, what is even more dangerous than Arjuna's befuddlement about his responsibility for his own actions is how the epic treats Karṇa's killing and how tradition portrays it. While the immorality of Bhīṣma's killing is made retributive, and Arjuna suffers its consequences at the end with his own son felling him, the transgression of Karṇa's killing is swept under the rug of *niyati*, and Arjuna suffers no retribution for it. This is, of course, because Bhīṣma is portrayed as a good and righteous man and Karṇa sides with Duryodhana—the supposed evil. Hence, the implication is that dharma sanctions the killing of those who are perceived as evil. The Mahābhārata offers no clarity on this issue; even the Gītā does not address it. This is another problem of evil that is filed away under the pretext of ambiguity of dharma, but what is not ambiguous are the ethical questions that Arjuna's actions raise.

In this sense—the fact that Arjuna's character invokes enquiry into dharma—he fits the role of everyman, because this is what every person on the path of realization should be doing: enquiring into the nature of self and dharma. However, once the kṣetra of enquiry is laid out and Arjuna's character is examined, he is hardly an exemplar. He fails the test of almost every enquiry. But then, as Indrani Sanyal (2010) says, 'Arjuna is not the ideal man. He is an ordinary person who aspires to fulfil his ideals, just as every man'. However, as mentioned earlier, while Arjuna pursues his ideals like every man, he is not an ordinary person; he is a privileged semi-divine who is constantly favoured by the gods. Therefore, he is a poor choice for an everyman warrior because, firstly, his life does not include the struggles of an everyman, and secondly, his escapism, despite all the odds being in his favour, make him less than an ordinary man.

The key reason for which Arjuna is considered everyman and is made representative of the human experience is his moral dilemma at the beginning of the war, which resonates with all moral agents. Arjuna does redeem himself through this dilemma. His sentiments are genuine and human (not heroic), and they are based in human qualities of love for his elders, compassion for humanity, and desire for the sustenance of society. Also, the fact that Arjuna is the recipient of the Gītā proves that he is chosen as the quintessential everyman, because Kṛṣṇa, while acknowledging Arjuna's human weakness, evokes his true kṣatriya/hero dharma, and it is on this ground that he declares this war a dharmayuddha and this kṣetra a dharmakṣetra. Hence, the question is: does Arjuna sustain this kṣetra as a dharmakṣetra and does he truly fight a dharmayuddha to remain true to the legacy? This question can only be answered by examining whether Arjuna resolves his moral dilemma. For it is only after he resolves this moral dilemma and acts accordingly that he can be considered the deserving recipient of the Gītā's message and be representative of everyman (who can also elevate himself with this knowledge). M.M. Agrawal, in his essay 'Arjuna's Moral Predicament' says that a true resolution of a moral dilemma is not simply when a moral agent makes one choice over another or realizes the benefit of one choice over another or even understands the rationality of one choice over another. A true resolution is when a 'radical conversion of enlightenment' occurs in the mind of the moral agent, and his mind is ready to 'embrace only *one* set of values, and that one set of values must be internally coherent, and must somehow reflect the true and eternal order in nature' (Agrawal 1989:139–41). This 'moral monism' (Agrawal 1989:137) in Arjuna's case would be his realizing, to the exclusion of everything else, that his true kṣatriya dharma is to fight—to war with his opponents without feelings of remorse, anger, or revenge, and without anticipating or relishing the victory. In addition, he must align his self with his inner self, and even as his self is involved in battle, he must remain equanimous, which is the nature of his true self. Then and only then can the battle be righteous. Only then would the kṣetra be a dharmakṣetra, and this yuddha, a dharmayuddha. Agrawal (1989:137) thinks Kṛṣṇa is able to bring about just such a conversion in Arjuna through the lessons of the various aspects of the Gītā.

However, Arjuna's moral dilemma is never actually resolved, because this conversion that Agrawal confers on Arjuna never occurs. In the fray of battle, Arjuna is not only riddled with conflicts, egoism, anger, revenge, and grief, but in some instances, he even regresses to a state of such *tamas* that he loses his humanity; for instance when he threatens to kill Yudhiṣṭhira or when he slices off Bhūriśravas' arm for no reason at all. In fact, Arjuna's behaviour in the war negates every lesson of the Gītā; it is as though the sermon never happened (which may prove that the Gītā was a later interpolation). Even Kṛṣṇa himself doubts whether the Gītā has had any impact on Arjuna, and tells him 'O son of Pāṇḍu, you are destitute of faith and your understanding is not good' because 'you did not from folly receive what I gave' (*Mbh* 14.16.10–11). Most importantly, Arjuna himself professes to Kṛṣṇa that he has forgotten the lessons of the Gītā (*Mbh* 14.16.6–7). If his moral dilemma had been resolved and his mind had embraced only one set of values—the Gītā's—would the question of his remembering these values even arise? These values would have become part of his being, his very motive of thought and action. Therefore, in actuality, Arjuna even bungles the moral dilemma he so famously represents, thus foiling the kṣetra which Kṛṣṇa tries to establish as a dharmakṣetra through his Gītā.

Yet, in the tradition of the Mahābhārata, Arjuna is upheld as the ideal, an everyman warrior battling the dilemmas of life, demonstrating the lakṣaṇa of dharma, making dharmic choices over adharmic enticements and desires, and connecting everyman to the divine through Nara–Narayana co-relations. The fact is that Arjuna fails everyman and, most importantly, his failures are not honest; they are treacherous and misleading.

HOW YUDHIṢṬHIRA DEFINES THE KṢETRA

Yudhiṣṭhira is the embodiment of dharma, and just by this virtue, his very presence in the kṣetra would make the Mahābhārata a dharmakṣetra and the yuddha a dharmayuddha. Not only does Yudhiṣṭhira have the knowledge of dharma by merit of birth, he also receives this knowledge through various deliberate means such as Vidura *nīti* and Bhīṣma's lessons in the *Śāntī* and *Anuśāsana Parvas*. However, Yudhiṣṭhira commits two key sins: his lie to Drona, which causes him to lose his own tējas, and his actions in the dice game, which not only cause the war, but also shake the very foundation of a dhārmic society. Scholars like Hiltebeitel also consider Yudhiṣṭhira's request of Śalya to play Karṇa false and cut down his energy as one of Yudhiṣṭhira's grave adharmas. However, while this adharma is definitely a slippage of Yudhiṣṭhira's tējas, it can be considered more of an infraction that results from his very human and debilitating fear of Karṇa, which he reveals in the incident of his exchange with Arjuna in *Karṇa Parva*. Of course, as the dharmarāja, who claims that his constant adherence to dharma makes him equanimous, his feelings of fear falsify his claims. But he is also human, and while fear makes a kṣatriya weak, it does not necessarily make him immoral, depending on how he combats this fear and what are its consequences. Yudhiṣṭhira's fear injures not only Karṇa but also Arjuna (as explained earlier), which make Yudhiṣṭhira's request to Śalya immoral. But, from the perspective of cause, it is more of a human emotion that Yudhiṣṭhira cannot control. However, the other two incidents of marked adharma are completely within his control, and he makes a conscious choice to commit them. Therefore, these incidents truly mar his dharmarāja image. Despite this, Yudhiṣṭhira's place in the Mahābhārata and, consequently, in Hindu society, is one of dharmarāja. Is that title deserved? And can Kurukṣetra be considered a dharmakṣetra because of him?

The prophecy of the invisible heavenly voice at Yudhiṣṭhira's birth declares him a greatly virtuous man: '... the best of men and the foremost of all the virtuous. He will be truthful and greatly powerful; he will be the ruler of the earth ... He will be endued with splendor, fame and vows' (*Mbh*1.123.7–8). And true to the prophecy, Yudhiṣṭhira's life is an epitome of virtue and sātvic qualities. He says this about himself: 'My mind and nature ... are naturally bent on virtue ... I act piously not for getting [the] fruits of virtue but for not transgressing the *Vedas* and serving the conduct of the pious' (*Mbh* 3.31.3–4). Hence, for him, all his actions are desireless. In fact, if any character from the dramatis personae of the Mahābhārata can be seen on the path of mokṣa, it is Yudhiṣṭhira. In addition, he is also the one who, through his experience of heaven and hell, conveys the philosophy of the illusion of these states of being. These qualities of virtue give Yudhiṣṭhira such ascetic tējas that if he is moved to anger, he has the power to 'consume men' (*Mbh* 1.80.13) and his spilled blood (except in battle) has the power to destroy kingdoms (*Mbh* 4.68.41 & 63). Thus, Yudhiṣṭhira embodies dharma, ascetic tējas, and the ideological message of the ultimate knowledge of mokṣa. For these reasons, Yudhiṣṭhira certainly has the potential to make the Mahābhārata a dharmakṣetra.

However, Yudhiṣṭhira's ascetic qualities also detract from his kṣatriya dharma. His own brothers and wife also question his varṇadharma and blame him for the consequences that follow such caste transgressions. Bhīma even says to him that it is because of his desire for virtue that they have all sacrificed themselves. He calls Yudhiṣṭhira a weak man: 'Attached with your vow you always cry, "Virtue, virtue". O king, have you from despair become a man of no manliness' (*Mbh* 3.33.13)? He blames Yudhiṣṭhira's virtue for all the miseries that the Pāṇḍavas have to suffer and tells him that none of his brothers approve of his behaviour. Draupadī, too, admonishes him that if 'a man, who though capable of work, does not work, he does not live long, for his life is one of weakness and helplessness' (*Mbh* 3.32.15), and, of course, the action that she wants him to take is to fight the Kauravas. She also considers his lack of action as being uncaring of her misery and tells him, 'O foremost of Bhāratas, you have no anger, since beholding me and your brothers your mind is not pained ... This is the saying of Smṛti that in this world there is not a kṣatriya who is without anger, but in you do I behold today the contradiction' (*Mbh* 1.27.37–38). Thus it is clear that in epic society Yudhiṣṭhira's virtue, while greatly admired for its moral value, is not considered practical; in fact, it is injurious to others. However, despite his un-kṣatriya-like behaviour and inclination, there is no denying that everyone, including his brothers, consider him an epitome of dharma, and because of this, they consider the yuddha to be a dharmayuddha and believe that they deserve victory because, as Vyāsa says, 'yato dharmas tato jayaḥ' (*Mbh* 7.184.66).

Yudhiṣṭhira is so devoted to dharma that he even pursues it in deprivation. For example, he not only fulfils the terms of his exile with grace, but also sustains his rājadharma in the forests by hosting brāhmins and by visiting pilgrimages. Yudhiṣṭhira accepts his exile as part of his fate, harbouring no desire for revenge or bitterness against Duryodhana, as is evident from his demeanour when he facilitates Duryodhana's rescue from the Gandharvas. And, when the time is right, he does prepare for war, but even that he does in the most virtuous manner, allowing for peace before he takes up arms. His words to Saṃjaya and to Kṛṣṇa clearly express his honourable attitude. He tells Saṃjaya that he is not desirous of war and if Duryodhana is willing to give up the kingdom, he would let bygones be bygones (*Mbh* 1.26.3); but he warns him that he is also not afraid of war, because, for him, it will be a virtuous war. Also, he tells Kṛṣṇa that he does not want to destroy his enemies, because it would be cruel, but he cannot give up his claim to Hāstinapura, because it would mean the extinction of his family; hence he is willing to negotiate with the Kauravas and will be satisfied with just five villages (*Mbh* 5.72.16). Of course, Duryodhana refuses to give up even a needle tip's worth of land, because he too believes his claim is righteous. Consequently, on Kṛṣṇa's advice, Yudhiṣṭhira agrees to war, which he believes will be a dharmayuddha because his claims are legitimate.

It is because Yudhiṣṭhira is portrayed as someone with high moral fibre that his adharmas, in contrast, are not only thrown in sharp relief, but they also become the barometer for society's system of ethics. One egregious adharma that he commits is his lie to Drona. The incident occurs in the *Drona Parva* (*Mbh* 7.191.11–13), when Drona, as a Kaurava commander, proves to be a force so powerful that the Pāṇḍavas fear total destruction at his hands; hence, Kṛṣṇa advises the Pāṇḍavas to 'abandon virtue' and take recourse to trickery. He tells the Pāṇḍavas to lie to Drona and inform him that his son Aśvatthāman is dead, so that Drona will give up his weapons as per a vow he has taken. When Yudhiṣṭhira agrees, although with reluctance, Bhīma kills an elephant named Aśvatthāman and tells Drona that Aśvatthāman is dead. Not believing Bhīma, Drona asks Yudhiṣṭhira to confirm this, because he knows that the son of dharma will not lie—'not even for the sake of getting the earth of the three worlds'

(*Mbh* 7.191.43). At this time, Kṛṣṇa influences Yudhiṣṭhira by advising him that if Drona is not killed, he will destroy the Pāṇḍava army; Bhīma too impresses upon him the need to lie. And thus, Yudhiṣṭhira lies, although he also adds the truth, but in a whisper. However, this lie becomes momentous, especially because it is told by a man who is an exemplar of truth. This lie raises many ethical questions about Yudhiṣṭhira's own integrity and the place of untruth in the concept of dharma.

The first point to note is how this lie is treated by the authors of the narrative. Even as Yudhiṣṭhira prepares to utter the lie, the authors, as though through the reflex of favouring the Pāṇḍavas, pass this off as 'the inevitability of fate' (*Mbh* 7.191.54), thus exonerating Yudhiṣṭhira even before he commits the adharma. But it is also made clear that Yudhiṣṭhira is 'afraid' of speaking the lie, although he is 'anxious to obtain victory' (*Mbh* 7.191.54). Therefore, it can be surmised that, even though Yudhiṣṭhira tries to fool himself that he is not openly lying by whispering the word '*kuṃjara*' (elephant) at the end of the lie to counter it, he is fully aware that he lies, or he would not have been afraid to utter it. However, at that time, Drona does not pay attention to his whisper, or he does not hear him, and perhaps, in that moment, Yudhiṣṭhira believes that since he has at least whispered the truth, he has technically been truthful. Or perhaps he believes that if Drona hasn't heard his words, it is not his fault. No matter what Yudhiṣṭhira's inner struggle is, the cosmos considers this a clear act of adharma because, at the moment when Yudhiṣṭhira utters the lie, his chariot that used to ride four fingers above the earth now touches the ground (*Mbh* 7.191.55). There is no question then that Yudhiṣṭhira's integrity as dharmarāja suffers a huge blow.

Yudhiṣṭhira's lie evokes an enquiry into the ethics of truth-telling. Kṛṣṇa and Bhīṣma state many times that truth is alterable in certain circumstances, one of them being the fear of losing an entire fortune (*Mbh* 8.69.31). If Yudhiṣṭhira did not ensure Drona's death, the Pāṇḍavas were sure to lose the war and hence their fortune. Therefore, by deceiving Drona into believing that his son was dead, Yudhiṣṭhira did not violate ethics. However, in this instance, the ethical norm of treating the truth as a malleable value misaligned with Yudhiṣṭhira's personal sense of morality. Why is his alteration of the truth immoral, and why is this breach of morals so significant for society's ethics? There are two main reasons for this. The first reason is that this lie is spoken by a person who is the epitome of truthfulness—a person for whom truth cannot be altered, no matter the circumstances. When a person alters the truth, he engages a whole gamut of adharmas and foregoes virtue on many levels. He alters the truth for selfish reasons, even if those reasons may be to benefit others. Additionally, he hopes to attain a certain goal; therefore, he is engaged in sakāma karma, and his lie, even if it benefits another, is for a desired consequence. It also has the potential of either injuring the one to whom the lie is told, or someone else who may be inadvertently caught in the crossfire of the lie. Moreover, whoever tells a lie is inevitably caught in the moral dilemma of whether or not to tell the lie, and this causes a separation of the self from the inner self, a self mired in pravṛtti, removed from the equanimity of the true self. The lie also creates a double image: something that is and something that isn't. For Yudhiṣṭhira, truthfulness is like a mirror that reflects only what is. It affirms that the nature of truth is such that it creates no false reflection and definitely no contradictions. Something is either truthful or it isn't. Hence, by telling this lie, Yudhiṣṭhira has played himself false by validating Kṛṣṇa's manner of paradoxical truth-telling, which no doubt sustains the trivarga of dharma, artha, and kāma, but it creates a karma *phala* which mars the ascetic self and prevents it from reaching mokṣa.

The other significance of this incident of Yudhiṣṭhira's untruth is that it raises the very important ethical question of what constitutes a lie: words that controvert a fact and/or the intent of the speaker of the words. For example, let's say that Bhīma and Kṛṣṇa had not consulted Yudhiṣṭhira about tricking Drona into believing that his son is dead but had themselves killed the elephant and simply told Yudhiṣṭhira that Aśvatthāman is dead. In that case, when Drona asked Yudhiṣṭhira, he would have been able to say that, yes, Aśvatthāman, Drona's son, is dead, because he would have been ignorant of the truth. His words still would have been false, but not a lie, because he wouldn't have known that the Aśvatthāman that died was an elephant. In this case, would Yudhiṣṭhira still be liable for the falsehood? The answer is, no he would not, because his intent would not have been to deceive Drona, and even if the consequence would have been Drona's death, Yudhiṣṭhira would not be responsible for that injury. So, a lie is only a lie when a person knows that it is a twisting of the facts, and that by telling it, the other person will believe something different than the fact. Hence, it is the intent to lie that makes a person accountable, and the intent can be of any kind: to cheat and hurt the other person, to gain something, even the good of the other, to cover up one's own shortcomings, to avoid unaccountability, etc. In fact, the latter two instances are of self-deception, which is a lie in itself; therefore, any time a person, instead of owning up to an action, calls it fate, he is lying. This makes the very concept of fate an accomplice of adharma, and it renders almost all characters in the Mahābhārata who justify the distressing consequences of their actions as niyati or daivya—from Yudhiṣṭhira to Bhīṣma, from Dhṛtarāṣṭra to Kṛṣṇa—liars.

In Yudhiṣṭhira's lie, while the authors see it as fate, Yudhiṣṭhira himself knows he has lied. And, because the lie is told by dharmarāja himself, it is pivotal; it results in dire consequences that expose the adharma of each character and also creates a whole new vendetta in the war. Even after hearing about his son's supposed death, Drona continues to fight in a frenzy, 'consuming hosts of kṣatriyas' like a 'blazing fire without even a curl of smoke' (*Mbh* 7.193.23–5) and wounds Dhṛṣṭadyumna, his nemesis from an earlier vendetta. But when Bhima grabs his chariot and impresses upon him Yudhiṣṭhira's words that his son is dead, Drona finally lays down his weapons and, through yoga, ascends to heaven. Dhṛṣṭadyumna then seizes the 85-year-old dead man by the hair, drags his body the dust, and then cuts off his head, feeling exultant at the deed (*Mbh* 7.193.62-63). Aśvatthāman reviles the unfairness and adharma of his father's death, especially the humiliation that Dhṛṣṭadyumna heaps upon him. He then swears to destroy the Pāñcālas through any means possible (*Mbh* 7.196.14). But it doesn't end here. Adharma begets more adharma, and the dharma of the very kṣetra is put in jeopardy, because all the actors in this kṣetra become divided on the issue of the righteousness or unrighteousness of Dhṛṣṭadyumna's and Yudhiṣṭhira's actions. Thus, whereas earlier the kṣetra was divided among the Kauravas and the Pāṇḍavas, now the Pāṇḍavas themselves become fragmented, and the blanket illusion of dharma and unity which the Pāṇḍavas have created unravels. After Aśvatthāman decides to use his Nārāyaṇa weapon to avenge his father's death, Arjuna berates Yudhiṣṭhira for his sinful lie and says that his lie has brought ignominy to them forever (*Mbh* 7.197.34). But then Dhṛṣṭadyumna comes on the scene and, verbally attacking Arjuna, claims that his cutting off of Drona's head was his dharma, because it fulfilled his purpose of being born (*Mbh*1.198.30–40). He calls Drona sinful for having abandoned his caste and for taking up kṣatriya duties, and he questions Drona's very purpose of being a guru, accusing him of treating his students inequitably. Then he accuses Arjuna for his own sinful killings—of Bhagadatta and Bhīṣma—which propels Sātyaki into reviling Dhṛṣṭadyumna for killing a brāhmin and berating Arjuna. Dhṛṣṭadyumna then condemns Sātyaki for the unrighteous killing of Bhūriśravas. Basically, each Pāṇḍava warrior exposes the adharma of the other till all are revealed to have sinned. Ultimately, Dhṛṣṭadyumna's final words in this blame-game unmask the true adharmic nature of the kṣetra. He very clearly states how both the Pāṇḍavas and Kauravas have gone against morality, even though both have knowledge of morality. But, he says, morality is mysterious, and all one can do is fight on (*Mbh* 7.199.44–45). In the final analysis then, the kṣetra is revealed as just that—a kṣetra that had the potential of being a dharmakṣetra if the warriors had followed morality, but immorality has polluted the kṣetra, and changed it to an adharmakṣetra.

The other crucial adharma that Yudhiṣṭhira commits is in the dice game. In fact, in this game, he commits not one but multiple adharmas which shatter all the key aspects of dharma in his life—rājadharma, kuladharma, *bhrātadharma*, *patidharma*, and svadharma—and these adharmas, consequently, pollute the whole system. The only way to save society then is to bring about its total destruction through pralaya so that it can be restored to some semblance of dharma in the new yuga. Therefore, perhaps, the only dharma Yudhiṣṭhira inadvertently performs in this game is yugadharma; but it is highly ironic that a dharmarāja would be responsible for bringing dharma to its knees, or, more aptly, to make it hobble on a single hoof.

Aside from expediting Kali Yuga, the dice game itself, on a mythopoeic level, is a symbol of the changing yugas. This fact has already been established from Śiva's dice game in *Sabhā Parva*, in which the dice are named after the four yugas. In addition, some of the key Kauravas are incarnations of the yugas themselves. For example, Śakuni is incarnation of Dvāpara and Duryodhana himself represents Kali. However, it is interesting to note that in the play between Śakuni and Yudhiṣṭhira, Śakuni throws the best dice—Kṛta, which is the golden age, when dharma is at its zenith, and Yudhiṣṭhira's throws are Kali. Admittedly, Śakuni's play is a result of his cheating, but the yuga names of dice also seem to indicate that it is Yudhiṣṭhira who reduces dharma, bringing Kali Yuga closer with each of his throws.

However, no matter the yuga, dicing is clearly a condemnable activity in all ages. As Vidura says to Dhṛtarāṣṭra, 'Gambling is the root of dissensions. It brings about disunion. Its consequences are frightful' (*Mbh* 1.63.1). Therefore, trying to justify Yudhiṣṭhira's involvement in this activity is like trying to prove the innocence of a murderer who has been caught in the act. The danger of dicing is recognized numerous times in the epic and the Purāṇas. For example, Nala is destroyed by the dice which Kali has possessed (*Mbh* 3.59.1–18). In Virāṭa's court, Yudhiṣṭhira himself as Kaṇka associates gambling 'with many evils' (*Mbh* 4.68.26). By Parikṣit's time, when Kali Yuga has already set in, dicing is considered equivalent to the demon Kali who injures both dharma and the earth (*BP* 1.171.45). In addition, at this liminal time between yugas, when Kṛṣṇa has incarnated to restore the dwindling dharma, even he condemns dicing. When he meets the Pāṇḍavas in exile, he tells them that he considers gambling the most contaminating of desires, and he calls it the most evil out of the four evils of women, hunting, drinking, and gambling. He wishes he had been present at the game, because he would have told Dhṛtarāṣṭra to stop his sons from gambling (*Mbh* 3.13.3). Of course, Kṛṣṇa heaps blame on the Kauravas, as do most Hindus and many scholars, because Yudhiṣṭhira's vice is passed off as (1) his intoxication; hence he has no control, and (2) his oath of never refusing a challenge.

It is clear that Yudhiṣṭhira is intoxicated, and there is no doubt that he is addicted to gambling, so control of senses is a key factor in dharma, and addiction is an extreme form of loss of control. So, how is it that Yudhiṣṭhira, a strict adherent of virtue, is not able to control his addiction? It can be argued that he does not know he is addicted, but this argument does not ring true because that would steep Yudhiṣṭhira in the ignorance of a deep tamasic nature; the first step to realization is awareness of one's shortcomings or adharmic inclinations. And, since Yudhiṣṭhira's character is of a stalwart in ascetic self-analysis, there is no doubt that he knows about his addiction. In that case, why does he allow himself the temptation of the game when it is a known fact that the best way for an addict to avoid indulging in his addiction is to stay away from temptation? But then, of course, there is the question of his oath, which will be discussed below. In this particular argument about his addiction, the question must also be raised: What about the inaction of Yudhiṣṭhira's well-wishers? Why don't they break him away from this addiction? Even in modern times of extreme indulgences and addictions, friends and well-wishers who, without having any personal or material stake in the well-being of their addicted friend, consider it their responsibility to stage an intervention to save their friends from destructive behaviour. It seems that all of Yudhiṣṭhira's well-wishers, like Bhīṣma and Vidura, are really false friends, since they watch him suffer in his addiction without doing or saying a thing. Even Vidura acknowledges that Ajātaśatru (Yudhiṣṭhira) is intoxicated with dice (*Mbh* 2.63.8). Not only is it ironic that he refers to him as Ajātaśatru here, which means 'having no enemy' when clearly dicing is his enemy, but, also, instead of admonishing Yudhiṣṭhira, Vidura castigates Duryodhana repeatedly for indulging in the game, calling him a 'wicked man'. He does not, however, say a word to stop Yudhiṣṭhira, not even when he stakes Draupadī.

There *is* one person who continuously warns Yudhiṣṭhira about the evil of indulging in his addiction, and that person, quite surprisingly, is Śakuni. Śakuni warns Yudhiṣṭhira that he is intoxicated and alerts him immediately after he has his first big loss—Nakula and Sahadeva. Śakuni says, 'O king, one who is intoxicated falls into a pit and remains there, being deprived of his power of motion. O best of the Bhārata race ... know that gamesters in the excitement of play utter such ravings as they would never do in their waking moments or in their dreams' (*Mbh* 2.65.19-20). Yet, Yudhiṣṭhira, in his subsequent moves, stakes Arjuna, Bhīma, himself, and then Draupadī.

By losing his brothers, Yudhiṣṭhira's loses his dharma as an elder brother, but there is the question of the dharma of the other Pāṇḍavas themselves in relation to Yudhiṣṭhira's addiction. Since intoxication or addiction, even in epic times, was recognized as addling the brain, then how is it that the other Pāṇḍavas continue to follow their dharma to their elder brother, knowing that it is not their elder brother who plays but a man under the influence of an addiction? Is dharma to be considered blind—a blind observation of duty without any free will or rationality? This negates the very meaning of dharma which necessitates the doer to *recognize* the singular righteousness of the act before it is performed. Thus the fact that the Pāṇḍavas abandon their wife in their mute acceptance of their brother's addiction is clearly a total lack of dharma.

The other justification that is often given for Yudhiṣṭhira's dice playing is that he is under oath to never refuse a challenge; hence he cannot refuse to play in the dice game, even though he knows that it is rigged and that Śakuni will cheat. Śakuni tells him that the purpose of a game is to win by any means possible (*Mbh* 2.59.6), and Yudhiṣṭhira himself specifically acknowledges this. His exchange with Vidura before the game proves that he is quite aware what nature of dyūta will occur in the game: Vidura tells him 'O king, you will see there all those gamblers, those cheats ... and I have come here [to warn you] about this', and Yudhiṣṭhira responds, 'It appears that some of the most desperate and terrible gamblers who always depend on deceit are present there' (*Mbh* 2.58: 9 &14). Yet, he decides to play, all because of his oath. Does this mean that thanks to his vow to never refuse a challenge he must accept and perpetrate evil action? Doesn't this negate his superior air of always favouring virtue? However, a true ascetic is one who remains undeterred and equanimous in both good and evil situations, and this, indeed, is a noble comment on Yudhiṣṭhira's character, but the question is, does it apply to Yudhiṣṭhira in this instance? Can he remain undeterred and equanimous when he knows that he is addicted to dicing? The dice game and its consequences are evidence that he cannot, and the events subsequent to the dice game prove the falsity of his words and nobility.

The fiasco of Yudhiṣṭhira's conduct continues after losing the first game, when he accepts the challenge of the second game knowing full well that this too will be rigged, and sits down to play 'from shame and sense of his kṣatriya duty' (*Mbh* 2.76.18). How strange it is that the words 'shame' and 'kṣatriya duty' be combined in this sentence and juxtaposed. Is Yudhiṣṭhira ashamed because he is aware that he will lose but he cannot refuse a challenge, or is he aware of his addiction and is ashamed of it? In the former case, where is the pride in the kṣetra of kṣatriyas where loss and victory are irrelevant and only the yuddha is important; and in the latter case, his oath itself is adharmic because it leaves open the potentiality of temptation and of steeping him in shame. Yudhiṣṭhira behaves as though he has no choice—that it is his duty to accept the challenge. But apparently there is a choice, otherwise the people present in the court would not have continued to say that someone in the court should warn him of the danger of the second dice game. They think he has not understood the implications (*Mbh* 2.76.14). If his vow was unbreakable, they would have uttered words of sympathy for Yudhiṣṭhira for having no choice but to play. But the truth is Yudhiṣṭhira has a choice. He has a choice to break his vow or find some way around it, as Arjuna does in the *Karṇa Parva* to help him circumvent his oath that impels him to kill his elder brother. Similarly, Yudhiṣṭhira also has a choice to weigh the dharma of an oath against the dharma of not allowing himself to fall into temptation, and that too a temptation that could destroy not just himself but also his family, his kingdom, and his subjects. This is especially significant, because while the latter choice of preventing the destruction would have been unselfish and saved many, his refusal to break the vow assures pain and suffering for many. It also seems nothing more than a way to massage his own ego: he is so kingly that he will not refuse a challenge. Or perhaps his choice to keep the vow is a lie of self-deception, a disguise for his addiction that justifies his gambling.

In actuality, Yudhiṣṭhira *is* in control in the dice game and he *does* make a choice, and that choice is to play and to continue playing. He chooses to gamble, not so much because he must keep his oath, but because he has another ulterior motive; a motive he has consciously thought out. He reveals this himself in the *Vana Parva* when he tells Bhīma: 'I was engaged to play dice with the desire of snatching from Dhṛtarāṣṭra's son his kingdom with his sovereignty' (*Mbh* 3.34.3). In addition, he admits to losing control when his motive was thwarted: 'Seeing the dice obedient to the wishes of Śakuni in Abuja and Yuma [odds and even], I could have controlled my mind, but anger drives off a person's patience' (*Mbh* 3.34.5). What Yudhiṣṭhira admits to is that his very motive to play the game was immoral, and that during the dice game he not only lost his sense of dharma, but he knowingly made choices that were adharmic.

Whatever it is that impels Yudhiṣṭhira to play the dice game, the fact is his actions injure his brothers and his wife grievously. Everything that follows the dice game certainly attests to this, but what makes Yudhiṣṭhira's culpability clear is Kṛṣṇa's words at the end of the war when the Pāṇḍavas find Duryodhana in Dvaipāyana Lake and Yudhiṣṭhira challenges him to accept one last win-or-lose battle. Yudhiṣṭhira once again gambles with the Pāṇḍavas' lives and fortune by giving Duryodhana a choice of adversary in single combat. At this time, Kṛṣṇa, worried that Duryodhana may win, tells Arjuna that Yudhiṣṭhira was wholly to blame for the dice game, for he says, 'It is through the fault of king Yudhiṣṭhira alone that danger has once more befallen us' (*Mbh* 9.58.10). The key words here are 'once more'—that danger has fallen upon the Pāṇḍavas again through Yudhiṣṭhira's addiction to the game of chance.

In Yudhiṣṭhira's culpability, the one to suffer the greatest injury is Draupadī. She is also the one who poses a question that not only mocks her husband's relationship with her, but also puts to shame all those keepers of dharma who claim the kṣetra to be a dharmakṣetra. In addition, Draupadī's question casts real doubt on the charges of evil behaviour that are heaped on the Kauravas, who are ultimately and forever blamed for her humiliation. Her question at being staked by Yudhiṣṭhira is: 'Whose Lord was [Yudhiṣṭhira] at the time when he lost me in play? Did he lose himself first or me?' (*Mbh* 2.67.10). By asking this question, Draupadī shows the farce of the keepers of dharma and also of the dharmakṣetra. She says to the assembly of noble Kurus, 'All the Kurus in this assembly look silently on this act which transgresses the shore of the Kuru morality; the morality of the Bhāratas has certainly been destroyed and the usage of those conversant with the kṣatriya practices have surely disappeared' (*Mbh* 2.67.40). And all Bhīṣma can say to this is, 'I am unable to decide properly the point put forward by you. The ways of morality are subtle' (*Mbh* 2.67.47). Furthermore, instead of condemning Yudhiṣṭhira, Bhīṣma reiterates that Yudhiṣṭhira will abandon all the wealth of the world but not morality (*Mbh* 2.67.48). The irony of this statement is inescapable, because not only has Yudhiṣṭhira lost all the wealth of the world but he has also done so with extreme immorality, the gravest of which is expressed in Draupadī's question.

Hiltebeitel (2001: 244) suggests that when Yudhiṣṭhira orders Draupadī to 'come before [her] father-in-law in soiled clothes, it is "preposterous marital cruelty."' In fact, this is not just marital cruelty; it is a thorough demeaning of women and the very institution of marriage. Moreover, what Yudhiṣṭhira says prior to staking Draupadī is more damaging to her and, by extension, all women, than even this cruel order. Before staking her, Yudhiṣṭhira describes Draupadī's womanly attributes in front of an assembly full of males, half of whom are fathers and grandfathers and the other half who look upon her lecherously. Yudhiṣṭhira describes Draupadī as a woman 'who is neither short nor tall, neither lean nor corpulent, who possesses blue curly hair, and eyes like the leaves of autumn lotus, and fragrance like that of the lily, who is like Śrī herself in symmetry and grace ... Whose face when covered with sweat looks like the lotus or the wasp, who possesses long flowing hair, red lips, and body without down ... The slender-waisted Draupadī' (*Mbh* 2.65.33–9). Whatever Yudhiṣṭhira's intention may have been in extolling his wife's qualities at this time, the sensual description sounds like that of a pimp describing a whore to a customer, and this enflames the Kauravas to react the way they do: Karṇa calls Draupadī a whore and Duryodhana orders her to be disrobed.

Draupadī's prostitution begins with her birth on earth, when Viṣṇu 'hires' her as Śrī to the five Indras so that they can redeem themselves. Four of these Indras had committed the sin of arrogance, and the sin of the fifth—the Indra of the current eon—was his killing of Vṛtra, which cost him to lose his tējas, *balam, vīryam*, and *rūpam*. It is these losses of the fifth Indra that caused the birth of the Pāṇḍavas and Śrī is sent to Indra/Pāṇḍavas to restore his/their dharma. Hiltebeitel (1991: 221) points out that Śrī is Earth, which is not just land, but also vegetation, wealth, and prosperity; in other words, Śrī is everything that will restore the dhārmic order and well-being of society. In this birth of Draupadī's, Hiltebeitel (1991: 225) gives Kṛṣṇa the role of Gālava, the ṛṣi who hires Mādhavī's womb out to gain the horses he has to gather for his gurudakṣiṇā. The only difference between Mādhavī and Draupadī's situation is that Draupadī's further prostitution in the dice game robs the Pāṇḍavas of their prosperity. Perhaps Mādhavī is able to restore royalty because she accepts her prostitution mutely, whereas Draupadī is vociferous in her objection. But does this mean the authors of the Mahābhārata are suggesting that if women consent to their oppression by men, society can continue to function smoothly, but if women begin to stand up for their rights, society will be thrown into chaos? Or perhaps the reason Mādhavī is able to restore royalty but Draupadī isn't is that while Gālava is seemingly unaware of the immorality of his action, the Pāṇḍavas are fully aware of the utter humiliation to which they have subjected Draupadī.[8]

Draupadī is played like a puppet or a doll, and she is wagered like property, her bodily attributes described as one would a piece of property (Hiltebeitel 2001: 263). Hiltebeitel (2001: 263) considers this an indication of the problematic role of women in a broader perspective: 'A Sāṃkhya problematic underlies the *Mahābhārata* portrayals of heroines ... the heroine-goddess represents prakṛti as unconscious matter, blind ignorance given to "obstinacy"; matter that unknowingly yet somehow inerrantly works on behalf of puruṣa ...through "blind initiatives"; heroines whose ignorance is unknowing, in particular about dharma'. This ignorance may be true of some other heroines; the fact is that *this* heroine (Draupadī) is fully knowledgeable of her dharma status. Moreover, not only is her defiance of prevalent practices open and obvious, it also reverses the ignorance, attributing it to the males instead. It is as though she takes on the evolvement of all womanhood. Hiltebeitel (2001: 242) says that Draupadī telling the Sūta to ask this question in court makes her 'clever', making it clear to the readers that this is a question worthy of being discussed in a sabhā—a question that must be decided by the highly respected members of the

[8] Draupadī's disrobing, especially during her menstruation, is considered so heinous in certain communities that it has resulted in many narrative changes in the Mahābhārata tradition. For example, Mahābhārata drama festivals in some places in South India omit the whole disrobing scene from the dice game (Hiltebeitel 2001: 251). In his book, *The Cult of Draupadī*, Hiltebeitel suggests that later sectarian interpretations even omit Kṛṣṇa's direct intervention in this scene to 'rescue *him* from "textual contact" with her impure single garment' (Hiltebeitel 2001: 251). T.S. Rukmini also describes the *therukoothu* (street play in Tamil tradition) *Vastrāpaharaṇa* in which, when the moment of Draupadī's disrobing is to begin, there is a dramatic pause, and the *kattiyakaran* (chorus) 'does *arati* to the character playing Draupadī and the entire troupe prays to be forgiven for indulging in this despicable act' (Rukmini 1993: 189).

assembly. Therefore, this question that Draupadī asks in the assembly does not just pertain to Draupadī, but transforms the issue of mistreatment of women from being a private matter within a family to the legality of a societal question.

It is clear from the responses of the males in the assembly hall that either they are ignorant of this issue of women's mistreatment or they are pretending ignorance. What is more likely is that they are fully aware but not willing to change the status quo. Hence, none of the elders have an answer to Draupadī's question, and Bhīṣma evades the issue by calling it a subtlety of dharma, which is clearly indicates that he is aware of the dharma violations that have occurred but is not willing to admit it. Only Bhīma acknowledges the fact that Yudhiṣṭhira has done wrong, and he threatens to burn his hands (*Mbh* 2.68.5). But Bhīma does not mean to end the mistreatment of all women, only that of his beloved wife. And Arjuna appears even more 'ignorant' because he admonishes Bhīma and tells him that it is not virtuous to oppose an older brother (*Mbh* 2.68.7); he thus completely disregards not just the plight of women but also of the wife he has sworn by Vedic rights to protect and cherish. Thus, even if it is accepted that Arjuna is ignorant of the former, in no way can he be considered ignorant of the latter. And since, in this incident, the two issues are interrelated, his flagrant disregard of his patidharma translates into his adharma towards all women and their status in society.

There is one person in the assembly who does attempt to answer Draupadī's question, and he appeals to the elders to consider what he has to say. This person is Vikarṇa, a younger brother of Duryodhana. Scholars like Hiltebeitel and Shah believe that Vikarṇa only gives a weak answer. Citing Shah, Hiltebeitel (2001: 248) says his 'defence does not turn out to be a defence at all but a mere debate on technicalities'. However, Vikarṇa's arguments are not weak. Admittedly, they do not redeem the status of womankind, but they do condemn the males who indulge in vices that can result in the mistreatment of women. Vikarṇa points out: 'It has been said that hunting, drinking, gambling, and enjoying women are the four vices of the kings. The man who is addicted to those vices lives by forsaking virtue. People do not consider the acts done by a person who is thus improperly engaged as of any authority' (*Mbh* 2.68.20–2). Very clearly Yudhiṣṭhira has indulged in just such a vice; hence, he has not only lost his authority as king and as dharmarāja, he has also abandoned the dharma that Draupadī has evoked. Vikarṇa also makes the significant point that Draupadī is the common wife of all five Pāṇḍavas; hence she is not only Yudhiṣṭhira's possession but also belongs to the other four brothers. Most importantly, Vikarṇa states what everyone is ignoring: that Yudhiṣṭhira first lost himself. Hence, Vikarṇa declares that Draupadī is not won (*Mbh* 2.68.23–4). However, Vikarṇa is but a youth and of no consequence and no one pays much attention to his words.

On the other hand, the Kauravas not only seem to have more knowledge of the issue of women but also give Draupadī's question due consideration, thus giving her a respect that the elders and her husbands fail to give. But perhaps Duryodhana does so only to twist the situation to his advantage. He tells Draupadī that he will give Yudhiṣṭhira another chance to answer the question; he even promises Draupadī that if the four younger Pāṇḍavas, 'for [her] sake declare in the midst of these most noble men (present here) that Yudhiṣṭhira is not their lord and that he is a liar; [she] will be freed from slavery' (*Mbh* 2.70.4–5). Ironically, and perhaps unwittingly, by his words, Duryodhana gives Draupadī the same status as the other Pāṇḍavas—he regards both Draupadī and the four remaining Pāṇḍavas as Yudhiṣṭhira's property, a status that Yudhiṣṭhira himself has reduced them to by staking them. Duryodhana even gives Yudhiṣṭhira a chance to redeem himself and admit that he was wrong in playing his brothers and his wife as though they were property; but Yudhiṣṭhira remains silent. Is it his ego that prevents him or his blindness to his own fault, or does he, as king and older brother, really see everyone else as his property? Whatever the case may be, the fact is that in an instant, Yudhiṣṭhira has decimated all his roles—his rājadharma, his bhrātadharma, his patidharma, and, most importantly, his role as dharmarāja.

Ultimately, when no one else answers Draupadī's question, the cosmos intervenes as though in frustrated wrath at the rupture of dharma, and bad omens occur. Suddenly, finding themselves cornered, the elders look for a scapegoat and, as always, point fingers at the most obvious culprit—Duryodhana—thus once again using the blanket of self-deception to cover up all adharmas. They blame Duryodhana for bringing the destruction of the Kurus closer by holding the dice game, by instigating Śakunī's cheating, and by humiliating Draupadī. And Dhṛtarāṣṭra, afraid of the omens and guilt-ridden at his own inaction, grants Draupadī three boons; she uses two of these to get Yudhiṣṭhira and then the other four of her husbands released. But she refuses the third boon, saying that according to ordinance a kṣatriya woman may ask only two boons, and that she does not deserve a third boon because 'covetousness destroys virtue' (*Mbh* 2.71.35–6). S.M. Kulkarni (1989: 155) suggests that by asking only for the release of her husbands, Draupadī herself answers her question. Because she does not consider herself enslaved, she does not need to ask for her freedom. And everyone, even Duryodhana, accepts this resolution.

The fact is that while Duryodhana and his cohorts can certainly be blamed for rigging the dice game and for humiliating Draupadī, they cannot be blamed for Draupadī being played as a stake. That is entirely Yudhiṣṭhira's own doing. He voluntarily, and without urging, begins to first stake his brothers and then, with just a tiny nudge from Śakuni, who actually suggests that Draupadī may help Yudhiṣṭhira win back his whole wealth, Yudhiṣṭhira places Draupadī in the game. Hence, Draupadī is victimized not just by Duryodhana but also by Yudhiṣṭhira and her other husbands.

Surprisingly, the man who salvages Draupadī's respect, and in consequence all of womanhood, is Karṇa. It is he who raises Draupadī to the status of the one who provides salvation—not just to the Pāṇḍavas but also to the Kauravas. After Draupadī frees her husbands through Dhṛtarāṣṭra's boons, Karṇa says,

> We have not heard of such an act performed by any women who are noted in this world for their beauty. When the sons of Pāṇḍu and Dhṛtarāṣṭra were excited with anger, this Kṛṣṇā, the daughter of Drupada, became their salvation. The sons of Pāṇḍu were sinking

boat-less in an ocean of distress, this Pāñcālī, becoming a boat to them, brought them safely to the shore. (*Mbh* 2.72: 1–3)

Once this question about the rights of women is posed and left unresolved, the narrative moves on as before, as though it was never asked. Even Draupadī resumes her conventional role of a wife who sees no fault in her husbands. She, too, blames Duryodhana and Śakuni, and affirms her belief that 'though Yudhiṣṭhira does not possess any skill in dice, yet he was made to play with skilful, wicked deceitful and desperate gamblers. How then can he [Yudhiṣṭhira] be said to have staked voluntarily' (*Mbh* 2.67.40). However, what Draupadī does not forget is her abandonment by her husbands, which she continues to question. Crying before Kṛṣṇa, she shames the prowess of Bhīma and Arjuna by accusing them of not protecting her when she needed protection. She also cites śāstras:

> [It] is the eternal course of morality—a husband should protect his wife because by protecting his wife a man protects his offspring and by protecting the offspring, he protects himself. His own self is begotten on his wife and therefore the wife is called Jaya. Similarly a wife should also protect her husband remembering that he would take his birth in her womb. (*Mbh* 3.12.68–70)

But even Kṛṣṇa has no answer for Draupadī's distress, just as no one had an answer for her question in the dice game.

Scholars believe that Draupadī's question is never really answered except, perhaps, by Vikarṇa. In actuality, Yudhiṣṭhira *does* answer Draupadī's question, though not at the dice game, but later, at the end of the war. This is when Duryodhana is dying and he offers Yudhiṣṭhira the kingdom. At that time, Yudhiṣṭhira tells Duryodhana that he will not accept the earth from Duryodhana as a gift. He says, 'You are not now lord of the Earth. Why then do you wish to make a gift of that over which you have no right (*Mbh* 9.31.51)?' Considering that Draupadī is Śrī, Yudhiṣṭhira has just implicated himself. He staked his 'Earth'—Draupadī—when he had no right over her. He had lost himself in the dice game before he staked her; therefore he was not then 'Lord of the Earth' (Draupadī) at the time of the dice game. On, the other hand, Duryodhana might have lost the war, but he is still king. At the time he offers the kingdom to Yudhiṣṭhira, he has not yet given up the kingdom; hence, he still has a right over *his* earth. In addition, while Duryodhana at least sees Earth/Śrī as a gift to 'give away', Yudhiṣṭhira saw Earth/Draupadī only as a stake to be played in a dice game. Who, then, does the feminine aspect of the kṣetra more injustice? In addition, since according to *Manu Smṛti*, women are the source of three out of the four puruṣārthas (dharma, artha and kāma) and the Pāṇḍavas and Kauravas have both violated this 'source' with so much adharma, what dharma remains in this kṣetra?

Hence, in the Mahābhārata, Dharmavīra himself ruptures two of the most significant functions of dharma: sustenance of society through the preservation of the feminine principle and sanctity of trust through the observance of truth. Sadly, society was never able to repair these ruptures, perhaps, because tradition never really acknowledged the damage.

HOW KṚṢṆA DEFINES THE KṢETRA

The character who can be considered truly capable of delineating the kṣetra as a dharmakṣetra is Kṛṣṇa, because the sole reason for his incarnation is to restore dharma:

> *yadā yadā hi dharmasya glānir bhavati bhārata*
> *abhyutthānam adharmasya tadātmānaṃ sṛjāmy aham*
> [Whenever, O Bhārata, virtue languishes and sin predominates, I create myself.] (*Mbh* 6.28:7)

Hence, it is Kṛṣṇa who must ensure that the opposing sides on the kṣetra are clearly defined as dharma and adharma according to their lakṣaṇa, because it is he who ensures that victory is on the side that adheres to dharma. That is how Kṛṣṇa, as the preserver of dharma, becomes equivalent to dharma, and hence to victory: 'Yataḥ kṛṣṇas tato jayaḥ'—where there is Kṛṣṇa, there is victory (*Mbh* 5.68.9). But

Kṛṣṇa plays two roles in the Mahābhārata: he is a mortal, the Yādava chief, Vāsudeva Kṛṣṇa, cousin of the Pāṇḍavas, and brother-in-law to Arjuna; and he is the eternal supreme being, Nārāyaṇa, the *saguṇa* brāhman of Vaiṣṇavism, the mythic reincarnation of Viṣṇu. In the first role, he is a moral agent, accountable for his dharma like any mortal, in his second role, especially that of Viṣṇu's reincarnation, he himself is the preserver of dharma. However, because he slips in and out of both roles, his character is full of ambiguities, and because he uses both roles to suit his purpose, he often fails dharma in both.[9]

As a mortal, Kṛṣṇa is subject to human frailties and worldly bindings, such as karma, puruṣkāra, niyati, daivya, and kāla; and in this role, he displays all the qualities of a mortal with human inclinations to adharma and moral dilemmas. Therefore, in this role, he cannot be seen as equivalent to dharma. In fact, in this role, he not only violates moral and ethical codes, but he also uses the excuse of his divinity to justify his mortal behaviour, thus controverting even his role as preserver or restorer of dharma. As the supreme being, he is the guardian of both *śāśvata dharma* and transient dharmas of *deśa* and *kāla*; but in this role, in the paradigm of supreme divines, he is unbelievable, because this role would either put him beyond all temporal limitations of dharma or invest him with lakṣaṇa of absolute dharma that is expected of a supreme divine in a theocracy. Instead, what we see is an archetype of a divine, glossing over situations where dharma seems to be ambiguous or in jeopardy. Perhaps the reason for this ambiguity is that at the time of the Mahābhārata, Kṛṣṇa as a supreme being had not quite come into his own. V.S. Sukthankar (1998: 67) says that although Kṛṣṇa as a supreme being underlies everything in the Mahābhārata, the Kṛṣṇa element is only incidental.

The reason why the Kṛṣṇa element in the epic is difficult to categorize is because Kṛṣṇa's history is quite unknown. He may have

[9] The dharma referenced here is of puruṣārtha and varṇa and does not include the dharma of ultimate realization that Kṛṣṇa teaches Arjuna in the Gītā.

been a Yādava chieftain who was elevated to divine status through legend and folklore to bring together divergent communities. Thapar (2004: 147 & 150) suggests that Kṛṣṇa may have belonged to a pre-Aryan tribe or at least to a *gaṇasangha*, much like the gaṇasanghas of Mahāvīra and Gautama. The rise of Kṛṣṇa was probably heterogeneous, just like Buddhism, but it was also, perhaps, the brāhmin answer to reclaim its identity against heterodoxies like Buddhism and Jainism. Bhattacharji (2000: 301–6) suggests that the 'cultic' and 'mythological' hostility between Indra and Kṛṣṇa may have been the result of an aboriginal sect who worshipped Kṛṣṇa, and there may have been an actual contest between the Aryans and a tribe who had a leader named Kṛṣṇa. It is also possible then that the victory of this tribal leader against the all-powerful Aryans gave Kṛṣṇa the validity he needed to rise to the forefront and claim a three-dimensional substance, such as what we see peripherally in the Mahābhārata but fully realized as a solar hero in the Harivaṃśa. And, as Kosambi (1965: 117) points out, helping him along were his supposed exploits of marrying 16,108 wives, some of whom were apsarās and others women of local cults, thus allowing inclusion and spread. Kṛṣṇa's close association with fertility was most important for his rise and also spread of the Kṛṣṇa cult, because fertility pertained to both factions—Aryan and indigenous.

Kṛṣṇa himself postulates as a theistic divine with a history of theism that goes back to the Vedas, pervading all time as the primary cause:

> pitāhmāh asya jagato mātā dhātā pitāmahaḥ
> vedyaṃ pavitram oṃkāra ṛk sāma yajur eva ca
> [I am the father of this universe, the mother, the support and the grandsire.
> I am the object of knowledge, the purifier, and the syllable om. I am also the *Ṛg*, the *Sāma* and the *Yajur Vedas*.] (*BG* 9.17)

However, there is no evidence of Kṛṣṇa's divinity in the Vedas. The only mention of a Kṛṣṇa in Vedic literatures is in *Chāndogya Upaniṣad*—a son of Devaki, a pupil of Ghora Angiras, initiated to the 'secret doctrine' of 'man as sacrifice' by his guru (*CU* 3.17.6, quoted in Gupta: 1991–2008, 5. 4, 279–280). Admittedly, Kṛṣṇa assumes the persona of Viṣṇu, the god who is present in the Vedas, but even Viṣṇu is only a minor god in the *Ṛg Veda*, with just five hymns devoted to him. He is also not very 'godly' in his attributes. The only great feat that raises his status is his three wide strides that 'measure the earthly regions' and within which 'all living creatures have their habitation' (*RV* 1.155.1–2). These Vedic hymns do suggest his overlordship over all creatures, but then, in the henotheistic nature of Vedic hymns, so do the hymns devoted to most other Vedic gods. Perhaps Viṣṇu's lack was his greatest advantage, because, unlike gods like Indra who already had full-fledged histories and backgrounds, Viṣṇu could be moulded to suit the purpose of the new order. However, it is not at all clear how the transformation from Viṣṇu to Kṛṣṇa occurred.

Whatever his historical background may have been, Kṛṣṇa was certainly a phenomenon in post-epic society, probably beginning as legend and folklore, then burgeoning into fully fledged myth and divinity, and finally as an incarnation of Viṣṇu, morphing into the supreme divine. Sukthankar (1998: 67) says, 'We must ... be content with taking Śrī Kṛṣṇa to be a person of the same order of reality as the other heroes of the epic ... Just as the [Pāṇḍavas and Kauravas] are uniformly treated as incarnations of minor gods and anti-gods of the Hindu pantheon, so Śrī Kṛṣṇa is also consistently treated as the incarnation of the Supreme Being'. However, the idea of an incarnating supreme divine lacks credence, because, as Matilal (2007: 413) says, there is no precedence to authenticate the lakṣaṇa of such a divine. The concept of the infinite supreme god is so abstract that it could not have been born in the material, henotheistic world of the Vedas. Hence, not only do Viṣṇu and Kṛṣṇa lack qualities that would qualify them as supreme in a theocracy that commissions or restores standards in society, but also the very idea of a theocracy was foreign in Hindu society (Matilal 2007: 413). If this society was founded under the aegis of a supreme god, why would he have been absent in the Vedas? If he was the infinite, surely he would have existed from the beginning of time and eulogized in the Vedas. In actuality, this concept of a supreme being was a new phenomenon—an *idea* that caught on, but one that was still in its formative stages in the epic. Therefore, in the Mahābhārata, when Kṛṣṇa does assume his supreme divine form, it is simply a static, archetypal form with no demonstrable lakṣaṇa; it is mainly to establish a sectarian scheme, which, as explained earlier, is neither dhārmic nor adharmic; it is simply the call of a new order. Hence, Kṛṣṇa's divinity is not exemplary of dharma and goodness; it is, at the very most, a leap of faith which negates a knowledge-based realization of the kṣetra as being a dharmakṣetra. When he is in dynamic form, it is mostly to give credence to his own or the Pāṇḍavas' intent or actions, some of which are so duplicitous that, without the mantle of divinity, they would cause society's ethical structure to crumble.

A key incident which is representative of Kṛṣṇa's ambiguity of roles is his Embassy to the Kaurava court to negotiate peace prior to the war. In this incident, Kṛṣṇa's surface role seems to be of a mortal—that of adviser to the Kauravas and Pāṇḍavas and of Yudhiṣṭhira's envoy of peace. However, because at the end of this incident Kṛṣṇa reveals a theophany, he must also be perceived as a divine reincarnate whose purpose it is to secure dharma. Both roles require him to make an honest bid for peace, because war can only result in the pain and suffering of many, a breakdown of societal values, and a devastation of families. Therefore, if Duryodhana is on the path of adharma, it is Kṛṣṇa's duty as adviser and ambassador of peace and as a dharma divine to make a genuine effort to convert him to goodness and dharma, so that he realizes the adharmic consequences of war. And if, on the other hand, Kṛṣṇa sees Duryodhana as unconvertible to dharma and as an embodiment of evil, hindering the victory of dharma, it is his duty to destroy Duryodhana so that war can be prevented. But Kṛṣṇa does neither; instead, he adds fuel to Duryodhana's desire for war. Why, then, this pretense of negotiation for peace? And it certainly appears to be pretense, because even before Kṛṣṇa leaves on the Embassy, he defines Hāstinapura as the enemy camp, where peace is not possible. This is, ironically, made more so by Kṛṣṇa's own prior actions as the chieftain of the Yādavas. He has made enemies of kings by taking their wealth, and those kings have now joined the Kauravas in support and solidarity against Kṛṣṇa. This is a fact that Vidura confirms (*Mbh* 5.92.25). Hence, even as Kṛṣṇa leaves for the embassy, he is convinced that peace is unattainable. He tells Yudhiṣṭhira that 'whatever is capable of being done by me by speech or by deed, O Pāṇḍava, shall be done by me, but do not expect peace with the enemy' (*Mbh* 5.79.18).

The Kauravas, too, are aware of the hypocrisy of the peace negotiations. However, Dhṛtarāṣṭra, who is aware of Kṛṣṇa's growing popularity as a divine, decides to honour Kṛṣṇa with wealth, which Vidura believes to be a bribe to win him over and to possibly draw him away from the Pāṇḍavas. If Kṛṣṇa's divinity were an accepted fact, would Vidura, who is an ardent Pāṇḍava supporter, attribute to Kṛṣṇa the human evil of being tempted by a bribe? Duryodhana too acknowledges Kṛṣṇa's possible divinity, but he shuns the hypocrisy of honouring him, because, as he says: 'He [Kṛṣṇa] will think on receiving our worship ... that we are honoring him out of fear' (*Mbh* 5.88.3). Duryodhana also believes that nothing should be given to him, because it will not turn war into peace (*Mbh* 5.88.6). However, since Kṛṣṇa is also a relative and a guest, Duryodhana is happy to offer him hospitality in that role, and Kṛṣṇa refuses Duryodhana's hospitality on this human basis, because, as he says, 'One should eat others' food when there is love [between them] or again it should be taken when one is in distress. O king, neither do you please me, nor am I in distress' (*Mbh* 5.91.25). Here, not only are Kṛṣṇa and Duryodhana dealing on a purely human level, but also this indifference that Kṛṣṇa displays hardly inspires trust—a necessary quality for successful negotiations. To make matters worse, he openly declares his bias, claiming allegiance to the Pāṇḍavas by making statements such as: 'He who bears them [Pāṇḍavas] malice bears me malice ... know that I am merged with the Pāṇḍavas' (*Mbh* 5.91.28). Clearly Kṛṣṇa belies his role as impartial adviser and as dharma divine, and Duryodhana points this out to him, telling him that since he is related to both the Pāṇḍavas and the Kauravas, he should be impartial in his treatment of both.

The purpose of the Embassy is to give the opposing side the option to choose peace and, to give Kṛṣṇa credit as a human ambassador, he does make an occasional attempt to fulfil it. He does talk about peace so that the world can be saved from destruction, but then he falsifies his own words by telling Duryodhana the story of Daṃbodbhava who was so intoxicated with his own power that he thought no one could defeat him, but was defeated by the Ṛṣis Nara and Nārāyaṇa (*Mbh* 5.96.5–37). Then he reveals that Arjuna is Nara, and he himself is Nārāyaṇa, and together they are undefeatable. He further provokes the war by telling Duryodhana that the Pāṇḍava brothers are gods whose strength he will not be able to bear in battle. Making divine claims such as these and spreading rumours about the miraculous powers of one's supporters in war was a war strategy that was quite in use at that time. This is attested in Kautilya's *Arthaśāstra*. In fact, Kautilya specifically advised using reciters of the Purāṇas to claim association with divinities to boost the morale of one's own troops and to dishearten and frighten the enemy (Boesche 2003: 35). The possibility that Kṛṣṇa's divinity was no more than a strategic ploy not only further shatters his dharma role, but it also weakens the supposition of his reincarnation.

Even if the possibility that Kṛṣṇa's divinity was simply a strategic rumour is discounted, the fact remains that, here, when Kṛṣṇa is required to forward the cause of peace, his attitude, both as a mortal and divine, is hardly conciliatory. His words sound more like a challenge that would goad the pride of any warrior, regardless of whether it was issued by a mortal or a divine and, as expected, Duryodhana's response is of a true kṣatriya, one who is filled with the motive of svadharma: 'Since I have been created by God, I am what he has made me; what will happen must happen and so must my course be shaped' (*Mbh* 5.105.40). In addition, Duryodhana proudly announces that if he dies in battle, he will be fulfilling the greatest of kṣatriya dharma; but, if he cowers before his enemies, it will be against kṣatriya dharma (*Mbh* 5.127.6). Moreover, he does not see himself as the cause of war and tells Kṛṣṇa that in his own estimation, he has not committed any adharma in the catalytic dice game. Yudhiṣṭhira played the dice game and staked his kingdom of his own free will. He reiterates that he will not give away land as much as the point of a needle because he believes himself to be the true king of Hāstinapura, so why should he give away his wealth to his enemies? Duryodhana is certain that he is upholding his dharma and questions Kṛṣṇa's interference; especially in the circumstance of karma which makes the cause and effect of Duryodhana's dharma and adharma his own prerogative—whether his actions are dhārmic or not, his karma will decide. Thus, in one stroke, Duryodhana drills holes in all of Kṛṣṇa's roles: that of ambassador of peace, of a reincarnation of Viṣṇu governing dharma, and of facilitator in the scheme of metempsychosis.

As expected, the peace talks break down completely after this exchange that Kṛṣṇa triggers and manipulates. But Kṛṣṇa condemns Duryodhana for this failure, and also threatens to pay him back for all the injustices he has meted out on the Pāṇḍavas from the time they were children. Since the dialogue has opened animosities, it is no wonder then that Duryodhana decides to make Kṛṣṇa captive with the help of Duḥśāsana, Śakuni, and Karṇa, especially since Kṛṣṇa himself advises the Kuru elders to bind Duryodhana and make him captive so that he is not able to carry out his 'dark' designs (*Mbh* 5.130.4–5). And how does Kṛṣṇa escape the situation? He awes everyone by showing his Kṛṣṇized universal form in which the Pāṇḍavas emerge from his body (this theophany has been described earlier in this text).

Clearly, this divine form is creational; hence, it is not clear why Kṛṣṇa reveals it; it is not meant to convert Duryodhana. What this theophany does is to establish Kṛṣṇaism and impress upon Duryodhana that the Pāṇḍavas are part of Kṛṣṇa's divinity. However, on an extended level, it does invoke a Śaivic form or pralaya, because it provokes Duryodhana to engage in an extreme war that will cause the destruction of the world. Not only is this minimally suggested, this representation is also only archetypal. Furthermore, adding another level to the archetype, Matilal (2007: 414) says that here Kṛṣṇa is also Kāla, which creates and destroys. But Kāla is passionless. Admittedly, it destroys to restore justice, but in the scheme of Kāla, the ends justify the means. From this perspective, Kṛṣṇa's role, as revealed in this theophany, not only makes karma impotent by removing causality, but it also negates the purposefulness of the yoga to achieve the ultimate dharma that Kṛṣṇa teaches Arjuna in the Gītā.

The most evident summation of Kṛṣṇa's behaviour in the Embassy is that he is a politicking mortal, which he actually confirms when he conveys to the Pāṇḍavas the happenings at the Embassy. He admits that he tried to break up the Kauravas to create disunity among them by using fear tactics, by ridiculing Duryodhana, and by any means possible. He even admits that he used his divine form to bring about this end (*Mbh* 5.150.7–14). Thus, by his own admission, this theophany of Kṛṣṇa's becomes one of strategy. It is also obvious that Kṛṣṇa uses his divinity for the benefit of his mortal shortcomings, hence absolving himself of his moral obligations. Such mortal political maneuvres hardly fit the lakṣaṇa of a pure divine, and they also cast doubt on Kṛṣṇa's role as impartial preserver of dharma. Kṛṣṇa's partiality towards the Pāṇḍavas is so blatant that it is cannot be seen as anything but a mortal trait, so much so that it strikes even Balarāma as unfair. In the *Udyoga Parva*, he admonishes Kṛṣṇa for not heeding his repeated warnings to remain impartial to both the Pāṇḍavas and to Duryodhana. Kṛṣṇa, however, is predisposed to serve only the interests of the Pāṇḍavas, especially Arjuna (*Mbh* 5.157.31–2). As a consequence, Balarāma believes that victory will come to the Pāṇḍavas only because Kṛṣṇa is partial to them and not because they deserve the victory.

What is also most interesting is that Balarāma displays no awe of Kṛṣṇa's divinity and continues to reprimand his younger brother for his deceitful behaviour. For instance, after Kṛṣṇa incites Bhīma to treacherously strike Duryodhana on the thigh, Balarāma tells Kṛṣṇa that he feels ashamed to have witnessed this adharma. Kṛṣṇa's circuitous response to his elder brother's admonishment also detracts from his credibility. First he tries to justify this adharmic killing by stating that Pāṇḍavas are relatives and that he needed to ensure that Bhīma kept his vow of breaking Duryodhana's thigh; then he resorts to the human insurance of daivya by insisting that fate had already ordained this through Ṛṣi Maitreya's prophecy that Bhīma would carry out this act. But when Balarāma is not convinced and bemoans the violation of dharma, Kṛṣṇa resorts to his divine archetypal role, stating that Kali Yuga has arrived and such violations of dharma are to be expected (*Mbh* 9.60.9–25). With this statement, Kṛṣṇa not only justifies the deceit but also establishes himself as the divine whose purpose is yugadharma. However, this is especially damaging for Kṛṣṇa's credibility as a reincarnating dharma divine, because both Balarāma and Kṛṣṇa are supposed to be reincarnations of Viṣṇu, created from two hairs—one white and one black—from his body to assist the fallen Indras in their redemption and to restore dharma in the world (*Mbh* 1.197.34). Hence, Kṛṣṇa as a divine facilitating a decline in dharma as per yugadharma is at variance with the purpose of his incarnation.

The incident in which Kṛṣṇa is introduced in his fully supreme divine role in the Mahābhārata is in the *Sabhā Parva* when he kills Śiśupala of Cedi. Śiśupala objects to Kṛṣṇa being chosen by Bhīṣma as the foremost to receive the first arghya in Yudhiṣṭhira's Rājasūya, and he believes that the dharma of kingship and of the Rājasūya are violated by this choice. Yudhiṣṭhira, however, refutes Śiśupala and declares that Kṛṣṇa should be 'worshipped by all the pious men on earth, [because] he is the source of all happiness, the origin of the universe, and that in which the universe is to dissolve. This universe of mobile and immobile creatures has sprung into existence from Kṛṣṇa alone' (*Mbh* 2.38.21–23). Nārada validates Yudhiṣṭhira's words by announcing: 'Those men, who will not worship the lotus-eyed Kṛṣṇa should be considered as dead though living' (*Mbh* 2.39.9). This is a very revealing exchange in terms of Kṛṣṇa's history. This is the first bid to establish Kṛṣṇa theocracy, and revered characters like Yudhiṣṭhira, Bhīṣma, and Nārada are used as spokesmen for this new and emerging system. However, Śiśupala, who is a Śiva devotee, denounces Kṛṣṇa's divinity, and for this Kṛṣṇa cuts off his head with his *chakra*. The reason Kṛṣṇa gives for this action is a combination of human imperative and divine destruction. He announces to everyone that he had promised Śiśupala's mother, his aunt, that, as a divine, he would forgive his human cousin, Śiśupala, a hundred evils. And now that Śiśupala has exhausted his quota, as a dharma-preserving divine, it is his duty to destroy him. However, on a human level, Śiśupala's death at Kṛṣṇa's hands cannot be seen as a dharmic act because Kṛṣṇa's violent retaliation to Śiśupala's insult is shocking; no mythical justification, such as the promise Kṛṣṇa has made to his aunt, excuses it.

Another possible reason for why Kṛṣṇa kills Śiśupala is not cited in this incident in the Mahābhārata, but it is narrated in the *Viṣṇu Purāṇa,* and it further implicates Kṛṣṇa as no better than a mortal filled with jealousy (*VP* 4.15): Rukmini, Kṛṣṇa's favourite wife, was, at one time, pledged to Śiśupala by her brother Rukmi, but Kṛṣṇa kidnapped her and married her. Śiśupala never let Kṛṣṇa forget that Rukmini was once his betrothed; in fact, even in this Rājasūya assembly in the Mahābhārata, Śiśupala mocks Kṛṣṇa about it. For the human Kṛṣṇa, this fact has always rankled, and now, given the occasion and opportunity, Kṛṣṇa gets his revenge. This incident and the manner in which it concludes in the Mahābhārata adds a whole different divine and metaphysical dimension to it. As Śiśupala dies, his energy merges with Kṛṣṇa (*Mbh* 2.45.27). Neither the Purāṇas nor the Mahābhārata give any explanation for this strange occurrence. However, this event gives an insight into an array of concepts prevalent and evolving at this time. Drawing on the allusion of the Viṣṇu mythos, it can be said that since Rukmini is Śrī, Śiśupala, who was once betrothed to her, is a portion of Viṣṇu, hence it is fitting that he should merge into Viṣṇu. It also concretizes Kṛṣṇaism and defines Kṛṣṇa's role in the metaphysical polemic rife at this time. This display is one of the few occasions in the Mahābhārata when Kṛṣṇa is identified with the ultimate self, absorbing the lesser selves in mokṣa. But what is most noteworthy is that Śiśupala is not a Kṛṣṇa devotee; in fact, he bears great enmity towards Kṛṣṇa; then how is it that he achieves salvation through Kṛṣṇa? There are a number of possible answers to this question, and they all point to the fact that this incident aptly establishes Kṛṣṇa's supreme divinity. Firstly, the incident occurs in the *Sabhā Parva,* and it is early enough in the epic that Kṛṣṇa is still more the mortal Vṛṣṇi chieftain than a divine. Hence, the epic uses this occasion to introduce Kṛṣṇa as a divine by having him eulogized by the Kuru elders and celestial brāhmins like Nārada. Secondly, the pointed references to the *Viṣṇu Purāṇa* myth in which Śiśupala is a reincarnation of the demons Hiraṇyakaśipu and Rāvaṇa, asura arch-enemies of Viṣṇu from earlier yugas, also popularizes the concept of mokṣa in Sāṃkhya, which was still relatively new in the soteriology debate. According to the above cited *Viṣṇu Purāṇa* myth, at his death, Rāvaṇa earned the privilege of merging with Viṣṇu by virtue of being killed by Rāma. As he could not complete his mokṣa journey, he was reborn as Śiśupala to fulfil it. In this context, then, the hundred sins that Śiśupala is allowed can be seen as synecdochical—that when a person's sins become too numerous to be counted, they lose the right to enjoy a life of puruṣārthic materiality. However, all is not lost, because there is another path—of life negation—which promises ultimate salvation. But this goal has to be realized through wisdom, which, in the symbolic context of mythology, is often connoted when a divine weapon destroys a being, such as Kṛṣṇa's chakra destroying Śiśupala. Thus, rather than being a literal destruction, it is a destruction of ignorance; therefore, here, the implication is that Śiśupala's ignorance has been destroyed and he has attained the wisdom of self. Then there is the path of bhakti, which was also an emerging element of the Kṛṣṇa theocracy. In bhakti, just the total remembrance of the divine is salvation. The Purāṇic myth of Śiśupala's vadha suggests that because Śiśupala has repeated Kṛṣṇa's name so often, even if in enmity, despite himself, his heart is filled with Kṛṣṇa; hence, he has earned the privilege of merging with the divine.

Obviously, the most significant role that Kṛṣṇa plays in this incident is of the ultimate divine, but the nature of the kṣetra that is established in the context of Śiśupala's mokṣa is neither dharma nor adharma, because mokṣa is beyond both. Thus, neither is Śiśupala's destruction a consequence of his evil, nor is Kṛṣṇa's killing of him an act to sustain ethical codes of goodness. It is simply a negation of dualities—a necessary condition of realization. On a smaller scale, this uncategorized kṣetra is also defined by the deva–asura archetypes that are apparent in this incident. Śiśupala is an archetypal asura by virtue of being outside the Vaiṣṇava fold, and by parallelism, Kṛṣṇa's divinity, too, is archetypal. Admittedly, in this view, Kṛṣṇa's ultimate divine role as facilitator of mokṣa creates a causative of overcoming the polarities of good and evil, and this promises a new human–divine relationship.

The dynamism that is established though the man–divine paradigm defines the kṣetra of the entire war. Although Kṛṣṇa plays the role of Arjuna's unarmed charioteer in the war, he is most vigorous as a divine, and in his divinity, not only does he direct the Pāṇḍavas to commit many adharmic killings, but he also uses his divine māyā in the whole war. However, in each key incident in which he participates, the dharma of the kṣetra becomes suspect. A good example is in *Drona Parva*, when Bhagadatta, king of Prāgjyotiṣa, son of Narakāsura, throws the Vaiṣṇava weapon at Arjuna, but Kṛṣṇa shields Arjuna, taking the weapon on his own breast, and turning it into the Vaijayantī garland (*Mbh* 7.29.18). Thus, not only is a fair fight foiled by the excuse of Kṛṣṇa as divine, but also Kṛṣṇa breaks his vow of unarmed alliance; even Arjuna criticizes him for this (*Mbh* 7.29.19). But Kṛṣṇa has a justification: He tells Arjuna the history of the Vaiṣṇava weapon and how he had given it to Bhūmī's asura son, Naraka, as a boon. Bhagadatta, Naraka's son, who Kṛṣṇa himself declares is full of dharma, acquired it from his father. At the time of the Kurukṣetra war, Bhagadatta is an old man who keeps his eyes open with a strip of cloth, and the Vaiṣṇava weapon is his strength. Once Bhagadatta loses this weapon, he becomes weak and an easy target for Arjuna, who shoots at him, completely blinding the old man (*Mbh* 7.29.44-46). Hence, Kṛṣṇa's interference is of a deva destroying an asura and fulfilling his daivic role, but in the guise of this archetype, he compels Arjuna to commit an act of adharma.

Another example of Kṛṣṇa orchestrating events in the war with his divine powers is his manipulation of Jayadratha's death, which Arjuna has sworn to accomplish before sundown of the day after Abhimanyu's death. As the sun begins to dip on that day, Jayadratha is nowhere to be seen: knowing the vow that Arjuna has sworn, he has gone into hiding. To trick Jayadratha into showing himself, Kṛṣṇa darkens the sky so that it seems that the sun has set; Jayadratha comes out of hiding, and Arjuna kills him (*Mbh* 7.146.66–72). Kṛṣṇa's divine manipulation in this killing is not only obvious but also ironic because Yudhiṣṭhira praises Arjuna for executing an act so rare that even Indra could not have accomplished it. And Arjuna himself thanks Kṛṣṇa for helping him keep his vow—a vow, he says, that even the celestials would have found difficult to keep (*Mbh* 7.148.41). Therefore, Arjuna accepts credit for an act in which he hardly played a part, and it is also an adharmic act of treachery that is falsely portrayed as heroic.

Kṛṣṇa's deceits as an active divine are very difficult to reconcile with his role as sustainer of dharma; in fact, from the perspective of morality, these are hard to justify. Matilal (2007: 416) says that we, as readers, are actually 'embarrassed' and 'definitely shocked' at Kṛṣṇa's conduct because 'our expectations were high and he disappoints us'. Occasionally, Kṛṣṇa does try to explain his behaviour and actions, especially to mortals who question him, but he fails to convince. For example, after the Aśvamedha, as Kṛṣṇa is returning home, he meets Ṛṣi Utanka, who, unaware of the war's conclusion, asks him if he has been able to avert the war. Kṛṣṇa apologetically tells him that he tried to negotiate peace but the Kauravas disregarded what he had to say, and so both the Pāṇḍavas and Kauravas were almost wiped out in the war. Utanka is so upset at Kṛṣṇa for not rescuing the world when he was fully capable of doing it that he begins to curse Kṛṣṇa; but Kṛṣṇa reveals his divine form to Utanka, telling him that he is supreme god and has been born in mortal form to restore dharma. It was because the Kauravas were unwilling to listen that they had to be *righteously* killed in battle (*Mbh* 14.54.1–14). This declaration of Kṛṣṇa's divine yugadharma is repeated in the epic many times to justify his deceptions; moreover, this role makes him a one-dimensional divine; hardly the Saguṇa Brāhmaṇa with infinite attributes that he is supposed to be.

Hiltebeitel (1991: 47) suggests an explanation of Kṛṣṇa's dichotomous actions. He says, gods' 'assorted crimes ... are pure deeds. They invite no moral investigation. The gods act out of their own essential nature ... but when a hero sins, whether implicit or explicit, one finds a dilemma, a matter of choice, which gives the act its special finality and tragedy, and which leaves it open to investigation from every angle.' This is certainly a valid approach to dharma enquiry, and it can be applied to Kṛṣṇa. Because Kṛṣṇa in the Mahābhārata is playing both roles—that of a god and a mortal—he must be judged in his latter role on the grounds of morality, and he must be accountable for his dharma and adharma, which must be open to investigation from every angle. Also, as Hiltebeitel says, as a god, his own actions may not invite moral investigation; however, when the god impels a human hero to commit an adharma, as Kṛṣṇa does to Arjuna, then both the god and the hero must be morally investigated.

Kṛṣṇa as the archetypal divine may have been an interpolation to meet the needs of an evolving society in which tribal communities were forming small kingdoms, the practice of war was changing, and deceits, such as those committed by the Pāṇḍavas, were considered strategy. Hence, perhaps, the dharma he came to preserve was of a polity (*rājanīti*), which according to Katz, requires more strategy than dharma in Kali Yuga. In fact, in Kali Yuga, the policy he would use would be more related to āpad dharma (dharma during a situation of emergency), and 'Kaliyuga is a prolonged period of emergency' (Katz 1990: 181); hence, it can be said that Kṛṣṇa's trickery is to preserve kingdom and society.

Additionally, the Mahābhārata is a text of Kṛṣṇa theism and the absolution that his bhakti promises. But if Kṛṣṇa bhakti is the new order of victory, this new form of dharma is in opposition to earlier puruṣārthic and Vedic values. And since the Kauravas represent the earlier morality, this dharmayuddha becomes a battle of Vedic dharma against a new emerging form of dharma. However, considering that both adversaries are adherents to systems of dharma, is adharma then inconsequential in this battle? Actually, it appears that in this new order, both dharma and adharma are inconsequential because values of right and wrong are hardly made indicators of victory and defeat. In that case, is the dharmakṣetra itself made irrelevant?

Furthermore, in this evolving order, fate (daivya) and human effort (puruṣkāra), are not always in harmony (Katz 1990: 178); very often daivya defeats puruṣkāra. This is tantamount to saying that victory is purely plain old luck; this is reinforced by Yudhiṣṭhira who says to the Pāṇḍavas after the war: 'By good luck you have paid off your debt to your mother, and to your wrath! By good luck, you have been victorious, and by good luck, your enemy has been defeated' (*Mbh* 9.60.48). Perhaps fate and luck are the only victories that are possible in this new kṣetra, because it is clear from the immoral behaviour of the moral agents that they hardly allow dharma values to interfere in their actions. In a kṣetra where exemplary warriors, dharma heroes, and supreme divines fight for materialistic sovereignty, indulgence of wrath, ignorance, addiction, satisfaction of blind egos, and just plain old revenge, victory can only be through deceit or a lucky draw.

There is no doubt that the war has let loose many forms of adharma in which both the Pāṇḍavas and Kauravas are mired. Firstly, out of eighteen combined *akṣauhiṇī* (Kauravas' eleven and Pāṇḍavas' seven) amounting to about four million warriors (*Mbh* 5.155.1-21), only twelve warriors survive. Secondly, even if these numbers are passed off as casualties of war, it cannot be denied that in much of the war, dharma itself has been a casualty. Even Yudhiṣṭhira acknowledges this at the end of the war and feels that in order to continue with his life and to take over the reins of the kingdom as a dharma-following king, he needs to expiate his sins. Thus, Vyāsa advises him to perform an Aśvamedha Yajña. Hiltebeitel (1991: 296) suggests that here, not only are Vyāsa and Kṛṣṇa one, but also Kṛṣṇa is Viṣṇu, and in this instance his divinity is not static, it evokes dhārmic human effort because Kṛṣṇa/Viṣṇu makes atonement possible for sacrifices badly performed, as the sacrifice of war has been. However, the fact is that Kṛṣṇa himself has been the one to corrupt the sacrifice in the first place. Moreover, in the Aśvamedha, even Kṛṣṇa's redemptive qualities are cast in doubt, because a half golden mongoose appears at the sacrifice in the hope that the virtue of Yudhiṣṭhira's yajña will turn the other half of its body golden, but it leaves disappointed (*Mbh* 14.90.5–117). Admittedly, this mongoose story is a narrative about changing times when the Vedic vidhi of large-scale sacrifices was being denounced. But it is also about those values of dharma, such as 'abstention from injury to all creatures, contentment, sincerity, penances. Self-control, truthfulness ...' (*Mbh* 14.90.120), which are normative for all systems, including puruṣārtha and varṇāśrama expounded in the Mahābhārata and the new emerging system of Kṛṣṇaism. It is the violation of these sustaining values that disappoints the mongoose. Hence, because of the mongoose's verdict, it would seem that Yudhiṣṭhira's Aśvamedha would be a failure of expiation, but it is not. The yajña still redeems Yudhiṣṭhira and wipes clean all the adharmas committed in the war; Yudhiṣṭhira not only becomes king, but, also after thirty-two years of kingship, he ascends to heaven.

It is ambiguities and contradictions such as these that have survived in the Mahābhārata's tradition, and these evoke a few questions: Whose dharma is good and whose evil? Which action is dharma and which adharma? Is the dharma of the new system of Kṛṣṇaism better than that of the old Vedic system? It is obvious from the epic that since dharma is both constant and shifting, absolute judgment about its implementation cannot be made in contextual paradigms. In that case, perhaps the only true measure of good and evil is the consequence of an action or behaviour, provided the consequence itself is measured in terms of a priori human values, such as happiness and freedom. Hence, to put Kṛṣṇa and his 'new order' to the test, the consequence of his actions and behaviours must be examined in terms of the greater good. Matilal (2007: 416) wonders if Kṛṣṇa can be called a 'utilitarian consequentialist'. He says that the consequentialist would make sure that the consequence was better than the situation—it was for the greater good. But in this epic war, no one benefits, not even the victors themselves; hence Kṛṣṇa fails in this as well. Matilal suggests that the only logic behind Kṛṣṇa's deceits is that 'Kṛṣṇa as a moral agent [gives] up moral integrity to avoid total miscarriage of justice in the end'. Thus, he says, Kṛṣṇa formulated a 'new paradigm' in the social codes of society—'a paradigm in which there are limitations of such generally accepted moral codes of truth-telling and promise-keeping' (Matilal 2007: 416–17). In other words, in the new paradigm of dharma, through

Kṛṣṇa as a moral agent, instead of progress and evolvement for the better, there is degradation of human values of truth-telling and promise-keeping.

And Kṛṣṇa as a divine fares no better, because when he actively engages in dharma circumstances, he sabotages human effort and promotes unethical values, and when he does not actively engage, he only recalls mythic archetypes which are unrelated to the evolving values of puruṣkāra and dharma. His divinity, instead of creating a new order of an infinitely good and pure divine (as he is offered up to be), corrupts a pre-existing system that sustained an order for centuries. If this is the new paradigm, then Gāndhārī's curse on Kṛṣṇa that, for his indifference to the massacre of Kurus and Pāṇḍavas, he will be the destroyer of his own kinsmen and die an inglorious death (*Mbh* 11.25.41–3) is apt fate for both humans and divines, because obviously the paradigm that has been created is degenerative. Matilal (2007: 415) tries to rescue the value of this paradigm by saying that the question is of realism vs. idealism, and in this effort what is revealed is that the world is imperfect. Is Matilal suggesting that in realistic terms we should not expect a supreme divine to establish ideal dharma? Or is he suggesting that the ideal dharma which a supreme divine should ensure is foiled by the realistic circumstances of an imperfect world? In this case, how credible is the supremacy of the divine and how credible is he as a protector of dharma and dharmakṣetras? The fact is that not only is Kṛṣṇa an imperfect divine but his imperfection makes this kṣetra and all Kṛṣṇized kṣetras to become imperfect. Not only does he falsify the absolute good that ultimate divines of theodicy are meant to embody, but also his actions fudge the ethics that *did* exist in pre-epic society, thus augmenting the situation that was already wrought with ideological problems of ethics and morality. And, as Kṛṣṇaism became more ensconced in Hinduism, his immoral and unethical actions also became more entrenched till their description came to be seen as the norm, and the slippage in ethics and morality became continual and irreversible.

Despite the distortions that are wrought by Kṛṣṇa and the warrior heroes in the kṣetra of Mahābhārata, this mahā kṣetra can be seen as a dharmakṣetra on many levels. It is the archetypal battle of the incarnate gods and demons on earth, in which devas fight to alleviate the earth of dānava oppression. It is also a dharmakṣetra because it facilitates the changing of yugas through the pralaya of the Great War. In addition, the text of the Mahābhārata, by its own admission, is a dharmaśāstra designed to illuminate the kṣetra of people's minds with its light of didactic discourses. And finally, this *kāvya* is a dharmayuddha kṣetra because, through the metaphors of the field of war and the weapon of Bhagavad knowledge, it shows how the self must battle to win victory of the self's ultimate dharma. However, in all these dharmakṣetra functions, there is no praxis of the kṣetra. The practice of a dharmakṣetra can only be learned through the lakṣaṇa of moral agents who act in the kṣetra and whose moral deeds must define the kṣetra as a dharmakṣetra. In this function—a function that truly teaches people how to act and behave—the Mahābhārata tradition fails. In fact, not only does it fail to ascertain the paradigms of dharma though the lakṣaṇa of the characters, it also foils the lakṣaṇa of those characters whose dharma is discernible. The text presents the Pāṇḍavas and Kṛṣṇa as exemplars of dharma, but all these characters are deeply deficient dharma heroes. Yudhiṣṭhira, the incarnate of Dharma, violates and demeans each one of his human relationships; Arjuna, the hero who is the conduit for everyman warrior to realize dharma, not only enjoys a life that is unlike any man's, but he also betrays everyman by forgetting the very legacy with which he is entrusted; and Kṛṣṇa, who has reincarnated to preserve dharma changes the whole structure of truth values. On the other hand, Duryodhana, who, flawed though he is, embodies every puruṣārthic value that the epic prescribes and extols, is reviled and denounced for besmirching the kṣetra by practising these values. Perhaps the text of the Mahābhārata can be forgiven these ambiguities and contradictions, because it was composed in a transmutable context when ideas were in flux and people were grappling to arrive at some sort of stable belief system. However, what cannot be accepted is the tradition that evolved as a consequence. Instead of establishing a terra firma in which people can ground their sense of morality, the tradition of the Mahābhārata creates a precarious kṣetra in which people are always in danger of moral slippage.

5 The Ideal of *Dharmayuddha* and its Practicability

The Mahābhārata is hailed as a prototype of a dharmayuddha—not just in terms of a lawful war in the battlefield of Kurukṣetra, but also in its entirety; the whole text is considered a paradigm of dharma's battle against adharma and the victory of dharma. In its most simplistic sense, it is a battle of good against evil; however, as has been argued in the previous chapters, dharma and adharma and good and evil are not categorical. Therefore, to erect them on opposite sides of a yuddha and to claim the victory of one over the other is not only arbitrary, it is also impractical. To add to the confusion is the word 'yuddha' itself. The meaning of this word is to fight, wage war and/or engage in battle, overcome in battle, subdue, and conquer. All these words, 'fight', 'subdue', 'battle', are conceptually related to 'violence'. Moreover, the essential nature of yuddha is strategy, which necessarily requires deception, as Sun Tzu says in his sixth century BCE treatise, *The Art of War* (2007: 18). Hence, yuddha, deception, and violence have a relationship of causation. As the Mahābhārata calls its war a dharmayuddha, it does attempt to imbue this relationship with some righteousness; for example, as per Kṛṣṇa, truth is a shifting value based on circumstance; therefore deception (arising from untruth) is also moral or immoral based on the situation. Furthermore, while the consequence of violence is always hiṁsā (both internal and external), the epic makes a teleological distinction between good or necessary violence and bad violence. Thus, violence sanctioned by dharma is dhārmic, and it is condoned with maxims of victory of good, implying that when forces of good or light are involved in violence or conflict, the destruction is for the general good, that is, sustenance of dharma; whereas, when forces of darkness or evil are involved in the same violence or conflict, it is unnecessary hiṁsā and baneful, making it a threat to dharma. In Kurukṣetra, the violence that is carried out by the forces considered to be good is to conquer the forces that are perceived as evil—and that is why it is considered good violence. Therefore, the war in Kurukṣetra is made out to be a dharmayuddha.

However, what is the cognitive proof that the Pāṇḍavas are forces of good, and that their victory is the victory of the good? In fact, in the Mahābhārata, it is difficult to tell who is good and who is evil because both sides perpetrate many adharmas of action and behaviour. The Pāṇḍavas cannot be seen as epitomizing dharma simply because they have Kṛṣṇa, the divine, on their side, and the Kauravas cannot be perceived as adharmic and evil simply because they belong to an earlier form of dharma or, more significantly, because they are the 'others'—outside the fold of Vaiṣṇavism. The fact is that both the Pāṇḍavas and Kauravas are three-dimensional moral agents and not simply archetypes of good and evil. Therefore, neither side is categorically good nor evil; consequently, no victory can be called an unequivocal victory of dharma, and no defeat can be labelled a defeat of evil.

Furthermore, what violence *is* good violence? Should any violence be considered good when the consequence of all violence, good or bad, is hiṁsā because it causes pain and suffering not only to the recipient but also in the mind of the perpetrator? Hence, the very idea that a yuddha, even if termed a dharmayuddha, can indubitably be a dharmayuddha is erroneous—a contradiction in terms—and to term any yuddha as a dharmayuddha is to sanction the adharma of violence. However, because the Mahābhārata is considered a prototype of dharmayuddha and is cited as model praxis, it becomes important not only to examine whether it is in fact a dharmayuddha, but also to evaluate the practicability of such a dharmayuddha. Furthermore, since societies today are interconnected in all respects, practicability can no longer be measured in the isolated environment of a single society; therefore, the dharmayuddha that the Mahābhārata delineates must be seen in the context of today's world.

Moreover, the everyman warrior today is more complex than the Kuru warriors of the Mahābhārata; not only is he a composite of good and evil traits, he is also a product of good and evil influences of his own culture and the cultures of the world. How can this everyman warrior distinguish, without a doubt, between what is good and what is evil? And even if he knows this distinction by basing his judgement in the dharma values of his own society, how does he judge whether his dharmayuddha is more justified and righteous than the other man's, who may also be practising a form of dharma that is valued in his society? In short, whose yuddha can be called good violence and whose should be condemned as bad violence?

In the Mahābhārata, dharmayuddha has four meanings: fighting for the victory of general dharma principles against adharma; fighting for one's legitimate right, as Kuntī advises Yudhiṣṭhira to do; rules of the actual war; and the dharmayuddha that everyone has to fight within.

DHARMA'S IMPRACTICABILITY

Relationships of Self Versus Universal Values

Dharma was ambiguous even at the time of the Mahābhārata and, although this ambiguity remains unresolved, Hindu ethics are based on this concept, and it is considered the obligatory duty of a Hindu to participate in a yuddha to protect dharma's ideals. However, to fight a yuddha, the issues of contention must be clear and definable. Dharma cannot be defined:

> whether we know or do not know it, whether we determine it or not, [dharma] is finer than the finest edge of a sword and grosser than a mountain. At first it appears in the form of the romantic house of

vapour seen in the distant sky. When, however, it is examined by the learned, it disappears. (*Mbh* 12.260.12-13)

This is Yudhiṣṭhira's analysis of dharma, and what he is saying is that the ideals of dharma can, at best, only be romanticized because when they are scrutinized, they are incapable of being understood even by those people who are recognized as śiṣtas. Thus, dharma was unknowable even by dharmavīra himself; and, over the centuries, instead of gaining more comprehension, the ideals of dharma have become more indefinable. As Badrinath (2006: 78) says, 'there is in the history of mankind no other word like *dharma*, a word into which so much has been poured, and yet which is so restricted; which is so clear, yet so vague; so straight, yet so tortuous; so much like a rock, yet so wax-like'. Hence, how can a yuddha to protect dharma be practical when it is not even clear exactly what needs to be protected?

One reason why dharma has become even more ambiguous today is because the actions and behaviours of moral agents are guided more by their relationships of self than by ideals that are universal. Instead of self-aggrandizement and individuation, if moral agents recognize what is universally good—meaning that the same 'good' action by a moral agent in a relationship in one system would also be 'good' if performed by another moral agent in another social structure—then fighting for and protecting a universal good would be dharmayuddha.

However, while acknowledging dharma's universal value in relationships of self is definitely a method to resolve the issue of dharma's ambiguity, it is an impractical cause for yuddha because not only are these values more idealistic than practical, they are also transmutable according to relational circumstances of deśa, kāla, and varṇa, which are attributes of dharma itself. This means that every change would evoke a new dharmayuddha, and each dharmayuddha may be nothing more than a fight against a prior form of dharma. This would make dharma its own enemy. For example, one universal a priori value that Badrinath cites is 'goodness'. But the principle of 'goodness' has always been changeable; for instance, in Ṛg Vedic times, sacrificial rituals involving the killing of animals were considered 'good' because the self in these rituals related to natural and celestial phenomena, which, in turn, upheld a good life for everyone involved in the ritual. But, in the time of the epic, animal sacrifices came to be seen as adharmic, because the relationship of self with natural phenomena was no longer key to survival. Also, people began to explore the human psyche and discovered that it suffered internal conflicts by the act of animal sacrifice; hence, in epic times, '*ahiṁsā paramo dharma*', nonviolence as the foremost dharma, became the dictum. Therefore, the value of goodness changed as people's relationships changed from alignment with nature to alignment with self.

Additionally, even if an ideal is established in society, it does not mean that people will abide by it in their personal relationships, thus reducing its value of 'general good'. So, an ideal about what people ought to do may exist in society, but it is what people actually do that substantiates the ideal. Badrinath (2006: 114) himself attests to this by using the example of hiṁsā: The most important thing, he says, is that because 'ahiṁsā paramo dharma' is repeated so many times in the Mahābhārata, it is obvious that 'to legislate against an offence, or a crime, presupposes its existence. When a great emphasis is placed upon *ahiṁsā*, or not to do violence, and upon *satya*, or truth, it can be safely concluded, *from the emphasis alone*, that both violence and falsehood must be widespread in human relationships'. In this case, a dharmayuddha to protect the established ideal is a valid action but, in actuality, when a practice is widespread (even if it is a false value), the system itself begins to adapt the ideal to accommodate the contraventions; therefore, a dharmayuddha in this case would be counterproductive. For example, despite making ahiṁsā an integral value of dharma, the Mahābhārata not only sanctions hiṁsā in the form of individual and collective good violence, it also enforces it as necessary violence.

To counter the changeability of the general values of dharma, the lakṣaṇa of these values, such as non-injury, respect, tolerance, etc., can be established as ideals. However, these lakṣaṇa, although concrete guides to behaviour, can also be subject to change, especially in situations of āpad. For example, in the āpad time of the Mahābhārata war, 'depriving, starving, hurting, ... doing violence, debasing, and degrading the other'—actions that Badrinath (2006: 89) sees as against the value of goodness, were all necessary and approved modes of action for the kṣatriya following his kṣatriya dharma or rājadharma. The lakṣaṇa of goodness have always been in flux, and today the same is still true, especially as they are more self-oriented.

Another way to ensure dharma can be to measure one's actions in terms of definable outcomes for the general good, such as freedom. However, definitions are a matter of perspective; how one individual perceives a value and construes its meaning is often different from another's. For example, freedom can mean something completely different to a bonded labourer than to a landowner (Jhingran 2001: 9). Also, the understanding of the term itself can be a matter of perspective. For example, Satyagraha for Gandhi had no scope of physical force; whereas for some others it meant 'passive resistance'—the weapon of the weak—only because they lacked other weapons, and only till the time they could acquire weapons. Hence, while the purpose of both Satyagraha and passive resistance is freedom through resistance, they are, in fact, so different that one (Satyagraha), a 'soul force', is a true dharmayuddha, and the other (passive resistance) is simply acknowledgement of weakness, an adharmayuddha (Gandhi 1969: V.5.396–400).

Dharma values are bound by many other factors of self as well, such as a person's character, his/her circumstances, fears, insecurities—and many of these cater to self-interest. In fact, as Agrawal (1998: 5) says, the 'self' is nothing but a bundle of self-interests. While some of these are external factors, such as social and political situations, others are internal. The external may be changed to align with the ideal values of a society, but the internal values that relate to a person's psyche cannot easily be changed. Although much of a person's psyche is formed and moulded by external factors, many of the psychological issues are deeply rooted in or relate to circumstances of an earlier time, such as childhood. Therefore, even if the external factors change to an environment of goodness and dharma, a person's psyche will recreate the same conflict situation in the new environment. So, this person is caught in a never-ending relationship with a self that does not allow him/her to adopt universal values of good.

Agrawal (1998: 9) suggests that the only way to break the cycle of conflicts with the self is to discover what is good and right and what causes happiness for one's self, and then to live in those discoveries. This, Agrawal calls spirituality and says that there is a close relationship between morality and spirituality. What he is suggesting is an internal dharmayuddha which, in actuality, is the truest form of dharmayuddha—one that is not only valid but also necessary in today's world. However, the recognition of one's own happiness and spirituality can sometimes conflict with the ethics of a social system because even though societal ethics and individual morality may overlap, they play out differently. While ethics form the social structure of a society, morality is how people within that social structure play their roles according to their own perception of happiness and spiritual relationships of self. This conflict of ethics and morality can juxtapose an internal dharmayuddha against an external one. A good example of this is Yudhiṣṭhira. His telling a lie to win a victory is ethical because it favours his kṣatriya dharma and his goal is victory, which is also ethical. Therefore, Yudhiṣṭhira's facilitation of Drona's death is ethical and a valid dharmayuddha, just as is his manipulation of the truth according to the situation—because, at this time, his relationship is with his co-warriors for whom he must win victory. On the other hand, Yudhiṣṭhira's act is immoral in his self's relationship with supreme self, because he abhors untruth and his personal karma is hurt by his lie. Therefore, while Yudhiṣṭhira wins the external dharmayuddha by defeating Drona, he loses the internal dharmayuddha. Thus, because dharma encompasses both ethics and morality, it becomes a problem, and when ethics and morals cannot be synchronized, moral dilemmas occur which undercut the decisiveness of intent required for a yuddha.

Today, moral dilemmas are the norm, especially because emphasis is placed on the human psyche and its connectedness with human relationships rather than on rationality and/or recognition of universal ideals. M.M. Agrawal (1998: 11) says everything has changed, even relationships, and what were simple ethical situations earlier are now dilemmas: 'Virtue ethics turned into Quandary ethics'. It can be argued that moral dilemmas can be resolved if there is a strong enough conviction. However, Agrawal (1998: 138) warns that in a moral dilemma, one cannot simply be swayed to choose one over the other. Our present conviction does not prove that our earlier conviction was morally inferior. For the dilemma to be truly resolved or dissolved, one part of the conflict must be totally purged. But how is this purging possible without also destroying relationships of the self? Conflict necessarily arises when at least two such self-relationships cannot be reconciled. And to purge any one of the conflicts, a person must necessarily destroy all factors connected to it, including human relationships. Ideally, moral dilemmas would be resolved with the conviction of rationality, but in the scope of relationships, rationality is impossible. It would mean negating emotions and feelings—in other words, one's self.

This current-day quandary is also evident in the Mahābhārata in its key moral dilemma: that of Arjuna laying down his weapons at the beginning of the war, because he is unwilling to kill his relatives and loved ones. Although Kṛṣṇa shows Arjuna the cosmic vision, and it appears that Arjuna is 'free from *moha*' and is ready to fight after realizing the inner self is immortal and that he will not personally be killing anyone and, hence, there is no cause for grief (*Mbh* 6.42.73); the fact is that Arjuna is *not* purged of moha (and neither is it made clear that his understanding of the Gītā is absolute). In the war, he hesitates to kill Bhīṣma and Drona, and he grieves for his son Abhimanyu because he is unable to sever his relationships of self. He does finally kill his blood relations, but it is not because his moral dilemma has been resolved; therefore, he gains neither freedom from doubt nor victory of unequivocal dharma. Consequently, while he kills all his opponents, he cannot kill his self. It can be thus concluded that when even Arjuna, who is favoured with a divine epiphany to resolve his moral dilemma, fails to resolve this dilemma, how then is it possible for ordinary mortals to resolve moral dilemmas in the modern world that has so distanced itself from the divine? For today's everyman, changing a course of action or gaining total cognition opens up a whole new chain of causes and effects, giving rise to whole new dilemmas. Thus, today, people are persistently caught up in the dilemmas of self and, trying to grapple with those, they constantly face moral dilemmas which force them to continually revise their sense of dharma. Therefore, because in a dharmayuddha the ideal of dharma must be single-minded and unequivocal, to use dharma as a clarion call for yuddha is to nullify the reality of self.

Relationships of self and consequent actions and behaviours also develop from the mores of a society's own cultures and traditions. Jhingran (2001: 6) says,

> All our beliefs, attitudes, patterns of behavior are learnt from our social environment. Even our deepest convictions about moral rightness or wrongness of certain kinds of acts practices or patterns of behavior are but introjected and interiorized views of our culture. Our very conscience is formed by internalizing of sanctions used by our society to support moral norms.

In other words, these moral norms and traditions are deeply rooted in people, so much so that their practice becomes a reflex. Therefore, even if a tradition or a norm opposes goodness or is unjust, people continue to practise it, often without examining its goodness or evilness. Sometimes these traditions pit one section of society against another, which means that a dharmayuddha in such a situation would create internal conflicts in a society. In fact, these traditions can sometimes be so categorical that in order to hold up universal standards of goodness, a society would need to prevent dharmayuddhas rather than encourage them.

VARṆĀŚRAMA AND DHARMAYUDDHA

One such moral norm of dharma that creates a significant problem of practicability in Hindu society is varṇāśrama dharma, especially because it is so pervasive in a Hindu's life. In fact, whatever else dharma may be—pravṛtti-dharma and nivṛtti-dharma, kula-dharma, rāṣṭra-dharma, yugadharma, puṇya, Vedic-vidhi, nyāya, svabhāva, āchār, sva-dharma, sādhārana-dharma, etc., it ultimately all subsumes in varṇāśrama (Badrinath 2006: 81–2). According to P.V. Kane (quoted in Badrinath 2006: 79), within this āśrama, the meaning of the word 'dharma' could be taken to be 'fixed principles' or 'rules of conduct' which pertain to one's privileges, duties, and obligations, or one's standard of conduct as a member of the Aryan community, as a member of one of the castes, and as a person in a particular stage of life. Varṇāśrama dharma, then, creates an institutional social structure that defines the ethics of Hindu society. This structure can be considered normative because it determines how people ought to act in order to sustain it. For example, a kṣatriya ought to be involved in honourable yuddha, or a brāhmin ought not to perform the duties of a kṣatriya, and this belief that people should act according to their varṇa is considered to be right and good. By the same standard, if peoples' acts oppose the codes of conduct of their varṇa, it is adharma and evil. In addition, varṇāśrama dharma establishes dicta of how people should act in relationships with people of other varṇa. Furthermore, and most significantly, this dharma specifically governs how people of the lowest varṇa and those who are outside the varṇāśrama fold must be treated by people of the upper castes. Hence, because this āśrama dharma makes the preservation of the purity of varṇas a moral obligation, it sets up people of one varṇa against those of other varṇas. During the time of the Mahābhārata, this dharma actualized the concept of 'the other', and in subsequent eras it instituted varṇa-based dharmayuddhas, which not only victimized people but also endorsed criminal actions.

The fact is that any yuddha to preserve varṇāśrama is highly questionable, especially when it is not even clear what ideal it preserves. It is not known how this varṇa system originated and for what purpose. The origin of caste has been attributed to the *Puruṣa Sūkta* hymn by Ṛṣi Nārāyaṇa, which appears in the *Ṛg Veda* (*RV* 10.90.12) and is mentioned in the *Atharva Veda* (AV 19.6.6). The hymn states that the brāhmin came from the mouth of Puruṣa, the kṣatriya from his arms, the vaiśya from his thighs, and the śūdra from his feet. Therefore, it came to be believed that the Vedas ranked the four varṇas as per the ascendency of the body parts, with the brāhmins being the highest in status and the śūdras the lowest. However, while some scholars refute the ranking of the body parts, many others refute the very suggestion that the hierarchy of caste derived from the *Puruṣa Sūkta*. Still others suggest that even if its origin can be traced to the Ṛg Vedic hymn, it is more appropriate to think that the varṇas in the *Puruṣa Sūkta* meant division of labour.

Numerous scholars over the years have proposed many reasons for the caste stratification in Indian culture, ranging from keeping the Aryan invaders superior to the indigenous invaded people of the Indus Valley; differentiating between colour; keeping the purity of races; sustaining economic structures by sustaining different occupations; brāhmanization of the Aryan culture; exogamy and endogamy; etc.—the list is endless. But, as early as the *Atharva Veda*, the differentiation of varṇa began to mean distinction in class. Also, at that time, varṇas began to exclude those outside the Aryan fold who could not participate in the sacrifices. Therefore, it can be surmised that the varṇa structure was already a subversion of equality and tolerance in early Hindu society.

In the Mahābhārata too varṇa division between classes is on many levels: occupation, conduct, character of people, and even colour symbolism as per guṇas: brāhmin is white, kṣatriya is red, vaiśya yellow, and śūdra is black (*BG* 4.13). In the *Śāntī Parva*, Bhīṣma describes to Yudhiṣṭhira the duties of each varṇa: brāhmins study the Vedas and practice austerities; kṣatriyas perform sacrifices under the officiating brāhmin, have knowledge of the Vedas, and win victories in war; vaiśyas have knowledge of the Vedas, look after the cattle, trade, farm, and earn their living; and śūdras service the three other varṇas. In addition, śūdras should never pursue wealth. They should wear clothes discarded by the upper three castes, and must never leave their masters, even if they suffer under their tyranny (*Mbh* 12.60.8–34). But, despite these discriminatory norms, there continued to be doubt about the origin of the varṇas and their method of categorization.

For example, Bhīṣma also says that all four castes are 'holy' and have originated from Brāhmaṇa, the supreme creator (*Mbh* 12.60.47). Also, Bhṛgu declares that there is no distinction between the different castes and that everyone was a brāhmin at first, but they were divided later according to their acts: those who lived their life in pleasure and possessed anger, but also courage, became kṣatriyas; those who had both goodness and darkness became vaiśyas; and those brāhmins who lied and cheated became śūdras, as did those who lived their life in ignorance and adharma (*Mbh* 12.188.10-15).

Despite doubts about the origin of the varṇas and the status of the people, not only did character and karma classifications of caste begin to lose ground, but lower caste people began to be strongly condemned by the upper castes. This is evident in the words of many of the characters in the epic. For example, Karṇa tells Śalya: the races who are ignorant of the Vedas, like the Piśācas, Kāraskaras, Mahiṣkas, Kuraṇdas, Keralas, Karkoṭakas, Vīrakas, and the people who do not perform yajñas are fallen and have been begotten by śūdras. Hence, 'the gods never accept gifts from them'. They are outside the Āryan fold (*Mbh* 8.44. 42–7). Bhīṣma lists for Yudhiṣṭhira the sinful races: Andhakas, Guhas, Pulindas, Śabras, Cūcukas, Madrakas of the southern region and Yaunas, Kāmbojas, Gandhāras, Kirātas, and Barbbaras of the northern region. 'All of them are sinful and live on this earth acting like Candālas, ravens and vultures,' and with degradation that came in the Tretā, 'they sprang and began to multiply' (*Mbh* 12.207: 42–5). Thus, Bhīṣma's naming of races suggests that in Tretā Yuga, caste had begun to be hereditary. Hence, varṇa dharma in the Mahābhārata not only created demarcations among the people, it also began to establish the concept of 'the other' based on people's birth.

In post-epic texts, such as in the Dharmasūtras, the caste system devolved further as birth became the sole determinant of caste and laws were made to prevent mixing of castes so as to preserve the purity of the upper castes. *Manusmṛti* finally cemented the apartheid that the caste system initiated, declaring that overreaching one's varṇa led to dire consequences, the least of these being excommunication. Such abasement of humanity not only created a culture of grave inequity, but also ingrained in people a fear of losing their caste. Therefore, it was natural for people to try to preserve their caste in any way possible, even yuddha.

This fear of caste corruptions was so much a part of the Mahābhārata's environment that a warrior like Arjuna is even prepared to cease a dharmayuddha so as not to perpetrate the adharma of killing kṣatriyas and causing imbalance in society. Arjuna himself states this fear to Kṛṣṇa at the beginning of the war. He says, 'From the predominance of sin, O Kṛṣṇa, women become corrupt, and then O descendant of Vṛṣṇi, cross-breeds [mixed races] are born. Such cross-breeding leads both the exterminator of the race and the race itself to hell ... Both the caste and family rites of the exterminators of the race [that is] guilty of the sin of cross-breeding are destroyed. (*Mbh* 6.25.41–4). He refuses to perpetuate this sin of intermingling of castes 'even for the sake of sovereignty over the three worlds!' (*Mbh* 6.25.32). Thus, maintaining purity of caste is more important than fighting for kingship, even for a consummate kṣatriya like Arjuna.

However, ceasing a war of succession to the throne to prevent caste contamination does not mean peace; it is tantamount to a dharmayuddha of a different kind—one that is more destructive because it ravages human value. This division of people into castes deteriorated into a perpetual war of the upper caste against the lower, depriving the latter of human dignity. Sadly, this unjust yuddha is one of Hindu society's harmful legacies from epic and dharma literatures, and it continues to sanction a norm that not only creates inequity and discrimination among Hindus, but it is also responsible for terrible violence. By following, or rather, misinterpreting varṇāśrama, people in India have been misusing this institution of dharma for millennia, keeping the system constantly on the brink of violence.

Furthermore, when these dharmayuddhas of one varṇa against another become widespread or are carried out against whole communities, it can take a very dangerous shape. An extreme but apt example is Hitler's persecution of the Jews, one of the most evil crimes against humanity in recorded history, which was carried out in the name of varṇa. It can be argued that what happened in Nazi Germany has no bearing on cultural and societal norms in India. But the fact is that there is a disturbing similarity between the ideas Hitler used in his *Mein Kampf* to forward his race theory and Arjuna's fear of mixing castes. In fact, Hitler's words almost mirror Arjuna's warning about deterioration of Aryanism as a result of caste corruption. For example, Hitler (1.11) says:

> The Aryan gave up the purity of his blood and, therefore, lost his sojourn in the paradise which he had made for himself. He became submerged in the racial mixture, and gradually, more and more, lost his cultural capacity ... then petrifaction set in and he fell a prey to oblivion ... Blood mixture and the resultant drop in the racial level is the sole cause of the dying out of old cultures; for men do not perish as a result of lost wars, but by the loss of that force of resistance which is contained only in pure blood.

These ideas of Hitler continue to reflect the mindset of the *dvija* Hindus, who perpetrate violence against lower castes to preserve their 'pure' castes, all in the name of their dharma. In fact, current incidents of caste violence even negate the checks and balances of deśa and kāla transmutations in dharma conventions. This flexibility can ensure that practices remain current and people-friendly, rather than coldly fettered by the rigidity of traditions that may no longer be viable in a society; however, this is so only if changeability does not oppose the authority of the śāstras. The problem is further compounded, because, as Jhingran (1999: 209) points out, 'Hinduism seems to demand only that new norms should come from men who are śiṣtas, that is, are both learned and morally upright people'. This further opens the scope for all kinds of corruption. How can the authority of these moral and upright people be proved? How can it be proved that these people are free of prejudices? They may be morally upright publically, but they may hold prejudices, passions, emotions, and personal beliefs which may influence their decisions; this is especially so because śiṣtas necessarily belong to the upper castes. Therefore, attributes of dharma (deśa and kāla) that have the propensity of good can become evil when manipulated by people. The evidence of this is in the rootedness of varṇāśrama dharma in Hindu society, which still exists without much scope of change despite it being prohibited by law. The consequence is that this norm is still misinterpreted and misused to push agendas of personal aggrandizement and hegemonies, just as it did during the time of the Mahābhārata. And today, too, people continue to provoke dharmayuddhas to protect its conventions, which are neither just nor dhārmic. These have instituted discriminatory practices that continue to be highly injurious to large sections of society. In fact, a dharmayuddha in the name of varṇa is a dangerous concept.

Sectarian Religiosity and Dharmayuddha

Another modern-day dharmayuddha that the dharma ideologies of the Mahābhārata have shaped is that of sect-based religiosity. This sectarianism existed in pre-epic society when there was a labyrinth of belief systems with a multitude of traditions and ideologies which co-existed but often came into conflict. For example, Vedic traditions opposed Śramaṇic traditions and Vaiṣṇavism contested Śaivism. S.D. Joshi (quoted in Thapar 2004: 336) notes that even Patañjali refers to the hostility between the brāhmins and the other sects 'as innate as is that between the snake and mongoose'. Although many of these systems accepted the social hierarchy of dharma, often the conflicts were about *how* dharma should be executed. In the theistic Smṛtis (which drew attention away from the Buddhist–Brāhmanical polemic), the sectarianism of Śaivic and Vaiṣṇava ideologies contended with each other, creating distinct Śaivic, Vaiṣṇava, and Śakta sects; and the conflict between them became more yuddha like. Sometimes narrative texts such as the Mahābhārata did attempt to neutralize the conflict by bringing the sects in alignment, especially by creating unifying hymns of eulogy for Viṣṇu/Kṛṣṇa, Śiva, and Devī, but sectarianism did not disappear.

The main cause for this yuddha phenomenon was the practices of belief, but the immediate and most exigent causes for these sectarian contentions may also have been regional and political difference, and even economic needs. For example, Romila Thapar (2004: 345) cites at least two historical incidents about the violent conflicts between Śaivas and Śramaṇas that may have been caused by economic exigencies. Citing Hsüan Tsang and his seventh century visit to Kashmir, Thapar refers to the destruction of Buddhist monasteries by the Huna Śaiva King Mihīrakula, which may have been caused by the material prosperity of the Buddhist Sangha, resulting from Buddhist commerce between India and Central Asia. Another evidence that Thapar gives is of Tamil Nadu and Karnataka where, in the seventh century, Śaivas attacked Jain establishments, perhaps because of the control Jains had over commerce and also their high standards of literacy, which gave them more opportunity of royal patronage. Thus, both underlying sectarian differences and pressing economic and political needs contributed to situations of conflict. More often, the provocateurs of these conflicts were adherents of the Vaiṣṇava sect, because it was the largest sect with more at stake in terms of the socio-political power struggle than the other sects. And, later, when this sect came to be identified as 'Hindu', and 'Hindu' became equated with dharma, the contentions became more religion-based and more pronounced.

However, dharma is not religion. Religion, as Shyam Ranganathan (2007: 91) says, 'is a complex of *deontic* and *aretaic* concerns organized around the goal of soteriology'. It is wholly definable as an extraneous system, while 'in contrast, *DHARMA* is an *intentional* concept' (Ranganathan 2007: 92). Hence religion is extensional and dharma is intentional. This meaning of religion and its distinction from dharma is furthered by Badrinath (2006: 83–4) who says that

> 'Religion' implies a central code of commandments, a corpus of ecclesiastical laws to regulate thought and relationships in the light of these; and a hierarchy of priesthood to supervise that regulation and control.... *Dharma* has none of these elements as any essential part of its meaning. It does not require as a presupposition even 'belief in the existence of God', which all religions do ... Religion in its institutional form is divisive; *dharma* unites. A religion excludes all that is not; *dharma* includes every form of life.

The danger of perceiving dharma as organized religion is very obvious, especially in today's context. It excludes those outside the fold of the religion, because religion, to keep itself protected and to prevent its members from leaving the congregation, breeds suspicion of all those outside the fold, considering them a threat. Just as enemies in war. Moreover, keepers of the religion use the excuse of religion in jeopardy and employ fear tactics of damnation or excommunication to incite people to dharmayuddhas against 'enemies'. Consequently, moved by the zeal of protecting the religion, people blindly follow the commandments, losing the propensity to consciously experience their own truth values. These dharmayuddhas, then, are not only blindly fought for fixed, external values that were never a part of dharma, but they also destroy the scope of a unified and secular society.

Moreover, the concept of a dharmayuddha suggests that one side must necessarily be right and good, and the other side be necessarily wrong. In a religion-based dharmayuddha, it is never the case that one side would be right and the other would be wrong. This would mean falsifying a whole religion that is 'the enemy'. And, in today's context, since dharma has been transformed to mean Hindu, it suggests that in a dharmayuddha the Hindu side is the good side and any religion or system (Islam, Christianity, Judaism, etc.) against whom the dharmayuddha is carried out must be the bad side. What this definition discounts is that, by the same standard, to a Muslim, or a Christian, or a Jew, his/her religion or system of beliefs is also good. Thus, in a world where religion has become the cause of war, we have a world in a perpetual state of dharmayuddha, with each side fighting on and for the good side against a supposed evil side. How can this perpetual state of war be practical?

LEGITIMACY OF OWNERSHIP AND ITS IMPRACTICABILITY

If the concept of dharmayuddha in the Mahābhārata is used as a paradigm, then the following three conditions must be met in order for a yuddha to qualify as a dharmayuddha: legitimate cause, necessary and sufficient conditions, and unequivocal knowledge of the enemy's wrongness. In other words, a dharmayuddha must be fought for a cause that at least one party knows as a fact is legitimately dhārmic. The time and circumstance of the yuddha must be such that there is no other recourse but war. And, most importantly, this party must know, as a fact that those against whom they fight are not fighting for dharma; hence the opposition must be clearly adharmic. In addition, the yuddha must be a moral obligation placed on the yoddhās by their system of beliefs; but it is not necessary that the cause be theistic. If these conditions are fulfilled, then in this battle of dharma against adharma, dharma will be victorious because this is a yuddha of truth.

The Mahābhārata proves that the legitimate cause of a dharmayuddha can be a claim to ownership. This is established by Kuntī in the *Udyoga Parva*, when she declares the Pāṇḍava yuddha for the throne of Hāstinapura as a dharmayuddha. In a message Kuntī relays through Kṛṣṇa to her sons, and especially to Yudhiṣṭhira, she says, 'O you of long arms, earn again your paternal wealth which is lost, by means of conciliation, dispute, gifts, punishment, or by diplomacy' (*Mbh* 5.132.32). And, to drive home her point, she uses the analogy of Vidulā and her son, Saṃjaya, who is dejected after being defeated by the Sindhus. Vidulā tells her son to be wrathful and unforgiving, because a kṣatriya without these qualities is no better than a woman. Vidulā also tells her son 'to have a heart of steel and hunt the enemy and recover his lost wealth' according to 'ordinary rules of prudence' (*Mbh* 5.133.32–5). These words of Vidulā to her son become Kuntī's call to her own sons for a dharmayuddha.

Four key factors become evident in Kuntī's advice: (1) fighting to win back lost wealth is dharma for a kṣatriya because, legitimately, this wealth belongs to said kṣatriya; (2) he should fight only with a goal in mind, which is pre-established; (3) a kṣatriya cannot show compassion to his enemy and must fight with anger and an unforgiving heart; and (4) he should fight with ordinary rules of prudence (as opposed to virtue). This, according to Kuntī, is the cause and nature of a dharmayuddha, and this is the lesson that Yudhiṣṭhira takes to heart before preparing for war against his Kuru cousins. But it is important to thoroughly examine if these four factors are genuine in the context of the necessary conditions of a dharmayuddha; otherwise the dharma causality of the Pāṇḍava yuddha is falsified.

In the war that Yudhiṣṭhira incites, firstly, the legitimacy of the paternal wealth Kuntī talks about is never proved, because the issue of who is the legitimate ruler of Hāstinapura is never resolved. Therefore, in the very first proof of the cause's truth, the Pāṇḍava dharmayuddha is negated; hence, the claim that this is a dharmayuddha is also invalidated. However, since the Mahābhārata professes to be an itihāsa of the victory of good over bad, and since the victors are the Pāṇḍavas, they are considered legitimate by virtue of being 'good'; therefore, the Pāṇḍavas' yuddha is presented as a dharmayuddha. But, if the Pāṇḍava cause of legitimacy is proved invalid, then the statement that their yuddha is a dharmayuddha becomes a non sequitur: being 'good' does not mean being legitimate. A person may have a legitimate right to something, but he may be a person without virtue or, vice versa—he may be a good person, but his claim may have no verifiable grounds. Therefore, the question of dharma being on the side of the 'legitimate heir' to the throne does not arise. Hence, on this level, the yuddha that occurs in the epic is erroneously termed a dharmayuddha.

On the other hand, disregarding the question of legitimacy, even if the words 'lost wealth' are removed from Kuntī's statement, then it can be said that Kuntī's advice to her son is that a kṣatriya must simply fight his enemies because it is his moral obligation, just as Kṛṣṇa advices Arjuna in the Gītā. In that case, the Mahābhārata can be termed a dharmayuddha, because kṣatriya dharma requires the kṣatriya to fight the enemy, whoever that may be—a person justified in his opposition and following his dharma, or a person not following any dharma and simply wishing harm on said kṣatriya. The causes for the enmity are not important; what is relevant is that he is an enemy. But, if this argument is accepted as a true statement, then it contravenes the sufficient and necessary condition of a dharma yuddha that the enemy be adharmic.

However, let it be assumed that both Kuntī and Yudhiṣṭhira know it as a fact that the rulership of Hāstinapura legitimately belongs to the

Pāṇḍavas, and they know for a fact that the Kauravas are adharmic, and they also know that it is the moral obligation of the Pāṇḍavas in the system of kṣatriya dharma to fight the Kauravas. On these assumptions, the Mahābhārata becomes a dharmayuddha, but the question that still remains is whether this assumed dharmayuddha is practical or not. To examine this practicability, the other three factors that Kuntī conveys to her sons must also be examined. Kuntī's second piece of advice to her son is to fight with a pre-established goal in mind, as per Vidulā's last words. This opens up a whole gamut of gaining a desire without being mindful to the means used to acquire that end. This lesson of ends justifying means is clearly conveyed in Kuntī's third and fourth factors: a kṣatriya cannot show compassion to his enemy and must fight with anger and unforgiving heart; and the means he uses should, at the most, be only in accordance of 'ordinary prudence', that is, not especially prudent and not necessarily virtuous.

There is no doubt that the war between the Pāṇḍavas and Kauravas for their supposed legitimacy to the kingship of Hāstinapura is accomplished by whatever means that are prudent for victory: cheating, lying, deceit, violence without reason, etc. In actuality, in the process of fighting this dharmayuddha, the Pāṇḍavas commit so many acts of adharma that even if they are fighting a dharmayuddha on the basis of true and unequivocal legitimacy, their individual adharmas far outweigh the dharma of the battle.

These indiscriminate means of war to achieve victory also create the scope for an eye-for-an-eye form of justice. Just the execution of any yuddha creates *śatru*, a fact which itself sets up a scope of reciprocal hostility and corrupts unequivocal victory. Also, this word is clearly irreversible; in other words, once an enemy has been declared an enemy, he does not become a friend just because he is defeated. When unjust means are added to this equation, the potential of enemy retaliation becomes greater because this enemy waits for his opportunity to avenge himself of the injustice he has suffered. This is his dharma—his moral obligation.

Notwithstanding this prospect of revenge, the Mahābhārata does lay out conciliatory rules for treatment of enemies. For example,

Bhīṣma advices Yudhiṣṭhira that after the war is over, the king should forgive all, but with both severity and mildness—like a father castigating his child. Also, after victory, a victorious king should show the people he grieves for their dead and not malign them. Further, during war, a king should not wound the enemy in such a way that it wounds his heart, such as using demeaning and degrading words or actions (*Mbh* 12.102.32–8). But the Mahābhārata also abounds with other contradictory rules that deal with enemies more ruthlessly. For example, in the very next piece of advice, Bhīṣma tells Yudhiṣṭhira that if the enemy is suffering a miserable plight, a king should take advantage of the situation and send his troops against him and defeat him. Or, if the enemy is strong, one should not adopt the policy of conciliation; instead, secret means should be used to weaken him, using hypocrisy and discreet agents to learn about the inner working of the state, which then later can be used against him. Also, one should not feel a false sense of security but should harbour a secret desire for the enemy's destruction (*Mbh* 12.103.13–18). These, and many more, are the strategies about enemy treatment that Bhīṣma teaches Yudhiṣṭhira in the *Śāntī Parva*.

These strategic rules hardly advocate making friends out of enemies. In fact, these rules clearly prove that war does not end with the defeat of an enemy, because once an enemy, always an enemy. Therefore, a wise yoddhā, even after defeating the enemy, should always prepare for retaliation. These strategies describe the perfect storm for an eye-for-an-eye kind of justice, because when the defeated enemy is able to, he too will strike back with equal intent and with similar strategies of deception, as revenge for him will be a means to right the wrong he has been dealt. In fact, to right his wrong is *his* legitimate right—his dharma. Therefore, a war to claim legitimacy can plunge the community in cyclical yuddhas of supposed right action, a.k.a., dharmayuddhas. And soon there are situations that are best summed up by the adage that is sometimes attributed to Mahatma Gandhi: 'eye for eye—soon the world will be blind'. The Mahābhārata is full of incidents of such eye-for-an-eye forms of blind justice, from beginning to end, from the battle of gods and demons to the destruction of the

Kuru warriors and the Yādavas to the snake sacrifice. And, in most cases, the end result of each cycle of such justice is the destruction of a whole race or community. In fact, there is such a vast number of such incidents and stories that they form concentric circles. Perhaps it is for this reason that scholars label all such cyclical battles in the Mahābhārata as repetitions of the archetypal battle of gods and demons. However, in most instances, while the pattern of the battle is the same, the agents involved in the battles are not the stick figures of gods and demons. They are living, breathing moral agents who are bound by the causality of their actions and who believe that striking back is their moral obligation as warriors. The following are just a few of these vendettas:

- The serpents are sacrificed by Janamejaya in a snake sacrifice because he is avenging his father Parikṣit's death from Takṣaka's snake bite, but Takṣaka himself is avenging his son, Aśvasena's death, who Arjuna, Janamejaya's grandfather, kills in the war (*Ādi Parva*: *Pauṣya, Pulomā,* and *Āstīka* Parvas). Aśvasena, too, was avenging his mother's death in the Khāṇḍava fire that Arjuna and Kṛṣṇa had caused (*Ādi Parva*: *Khāṇḍava-dāha* Parva).
- Then there is the cyclical conflict of Drona and Drupada. Drupada rejects Drona's request for a gift, and a humiliated Drona commands his students to defeat the Pāñcāla king. He also humiliates him and usurps half his kingdom (*Ādi* Parva: *Sambhava* Parva 138). To teach Drona a lesson, Drupada performs a sacrifice and begets Dhṛṣṭadyumna, whose very purpose in life is to bring about Drona's death (*Ādi* Parva: *Sambhava* Parva 167). When Dhṛṣṭadyumna succeeds, Aśvatthāman kills Dhṛṣṭadyumna and other Pāñcālas, including the foetus in Uttarā's womb (*Sauptika Parva:* 7).
- Even incidents that are not part of the frame story echo this cycle of justice; for example, the Bhṛgu cycle of tales includes the enmity of Viśvāmitra and Vasiṣṭha, and their quarrel over Ayodhyā's king Kalmāṣpāda, who Vasiṣṭha turns into a rākśasa. This rākśasa devours Vasiṣṭha's son Śakti, and, consequently, Śakti's son Parāśara performs a sacrifice to kill all rākṣasas. Within this cycle is embedded

another vendetta: Trying to appease Parāśara's wrath, Vasiṣṭha tells him the story of the Bhṛgu Aurava who bears wrath towards kṣatriyas. His mother had kept him hidden in her thigh as a foetus for a hundred years because the kṣatriyas were destroying all of the Bhṛgu embryos. When he is born, Aurava wants to destroy the entire warrior race (*Ādi* Parva: *Citraratha* Parva 175–81).

- The dharmayuddha of the frame story itself is a cycle of revenge: Dhṛtarāṣṭra and his sons are cheated of the kingship of Hāstinapura because of Dhṛtarāṣṭra's blindness, and Pāṇḍu's sons become claimants for the throne. To avenge themselves of this injustice, the Kauravas cheat the Pāṇḍavas of their wealth and insult Draupadī in the dice game. So the Pāṇḍavas declare war and, in the war, each of the key Kauravas is killed for some past insult or injury he has done the Pāṇḍavas. To avenge the death of Kauravas, Aśvatthāman kills all the surviving Pāñcālas in a treacherous and bloody night raid. To avenge the death of her sons, Draupadī seeks to destroy Aśvatthāman and reduces him to wander the earth forever. And in a stretch of interpretation, Takṣaka (a Śaiva by virtue of being a snake), avenges the destruction of Aśvatthāman, a co-Śiva-bhakta, by biting Parikṣit, the progeny of the Pāṇḍavas, who are Vaiṣṇavas. In turn, Parikṣit's son, Janamejaya, organizes a sacrifice to immolate all serpents.

Hence, the whole Mahābhārata war is a series of so many blood feuds that it reduces the ideology of a dharma war to gratuitous war-mongering.

A dharmayuddha to fight for legitimacy was a questionable prospect even in the time of the Mahābhārata. And, today, when the world has become so much more complex, all the negative factors—a nebulous legitimacy, adharmic means to achieve an end, eye-for-an-eye justice, and consequential human suffering—have become compounded. Today, absolute legitimacy can never be proved on any single basis. How can it be? No people live by a single principle or resource; societies function as a consequence of a favourable combination of many factors: economic, religious, political, geographical, cultural, historical, and demographical. Hence, it is difficult for any one party to extract just one factor and hold it up as the only legitimate claim. Therefore, the dharmayuddha of legitimacy is not at all practical in today's world because it is a power struggle. While one side may have a legitimate political claim, the other may have a valid religious claim. Most importantly, what results in this power struggle is the suffering of innocent people because all legitimate parties only have their eye on the goal of winning victories by any means possible, which normally involves hurting innocent people to maximize the impact of their cause. And when a victory is achieved by one, the other side retaliates by once again targeting innocent people so that they can undermine the victory. This form of war not only keeps a region in a constant state of war, but also robs perpetrators of their very humanity and strips the victims of their lives and identity. Therefore, evoking dharmayuddha on the basis of legitimacy of ownership is one of the most dangerous forms of yuddha today.

THE RULES OF WAR AND THEIR IMPRACTICABILITY

The Mahābhārata makes an attempt to keep the means of warfare ethical by establishing rules of engagement. Because the battlefield Kurukṣetra is considered sacred ground and the war itself is considered a sacrifice, it would follow that, just as the dhārmic vidhi of a sacrifice, the rules of the war would be in adherence to absolute dharma so that the sacrificial ritual of war can be successful. Bearing testimony to this ritualization of war are dharma warriors like Bhīṣma, Karṇa, and Kṛṣṇa. Bhīṣma calls it *yuddhayajña*, and Karṇa gives an elaborate description of this yajña to Kṛṣṇa, calling the war, 'a sacrificial ceremony of weapons' (*Mbh* 5.141.26–54). In addition, he calls Kurukṣetra the holiest of spots and sees his own liberation through this sacrifice, and Kṛṣṇa promises him the fulfilment of this desire (*Mbh* 5.142.18–20). Even Indra attests to the moral nature of such a sacrifice. Explaining the nature of the place warriors have in heaven, he says: 'Every warrior clad in coat of mail by advancing against enemies in battle becomes installed in that sacrifice. Indeed, it is settled that such a person, by acting in this wise, is regarded as the performer of the sacrifice of battle' (*Mbh* 12.98.13). Kṛṣṇa, too, infuses the war with dharma by stating that it emulates Durgā's battle, a goddess who is the epitome of waging a fair battle (*Mbh* 6.23.3), and he sees the field of battle as glorious. Describing the battlefield to Arjuna prior to Karṇa's death, he calls it 'most wonderful'—a superlative that would result only if war were considered fair and just, like a ritual. Describing both the jewels and diamonds embedded in armours and carriages lying broken on the field and the faces of the dead warriors, Kṛṣṇa compares them to stars and moon, or like a lake strewn with lilies. In fact, Kṛṣṇa considers the yuddha in Kurukṣetra so elevated that he tells Arjuna, 'deeds that have been wrought by you today in this battle are proper for you or for the lord of the celestials in heaven' (*Mbh* 8.19.40–8).

However, the reality of the war hardly lives up to this romanticized picture that Kṛṣṇa paints. A more accurate picture is drawn by Saṃjaya, who can be considered the only true and objective observer of the war: '... the earth soon assumed a dreadful repulsive aspect being strewn over with numerous horses and their riders all lying dead ... with their body parts all over the place' (*Mbh* 7.50.7–8). Thus, metaphorically, just as Kṛṣṇa's description of a beautiful battlefield could mean a fair and just war, Saṃjaya's description of a dreadful battlefield can be interpreted as one where fairness and justice died a terrible death. Perhaps the reason why Kṛṣṇa disguises the truth of the battlefield in the righteousness of ritual is because, being a dharma avatār, he needs to emphasize the dharma of the war he has helped initiate, and 'ritualizing violence ... along these lines [is] one way of solving moral problems connected with the ethics of war' (Brekke 2005: 71).

Another way to tout ethics was to clearly establish rules of war, and the Mahābhārata war was no exception. Hence, an examination of the factors defining this war as dharmayuddha must take into account not just the established rules of war, but also how these rules were actually executed. In addition, to judge if a yuddha based on a code of honour is practical or not, these ancient rules of warfare must be examined in the modern context.

M.A. Mehendale (1995: 6) divides the rules of the Mahābhārata war into two segments: general and specific. The former were rules that probably governed all practices of warfare in epic times, and the latter are rules that the Kurus and Pāñcālas establish just prior to the war as a code of conduct specific for the Kurukṣetra war. Vaiśaṃpāyana describes these specific rules to Janamejaya at the beginning of *Bhīṣma Parva* (*Mbh* 6.1.27–34):

- Only men of equal status and situation should engage in battle and, it is preferable, if one, having fought with fairness, withdraws.
- A battle of words should only be fought with words, and if one withdraws, he should be spared.
- A chariot warrior should fight only with a chariot warrior, or an elephant rider with an elephant rider, and horse rider with a horse rider, foot soldier with a foot soldier, etc.
- Before engaging in a battle, a challenge should always be issued and no one who is fearful or in a panic should be struck.
- One fighting with another, one seeking refuge, one retreating, one whose weapon is broken, and one who is not clad in armour should never be struck.
- Charioteers, animals, those who carry weapons, and those who play drums and conches should never be struck.

Most of these rules are quite apparent in the text, and most warriors adhere to them throughout the war. Aside from these, there are certain regulations which were probably prevalent dharma standards of warfare at that time and are therefore, not stated, but whenever someone plays foul, the character against whom the act has been committed cites them (Mehendale 1995: 6). The first instance when these general rules are cited occurs in the *Karṇa Parva* when Yudhiṣṭhira tells Arjuna to give up his Gāṇḍīva and Arjuna begins to draw a sword on his brother to keep his secret vow. At this time, Kṛṣṇa admonishes Arjuna and cites a general rule of war: 'O Bhārata, the slaying of a man who is not engaged in a fight or is unwilling to fight, or takes to flight, or seeks shelter, or joins his hands, or gives himself up to you, or is insane, be he even a foe, is never upheld by the righteous' (*Mbh* 8.69.26).

The second instance of a general rule coming into play is also in the *Karṇa Parva*, when Arjuna prepares to kill Karṇa even though that warrior's wheel is stuck in the mud. At this time, Karṇa calls upon the rule that 'brave and pious heroes never shoot their arrows at person with disheveled hairs, at those who fly away from the battle-field, at a brāhmin, at him who clasps his hands, at him who surrenders, at him who prays for quarter, at one who throws off his weapon, at one whose arrows are all gone, or at one whose weapon has fallen off or been broken.' Karṇa tells Arjuna, 'You are brave and pious of all in the world. You know all the rules at warfare ... you are stationed on your chariot and I am standing helplessly weak on the earth. You should not kill me now' (*Mbh* 8.90.114).

The third time a general rule which is also reiterated for this war is violated is in the *Drona Parva* when Arjuna, covertly, at Kṛṣṇa's instigation, severs Bhūriśravas' arm when the latter is engaged in single combat with Sātyaki, and has the upper hand. Bhūriśravas rebukes Arjuna: 'Alas O son of Kuntī, you have committed a cruel and heartless deed, in as much as, not being engaged with me and covertly, you have cut off my arm ... The righteous never strike him who is careless or who is frightened or who is made careless or who implores mercy or who is involved in a calamity' (*Mbh* 7.143.4–7).

In addition to the general and specific principles that govern the battles in Kurukṣetra, the whole Mahābhārata itself should also be considered a treatise on war, because what comes prior to war is the cause of war and preparation for war, and what comes after—in the post-war Parvas—are lessons of war and reparations of war. These pre- and post-war strategies are mostly based on the overarching practices that Bhīṣma enumerates in the *Śāntī* and *Anuśāsana Parvas*. Some of these are clearly guiding lessons of rājadharma and anuśāsana, but others appear statutory, such as the treatment of the aged and children, the wounded, sick, and those seeking refuge; or the use (or not) of poisoned arrows, armours for animals, etc. Other rules seem to be contradictory; for example, one rule regarding enemies is fighting deceit with deceit, and another is fighting the enemy with fair means. The reason for these inconsistencies is simple: war is a situation of āpad in which rules are abandoned to gain advantage over the enemy. This is 'political realism' as attested in the *Arthaśāstra* (Boesche 2003: 14).

In fact, Kautilya's *Arthaśāstra* is a perfect text to gauge the practicability of the war of the Mahābhārata, because it provides a historical and realistic basis to the mythical events of the epic. Some scholars believe that the *Arthaśāstra* and the *Mahābhārata* cannot be compared on the basis of a dharmayuddha, because the war that Kautilya describes is utilitarian, and the war in the *Mahābhārata* is deontological. Kautilya was not concerned about the 'morality' of policies—in war, politics, or diplomacy. The only morality he was concerned about was the common good (Boesche 2003: 14). Therefore, scholars believe that Kautilya's war policies are not suitable for a dharmayuddha, whereas the Mahābhārata's lessons are. However, since both texts are roughly contemporaneous, originated in about the same region, and share subject matter commonalities, the war strategies enumerated in the *Arthaśāstra* can shed significant light on the Mahābhārata.

For example, the yuddha nīti and rājanīti that Kautilya expounds is similar to what Bhīṣma teaches Yudhiṣṭhira, and these are the very same policies that the Kauravas and Pāṇḍavas follow as their rājadharma, and to prepare for war. Kautilya's strategies of weakening the enemy are also what Bhīṣma suggests to Yudhiṣṭhira: 'Secret agents should be sent for creating disunity amongst the allies of the enemy' (*Mbh* 12.102.27). Also, 'A king should ... corrupt the forces of his enemy, determine everything by positive evidence, creating disunion, making gifts, and administering poison' (*Mbh* 12.103.16-17), even going to the extent of '[destroying] crops and poisoning of wells and tanks' (*Mbh* 12.103.40). Additionally, like Kautilya, Bhīṣma suggests a systematic process of breaking the enemy by becoming close friends with them, then getting them addicted to luxuries and pleasures, such as costly prostitutes, beds, chariots and houses, and other pleasures, and then having them celebrate costly sacrifices, such as *Viśvajīt*, to drain their treasury (*Mbh* 12.105.11–22).

It is noteworthy that while Bhīṣma categorizes some of these devious methods to gain advantage over the enemy, he impresses upon Yudhiṣṭhira that a king who wins a war by unrighteousness means weakens himself and his kingdom, and so a king should never conquer through deceit or trickery or magic (*Mbh* 12.100.5-6). Also, Yudhiṣṭhira, the dharma king, rejects these strategies because they are connected with fraud (*Mbh* 12.106.1). Kautilya, on the other hand, upholds these deceitful practices. However, just the fact that Bhīṣma mentions these strategies attests that they were an acknowledged part of statecraft at that time.

Most scholars believe the *Śāntī* and *Anuśāsana Parvas* may have been later interpolations, and that the earlier versions of the Mahābhārata may not have enumerated these nītis. But, from the actions of both the Pāṇḍavas and Kauravas, it is quite evident that these were well-known rājadharma strategies practised by rulers, because both seem to be very familiar with them. Duryodhana uses these methods to rid himself of the enemy even before the question of the war arises. He tries to poison Bhīma and uses arson to kill the Pāṇḍavas in the house of lac. In fact, even his treatment of Draupadī in the dice game can be categorized as one such strategy—to create dissension in the enemy and divide the Pāṇḍavas. Admittedly, Bhīṣma's and Kautilya's advice about using women as a weapon of dissension pertains to prostitutes and not wives, but Karṇa's words in the dice game prove that in the eyes of the Kauravas, Draupadī's is a prostitute because of her polyandrous marriage. Of course, in the epic, this fails as a strategy because, aside from a brief altercation between Bhīma and Arjuna over Yudhiṣṭhira's actions, it does not create much discord among the brothers. However, it is, perhaps a consequence of the strategy's failure that the Pāṇḍavas are able to claim Draupadī's unjust treatment as a reason for war and a reason for foul play; and, thus, from the viewpoint of warcraft, their claim can be considered a counter strategy. Hence, the Kauravas' behaviour in the dice game can be seen as tactics—for though these strategies were immoral, they were part of the dharma of war.

Another very significant war strategy that Kautilya advises and the Pāṇḍavas clearly use further vindicates the perception that

Duryodhana was pure evil and provides new insights into how tradition may have wronged the Kauravas. Kautilya advises that one effective way of breaking the enemy or creating dissension in his ranks is by constantly berating him for being wicked and full of adharma. He says that the enemy should be shown the 'immorality of his ways by constantly being told that he is morally wrong or that because of him innocent people will die, or that the enemy is strong and that he will surely lose' (Boesche 2003: 25). Bhīṣma, too, suggests this by advising that a king's envoys should go into enemy cities and 'proclaim that the king and his cohorts are wicked men who have suffered for their own misdeeds' (*Mbh* 12.102.43). The Pāṇḍavas, and especially Kṛṣṇa and Vidura, use this strategy extensively, almost throughout the text. They continually call Duryodhana wicked and berate Dhṛtarāṣṭra for his evil sons who want to retain the kingship illegitimately. So, this persistent maligning of the Kauravas may actually have been just a strategic war tactic. However, its purpose may have been misconstrued in tradition and perceived as a literal fault in Duryodhana's character.

This vilification of Duryodhana as a war strategy is also evident from Kṛṣṇa's conversation with Karṇa in the *Udyoga Parva*. His words in this incident are devoid of any such negative remarks about Duryodhana. If Duryodhana were truly evil, wouldn't Kṛṣṇa have used this opportunity to persuade Karṇa about his evilness? On the contrary, just before parting with Karṇa, Kṛṣṇa promises him that 'The kings and princes, who are under the leadership of Duryodhana will, by coming into contact with weapons, meet with death and attain to very excellent salvation' (*Mbh* 5.142.20). Kṛṣṇa does not defame Duryodhana in his meeting with Karṇa because there is no point. Karṇa knows the truth about Duryodhana.

Another very meaningful strategy that Kautilya cites to frighten and weaken an enemy is to spread rumours about one's own force—that it possesses miraculous powers and has celestials in its ranks. In fact, Kautilya specifically advises the use of reciters of the Purāṇas to tell one's own troops and the enemy that the king is associated with divinities and hence cannot lose because he will have divine powers working for him (Boesche 2003: 35). Bhīṣma does not specifically state this strategy because, obviously, it would have undercut his greater purpose of establishing Kṛṣṇaism. However, this is clearly the key strategy of the Pāṇḍava camp from day one. They boast of divine connections and they claim an association with Kṛṣṇa, who they claim is divine himself. Thus, it is possible that Kṛṣṇa's divinity, too, is just a strategy that the brāhmin policy experts on the Pāṇḍava side developed to frighten the Kauravas. In fact, not only is this strategy used to awe the Kauravas, but it is also used to instil awe in the Pāṇḍavas themselves, especially in Arjuna, to empower him and impel him into action, making him believe that he is not only supported by Kṛṣṇa, who is the supreme divine, but that he himself is divine. As the composers intended, Kṛṣṇa's legend proved so effective that the idea concretized and gave birth to the divine Kṛṣṇa we know in post-Mahābhārata texts.

Kautilya's idea of dharma was practical; it signified economic prosperity of a state, and he believed that to achieve that end, war was a realistic means. From this perspective, the puruṣārthic trivarga that the Mahābhārata touts over and over again is sustainable through war; and in war, ideal dharma must necessarily be the first casualty. Kautilya's aim was utilitarian; therefore, for him, war was for the common good, and this makes his treatise dhārmic. In contrast, the Pāṇḍavas' war becomes adharmic because, as Kautilya states, a king whose kingdom is strong and the people are happy should not be attacked, because it will result in bringing unnecessary pain and suffering to the people and victory against that king is not possible (Boesche 2003: 29). In the Mahābhārata, the people of Duryodhana's kingdom are happy. Duryodhana states this himself when he is dying and the people of Hāstinapura attest to this fact too when they meet Dhṛtarāṣṭra in his forest retirement. Additionally, Duryodhana is certainly more powerful and has a larger force, yet the Pāṇḍavas attack him. The consequence (just as Kautilya foretells) is immense and unnecessary pain and suffering to the people of Hāstinapura. Considering this factor, it is irrelevant whether, technically, the Mahābhārata is a dharmayuddha and whether the rules of war have been followed, because just the fact that the Pāṇḍavas destroy the peace and happiness of an entire land proves that their yuddha is an adharmayuddha.

Although the Mahābhārata text treats the subject of rules of war extensively, and it posits the war as one in which the rules are followed as per yuddha dharma, the fact is that many rules are only theorized. In practicality, what is revealed are strategies of war that not only breach the rules but are also unethical. The main reason for this lack of adherence to dharma rules is that war is an āpad situation in which securing a quick victory is more important than observing conventions. Therefore, if the Mahābhārata war is a dharmayuddha, then it is only so from the perspective of āpad dharma, which is impractical in all other situations.

Modern wars, even if they qualify as dharmayuddhas, do not follow the prototype of the dharmayuddha in the Mahābhārata. They follow international laws which are based on international conventions, declarations, and treaties on the laws of war, and are mostly concerned with justified causes to engage in war *(jus ad bellum)*, and just and humanitarian conduct in war *(jus in bello)*. An early source for these modern principles is the Just War Theory *(jus bellum iustum)* shaped by the Roman philosopher Cicero and moulded by the Christian principles of Thomas Aquinas and Augustine of Hippo, which addresses not just *jus in bello*, but also *jus ad bellum*, and *jus post bellum*, ensuring military ethics in all three eventualities of war. This theory—although critiqued by most modern scholars—in a practical sense, accepts that war is necessary in certain circumstances, similar to what the epic suggests. But many of the rules of Just War and of modern international laws not only contradict the Mahābhārata's rules of war, they are also more moral in terms of universal values. Therefore, in principle, today, most wars can be considered dharmayuddhas, because they generally have the oversight of international peace-keeping bodies. In addition, these rules are improved upon every time there is a violation of human rights. For instance, following the atrocities of World War II, the laws of war were made rigid, and a number of protocols and conventions by international bodies were formed to protect human rights; and after the atrocities in Yugoslavia and Rwanda, the UN Security Council mandated International Criminal Tribunals such as the 1949 Conventions and Additional Protocols in 2005.

One would think that with the world keeping watch on war and ensuring that wars remain dharmayuddhas, such dharma wars would serve only the practical purpose they should—righting a wrong and protecting people. However, these rules of *jus ad bellum* and *jus in bello* are also constantly violated by warring nations, simply because war is never just an endeavour to right a wrong; it is ultimately a show of power and superiority, and power involves subjective agendas of warring parties. Hence, in the final reckoning, no war can be a dharmayuddha, and no theory or rules of war prove practical because, to use the phrase attributed to Cicero, *inter arma enim silent leges*—in times of war the law falls silent.

THE MAHĀBHĀRATA AS INTERNAL DHARMAYUDDHA

Aside from being a narrative about a literal yuddha, the Mahābhārata is an allegory of an internal war that each individual experiences. This yuddha of self is an inner conflict about the self's relationships with the world in all aspects of life. In fact, this battle is constant and the self as warrior is always a dharma warrior because, inherently, simply by virtue of being human, a person intuitively knows right and wrong and the dharma of humanness. However, his needs and desires often sway him from the right path, and he therefore has to constantly do battle with his self for the victory of what he knows to be his dharma. Admittedly, the values of right and wrong are relative to deśa and kāla, and they are subjective. But, because they are determined by environment and familial, cultural and societal perceptions and experiences, these values are most relevant to his wellbeing. The battle ensues because these very same value determinants are the forces in the battle—as either opponents or allies of the self. Sometimes these battles occur when the self has no moral justification for one course of action but is impelled by desire, greed, anger, and other such negative impulses. In this case, the self is aware of the evil inherent in the path, but the pull of the evil is so strong that the individual has to battle with his own self to resist it. Sometimes these battles are moral dilemmas where the self has moral reasons to justify each of the paths. In this case, the moral agent has to battle with himself to determine which path is best suited for his own wellbeing, the wellbeing of his family and society, and the evolvement of his self.

From the perspective of this internal dharmayuddha, the Mahābhārata is a guide for everyman, because its characters and their actions and behaviours are representative of everyman. Through the morality and immorality of its characters, the text shows that everyman is a moral agent with free will, and everyman is fighting a yuddha for which the puruṣkāra is geared towards a goal that the individual perceives as dharma. The text also shows how, in the process of this yuddha, moral agents do sometimes veer into adharma because their self is not strong enough to resist it; but then that is the lakṣaṇa of a true moral agent—one who faces evils and battles to overcome them, and one who seeks to resolve moral dilemmas. While in the former case the self of the moral agent sometimes loses to adharmic behaviour and indulges in evil, in the latter case, there is no adharma. It is not a sin to be caught in a moral dilemma; it is also not a sin to make the wrong choice to resolve a moral dilemma. The sin would be *not* to fight these inner battles; therefore, conversely, to fight these battles is dharma. In addition, every time dharma is victorious in these inner battles, the self of the moral agent takes one step closer to align with his divine self. Hence, from this perspective, the whole Mahābhārata is a dharmayuddha. Not only does it visibly portray the inner battles that its characters fight but, through them, it also conveys every person's necessity of the battle which, at its core, is a battle that a person's higher self fights to gain victory over his baser self.

Some of the most revered scholars see the true tradition of the Mahābhārata as a metaphor for this inner battle. For example, Gandhi believed that '[The Gītā] was not a historical work but that under the guise of physical warfare it described the duel that perpetually went on in the hearts of mankind, and that the physical warfare was brought in merely to make the description of the internal duel more alluring' (quoted in K.N. Upadhyaya 1969: 1). Similarly, Dr Radhakrishnan said, 'The life of the soul is symbolized by the battlefield of the Kurukṣetra ... The chariot stands for the psychological vehicle.

The steeds are the senses, the reins their controls, but the charioteer, the guide is the spirit or real self, atman. Kṛṣṇa, the charioteer is the Spirit in us' (quoted in K.N. Upadhyaya 1969: 1).

The Mahābhārata itself claims to be a text about the metaphysics of the soul. For example, when introducing the epic to the ṛṣis at Naimiṣāraṇya, Ugraśravas says that this work has 'opened the eyes of the world, which were covered by the darkness of ignorance. As the sun drives away darkness so does this Bhārata, by its discourses on *dharma, artha, kāma* and *mokṣa*, to drive away the ignorance of men' (*Mbh* 1.1.84–85). From the implication that the Mahābhārata drives away darkness, it can be surmised that the 'darkness' is created by a person's baser self and, by striving for knowledge and realization, he can aspire to connect with his higher self. Thus, the Kurukṣetra war is metonymic for the dharmayuddha that the whole text implies, and amongst the many types of dharmayuddhas, an internal dharmayuddha is one of the most significant. In this dharmayuddha, all key characters become allegories for the good and evil that the self is constantly battling—those that are allies of the self's pursuit of highest dharma and those that oppose it. Furthermore, in this allegorical perspective, even destruction and violence are the means to a soul's evolution, because what is being destroyed are the desires of the baser self. Hence this internal dharmayuddha is necessary in the journey towards self-realization, and it is only in this dharmayuddha that the Mahābhārata tradition is successful.

The most obvious proof that the Mahābhārata is a guide to realization and liberation is that it houses the Gītā and Kṛṣṇa is a metaphoric charioteer in the war. But, from the perspective of the soul's metaphysics, the Mahābhārata rises even above Kṛṣṇa and his divinity. Matilal (2007: 413–14) aptly points out that Kṛṣṇa-theology or 'Kṛṣṇalogy' in Hindu philosophy does not make Kṛṣṇa a god. He adds that in early Sāṃkhya, the very 'category of God was declared as redundant'. God was only the goal of yoga—a god whose will it is to bring the already existent atoms together in a gross universe. But human beings have the ability to act freely within this universe and ultimately realize a god that has all kinds of lovable qualities of humans. Therefore, in the internal dharmayuddha, it is irrelevant whether Kṛṣṇa is a man or a god. His historicity is inconsequential and his incarnation is only important on a mythic level. What is relevant is the knowledge that Kṛṣṇa exists, because Kṛṣṇa is really a person's Self, which every individual must realize. He is a being's higher self, the Self with the most lovable human qualities, and which is unborn and infinite. It is for this reason that, over the course of the Mahābhārata, the understanding 'where dharma is, there is victory' transforms into 'where Kṛṣṇa is, there is victory'. Sukthankar (1998: 108–9) adds to this truth about the correlation of Kṛṣṇa and everyman by suggesting that '[Kṛṣṇa] is manifestly a God who has become a Man. How little difference, if any, would there be between God who has become Man and Man who has become God. Must it not be a reversible equation?'

In this indiscriminate realm, where god and man are the same,

> the relation of God in man to man in God [is represented] by the double figure of Nara-Nārāyaṇa. Nara is the human soul, the eternal companion of the Divine, which finds itself only when it awakens to that companionship and begins, as the *Gītā* would say, to line in God. Nārāyaṇa is the divine Soul always present in our humanity, the secret guide, friend and helper of the human being. (Aurobindo 1997: 14)

Aurobindo suggests that the historicity of the Gītā, or of Kṛṣṇa, or of Arjuna does not matter, just as long as an individual knows from spirituality the inner Arjuna or the inner Kṛṣṇa (Aurobindo 1997: 15). And ultimately, Arjuna and Kṛṣṇa are also one. Sukthankar (1998: 108) explains how this is so: 'Arjuna appears different and acts differently from Śrī Kṛṣṇa merely because his *essential* identity on the transcendental plane is realized neither by Arjuna himself nor by others around him'. However, Kṛṣṇa tells Arjuna to realize this oneness; therefore, they are both called Kṛṣṇa, because after realization, Arjuna *will* be Kṛṣṇa, just as anyone who has realized the oneness will be Kṛṣṇa.

Arjuna is that everyman who Aurobindo classifies as a man of action, who has lived morally according to the codes of society and dharma but is not a thinker. He has never internalized his actions; it is only in the moment that he faces his relatives on the battlefield that he is suddenly thrown into this kṣetra where he must now think. He must think beyond the action, because action at this point will result in everything immoral—loss of moral value, sin, society, the mixing of races, the annihilation of family, etc. But without action he feels lost and bewildered. In fact, he is so lost that he is willing to die without any further action. Aurobindo names this state of Arjuna 'bankrupt' (1997: 23–6). In this bankrupt state, Kṛṣṇa advises Arjuna not so much to change the state of action, but the knowledge behind the action and to 'yoke' knowledge and action. This union is termed 'yoga'. Hence, Arjuna is the *narottam*, the ideal man who is closest to realizing this truth. In this state, Arjuna is representative of the higher self that understands, but he is also like the tamasic self that needs to understand. He is Kṛṣṇa, the realized Self, and he is also Dhṛtarāṣṭra—vacillating, unsure, listening to Vidura's advice about following his true self, but often rendered blind to the advice. Sometimes he listens to the Gītā and understands, and sometimes he forgets the lessons he has heard. When he is given special insight to see the theophany of truth, he is amazed by it, but once it is gone, he is back to being his blind and deaf self again. But Arjuna, unlike Dhṛtarāṣṭra, has the capability to rise above it all to reach his higher self and fully realize the Kṛṣṇa that he is. Therefore, the key lesson of Mahābhārata's dharmayuddha for everyman Arjuna is to recognize the blind Dhṛtarāṣṭra within, and battle him to strive to be a true Arjuna who is capable of being Kṛṣṇa.

The opponents that hold an individual back from seeing and hearing the voice of the inner Self are those aspects of his being that prevent knowledge and realization, and because these aspects of ignorance hinder realization, they are evil. However, these opponents do not always appear evil; in fact they appear to be good allies aiding the person in his path of righteousness. For example, they can be the kṣatriya desire to prove valour, as is Karṇa's desire; they can be adherence to tradition to the exclusion of everything else, just as Bhīṣma's motives are; they can also be attachment to progeny, just as

Drona is. These are not 'evil' opponents in the sense that they force a person to commit sin, but they are opponents that bind and prevent the individual from transcending to a higher place, because they generate attachment to action. These opponents may also simply be external dharmas that are a society's ethics, such as the pursuit of puruṣārthic goals of artha and kāma. But these too bind a person. Therefore, the first battle in the dharmayuddha of self is to abandon the limitedness of an externalized dharma. Because adhering to the normative duties and desires of dharma, individuals forget to listen to their Self. This is the dharma that Kṛṣṇa in the Gītā advises when he says: *sarva-dharmān parityajya*, 'abandon all dharma' (*BG* 18.66). Ultimately, what must be realized is that moral law is above social law (Aurobindo 1997: 35), only then will dharma become internalized, and the self will understand what Kṛṣṇa means when he says, '*mām ekaṁ śaraṇaṁ vraja*' [just surrender unto Me] (*BG* 18.66).

A good analogy of this internalization of moral law is in the Upaniṣads that internalized sacrifice. The Upaniṣadic seers 'synthesized the plurality of the Vedic gods into one Ultimate Reality', translating 'the heavens from beyond the skies into the case of man's own heart' (Sukthankar 1998: 94). By doing so, the lokas and the old devas became merely levels of reference and symbolic entities that are neither individuals nor planes (in the theosophic sense) but states of being, realizable within oneself. Similarly, internalized dharma can make a person's very self the Kurukṣetra—a symbolic battlefield in which his ultimate dharma will be to fight a dharmayuddha to make the Self victorious against the opponents of the lower self.

It is important to realize that externalized dharma opponents that appear good are illusions of the lower self, but because these opponents disguise themselves as goodness, they are hard to identify and destroy. Therefore, often, the only means possible for their destruction is through deceit and trickery. In fact, the rule of war that Bhīṣma cites to fight deceit with deceit, which is adharmic in the literal sense, becomes a person's greatest ally in the internal dharmayuddha. To 'kill' these opponents that are deeply entrenched, a person must trick them to destroy them. He must strike them on the thighs, as

Bhīma does Duryodhana; strike them while they are hiding behind a Śikhaṇḍin, like Arjuna; strike them while their wheel is stuck, as Karṇa's is. A person must even 'lie' to them to deliver the strike. No matter what the means, these opponents of the lower self must be destroyed for the individual to reach a higher plane.

In addition, in this battlefield, even violent destruction is necessary. Aurobindo (1997: 39–46) says that, most importantly, man must first realize that the self-soul is the creator and the destroyer. Death is the law of life, and an individual must preserve his higher self by destroying his baser self. In material terms, this is actual physical violence, but in metaphysical—soul-force—terms, it is figurative violence. For example, the patriot dies—kills himself and his enemy, but what has his spiritual Self destroyed? Perhaps the aggressor. The physical violence seems extreme, and it appears evil to those who don't believe in war, but what is it preserving? Similarly, Christ may die, but Christianity will live. It is important to recognize that the Self is both Durgā the mother and Kālī the destroyer. Both are equally to be adored. Hence,

> [a person] must acknowledge Kurukṣetra; [he] must submit to the law of Life by Death before [he] can find [his] way to the life immortal; [he] must open [his] eyes with a less appalled gaze than Arjuna's to the vision of [the] Lord of Time and Death and cease to deny, hate or recoil from the universal Destroyer. (Aurobindo: 1997: 46)

To explain the necessity of this metaphoric violence, the Gītā is the perfect guide, as is the occasion of the Gītā: poised between the two sides—the catalytic moment—an individual can make a breakthrough. Either the individual succumbs to the warriors that are guarding his lower self, or he can kill them violently to gain victory of the Self. Because the opposing warriors are a person's means of joy, pleasure, and enjoyment, destroying them will be very painful. Also, these opponents of pleasures and indulgence have taken root deep in the consciousness and subconsciousness of a being; therefore to dig them out, he will bleed—emotionally, mentally, and psychologically. However, this violence is necessary to transcend the conflict and achieve realization. The Gītā can guide a person through this conflict by leading the individual through the triune path of karma, jñāna, and bhakti. But, before a person chooses a path to realization, before the battle begins, it is important to acknowledge the state of poise because, in this state, he needs to do a systematic analysis of the forces of both sides: those which bind him to the lower self, and those which will help him transcend. This, too, can be accomplished through the guidance of the Gītā, because the Gītā is 'a document of self-analysis or psycho-analysis .... The cosmic mind, symbolized as Bhagavān Śrī Kṛṣṇa analyses by introspection with the *Gītā* the conscious mind, symbolized as Arjuna, who determines and eliminates its complexes and synthesizes it' (Sukthankar 1998: 119–20).

However, most people never reach that stage of facing the opposing forces because they never even realize that these are all forces within them. And even if they do realize this, most people skip over that perfect state of poise between opposing forces, when they should perceive them and analyse them before they attempt to destroy them. Even for a person who has recognized the power of these forces, the tendency is to skip over this stage of being poised on the verge of yoking action and knowledge, and jump right into the fray of the Kurukṣetra—the battle itself. But, in this impulse of battle, the chances of achieving victory of the higher self are less likely, because the forces allied with the lower self are too strong. Arjuna himself is a good example of this failure. He is poised between the two opposing forces. He also receives the knowledge of the nature of the two forces, and he is shown by Kṛṣṇa the transcendence that is possible. However, he does not analyse, and he does not yoke this knowledge to action. Instead he jumps right into the fray of battle and is not able to root out the forces of the lower self. Therefore, even while acting as per Kṛṣṇa's advice, he remains attached to his love for his grandfather, his son's sorrow, his egoity, and his material victory.

But why must a person engage in an arduous battle to win victory over his or her empirical self? It is to be free from the constant tension of experiential polar realities of *sukha* and *dukha* (pleasure and pain), which are the basis of a person's whole existence (Badrinath

2006: 225). What causes pain are a person's own behaviours (be it greed, ignorance, or anger) and relationship with others, which evoke expectations; and when expectations are thwarted, there is pain. Another, greater reason for pain is a person's awareness of decay and death, which cannot be ignored even in the midst of sexual and material pleasures; therefore, even an individual's sukha is shadowed with pain. These facts of life are so potent that even Kṛṣṇa's mortal self experiences it. For example, in the *Ādi Parva*, Kṛṣṇa tells Nārada about this unhappiness and laments about how helpless he feels in his relationships with his kinsmen. He says, 'Saṃkarṣaṇa is powerful, Gada is mild, Pradyumna is beautiful but no one seems to get along with each other.' Therefore, Kṛṣṇa feels caught in the middle and feels hurt when they utter cruel words to him (*Mbh* 1.81.8–14).

There are many other apt examples in the Mahābhārata about the constant dukha that plagues a human being's life. For example, in the Śāntī Parva there is a story of Senajīt, a father who is sorrowful at losing his son, and he cannot seem to alleviate the sorrow. A brāhmin then tells Senajīt a whole host of reasons for his grief: attachment to children and to spouse; loss of wealth, son, or relative; having friends or having no friends; having enemies, etc. The brāhmin tells Senajīt that even wisdom and intelligence do not drive away sorrow (*Mbh* 12.174.23–33). It can be concluded from the brāhmin's words that the very relationships of self are a cause of dukha in the world. And this truth—that life is persistent sorrow—when perceived in reverse, presents itself as sukha: that every relationship of self that does not cause dukha causes sukha. But that sukha too, ultimately and inevitably, causes dukha because the material objects and relationships of self that bring sukha are never permanent; they are transient and subject to decay.

The only true happiness is to be free from both sukha and dukha—pleasure and pain (*Mbh* 12.174.35). In order to accomplish this, a person needs to eradicate the kāma, or desire, in which the self is mired; and once that is accomplished, even living in the material world, a person can rise above it. Thus, for a *karmayogi*, the true dharmakṣetra is one in which the material is combined with the spiritual—a life governed by the discipline of yoga. This, then, is the key battle in life's dharmayuddha: eradicating desire or kāma from all action. This internal yuddha, as opposed to outward conflict, is ultimate dharma. Consequently, victory achieved in this dharma is absolute, because it is through total cognizance. This internal yuddha is not only good, but it also leads to an individual's most natural holistic state. Ordinarily, people are constantly engaged in conflict, which implies that life is a struggle of good and evil and is full of unrest. But, in an individual who has realized the highest good, the struggle ends, because the state of good becomes constant, and quiescence becomes a natural state. In addition, this good or *śreyas* is amoral, because morality also implies that there is an opposite, conflicting value—immorality. On the other hand, in this individual, there is no remainder that can be classified further as morality or immorality. Therefore, this realized person is not only devoid of morality, but also of the polarities of sukha and dukha.

For those who aspire to achieve śreyas, engaging in dharmayuddha is normal because when their social self, the self that interacts with the world, relates to others, their social dharma comes into play, which is always changing and inconstant, depending on deśa and kāla, and their own subjectivity. For this reason yuddha is normal in the inner self, which strives for the constancy of the higher self. This struggle is what Arjuna's dejection at the beginning of the war is about; and Kṛṣṇa shows him how to allow his constant inner Self to gain victory over his social, inconstant self. Therefore, even after Arjuna learns the truth, the conditions of war remain the same, that is, Arjuna still has to do battle with his relatives and his duty as warrior still remains the same; however, the motivation of doing battle ceases to be victory or gaining his lost wealth. Instead it becomes an extension of his śreyas. On the other hand, as compared to Arjuna, Duryodhana is considered 'evil' not because his actions are evil or sinful, but because his social self is the only one he knows. He knows no inner struggle and only glories in an outward, physical yuddha in which he seeks dharma and victory only for his social self.

If an individual has to engage in a physical dharmayuddha, the ideal condition to do so would be only after he has battled with his self and won the internal dharmayuddha. Only then should he turn the yuddha outwards. In fact, it is necessary to emphasize that it is *mandatory* to win the internal dharmayuddha before attempting any external dharmayuddha; otherwise the external dharmayuddha will have an evil causality. The individual who is engaged exclusively in this external war will act in accordance with his desires, attachments, and aspirations, not even realizing that he is being impelled by these forces of evil, and the consequence, too, will be injury to self and others. Therefore, even if he wins victories, they will only be victories of the lower self. On the other hand, if a person wins the internal dharmayuddha first, he will have gained equanimity, and the external war will simply be a duty that must be fulfilled. In this case, victory will be assured, even if the war results in a defeat, because the victory over the self will become the victory outside, and the truth of 'yato Kṛṣṇa tato jayaḥ' will be realized. This victory of Self—Kṛṣṇa—will then be victory on all levels.

However, notwithstanding its truth and value, is an internal dharmayuddha practical in the contemporary world? The fact is internal dharmayuddhas, although necessary for all human beings, are hard to accomplish today because they require the recognition of metaphysical truths that go beyond the everyday practical human experience. While the dharma of the lower self is based in empiricism and practicability, a true dharmayuddha requires a yoking of practical dharma and absolute dharma. The problem is that, today, any one unified concept cannot be applied to man's total cognition, because this totality requires all knowledge necessary for existence, including practical, material, and truth knowledge. It is true that dharma concerns itself with both practical and truth-oriented knowledge, but while practical dharma defines rules of action and behaviour for dealing with man's practical problems of life, absolute dharma of knowledge remains unexplained.

Additionally, for most people, while knowledge is important, truth knowledge is not; it is not what people seek today. Or, the only truth knowledge they seek is the truth of scientific knowledge, and unless absolute truth knowledge can correspond with empirical knowledge, it is not considered important. On the other hand, material values like ambition, individual aspiration, etc. are what nurture a successful life today. And if this promises a good life, what is the need for individuals to detach themselves from this life? In fact, most often, only the unhappy seek release, and that too only till the point where they can secure material happiness again. In other words, people are not concerned with the metaphysics of dukha, but are simply interested in a quick release from it.

A significant factor that contributes to the failure of self-realization is the actualization of the self. This is a person's desire for personal external success—in a career, in relationships, and in personal life. However, in order to achieve this success, a person has to often engage in manipulation, cheating, and deception. Also, the more fragmented and disorderly the world becomes, the more individuals need this self-actualization, and the more they strive to attain it. This striving then leads them to more manipulation, cheating, external violence, etc., because the odds are stacked against them. The dharmayuddha with one's self is most difficult in these strained circumstances, because people persist in this process of achieving desires and push themselves into deeper striving, using free will. In other words, free will is constantly catering to a person's desires. Thus, 'freedom is not freedom—to choose, but freedom from having to choose under impelling force of desire. In the natural condition, therefore, we do not find true freedom' (Agrawal 1998: 41).

This conflict with desire is yuddha, and the self's effort of deliverance from it would be victory of dharma. In this victory, there would be holistic transformation. In its evolved form, it would also be free from the slavery of free will and choices, because the very natural condition would change. But the process is a difficult one, requiring a negation of the 'I' through understanding oneself as a total process—'an understanding that reveals the truth about self, about what lives *qua* self and why it gets engaged in life the way it does' (Agrawal 1998: 41). This negation of self and its endeavour, when it pertains to personal consciousness, is what Agrawal (1998: 51) terms as 'spiritual' and when it pertains to relationships, he terms it as 'ethical'. However,

Agrawal also warns that these solutions that give a person the ability to understand and recognize the truth of the self are idealistic. The biggest hurdle to this comprehension is that this need for self-consciousness only arises when a person is disenchanted with the natural conditions of the self's desires, and with material gains, which is almost an impossibility in today's world.

The Gītā offers an easier path to overcome the hurdles to self-realization—the path of bhakti, which even Kṛṣṇa establishes as being accessible to everyman in today's world. He tells Arjuna, 'For those who worship Me, giving up all their activities unto Me and being devoted to Me without deviation...having fixed their mind of Me, O son of Pṛthā—for them I am the swift deliverer...' (*BG* 12.6). Thus bhakti is a recognition of a personal god and devotion to him or her, and, through this path, a person can also aspire to a realization of self.

However, it is important to point out that unless bhakti is practised in its purest form of total and absolute devotion, rather than freeing the self, it can bind it even more because bhakti, today, is most often practised with the help of organized religion, and it concretizes the self even more. When bhakti is practised through social institutions, the danger is that the self begins to see its continuity through visiting the temple, giving to charity, worshipping the idol, and performing rituals—pursuits for the acquisition of personal goals and desire for materiality. The only difference between following the path of this 'false' bhakti and not following any path of self-realization is that bhakti gives a person a tangible sense of a personal 'god' to whom he or she can turn to. But then people can also blame their insecurity and failures on this personal god; thus, some of the suffering and dukha that causes these fears of self are given a cushion. But in this false sense of security, the attachment and the desires remain the same; or worse, they become keener, because now the self has someone other than its own striving to fulfil desires. And if there is failure, it is not a failure of self, but a failure of the divine. Furthermore, if material success is achieved, it is even more dangerous because the devotee believes this success is a result of his devotion being 'true'. Consequently, this person sees no need for any other form of transcendence. Hence, self-knowledge remains as elusive as ever. Admittedly, the form of bhakti described above is not the pure bhakti that Kṛṣṇa offers Arjuna, which involves love for all and is life-negating. But that form of bhakti is also not practical for the person who lives a life of affirmation in today's world.

Despite their impracticability, the ideal to achieve ultimate dharma and the aspiration for internal dharmayuddha still exist in Hindu culture and tradition. And Hindus know, through texts like the Mahābhārata, that internal dharmayuddhas are not only possible but also exigent. There is also no denying that even when faced with the dangers of fact-based truth and theology, a Hindu strives for a way of life that adheres to both material dharma and absolute dharma. And, perhaps, that is where the greatest tragedy is, because in this complex time when people need the clearest guidance, they are presented with ambiguities that the Mahābhārata tradition has created. In an earlier time, the ambiguities prompted people to think for themselves; but today, with all the other concerns of competition and survival, they are only confused by this equivocacy which creates moral dilemmas to which they have no answers.

There is no doubt that the Mahābhārata is a paradigm of a dharmayuddha, both internal and external. As the latter, it establishes moral and ethical parameters to contain the anarchy that war can unleash. Through didactic means, it indicates preservation of the dharma principle, ensures the legitimacy of war, and emphasizes the rules of war. However, it fails to adhere to these very same codes in its exemplification, because all its characters—both the supposed villains and dharma heroes—violate them in the praxis of the war. Further negating the dharmayuddha paradigm, the text sanctions dangerous practices such as personal vendettas, eye-for-an-eye justice, and unlawful means to justify ends. Not surprisingly, when this exemplar is used in today's context, the consequences are just as devastating as described in the Mahābhārata. In fact, the Mahābhārata's yuddha dharma is so apocalyptic that, despite being hailed as a śāstra and a tradition, this scriptural text is not recited during pious events in many parts of India. Some Hindus consider it an ill omen to even keep this text in their homes for fear of evoking its spirit of disunity, extreme violence, and pralaya. Thus, considering these evidential perceptions, the Mahābhārata's dharmayuddha can hardly be touted as a yuddha of practicability.

On the other hand, the internal dharmayuddha symbolized in the Mahābhārata is not only applicable in today's world, but it is also exigent for the everyman caught up in tensions, anxieties, ambitions, and fulfilment of desires. However, this internal dharmayuddha is not only arduous, it also requires edifying guidance. The Mahābhārata tradition poses as a lucid guide to lead everyman through internal conflicts to the victory of Self. In actuality, it convolutes the path even more with its ambiguities and contradictions. Therefore, even in this respect, the dharmayuddha of the Mahābhārata fails in its practicability.

Conclusion

Questioning the Tradition of the Mahābhārata

The Mahābhārata is 'sacred history' (*Mbh* 1.62.17) about events in the past that relate to all aspects of life and pertain to both good and evil. It also portrays divine and human characters that were engaged in both ethical and unethical behaviours. And, most importantly, it presents issues of ethics and morality with which people at that time were grappling. However, around the first century CE, when the Mahābhārata's oral narrative was written down in Sanskrit, it came to be considered as not just a purāṇa, but also as a śāstra in the tradition of other śāstras, such as the *Mānava Dharmaśāstra*. One prominent factor resulting from this formalizing of the Mahābhārata was that its narrative was concretized, which meant that it was no longer open to accretions and interpolations, and this, in turn, meant that all its good and evil, and moral and immoral facets were established as tradition. Another, and perhaps the most significant factor was that, as a śāstra, it came to be seen as a scripture. Wendy Doniger (2009: 309) explains that the word śāstra comes from '*shas*', which means 'discipline', which in turn is derived from '*shams*', a verb meaning 'to injure', and the root of the noun, meaning 'cruelty'. Therefore, the word śāstra is related to disciplining by 'chastening' or 'chastising'. Thus, as a śāstra, the Mahābhārata was no longer just history that presented life as it was, with all it perfections and flaws; instead it became a text that taught how life should be lived according to ethics of doctrinal traditions. This also gave the brāhmins, who were creators of the śāstra, and the śiṣtas, who were keepers of the śāstra, sanction to discipline those who violated its traditions.

In actuality, the Mahābhārata is not a text that creates tradition; it is, in fact, a text that questions tradition. Therefore, the only tradition the Mahābhārata actually institutes is one that makes enquiry customary. It raises questions about all conventions of behaviour and ideology—from divine to human, from past to present to future, and from existence to non-existence. It interrogates the Vedas, Upaniṣads, and Vedāṅgas; Ṛg, Saman, and Yajur; celestial and human births; the art of war, and tolerance and intolerance towards different people; *Kāla* and the *yugas* and *kalpas*; the earth, the sun, and the moon; pilgrimages and rituals; death, decay, and disease; modes of life, castes, asceticism and the goals of dharma, artha, kāma, and mokṣa (*Mbh* 1.1.62–7). Altogether, it evokes such questions about these 'mysteries' that even the self-knowing Gaṇeśa had to pause to consider his own answers before scribing the verses that Vyāsa recited to him (*Mbh* 1.1.78–80).

Gaṇeśa, being self-knowing and wise, may have been able to find answers to his questions within his all-knowing self so that he could proceed with the scribing, but the ordinary mortal is not so equipped, and the text itself offers no answers because the questions it raises have no clear-cut explanations. These questions, such as the one Draupadī asks the Kuru assembly in the dice game, or the ones Arjuna asks Kṛṣṇa at the beginning of the war, or the questions of dharma that every character raises, receive only one answer from the authors of the text—that dharma is subtle. This equivocacy is no answer at all; in fact, it compounds the challenge for moral agents grappling with problems of right and wrong and good and evil, because no matter what they do or say, or how they behave, they are never sure whether they are fulfilling dharma or violating it. Only the consequence of their behaviour reveals its right and wrong and, often, this consequence is actually at variance with what the moral agents expect. Perhaps this is the reason why most actions of good and evil intent in the Mahābhārata do not reach their expected completion, because the authors themselves were not sure of the moral and immoral veracity of these actions.

There are many key incidents of good and evil intentions in the Mahābhārata that don't reach absolute fruition. To cite just a few: Bhīṣma takes the vow of celibacy to gain merit of asceticism and protect Hāstinapura, but both he and Hāstinapura are ruined as a result of it. Hāstinapura erupts in a war of legitimacy and Bhīṣma himself is destroyed by Ambā, who condemns him for his vow. Then, there is Draupadī's situation: The Kauravas drag her into the assembly hall with the evil intent to strip her of clothing and dignity but, at the last minute, her garment and dignity are mysteriously restored. Another example of an incomplete action is the burning of the Khāṇḍava in which Arjuna and Kṛṣṇa annihilate the forest and all the forest creatures to help Agni. But not all creatures are destroyed; four Śārngaka birds, the asura Māyā, and Takṣaka's son, Aśvasena, escape. (The survival of the latter two is especially significant, because they are both instrumental in inciting future evil. Māyā builds a māyāvi palace which hastens the war, and Aśvasena intensifies Takṣaka's vendetta.) Another unfinished evil is Aśvatthāman's night raid in which he wants to wipe out the Pāṇḍavas; however, not only are the five Pāṇḍavas and Kṛṣṇa preserved, but Kṛṣṇa also ensures a Pāṇḍava heir by restoring the life of Uttarā's foetus. Then, there is Janamejaya's snake sacrifice which, in itself, is morally ambiguous, but it is a result of Janamejaya's vow to avenge his father's death. However, the nāga race is saved by the sage Āstīka.

Another unfulfilled intended action of moral ambiguity is the war itself. The Pāṇḍavas declare the war a dharmayuddha by claiming legitimacy to the kingship of Hāstinapura as the dharma for which they must fight. However, when the war is over, even Yudhiṣṭhira, the victor, bemoans the adharmas that the Pāṇḍavas committed, and he calls his victory his defeat (*Mbh* 12.1.14). In addition, and ironically, the actual heir to the Pāṇḍava legitimacy, Karṇa, is killed illegitimately by the Pāṇḍavas themselves. Moreover, at the end of the war, Yudhiṣṭhira performs a grand Aśvamedha with immense wealth to gain the merit of this Vedic sacrifice and expiate his guilt, but his ostentatious yajña is declared unmeritorious by Dharma disguised as a mongoose (*Mbh* 14.90. 7 & 114). These are just a few examples of the many incidents of good and evil in the Mahābhārata that are inconclusive. This failure to complete moral and immoral actions is so indicative of the questionable nature of these values that even the consequentiality of heaven and hell is made dubious when Yudhiṣṭhira's sojourn to these places is revealed as no more than an illusion.

In addition to the unrealized intentions of the characters, the ideologies that the text presents are also not uniform or absolute. For example, ahiṁsā is emphasized as param dharma for everyone; yet, the kṣatriya's highest dharma is to engage in violence. Similarly, the characters in the text clearly recognize a hierarchy of varṇa and act according to set standards towards people of different varṇas; yet all varṇas are stated as equal, because they all arise from Nārāyaṇa. In the same way, people of each varṇa are enjoined to perform the duties of their own respective varṇas; yet some of the most respected brāhmins in the text, such as Drona and Rāma Jamadagni, behave like kṣatriyas. But if people of the lower varṇas, like Ekalavya, aspire to the actions of a higher varṇa, they are punished. Then there is the credo of puruṣārtha, which is stated as the ideal way to live a life. But puruṣārtha's fourth ideal of mokṣa is in direct contradiction to the other three goals of artha, kāma, and dharma, because while the goals of trivarga are life-affirming, the former requires life negation. To add to the inconsistencies is the philosophy of karma. While there is an underlying sense of karmic consequentiality in the actions of the characters, in most of the text, karma is portrayed as daivic design over which humans have no control.

These incomplete executions of good and evil action and the ideological paradoxes in the Mahābhārata appear either like narrative and editorial flaws in the text, or like ethical contradictions that the authors of the text did not know how to resolve. But neither of these conclusions is accurate. Doniger (2009: 264) says, 'The contradictions [in the Mahabharata] ... are not mistakes of a sloppy editor but enduring cultural dilemmas that no author could ever have resolved'.

Therefore, a more accurate assumption seems to be that the authors of the text used this equivocation to show that morality and immorality can never be absolute or fully executed, because these values are always subjective and always questionable. But most importantly, while these values are inherently subject to enquiry, the specificity of the questions they invoke cannot be instituted for all time. Each yuga, each phase of human development, and each stage of social and cultural evolvement must mould its own enquiry and ask its own questions. Therefore, what is provided in the text are not answers, but ways that moral agents can contextualize the enquiry in their own deśa, kāla, and āpad imperatives.

The Mahābhārata itself is a true product of its own time. When it was composed (between 900 BCE– and 1st century CE, which are the most accepted dates), it was a time of social, political, and ideological flux. Added to that is the fact that the story of the war is set in a time which is nebulous in terms of historical evidence (approximately 900–600 BCE), but this period was witness to rapid changes in religious outlook. Consequently, the Mahābhārata is a reflection of both an ideological metamorphosis and a social, political, and cultural transformation that occurred from the time of the story's backdrop to the time of its composition. During the period of its composition, the four powerful and influential kingdoms of Kosala, Magadha, Vatsa, and Avanti had eclipsed the old Kuru land. While not many records of Vatsa and Avanti survive, there is historical evidence that Kosala and Magadha were themselves in turmoil because of either ineffectual rulership or wars of succession. This was also a time when the old tribal organizations that had provided people a sense of community and belonging were breaking up and consolidating into little kingdoms with despotic kings who ruled with absolute power. The only limitation to the rulers' power was the dictates of the brāhmins—who were themselves autocratic—and they weighed even heavier on the people with their strictures of tradition and enforcement of ritual and sacrifice. At this time also, a new philosophical order was coming into existence, advocated by texts such as the Brāhmaṇas and Upaniṣads, which negated the good life in heaven and gave prevalence to practices of asceticism and aspirations of mokṣa and liberation from saṃsāra.

Added to this mood was the new thought of Buddhism and Jainism, which were propagating nonviolence; hence even what the Vedas perceived as 'necessary violence' was being questioned. Additionally, Upaniṣadic ideas of karma and transmigration were sweeping the scene and taking the very gods into their fold. Therefore, myths of revered gods like Indra were being re-examined. For example, while Vṛtra in the Vedas was seen as an evil asura, holding back the waters, and Indra's slaying of this asura was hailed as good; in the new era, this same Vṛtra became a brāhmin, and his slaying was deemed as Indra's treachery. Furthermore, even low-born people, like woodcutters, were allowed to question Indra's morality. For example, in one retelling of this myth in the Mahābhārata, when Indra slays Vṛtra and asks the woodcutter to cut off his head, the woodcutter wants to know who Indra is: 'I must know who you are and I want to hear why you have done this cruel deed today. Tell me the truth.' And when Indra tells him that he is king of gods, the woodcutter questions, 'How is it that you are not ashamed at this cruel deed?' (*Mbh* 5.9.32–4). In fact, this was such a time of turmoil and change that a mortal like Nahuṣa could replace Indra as king of gods and question the authenticity of the Vedas and the actions of the solar gods. In this myth, when Nahuṣa becomes king of devas, he asks the gods why they did not prevent Indra 'in bygone days, [when he committed] many deeds of cruelty and viciousness and deceitfulness' (*Mbh* 5.12.7). And when the brahmarṣis and devarṣis ask Nahuṣa 'if the hymns prescribed to be chanted by Brahmā are authentic,' he replies, 'They are not' (*Mbh* 5.17.9–10). Clearly, at this time, nothing was sacrosanct—not the gods, not the Vedas, and not traditions.

People's disenchantment with old ideas and beliefs created a cultural and ideological vacuum; this was the reason why kings and brāhmins were able to impose their own form of stability through *rāja* and *daṇḍa nīti*. But, instead of appeasing the tension, the social structure created by kṣatriya kings and brāhmin śiṣtas was oppressive for ordinary people, especially for people of the lower varṇas and women. In fact, in such a repressive environment, even the upper castes were no longer sure about what was right and what was wrong, or what path would ensure them a happy and righteous life and a good afterlife.

In this climate of chaos, there were no clear answers to questions of ethics and morality—answers that could be a continuum of tradition in the coming eras. Therefore, it is possible that to depict how ethical degradation was thrusting society into a dire state, the authors of the Mahābhārata created a narrative of an annihilating war in which everyone and everything would be wiped out. This was to warn people that such āpad situations force people into committing grievous acts of immorality that can destroy a society and cause widespread sorrow. The authors also cautioned that the degradation would reach so deep that even after the war, even among the few who survived, morality would take a further dive and 'men...would deceive their fellow men by spreading the [false] net of virtue, and men of false pride would make truth concealed' (*Mbh* 3.190.10). To help them convey this cautionary tale, the authors also created characters that were representative of the problematic times. This new breed of heroes—the Pāṇḍavas—had no historical precedence and may have been fictitious characters superimposed on existing warriors (Katz 1990: 38, 51 & 134). That is also why heroes of thorough Indra-like warriorship, such as Duryodhana, were examined, deemed no longer viable, and discarded. Also instituted was a new divine—Kṛṣṇa—who not only encapsulated the pantheon of Vedic solar gods but also set a new convention of divine execution—one of machinations to achieve a desired end. Deviously manipulating situations, he unified conflicting beliefs—Vedic, Upaniṣadic, and folk—to give people a new direction. Thus, though the Mahābhārata is a war text, at its core, it is actually 'passionately against war [and] vividly aware of the tragedy of war. (Doniger 2009: 283). By advocating a war, the authors hoped to use the metaphor of war as a catalytic goad to elicit deep questioning about moral and immoral behaviours. They hoped that by showing how certain conduct can lead to a gory war that can plunge society into a Kali Yuga, they could make people cognizant of their own actions and behaviours.

This purpose of the Mahābhārata, as a text invoking enquiry, is quite evident from Sauti's proclamations about it. At the very beginning of the narrative, Sauti tells the ṛṣis in Naimiṣāraṇya that the wisdom of this text is 'like a stick used for applying collyrium and it has opened the eyes of the world which were covered by the darkness of ignorance' (*Mbh* 1.1.84). By this statement, Sauti does not mean that the knowledge contained in the Mahābhārata has cleared away all doubts and evils, or that the knowledge that this text expounds must be established as society's traditions of *śiṣṭācāra* and *sadācāra*. Instead, what Sauti means is that when the wisdom of this text is applied like collyrium in the eyes, people can discern right from wrong. In other words, the collyrium is the wisdom of *questioning* what is right and what is wrong, and the cognizance derived from this questioning is what clears away the darkness of ignorance. Therefore, it is evident that if any tradition is established by this text, it is the tradition to eradicate the ignorance of narrow-mindedness so that people can open themselves to potential knowledge that may be revealed through enquiry. Sauti then continues to clarify this purpose of the Mahābhārata further by using more similes: 'As the full moon with its mild light opens the buds of the water-lily, so does this *Purāṇa* with the light of *Śruti* expand the human intellect.' And 'The whole house of the womb of nature is properly and completely lighted by the lamp of history which destroys the darkness of ignorance' (*Mbh* 1.1.76-7). All these declarations of the Mahābhārata's significance clearly indicate that the history it contains sheds light on all aspects of life and expands people's minds so that they can better understand their world, their selves, and their truth values. However, in order to receive this light, people must open themselves to questioning and self-analysis, which is only possible when they are not bound by restrictive and disciplinary traditions.

Arjuna in the Mahābhārata is a good example of how this emergence from ignorance can occur through enquiry. His character is full of questions about how to resolve ethical dilemmas so as to follow the path of dharma. Therefore, he is a representative of what the authors hoped would occur to everyman—that by relating to the ethical situations portrayed in the Mahābhārata, people would come face to face with their own sense of right and wrong and question these values in the contexts of their own deśa and kāla. They hoped that this enquiry may lead people into such depth that it would help them emerge from ignorance to arrive at the realization of the absolute and unchanging dharma of the self that Kṛṣṇa teaches Arjuna in the Gītā. Admittedly, Arjuna does not experience any significant realization or transformation; but, perhaps, this too was by design—to show that although people don't always learn what they are taught, if there is a tradition of enquiry, there is always scope for questioning and learning. Perhaps this is why Vyāsa taught the Mahābhārata to five different disciples so that they could venture out among diverse people, elicit diverse enquires, and show how the wisdom of the Mahābhārata pertains to all who are open to self-development.

However, instead of keeping the spirit of diverse enquiries alive, the 'Brahmins perceived this same diversity as a threat and therefore set out to hierarchize, to put together in its proper place, to form, to mold, to repress, to syncretize—in a word discipline (*shas*) the chaos that they saw looming before them' (Doniger 2009: 309). The consequence was that, instead of eradicating or finding solutions to the problems of evil that were revealed in the groundswell of social, political, and ideological change, the brāhmins, to ensure their own hegemony, not only eradicated all enquiry, but also conventionalized these very problems as norms. Therefore, the tradition of the Mahābhārata that was concretized as a śāstra still retains ethical problems of a bygone era, and these continue to harm Hindu society.

There are numerous problems of evil in this śāstric tradition of the Mahābhārata. For example, unethical behaviours, such as those of Kṛṣṇa, that even in the time of the epic had evoked questions about good and evil, were authorized as a legitimate means to restore dharma. Ironically, in the Mahābhārata, dharma is so ambiguous that its preservation or restoration is a moot point. However, this fact was overridden when the principle that dharma *is* ambiguous was regularized, and, henceforth, accepting dharma's vagueness as the mysterious 'subtlety' of dharma became the mark of śiṣṭācāra. And dharma's amorphousness became a vehicle in the hands of the śiṣtas, who interpreted dharma situations to their own advantage, mostly for self-aggrandizement and oppression.

Furthermore, despite this equivocation of good and evil within the construct of dharma, the yuddha kṣetra that was drawn in the Mahābhārata was classified as a dharmakṣetra, demarcating one side as good and the other as necessarily evil. In actuality, neither was the kṣetra a dharmakṣetra, nor was it an adharmakṣetra. And, by extension, neither was the yuddha a dharmayuddha, nor was the victory in the war dharma's victory. This was a political war between two parties battling over legitimacy of a kingship. Admittedly, there was a dharma factor involved in the conflict, but it was not of good and evil. It was simply a conflict between the old-style Vedic dharma of warriorship and the new form of Kṛṣṇized dharma. But the conflict was mirrored as the archetype of deva–asura battles and portrayed in the symbolic mould of archetypal good and evil. Consequently, this misrepresentation created the concept and scope of dharma-based yuddhas in society which, even today, can be invoked by anyone who feels a threat to his or her dharma values, and pit one side against another in a good versus evil paradigm.

Another example of an evil that continues to be problematic in Hindu cultures is the concept of the 'other', which, in the Mahābhārata, is represented by the nāgas, the Niṣādas and other aboriginals, the Mlecchas, and, sometimes, the asuras. The Mahābhārata presents numerous incidents in which these 'others' suffer grievous injury at the hands of the Aryans. However, this problem of violence against 'the other' had already been examined in the Mahābhārata's ethical context, and it had actually been condemned in the face of new ideas of ahiṁsā, a fact that is clear from Āstīka's intervention in the snake sacrifice and Janamejaya's acquiescence to stop the genocidal sacrifice. In fact, not only had the epic Aryans realized the evil of injuring 'the others', they had also accepted the Nāgas into the fold of their society. This is evident from many Mahābhārata myths; especially noteworthy is the final myth in the *Śāntī Parva* of the Nāga king Padmanabha, who is portrayed as having the knowledge of both an Aryan householder's dharma and the ultimate dharma of mokṣa. In fact, Padmanabha even instructs a brāhmin about the wisdom of the soul (*Mbh* 12.364.7). However, the śāstric tradition curtailed these progressive ideas about tolerance, acceptance, and assimilation of 'the other'. Instead, the concept of the non-Vedic, an-Aryan 'other' (which became un-Hindu in later times) was re-instituted, and anyone outside the Aryan fold was once again labelled 'evil'. The problem was further exacerbated by dharmaśāstric laws, which drew indelible lines between Aryan and an-Aryan, and not only sealed the fate of 'the other', but also created a divided Hindu society.

Another similar problem that the authors of the Mahābhārata wrestled with but could not resolve was the idea of varṇa and the role different varṇas played in society. However, in the śāstra tradition of the text, instead of examining the questions on varṇa that were raised, discriminatory practices of varṇāśrama were rigidified, creating a caste system that left no scope for enquiry or flexibility. Consequently, strict adherence to, and the preservation of varṇa dharma became social law, and anyone crossing over caste lines was penalized. But, once again, the law was inequitable, because while the upper castes were given leeway to practise the dharma of other varṇas if it suited their purpose, the lower castes suffered grievous injury if they attempted a crossover.

Another problem of evil that can be traced to the epic's śāstric tradition is the misuse of the puruṣārthic goals of artha and kāma. The Mahābhārata's ideal practice of these two goals was their pursuit within the limitedness of dharma. But because dharma's parameters were malleable, these goals were often abused for selfish gain. That is why ascetic and ethical characters like Yudhiṣṭhira question them. However, in the tradition that formed, Bhīma's and Arjuna's response to Yudhiṣṭhira's questioning became the norm. Bhīma chastises Yudhiṣṭhira for focusing only on virtue to the exclusion of all else and tells him that to live a happy life, 'All three [virtue, profit, and pleasure] should be equally pursued' (*Mbh* 3.33.40). And Arjuna advises Yudhiṣṭhira that 'poverty is a sin'. And 'From wealth originates all religious acts, and pleasures and heaven itself. He who has wealth is regarded as a sincere man. He who has wealth is regarded as a learned man ... He who is without wealth has neither this world nor the next' (*Mbh* 12.8.13–23). Therefore, pursuit of wealth was validated as a moral necessity of life, because it facilitated not just a prosperous life and afterlife but also sacrifices and charity, whose beneficiaries, needless to say, were the brāhmins.

Kāma, too, was questioned in the history of the Mahābhārata—especially its abusive practices against women. For example, it is Yudhiṣṭhira's lust to gamble that causes him to stake Draupadī, and the interrogative custom of the Mahābhārata not only questions Yudhiṣṭhira for this act through Draupadī's remonstration, but it also condemns him by showing his ruin. Moreover, by depicting Draupadī's injury at being treated like property, all of society is asked to account for its norms about the treatment of women. Similarly, it is Pāṇḍu's desire to acquire sons that makes him prostitute his wives; hence the birth of the Pāṇḍavas is always cast in doubt and raised in enquiry. Additionally, narratives of women like Oghavatī and Mādhavī were included so that they could invoke investigation about such reprehensible practices. However, when śāstric traditions about kāma evolved from the Mahābhārata, they were not about condemning crimes against women. Instead, what came to be sanctioned by tradition was the justification of men's pursuit of kāma and a condemnation of the same pursuit by women. Additionally, in a twist of irony, pronouncements were made against women that further curtailed their freedom and desires, such as the one Jamadagni makes when he tells his sons to kill their mother, Reṇukā, who experiences a fleeting moment of lust for another man (*Mbh* 3.116.5–15). Furthermore, misogyny was disguised as wisdom by making characters like Bhīṣma denounce women as 'sunk in the quality of darkness' who 'stupefy' the wisdom of men (Mbh 12.213.9). Thus, tradition not only reduced women to no more than objects to serve the interests and desires of men, it also blamed them for the immoral acts that men committed. Essentially, tradition robbed women of their character and humanness.

The fact is that Mahābhārata's history is replete with problems of evil. Yet, it is also evident that the authors were not only aware of these evils, they were grappling with them and trying to find solutions so much so that they had created a tradition of fluid enquiry that would promote a questioning of these evils in every era. Perhaps if this tradition had remained fluid, the questions that were raised may have been answered, and these problems may have been resolved. However, when the Mahābhārata became a śāstra, not only did its evolution cease, its problems of evil transformed into the customary way of life.

Admittedly, over the centuries, there have been some attempts to continue to address the problems and to question the conventions of good and evil that were established, but these attempts have been more in the folk and literary tradition rather than in the social and ethical spheres. For example, Draupadī's humiliation in the dice game led to the creation of the folk tradition of Therukoothu plays in Tamil Nadu in south India, in which Draupadī is raised to the status of a goddess and worshipped, so as to compensate her for the insult she suffered at the hands of her husbands and the Kauravas. In literature, too, the enquiry about what is rightful behaviour and what behaviour causes injury to others continued. For example, in Kālidāsa's *Abhijñānaśākuntalam*, Duśyanta's abandonment of his wife and child is questioned by Śakuntalā herself, who berates Duśyanta for violating his patidharma, just as she does in the original version in the Mahābhārata, even though Kālidāsa's Śakuntalā herself is rendered powerless through convention and Ṛṣi Durvāsa's curse. In Bhāsa's plays, the questions of who is good and who is evil and what is rightful behaviour in relationships are re-examined. For example in *Urubhangam*, Duryodhana is portrayed as a sympathetic noble king, and Bhima's breaking of his thighs by violating a code of war is examined. *Pañcarātram* is about honouring promises, and it once again establishes Duryodhana as an honourable king who fulfils the promise he makes—that if the exiled Pandavas are discovered within five nights, he will hand over the kingdom. *Karnabhāram* explores Karna's relationship with his charioteer, Śalya—through the incident in which

Indra tricks Karna to give up his kavaca and kuṇḍala. Bhāsa's Śalya, unlike in the Mahābhārata, where he plays Karna false, advises the warrior like a true charioteer. There are other similar portrayals in literature that raise questions about right and wrong; however, though these attempts make a strong statement about the dynamic nature of the Mahābhārata, they have not been enough to keep the tradition fluid.

The Mahābhārata tradition that was established when the text was written in Sanskrit is the tradition that has dictated śiṣṭācāra and sadācāra in Hindu cultures; therefore the problems of evil that were inherited became a part of Hindu conventions. The only way to break from these problems of evil is to re-examine the text as a chronicle of its time and re-interpret its myths for what they really are—not binding traditions but metaphors of enquiry into the changeable human condition.

Bibliography

Agrawal, M. M. 1989. 'Arjuna's Moral Predicament', in B. K. Matilal (Ed.), *Moral Dilemmas in the Mahābhārata*, pp. 129–42. Delhi: Indian Institute of Advanced Studies and Motilal Banarsidass.

———. 1998 [1997]. *Ethics and Spirituality*. Shimla: Indian Institute of Advanced Study.

Aurobindo, S. 1997 [1922]. *Essays on the Gita* (9th Edition). Pondicherry: Sri Aurobindo Ashram Trust.

Badrinath, C. 2006. *The Mahābhārata: An Inquiry in the Human Condition*. New Delhi: Orient Longman.

Bali, D.R. 1993. 'Folk Version of *Mahābhārata* in Jammu Region', in K. S. Singh (Ed.), *The Mahābhārata in the Tribal and Folk Traditions of India*, pp. 28–31. Shimla: Indian Institute of Advanced Studies.

Basham, A. 1989. *The Origin and Development of Classical Hindusim*. New Delhi: Oxford University Press.

———. 1995 [1954]. *The Wonder That Was India*. Noida: Rupa & Co.

Bharadwaj, O.P. 1991. *Ancient Kurukṣetra*. New Delhi: Harman Pusblishing House.

Bhāsa. 2008. 'Panchrātram', in A. Haksar (Ed.), *Bhasa: The Shattered Thigh and Other Plays*, pp. 19–56. New Delhi: Penguin Books.

———. 2008. 'Urubhangam', in A. Haksar (Ed.), *Bhasa: The Shattered Thigh and Other Plays*, pp. 107–25. New Delhi: Penguin Books.

Bhattacharji, S. 2000. *The Indian Theogony: Brahma, Viṣṇu & Śiva*. New Delhi: Penguin Books.

Bhattacharya, A.N. 1992. *Dharma, Adharma and Morality in the Mahābhārata*. Delhi: S.S. Publishers.

Boesche, R. 2003. 'Kautilya's "Arthaśāstra" on War and Diplomacy in Ancient India', *The Journal of Military History*, 67(1): 9–37.

Brekke, T. 2005. 'The Ethics of War and the Concept of War in India and Europe', *Numen*, 52(1): 59–86.

Bryant, E. 2001. *The Quest for the Origins of Vedic Culture*. New York: Oxford University Press.

Chakravarti, U. 2009. *Of Meta-narratives and 'Master' Paradigms: Sexuality and the Reification of Women in Early India*. Delhi: Center for Women's Development Studies.

Chatterjee, B.C. 1991 [1886]. *Krishna Charitra* (Trans. P. Bhattacharya). Kolkata: M.P. Birla Foundation, Research & Publication Unit.

Coomaraswamy, A.K. 1935. 'Chāyā', *Journal of the American Oriental Soceity*, 55(3): 278–83.

Dasgupta, S. 2004 [1967]. *A History of Indian Philosophy*. Delhi: Motilal Banarsidass.

———. 2008 [1967]. 'The Individual in Indian Ethics', in C.A. Moore (Ed.), *The Indian Mind: Essentials of Indian Philosophy and Culture*, pp. 341–58. Delhi: Motilal Banarsidass.

Deshpande, M.M. 2005. 'Vedic Aryans, Non-Vedic Aryans, and Non Aryans', in T.R. Trautmann (Ed.), *The Aryan Debate*, pp. 84–105. New Delhi: Oxford University Press.

Doniger, W. 1981. *The Rig Veda*. London: Penguin Books.

———. 2009. *The Hindus: An Alternative History*. London: Penguin Books.

Dutt, P. N. (n.d.) [1934]. *The Mahabharata: A Critical Study 1934* . USA: Kessinger Publishing.

Eliade, M. 1959. *The Sacred & the Profane* (Trans. W.R. Trask). Germany: Rowohlt Taschenbuch Verlag GmbH.

———. 1998 [1963]. *Myth and Reality* (Trans. W.R. Trask). Illinois: Waveland Press.

Gandhi, M.K. 1969. *Selected Works of Mahatma Gandhi* (Ed. S. Narayan). Ahmedabad: Navjivan Publishing House.

Gotimer, D. 1992. 'King Duryodhana: The *Mahābhārata* Discourse of Sinning and Virtue in Epic and Drama', *Journal of the American Oriental Society*, 12(2): 222–32.

Gupta, S. 2005. 'The Indus-Sarasvatī Civilization Beginnings and Development', in T.R. Trautmann (Ed.), *The Aryans Debate*, pp. 157–204. New Delhi: Oxford University Press.

Gupta, S.R. 1991–2008. *The Word Speaks to the Faustian Man*. Delhi: Motilal Banarsidass.

Hale, W.E. 1999 [1989]. *Ásura in Early Vedic Religion*. Delhi: Motilal Banarsidass.

Haksar, A. 2008. *Bhasa: The Shattered Thighs and Other Plays*. New Delhi: Penguin Books India.

Hiltebeitel, A. 1980. 'Śiva, the Goddess, and the Disguises of the Pāṇḍavas and Draupadī', *History of Religions*, 20(1/2): 147–74.

———. 1984. 'The Two Kṛṣṇas on One Chariot: Upaniṣadic Imagery and Epic Mythology', *History of Religions*, 24(1): 1–26.

———. 1991. *The Ritual of Battle: Krishna in the Mahābhārata*. Delhi: Sri Satguru Publications.

———. 2001. *Rethinking the Mahābhārata, A Reader's Guide to the Education of the Dharma King*. Chicago: The University of Chicago Press.

Hindery, R. 2004 [1978]. *Comparative Ethics in Hindu and Buddhist Traditions*. Delhi: Motilal Banarsidass.

Hitler, A. (n.d.). *Mein Kamf by Adolf Hitler*. Retrieved January 2, 2011 from http://www.hitler.org/writings/Mein_Kampf/

Hopkins, E.W. 1968 [1924]. *Ethics of India*. Port Washington: Kennikat Press.

Griffith, Ralph T.H. (Trans.). 2004 [1896]. *The Hymns of the Rigveda*. (Vols. 1 & 2). Delhi: Low Price Publications.

International Committee of the Red Cross. 2005. '1949 Conventions and Additional Protocols in International Humanitarian Laws—Treaties and Documents.' International Committee of the Red Cross. Available at http://www.icrc.org/ihl.nsf/full/470?opendocument (accessed on 3 March 2012).

Jhingran, S. 1999 [1989]. *Aspects of Hindu Morality*. Delhi: Motilal Banarsidass.

———. 2001. *Ethical Relativism and Universalism*. Delhi: Motilal Banarsidass.

Johnson, W. 1998. *The Sauptikaparvan of the Mahābhārata*. Oxford: Oxford University Press.

Karve, I. 2008 [1969]. *Yuganta: The End of an Epoch*. Chennai: Orient BlackSwan.

Katz, R.C. 1990 [1989]. *Arjuna in the Mahābhārata; Where Kṛṣṇa Is, There Is Victory*. Delhi: Motilal Banarsidass.

Kinsley, D.R. 1988. *Hindu Goddess*. Berkeley: University of California Press.

Klostermaier, K. 2007. 'The Original Dakṣa Saga', in A. Sharma (Ed.), *Essay on the Mahabharata*, pp. 110–29. Delhi: Motilal Banarsidass.

Kosambi, D. 1965. *Ancient India*. New York. Pantheon Books.

———. 1967. 'The Vedic "Five Tribes"', *Journal of the American Oriental Society*, 87(1): 33–9.

Krishan, Y. 1989. 'The Meaning of the Puruṣārthas in the *Mahābhārata*', in B.K. Matilal (Ed.), *Moral Dilemmas in the Mahābhārata*, pp. 53–68. Shimla: Indian Institute of Advanced Studies.

Krishan, Y. 1997. *The Doctrine of Karma*. Delhi: Motilal Banarsidass.

Kulkarni, S. 1989. 'An Unresolved Dilemma in "Dyūta-Parvas": A Question Raised by Draupadī', in B.K. Matilal (Ed.), *Moral Dilemmas in the Mahabharata*, pp. 150–7. Shimla: Indian Institute of Advanced Studies.

Matilal, B.K. 1989. 'Moral Dilemmas: Insights from Indian Epics', in B.K. Matilal (Ed.), *Moral Dilemmas in the Mahābhārata*, pp. 1–19. Shimla: Indian Institute of Advanced Studies.

———. 2007. 'Kṛṣṇa: In Defense of a Devious Divinity', in A. Sharma (Ed.), *Essays on the Mahabharat*, pp. 401–18. Delhi: Motilal Banarsidass.

Mehendale, M. 1995. *Reflections on the Mahābhārata War*. Shimla: Indian Institute of Advanced Study.

———. 2005. 'Indo-Aryans, Indo-Iranians and Indo-Europeans', in T.R. Trautmann (Ed.), *The Aryan Debate*, pp. 46–61. New Delhi: Oxford University Press.

Minkowski, C. 1989. 'Janamejaya's Sattra and Ritual Structure', *Journal of American Oriental Society*, 109(3): 401–20.

———. 2007. 'Snakes, Sattras and the *Mahabhārata*', in A. Sharma (Ed.), *Essays on the Mahābhārata*. Delhi: Motilal Banarsidass Publishers.

Monier-Williams, M. 2005 [1899]. *A Sanskrit-English Dictionary*. Delhi: Motilal Banarsidass Publishers.

Müller, F. M. (Ed.) *The Laws of Manu* (Trans. G. Buhler). 2006 [1886]. *Sacred Books of the East* (11th ed., Vol. 25). Delhi: Motilal Banarsidass.

Nayak, G.C. 1973. *Evil, Karma and Reincarnation*. Santiniketan: Centre of Advanced Study in Philosophy Visva-Bharati.

O'Flaherty, W.D. 1988 [1976]. *The Origins of Evil in Hindu Mythology*. Delhi: Motilal Banarsidass.

O'Flaherty, W.D. 2007 [1983]. 'Karma and Rebirth in *Vedas* and Pūraṇas', in W.D. O'Flaherty (Ed.), *Karma and Rebirth in Classical Indian Traditions*, pp. 3–37. Delhi: Motilal Banarsidass.

Olivelle, P. (Trans. and Anno.) 2000. *Dharmasūtras: The Law Codes of Āpastamba, Gautama, Baudhāyana, and Vaṣiṣṭha*. Delhi: Motilal Banarsidass.

Olivelle, P. (Trans.). 2004. *The Law Code of Manu*. New York: Oxford University Press.

Parpola, A. 2002. 'Πανδαιη and Sītā: On the Historical Background of the Sanskrit Epics', *Journal of the American Oriental Society*, 122(2): 361–73.

Patil, S. 1974. 'Earth Mother', *Social Scientist*, 2(9), 31–58.

———. 1976. 'Myth and Reality of Rāmayana and Mahabharata', *Social Scientist*, 4(8), 68–72.

Swami Prabhupāda (Trans.). 1983. *Bhagavad-Gītā As it Is*. Los Angeles: The Bhaktivedanta Book Trust.

Poruvazhy Peruviruthy Malanada Temple. Available at https://www.malanada.com/ (accessed on 1 September 2017).

Puhvel, J. 1989 [1987]. *Comparative Mythology*. Baltimore: The Johns Hopkins University Press.

Raina, R.L. 1993. 'Mahābhārata Traditions and Kashmir's Links with the rest of India (Bharat)', in K.S. Singh (Ed.), *The Mahābhārata in the Tribal and Folk Traditions of India*, pp. 22–7. Shimla: Indian Institute of Advanced Studies.

Ranganathan, S. 2007. *Ethics and The History of Indian Philosophy*. Delhi: Motilal Banarsidass.

Rukmani, T.S. 1993. 'Folk Tradtions Related to the *Mahābhārata* in South India', in K. Singh (Ed.), *The Mahābhārata in the Tribal and Folk Traditions of India*, pp. 184–96. Shimla: Indian Institute of Advanced Studies.

Saksena, S.K. 2008. 'Relation of Philosophical Theories to the Practical Affairs of Man', In C.A. Moore (Ed.), *The Indian Mind*, pp. 1–18. Delhi: Motilal Banarsidass.

Santina, P.D. 1989. 'Conceptions of Dharma in the Śramanical and Brāhmnical Traditions: Buddhism amd the Mahābhārata', in B.K. Matilal (Ed.), *Moral Dilemmas in the Mahābhārata*, pp. 97–115. Shimla: Indian Institute of Advanced Studies.

Sanyal, I. (n.d.). Personal Lectures, 2010–12.

Shamasastry, R. (Trans. and Ed.). 1915. *Kautilya's Arthashasta*. Available at https://archive.org/details/Arthasastra_English_Translation (accessed on 3 September 2017).

Sharma, A. 1978. 'The Puruṣasūkta: Its Relation to the Caste System', *Journal of the Economic and Social History of the Orient*, 21(3): 294–303.

———. 2002. 'On Hindu, Hindustān, Hinduism and Hindutva', *Numen*, 49(1): 1–36.

Sharma, I.C. and O.N. Bimali (Eds). 2006. *Mahābhārata* (Vols 1–9) (Trans. M.N. Dutt). Delhi: Primal Publications.

Shastri, C.B. (Ed.). 1999 [1976]. *The Bhāgavata-Purāṇa* (Part 1) (Trans. G.V. Tagare). Delhi: Motilal Banarsidass.

Shiva, R.S. and Ganesha Murthy, (Eds). 2004. *The Vāmana-Purana: Ancient Indian Tradition and Mythology Series* (Vol. 72). Delhi: Motilal Banarsidass.

Singh, Nag Sharan (Ed.). 2003. *The Viṣṇu Purāṇa* (Vol. 1 & 2) (Trans. H. Wilson). Delhi: Nag Publishers.

Sinha, B.M. 2007. 'Arthaśāstra Categories in the Mahābhārata: from Daṇḍanīti to Rājadharma', in A. Sharma (Ed.), *Essays on the Mahābhārata*, pp. 369–83. Delhi: Motilal Banarsidass.

Sivaraman, K. 2001. *Śaivism in Philosophical Perspective.* Delhi: Motilal Banarsidass.

Smith B.K. and W. Doniger. 1989. 'Sacrifice and Substitution: Ritual Mystification and Mythical Demystification', *Numen*, 36(2): 189–224.

Solomon, T.J. 1970. 'Early Vaiṣṇava Bhakti and Its Autochthonous Heritage', *History of Religions*, 10(1): 32–48.

Sudh Mahadeva. Available at http://www.jammu.com/jammu/temples-shrines-sudh-mahadev.php. (accessed on 11 January 2016).

Sukthankar, V.S. 1998 [1957]. *On the Meaning of the Mahābhārata.* Delhi: Motilal Banrsidass.

Sullivan, B.M. 1999. *Seer of the Fifth Veda, Kṛṣṇa Dvaipāpana Vyāsa in the Mahābhārata.* Delhi: Motilal Banarsidass.

Sutton, N. 2000. *Religious Doctrines in the Mahābhārata.* Delhi: Motilal Banarsidass.

Thapar, R. 1989. 'Epic and History: Tradition, Dissent and Politics in India', *Past and Present*, 125: 3–26.

———. 1995 [1992]. *Interpreting Early India.* Delhi: Oxford University Press.

———. 1996. *History of India*, (Vol. 1). London: Penguin Books.

———. 2004. *Early India.* Berkeley: University of California Press.

———. 2005. 'Some Appropriations of the Theory of Aryan Race Relating to the Beginnings of Indian History', in T.R. Trautmann (Ed.), *The Aryan Debate*, pp. 106–31. New Delhi: Oxford University Press.

———. 2010. *The Epic of the Bharatas.* Available at http://www.india-seminar.com/2010/608/608_romila_thapar.htm (accessed on 15 February 2011).

Tzu, S., translated by L. Giles. 2007 [1910]. *The Art of War*. Kindle Books.

Upadhyaya, K.N. 1969. 'The Bhagavad Gītā on War and Peace', *Philosophy East and West*, 19(2): 159–69.

van Buitenen, J.A.B. (Trans.). 1973–8. *The Mahābhārata* (Vols 1–3). Chicago: The University of Chicago Press.

Vogel, J. 1995. *Indian Serpent Lore or The Nagas in Hindu Legend and Art* (Rare Reprint ed.). USA: Kessinger Publishing.

Zimmer, H., J. Campbell (Ed.). 1972. *Myths and Symbols in Indian Art and Civilization*. New Jersey: Princeton University Press.

Index

About the Author

Meena Arora Nayak is a scholar of mythology and a novelist. She is the author of *In the Aftermath* (1992), *About Daddy* (2000), *The Puffin Book of Legendary Lives* (2004), and *Endless Rain* (2006), and a forthcoming book on myths and folktales of India. She is a Professor in the Department of English at Northern Virginia Community College and lives in Virginia, USA.